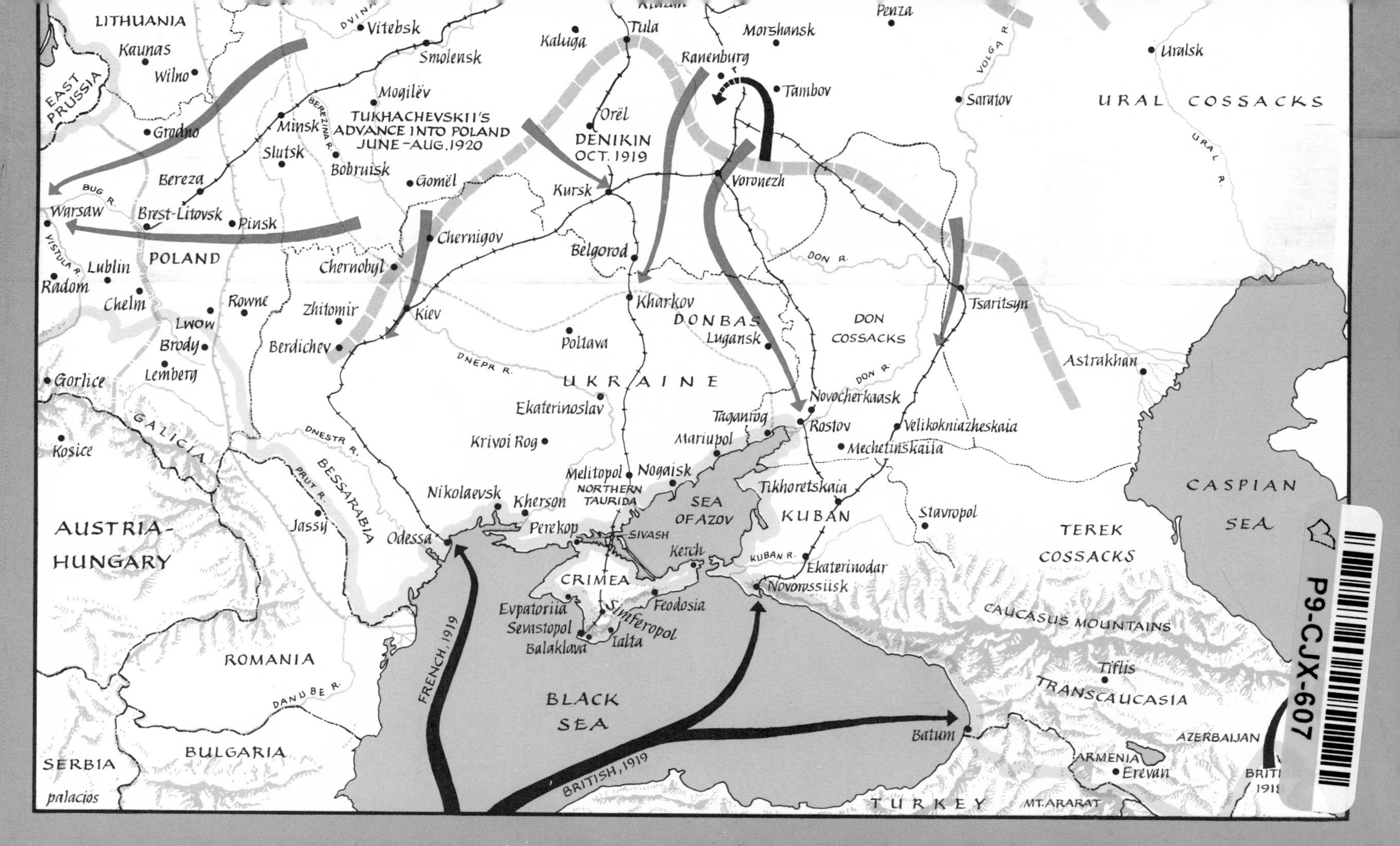
LITHUANIA
Kaunas
Wilno
EAST PRUSSIA
Grodno
Vitebsk
Smolensk
Mogilëv
Minsk
BEREZINA R.
TUKHACHEVSKII'S ADVANCE INTO POLAND JUNE-AUG. 1920
Slutsk
Bobruisk
Gomël
Bereza
BUG R.
Warsaw
Brest-Litovsk
Pinsk
VISTULA R.
POLAND
Lublin
Radom
Chelm
Rowne
Lwow
Brody
Lemberg
Gorlice
Kosice
GALICIA
AUSTRIA-HUNGARY
ROMANIA
DANUBE R.
BULGARIA
SERBIA
palacios
Kaluga
Tula
Orël
DENIKIN OCT. 1919
Kursk
Chernigov
Chernobyl
Zhitomir
Kiev
Berdichev
Belgorod
Kharkov
Poltava
DNEPR R.
UKRAINE
Ekaterinoslav
Krivoi Rog
DNESTR R.
BESSARABIA
PRUT R.
Jassy
Nikolaevsk
Kherson
Odessa
Melitopol
Nogaisk
NORTHERN TAURIDA
Perekop
SIVASH
CRIMEA
Evpatoriia
Sevastopol
Balaklava
Simferopol
Ialta
Feodosia
Kerch
SEA OF AZOV
BLACK SEA
FRENCH, 1919
BRITISH, 1919
Morshansk
Ranenburg
Tambov
Penza
Voronezh
DON R.
DONBAS
Lugansk
DON COSSACKS
Taganrog
Mariupol
Novocherkaask
Rostov
Tsaritsyn
Velikokniazheskaia
Mechetinskaia
Tikhoretskaia
KUBAN
KUBAN R.
Ekaterinodar
Novorossiisk
Stavropol
Saratov
VOLGA R.
Uralsk
URAL COSSACKS
URAL R.
Astrakhan
CASPIAN SEA
TEREK COSSACKS
CAUCASUS MOUNTAINS
Tiflis
TRANSCAUCASIA
AZERBAIJAN
ARMENIA
Erevan
MT. ARARAT
TURKEY
Batum

Excessive verbosity and too much detail of political disputes & attitudes of protagonists. This book was researched too much & author trys to show all of it. A good example of too much information about people, politics, and not simple reporting of facts. Probably shows & emphasizes just available sources. Lincoln must have been paid by the word.

J. A. BALL
JAN '90

ALSO BY W. BRUCE LINCOLN

NIKOLAI MILIUTIN:
An Enlightened Russian Bureaucrat

NICHOLAS I:
Emperor and Autocrat of All the Russias

PETR SEMENOV-TIAN-SHANSKII:
The Life of a Russian Geographer

THE ROMANOVS:
Autocrats of All the Russias

IN THE VANGUARD OF REFORM:
Russia's Enlightened Bureaucrats

IN WAR'S DARK SHADOW:
The Russians Before the Great War

PASSAGE THROUGH ARMAGEDDON:
The Russians in War and Revolution

RED VICTORY

A History of the Russian Civil War

W. Bruce Lincoln

SIMON AND SCHUSTER
NEW YORK · LONDON · TORONTO · SYDNEY · TOKYO

SIMON AND SCHUSTER
Simon & Schuster Building
Rockefeller Center
1230 Avenue of the Americas
New York, New York 10020

Designed by Edith Fowler
Manufactured in the United States of America

10 9 8 7 6 5 4 3 2 1

Library of Congress Cataloging in Publication Data

Lincoln, W. Bruce.
Red victory: a history of the Russian Civil War / W. Bruce Lincoln.
p. cm.
Includes bibliographical references.
1. Soviet Union—History—Revolution, 1917–1921.
I. Title.
DK265.L449 1989
947.084'1—dc20 *89-21721*
CIP

ISBN 0-671-63166-7

A leatherbound signed first edition of this book has been published by The Easton Press.

For Mary, with love

Contents

Preface

CIVIL WARS are tragedies that shape the histories of nations. They mark those pivotal moments when men and women choose death before compromise in the belief that their vision of the future can survive only at the cost of eradicating all others. Such national tragedies leave lasting scars, for defeat in civil war obliterates the principles for which the vanquished fought, just as victory elevates the beliefs of the victors into new, self-evident truths that reshape a nation's destiny. No nation has ever set aside the principles that triumphed in its civil war, nor has any ever erased the imprint from its national character. Nowhere has this been more true than in Russia, where, between 1918 and 1921, civil war set an exhausted nation upon a course yet untried by any other. Unable to chart their path by the experience of others, the Russians found themselves alone. In an important sense, the history of the Soviet Union has become the story of the Russians' efforts to complete the passage through unknown waters that their civil war had begun.

The Russian Civil War grew out of two revolutions in 1917, which, in turn, grew out of Russia's disastrous defeats in the Great War of 1914–1918. The violent background heightened the Civil War's tragedy and deepened its turmoil, for war and revolution had claimed the lives of more than seven million Russians before Red began to fight against White. Before they fell into the abyss of civil conflict, the Russians already had overthrown the dynasty that had ruled their land for more than three hundred years. They had tried democracy and failed. Their army had collapsed, and so had those political institutions and industrial establishments upon which nations depend to sustain them in war. Weakened by the attacks of foreign enemies, her stability shattered, and her economy in ruins, Russia in 1918 entered upon one of the most bitter civil wars of modern times. Combined with the revolutionary turmoil of 1917, that terrible conflict makes up the Soviet Union's revolutionary heritage.

The Bolsheviks' desperate struggle to survive during the Russian Civil War shaped the Soviet system of government and dictated its future course. Only by placing all human and natural resources within reach at the service of a government that spoke in the name of the people but acted in the interest of the Communist Party did Lenin and his comrades defeat their enemies. These included soldiers from fourteen foreign countries, the armed forces of nearly a dozen national groups that struggled to establish independent governments upon the lands that once had been part of the Russian Empire, and a half-dozen White armies that formed on Russia's frontiers between 1918 and 1920. To comprehend the Soviet Union of today, it is important to understand how the Bolsheviks triumphed against such crushing odds and how that struggle shaped their vision of the future.

Red Victory tells the story of Russia's terrible civil war. Here, sons fight against fathers, and brothers kill brothers as they come to learn the full dimensions of the revolutionary course upon which they had embarked in 1917. Before the struggle reached its end, hundreds of battles and tens of thousands of executions combined with epidemics and mass starvation to claim millions more lives on both sides. Uprooted by the conflict that had torn their homeland for so long, millions of Russians struggled to build new lives far from home in those parts of the Soviet Union into which the war's turmoil had cast them, and hundreds of thousands more men and women fled abroad lest they be added to the Civil War's list of casualties. Yet the end of the fighting did not end the suffering, for the brave new world that the Bolsheviks had envisioned proved more difficult to shape than they had imagined. From their victory emerged a state in which despotic Party officials terrorized their nation's citizens while a growing army of petty bureaucrats tyrannized those whom they were supposed to serve. Such despotism created a society permeated with illegality, and although time has moderated that heritage, the Soviet Union's Civil War experience continues to determine the framework within which its people think and govern. Only by understanding that experience can we start to unravel the mystery of the Soviet Union and begin to estimate its future course.

Although by no means as complete as an historian might wish, the sources for a book about the Russian Civil War are extremely rich, and no single volume can do justice to the many fascinating tales that constitute the story of Russia during that terrible conflict. More needs to be written about the inner history of the Bolshevik Party during these years, just as the full extent of other socialists' efforts to oppose the Bolsheviks and their monolithic state needs to be better understood. As in the first two volumes of this trilogy, I must beg readers' indulgence for giving too little attention to the immensely complex nationality problems that plagued the Russian Empire and Soviet Union. The successful struggles of Finns, Poles, Estonians, Latvians, and Lithuanians for independence—and the failed attempts of Ukrainians, Georgians, Armenians, and the peoples of Central Asia to follow their example—still require more study before they can be fully explained. Much more will be known about these problems a decade hence, after a new generation of young historians has taken up their study in universities across America and the Soviet Union. Yet, other parts of Russia's Civil War story will almost certainly never be told, for the documents needed to do so remain locked away in Soviet archives.

As in the earlier volumes of this trilogy, I should remind readers that, until February 1, 1918, when Lenin's government adopted the Western Gregorian calendar, the dates in this book are cited according to the Julian calendar. In the twentieth century, this is thirteen days behind that used in the West. To note this change, I have marked the first date cited according to the Gregorian calendar with an asterisk. Russian names and place names continue to pose the usual problems, but I shall spare readers additional explanations and refer them to the rules I have followed in my previous books.

Few historians have the good fortune to study Russia's past in archives and libraries halfway around the globe, and I should not have been able to do so had it not been for the financial and logistical support so generously provided by archives, libraries, research foundations, and academic institutions that stretch from California to Moscow. Among those to whom I am grateful are The Academy of Sciences of the U.S.S.R., Leningrad; Archives de la Guerre, Service Historique de l'Armée de la Terre, Château de Vincennes, Vincennes; The Bakhmetieff Archive, Columbia University, New York; Bibliothèque Nationale, Paris; The British Museum, London; The Central State Historical Archive, Leningrad; The Fulbright-Hays Faculty Research Abroad Program, U.S. Department of Education, Washington, D.C.; The Harriman Institute, Columbia University, New York; The Hoover Institution, Stanford, California; The Imperial War Museum, London; The International Research and Exchanges Board, Princeton, New Jersey; The Kennan Institution, Woodrow Wilson Center, The Smithsonian, Washington, D.C.; The Library of Congress, Washington, D.C.; The Lenin Library, Moscow; The National Endowment for the Humanities, Washington, D.C.; Northern Illinois University, DeKalb; The Public Records Office, Kew, England; The Russian and East European Center, University of Illinois at Urbana-Champaign, Urbana; The Regenstein Library, University of Chicago; The Saltykov-Shchedrin Public Library, Leningrad; The Slavic Library, University of Helsinki; Stanford University, Stanford, California.

Beyond the acknowledgments listed above, the University of Illinois Library deserves a special added note of thanks. Without access to its outstanding Slavic Collection, and without the generous help given by Susan Burke, Marianna Choldin, Laurence Miller, and Helen Sullivan in its Slavic Reference Service, my research would have gone more slowly and my task would have been more difficult. As always, I owe a particular intellectual debt to Marc Raeff, recently retired as Bakhmetieff Professor of Russian History at Columbia University. Although the list of other scholars who have been generous in helping me by discussing some of the problems relating to Russia's history during this complex and confusing era is, regrettably, too long to include here, I should mention at least Michael Hickey and John Long, who read nearly all of the manuscript in an earlier form.

Among the people at Northern Illinois University who helped me while I was writing this book, Jerrold Zar, Dean of the Graduate School and Associate Provost for Research, came to my aid on several occasions, as did James Norris, Dean of the College of Liberal Arts and Sciences, whose dedication to supporting research among his faculty made the task of writing this book both easier and more pleasant.

I continue to be grateful to Robert Gottlieb, who has played a part in my work for over a decade as one of those rare literary agents whose talent for providing proper measures of enthusiasm, encouragement, and reassurance grows more amazing with the passage of time.

Most of all, I owe more than I can express here to my wife Mary, whose critical judgment and generous spirit have made my life so much richer than it would have been without her. Dedicating this book to her is but another small payment against a debt that grows larger with each year that passes.

W. Bruce Lincoln

DeKalb, Illinois
September 6, 1988

Major Characters

ALEKSANDRA FEODOROVNA (1872–1918): Russia's last Empress. Born Alix of Hesse-Darmstadt, married Nicholas II in 1894, and executed by the Bolsheviks in Ekaterinburg.

ALEKSEEV, MIKHAIL VASILEVICH (1857–1918): Chief of Staff when Nicholas II commanded Russia's armies, Supreme Commander from May to June 1917, and a key figure in forming the first White Army in South Russia after the October Revolution.

ANTONOV, ALEKSANDR (date of birth and death unknown, though probably killed in June or July 1922): A Socialist Revolutionary who, after a brief alliance with the Bolsheviks, led a massive uprising against them in Tambov province in 1920–1921.

ANTONOV–OVSEENKO, VLADIMIR ALEKSANDROVICH (1884–1939): Led the Bolsheviks' assault on the Winter Palace in October 1917, commanded the Red forces in South Russia in late 1917–early 1918, and played an important part in suppressing the Antonov uprising before perishing in the Great Purge.

ARMAND, INESSA [née ELISABETH D'HERBENVILLE] (1874–1920): A staunch advocate of female liberation who joined the Bolsheviks in 1904, worked closely with Lenin, and, after the October Revolution, headed the Bolsheviks' *zhenotdel* until her death.

BUDËNNYI, SEMËN MIKHAILOVICH (1883–1973): Tsarist sergeant-major who joined the Bolsheviks in 1918 and rose quickly, as an ally of Stalin and Voroshilov, to command the famous *Konarmiia* in South Russia, the Ukraine, and Poland. With Tukhachevskii, he became one of the first to be named a Marshal of the Soviet Union in 1935. Two years later, he sat on the tribunal that condemned Tukhachevskii to death.

BUKHARIN, NIKOLAI IVANOVICH (1888–1938): Leading Bolshevik theorist, head of the Left Opposition (1918), and, with Lenin, chief author of the 1919 Party program. After supporting Stalin against Trotskii, he was executed during the Great Purge.

CHAIKOVSKII, NIKOLAI VASILEVICH (1850–1926): Active in the Russian revolutionary movement from the 1870s, Chaikovskii remained an unyielding opponent of the Bolsheviks after the October Revolution, headed (with Allied support) the anti-Bolshevik Supreme Administration of the North, and, in 1919, emigrated to Paris.

DENIKIN, ANTON IVANOVICH (1872–1947): Commander-in-Chief of Russia's Western Front in the summer of 1917, Denikin took command of the White forces in South Russia after Kornilov's death. After his march against Moscow failed, he resigned his command in March 1920 and left Russia for a life in exile in Europe and the United States.

DZERZHINSKII, FELIKS EDMUNDOVICH (1877–1926): Head of the Cheka and, later, GPU, as well as (beginning in 1924) chairman of the Supreme Economic Council.

EGOROV, ALEKSANDR ILICH (1883–1939): A metalworker with socialist-revolutionary sympathies who rose to the rank of lieutenant colonel during World War I. After joining the Bolsheviks in 1918, he commanded their South-Western Front against Denikin and the Poles. Along with Budënnyi, Voroshilov, and Tukhachevskii, he received the rank of Marshal of the Soviet Union in 1935.

FRUNZE, MIKHAIL VASILEVICH (1885–1925): Bolshevik mill hand who commanded the Red Army's campaigns against Kolchak and Wrangel. A sometime ally of Stalin, he replaced Trotskii as Commissar for Military and Naval Affairs at the beginning of 1925 and died soon after, probably from an overdose of chloroform.

GRAVES, WILLIAM SYDNEY (1865–1940): Commander of the United States army units in Siberia.

IRONSIDE, WILLIAM EDMUND (1880–1959): Commander of the Allied forces in North Russia.

IUDENICH, NIKOLAI NIKOLAEVICH (1862–1933): Commander of the Caucasus Front in 1917, and leader of the nearly successful White attack against Petrograd in October 1919.

KALININ, MIKHAIL IVANOVICH (1875–1946): A peasant-turned-metal-worker who replaced Sverdlov (in 1919) as chairman of the All-Russian Central Executive Committee of the Soviets. Kalinin held that office until 1937, when he became chairman of the Presidium of the Supreme Soviet of the U.S.S.R.

KAPLAN, FANIA EFIMOVNA (1890–1918): Terrorist and close ally of Spiridonova who spent eleven years in tsarist prisons. Bitter at what she considered the Bolsheviks' betrayal of Socialist principles, she wounded Lenin with two pistol shots in 1918 and was executed soon afterward.

KERENSKII, ALEKSANDR FEODOROVICH (1881–1970): Minister of Justice, Minister of War and Navy, and Prime Minister in the successive provisional governments that ruled Russia from March to October 1917 after which he fled into exile in France and the United States.

KOLCHAK, ALEKSANDR VASILEVICH (1870–1920): Admiral and Arctic explorer before 1917, Kolchak became Siberia's Supreme Ruler and commander of its White forces.

KOLLONTAI, ALEKSANDRA MIKHAILOVNA (1872–1952): The Bolsheviks' leading apostle of women's liberation, Commissar of Public Welfare in the first Sovnarkom, Inessa Armand's successor as head of *zhenotdel*, and, later, a leading member of the Workers' Opposition.

KORNILOV, LAVR GEORGEVICH (1870–1918): Commander-in-Chief of Russia's armies (August 1917), Kornilov commanded the first White forces in South Russia until he was killed in battle near the end of the famed Icy March.

KRASNOV, PETR NIKOLAEVICH (1869–1947): Commander of the Whites at Pulkovo a few days after the October Revolution and Kaledin's successor as Commander-in-Chief of the Don Cossacks, Krasnov went into exile in Germany in 1919 when he could not resolve his differences with Denikin. After the Second World War, he fell into Soviet hands and was hanged as a traitor.

KRUPSKAIA, NADEZHDA KONSTANTINOVNA (1869–1939): Close associate and wife of Lenin, she played an important role in the development of Soviet education after the October Revolution.

LENIN [ULIANOV], VLADIMIR ILICH (1870–1924): Founder of the Bolsheviks and, after the October Revolution, Chairman of the Sovnarkom.

LUNACHARSKII, ANATOLII VASIL'EVICH (1873–1933): Bolshevik literary critic and friend of Lenin who served as the Soviet Commissar for Public Enlightenment until 1929.

MAKHNO, NESTOR IVANOVICH (1889–1935): Ukrainian peasant anarchist who fought against both Reds and Whites from 1918 until his defeat in 1921, after which he fled to France.

MILIUKOV, PAVEL NIKOLAEVICH (1859–1943): Noted Russian historian, leader of the Kadet Party, and Foreign Minister in Russia's first provisional government who became a prominent figure among the Whites in South Russia before he fled to Paris and London.

MILLER, GENERAL EVGENYI KARLOVICH (1867–1937?): Commander-in-Chief of the White forces in North Russia, who fled to Paris in February 1920. The suspected victim of an NKVD kidnapping, Miller disappeared in 1937.

NICHOLAS II (1868–1918): Russia's last Emperor who ruled from 1894–1917. Executed by the Bolsheviks in Ekaterinburg.

PETRICHENKO, STEPAN (date of birth and death unknown): Leader of the Kronstadt uprising against the Bolsheviks.

PETLIURA, SIMON VASILEVICH (1879–1926): Ukrainian nationalist and head of the Directory before he fled into exile in Poland and Paris, where he was assassinated.

PILSUDSKI, JOZEF (1867–1935): Anti-Russian Polish revolutionary who served as head of his nation's first government after Poland declared her independence in 1918, and commanded her armed forces in the Russo-Polish War of 1920.

SKOROPADSKY, PAVLO (1873–1945): Closely connected to the Russian court and the German High Command, Skoropadsky was one of the wealthiest men in the Ukraine and one of its greatest landowners. After seizing power from the Rada in April 1918, he was overthrown by Petliura in December, after which he fled to Germany.

SPIRIDONOVA, MARIA ALEKSANDROVNA (1884–1941): Terrorist and assassin before 1917, Spiridonova became a leader of the Left Socialist Revolutionaries after the Bolshevik seizure of power and was one of the key figures in the Left SR Moscow uprising in July 1918.

STALIN [DZHUGASHVILI], IOSIF VISARIONOVICH (1879–1953): A shadowy figure in 1917, Stalin became the first Commissar for Nationalities (1917–1923) and General Secretary of the Party (beginning in 1922). After Lenin's death, he destroyed all rivals and ruled unchallenged until his death.

SVERDLOV, IAKOV MIKHAILOVICH (1885–1919): One of Lenin's closest collaborators in 1917–1918, who served as chairman of the All-Russian Executive Committee of the Soviets until his premature death.

TROTSKII [BRONSTEIN], LEV DAVIDOVICH (1879–1940): Chief architect of the Bolsheviks' seizure of power, Commissar for Foreign Affairs (briefly), and then Commissar for War. Assassinated, almost certainly on Stalin's orders, in Mexico.

TUKHACHEVSKII, MIKHAIL NIKOLAEVICH (1893–1937): A Russian nobleman who joined the Bolsheviks in 1917 and enjoyed a spectacular career in the Red Army. During the Civil War he won key victories on the Volga, in Siberia, in the Trans-Caucasus, against Poland, and at Kronstadt. A Marshal of the Soviet Union at the age of 42, he was executed as part of Stalin's purge of the Red Army's High Command.

VATSETIS, IOAKIM IOAKIMOVICH (1873–1938): Son of a Latvian farm laborer, who rose to the rank of colonel in the tsarist army and joined the Bolsheviks in 1918. Vatsetis crushed the Left SR uprising in Moscow in July 1918 and went on to command the Red Army's Eastern Front (briefly) and, for nearly a year (1918–1919), served as Commander-in-Chief of the Red Army.

VOROSHILOV, KLIMENT EFREMOVICH (1881–1960): A metalworker from the Donbas, one of Stalin's first allies, and chief political officer of Budënnyi's *Konarmiia*, Voroshilov became a Marshal of the Soviet Union in 1935, Commissar of Defense on the eve of World War II, and Deputy Prime Minister. After Stalin's death, he became Chairman of the Presidium of the U.S.S.R.

WRANGEL, BARON PETR NIKOLAEVICH (1878–1928): A fighting general in World War I and a leading figure in the White movement who took command of the White forces in South Russia after Denikin's resignation.

Part One

1918

Prologue

CHRISTMAS 1916 found the people of Europe weary of war and sick at heart. Gone was the romantic thirst for glory that had inspired millions of young men all across the continent to take up arms at the outbreak of the Great War twenty-nine months before. Gone, too, was the belief that a better, brighter world would somehow emerge from the Great War's carnage. In its place, a morbid fatalism that saw a future filled with death and dying reigned supreme. Men now concluded, as a young English officer confessed, that "Armageddon was too immense" for anyone's "solitary understanding."[1] The Great War seemed destined to be with them always. George Bernard Shaw had come away from a visit with England's Commander-in-Chief Sir Douglas Haig at the front that fall feeling certain that "the war would last thirty years." Even *The Times* of London set aside its usual rose-colored optimism on New Year's Day 1917 to remark that "after 29 months of fighting, which has involved nearly all the States of Europe, anything like a definite decision seems far distant." England's enemies feared the same. "I see no end to it," a captured German army doctor told an English writer. "It is the suicide of nations."[2]

The exalted hopes with which Europeans had greeted the Great War's coming now made their disillusionment more bitter still. Before the guns of August had shattered the peace of Europe in 1914, Germany's great novelist Thomas Mann remembered, young men had believed that a great war would come as "a purification, a liberation, an enormous hope."[3] In those days of peace, some had thought war inevitable, others had thought it desirable, and General Friedrich von Bernhardi of the German General Staff had even insisted (in his widely read *Germany and the Next War*) that it was a "biological necessity." War, the straight-backed Bernhardi had explained loftily in 1911, was "an indispensable factor of culture" because it evoked "the noblest activities of the human nature."[4] On the British side, one of the characters in Richard Aldington's autobiographical *Death of a Hero* spoke more simply. "We're getting stale," he muttered. "Too much peace. Need a bit of blood-letting."[5] As the Western world had moved through its last days of peace in the summer of 1914, many men and women thus had come to believe that a great war would invigorate nations whose people had become too lethargic and complacent. Russia's Empress Aleksandra had even insisted that such a war would be "healthy . . . in the moral sense."[6] Now, in the final days of 1916, everyone who had seen the modern god of war face to face knew otherwise.

It had cost Europe's great nations several million lives and billions of pounds, francs, marks, schillings, and rubles to discover how false their grand illusions of 1914 had been. During 1916 alone, more than a million men had fallen during General Brusilov's summer offensive in Galicia, and even more had died in the great battles that stretched across most of that year at Verdun and along the Somme. Thinking men no longer cared to remember that they once had sought purification in war's cleansing flames. Now they thought only of the awful devastation that war wrought upon the minds and souls of those who survived its terrors. Everywhere the Great War had become a curse that touched everyone.

Men now knew that they never would find "the highest expression of strength and vitality"[7] that von Bernhardi had promised anywhere in the thirty thousand miles of stinking trenches that zigzagged across northern France, Belgium, and western Russia. "The poetry of the trenches is a thing of the past," a German theology student in uniform explained bitterly. "The spirit of adventure is dead. We are oppressed by the reflection that we have seen what battle is like and shall see it again."[8] Such disillusionment came not so much from the agony and dying that filled the third year of the Great War as from the cold impersonality with which its machines took men's lives. Chivalry, bravery, the exaltation of testing oneself in combat, all counted for very little in trenches where the instruments of death fell unseen from the sky, or in no-man's-land, where massed machine guns spewed death as each "hosed" the advancing enemy (the term then in popular use) with several hundred bullets every minute. "That is the disgusting part of this war: it's all so mechanical," a young graduate from one of Germany's technological academies exclaimed. "One might call it the trade of systematic manslaughter."[9]

With its killing machines and poison gases, the first great war to employ the fruits of modern technology thus became what one commentator called "a blindly crushing mechanism which was kept in motion by an army of hirelings, some of them skilled mechanics but all of them soulless men."[10] Men in battle no longer even remotely resembled the stalwart warriors who, in bygone days, had marched tall, straight, and brave for the glory of God, King, and Country. Fighters of the new technological age appeared in dehumanized form, as instruments bound by some common technological heritage to the death-dealing machines they tended. "They filed by," England's Richard Aldington wrote of his comrades during a German gas attack, "grotesques with india-rubber faces, great dead-looking goggles, and long tubes from their mouths to the box respirators [that hung from their sides]."[11]

During the great slaughters of 1916, men lived, made ready to kill, and prepared to die below ground, with the slit of sky that hung over their trenches the only proof that they had not already crossed into the world beyond the grave. "Hideous landscapes, vile noises, foul language . . . everything unnatural, broken, blasted," the young English poet Wilfred Owen wrote to his mother in describing the "most execrable sights on earth"[12] that he found in the "troglodyte world" of the trenches.[13] There, only rats flourished as they gorged themselves on the rotting cadavers of men that had lain for months unburied in the no-man's-land beyond the trenches. "No pen or drawing can convey this country," the artist Paul Nash wrote to his wife then. "The black dying trees ooze and sweat. . . . It is unspeakable, godless, hopeless." Cynically, Nash later gave the title "We Are Making a New World" to a painting in which those nether regions resembled more the moon's barren surface than anything ever touched by the hand of man.[14] No longer heroic, no longer glorious, war and death thus had become the depersonalized products of the same great technological age that, in a touch of supreme irony, had provided man with the means to preserve life through the wonders of immunology and sterile surgery at the very moment it had given him the means to destroy it on an unprecedented scale. "Man, as it were, is shoved into the background [in modern war]," one critic wrote, "even though it is ultimately his destruction which is at stake."[15]

Nowhere was that truth more certain than on Europe's eastern front, where thousands of unarmed Russian soldiers stood defenseless in reserve trenches awaiting the moment when they could charge forth to seize the rifles of their fallen comrades and continue their attack. While they waited "until casualties in the firing-line should make rifles available," Britain's General Sir Alfred Knox reported in outraged amazement, they were "churned into gruel" by the Germans' heavy guns.[16] Such men never faced their enemies on the field of battle. Death came to them unseen, inflicted by foes who, from their positions far beyond the horizon, never once glimpsed their victims but merely adjusted the elevation of their heavy guns according to numerical coordinates set down on their gunnery maps.

Much more than on the western front, the Germans had tested their killing machines in the east during 1915, the year before the great battles in the west. First along a narrow thirty-five–kilometer front between Tarnów and Gorlice in May, and again, as he drove northward toward Lublin, Cholm, and Brest-Litovsk two months later, the hard-eyed General August von Mackensen perfected his "Mackensen wedge," in which massed heavy guns hurled more than a thousand high explosive shells a minute onto the enemy's positions before his soldiers began to advance. Mackensen's was a strategy calculated not to challenge his enemies but to eradicate them. "Creeping like some huge beast, the German army would move," one Russian general remembered. "[Their] heavy guns would start to shower their shells on the Russian trenches . . . until nothing of the trenches remained and their defenders would be destroyed. Then the beast would cautiously stretch out its paws, the infantry units, which would seize the demolished trenches."[17]

Again and again during Russia's Great Retreat in the summer of 1915, Europe's eastern front witnessed this unequal confrontation between technology and man as the heavy weapons of the German army battered their way ahead. "The Germans literally plow up the field of battle with a hail of metal and level our trenches and defenses, often burying their defenders in the process," one desperate Russian division commander reported. "They use up metal," he concluded bitterly. "We use up human life."[18] As the cost in lives soared, Russians' disillusionment with modern warfare turned to outright defeatism that demanded an end to the war at any price. "Complete demoralization is in progress," a member of one of Russia's most prominent civic groups reported in the fall of 1916. "Soldiers began to demand peace a long time ago, but never was this done so openly and with such force as now."

The Tsar's secret police, the fearsome Okhrana, whose business it was to report on Russians' attitudes toward their government and its policies, understood the sentiments of the country and sensed the danger of revolution all too clearly. "Everybody is impatiently waiting for an end to this 'damned war,' " one of its senior officials stated in a secret report in October 1916. "There is a marked increase in hostile feelings among the peasants [from whose midst most of Russia's soldiers came], not only against the government but against all other social groups."[19]

No one expressed Russians' hatred for the war more forcefully than Vladimir Maiakovskii, the twenty-three-year-old Futurist poet who had become a revolutionary at the age of fifteen and had been in tsarist jails on three separate occasions before his sixteenth birthday. Like so many others who had been caught up in the war's first surge of patriotic enthusiasm, Maiakovskii in 1914 had cursed the Germans for their barbarity and had tried to enter the army as a volunteer. More quickly than most of his countrymen, however, he had shifted to a broader indictment of the war itself in which he condemned everyone in any country who supported it. "Every person,/ Even someone who is of no use,/ Has the right to live," he raged in *Voina i Mir* [War and the World]. "You can't,/ Simply cannot/ Bury him alive/ In trenches and dugouts—/ Murderers!" For Maiakovskii, the war had taken on a life of its own by 1916, and he feared it would consume victors and vanquished equally. Not even victory, he insisted, could justify war's cost in lives and treasure lost. "To an armless stump left over from the bloody banquet," he exclaimed angrily, "what the hell good is it?"[20]

Filled with hatred for the politicians and generals who continued to send men to their deaths in the uneven struggle against the killing machines of Germany, Maiakovskii's indictment of the war nonetheless contained a flash of optimism that accorded strangely with the pessimism overwhelming East and West as 1916 neared its end. For if Russia's angry young poet remained second to none in his outrage at the Great War's brutality, he nonetheless closed *Voina i Mir* with a rare vision of a new and better world that might emerge from its carnage. At the end, Maiakovskii promised, his brave new world would bring freedom: "The free man,/ About whom I shout/ Will come," he concluded. "Believe me!/ Believe me!/"[21]

Behind Maiakovskii's new vision of a world of freedom lay his belief that "the thorny crown of revolution" soon would settle upon Russia and its people. For, if the Great Retreat of 1915 marked the low point in Russia's military effort, 1916 brought political crises of equal magnitude. Ever since the Emperor Nicholas II had taken command of his country's collapsing armies in August 1915, he had allowed his neurotically introspective Empress to turn his empire onto one of the most bizarre courses ever taken by a nation at war. A woman who believed that God had chosen her as His instrument, the Empress Aleksandra surrounded herself with an assortment of prattling holy men and corrupt hangers-on who flattered her belief that God had chosen her to save Russia. With an urgency that proved all but impossible to resist, she pressed her weak-willed husband to appoint ineffectual nonentities and gross incompetents to high office and changed their appointments so rapidly that one sharp-tongued conservative politician dubbed the entire farce "ministerial leapfrog."[22]

Aleksandra praised Aleksei Khvostov, a corrupt influence peddler whose lust for food and drink was exceeded only by his greed for power, as a man whose soul was "light and clear,"[23] when she insisted, in the fall of 1915, that his appointment as minister of internal affairs could not be delayed for a moment. A few months later she urgently pleaded for the "honest and excellent"[24] Boris Stürmer, a man whom others described as "worse than a mediocrity, with limited intelligence, mean spirit, low character, questionable honesty, no experience and no idea of statecraft,"[25] to be named prime minister. Not long after, she concluded that "the devil had somehow got hold of" Khvostov,[26] and championed as his replacement Aleksandr Protopopov, a man who, according to rumor, once claimed that he had seen Christ standing behind her[27] and whose ailments—recurrent paresis, hallucinations, and "tubercular" leg ulcers—bore a disturbing resemblance to the symptoms of advanced syphilis.[28] Protopopov proceeded to insult Russia's national assembly, the Duma, by appearing before it dressed in the uniform of the repressive imperial gendarmerie, while Aleksandra calmly insisted that "Protopopov is honestly for us" and that his efforts "will be blessed."[29]

One of Protopopov's great virtues as a statesman, Aleksandra assured Nicholas, was that "he venerates our Friend [Rasputin],"[30] the sinister pseudo-saint, whose every word, she thought, bore God's imprint. From all of the men she chose to direct Russia's affairs, Aleksandra demanded unswerving devotion to Rasputin, whose "prayers and wise councils," she insisted, were the "rock of faith and help" that would save Russia.[31] A charlatan who pretended to stand close to God and the Russian people, Rasputin had, for more than a decade, used his strange, hypnotic ability to stem the bleeding of Russia's hemophilic Tsarevitch to gain the Empress's unreserved confidence. In the Tsar's absence, he readily used that trust to raise to high office men who paid handsomely for his favor, and through them he seems to have pursued an array of unsavory schemes that boded ill for Russia and his imperial patrons.

Rasputin's widely reported sexual excesses and outrageous public behavior angered the very men and women who had formed the bulwark of Russia's throne for centuries. Yet no amount of pleading from statesmen, courtiers, and even members of the imperial family could shake Aleksandra's belief that God spoke through the man whom one disgusted conservative branded a "filthy, depraved, corrupt peasant."[32] Rasputin thus became a symbol of ominous "dark forces" lurking behind the throne, which, too many Russians feared, would drive their nation into the chaos of revolution and defeat. "Oh, how terrible an autocracy is without an autocrat!" a loyal monarchist confided to his diary as 1916 came to an end. "The Tsar offends the nation by what he allows to go on in the Palace . . . while the country offends the Tsar by its terrible suspicions."[33]

As Russia's old-fashioned Julian calendar passed Christmas 1916 and turned toward the New Year thirteen days after Western nations had celebrated those events, many sober-minded citizens thought revolution had become a near certainty. "We're heading for revolution," former Prime Minister Vladimir Kokovtsev had warned France's ambassador Maurice Paléologue some months earlier while they had sat at dinner with the great Petrograd industrialist Aleksei Putilov. Putilov expected something even worse. "We're heading for anarchy," he insisted. "There's a vast difference. The revolutionary has the intention to reconstruct; the anarchist thinks of nothing but destruction."[34] As the New Year opened, Paléologue thought for a moment that anarchy already had come, but from the right, not the left. "Anything is preferable to the state of anarchy that characterizes the present situation," he reported, as he described to his superiors at the Quay d'Orsay the outrageous flounderings of Protopopov and Aleksandra's other favorites. "I am obliged to report," he concluded in amazement, "that, at the present moment, the Russian Empire is run by lunatics."[35]

Many Russians no longer even bothered to ask *if* there would be a revolution, but only debated *when* it would break out. "The revolutionary path of struggle is inevitable," one influential liberal politician concluded. "The only question is when to start the fight."[36] Even members of the imperial family saw the danger. "We are watching an unheard-of plot," one of the Emperor's cousins lamented on New Year's Day 1917. "We are looking on while the revolution comes from above, not from below."[37] Then, for a brief moment at the beginning of February, a false calm settled upon Russia. As subzero temperatures slowed the pace of life and blizzards piled the snow in deep drifts across the land, men, machines, and political conflicts all came to a standstill and Russia's rulers took heart. "You are exaggerating the danger," Aleksandra confidently chided Grand Duke Aleksandr Mikhailovich when he warned that revolution lay just beyond the horizon. "When you are less excited, you will admit that I knew better."[38]

Few besides Aleksandra were deceived. As snow-clogged railways and disabled locomotives halted vital food and fuel shipments, Russia's cities froze and people went hungry. Bread prices climbed by more than two percent each week after the first of the year, potatoes and cabbage by three, milk by five, meat and sausage by seven, and chocolate and sugar by more than ten.[39] As in earlier less prosperous times, workers no longer ate eggs, meat, milk, and fruit and settled for watery cabbage soup and bits of black bread that were increasingly hard to come by. In Moscow and Petrograd, breadlines began to form, even though the temperature stood well below zero. "Children are starving in the literal sense of the word," an Okhrana agent reported as he grimly warned his superiors to prepare for hunger riots that could turn all too easily into revolution.[40] "Underneath, everything is seething," a worried Moscow newspaper editor wrote. "The tighter the government screws down the top on the caldron, the bigger the explosion is going to be."[41]

Although thoughtful Russians sensed that an explosion was all but certain, they remained as innocent about the nature of modern revolution at the beginning of 1917 as they had been ignorant about the terrors of modern warfare when they had sought national regeneration on the Great War's first battlefields. Certainly, they knew the history of Europe's revolutions, but even the most recent of those, in 1848, had come during the early days of the Industrial Revolution, when men and women still thought mainly in preindustrial terms. During the great French Revolution of 1789, the absence of modern transportation and communications had kept the angry masses of town and country apart, and Europe's nineteenth-century revolutions had been staged by city crowds for the same reason. In 1917 no one knew what might happen when modern transportation and communications allowed the urban and rural mobs to unite in common cause. Nor could anyone imagine what a revolution would be like when each side had modern weapons at its disposal and the insurgents numbered in the millions. No one, in fact, could even envision what sort of government such a revolution might produce.

Hopeful, perhaps, that they might find in the revolutionary abyss the uplifting forces they had failed to find in the Great War's carnage, less timid men and women moved toward the events that forced the abdication of Nicholas II on March 2, 1917, with a thrill of anticipation. Yet, despite their clear sense of its inevitability, they at first did not recognize the revolution when it began. Starting as a protest by seven thousand underpaid female textile mill workers on the morning of Thursday, February 23, 1917, the ranks of Petrograd's revolutionary demonstrators swelled to over seventy thousand by nightfall. The mob doubled the next day. On the next, it almost doubled again until it numbered more than a quarter-million. On Sunday, the fourth day, the Petrograd garrison joined the revolution, and only the city's police force of less than two thousand remained to defend the government. Now far stronger than the police, and with the army's machineguns and armored cars on their side, Petrograd's working men and women opened the city's prisons and called the first Soviet of Workers' and Soldiers' Deputies into session. Although some of the Duma's most prominent politicians desperately tried to regain control by forming a Provisional Committee "for the restoration of order," they could do little but preside over the demise of Imperial Russia. Less than a week after Petrograd's angry women first took to the streets, Nicholas II abdicated, and the Duma's Provisional Committee became Russia's first Provisional Government.

Joyfully Petrograd's crowds felt the weight of the fallen imperial government drop from their shoulders. "The government no longer gives any signs of life," one of the city's most celebrated poets confided to her diary one evening. "Someone, somewhere, something, is giving orders," she went on. "It's like some gigantic corpse is suffocating. And that's all. A strange sensation."[42] Almost as Maiakovskii had predicted in the closing stanzas of *Voina i Mir*, freedom came suddenly upon the men and women of Russia. "We have triumphed!" the young poet exclaimed as cheering crowds tore Russia's famed two-headed imperial eagles from buildings all across Petrograd. "Glory to us all! Glo-o-or-r-y to us all!"[43]

Freed from symbols too long associated with oppression, the Russians now set out upon a path as yet untrod by any modern nation. No one yet knew who would govern, nor did they know to whom their as yet unnamed leaders would be responsible. Men like the loyal monarchist Vasilii Shulgin hoped that sober statesmen, industrialists, and professional men and women would unite to lead Russia's foundering "state formation without a name" along the moderate political path that the nations of Western Europe had taken after the revolutions of 1830 and 1848.[44] Others, like Maiakovskii, hoped that the revolution of February 1917 marked only the first step on a journey that would carry Russia through a socialist revolution to a brave new world shaped not by the example of Europe's democracies but according to the vision of proletarian democracy in which workers' rights to food, housing, and medical care replaced the sacred Western freedoms of speech, religion, and assembly.

Unable to predict which of these courses Russia might take, the men of substance who made up the first cabinet of the revolutionary Provisional Government at the beginning of March 1917 dedicated themselves to Shulgin's more moderate course and insisted that newly liberated Russia must remain loyal to her allies. Victory in the Great War, they said, must be won before the government could turn to the urgent domestic crises that had made possible the Romanovs' overthrow, and the Russians therefore must prepare for the new and bloodier battles to come that spring and summer. Together with her common soldiers, Russia's working men and women thought differently. Although they remained uncertain about taking power into their own hands and continuing Russia's march toward a socialist revolution, Petrograd's Soviet of Workers' and Soldiers' Deputies bitterly opposed any effort to set aside the issues that had driven their comrades to overthrow the Romanovs.

Formed at the end of February to represent the city's workers and soldiers, Petrograd's Soviet of Workers' and Soldiers' Deputies became the assembly to which the civilian and military masses of the capital gave their first allegiance, and it was within its walls that Russia's revolutionary workers, soldiers, and sailors took their first steps to seize political power. Ironically, they did so in spite of their leaders' calls for caution. Too long used to debating the complexities of revolutionary theory while they remained unschooled in revolutionary practice, the men who stepped forward to lead the Petrograd Soviet during the revolution's first weeks proved to be timid advocates for Russia's proletarians. Content for the moment with the Provisional Government's promise of "complete political freedom," these halting theorists preached that the revolution neither had "the practical strength to bring about the rapid socialistic transformation of Russia, nor were the conditions yet ripe" for doing so.[45] Political power, they insisted, must be delivered first into the hands of those sober politicians who represented Russia's men and women of property, and they moved with unseemly haste to see that accomplished.

Petrograd's workers and soldiers proved much less willing than the Soviet's leaders to surrender their newly won revolutionary victories. Led by representatives of Russia's common soldiers, they approved Prikaz No. 1—"Order No. 1"—the most fateful document to emerge from the February Revolution. "Only in those cases where they do not conflict with the orders and resolutions of the Soviet of Workers' and Soldiers' Deputies," Prikaz No. 1 decreed, should the soldiers and sailors in Russia's armed forces execute the orders of the Provisional Government.[46] Russia's newly established Provisional Government thus remained responsible for governing on a day-to-day basis, but could enforce only those policies that the Soviet sanctioned. The awkward and contradictory result—what politicians and historians have called *dvoevlastie*, or dual power—left both the Provisional Government and the Soviet unable to govern effectively, while each struggled desperately to prevent the other from accomplishing its revolutionary vision.

While Russia's crises deepened that spring and summer, men and women debated their nation's future. "Across the entire country, an unending, disorderly meeting went on day and night," one young journalist wrote as he remembered how the February Revolution had loosened Russians' tongues beyond anyone's expectations.[47] Although prices had begun to soar, talk became incredibly cheap. For the moment, to speak openly, to write freely, and to disagree became ends in themselves for men and women who had been kept in silence for centuries. Everywhere, people spoke of hopes, and plans, and dreams to be fulfilled in an unceasing orgy of words. Faith in the future, as yet uncertain and undefined, captivated Russians' imaginations. "Everyone is overcome by a recognition that a miracle has occurred, and, consequently, that more miracles will follow," wrote Aleksandr Blok,[48] the passionate Symbolist poet whose verse, one admirer later confessed, had affected Petrograd's avant-garde "as the moon affects lunatics" in the days before the Great War.[49] "Freedom is extraordinarily majestic!" he exclaimed as he welcomed Russia's new revolutionary future. "Everything [now] is possible."[50]

No one personified the verbal tempest that swept across Russia in those days more vividly than Aleksandr Kerenskii, the obscure provincial lawyer who rode the crest of the revolutionary wave to become prime minister of Russia. Kerenskii had first come to Petrograd as a deputy to the Duma in 1912, where his virtuosity at shaping words to accommodate his listeners' moods and preferences had won him enthusiastic supporters among several left-wing groups. During the Great War he had nurtured his following with such success that the Okhrana identified him as the man most likely to unify Russia's badly splintered revolutionary movement long before the revolution actually broke out.[51] After the February Revolution, Kerenskii's rising star soared as he used his sensitivity to the revolution's progress to further his quest for political power. "Only Kerenskii," Shulgin concluded with reluctant admiration, "knew how to dance upon the revolutionary quagmire" in those days.[52] For several months he did so with unmatched virtuosity as he stirred crowds to anger, fierce patriotism, revolutionary zeal, or charity for the vanquished statesmen of the Old Regime as it suited his purpose.

With consummate skill, Kerenskii maneuvered to become the only person in Russia who could move freely across the barrier that *dvoevlastie* had erected between the Soviet and the Provisional Government. As vice-president of the Petrograd Soviet, he claimed to be "the hostage of revolutionary democracy" in the camp of the "bourgeoisie,"[53] while as minister of justice in the Provisional Government's first cabinet he announced his moral mission to "keep the revolution undefiled by shameful bloodshed" and prevent revolutionary extremists from taking revenge against their former oppressors.[54] One contemporary recalled him "pallid, and with an outstretched arm," striding forth "like the flaming sword of revolutionary justice"[55] to save fallen tsarist statesmen from crowds of vengeful proletarians. In factories, at street rallies, and in the Soviet, Kerenskii preached the doctrine of Russia's revolutionary rebirth. Everywhere he summoned men and women to believe in the future, never telling its content or offering a clear program, but always speaking with a passion that infected his listeners with his enthusiasm for the new order that would, by definition, be better than the past or present.

Unleashing verbal torrents upon his audiences as he struggled to keep the revolution's natural anarchy from diverting its progress, Kerenskii always gave the impression that he stood at the revolution's vortex. Konstantin Paustovskii, a young streetcar conductor in tsarist Russia whose literary portrayals of the agonies that men and women suffered during wartime eventually won him the Lenin Prize, remembered Kerenskii's "lemon-colored puffy face . . . reddened eyelids, and . . . close-cropped, thinning, grayish hair," as he struggled to "knock the broken pieces of Russia back together with his ecstatic eloquence."[56] Ambassador Paléologue thought Kerenskii acted "like a monomaniac or one possessed" and reported that, at certain moments, "a mysterious or prophetically apocalyptic inspiration . . . radiates around him in magnetic waves."[57] Some fifteen years later, Robert Bruce Lockhart, Britain's vice-consul in Russia during 1917, still recalled an "epic performance" by Kerenskii in Moscow as being "more impressive in its emotional reactions than any [early] speech of Hitler."[58] Proclaiming that "I am sent by the Revolution!" Kerenskii thus became the personification of the new order for many Russians during the spring and summer of 1917.[59] He promised his listeners everything but gave them nothing, and people always found it easier to recall how he had spoken than to report what he had said. One of his arch enemies concluded at the time that Kerenskii "expressed more completely than anyone else the first epoch of the revolution, its 'national' formlessness, [and] the idealism of its hopes and expectations."[60]

What Kerenskii's enemies called his "formless radicalism of phrase"[61] worked its magic upon the hearts of men and women ready to be captivated by a golden tongue, but it could do nothing to feed, clothe, house, or protect them. Even before the Revolution, inflation had begun to drive too many men and women who had clawed their way into the lower middle class back into the depths of poverty. Now the shortages grew worse, and prices soared until inflation threatened Russia's workers with starvation. In 1914, a single ruble had bought enough food to produce 1,400 calories; now, it bought a mere 168![62] "A terrible war, an acute food shortage, a paralyzed transportation system, an empty treasury, and a population in a state of furious discontent and anarchic disintegration" was the heritage that Nicholas II's fallen government had bequeathed, Kerenskii later explained. Although gross efforts at self-justification were to mar much of what he published after the Revolution, in that instance, Kerenskii wrote the simple truth.[63]

Throughout 1917, people spoke of the "broad Russian nature" and its potential for exploring untried courses. Yet it was self-discipline, not revolutionary enthusiasm, that was needed to save the Russians from themselves that spring. Clearly, the Revolution's anarchistic turbulence had to be brought under control. Workers had to be gotten back to their looms and their lathes, peasants had to be urged to get on with their spring planting, and trains had to be made to move again. At the front, where soldiers had taken to electing their commanders and voting about whether to obey orders to attack, discipline had to be restored. In the rear, the rule of law had to be reestablished among peasants who felt free to seize others' lands and workers who demanded control of the factories in which they were supposed to work. "What was wanted," England's acid-tongued military attaché to Russia later remarked, "was a little narrow common sense."[64] Yet there seemed to be no way to bring Russia's unruly masses to heel without betraying the Revolution's most cherished principles. Failing to understand, as Paustovskii later wrote, that "the establishment of justice and freedom was going to require a great deal of hard work and, even, some brutality,"[65] Russians continued to celebrate their newly won freedom in a manner certain to destroy it. Moscow's thieves held mass meetings to discuss "liberty, equality, and brotherhood," while they plied their trade with greater enthusiasm than ever. So did the city's prostitutes.[66] That summer, as the Russians prepared to launch a new offensive with divisions whose discipline had crumbled, the Petrograd Soviet abolished the death penalty for deserters and for soldiers who refused to attack.

Worst of all, the Great War continued. In addition to more than a million refugees who had perished from starvation and disease, Russia's losses in men killed, wounded, and taken captive had passed the six million mark before the revolution had broken out in February. Enemy victories had cost Russia half a million square miles of territory that had produced a tenth of her iron ore, a fifth of her coal, and two-thirds of her chemicals before the war. The great industrial centers of Warsaw, Radom, Lublin, and Łódż all lay behind enemy lines, as did some of Russia's mostfertile farmlands.[67] War had touched the life of each Russian directly, and there was not the comforting sense of isolation from the fighting as there was in England, where such fashionable London shops as Fortnum and Mason's and Harrod's sent special gift packages of gingerbread, cakes, tarts, and even fresh flowers to men who fought beyond the English Channel.[68] For Russians in 1917, the Great War had become too frightful, too pervasive, and too near.

Although the Petrograd crowd that had toppled the government of Nicholas II in February 1917 had borne placards that proclaimed "Down with the War," the statesmen who replaced the Tsar's fallen ministers failed to take their message seriously. Pavel Miliukov, leader of Russia's liberal Constitutional Democrats and a long-time student of his nation's policies in the Near East, insisted that it was "necessary to save Russia by carrying on the war to victory,"[69] and as the Provisional Government's stern and professorial minister of foreign affairs, he had promised his nation's allies that Russia would continue to fight "against the common enemy until the end, without cessation and without faltering."[70] In doing so, he enraged the Petrograd Soviet, whose representatives had called upon the "toilers of all countries . . . [to] refuse to serve as an instrument of violence and conquest in the hands of kings, landlords, and bankers" and had promised that, "by our united efforts, Russia's workers would put an end to this frightful carnage."[71] When Miliukov insisted that "Russia would fight to the last drop of her blood"[72] and spoke of her firm resolve "to bring the World War to a decisive victory,"[73] Petrograd's workers and soldiers stormed into the streets. Armed and angry, they provoked the April Crisis that drove Miliukov and his supporters from office.

That Miliukov's determination to continue the war had cost him the Foreign Ministry did not mean that Kerenskii, whose voice dominated the new cabinet, was prepared to make peace. As Russia's new minister of war and navy, he insisted that his nation must fight on, not for the annexations and indemnities with which her allies had promised to reward her, but to protect the Revolution and avoid the great territorial losses that defeat would bring. "For the sake of the nation's life," he later explained, "it was necessary to restore the army's will to die."[74] Soldiers must be convinced to fight again, and commanders must be given the authority to order men into battle if Russia was ever to have an efficient fighting force.

Kerenskii knew that "an unshakable, almost automatic conviction of the inevitability and necessity of sacrifice must rule the hearts of Russia's soldiers" if Russia was not to be left standing defenseless before her enemies. Determined to "make it possible again for everybody to look death in the face calmly and unflinchingly," he stormed back and forth along the front that spring and summer. "Forward to the battle for freedom!" he proclaimed in his grandest manner. "I summon you not to a feast but to death!"[75] To him it seemed certain that soldiers who had fought for a tsar and society that had offered them so few material rewards now should gladly sacrifice their lives for the Revolution that had given them freedom. "Let the freest Army . . . in the world prove that there is strength and not weakness in Liberty," he exclaimed. "Let them forge a new iron discipline of duty."[76]

As the commander-in-chief of the forces on Russia's western front explained some years later, "the *word* created hypnosis and self-hypnosis,"[77] and, for a brief moment, it seemed that Kerenskii's ringing summons to war had stirred the hearts of men long wearied of the Great War's killing. But it was one thing to stir men's hearts and quite another to convince them to face machine-gun bullets and artillery shells. Russia's millions of peasants in uniform defined freedom in the very concrete sense of being free to seize for themselves the land that belonged to aristocrats and landlords, and that posed a dilemma that no amount of golden rhetoric could resolve. "What's the use of the peasants getting land," one peasant soldier asked, "if I'm killed and get no land?"[78] Given the choice between answering Kerenskii's summons to die for freedom and seizing the lands that they and their ancestors had looked upon with such longing for so many years, Russia's land-hungry peasant soldiers walked away from the war by the tens of thousands during the summer of 1917. "They recalled to mind a vast migration of peoples," the Menshevik memoirist Nikolai Sukhanov wrote in amazement.[79] Always, this ever-growing wave of humanity flowed eastward, anxious to forget the fighting and the killing in order to return to their villages and seize whatever lands opportunity might put in their way. "The war was becoming more and more unbearable," Sukhanov remembered. "The elemental forces against the war, against its support, and against its entire organization were accumulating."[80]

As hordes of soldiers left the front and public opposition to the war deepened in the rear, Kerenskii announced a new offensive. Thanks to the Allies' efforts, the Russians' heavy guns outnumbered the enemy's, and they had enough shells to support their advancing troops properly for the first time since the first days of the war. Too quickly, Kerenskii rushed to proclaim a handful of successes as a "great triumph of the Revolution,"[81] only to see his nation's war-weary soldiers turn their backs on victory. When some units received orders to attack, they elected committees to discuss them. Others retreated even before the Germans and Austrians launched their first counterattacks, and still others actually overran enemy positions and then withdrew without a shot having been fired in their direction. "The army is on the run," one commander reported. "It is hard to conjecture where the enemy might be stopped."[82] The army remained "nothing but human dust," one disgusted commander concluded less than a month after Kerenskii's offensive. Another estimated that, if all the men who had retreated were brought to trial, "half the army would end up in Siberia."[83]

As summer neared its end, men at both ends of the political spectrum acted upon visions of Russia's future that diverged sharply from Kerenskii's own. As Kerenskii himself later confessed, that summer's defeats had caused many of his countrymen to yearn for "a general on a white horse"[84] to weld their nation's human and institutional shards back together. To some, General Lavr Kornilov, the daring son of a Siberian Cossack, whose "courage, coolness, and contempt for death,"[85] General Denikin later explained, had made him a legend in a nation starved for heroes, seemed to be the man to do so. While Kerenskii hesitated to take the stern measures required to halt the army's collapse that summer for fear of angering his supporters in the Petrograd Soviet, Kornilov had unashamedly hanged deserters at every crossroads in the rear of his Eighth Army. The lives of "a few cowards and traitors," he had stated bluntly when criticized for his action, was a small price to pay to "save many innocent lives."[86] Now, perhaps hoping that Kornilov's hero's aura would brighten his own dimming star, Kerenskii appointed him supreme commander of Russia's armies in mid-July, only to find that Kornilov was neither biddable nor cooperative when it came to allowing politics to moderate the stern principles that ruled his life.[87] The two men were bound to clash.

Kornilov's first direct confrontation with Kerenskii came in mid-August, when both addressed the State Conference in Moscow, where, in sharp contrast to Petrograd, a more moderate political atmosphere prevailed. As men and women spoke of property, order, and security in words not heard since the February Revolution, Kornilov 's flatly-stated warning that "only an army welded together by iron discipline" could save Russia from disaster provoked an enthusiastic response,[88] while the theatrical rantings with which Kerenskii had so often delighted Petrograd's proletarians received a less sympathetic reception. After their meeting in Moscow, neither man trusted the other, and their mutual antagonism soon led to an open break between them. At the end of August, Kerenskii's suspicion that Russia's supreme commander was about to seize the reins of government, and Kornilov's certainty that Kerenskii had betrayed his vow to restore order in the army, culminated in the "Kornilov Revolt," in which Kornilov marched upon Petrograd to save the city from the pact he believed Kerenskii had struck with the Bolsheviks. With the resources of Russia's front-line commanders at his disposal, Kornilov's victory seemed certain, yet, to the unanimous surprise of Allied diplomats and military attachés in Petrograd, Kerenskii triumphed. In less than a week he took near-dictatorial powers and the title of supreme commander of Russia's armed forces, while Kornilov and several of the generals who had stood closest to him found themselves imprisoned on charges of treason.[89]

With Kornilov's arrest, the last remnants of discipline in Russia's armies collapsed. Bitter, disillusioned, and tired of living "facing machine guns while machine guns pointed at their backs," as Aleksei Tolstoi explained in his great novel about the Revolution and Civil War, Russia's peasant soldiers moved eastward toward peace and home, "home to the land, home to their women." The great tide of deserters that flowed away from the front that summer now swelled into a human flood so vast that none could count its numbers. Tolstoi described the herds of crawling troop-trains—their windows shattered, their doors torn from their hinges, their roofs and couplings cluttered with men unable to force their way inside—cutting their way across the great Russian steppe "like plowshares, leaving in their wake a trail of battered railway stations, smashed rolling-stock, and looted towns." Nothing deterred them. "They froze to death," Tolstoi wrote. "They were killed under the wheels and smashed their heads against the cross-girders of bridges," but still the human tide continued to flow, "home to divide up the lands" that they had looked at with such longing for so long.[90]

As her armed masses flowed homeward in the days after the Kornilov Revolt, Russia's political horizon darkened. Never had Russian workers had so many weapons in their hands; never before had so many been trained to use them. "All the dark instincts of the crowd, irritated by the disintegration of life and by the lies and filth of politics, will flare up and fume, poisoning us with anger, hate, and revenge," the dean of Russia's proletarian writers, Maksim Gorkii predicted that fall. "People will kill one another, unable to suppress their own animal stupidity," he warned. "They will fire . . . [at each other] only because . . . [they] want to kill their fear."[91] Unlike Gorkii, Lenin and Trotskii were delighted by that course of events. As the Bolsheviks won their first majorities in the soviets of Moscow, Petrograd, and the Ukrainian capital of Kiev in early September, Lenin rejoiced that "all the objective conditions exist for a successful insurrection,"[92] and he shifted course dramatically. In contrast to those revolutionary leaders who continued to insist that Russia's workers ought to leave the business of government to others for some time to come, he now insisted that "the present task must be an *armed uprising* in Petrograd and Moscow, the seizure of power, and the overthrow of the government."[93] "The crisis has matured," Lenin insisted as he thrust aside the pleas of his shocked comrades on the Bolsheviks' Central Committee that they had not yet the strength to overthrow Kerenskii's government. "The whole future of the revolution is at stake."[94]

On the night of October 10, at a secret meeting in an out-of-the-way apartment on the outer edge of one of Petrograd's working-class districts, the Bolsheviks settled their differences and agreed to an uneasy peace that committed the majority of the Central Committee to Lenin's daring revolutionary course. Obliged to remain in hiding because Kerenskii had ordered the police to arrest him on sight, Lenin now looked on while Trotskii led the Bolsheviks toward the armed uprising that he believed to be "inevitable and imminent."[95] Blessed with a gift for bending crowds to his will, Trotskii set out to make Lenin's prediction come true. "The time for words has passed," he thundered. "The hour has come for a duel to the death between the revolution and the counterrevolution."[96] In a fortnight, Trotskii's followers were ready. On the afternoon of October 24, two of his agents, both of whom had forgotten to bring weapons, took command of Petrograd's Central Telegraph Office to signal the beginning of the armed insurrection that Lenin had promised. In less than forty-eight hours the Bolsheviks had driven Kerenskii from office, seized control of Petrograd, issued their famous decrees on land and peace, and established Russia's first government of people's commissars. So quickly had the October Revolution succeeded that even Lenin seemed stunned for a moment. "You know," he confided to Trotskii on the evening that Kerenskii's government fell, "to pass so quickly from persecutions and living in hiding to power—*es schwindelt*—it makes one's head spin!"[97]

The moment he had arrived in Petrograd in April 1917, Lenin had promised the Russians "peace and land." These stood at the center of the masses' hopes and dreams, although every cabinet of the Provisional Government that had ruled Russia between March and October had failed to understand that obvious fact, and each had fallen for that simple reason. No longer could peasant soldiers be coaxed into battle by promises too often postponed. Nor could they be denied their share of the Revolution's fruits. Without peace and land, Russian soldiers refused to give their lives to defend either the Revolution or Russia. As Kornilov had warned his listeners at the Moscow State Conference in August, the events of 1917 had "transformed [the army] into a mindless mob, valuing nothing but its own life."[98] No one understood that better than Lenin, and he therefore spoke of peace the moment the Bolsheviks overthrew Kerenskii's government. "The question of peace is a burning question," he told the Second All-Russian Congress of Soviets on the evening of October 26. "The overwhelming majority of the working class and other working people of all the belligerent countries," he continued, "are craving . . . an immediate peace," and Russia must therefore take the lead in calling for a peace "without annexations . . . and without indemnities." Her victorious proletariat must stop at nothing to bring the fighting to an end.[99]

For the first time in thirty-nine months, Russians began to believe that peace had become possible, but the war's end proved to be much more elusive than Lenin or his listeners had expected. Even as Lenin addressed the Second All-Russian Congress of Soviets on October 26, a new and more terrible conflict already had begun as men and women who stood to lose too much under Lenin's revolutionary socialist government vowed to fight to regain what the October Revolution promised to take from them. On the Pulkovo Heights, within sight of revolutionary Petrograd, Trotskii's Red Guards fought against the Whites for the first time on the morning of Monday, October 30, 1917, and the confrontation sowed new seeds of hatred whose bitter harvest Russians were destined to reap for four long years. "Oh God, we haven't seen the end of it yet!" the poet Zinaida Gippius exclaimed as the men she called Lenin's "pack of scoundrels"[100] began to tighten their grip on the prize they had won. This one-time lioness of Petrograd's avant-garde salons, now middle-aged, stared into "a nocturnal void filled with black, clotting blood"[101] to learn the shape of Russia's future. Then she confided her worst fears to her diary: "*Civil war without end and without limit!*"[102]

Others felt the same and began to prepare. Several hundred miles to the southwest, where a long-abandoned Roman Catholic monastery in the ancient western Russian town of Bykhov had been converted into a small prison, General Kornilov and the comrades who had stood with him against Kerenskii had spent a tedious fall under arrest. There, under the monastery's low roof, behind deep-set windows whose ancient iron bars remained still in place, Russia's former quartermaster general Ivan Romanovskii shared a spartan second-floor room with Anton Denikin, former commander-in-chief of Russia's western and southwestern fronts, and Denikin's long-time friend and faithful chief of staff General Sergei Markov. General Aleksandr Lukomskii, an officer of scrupulous honesty who had refused Kerenskii's offer of his fallen chief's position, occupied a solitary room next door to Kornilov, who also enjoyed the comparative luxury of a small room to himself. Kornilov's guards still called him *verkhovnyi* (a title held in particular esteem and reserved for the Supreme Commander of Russia's armies) and treated him and his comrades with all the deference that their high positions had commanded before their arrests. "We had the impression," General Denikin recalled, "that everyone was embarrassed about having to act as our 'jailers.' "[103]

Guarded by Kornilov's Tekintsy, the fierce Central Asian tribesmen who had been his protectors during his days as Russia's supreme commander, these five generals had spent the fall of 1917 waiting for the public trial they had demanded to prove their innocence. Despite their guards' repeated urgings, they had made no effort to flee during those crucial October days when Kerenskii's frantic efforts to stem the Revolution's leftward march had collapsed into futile self-delusions and outright political paralysis.[104] Nor did they join the fight of Krasnov's Whites against the Reds on the Pulkovo Heights at the end of October. Only after Lenin's supporters seized Moscow, sent a Bolshevik ensign to take command at Supreme Headquarters, and began to extend their authority throughout Central Russia did Kornilov and his comrades conclude that they must escape because they—and the Russia in which they believed—could survive only if they declared war upon their enemies.

In that thought they were not alone. During the winter of 1917–1918, many of the moderate and sober men who had led Russia's government and armies during the first eight months of the Revolution made their way southward from Petrograd and Moscow toward Novocherkassk, the capital of the lands of the Don Cossacks, in search of the means to overthrow the Bolsheviks. Mikhail Rodzianko, the loyal monarchist who, as president of the Duma, had pleaded in vain with Nicholas II to rule wisely before revolution devoured them all, went there in mid-November after traveling the entire 740 miles from Moscow disguised as an invalid whose vast 280-pound bulk had to be confined to a wheelchair. Miliukov, who had always preferred monarchies to republics, followed him, and dozens more arrived closely upon their heels. Some came alone; others traveled in small groups. One clever army nurse escorted several hundred able-bodied White officers from Moscow to Novocherkassk by disguising them as sick and wounded soldiers.[105] In the past some had been rivals, even enemies. Now united by their hatred of the Reds, they stood together as Whites who pledged themselves to free Russia from her Bolshevik rulers.

Many of these weary political refugees dreamed of a "White General"—a man of fierce patriotism, legendary daring, and iron will who would free them from the tyranny of the mob, save Russia from destruction, and somehow restore their nation's lost greatness—to lead them against the Reds.[106] Some hoped to find him in General Mikhail Alekseev, who, for all practical purposes, had commanded Russia's armies between August 1915 and February 1917 as Nicholas II's chief of staff and had become revolutionary Russia's first supreme commander after his emperor had lost his throne. But Alekseev was far too quiet, plain, and modest to project the aura of authority expected from Russia's White savior. Many influential men and women therefore looked to the Bykhov generals. They looked to Kornilov most of all.

By mid-November Bykhov's imprisoned generals knew that they must join the White migration to Novocherkassk or face certain death at the hands of the Red Guards who were marching in their direction.[107] Disguised as an ensign, and armed with forged documents, Romanovskii set out directly for Novocherkassk by train on November 19, while the elegant, fastidious Markov transformed himself into a swaggering, cursing private to travel as his orderly. As Markov and Romanovskii began their journey south, Lukomskii traveled east. His impeccably groomed Vandyke beard shaved clean and his general's overcoat replaced by a peasant's sheepskin, Lukomskii slowly made his way to Moscow aboard trains packed with deserters before he turned toward the Don lands. Posing as the civilian assistant to the director of a Polish first aid unit, Denikin in the meantime made his way southeast to Kharkov and Rostov. Then, like his comrades, he too turned toward Novocherkassk.

More than any of his comrades, Denikin sensed the pulse of the new Russia during his journey and felt the depths of the anger that overflowed from its trenches, factories, and peasant huts into its cities and villages. Wherever he turned, Denikin saw the enraged masses smashing whatever symbols of the old order had survived Russia's first nine months of revolutionary turmoil. No one and no thing escaped. Officers who reprimanded privates for being drunk, businessmen and aristocrats whose better manners spoiled their efforts to travel in disguise—even the velvet upholstery in the first- and second-class carriages from which their poverty had excluded them before the Revolution—all became targets of the primitive outrage of men and women oppressed for too long. "I saw clearly . . . unbounded hatred everywhere," Denikin remembered. "Only one desire reigned supreme—to seize or destroy. Its aim seemed to be not to better itself, but to drag down to its level anything that in one way or another stood out or seemed different."[108] A few months later, Trotskii explained the masses' anger differently. "Perhaps for the first time in his life, the exhausted, down-trodden Russian peasant . . . found himself in a first-class compartment and saw the velvet upholstery," he told a group of cadets at Moscow's new Military Academy in an effort to describe how the Revolution had brought Russia's masses to life. "In his own boots he had nothing but stinking rags to wrap his feet, and so he tore off the velvet saying that he too had the right to have something good."[109]

Although patrols of rude Red Guards checked their forged papers on several tense occasions and every railroad station displayed posters warning travelers to be on the lookout for them, it took the four fugitive generals from Bykhov only a few days to reach the safety of the Don Cossack lands. Only for Kornilov, who had scorned the disguises and forged papers upon which his comrades had chosen to rely and had marched away from Bykhov at the head of his Tekintsy, did the journey take longer. Such daring bordered upon foolhardiness, for four hundred red-coated Asiatic tribesmen could not pass unnoticed, even in a land where communications were as shattered as they had become in revolutionary Russia. Bolshevik Red Guard units quickly charted Kornilov's line of march and moved to the attack. For more than a week the Tekintsy fought off Red Guard assaults, but their resolve to continue broke before they had covered even half the distance to the Don. As the Tekintsy opted for peace, Kornilov hastily exchanged his general's uniform for peasant rags and continued his journey alone. On December 6 he finally limped into the railroad station at Novocherkassk, looking for all the world like the tattered old Romanian peasant refugee that his forged passport proclaimed him to be.[110]

Even before Kornilov reached Novocherkassk, the fighting began in South Russia. On November 26, Bolshevik factory workers in the nearby industrial center of Rostov revolted against the authority of the Cossack General Aleksei Kaledin and seized the city. As he recaptured Rostov with the help of a handful of officers from the fledgling White Army a week later, Kaledin was all too conscious of the battle's tragedy. "My heart is heavy," he told Rostov's citizens when he entered their city on December 2. "Blood was shed and we have nothing to be glad about."[111] He spoke a truth more bitter than he knew. Russia's Civil War, which would claim the lives of Kaledin, all the Bykhov generals except for Denikin and Lukomskii, and millions of men and women as victims of battles, executions, starvation, and disease during the next three years, had begun a full three months before Lenin freed Russia from the Great War's grip.

Raw cruelty and fanaticism unlike anything seen in those gigantic battles of the Great War became a part of Russia's Civil War from its beginning. On one occasion, Whites filled three freight cars with the bodies of Red Guards, their frozen corpses "placed in obscene positions," according to one observer, and returned them to their starving enemies marked "fresh meat, destination

Petrograd."[112] Some months later, General Denikin remembered, a diver found the bodies of a group of White officers whom the Reds had drowned in the harbor at Novorossiisk, their "livid, greenish, swollen, mangled corpses kept upright owing to the weights tied to their legs [so that they] stood in serried ranks, swaying to and fro, as if talking to one another."[113] All over Russia it was the same, as Red and White terror condemned men and women to suffer for what they were, not for what they had done.

Although the Reds' brutality stemmed in part from that instinctive hatred of privilege that Denikin had witnessed during his incognito journey to Novocherkassk, it grew much more from their desire to defend a vision of the future and a new order that offered broader opportunity and promised greater justice than they could have hoped to enjoy under any White government. For this they killed willingly and justified their cruelest acts by the self-righteous vow that (to quote a Bolshevik commissar for foreign affairs) "in Russia, violence is employed only for the sake of the sacred interests of liberation of the masses."[114] Thus, any amount of brutality could be justified in the name of the masses. "The bourgeoisie of international imperialism killed ten million and mutilated twenty million human beings in its war . . . to decide whether British or German robbers should rule the whole world," Lenin explained at one point. "If our war, the war of the oppressed and exploited against the oppressors and exploiters, will cost half a million or a million victims . . . the bourgeoisie will say that the former sacrifices were justified, [but that] the latter [were] criminal."[115]

While the Reds killed to implement Lenin's vision, the Whites' vicious treatment of Reds came from their certainty that a Russia founded upon Lenin's principles would deprive them of everything they had hoped to bring with them from the old Russia into the new. Always the Whites relied upon an elite to shape the future and lead the Russian masses to it. "Where does salvation come from in times like these?" General Lukomskii once asked. "Certainly not from any great deeds on the part of the masses, which are always gray, colorless, and small-minded," he went on, "but from the heroic deeds of the best and chosen men. . . . People, not the masses," Lukomskii concluded, "make history."[116]

In December 1917, the Russians therefore turned upon each other in deadly fury, certain that the Russian land could not accommodate Red and White together. Yet, as their leaders prepared for the bitter battles that would determine their nation's future course, others struggled to survive the present. At the beginning of 1918, Russia's people faced hunger on a scale more massive than any they had known in modern times. The hungry spring of 1918, when the food ration in Petrograd and Moscow plummeted to a tenth of the calories needed to sustain men and women engaged in manual labor, brought many within a hair's breadth of not surviving at all.

CHAPTER ONE

The Hungry Spring

DURING THE YEAR after the Petrograd crowd had driven the Romanovs from their throne, Russians had reveled in an orgy of proletarian self-indulgence. At the front, soldiers elected committees to discuss whether to retreat or attack; in the rear, factory workers demanded exorbitant raises, bonuses, and control over their employers. Peasants rampaged across the countryside, burned manor houses, killed landlords, and seized lands and livestock. Working men and women stopped cleaning streets, repairing trains, running lathes and looms, and plowing fields to take part in an endless succession of impromptu assemblies and political speeches. "Russia had started talking," the young revolutionary journalist Konstantin Paustovskii explained. "In a few months Russia managed to say all those things about which she had been obliged to keep silent for centuries."[1] In this new revolutionary world, Russians believed that anything was possible and that nothing stood beyond their reach. "With the 'broad Russian nature' experiments are possible that could not be tried in Western countries," they promised one another during those days. "Russia will find a Dostoevskii, not a Napoleon!"[2]

Bright promises for the future could not remove the danger of the present. With no traditional frame of reference within which to command obedience, the Provisional Government had worked at cross-purposes with Russia's soviets of workers' and soldiers' deputies as disasters far greater than any that had brought the Revolution loomed above them all. "Russia is not ripe for a purely democratic form of government," England's ambassador Sir George Buchanan warned his superiors at the Foreign Office. "The Russian idea of liberty," he wrote in disgust, "is to take things easy, to claim double wages, to demonstrate in the streets, and to waste time in talking and in passing resolutions at public meetings."[3] By the fall of 1917, Russia thus stood at the brink of defeat, starvation, and economic collapse. Only if order returned could her proletarians—"weak, ignorant people, with an inborn inclination toward anarchism" in the words of Maksim Gorkii[4]—hope to see the future of which they had dreamed and talked so eagerly throughout the year.

That some form of the stern authority to which the Russians had been accustomed to respond throughout their history must be restored thus was only too clear to Lenin and his Bolsheviks from the moment they overthrew Kerenskii's crumbling Provisional Government. "Learn discipline from the Germans," Lenin exhorted his followers during the weeks that followed. "We must produce order."[5] Trotskii echoed the same theme. "The only way to save ourselves is by dogged labor and revolutionary discipline," he insisted. "Work, order, persistence, self-sacrifice, and discipline—then we shall triumph!"[6] Discipline imposed from above had always distinguished the Bolsheviks' revolutionary organization from its rivals. Now it became a key element in their struggle against the chaos of 1917.

Nowhere was this chaos more clearly etched upon Russia's countenance than in Petrograd, where shortages of food, fuel, goods, and public services threatened to overwhelm the city. Never in Petrograd's two-hundred-year history had life been worse for its people, nor as uncertain, as the Bolsheviks' revolutionary egalitarianism erased all the traditional points of reference at once. Before the end of 1917, Russia's new government abolished church marriage and made divorce available on demand. Gold, silver, precious stones, large savings accounts, and certain factories all became state property, and so did large private homes, into which the Bolsheviks immediately began to move tens of thousands of former slum dwellers. "Everything was being canceled," Aleksei Tolstoi wrote at the beginning of *1918*, the second part of his Stalin Prize-winning trilogy about the Revolution and Civil War. "Ranks, honors, pensions, officers' epaulettes, the thirtieth letter of the alphabet, God, private property, and even the right to live as one wished—all were being canceled."[7] When he returned to Petrograd that winter, the young literary critic Viktor Shklovskii thought the atmosphere in the city seemed "like after an explosion, when it's all over, when everything's blown up."[8] Some felt that "the city of Peter the Great was dying."[9] For others, life in the capital of the new Russia took on a dullness that no amount of revolutionary fervor could enliven. Once the grande dame of the city's literary salons, the poet Zinaida Gippius now declared life in Bolshevik Petrograd to be boring above all else. "What I am going to say at this moment is very strange," she confided to her diary that winter, "but it is *boring* for me to write. Yes, even . . . among these loathsome and unprecedented horrors . . . it is boring."[10]

None who lived in Petrograd at the end of 1917 could doubt the speed with which the old Russia—the Russia of privilege, wealth, and grinding poverty—was breaking up. "All that was real, all that was vital—the best and the worst of men—lay close to the surface," one American journalist recalled as she described the uncertainty of those turbulent days.[11] Overnight, people of no experience or accomplishment rose to command, while men and women of rank and distinction fell into abject poverty. Revolutionary sailors turned the Stroganovs' gorgeous baroque palace, with which Russia's greatest eighteenth-century architect Rastrelli had adorned the corner of Nevskii Prospekt and the Moika Embankment, into an amusement center for their off-duty hours. "They smoke their cigarettes and spit out their sunflower seeds beneath the Claude Lorrains and the Poussins," the French diplomat Louis de Robien lamented. "They want to make openings in the wonderful paneling in the ballroom and turn it into a cinema!"

Everywhere, men and women who had stood on the peaks of old Russia slipped to its lowest depths, as Petrograd's new masters insisted that those they once had served now must serve them. "I saw an old general and a priest—the old Russia itself—clearing the streets of snow in order not to die of starvation," de Robien reported elsewhere in his diary.[12] Princess Obolenskaia was seen clearing snow from the Fontanka Embankment in the very center of the city, and Countess Sofiia Panina had to stand trial for embezzlement because she refused to turn over to the Bolsheviks a hundred thousand rubles entrusted to her by Kerenskii's government. "Our grandfathers, great-grandfathers, and fathers all had to clean up the shit and filth of your grandfathers and fathers," Trotskii exclaimed at one point. "Now you are going to do the same thing for us."[13]

Petrograd was awash with tales of lives broken and hopes lost. "Officers, barristers, school-masters, and engineers got employment as house-porters [and] as messengers . . . [while others] were breaking [up] the ice, selling newspapers, cigarettes, and chocolate," one sympathetic observer remembered.[14] Rumor had it that a former colonel in the elite Imperial Guards had been seen begging a bowl of soup from the head waiter who had served him in better times at the once-elegant Evropeiskaia Hotel.[15] Others found themselves in even more desperate straits, and more than a few formerly well-to-do wives and daughters turned to prostitution rather than see their families starve.[16] Perhaps nothing captured the sad spirit of the fallen in those days better than the watercolors of Ivan Vladimirov, one of which portrayed Prince Vasilshchikov sitting on a crumbling stone wall in an overgrown courtyard. Vasilshchikov's ragged trousers still bore the broad red stripe of a tsarist general, but the goat that stood tethered to his bony wrist spoke amply of the wretched plight of Russia's former lords, who faced poverty and physical danger at every turn.[17]

Violence—or the threat of it—seemed everywhere that winter, as mobs of armed soldiers roamed Petrograd's streets. Numbered at more than a hundred thousand at the beginning of 1917, the city's garrison had grown steadily as men joined it to "defend" the Revolution. Soldiers clustered on street corners, barged through the crowds that clogged Petrograd's sidewalks, and forced their way onto streetcars from which people hung by any available handhold. "There always were so many soldiers about in the streets of Petrograd that civilians were swallowed up by their greyish tidal-wave," one woman remembered. "Civilians hurried to hide themselves," she continued. "[They tried] to run away, to get into the shadow."[18]

War had long since rendered life cheap; now, too many gray-coated men with too many guns made violence a way of life. Soldiers and ex-soldiers killed for money, for such luxuries as furs and jewelry, for clothing, and for food. Sometimes they killed for no reason at all. Not more than five minutes' walk from the American Embassy, de Robien saw two soldiers shoot an old woman street-vendor rather than pay for two of the stunted green apples she offered for sale.[19] "When you recall that all this is going on in a country where human life is ridiculously cheap, where there is no respect for the individual and his work, and when you think that the 'simplicity' of killing becomes a 'habit,' an 'everyday occurrence,' you grow fearful for Russia," Maksim Gorkii wrote at the end of January. Himself risen from their midst, Gorkii feared the masses' dark, brooding violence and explained the "unspeakably foul" acts of Petrograd's soldiers as a product of Russia's sad past.[20] De Robien viewed the situation more generously. "These simple people, who for four years have been allowed to kill and be rewarded for it with crosses and decorations, now do it automatically," he explained sadly. "They know of no other rule than that of the rifle and the bayonet."[21]

As murder became commonplace on Petrograd's streets, robbery grew rampant, leaving no person safe, and no one's possessions immune. According to one estimate, almost eight hundred robberies occurred in Petrograd every day during January 1918, as the Russians stole from their government, their church, and each other with equal enthusiasm.[22] One winter night, Petrograd's robbers even dragged Moisei Uritskii from his sleigh, stole every stitch of his clothing, and left him to make his way home naked.[23] That Uritskii commanded the Petrograd Cheka, the Bolsheviks' newly established security police force, did not deter the thieves in the slightest. "As is well known, one of the loudest and most heartily welcomed slogans of our peculiarly Russian revolution has been the slogan: 'Rob the robbers!' " Gorkii wrote. "No doubt history will tell of this process of Russia's self-robbery with the greatest inspiration," he added with bitter sarcasm. "This is an 'original,' and we can be proud—there was nothing similar even in the era of the Great French Revolution."[24]

Nowhere did proletarians rob Petrograd's rich with more enthusiasm than in their assaults upon their wine cellars. During the October Revolution there had been scattered instances in which Red Guards and groups of workers had broken into stores of wine and spirits, but the full force of the storm—the so-called wine riots—broke only a month later, when Petrograd's workers invaded the cellars of the Winter Palace and then the cellars of grand dukes, great lords, rich merchants, and some of the city's best shops and restaurants. To the Bolsheviks' dismay, their hand-picked guards joined the workers all too readily. "The Preobrazhenskii [Guards] Regiment assigned to guard these cellars got totally drunk," one of Petrograd's senior Red Guard commanders wrote. "We sent guards from various other picked units—all got utterly drunk. We posted guards especially chosen from regimental committees [i.e. men long known for their dedication to the Revolution]—they succumbed as well. We dispatched armored cars to drive away the crowd. After patrolling up and down a few times, they also began to weave suspiciously. . . . We tried sealing up the entrances with brick—the crowd came back through the windows, smashing in the gratings and seizing what remained. We tried flooding the cellars with water—the firemen sent to do the job got drunk instead." Finally, a detachment of sailors, described as "men of iron, more used to killing than drinking" ended the orgy by smashing the casks and bottles that remained unemptied in the cellars of Russia's former tsars.[25] "It is sickening to see such good stuff thrown away," de Robien lamented to his diary. "There were bottles of Tokay there from the time of Catherine the Great."[26]

Bottles containing some of Château Mouton-Rothschild's greatest vintages perished in the mob's assault against Grand Duke Pavel Aleksandrovich's palace at nearby Tsarskoe Selo. Contant's elegant restaurant, the favorite of those diplomats who still remained in the city, only kept its wine cellars intact by hiring special detachments of machine-gun-carrying guards.[27] "[It was] as if guerrilla warfare was going on for the right of entrance to the kingdom of Bacchus," one observer remembered.[28]

Trotskii called for the sternest measures to bring Petrograd under control. "If you do not succeed in barring the path to drunken excess, all you will have left in the way of defenses will be the armored cars," he warned the Petrograd Soviet on December 2. "Remember this," he concluded. "Each day of drunkenness brings the other side closer to victory and us [nearer to returning] to the old slavery."[29] In desperation, Lenin's government gave a special military commissar of Petrograd for combatting drunkenness and pogroms the authority to shoot looters on the spot.[30] "Because experience has shown that less decisive measures have not had the desired result," the regiment assigned to restore order on Vasilievskii Island announced in a special proclamation, "storehouses of alcoholic beverages will be *blown up with dynamite* . . . [and] no advanced warning will be given before the explosions."[31]

The orgy of intoxication, robbery, confiscation, expropriation, and murder that filled the last days of 1917 left no doubt among Petrograd's former well-to-do that the old days would never return so long as the Bolsheviks ruled Russia. But the flood of decrees calculated to make life wretched for the men and women who had stood at the pinnacle of the old order did nothing to relieve the misery of the proletarians whose interests the new government now claimed to serve. As shipments of grain, coal, wood, and raw materials grew more erratic, shops and factories closed their doors and left tens of thousands of the city's proletarians without food and work. "Starving Petrograd . . . the city without coal or bread, with its factory chimneys gone cold," Aleksei Tolstoi wrote in *1918*. Russia's capital, he remembered, was "a terrible place at the end of 1917."[32]

To men and women whose labor counted for little, the passage of hours and days had little meaning, and for centuries Russians had moved according to their own sense of time. "Time was of so little value in Russia," one caustic observer explained, "that nobody had ever bothered to learn how to save it." In 1917 this meant that, although Russia's revolutionary upheavals produced shortages of everything else, they created a surplus of waiting. Every day brought longer lines in which people with shorter tempers waited more hours for less food and fewer goods. Petrograders stood in line for bread, meat, sugar, kerosene, cloth, tobacco, chocolate, and theater tickets. People even stood in line that winter to receive tickets that allowed them to come back to stand in line another day to buy such scarce items as shoes, boots, and galoshes. Because tradition dictated that mothers with infants be served first, Petrograd's women began to rent infants so that they could get to the head of the line more quickly. Men and women with nothing left to sell but their time began to post signs offering themselves "for queue work only," as they struggled to turn the hours spent in lines to some account.[33] The search for food became all-consuming. "Even in the drawing rooms," de Robien wrote, "[people] can only talk of the best way to get hold of a sack of flour or a few eggs."[34]

Vicious winter storms combined with food and fuel shortages to add to Petrograders' misery that winter. Four blizzards struck the city during the last ten days of December and piled mountains of snow upon streets and tramlines. As swirling and drifting snow in other parts of Russia slowed rail shipments of wood and coal, fuel became as scarce in Petrograd as the snow was plentiful. "Coal and firewood could be obtained only at the price of heroic effort," one of the Bolsheviks remembered many years later.[35] As the midwinter nights lengthened beyond eighteen hours, dwindling fuel supplies produced an acute shortage of electricity that plunged Petrograd's buildings into darkness for all but two or three hours each day and extinguished its street lamps for weeks on end. When anxious men and women hurried to replace electric lights with lamps, they found that they could buy no more than a paltry ounce and three-quarters of kerosene each day. Despite bitter rumors that Russia's new leaders lived in luxury while the masses froze and starved, the men who grappled with these crises suffered along with the rest. "We froze," one old Bolshevik remembered. "Our leaders froze in their offices. Even Lenin froze."[36]

In a nation where the masses' diet consisted mainly of bread, Petrograd's bakers had to knead and bake 725 tons of flour into bread every day to feed the city's two and a quarter million people. Because the trains that had made their way to the capital along Russia's crumbling railways during the fall of 1917 had carried less than a third of that amount, Petrograders' daily bread ration fell to a mere half pound, supplemented by trifling quantities of meat, sugar, fats, and one egg every sixteen days, several weeks before the Bolsheviks overthrew Kerenskii's Provisional Government.[37] Although experts estimated that a laborer required an absolute minimum of 2,700 calories to survive, a Petrograder's daily rations supplied 1,395 calories as the winter of 1917–1918 began.[38] As diligent Bolshevik Red Guards combed Petrograd for hidden reserves of food, they discovered some fifty thousand tons of provisions in freight cars that had been shunted to remote railway sidings and forgotten. More searches, careful planning, and the discovery of great stores of precious supplies that enterprising speculators had hidden away added another few weeks to the Bolsheviks' period of grace.[39] At the same time, Lenin ordered detachments of revolutionary soldiers, sailors, and workers into nearby provinces "to obtain grain through voluntary sales at fixed official prices" if possible, to barter previous reserves of cloth, thread, and tools if necessary, and to seize the grain from recalcitrant peasants by force if all else failed.[40] Such resolute action could not wipe away the crisis that hung over Petrograd, although it postponed the day when it would strike at full force. When the Soviet of People's Commissars—known by its Russian acronym Sovnarkom—increased the city's bread ration by half before the end of November, even the most hopeful among Russia's new leaders knew that workers would begin to starve soon after the new year unless other food reserves could be tapped.

Just when the December blizzards buried Petrograd beneath the heaviest snow of the year, workers' daily rations slipped to 1,038 calories and then plummeted to a pitiful 698 in January.[41] "For God's sake, use the *most* energetic and *revolutionary* measures to send *grain, grain*, and *more grain!!!*" Lenin telegraphed to his special agents in the provinces. "Otherwise, Piter [a slang term for Petrograd] may perish."[42] In a desperate effort to feed the city, the Bolsheviks sent small groups of dedicated workers, soldiers, and sailors to barter for grain in Russia's rich grain-growing provinces in western Siberia. Whatever the cost, Petrograd's citizens had to have grain.

During the first three months of 1918, goods-starved western Siberian peasants exchanged over a quarter million tons of grain reserves for more than sixty million rubles' worth of manufactured goods.[43] Yet the best efforts of the Bolsheviks' grain-gatherers could not free Petrograd from hunger's grip, for it proved to be nearly as difficult to transport food across hundreds (sometimes thousands) of miles of unruly lands as it was to find the food itself. A tenth of the freight cars and a third of the locomotives on Russia's railways had broken down even before the Bolsheviks inherited them from Kerenskii's government, and the blizzards that struck so frequently between December and March disabled many more. By the end of January, nearly half of Russia's locomotives no longer ran. Mechanical corpses of locomotives stripped for spare parts clogged rail sidings all across the land.

Without enough trains to move grain from the countryside to her cities, Russia's food crisis worsened. When the Bolsheviks moved their capital to Moscow in February, the city's daily bread ration had fallen below a quarter pound, and the workers' entire daily ration produced a pitiful 306 calories, less than a tenth of what experts thought necessary for "a healthy diet."[44] In Petrograd, the authorities raised the daily bread allotment to a quarter of a pound by ordering bakers to add more surrogates and moisture to the dough, only to cut that ration of "famine bread" in half a few weeks later.[45] Elsewhere, it was the same. In Novgorod, Pskov, Tver, Riazan, and Iaroslavl—in all the towns and cities in which the Bolsheviks ruled—hunger deepened as the winter of 1917–1918 turned toward spring.

To add to the Bolsheviks' difficulties, Russia's hard-drinking peasants continued to distill hundreds of thousands of tons of precious grain into raw *samogon* (moonshine) vodka throughout the winter. Thirsty country folk in one large Siberian province distilled an estimated quarter million tons of grain into *samogon* during the winter of 1917–1918, and the authorities discovered one village in south central Russia where peasants had distilled enough grain that winter to have fed a town of ten thousand people. Not yet able to extend their authority into each of Russia's hundreds of thousands of tiny peasant villages, the Bolsheviks could only lament the loss of such desperately needed food supplies and appeal to those poor peasants whose hunger had begun to rival that of their city brethren to take matters into their own hands. "Whole cities, entire provinces, are starving," one Bolshevik propagandist wrote. "Join together, all you poor folk in town and country, all you workers in field and factory! Remember: Russia's entire future—the fate of all her toilers—lies in your hands alone! You overthrew Tsar Nicholas. You dumped that petty 'tsarlet' Kerenskii. Did you do all that just so you could be defeated now by Tsar-Hunger?"[46] Clearly, the Bolsheviks hoped that Russia's poorest peasants would take their side against those who still held surplus grain, but the response of the Russian countryside proved to be far more complex than they had hoped.

The persistence of the *samogon* trade in time of famine stemmed in part from the most productive peasants' hatred for the government's wartime price-fixing policies and their hunger for hard-to-come-by farm implements and tools. When this comparative handful of prosperous peasants, or kulaks, had begun to hoard grain after the harvest of 1914, they had hoped to force the government to lift its controls, drive prices higher, and reap richer profits; but factors they had not foreseen undermined their plans. In order to manufacture more profitable war supplies, weapons, and ammunition, Russian factory owners had stopped producing for the civilian market, and the prices of scarce consumer goods had risen much faster than grain. When badly needed tools, iron, and boots no longer could be bought in Russia's provinces, the kulaks refused to sell their grain at any price, and during the winter of 1917–1918 they had begun to transform their reserves into more easily concealed *samogon*, which could be transported more conveniently and sold more profitably than grain. Such men stood to gain nothing from the Bolsheviks' October victory, and they continued to refuse all pleas to release grain for the common good.

While the Bolsheviks fought their battle against kulak distillers, the food shortages that had plagued the towns and cities of central Russia during the fall of 1917 therefore began to spread to hundreds of thousands of poor peasant households. Even in normal times, the last days of winter always had brought hunger to Russia's countryside, for only one peasant family in nine or ten usually had enough grain to last from harvest to harvest.[47] The first months of 1918 saw such shortages become unusually severe, and poor peasants in the provinces around Petrograd, Pskov, and Novgorod began to eat bark, straw, and moss long before the spring thaw.[48] At about the same time, peasants in the nearby province of Iaroslavl began to mix their last precious stores of coarse flour with corn husks, chaff, hay, and nettles. A few years later, one of them still remembered how "luxurious" bread baked from a mixture of potato bits, oat siftings, vegetable husks, a bit of rye flour had seemed during those hungry times.[49] As hungry crowds pleaded for food, violence flared. An angry mob in Taldom killed the local food commissar and stuffed his mouth full of ration cards. In Rybinsk and Pavlovskii Posad, hungry peasants burned the headquarters of the local soviet and beat several of its members to death. Fifty Red Guards had to be rushed from Moscow to disperse a mob at Zvenigorod that threatened to take matters into its own hands after it had swelled to nearly ten thousand. Always, hunger drove the masses on, and the promise of food dampened their outrage just as surely as useless ration cards stirred it. Not far from Petrograd, in the village of Kolpino, the authorities dispersed a starving mob with a promise to increase the bread ration to a paltry quarter pound a day.[50]

Such promises could not stave off death by hunger as famine began to take its deadly toll in Russia's towns and villages. By the thousands, and then by the tens of thousands, Russians began to bury their dead as the spring thaw came. To make matters worse, the Bolsheviks' enemies seized the very areas from which Lenin's hungry followers had hoped to draw more grain during the lean spring and early summer months. That spring, German armies occupied the north shore of the Black Sea and the Ukraine, easily the most productive of all grainfields in Russia and the breadbasket not only of the former Russian Empire but of much of Eastern and Central Europe. On the heels of that loss, victorious Whites seized Siberia, the trans-Volga region, and the rich lands that lay along the lower reaches of the Kuban and Don rivers. Before the hungry spring of 1918 had moved into midsummer, more than eight out of every ten bushels of the grain that Russia's peasants had stored after the harvest of 1917 lay beyond the Bolsheviks' reach. If there had been too little food in March, there was much less by June.[51]

Soaring unemployment made the plight of Russia's hungry proletarians more desperate still. In Petrograd alone forty large factories that had employed nearly eighty thousand millhands at the time of the October Revolution closed their doors before spring. Out of more than five thousand workers at the Franko-Russkii factory, only a handful remained as caretakers, and even the gigantic Obukhov and Putilov works laid off almost two-thirds of their workforce. Within four months after the October Revolution, the number of Petrograd's unemployed factory workers increased by more than a hundred thousand. Then, shortages of coal, electricity, and raw materials drove that number even higher. Before fall came in 1918, Petrograd's factories employed less than a third of the men and women who had worked there the year before.[52]

Ironically, unemployment struck hardest at the *metallisty*, those elite skilled metalworkers who had been among the most active supporters of Russia's revolutionary movement since the 1880s and had formed the core of the Bolsheviks' strength. *Metallisty* lost so many jobs during the Bolsheviks' first year in power that less than fifty thousand out of a wartime contingent of nearly a quarter million remained in Petrograd at the end of 1918. "Some have been killed in the struggles for freedom," Petrograd's metalworkers' union reported as it looked back upon the Bolsheviks' first year in power. "Others have gone off to fight [against the Whites], a third group left . . . at the time of the evacuation [to Moscow], and a fourth group has been scattered all across the country in search of food for themselves and their families."[53] So vast was the flight from Petrograd during the Civil War that seven out of every ten men and women who had lived there in 1917 no longer remained in the summer of 1920.[54]

Russia's factory workers thus turned their backs upon those urban centers that had been their beacons of hope ever since the Emancipation of 1861 had freed them from serfdom's heavy yoke and made their way back to the villages whence they or their parents had come. There they found traditional points of reference slipping away almost as rapidly as in the cities as their peasant relatives struggled to make sense out of Lenin's Decree on Land. On the evening after the Bolsheviks' revolutionary triumph, Lenin had proclaimed that "private ownership of land shall be abolished forever" and had promised that "the right to use the land shall be accorded to all citizens of the Russian state (without distinction of sex) desiring to cultivate it by their own labor." Yet he had purposely left vague his explanations about how those principles might be put into practice.[55] During the first months of 1918, Russia's peasants therefore moved to shape Lenin's promises to accord with their own understanding.

Almost everywhere, peasants had looted livestock, farm implements, and valuables from local manor houses in response to Lenin's Decree on Land. Yet, despite the sense of violence that emerges from memoirs and newspaper reports of that time, the number of such outbreaks remained small compared to the great number of landlords who were dispossessed.[56] The peasants' natural caution, common sense, and sense of fair play inevitably overbalanced their first impulse to give vent to centuries of accumulated anger, and instances in which they helped former landlords to find a place in the new order seem nearly as numerous as the incidents in which they looted their estates.[57] Far more frequently, hungry peasants directed their anger against local officials who met their pleas for bread with more regulations and more useless ration cards.

During the hungry spring of 1918, nothing spoke more dramatically of the hunger in town and country than the reports that poured into the People's Commissariat for Food Supply. None could doubt Russian masses' desperation as telegram after telegram chronicled their daily confrontations with hunger and death:

> WE HAVE NO BREAD. THE SITUATION IS HOPELESS. HUNGER REIGNS. (*May 19, from the village of Pokrov*)
>
> THE FOOD SITUATION IN KINESHMA HAS TAKEN AN OMINOUS TURN THAT IS LEADING TO CATASTROPHE. INDIVIDUAL RATIONS FOR APRIL AND MAY HAVE BEEN EQUAL TO ONLY TWO POUNDS OF FLOUR FOR AN [ENTIRE] MONTH. (*May 22, from the town of Kineshma*)
>
> IAROSLAV PROVINCE IS IN AN ABSOLUTELY, UNPRECEDENTEDLY IMPOVERISHED AND CATASTROPHIC CONDITION SO FAR AS FOOD SUPPLIES ARE CONCERNED. ABSOLUTELY NO SHIPMENTS OF GRAIN HAVE ARRIVED FOR TWO WEEKS. (*May 24, from the provincial capital of Iaroslav*)
>
> STARVING WORKERS ARE COLLAPSING AT THEIR MACHINES. EVERYONE WHO IS ABLE CONTINUES TO WORK AND WILL CONTINUE TO DO SO. WE BEG YOU TO SEND US BREAD. . . . THIS IS NOT A THREAT BUT A FINAL CRY OF DESPAIR. (*May 25, from the town of Vyksa*)[58]

The words "absolutely critical," "urgent," "desperate," "unprecedented," and "catastrophic" became commonplace in the telegrams that poured into the offices of the Sovnarkom and the Commissariat for Food Supply in Moscow. From all corners of the Bolsheviks' domains came word of the "last reserves" being eaten, of people collapsing from hunger, of men, women, and children dying by the thousands. In Moscow, grain shipments fell to a mere third of the amount needed to bake the quarter-pound daily bread ration that stood between its people and starvation, but news from Petrograd grew even worse. After desperate telegrams marked "Urgent, to Lenin" brought no new shipments of grain, officials cut workers' daily bread rations there to an eighth of a pound.[59]

Disease quickly joined the scourges that the Russians suffered during the hungry spring of 1918. The age-old traveling companion of famine in Russia, typhus, ran rampant, its spread facilitated by the chronic lack of toilet and bathing facilities for the hordes of demobilized soldiers and hungry city folk who made their way along the railways into the Russian countryside. Carried by lice that flourished amid the famine's filth and poverty, typhus rivaled starvation as Russia's greatest killer, for the bite of even one louse could mean death. Every Russian who knew that fact carried fear deep within his heart. "Today I caught an insect on my body," one perpetually apprehensive diarist wrote. "Is it a typhus louse or not? Let us wait a fortnight and see. If it is typhus, that means the end of me. I am too weak to live through the fever."[60] Without enough disinfectants, or even enough soap, few Russians could escape the deadly daily presence of such insects. An article in *Pravda* reported that dead lice became so thick on the floor of the disinfecting room where the clothing of Red Army soldiers was treated that they looked like a two-inch-thick layer of gray sand.[61]

Was starvation inevitable that spring? Or could the hoarded grain of the kulaks have fed the Russians? Although Bolshevik apologists crudely overstated their case and grossly underplayed the problems caused by their own disorderly assumption of power, their clumsy inexperience, and the collapse of Russia's railroads, there was an element of truth to what they said. Despite the loss of Russia's richest grainlands to the Whites and the Germans, kulak storehouses in the Bolsheviks' shrunken domains at midsummer probably still contained nearly three-quarters of a million tons of grain from the 1917 harvest plus a great deal more from earlier years.[62] "It is not because there is no grain in Russia that we face hunger," Lenin told Petrograd's workers that spring as he called upon workers and poor peasants to wrest the grain from those who would keep it from them.[63] The battle for grain had to be viewed not "merely [as] a struggle for bread," but as a conflict upon which the Revolution's very survival depended. Warning that "the entire future of socialism is at stake," Lenin thus summoned Russia's masses to battle against the kulaks.[64]

Convinced that only the most decisive measures could feed the Russians and save the world's first proletarian state, Lenin announced on May 9, 1918, that "those who have grain and fail to deliver it to properly designated rail stations and shipping points . . . are to be declared *enemies of the people*."[65] A fortnight later, he proclaimed a "great crusade against grain speculators, kulaks, bloodsuckers, disorganizers [and] bribe-takers,"[66] who, after growing "fat and rich during the war," he added in a separate note, "now refuse to give bread to starving people." Russia's toilers must join the "battle for bread," not only against those "nobles and great grain merchants" who had traded in grain in the old days, but, most of all, against the kulaks, the "village bourgeoisie." These "enemies of Soviet power," Lenin warned, planned to "bind the workers and poor peasants with the chains of capitalist slavery." As part of the "battle for Soviet power and for socialism," the "battle for bread" thus must become a "pitiless struggle"[67] in which no weapon could be too terrible and no tactic too brutal to crush those who sought to profit from the misfortunes of others.

Not all who believed in socialism advocated class warfare so readily. When the Bolsheviks asked the All-Russian Central Executive Committee of the Soviets to approve their plans for sending detachments of armed workers to confiscate the peasants' grain, the Menshevik leader Iulii Martov spoke angrily against it, just as he had stormed against their resolution to rule without the support of other socialists the previous October. "Martov's voice thundered from the tribune," one reporter remembered. "This is treachery! You've thought this up in order to get all the discontented workers—the finest flower of the proletariat—out of Moscow and Petrograd!" Martov's outrage quickly polarized the members of the Central Executive Committee, whose shouts of "Traitor!" and "Bravo, Martov!" shook the walls. Force, so often the Bolsheviks' favored course in moments of crisis, finally ended Martov's outburst, when the committee's Bolshevik president ordered the guards who stood outside the chamber to remove him. "The times were ominous, filled with murky predictions, expectations, brutal passions, and contradictions," Konstantin Paustovskii wrote when he recalled how Martov had stalked away, his boiling rage suddenly frozen into cold hatred. "The life of the country," Paustovskii concluded, "had been shaken right down to its thousand-year-old roots."[68]

With starvation looming on every corner of the horizon, Lenin and the Bolsheviks held firmly to their course despite the opposition of Martov and his allies. Firm in their belief that the higher goal of social justice justified the violence of class warfare, they called upon "all toilers and landless peasants" to "join together at once in a merciless struggle against the kulaks."[69] "Long live civil war in the name of bread for children and old people, for the workers and the Red Army, in the name of direct and merciless struggle with counterrevolution!" Trotskii announced to a workers' meeting in Moscow.[70] But class warfare could not solve the problem of too little land cultivated to feed too many people. "The civil war is not likely to induce the peasants to increase the area under cultivation," one of the Mensheviks warned grimly as he listened to the Bolsheviks' efforts to turn Russia's poor peasants against their slightly better off neighbors.[71] None with the power to alter Russia's course heeded that wise objection.

Instead, the Bolsheviks worked to deepen the conflict between those who had grain and those who did not in Russia's villages. "There remains only one solution," Lenin announced at the beginning of May. Russia's government must "meet the violence of grain owners against the starving poor with violence against the grain owners."[72] The Bolsheviks now insisted that all grain must be sold at the official price, which, at times, fell to less than a twentieth of what grain fetched on the black market. Anyone who refused to do so, or who was caught hoarding grain or distilling *samogon* after May 9, 1918, would have his grain confiscated and be sentenced to not less than ten years in prison. No longer would the government barter goods for grain as it had during the previous winter. "[Manufactured] goods," Lenin explained, "are to be distributed among the needy population . . . [as an incentive] to stimulate those who have no grain to force those that have [it] to hand it over."[73] Trotskii announced the Bolsheviks' new policy in more dramatic terms. "We Communists recognize only one sacred right—the right of the working man, his wife, and his child to live," he stated eloquently. "We did not hesitate to wrest the land away from the landlords, to transfer the factories, mills, and railroads into the hands of the people . . . and, by force of arms, to tear the crown from the stupid Tsar's head," he continued. "Why then should we hesitate to take the grain away from the kulaks?"[74] No longer a commodity to be sold, bought, or traded, grain became one of the chief spoils of class warfare to be "shared out in a fraternal fashion" (in Trotskii's words) among the starving masses in town and country.[75] Its distribution would be controlled, Lenin said, by "a dictatorship, a regime of violence against the exploiters."[76]

Such a dictatorship came into being several weeks before Russia's spring ended. Born in the same year as Lenin, a loyal Bolshevik for almost two decades, and the People's commissar for food supply ever since he had ousted his former chief from that office in February, the tough party infighter Aleksandr Tsiurupa was the ideal man to direct the "Dictatorship of Food Supply" that the All-Russian Central Executive Committee of the Soviets approved over the bitter opposition of Mensheviks and left-wing Socialist Revolutionaries on May 9.[77] As a graduate of the Kherson Agricultural Institute who had lived most of his early life in the provinces, Tsiurupa knew how the peasants lived, what they produced, and where to find it. "We are going to organize grain-requisitioning detachments," he explained to his colleagues on the Central Executive Committee, "not only for the purpose of collecting and requisitioning grain, but also . . . to demonstrate that grain will be taken by force."[78] *Pravda* hurried to underscore his stern position. "The war against hunger," it announced a few days later, "is the war against the bourgeoisie carried from the city into the countryside."[79] A "dictatorship of food supply," it added, would "support the poorest of the peasants and compel the rich, the village bourgeoisie, to surrender . . . their huge grain reserves to the starving people of Russia."[80] Only by turning the rural poor against those who stood above in the rural economic hierarchy could the Bolsheviks hope to solidify their authority outside Russia's cities. Iakov Sverdlov, the Bolsheviks' chief organizer during the Revolution and now, at the age of thirty-three, chairman of the All-Russian Central Executive Committee of the Soviets, summarized the situation in the bluntest terms less than two weeks after the supply detachments had been approved. "If we cannot split the villages into two irreconcilably hostile camps," he warned in a report dated May 20, "if we cannot unite the village poor against the rich, then we are going to live through some very bad days."[81]

For the manpower to fill the grain-requisitioning detachments that would fight the many battles with Russia's stubborn peasantry, Tsiurupa's Commissariat of Food Supply turned to the workers of Moscow, Petrograd, and other industrial centers. "The main task of the workers detachments should be to organize the toiling peasantry against the kulaks," its circulars announced. "If we smash the resistance of the village bourgeoisie immediately," another decree promised, "we shall be invincible and the socialist revolution will be established forever."[82] In such a struggle, the Bolsheviks insisted that the workers of Moscow and, especially, of "starving Petrograd," must lead the way. "Comrades! Time will not wait," the Petrograd Soviet warned. "Hundreds and thousands of honest workers are needed. We can't waste time!"[83] Immediately, Bolshevik-controlled committees of factory and mill workers spoke out as expected. "Let each factory, each workshop, each group of railroad workers, each group of service workers immediately select from its ranks three to five people out of every hundred," they urged. "Let the task of organizing grain-requisitioning detachments move forward at top speed."[84]

Yet words were one thing and action quite another, despite *Pravda*'s triumphant claim that "the working class of Petrograd is rising up in the masses' battle for bread."[85] As they had in 1917, when they had stood forth as heroic defenders of the Revolution so long as they did not have to face enemy gunfire, Petrograd's workers again proved hesitant to face hostile forces. They therefore "rose up" far more reluctantly than the Bolsheviks had hoped and required considerably more urging than expected. "To sit in Piter, to starve, to hang around empty factories, to amuse oneself with absurd dreams . . . is *stupid and criminal*," Lenin raged. If Petrograd's workers did not take the lead in the battle for bread, he warned, it would "mean the death of our revolution."[86]

While Trotskii and Lenin remained in Moscow, some of their most persuasive comrades hurried to organize the workers in Petrograd, now revered by Bolshevik propagandists as the cradle of the Revolution. Mikhail Kalinin (a peasant-turned-metalworker who spoke the language of humble folk and was affectionately known to them as "Papa"), People's Commissar of Public Enlightenment Anatolii Lunacharskii (a provincial clerk's son whose ready pen had spoken out in the workers' cause for the better part of a quarter-century), and Konkordiia Samoilova (a Siberian village priest's daughter who had devoted her life to the cause of proletarian women) all urged Petrograd's workers to defend the Revolution by enlisting in Tsiurupa's grain-requisitioning detachments. At first slowly, then with more enthusiasm, the workers joined the battle for bread, and Petrograd's detachment set out to do battle with the kulaks less than a week after Lunacharskii, Samoilova, and Kalinin arrived from Moscow. Within a month, four thousand more working men had joined their ranks.[87]

While workers from other cities followed the example of their Petrograd comrades, Trotskii summoned working women to join in the battle. "Our detachments . . . ought to take with them a few women, real proletarian wives and mothers, who know better than anyone else just what hunger means to a family where there are many children," he urged the Moscow workers. "Such toiling mothers," he added with grim satisfaction, "will really give the kulaks a piece of their minds."[88] By mid-June, workers from Moscow's great Prokhorov Cotton Mill, the even larger mills in Ivanovo-Voznesensk, the Riabushinskii factory in Vyshnii-Volochok, and scores of others had joined Tsiurupa's grain-requisitioning detachments.[89] "It was dangerous to go into the countryside then," a member of one detachment remembered, "but we had to have grain and we had to go and get it."[90]

Trotskii insisted that the rewards would far outweigh any dangers the grain-requisitioning detachments might face. "We shall find help everywhere, even in the most out-of-the-way places," he assured Moscow's workers as he reminded them that they and the poor peasants outnumbered the kulaks by at least twenty to one. "Can anyone think that the kulaks will dare to stand against [such odds]?" he asked. In almost all cases, he assured those who might doubt the readiness of village capitalists to capitulate so readily, "it will be enough to have several thousand politically conscious and disciplined workers appear along with honest, disciplined Red Army men and say: 'Moscow needs grain. Give it to us at the official price that has been set by Soviet authority.' Comrades!" he promised. "There will be grain!"[91]

By any calculation, workers and poor peasants outnumbered the kulaks by a huge margin, but as men and women whose hard work, stubbornness, and greater readiness to take risks had raised them to the top of the villages' pitifully low economic heap, the kulaks proved less willing to bow to superior numbers than Trotskii's optimistic promises indicated. Even before the grain-requisitioning detachments had been formed, scores of "kulak revolts" against Bolshevik authority were being reported in Russia's fertile grain belt, with more than fifty concentrated in just four provinces that spring.[92] When the grain-requisitioning detachments moved into Russia's villages, kulak resistance stiffened, and Tsiurupa had to take special measures to make certain that the grain-requisitioning detachments could defend themselves against all but the most overwhelming threats. "Every detachment is to consist of not less than seventy-five men and two or three machine guns," he ordered. "There should be continuous cavalry communication between different detachments," and, at the same time, senior commanders must distribute the forces under their command "in such a way that will make it easy for two or three detachments to unite in a short time."[93]

Every grain-requisitioning detachment thus had reinforcements near at hand when its searches provoked opposition. In some cases, entire villages resisted, making it clear that the Bolsheviks' definition of a kulak reached far down toward the bottom of the village economic pyramid. In other instances, Red Army units threatened to destroy entire villages unless those peasants whom they named as the resident "class enemies" surrendered a quota of grain.[94] Such choices of class enemies sometimes were made purely by chance. "Poor to the right, rich to the left," commanded one leader of a Bolshevik workers' detachment sent to seize grain from one village.[95] With rifles pointed at their heads, the "rich" did as they were told and found ways to settle scores afterward. Reports from commanders of the first grain-requisitioning detachments all across Russia left no doubt that the kulaks were ready and willing to defend their farms and grain against them. That July and August the number of "kulak revolts" in Russia's central provinces rose beyond two hundred.[96] Grain-requisitioning detachments therefore operated as if they were in enemy-held territory and supported their frequent house-to-house searches with machine gun fire, hand grenades, and even artillery shells. Such were needed, one commander explained, to produce the "necessary moral effect" upon the peasants.[97]

Men and women officially classified as the "village poor" formed a key element in the Bolsheviks' plans as the grain-requisitioning detachments moved through Russia's countryside. Established in response to Tsiurupa's direct orders, village committees of the poor were expected to help grain-requisitioning detachments uncover hidden supplies in return for part of the grain and desperately needed manufactured goods. Certainly, some of the poorest peasants hurried to join such committees, although it is by no means certain that they did so for any reason other than to take advantage of the food, tools, and clothing that Tsiurupa's Commissariat of Food Supply promised in return for their "energetic support in removing surpluses from the hands of the kulaks and the rich."[98] More frequently, committees of the poor were formed by units of the Red Army or by the grain-requisitioning detachments themselves.[99] Before fall came to an end, such "poor" peasants, assisted by large numbers of those city workers who had joined grain-requisitioning detachments and settled temporarily in the villages, had formed more than thirty thousand village and district committees; by the end of the year, that number had risen well beyond a hundred thousand.[100]

Even committees of the poor and grain-requisitioning detachments together could not feed the Russians. On the average, Tsiurupa's Commissariat of Food Supply collected a paltry thirty-six pounds of grain—not even enough to produce a daily bread ration of an eighth of a pound—for each person in Bolshevik Russia during 1918, and most city folk would have starved had they relied solely upon its efforts.[101] That most of them survived that year's dreadful food shortages was due in part (perhaps in large part) to a legion of itinerant peddlers known as bagmen who carried tools, hinges, nails, pipes, pots and pans, leather, and cloth to peasant villages and exchanged them for food products that they took back to sell in the city. Always buying and selling at prices far above those paid by the government, Russia's bagmen had reaped immense profits since the early days of the Revolution, yet all of Russia's provisional governments had tolerated them because they alone stood between the nation's collapsing food supply network and starvation in the cities.[102] A report issued in the fall of 1917 had spoken of "tens of thousands" of bagmen who plied their trade along the railroads and rivers that passed through Russia's most fertile provinces.[103] After the October Revolution, they continued to flourish despite the Bolsheviks' ideological hatred for their "petty bourgeois greed."

Even contemporary Soviet planners admitted that bagmen accounted for more than half of the grain consumed by city dwellers during the year after the October Revolution.[104] Because no one understood that fact better than Tsiurupa himself, the Commissariat of Food Supply issued special regulations which, under the guise of limiting the private transport of food into Moscow and Petrograd, allowed the bagmen to continue their work even after the Sovnarkom authorized special paramilitary units to stop trains and riverboats, search for bagmen, and confiscate the foodstuffs they carried.[105] But Tsiurupa's grudging awareness that the bagmen must be tolerated for the moment did not prevent the Bolsheviks from unleashing bitter propaganda attacks against them. Along with the grasping kulak, whose sinister image loomed so large in the Bolsheviks' decrees against "village capitalists," the bagman became the other "enemy of the people" during the summer and fall of 1918.[106] Now that regulations permitted the bagmen to function and forbade them from doing so, their fate depended upon the whim of the individual commanders they encountered. They thus began to operate in that vast twilight zone that Bolshevik rule brought to Russia, in which things were forbidden and permitted at the same time. Men and women now had to break the law to survive. "The real rule," one survivor wrote bitterly, "was: 'to each man nothing unless he gets it by transgressing the laws of the Communist government.' "[107]

With misplaced hopes that the harvest of 1918 would end the food shortages that had crippled their first efforts to govern Russia, the Bolsheviks intensified their campaign against the bagmen when peasant reapers began their work in the countryside that fall. In early September, Dzerzhinskii's Cheka warned Russians against "various types of marauders, speculators and professional 'bagmen,' " whose operations had thrown the nation's transport facilities "into chaos."[108] When it proved all but impossible to distinguish bagmen from genuine starving proletarians, Dzerzhinskii urged his colleagues on the Sovnarkom to close the loophole through which Tsiurupa had allowed them to operate their black market trade in Russia's largest cities. Significantly, the Sovnarkom did not issue its prohibition until the harvest was nearly finished in October. By then, the bagmen's illicit trade had kept Russia's cities alive during the worst months of that year's food shortages.[109]

The Bolsheviks' repressive methods during Russia's "hungry spring" provoked bitter criticism from the rapidly shrinking body of political adversaries who still remained at liberty in Russia. Just more than a month after the Menshevik leaders Dan and Martov had attacked Lenin's plans to organize armed grain-requisitioning detachments, the Bolshevik majority expelled the Mensheviks and all other socialists except for the left-wing Socialist Revolutionaries from the All-Russian Central Executive Committee. "The Soviet Government is living through its most difficult period," the committee's chairman Sverdlov warned on June 14. Because "the presence in Soviet organizations of representatives of parties which are obviously endeavoring to discredit and overthrow the Soviet Government is absolutely intolerable," he went on, the Central Executive Committee had found it necessary "to exclude [them] from its membership."[110] Nine days later, Cheka agents arrested thirty-nine moderate socialist leaders who had met to discuss how their parties should respond to the Bolsheviks' heavyhanded tactics.[111] By the end of June, only the Left SRs, who shared some of the Bolsheviks' views but rejected their decision to bring class conflict to Russia's villages as violently as they condemned their willingness to accept peace with Germany at any price, remained free to oppose their plans.

Within a month, the Left SRs, too, would be gone from the Central Executive Committee after their condemnation of the Treaty of Brest-Litovsk and their moral outrage at the Bolsheviks' readiness to incite Russia's peasants to war against each other culminated in a wild, romantic attempt to win in the streets of Moscow the revolutionary victory that had eluded them elsewhere. Yet the Bolsheviks' ability to crush the Left SRs' uprising and establish themselves as undisputed masters of Moscow in July 1918 did not assure their hold upon the Russian land, for they faced challenges on every side from men and women who considered the Bolshevik vision of Russia's future as abhorrent as their efforts to split Russia apart by means of class conflict. By the summer of 1918, thirty different governments functioned in the lands that once had been the Russian Empire, and twenty-nine of them stood against the Bolsheviks.[112] Their enemies pressing upon them from all sides, the Bolsheviks expected no quarter and gave none. "From the very beginning, the Bolsheviks defined the character of the Civil War in a single word: annihilation," General Denikin recalled in his memoirs. "Four years of war and the nightmare of revolution had left their mark on everyone," he continued. "There was heroism and brutality, compassion and hatred, social tolerance and class conflict."[113] Most of all, it seemed to Denikin that the Civil War's first battles heightened the tension between the "exalted and base tendencies" in the natures of men.[114] Absolutes began to rule men's minds as they never had during the Great War. As the Reds and Whites fought their first battles in the spring of 1918, neither thought simply of victory or defeat. Each planned the other's annihilation.

CHAPTER TWO

The Fighting Begins

MAROONED IN starving Moscow, near-sighted, impractical, frightened of automobiles and elevators, and without any means of support, the young Russian poet Marina Tsvetaeva looked southward as the winter of 1918 neared its end. Her husband already had enlisted in the embryonic Volunteer Army that soon would become the backbone of the White forces in South Russia, and she longed to join him. Yet the lines of battle between Red and White already had been drawn, and it would be four long years before she and her two small children could make the journey.[1] Anxious to escape the constraints of the new order that she found so deadening, but condemned by circumstances to spend the Civil War in the very center of Russia's red heart, Tsvetaeva saw a time to come when "thoughtful grandchildren" would ask their grandfathers: "Where were *you*?" during those dark and terrible days of 1918. "The reply," she wrote in neat, round, schoolgirl letters in a small notebook from the American YMCA, "crashes forth like thunder." For men who believed in duty, valor, and honor, she insisted, the place to be at the beginning of 1918 must be: "On the Don!"[2]

The Don! For centuries, those lands that stretched beyond the horizon in every direction to encompass more than 165,000 square kilometers of the great Don River basin in southern Russia, had stirred dreams of freedom in the minds of oppressed and restless men and women. Beginning in the fifteenth century, when Ivan the Great and his grandson Ivan the Terrible had begun to gather the far-flung Russian lands under Moscow's control, serfs and slaves from central Russia had fled to the Don lands, where they had found freedom from the tsars' relentlessly tightening grip. With their Cossack allies on the Dnepr's Zaporozhian Sich to the west and the lower reaches of the Kuban, Volga, and Iaik rivers to the east, thousands of fugitives had lived close to their horses and to nature free from want, servitude, and fear.[3] Theirs was the steppe, a land as vast as it was virginal, where the grass grew taller than a man on horseback and stretched as far as the eye could see. "Never had the plow cut through the immense waves of its grasses," a Russian novelist had written almost a century before the revolutions of 1917. "The entire surface of the earth was an ocean of green and gold, sprinkled with millions of different flowers."[4]

So it had been in the days of the fictional hero Taras Bulba. So, too, had it been when the rebel Cossack chieftains Ivan Bolotnikov, Stenka Razin, Kondratii Bulavin, and Emelian Pugachev had led their followers in some of the greatest uprisings ever known in the history of the Western world. On four occasions between 1600 and 1800 these Cossack leaders had challenged the authority of the autocrats who ruled from Moscow and St. Petersburg by forming hordes of oppressed peasants into formidable armies. Always their rallying cry had been freedom for Russia's poor and unfortunate. "Knights-errant of the Russian common people," the nineteenth-century radical Aleksandr Herzen once had called them, a race of "warrior-peasants"[5] who had lived free until the Empress Catherine the Great had tamed them by tempering the blows her armies dealt the forces of the Cossack Pugachev with promises of privileges and rewards.

Thanks to Catherine's artful cooptation of their leaders, the Cossacks became the Russian autocrat's most staunch defenders. Cossacks had ridden for Tsar, Faith, and Country against Napoleon in 1812, against the armies of England and France during the Crimean War, and against the Turks on at least four occasions after Catherine's death. Cossack squadrons had been the government's best weapon during the revolutionary disturbances of 1905, when they had ridden against striking workers, their slashing, weighted whips scattering their victims like so many flocks of frightened geese. In 1904 Cossack cavalry had traveled halfway around the globe to fight the Japanese. In 1914 they had struck terror into the hearts of even the superbly trained German armies, whose soldiers instinctively recoiled from the terrible cry: "*Kosaken kommen!*" which their ancestors had first learned to fear during the Seven Years' War a century and a half before.

As with all tales of knights-errant, legends of the Cossacks as freedom-loving fighters survived long after they had become autocracy's bulwark against revolution. For much of the nineteenth century, peasants in those parts of Russia where Pugachev had won his greatest victories in 1773 and 1774 dated events from the time of his revolt, instead of from the time of Christ, as they waited impatiently for his successor to appear. Revolutionaries in the twentieth century knew the importance of such Cossack legends to Russia's masses and tried to use them to political advantage. Even Lenin took care to stress his kinship with Stenka Razin in the struggle against oppression in Russia.[6]

Both Reds and Whites therefore looked to the Cossacks in 1918. The former recalled their deeds as long-ago champions in the people's struggle against Russia's tsars, while the latter drew comfort from their more recent exploits as the autocrat's first line of defense against revolution. Yet, neither Red nor White understood how seriously the turmoil of the First World War and the revolutions of 1917 had weakened the Cossacks' unity and eroded their sense of common purpose. Nor did they realize how bitterly divided the Cossacks had become among themselves. As they had done for centuries, younger Cossacks had ridden away from the Don in 1914 to add to the glory that their forebears had won in wars past. Yet the grinding brutality of war on Europe's eastern front had taken a bitter toll, and they had sickened of the killing as their elders never had. When these "men from the front" returned home in 1917, they were much more radical than those who had stayed behind. This produced a "confrontation between fathers and sons that frequently led to bloodshed," one observer wrote. It split families apart and brought bitter disagreements into the Cossack communities of the Don and Kuban lands.[7] To the chagrin of Red and White alike, the first months of the Civil War therefore saw groups with very contradictory aims and loyalties emerge among the Cossacks. Very quickly, the Don lands became a microcosm of the conflicts that divided men and women all across Russia.

None looked to the Cossacks and the Don lands with greater hope than General Mikhail Alekseev. Short and slight, his slender hands and wire-rimmed spectacles making him appear for all the world like a man who lived by his pen, not his sword, Alekseev at sixty was dying of cancer and had only eleven months to live when Lenin and Trotskii ousted Kerenskii from office. Scrupulously honest, and content to remain in the background while less deserving men basked in the public acclaim that was rightly his, Alekseev always had asked much less for himself than for others. During the trying months of the Great War, men better trained in the ways of the Imperial Court had gossiped about how this unassuming man of simple faith and simpler manners thought coffee should be drunk during meals rather than afterward, and many had raised their eyebrows in contempt when he left the dinner table before the Tsar in order to return to his workroom. "If you ever see before you a stern general looking every inch the part, whose countenance reflects his own great appreciation of the grandeur of his position," an admiring future Bolshevik correspondent once wrote, "then you are *not* in the presence of Alekseev."[8]

As the imperial chief-of-staff beginning in August 1915, Alekseev had regrouped Russia's shattered armed forces, rebuilt and rearmed its decimated divisions, and launched new offensives, while the inept and indecisive Emperor Nicholas II had posed as his nation's supreme commander. Solely as a consequence of his immense capacity for work and his single-minded dedication to his country, this son of a noncommissioned infantry officer had risen to take full command of Russia's armies in 1917 after the February Revolution had driven the Romanovs from their throne. Yet the revolution that Alekseev accepted had promised to lead Russia along the path to Western constitutional democracy, not reshape her around values he found politically dangerous and morally repugnant. Bitterly opposed to every principle for which Lenin and the Bolsheviks stood, Alekseev refused to accept their victory.

Certain that nothing short of military force could dislodge the Bolsheviks, Alekseev hurried to the South within hours after their victory in the hope that Novocherkassk, the capital of the Don Territory, could become a base from which to march against them. Relying upon the rich harvests and abundant natural resources of the region to support his effort, Alekseev intended to restore the order and regularity of civic life that the revolutionary year had destroyed. Still certain, as he had written some months earlier, that "the fate of Russia depends on the army," Alekseev planned to assemble fugitive officers, military cadets, experienced noncoms returning from the front, and "especially the Don Cossacks," who, he mistakenly thought, had "sufficient strength not only for defense but for an offensive," to form a Volunteer Army that would defend the Don and, one day, grow strong enough to defeat the Bolsheviks.[9]

At best, the Volunteer Army was a far cry from the military force that Alekseev had commanded from Russia's Supreme Headquarters earlier that year, for volunteers proved to be scarce, weapons and ammunition scarcer still, and money scarcest of all. "It was touching . . . to see how the former supreme commander of Russia's armies, so recently in command of millions of men and a billion-ruble budget, now scurried and bustled here and there and fretted about getting a dozen cots, a few sacks of sugar, and tiny sums of money," General Denikin wrote some years later. "Alekseev . . . forced the deaf to hear and those who slept to awaken," Denikin added in amazement. "[He] dedicated all his strength and energy to what he liked to call his 'last labor on this earth.' "[10] The obstacles seemed insurmountable. Nonetheless, Alekseev insisted that "the business of saving the state" could best be begun on the Don. "Russian state authority will establish itself here," he explained. "The fragments of the old Russian government that has just been shattered by this unprecedented storm will gradually be put back together into the nucleus of a healthy state here in the South-West."[11]

The prospects for Alekseev's success looked brighter in mid-November, when, in the elections for delegates to the Constituent Assembly, forty-nine out of every fifty Cossacks had cast their ballots against the Bolsheviks.[12] All too quickly, fugitive generals and politicians who had joined Alekseev in Novocherkassk began to dream about broadening their struggle against the Bolsheviks into a national movement. "Whoever controls the mineral fuels of the country," one of the refugees from Moscow explained at a meeting in Novocherkassk on November 11, "can exercise the greatest influence on all areas of national life." Thus, the coal of the Don and the wealth of its banks could be used to deprive Central Russia of the food and fuel that the Bolsheviks' government needed to survive. Then, if the mineral-rich Don could be allied with the grain-rich Ukraine, which already had declared its independence from Lenin's regime, they could pose a powerful threat to Bolshevik power.[13]

Although immensely seductive for men whose world had been shattered by the Bolsheviks' victories in Petrograd and Moscow, such a dream ignored the realities of life in the Don lands. Proud of their traditions of freedom and democratic institutions, the Cossacks resented those politicians from Moscow and Petrograd who had appeared so suddenly in their midst and spoke so readily as their representatives. Most of these politicians belonged to the Constitutional Democratic, or Kadet, Party, which had been founded in the wake of the Revolution of 1905 and had represented in Russia those basic traditions of European liberalism that emphasized proper legal procedure, civil liberty, and political democracy (as opposed to the class-leveling social democracy called for by the Bolsheviks).[14] Yet such politicians knew nothing of the Cossacks' own traditions and remained foreigners among them. So quickly did the Cossacks' ataman General Aleksei Kaledin regret his brief willingness to make common cause with the politicians and generals from the north, that he asked many of them to leave Novocherkassk before the end of November.[15]

Unfamiliar with the society of the Don lands, the Whites also failed to anticipate the animosity of the men and women of peasant stock who now worked in the factories of Rostov, labored in the coal mines of the Donbas, and eked out a marginal living on lands rented from Cossack landlords. Drawn by the prospect of richer soil and more temperate climate, Russian peasants had been making their way into the Don lands ever since Catherine the Great had pacified the Cossacks in the 1770s. Yet unlike those who had sought refuge on the Don in earlier times, these peasants had remained aliens. Called *inogorodnye* by the Cossacks and destined always to live and labor under heavy disabilities, they made up nearly half of the population in the Don lands in 1917 but owned only a tenth of the land, most of it broken up into tiny parcels of less than four acres. Beginning in the late nineteenth century, rising rents in the Don and the nearby Kuban[16] had driven many of the *inogorodnye* to seek work in nearby factories or mines. Bitter, poor, and rebellious, the *inogorodnye* stood ready to support the Bolsheviks against mine owners, factory managers, and Cossack landlords.[17]

Before the end of November, a growing bond of common interest among the *inogorodnye* who had remained on the land, the factory workers of Rostov and Taganrog, and the coal miners of the Donbas encouraged Bolshevik workers to seize control of Rostov and proclaim the Soviet Republic of the Don.[18] With typical Cossack disdain for men and women of proletarian background, Kaledin ordered his men to retake Rostov, only to have the younger "men from the front" refuse. Then Kaledin turned to Alekseev and the Whites for support. "Let us be like brothers and help each other," wrote the Cossack ataman who, a few days before, had been on the point of ordering Alekseev to leave the Don and build his Volunteer Army elsewhere. "Let us save whatever can yet be saved." Alekseev's reply reflected that unhesitating willingness to sacrifice personal interests for the general good that had characterized his lifelong service to Russia. "Everything that I have at my command," he told Kaledin, "I will gladly give for our common cause." At that point, Alekseev's Volunteer Army numbered about six hundred, yet he sent most of them to fight under Kaledin's command. With their help, the Cossack leader drove the Bolshevik Red Guards from Rostov on December 2.[19]

The role that the embryonic Volunteer Army played in Kaledin's victory convinced him that he must reach an agreement with those exiled politicians and fugitive generals who insisted that the time had come for the Whites to launch a "national crusade" against the Bolsheviks. To do so proved as difficult as restoring unity among the Cossacks, for if the exiles in Novocherkassk shared a common hatred for the Bolsheviks, they did not have much affection for each other.[20] The coldly professorial Kadet leader Pavel Miliukov remained unrepentantly arrogant as he insisted that civilians, not generals, must determine Russia's course.[21] To make matters worse, General Kornilov, who reached the Don four days after Kaledin's victory, continued to despise Alekseev for carrying out Kerenskii's orders to arrest him the previous September. As they searched for common ground upon which to unite during the second and third weeks of December, White and Cossack leaders knew that they could not build the Volunteer Army without Kornilov's great personal magnetism, but they knew for certain that Kornilov would never serve where Alekseev commanded.[22]

General Denikin long remembered the "distressing scene" on December 18, when generals spoke too bluntly and politicians spoke too glibly of self-sacrifice and "national need" after Kornilov had threatened to leave the Don and carry his battle against the Bolsheviks to Siberia unless he received undisputed command of the Volunteer Army. Only after long hours of bitter debate did the adversaries agree to form a triumvirate that gave Kaledin control of Cossack affairs, placed Alekseev in charge of civilian and diplomatic matters, and installed Kornilov at the head of the Volunteer Army.[23] General Kornilov therefore took command of the White forces in South Russia on Christmas Day, 1917. "Once again the Russian land must arise to defend its holy relics and rights that have been trampled upon as it did three centuries ago [during the Time of Troubles]," he proclaimed. "The Russian people, gathering in the South from all corners of our homeland, will defend to the last drop of their blood . . . this last bastion of Russian independence, this final hope for the restoration of a Free and Great Russia."[24]

Kornilov had pitifully little with which to support his heroic words.[25] When he took command, the Volunteer Army still numbered less than four thousand, most of them still without uniforms, winter clothing, or rifles.[26] Its first weapons came from troops who had abandoned the war on Russia's western front and were all too eager to discard the instruments of war, daring raids on Cossack arms depots, and, when their desperately limited funds permitted it, the black market run by greedy Cossack quartermasters.[27] On one occasion some of Kornilov's men boldly stole an entire battery of field guns. On another, they got a company of Cossack gunners drunk on bootleg vodka and bought their entire battery of guns for five thousand rubles. At one point, Volunteer Army officers simply "borrowed" two field guns to fire a ceremonial artillery salute and then claimed to have "lost" them.[28]

Such efforts could arm a handful of fighters, but they could not equip the modern army Alekseev hoped to put into the field against the Reds. Because Russia's weapons industries remained in territories under Bolshevik control, every field gun, rifle, and bullet had to be imported into the White lands, and each had to be paid for before it was delivered. Money thus became particularly crucial to the Whites' success. Mariia Nesterovich, an army nurse who served as a messenger for Alekseev, collected over seventy thousand rubles as she traveled clandestinely back and forth between Novocherkassk and Moscow, and sympathetic men and women all across Russia donated silver and gold objects ranging from military medals and teaspoons to serving dishes and jewelry. Larger sums reached the Volunteer Army only in mid-December, when anticommunist organizations in Moscow sent over a half-million rubles and South Russian banks donated several million more. Even these funds could do little but pay the Volunteer Army token wages.[29] To buy weapons and supplies for the army of twenty thousand men that they hoped to recruit, Kornilov and Alekseev needed the support of Russia's former allies, but these governments did not yet share their sense of desperation. While the Whites waited for help, the French, British, and Americans continued to debate whom to support and to search for the most effective channels through which to send their aid.[30]

Because Westerners still thought of the Cossacks as the staunch antirevolutionaries they had been before 1917, French, British, and American diplomatic and military circles continued to think that Kaledin, not Alekseev or Kornilov, could provide the best leadership for the anti-Bolshevik forces in South Russia. Despite strong protests from diplomats and military men knowledgeable about Russia, they continued to hold that view.[31] With too little understanding of conditions in Russia, the National City Bank of New York hurriedly transferred a half million dollars of Imperial Russian government assets to Kaledin,[32] while the chief of Britain's Imperial General Staff sent word that England would "grant Kaledin financial support up to any figure necessary," although his superiors in England's War Cabinet hurried to add that such sums would "be paid in installments [only] so long as the recipients continued the struggle."[33] Captivated by the vision that their francs, pounds, and dollars somehow would send divisions of raging Cossacks into battle against what they now perceived as an ungodly union of "Bolshevik forces assisted and controlled by the Germans,"[34] Russia's former allies still looked to Kaledin, even after Kornilov took command of the Volunteer Army.

How badly the Allies had misread the situation in the Don lands became clear at the end of January 1918. As Red Guards advanced, Kaledin's authority over the Cossacks collapsed.[35] On January 29, certain that he could not stem the Reds' victorious advance into the Don lands, the man whom the Allies had expected to lead the White armies to victory resigned as ataman of the Don Cossacks, bade his officers farewell, walked into an adjoining room, and shot himself through the heart.[36] That same day, the leaders of the Volunteer Army held a particularly acrimonious meeting in Rostov at which even Denikin lost his temper. "Only the devil knows," he exclaimed as he stormed out of the room, "why we have to have these discussions."[37] At that point the Whites' leaders were nearly as ready to fight among themselves as they were to confront the Bolshevik forces marching against them. For a time, only Alekseev's peacemaking held them together.

Although the Bolsheviks' military forces in those days were no more disciplined than Kaledin's turbulent Cossacks or Kornilov's hesitant volunteers, some of their commanders boasted military records that equaled the best of the White generals. Not all tsarist officers, and not even all tsarist generals, fought on the side of the Whites in Russia's Civil War, and a number of Russia's senior commanders—a majority of tsarist General Staff officers according to some reliable estimates—placed their talents at the Bolsheviks' disposal during the year after the October Revolution.[38] Certain that they were acting in the best interests of the land they loved, these men provided much of the organizational talent that transformed the unruly Red Guards into a highly disciplined Red Army before the Civil War ended.

The first tsarist general to join the Bolsheviks, General Mikhail Bonch-Bruevich had entered the Great War as quartermaster-general of the Third Army in Galicia and had risen to command the northern front at the time of Kornilov's "revolt." With a younger brother who had become one of Lenin's most dedicated disciples, Bonch-Bruevich readily transferred his loyalties to Russia's new order. Within a fortnight after the October Revolution he became the Bolsheviks' chief of staff and, in February 1918, took command of the defenses of Petrograd.[39] He was joined later by General Aleksei Alekseevich Brusilov, architect of the victorious "Brusilov offensive" that sent Russian armies storming into Austria's Galician lands in 1916 and commander-in-chief of Russia's armies between May and July 1917.

Brusilov had none of Bonch-Bruevich's ties to the new order, nor did his background mark him in any way as a potential leader in the Red Army. The son of a fighting general in the army of Nicholas I, educated as a courtier in the Imperial Corps of Pages, and married to the cousin of the renowned Imperial Prime Minister Petr Stolypin, Brusilov compiled an impressive record of victories while other commanders had suffered defeats. On the eve of the February Revolution he stood high in the confidence of the imperial government as commander-in-chief of Russia's southwest front. Sixty-four when the Bolsheviks seized power, he remained a dashing cavalry officer among proletarians, his body slim and straight, his mustaches still waxed and curled. Yet, aristocrat that he was, Brusilov could not share the Whites' belief that it was better to kill his countrymen than to allow them to live under Bolshevism. He therefore remained in Moscow after the October Revolution and, before the end of the Civil War, moved into the Red Army with several of his most trusted adjutants, the youngest of whom was to become a Hero of the Soviet Union during the Second World

War.[40] A man of conscience who loved his country above all, Brusilov in no way merited Denikin's scathing curse that he had lost "his honor and virtue . . . [by] entering the service of the enemies of the Russian people."[41]

Men such as Brusilov and Bonch-Bruevich entered the Red Army to organize and plan, not to command in the field. The Bolsheviks drew many of their best field commanders from the ranks of talented tsarist noncommissioned and junior grade officers whose plebian origins had slowed their promotions in an army that placed a premium upon birth and wealth. Other Bolshevik commanders had evaded military service during the Great War and only drew their first blood in revolutionary combat. Such was true of Vladimir Antonov-Ovseenko, the revolutionary street tactician who commanded the Bolsheviks' attack against the Winter Palace in October 1917. Antonov's rumpled clothing gave him the look of a down-at-the-heels provincial schoolmaster on the night he arrested the ministers of Kerenskii's fallen Provisional Government. "His collar and shirt and cuffs and hands," one of his fastidious prisoners remembered with disgust, "were those of a very dirty man."[42] Yet, Antonov's rusty, unkempt hair, wire-rimmed spectacles, and wispy mustache masked an instinctive sense for tactics and military organization that sometimes crossed the threshold of brilliance. Less than a week after his assault on the Winter Palace, he became commander of the Petrograd Military District and a member of the Central Committee of the People's Commissariat for Military and Naval Affairs. Early in December, Lenin and the Sovnarkom gave him command of the forces that were being assembled against the Whites in the Don lands.[43]

Bearing Lenin's promise that the land question in the Don region would be settled "in the interests of the toilers among the Cossacks and all working men and women on the basis of the program of the Soviets," Antonov-Ovseenko began his march to the South on December 8, 1917. Supported by Red Guards and detachments of revolutionary workers that had been sent from Petrograd, Moscow, and the coalfields of the Donbas, he not only expected to command the loyalty of those proletarians of Rostov, Ekaterinoslav, and Taganrog who had proclaimed the Soviet Republic of the Don in mid-November, but he hoped to win the Cossacks' land-hungry *inogorodnye* tenant farmers to his cause. From his headquarters at Kharkov, a city of about a quarter million, Antonov sent part of his force southeast along the Voronezh–

Novocherkassk railway against the Cossacks in Novocherkassk and the Volunteer Army in Rostov, while he took the remainder south against Ekaterinoslav and Taganrog.[44] Supported by more than a hundred machine guns, nearly twenty field guns, five airplanes, and an armored train, Antonov's Reds outnumbered the Whites by more than two to one when he began his advance on Christmas Day, 1917. By the time they approached the Don lands, the strength of his assault groups had nearly tripled to more than twenty thousand.[45] The one-time revolutionary propagandist and organizer thus faced the former Supreme Commander of Russia's Armies. Kornilov had tactical genius, long experience, and the advice of some of the best military minds that the Imperial Russian Army had produced. Although many of his soldiers had never before been subjected to military discipline and their readiness to obey orders remained completely open to question,[46] Antonov had the advantage of revolutionary fervor, greater numbers, and many more weapons.

Considering the disorderly nature of his forces, Antonov moved with surprising speed. Before Kaledin's suicide at the end of January, his Red Guards had taken Ekaterinoslav, Kupiansk, Lugansk, Mariupol, and Taganrog and stood ready to fall upon Rostov and Novocherkassk.[47] "The Red Army was advancing against Novocherkassk from the north and Rostov from the south and west," one young officer in the White forces remembered. "The Red troops were tightening a ring around these cities and the Volunteer Army found itself in its very center. . . . We didn't have the strength to hold out, but our commanders kept trying to shore up our lines by shifting exhausted groups of men from one critical point to another."[48] Briefly the Whites held, then they had to retreat.

These first battles showed all too vividly the type of fighting that would dominate Russia's Civil War, for terror coldly and brutally applied became a part of the struggle of Red against White from the very beginning. In contrast to the exalted notions of glory that had sent men to war in 1914, raw ideological passions that rivaled those of Europe's sixteenth and seventeenth century religious wars in their intensity spurred those Russians who now turned upon each other. Their followers either passionately drawn to the Bolsheviks' credo of class struggle or morally repelled by it, Kornilov and Lenin therefore both sanctioned terror more readily than commanders in Europe's Great War ever had. "The greater the terror, the greater our victories,"[49] Kornilov told his men as Antonov's Red Guards began their march. "We must save Russia!" he added later, "even if we have to set fire to half of it and shed the blood of three-fourths of all the Russians!"[50] The Bolsheviks spoke in similarly absolute terms. Trotskii demanded that measures be taken to "wipe off the face of the earth the counterrevolution of the Cossack generals and the Kadet bourgeoisie,"[51] while Lenin ordered Dzerzhinskii's Cheka to defend Russia's proletarians against "the most heinous crimes" of the Whites.[52]

Such passions led men to commit atrocities unheard of during the battles of the First World War. When a detachment of Whites trapped a handful of Bolshevik factory workers in the sleepy seaport town of Taganrog they blinded and mutilated them before they buried them alive.[53] Antonov's men repaid the Reds in the same coin. "I shall never forget the terrible impression it made on me the first time that they brought in the bodies of eight tortured Volunteers," Denikin later wrote. "They had been beaten and cut up so badly, and their faces so disfigured, that their grief-stricken relatives could scarcely recognize them." Elsewhere, Denikin's men found the body of a man whom Antonov's Reds had buried alive after they had cut off his hands and feet and slit open his abdomen. He had been tortured only because his son had joined the Whites.[54] No one emerged from three years of such cruelty and terror unscathed. "Not only did the experience cripple the body," Denikin confessed sadly. "It deformed the soul as well."[55]

As the Volunteer Army began its retreat on February 22,* Antonov's forces entered Rostov and Novocherkassk. "Madness came in our wake," General Denikin later wrote. "Reckless debauchery, hatred, robbery, and murder filled those towns and cities we had abandoned." Forced to leave their families behind, the men who followed Kornilov faced the certainty that their lives had veered onto a new course in which ranks held in earlier times counted for little. "Among us marched two former supreme commanders of the Russian armies, a former commander-in-chief of one of our [World War I] Fronts, former high-ranking chiefs of staff, corps commanders, and senior colonels," Denikin remembered. "Few in number, ragged, hunted, and surrounded, the Volunteer Army stood as the symbol of persecuted Russia as it wended its way across the wide expanses of the Don and Kuban steppe."[56] Still struggling to moderate Kornilov's dark, consuming hatred for Bolsheviks and politicians of any sort, Alekseev shared Denikin's sentiments. "We are retreating into the steppe," he wrote to a friend. "We must light a lamp so that at least one small flame will continue to shine through the darkness that has descended upon Russia."[57] Driven by "a sense of moral duty," one of his officers later remembered, Alekseev became "the spirit and the ideology of the . . . first campaign into the Kuban."[58]

For the next eighty days, the men of the Volunteer Army endured what its survivors remembered as the Icy March, which took them into the wilds of the Kuban steppe that lay to the east of the Black Sea. Tragically ignorant about the region into which they marched, the leaders of the Volunteer Army hoped to launch a new campaign against Antonov's forces from the city of Ekaterinodar, whose inhabitants included some twenty-five thousand turbulent workers sympathetic to the Bolsheviks. On March 14, 1918, as the Volunteer Army struggled south and southwest through freezing winds and swirling snow, the proletarians of Ekaterinodar seized the city, proclaimed their loyalty to Lenin's government,[59] and forced Kornilov to delay his attack while he awaited reinforcements. When he approached Ekaterinodar for a second time at the beginning of April, Kornilov found that the Bolsheviks had a force of some eighteen thousand (including armed women and teen-agers) ready to bar his way. For four days, weary White troops probed the Red's new defenses with little success.[60] Then, with food, ammunition, and medicines in desperately short supply, Kornilov ordered a final assault. "I see no way out except to take Ekaterinodar," he told a military council on April 12. "Therefore, I have decided to attack along our entire front tomorrow at dawn."[61] Retreat, Kornilov insisted, would bring the "slow agony" of certain defeat, while a final assault offered at least a slim hope for success. "We all may perish here," he concluded, "but, in my opinion, it is better to die with honor."[62] Always the proper aristocrat, the elegant General Sergei Markov, who once had described the purpose of the Kuban campaign as a march "to the devil, in quest of bluebirds,"[63] returned to his quarters after the meeting with few illusions about the difficulties the Whites faced. "Put on clean underwear if you have any," he told his staff with studied indifference. "We won't succeed in taking Ekaterinodar, but even if we do, we'll get killed anyway."[64]

Fate gave Markov two more months to live, but the next day's events radically changed the future of the Volunteer Army. When the Red artillery began to shell the Volunteer Army with particular ferocity, Denikin urged Kornilov to move his headquarters to a less exposed location, fearful that the whitewashed walls of the small farmhouse in which his chief had established his command post would present too easy a target to the Bolshevik gunners in the valley below. "It's not worth it," Kornilov replied with a shrug. "Tomorrow we're going to launch our final attack." Denikin left, intent upon the progress of the fighting. As the sun rose and warmed the morning air, he heard an explosion in a nearby grove. "I saw horses and men quickly scatter," he wrote later. "Then, there was another [explosion], this time very nearby." A Bolshevik gunner had fired a high explosive shell directly into the room in which Denikin had left his commander a few minutes before. "The door to Kornilov's room crashed open and a cloud of white plaster dust streamed forth," a staff officer who was in the corridor remembered. Kornilov lay on the floor, covered with dust, his right leg shattered. Only when they turned their general over did his aides see that a small piece of shrapnel had penetrated his left temple. The daring officer, who had defied death so many times during the great battles of the First World War, lay only moments away from death.[65] Still clad in the civilian overcoat he had worn ever since his escape from Bykhov, General Denikin took command of the Volunteer Army. "You have inherited a heavy burden," General Alekseev said with deep sadness when aides brought him to the farmhouse where Kornilov's body lay. "May God help you!"[66]

Certain that Ekaterinodar could not be attacked with any serious hope of success, Denikin led his men, "exhausted, filthy, and infected with every sort of parasite imaginable,"[67] in a torturous retreat. Desperately trying to preserve enough of the Volunteer Army to continue the Whites' struggle against the Bolsheviks in the South, he left most of his wounded behind and drove the survivors along forced marches of as much as fifty kilometers a day. Without telephone, radio, or telegraph, he and his men marched in ignorance of events in the outside world, as they circled back in the direction whence they had come in search of a haven in which to recoup their strength. Finally, less than seventy-five kilometers from Rostov, Denikin regrouped his forces in the large villages of Mechetinskaia and Egorlykskaia, and the Icy March, whose campaign medal would be a crown of thorns pierced by a sword, reached its end. Of the 3,685 men who answered muster on May 13, 2,368 had been officers before the Bolshevik Revolution and another 1,036 had served as corporals or sergeants. Clearly, Denikin still faced the awkward dilemma of sending into the fighting line as common soldiers men who once had held high commands. That so small a force included thirty-six generals (who had commanded divisions, corps, armies, and entire fronts during the First World War) and almost two hundred colonels (who had commanded regiments and brigades before they had joined the White forces in the South) would prove a mixed blessing. Men so long accustomed to giving orders found it nearly as difficult not to question commands as did Antonov's untrained and undisciplined legions.[68] Only Denikin's genius for welding men of volatile and diverse temperaments together would enable the Volunteer Army to survive into the summer.

Like Kornilov and Alekseev, Anton Ivanovich Denikin had risen from humble birth and poverty to a position of high command in the Imperial Russian Army. The son of a Polish Catholic seamstress and a Russian serf soldier who had fought in three wars before he retired with the rank of major in 1869, Denikin had entered the army at the age of seventeen and the General Staff Academy at twenty-two. A childhood spent in a shabby two-room apartment in the Polish industrial town of Włocławek had given him the tenacity to succeed where men of lesser will failed.[69] Just forty-five when he took command of the Volunteer Army, Denikin devoted all of his stubbornness, resourcefulness, and energy to building upon the foundations laid by Kornilov and the dying Alekseev. He needed time and resources. In the late spring and summer of 1918, rapid and unforeseen shifts in the course of events in Russia's southwest briefly gave him both.

While Denikin and his senior commanders struggled to keep the Volunteer Army alive, their enemies faced other problems. "Grinding its teeth," as its representative said, Lenin's government had signed the Treaty of Brest-Litovsk with Imperial Germany on March 3, 1918, just nine days after Kornilov had begun his Icy March.[70] Three hundred years of triumphs won by Russian arms and diplomacy dissolved in a single moment. Sixty million people and two million square kilometers of territory, including land that had produced nearly a third of Imperial Russia's crops, slipped from the Bolsheviks' grasp at Brest-Litovsk. When they moved their capital to Moscow in mid-March, their domains included only a seventh of the former Russian Empire's sugar beet fields, a quarter of its coal mines, iron foundries, and steel mills, and less than three-fifths of its population.[71] Russians "must measure to the very bottom that abyss of defeat, dismemberment, enslavement, and humiliation," Lenin announced bitterly. They must, he said, understand that "an epoch of most grievous defeats" was upon them.[72]

On the eve of the Brest-Litovsk treaty, Germany's jack-booted armies had marched into the Ukraine, the vast repository of natural wealth that had made up the southwest of the Russian Empire, in order to secure its iron, coal, and foodstuffs for their war effort. Advancing along rail lines, they received an enthusiastic welcome from anti-Bolshevik railroad workers and restored the Ukrainian national government that the Bolsheviks had driven into exile a scant three weeks before.[73] Soon afterward, they replaced the ineffectual Ukrainian national government with a more efficiently pro-German regime headed by General Pavlo Skoropadsky, a former aide-de-camp to Nicholas II and one of the wealthiest men in the Ukraine. Skoropadsky made no secret of his monarchist sympathies, met with Germany's Kaiser in Berlin, and, to the outrage of Ukrainian patriots, proclaimed his gratitude for the "powerful backing of the Central Powers," to whom the Ukraine owed its "salvation."[74] At the same time, the Germans continued their march east. Almost unopposed by Antonov-Ovseenko's inexperienced Red Guards, they entered Kharkov, Odessa, and, on May 6, Taganrog at the request of the anti-Bolshevik Ukrainian government they had just installed.

Clearly the Germans in May 1918 were in a better position to deliver military support to the Whites than any of Russia's wartime allies, although few among the Whites were so naive as to think that they would do so for any reasons other than their pressing short-term need to bring Russia's natural resources into the struggle on Europe's western front. On their side, White generals desperately needed weapons, and White politicians could not help but hope that the Germans would bring to South Russia the order and stability that they seemed to have established so easily in the western Ukraine. Could military aid from Russia's former enemies now be used against the Bolsheviks? That was the question that the Whites struggled to answer in the spring of 1918. The "law of national preservation," Kadet leader Miliukov insisted as he struggled to set aside four years of anti-German speeches, must take precedence over any "moral commitments" made in earlier times to former allies. Against the Bolshevik menace, Miliukov urged that the Volunteer Army accept an alliance with the Germans to bring about the "resurrection" of a true Russian government.[75]

Like too many politicians, Miliukov used semantic shadings to widen the gray area that separated right from wrong.[76] Yet for men of more straightforward views among the Don Cossacks, the prospect of German aid against the Bolsheviks also offered enticing prospects. Now led by Petr Krasnov, the Cossack general who had fought the Bolsheviks on the Pulkovo Heights a few days after the October Revolution, a special Cossack "Assembly for the Salvation of the Don" abolished all laws that had been issued in Russia since the abdication of Nicholas II.[77] Not at all troubled by the issues of principle and allegiance that Miliukov tried so deviously to explain away, Krasnov hurried to exchange Cossack grain for German weapons at the rate of one rifle and thirty cartridges for one *pud* (thirty-six pounds) of grain. Within eight weeks, the Germans delivered machine guns, artillery, shells, and more than eleven thousand rifles and eleven million cartridges to Krasnov.[78]

Although Krasnov and the Cossacks had no objections to exchanging Russian grain for German guns, Denikin and Alekseev remained stubbornly opposed to making agreements with the Germans. "Alliance with the Germans," Alekseev announced grimly, "is morally intolerable and politically inexpedient." In any union with Germany, he warned, Russians would be condemned to live as "political slaves and economic paupers."[79] Insisting upon "no relations whatsoever with either Germans or Bolsheviks," Alekseev announced that "the tasks of the Volunteer Army are, and will continue to remain, unchanged." There must be a "powerful, disciplined, and patriotic army" to wage an "unrelenting fight against Bolshevism" in order to establish a "unified and legal government."[80] Convinced that the leaders of the Volunteer Army must remain loyal to Russia's wartime allies, neither Denikin nor Alekseev would accept Miliukov's view that "treason" and "desertion" must take on new meanings in the struggle against the Bolsheviks.[81] Nor would they repeat Krasnov's assurances to the Germans that they would observe "complete neutrality" in the conflict that still raged in Europe.[82]

Denikin, Alekseev, and Krasnov could not agree about an alliance with the Germans, and they remained sharply at odds about the future of monarchy and democracy should Russia be liberated. Although convinced that, "in the normal course of events, Russia ought to come to a restoration of the monarchy," Alekseev feared that an open declaration of support for any political principle would split the Volunteer Army.[83] Wisely, Denikin supported him. "What right have we, a small handful of men, to decide the fate of the nation unknown to the Russian people and without their knowledge?" he asked. "The army ought not to meddle in politics," he concluded. "As far as I am concerned personally, I shall not fight for any form of government."[84] Yet Krasnov could not set his monarchist sympathies to rest so readily. Although he later claimed to have counseled the Cossacks "not to meddle in the affairs of the Russian State and leave it free to set up whatever form of government it preferred,"[85] he already had convinced his followers to repudiate the socialism of the October Revolution and the democracy of its February predecessor.[86]

Greatly outnumbered by their Bolshevik foes, the Whites desperately needed to settle their differences and unite their fragmented forces. On May 28, 1918, Krasnov and the high command of the Volunteer Army met for that purpose at the village of Manychskaia, yet their differences proved too broad, their personalities too much in conflict, and their aspirations too diverse. Krasnov and the Cossacks thought mainly of a war to liberate Cossack territory from the Bolsheviks, while Denikin and Alekseev called for a national struggle to create "a great, united and indivisible Russia."[87] For that reason, Krasnov never would subordinate his Cossacks to Denikin, nor would he allow them to fight outside the Territory of the Don. Most of all, he disdained the double standard that allowed Denikin to disdain all contact with the Germans but accept German weapons and ammunition so long as they first passed through Cossack hands. "The Volunteer Army is pure and without sin," Krasnov remarked bitterly some weeks later. "For it is I, the Don Cossack Ataman, whose filthy hands take the German shells and bullets, wash them in the waters of the Quiet Don, and, once cleaned, pass them on to the Volunteer Army."[88]

To their credit, Krasnov's Cossacks continued to supply Denikin's forces with German weapons and munitions, provide limited funds that had come into their hands from the banks of South Russia, and allow wounded volunteers to recuperate in Cossack hospitals in exchange for Denikin's promise to defend the Don against Bolshevik attacks from the Kuban. Yet they could come no closer than that to creating a common force against the Bolsheviks, for Krasnov resented Denikin's condescending view of him as an upstart commander. When Denikin launched his second campaign into the Kuban on June 22, Krasnov marched north and east against Tsaritsyn, the bastion on the lower Volga to which the Bolsheviks had retreated after the Germans had driven them from Rostov and Novocherkassk at the beginning of May. As one of the most important railroad centers in Russia, Tsaritsyn had become the home of new armaments and petroleum industries during the First World War. With these to support them, and spared from facing the full weight of the White armies by the failure of Denikin and Krasnov to unite their forces, the Bolsheviks built Tsaritsyn into a fortress to anchor their defenses in the southeast that summer.

Krasnov and Denikin did not command the only anti-Bolshevik forces in Russia during the spring of 1918, nor were theirs even the most significant. On May 25, three days before the disappointing meeting between Krasnov and Denikin at Manychskaia, the Czech Legion, a corps of thirty-five thousand Czechs and Slovaks, challenged Soviet authority along more than four thousand miles of the Trans-Siberian Railway and launched one of the most startling campaigns of the entire Civil War.

The force that history remembers as the Czech Legion began in the fall of 1914 as a brigade of less than a thousand men recruited by the tsarist government from among Czechs and Slovaks who had settled in Russia some years before. Originally formed to undertake reconnaissance and propaganda assignments behind the Austrian lines, this unit quickly became a focus for the political ambitions of those Czech nationalists who had fled to Paris from Austrian Bohemia at the war's outbreak. Encouraged by Tomáš Masaryk and Eduard Beneš, the Czech nationalist leaders who hoped to use its exploits as an allied force to bolster their efforts to wrest an independent Czechoslovakia from the Hapsburg Empire should the Allies triumph at the war's end, this Czech brigade fought bravely in the Third, Seventh, Eighth, and Eleventh Russian armies on Austrian territory.[89]

Instinctively fearful of all dissident nationalist movements, tsarist authorities refused the leaders of the Czech brigade permission to recruit replacements among the hundreds of thousands of Czech and Slovak prisoners taken in Russia's victories against the Austrians in 1914 and 1916. Only after Russia's new Provisional Government opened its prisoner-of-war camps to Czech recruiting officers in the spring of 1917 did new volunteers swell the brigade's ranks to the size of an army corps before the collapse of Russia's war effort left its future in doubt. Briefly, the enlarged Czech corps floundered in Russia's revolutionary tempest until Masaryk proclaimed it part of the Czech armed forces in France and called for its troops to be transported eastward across Siberia, the Pacific, North America, and the Atlantic to the battlefields of western Europe. On the surface, Masaryk's was a preposterous scheme that required not only Allied help but extensive cooperation from the Bolsheviks who had to face intense pressure from the Germans and Austrians to return the Czechs for punishment after they signed the treaty of Brest-Litovsk.[90]

Fearful that even the slightest Bolshevik betrayal could bring them before Austro-German firing squads, the Czech Legion's commanders viewed the safe-passage agreement that Masaryk negotiated with Lenin's government at the end of March 1918 with alarm because it required them to surrender most of their weapons. Hesitantly, and with much suspicion and great caution, they began their journey. Then, on May 25, they intercepted a telegram sent by Trotskii to soviets in the towns and cities along the Trans-Siberian Railway ordering that "every Czech who is found carrying a weapon anywhere along the route of the railway is to be shot on the spot."[91] Certain that they had been betrayed, the Czechs attacked the small Red forces that held the the Trans-Siberian stations of Marianovka and Mariinsk and made ready to fight their way to the Pacific port of Vladivostok.

The Czechs' victories against the disorganized Siberian Reds during the early summer of 1918 underscored the weakness of the Bolsheviks and showed that a comparatively small but well-trained and well-led armed force could be very potent in the chaotic conditions that prevailed in Russia. Within forty-eight hours, the Czechs seized the central Siberian cities of Novo-Nikolaevsk and Cheliabinsk and arrested the Soviet Commissar for Food Supply Tsiurupa, who had come to Siberia to speed shipments of grain to Petrograd and Moscow. Before the end of the month, they captured the Siberian provincial capital city of Tomsk and added Omsk, the largest city in western Siberia, with an armory that held a thousand rifles and 168 michine guns, and Samara, key to the middle Volga region, to their victories before the middle of June.[92]

That Siberia was honeycombed with anti-Bolshevik organizations made their task all the easier. During the months after the

October Revolution, hundreds of Socialist Revolutionaries and Mensheviks had made an unlikely alliance with thousands of tsarist army officers who had fled to Siberia, where the Bolsheviks' weak authority continued to be diluted by the region's vastness.[93] The estimated active anti-Bolsheviks in western Siberia alone approached seven thousand in mid-May, and these proved only too willing to join the Czechs.[94] In Novo-Nikolaevsk, one eyewitness remarked, their battle with the local Reds "was over in forty minutes."[95]

In June 1918, the Czech Legion found the Allies no better prepared for its first victories than the Bolsheviks, for no one in France, Britain, or the United States had expected its eastward march to revive the prospect for reopening a second front against the Germans. Indeed, the Brest-Litovsk treaty had made the Allies fearful that the Germans would force millions of Russians into industrial and military service to help their war effort on the western front. "Germany is not hampered, like the Western Powers, by any standards of Christianity," one British statesman insisted as he warned that his country's enemy would show no hesitation at using "starvation and flogging, backed by machine guns," to bring Russians in the lands occupied by the German army into the trenches of the Central Powers. Indeed, the author of one British government report in mid-May 1918 even had forecast a return in the German Empire to "the conditions of the ancient Roman Empire, with legionnaires fighting on her frontiers and slaves working at home, both recruited from subject races."[96] Then, Lord Robert Cecil, Britain's under-secretary of state for foreign affairs, had told Parliament, "the great foundation stone" of Britain's policy must be "to see Russia [remain] a great and powerful non-Germanic nation."[97]

In mid-May, Lord Cecil had urged his nation's allies to consider using the Czech Legion to reopen a second front against the Germans rather than transport them to the battlefields of France.[98] Angrily, the French had rejected his proposal and continued to insist, as they had since the Great War's outbreak, that all resources must be concentrated against the Germans in the West. "This is not the hour," France's Premier Clemenceau wrote indignantly, "for you to think of depriving us of soldiers who are courageous, well trained, and profoundly devoted to our cause." At the very moment when its final rupture with the Bolsheviks was in the making,

Britain and France thus agreed to keep in force the initial plan to transport the Czech Legion around the world to fight on the western front.[99]

The Czechs' unexpected victories all along the route of the Trans-Siberian Railway finally convinced the French that Allied intervention in Siberia could be of great value in their war against the Germans. In Allied headquarters all around the globe, anticipation of large-scale action hung heavily in the air, especially since Britain, China, and Japan already had landed token forces on Russian soil, beginning with the Chinese guards who had driven the Russians from the Chinese-Eastern Railway in December 1917. Early 1918 had seen the British dispatch small intervention forces to other parts of Russia at almost monthly intervals: at the end of January, General Dunsterville led the beginnings of "Dunsterforce" from Bagdad toward Baku; then, the Royal Marines landed at Murmansk at the beginning of March; and finally, fifty more marines marched into Vladivostok in conjunction with a larger Japanese contingent in early April. Although he had been unyielding in his insistence that the Czech Legion join the Allied forces on the western front, even France's Clemenceau had spoken of some form of Allied intervention in Siberia after receiving exaggerated reports of French citizens being killed in Irkutsk at the beginning of January.[100] Only the United States continued to stand resolutely against military intervention. Although America's Secretary of State Robert Lansing insisted that "the hope of a stable Russian Government lies for the present in a military dictatorship backed by loyal disciplined troops," President Wilson continued to resist committing troops against the Bolsheviks. Kaledin and the Don Cossacks, he remained convinced, would restore stable government in Russia.[101]

With President Wilson still refusing to support military intervention against the Bolsheviks at the beginning of 1918, his allies had placed their hopes for an anti-Bolshevik force in Siberia in the person of the corrupt and rapacious Siberian Cossack Ataman Grigorii Semenov, who, at twenty-seven, looked every inch the bandit he was. Colonel John Ward, commander of the forces the British eventually sent into Siberia, remembered most of all Semenov's eyes, "that belong rather to an animal than a man," when he wrote about him a few years later. "The whole pose of the man," he added, "is at first suspicious, alert, determined, like a tiger ready to spring, to rend, and tear."[102] Instinctively, Semenov understood that any man who commanded an armored train and a few hundred men had the strength of an army in the far-flung spaces of Siberia, and he used his armored trains in much the same fashion as a naval commander might use destroyers or battleships to subjugate enemy ports.[103] In all but the most desperate circumstances, legitimate governments shunned alliances with men of Semenov's type. During the first months of 1918, the French, British, and Japanese thought they had no other choice.

The Czech Legion's first successes allowed the Allies to shape their policy around a more legitimate and reliable military force than Semenov's, and even the United States began to think of exploiting the Legion's unexpected victories. "It would be a serious mistake to remove the Czecho-Slovak troops from Siberia," America's minister to Peking wrote to Secretary of State Lansing in mid-June. "If they were not in Siberia it would be worthwhile to bring them there."[104] The most dramatic policy reversal, however, came from France. In scarcely more than two months, Clemenceau turned from demanding that "all detachments of the Czech Corps should be transported with the swiftest means to the western front" (April 26) to urging that "all our efforts must now be directed to diverting the action of the Czechs to the . . . complete occupation of the Siberian Railway, in order to prepare quick progress for Japanese intervention (July 12)."[105]

Clemenceau had good reason to center his hopes for reopening a second front upon the forces of Japan. Of all the Allies with armed forces in the Far East, the Japanese stood most ready, able, and willing to render military and logistical support to the Czech Legion, and their efforts to achieve their national objectives in Siberia's eastern maritime provinces influenced the course of events more directly in 1918 than the actions of any other great power. Ever since the Sino-Japanese War of 1894–1895, Japan had pursued an aggressive policy on the Asian mainland that had brought her into direct confrontation with Russia and had produced important shifts in her alliances with the great powers of the West as the twentieth century moved toward the end of its first decade. Perhaps most important, Japan's expansion into Manchuria and Korea put her increasingly at loggerheads with American statesmen whose plans to expand their nation's commercial and political interests in the Far East included efforts to acquire a measure of control over the railways of China and Siberia. The Americans had looked especially to the opening of the Panama Canal in 1914 to strengthen their position in Asia, for they expected that monument to modern engineering to place their country at the very center of the world's shipping lanes. A scant fortnight before the canal opened, the outbreak of the First World War offered opportunities for the Japanese to expand onto the Asian mainland that even her most aggressive statesmen had not thought possible. While the storm that burst upon Europe drew the attention of the other great powers away from Asia, and with some of the most influential elements of Japanese public opinion insisting that "such an opportunity . . . will not occur [again] for hundreds of years,"[106] Japan moved quickly to occupy German territories in the Far East, strengthen her foothold on the mainland, and weaken the position of her American rival.

The Russian Revolution broadened the prospects for Japan to expand even further as her diplomats and military planners focused their attention upon the railways that connected European Russia, Manchuria, and the Far East.[107] Yet any movement by the Japanese into northern Manchuria and eastern Siberia threatened to bring them into conflict with those American financiers and politicians who continued to be fascinated by the prospect of linking their nation's Great Northern Railway with the Trans-Siberian by means of shipping lanes that stretched from Seattle to Vladivostok. Like the Japanese, these men hoped to profit from Russia's domestic turmoil, and, again like the Japanese, they identified their schemes with their nation's interests and pressed their government to support them.[108] In the spring of 1917, the United States therefore sent a Railway Advisory Commission to Vladivostok and Petrograd for the publicly announced purpose of helping the Provisional Government restore its collapsing rail system. Headed by John Frank Stevens, former chief engineer of the Panama Canal, and supported by the Railway Service Corps, which the United States sent later in the year under the command of the Great Northern Railway's General Manager George Emerson, this commission became the instrument of men dedicated to strengthening America's position in Asia. As they moved quickly from advising Kerenskii's government to managing Asiatic Russia's railways, their presence strengthened their nation's sphere of influence in eastern Siberia at the expense of the Japanese.[109]

Both Americans and Japanese thus looked to some form of intervention to strengthen their interests in the maritime provinces of Asiatic Russia, although each had different goals and very different types of intervention in mind. The Americans hoped that a restored railway network could help the Whites reestablish a strong Russia—"one mighty, aspiring democracy," President Wilson's envoy had said the previous summer[110]—that could prevent the Japanese from strengthening their foothold in the Far East, while the Japanese preferred a breakdown of Russia's railways that would enable them to broaden their influence on the Asian mainland. Both hoped to legitimize any intervention in the Far East by tying it to actions by other allied powers, yet, at the beginning of 1918, each hoped to prevent the other from seizing the initiative. While their allies debated what policy to adopt toward Russia's new Bolshevik government, the United States and Japan made preparations to intervene in Russia's Far Eastern lands, the Japanese by taking military action and the Americans by committing great sums of money and supplies to strengthen Siberia's railroads.

While insisting that "the success of any such undertaking [as military intervention] will depend largely upon the whole-hearted support of all the Great Powers,"[111] the Japanese had begun their preparations to march into Siberia nearly three months before the Czechs won their first victories. "Japanese military preparations are being completed rapidly," America's Ambassador Roland Morris reported from Tokyo at the beginning of March. "Troops are concentrating at west coast ports, [and] two divisions have already been sent to Korea."[112] At the beginning of April, some of these newly mobilized Japanese troops found themselves aboard the cruisers *Asahi* and *Iwami*, which stood at anchor in Vladivostok harbor alongside the U.S.S. *Brooklyn* and the H.M.S. *Suffolk*. In response to a small incident, in which the Russians killed three Japanese, Admiral Kato sent five hundred marines into Vladivostok on April 5, and the commander of Britain's *Suffolk* sent fifty British troops ashore to support them. Although the Japanese insisted that their marines would be withdrawn as soon as possible, the first military intervention in Siberia had been accomplished.[113] "It is . . . almost inevitable that the Japanese will advance," Lenin warned when he received news of their landing. "Undoubtedly, the Allies will help them."[114] That gloomy prediction proved all too accurate. Within six months, the handful of forces from the *Asahi*, *Iwami*, and *Suffolk* had swelled into invading armies. Before the end of 1918, 73,000 Japanese, 2,500 English, 1,000 French, 1,500 Italians, and over 8,000 Americans had entered Siberia to support the Czechs.[115]

While the Allies marched into Russia's Far Eastern provinces, those anti-Bolshevik forces that had made their way to Siberia after the October Revolution replaced local Bolshevik regimes with new governments. At first centered upon the intellectuals and politicians who had gravitated to the Siberian university city of Tomsk, the Provisional Government of Autonomous Siberia claimed its legitimacy from the Siberian Regional Duma dispersed by the Bolsheviks at the end of January 1918. First headed by an obscure Socialist Revolutionary by the name of Petr Derber, some of the dispersed Duma deputies formed an anti-Bolshevik government the moment they learned of the Czechs' first victories and raised a green and white flag as the symbol of the forests and snows of the autonomous Siberia they hoped to create.[116] Within a month this government had set up its headquarters in the western Siberian city of Omsk, moved sharply to the right, annulled all laws issued by the Bolsheviks, and restored all confiscated private property to its former owners.[117]

Typical of anti-Bolshevik movements all over Russia, Lenin's Siberian opponents squandered vital energy and resources in conflicts among themselves. None fought more bitterly with the Provisional Government of Autonomous Siberia during the summer of 1918 than the Committee of Members of the Constituent Assembly, known by its Russian acronym, Komuch, whose leaders proclaimed an independent government the moment that units of the Czech Legion drove the Red Guards out of the Volga River city of Samara.[118] Comprised mainly of Socialist Revolutionaries, the Komuch government proclaimed its support for a "United Independent Free Russia" and demanded that Russia's dispersed Constituent Assembly be restored.[119] Like the Provisional Government of Autonomous Siberia, the Komuch government returned privately owned factories to their former owners. "Repudiating all socialist experiments, the Committee [i.e. Komuch] considers that it is impossible to abolish capitalist forms of industry at the present time," its leaders announced. "Capitalist forms of industry must exist, and capitalists as a class must be allowed to direct them."[120] More dramatically than any other White government to date, Komuch promised to reopen the eastern front against the Germans and Austrians in return for Allied aid against the Bolsheviks and began to mobilize all men between the ages of twenty and twenty-three for military service in an army from which all political organizations, assemblies, and speeches were to be excluded.[121]

Like the Provisional Government of Autonomous Siberia further to the east, the Komuch government expanded its territory quickly during the summer of 1918. Led by Colonel V. O. Kappel, whose genius for using small detachments of land forces in conjunction with a fleet of river boats allowed him to strike far in the rear of his Red adversaries, the forces of the Komuch government seized the key cities of Ufa and Simbirsk, the birthplace of Lenin, before the end of July.[122] Then, on August 7, the Komuch army troops drove the Bolsheviks from Kazan, ancient capital of the Tatars and scene of Ivan the Terrible's great victory over them in 1552. Famed for the university that once had been the home of the great nineteenth-century mathematician Nikolai Lobachevskii, Kazan had long been a center of Russian learning, trade, and industry and stood as the last major military obstacle between the Komuch forces and Moscow. With their commander confessing to a "chaos of unpreparedness" among his forces in which many units "proved incapable of fighting in mass because of lack of preparation and discipline,"[123] the Bolsheviks fled Kazan so precipitously that they abandoned a gold reserve worth more than 650 million rubles that the tsarist government had stored in the city's State Bank.[124] Unlike the Volunteer Army in the South, or the Provisional Government of Autonomous Siberia to the East, the Komuch government thus emerged from its first battles in the summer of 1918 with the financial resources to fight a serious war.

If the Komuch government enjoyed the means that other Whites lacked, it also suffered a fatal flaw. "The government was Socialist Revolutionary, a party unconciliatory even with the Kadets," one of its leading generals pointed out, while its army "consisted of right-wing elements hostile to the Socialist Revolutionaries."[125] The men destined to fight and win the battles of the Komuch government therefore stood unalterably opposed to the politics of its Socialist Revolutionary leaders, who also failed to win the broad social base of mass support needed to sustain any successful long-term opposition against the Bolsheviks' government of workers and peasants.

The Whites' early successes only added to the Bolsheviks' fears. As fragile Bolshevik defenses collapsed in lands far from Russia's Red center, Lenin and his comrades faced the terrifying prospect that the Whites and their allies might weld their separate offensives into a solid ring that could squeeze the life from Russia's Red heart. White forces churned up the frontiers of the Russian land in a manner unknown since the troubled times of which Chaliapin had sung in Mussorgskii's *Boris Godunov*, and even Trotskii, the Bolsheviks' indefatigable commissar of war, wondered—at least for a moment—if the end had come.[126] Yet, the divergent aims of the Allied intervention, coupled with a volatile mixture of nationalist strivings, ideological rigidity, and political conflict that kept the Volunteer Army of Denikin, the Cossacks of Krasnov, the army of the Komuch government, and the forces of the Provisional Government of Autonomous Siberia at loggerheads spared the Bolsheviks from facing a united White movement. As the year neared its end, the balance of forces began to shift in Russia. War Communism, the system of mobilization compounded from the emergency of war and the dogma of socialism that Lenin proclaimed in the summer of 1918, gave the Bolsheviks the means to hold fast against their enemies and to exploit the antagonisms that began to separate the Whites.

CHAPTER THREE

"The Expropriation of the Expropriators"

NEITHER THE DISCIPLINE nor the dogma of War Communism had seemed much in evidence when Petrograd's leading Bolsheviks discussed the formation of a new government on October 26, 1917. Rejecting the title "minister" as "a foul, worn-out term,"[1] Lenin had seized upon Trotskii's suggestion that the men who would lead Russia's first revolutionary socialist government be called people's commissars—"a type born in the fires of revolution"—and that the government as a whole be known as the Soviet—that is, Council—of People's Commissars.[2] Between them, these fifteen men had spent more than two centuries in exile and tsarist prisons. Five among them had been imprisoned for their political activities within the previous three months, and Lenin had ended a life as a fugitive from Kerenskii's police a scant forty-eight hours earlier.*

* Chaired by Lenin, Russia's first Soviet of People's Commissars, or Sovnarkom, included Trotskii (Foreign Affairs), Aleksei Rykov (Internal Affairs), Vladimir Miliutin (Agriculture), Aleksandr Shliapnikov (Labor), Viktor Nogin (Industry and Commerce), Anatolii Lunacharskii (Education or Enlightenment), Nikolai Krylenko, Vladimir Antonov-Ovseenko, and Pavel Dybenko (as a committee of three to head the Commissariat of Military and Naval Affairs), Georgii Lomov-Oppokov (Justice), Ivan Skvortsov-Stepanov (Finance), Ivan Teodorovich (Food Supply), Nikolai Glebov-Avilov (Post and Telegraph), and Iosef Djugashvili-Stalin (Nationalities). Less than a month later, Aleksandra Kollontai (Public Welfare), Eduard Essen (State Control), Valerian Obolenskii-Osinskii (Supreme Economic Council), Nikolai Podvoiskii (Military and Naval Affairs), and Lenin's brother-in-law Mark Elizarov (Transportation) joined their ranks.[3]

Yet, finding men to bring down Kerenskii's government proved much easier than naming statesmen to replace it. If ever triumphant revolutionaries lacked experience in the business of governing, it was Russia's first Soviet of People's Commissars. None among them had ever held a government post or even worked in a government office, and none could claim any firsthand experience with the sorts of problems that their commissariats needed to resolve. "We did not even know how to set about the job, and we had to resort to the . . . [office] messengers who had worked in the department for two decades and had seen dozens of bosses change [for advice]," one Bolshevik confessed when he recalled his first days at the People's Commissariat for Internal Affairs. Such messengers, he added wryly, as if sensing the absurdity of the situation, "turned out to be quite well informed."[4] Thus many Bolsheviks moved bravely to build their new world with only a vague sense of what needed to be done or how to accomplish it. Lenin knew his comrades' failings all too well, yet, in the heady naiveté of victory, he believed that revolutionary dedication, boldness, and Bolshevik party discipline could offset the inexperience that afflicted them all. "How helpless, spontaneous, and incidental were our first steps," he wrote later. "[To govern] seemed to us [then] to be the easiest thing of all."[5]

Some weeks before, when he had spoken of the new institutions that would follow a Bolshevik seizure of power, Lenin had cautioned that "this new apparatus is bound to make mistakes in taking its first steps." Still, he remained certain that a quarter million Bolsheviks could govern Russia far better than "130,000 landowners who have . . . condemned the vast majority to inhuman toil and semi-starvation."[6] The mystique surrounding Russia's old bureaucracy must be shattered, "stripped of every shadow of privilege, of every semblance of 'official grandeur,' " and people made to understand that state administration had long since been "reduced to such exceedingly simple operations of registration, filing and checking that they can be easily performed by every literate person."[7] He promised that "the bold, universal move to hand over administrative work to proletarians and semi-proletarians will rouse such unprecedented revolutionary enthusiasm among the people . . . that much that seemed impossible to our narrow, old, bureaucratic forces will become possible."[8] When one of his comrades tried to refuse a post in the Sovnarkom, Lenin asked: "Do you think that any of us has any experience in this?"[9] The backgrounds of the men in the Bolsheviks' first government proved without any doubt that his question was far from rhetorical.

Aged between twenty-eight and thirty-three, and charged with commanding soldiers and sailors who walked away from the war without so much as a backward glance, People's Commissars Pavel Dybenko, Vladimir Antonov-Ovseenko, and Nikolai Krylenko had considerably less than a decade of military experience between them, and none had held a position of authority. After four years as a common seaman, Dybenko had been sent to prison for leading a mutiny on the battleship *Emperor Paul I*. A death sentence, commuted to twenty years in a prison from which he soon escaped, had cut short Antonov's brief career as an army ensign in 1906, and Krylenko, a student of history and law at St. Petersburg University, had served the Bolsheviks for a decade as a labor organizer before the tsarist authorities sent him to the front in the spring of 1916 as punishment for his revolutionary activities. When Antonov took command of Red forces fighting against the Whites along Russia's southern frontiers, and Krylenko assumed command of Russia's Supreme Army Headquarters at Mogilëv, Nikolai Podvoiskii took their place on the Sovnarkom. A man who had studied for the priesthood before he became a revolutionary, Podvoiskii had been wounded during a street battle in the provincial capital of Iaroslavl in October 1905, but he had held no post of military command before the night of October 25, 1917, when he and Antonov had commanded the Bolsheviks' assault against the Winter Palace.

Nor were the other appointees to the Sovnarkom any better prepared. The Bolsheviks expected Ivan Skvortsov-Stepanov, the schoolteacher son of a provincial factory worker, to face an urgent crisis of his nation's war-torn economy as people's commissar for finance with no experience in banking, and they looked to Viktor Nogin, a dedicated party activist whose only experience with anything related to trade and manufacture had been as a teen-age dyer, to avert the collapse of Russia's industry and commerce that the chaos of revolution had made all but certain. Aside from a childhood and adolescence spent in the Caucasus, and the fact that he had written an essay on the subject in 1912 that had caught Lenin's eye, Stalin had no claim to any expertise in dealing with the complex national antagonisms that threatened to tear the lands of the fallen Russian Empire asunder; and nothing in the long revolutionary career of Ivan Teodorovich, the son of a Polish surveyor from Smolensk, prepared him for solving the desperate problems that demanded his immediate attention as people's commissar of food supply.[10] These men and their comrades moved confidently during the first weeks of their victory nonetheless. "It seemed to them," one onlooker later explained, that "if one could liberate state life from the political domination of the bourgeoisie and its allies, then all questions arising in the government would become so clear and uncomplicated that . . . a small dose of ordinary everyday gumption would be more than enough to resolve them.[11]

From the start, however, they found it difficult to see to the day-to-day affairs of their offices. Civil servants and other white collar workers in Petrograd greeted the October Revolution by staying away from their desks, so that the Bolsheviks found many government offices empty when they arrived to take command. At the former Ministry of Internal Affairs, newly appointed Bolshevik officials found only "a heap of scrap papers, locked desks, and cabinets without keys," while Trotskii found mainly empty offices from which absent officials had removed all code books and keys to safes that held important documents when he took up his duties as commissar for foreign affairs. Elsewhere, sullen officials threw away their pens and poured out all the ink. Bank employees stubbornly refused payment on drafts signed by people's commissars, and diplomats who had represented the Provisional Government abroad refused to speak for the Sovnarkom in the capitals of Europe and America.[12]

Despite office workers' hatred for the Bolsheviks and the Bolsheviks' diatribes against bureaucrats who had served the old regime, neither dared to do without the other for very long. Lenin quickly conceded that it was "impossible to talk about destroying the bureaucracy immediately, everywhere, and completely,"[13] and Russia's old regime bureaucrats soon decided that even Bolshevik masters were preferable to none at all. "A longing for the routine to which they were accustomed," one observer explained, soon drove many of Petrograd's bureaucrats back to their desks to immerse themselves in the comforting and certain routines to which they had dedicated their lives. "One needed only to see the passion with which they seized upon . . . memoranda, reports, and the subtleties of office routine," he went on, "to understand that it would be more difficult for them to live without this atmosphere of papers and documents than without bread or boots."[14] Men who had rendered dedicated service to tsarist and provisional governments therefore returned to serve the Bolsheviks,[15] and the Bolsheviks, despite Lenin's insistence that "the remuneration of *all* servants of the state [should be reduced] to the level of workingmen's pay,"[16] soon began to buy the expertise of these experienced bureaucrats at premium wages.[17]

The Bolsheviks' efforts to govern from their revolutionary command post at Smolnyi added to the confusion of their first attempts to bring order to Russia. "All the world seemed to have business at Smolnyi," John Reed's companion Louise Bryant remembered. At Smolnyi, the "busy, humming hive, the heart and soul of the . . . Revolution," Russia's new people's commissars stood in the Revolution's vortex.[18] There, Trotskii had established the revolutionary command post from which the Bolsheviks had overthrown Kerenskii's government, and Lenin had taken his rightful place as the Bolsheviks' commander-in-chief. To all who shoved their way through the joyous jostling throng that guzzled caldrons of cabbage soup and wolfed great hunks of meat and black bread in Smolnyi's low-ceilinged basement dining room, it seemed certain that Russia's brave new world was being shaped in the crowded corridors above them. None among the Bolsheviks wished to stand apart.

Destined never to be forgotten as the command post of the Bolshevik Revolution, Smolnyi nonetheless could never become its general headquarters, and the Bolsheviks' failure to understand that simple truth proved to be one of the first tragedies of the October Revolution. Only the bureaucratic centers housed in Russia's former ministries stored the vital information needed to grapple with the nation's crises, and only those centers controlled the vital chain of command that could carry new laws and regulations into Russia's remotest corners. Every hour that the people's commissars rode the revolutionary whirlwind at Smolnyi therefore delayed their contact with the world beyond, where people continued to freeze, starve, and be shot by the tens of thousands.

Nor did moving the capital to Moscow, where newly arrived commissars and commissariats jousted for place and preference well into the spring of 1918 in what Trotskii once labeled "a fierce struggle" for office space, improve the Bolsheviks' understanding of the land and people they had to govern.[19] "What a mess we're in!" Lenin exclaimed as he struggled to maintain contact with feuding government offices that had scattered themselves all across the city.[20] For several crucial weeks, it seemed impossible to know what was going on in Moscow, let alone other parts of Russia. Combined with new and bitter rivalries in the Kremlin, such worries diverted Russia's revolutionary leaders from some of the most serious problems in the countryside. Unable to share the dreams and passions of rural folk, the Bolsheviks neither knew the ways of Russia's villages nor sensed their tensions. Too many among them remained urban revolutionaries to whom Fate had given charge of a nation of peasants.

While the Bolsheviks had struggled to seize their nation's industrial centers in 1917, rural Russia had seethed, its illiterate masses exhausted by war, overwhelmed by poverty, and bent upon revenge. For centuries, Russia's country folk had dreamed of sundering the chains of serfdom and claiming the estates held by men who did not share their labor in the fields. They had hoped in vain that the time for land and freedom had come after they had driven Napoleon's Grand Army from the Russian land in 1812, again after they had defended Russia's southern bastion at Sevastopol during the Crimean War, and yet again, in 1861, when the "Tsar-Liberator" Alexander II had decreed their emancipation. Always the lands their ancestors had looked upon with such longing had eluded their grasp. Now they would wait no longer. During the summer and fall of 1917, tens of millions of angry country folk stubbornly took control of Russia's woodlands, meadows, and farmlands.[21] Malignant discord—stubborn, silent, and deep—therefore held undisputed sway as rural Russia moved through its first revolutionary year. Outside the cities, no formulae applied save one: "The land belongs to those who till it."

Among Bolsheviks, who for a quarter-century had paid scant attention to the wants of Russia's "petty bourgeois" peasants, none sensed the deep urgency that seized rural Russia in 1917 more certainly than Lenin. "If the peasants take the land," he warned those who had opposed his demand that the Bolsheviks declare themselves in favor of transferring all land to the peasants' soviets immediately, "you can be certain that they will not ask us for permission to do it, nor will they give it back."[22] As one Provisional Government cabinet after another had met the rising violence in Russia's countryside with solemn insistence that any decision about dividing up the land must await the end of the war and the opening of a Constituent Assembly, Lenin had called boldly for "the abolition of private landed estates without compensation." "If power is [placed] in the hands of the soviets," he promised, "the landowners' estates will immediately be declared the inalienable property of the whole people."[23]

Certain that the peasants' call for land must be answered, Lenin spoke some of his first words after the Bolsheviks' victory to them at the Second All-Russian Congress of Soviets of Workers' and Soldiers' Deputies on the evening of October 26. Solemnly and deliberately, he set down the principles that "private ownership of land shall be abolished forever," that "all land . . . [shall] pass into the use of all those who cultivate it," and that "the right to use the land shall be accorded to all citizens of the Russian state (without distinction of sex) desiring to cultivate it." A number of other generally stated principles, most of them taken directly from the long-standing program of the Socialist Revolutionaries, filled out Lenin's brief speech. "We want no details in [this decree]," he explained. "We trust that the peasants themselves will be able to solve the problem correctly, properly, and better than we could do it." Peasants, not bureaucrats, must settle peasant affairs. Most of all, "the peasants should be firmly assured that there are no more landowners in the countryside" and that "they themselves must arrange their own lives."[24] In Smolnyi's great hall, the stale smells of tobacco smoke, damp boots, and human sweat contrasted strangely with the freshness of Lenin's words. Some years later, his wife recalled an elderly peasant whose "face shone with a peculiar waxen transparency" and whose "eyes glistened with a certain special light" as he had come to understand that, for the first time in Russia's thousand-year history, the land would belong to those who toiled upon it.[25] "So plunged the Bolsheviks ahead," the radical young American journalist John Reed concluded. "[They were] the only people in Russia who had a definite program of action, while others talked for eight long months."[26]

Lenin's words rekindled visions long held among his nation's peasants, and the people whom Gorkii once called "the half-savage, stupid, slow-witted folk of Russia's hamlets"[27] began the long awaited *chernyi peredel*—the "black repartition"—that promised justice, economic security, and the dawning of a new era to the poorest among them. Within a few months, Russia's peasants had increased their landholdings by something over fifty million acres,[28] yet, even fifty million acres—almost twice the size of modern-day East Germany—proved all too little when divided among nearly a hundred million peasants. *Chernyi peredel* therefore brought none of the economic improvements that the peasants had expected, and like so many of their dreams, the long-awaited panacea of the "lord's land" thus proved an empty hope. "If one were to divide all the lords' lands among the peasants," an expert had written from Orël province just a few months before the Bolsheviks seized power, "then each would get about a third of an acre."[29] Amazingly, that crudely formulated prediction, based upon the conditions in a single province in Russia's overpopulated black-earth center, proved sadly close to accurate for Bolshevik Russia as a whole. When it came to relieving the terrible poverty that had gripped Russia's villages for so many centuries, the peasants' determination to seize those lands that belonged to lords, church, or state counted for little.

During the winter and spring of 1917–1918, *chernyi peredel* undid more than a decade of careful government efforts to develop capitalistic agriculture in Russia by doing away with the peasant commune. Long regarded as a major reason for the primeval backwardness that ruled the Russian countryside, the peasant commune had come under heavy attack in the wake of the revolutionary events of 1905. After a year in which orderly crowds of peasants and workers had been shot down in front of the Winter Palace, mutiny had torn the Black Sea Fleet, and a general strike had blanketed the Russian Empire during October, Russia's statesmen had begun the complex task of transforming their nation's ancient autocracy into a constitutional monarchy. A critical part of that process had been an effort by the last great tsarist statesman, Petr Stolypin, to shape his nation's peasants into a conservative political force by encouraging a comparative handful of energetic peasant farmers to consolidate their scattered landholdings into separate farms and break away from the commune altogether. An unvarnished attempt to sharpen distinctions between "haves" and "have-nots" in Russia's villages, Stolypin's reforms thus had aimed to reward hardworking peasants at the expense of those who were not and to increase crop yields that ranked among the lowest in Europe. Soaring agricultural output had rewarded his efforts. On the eve of the First World War, Russian grain production reached a level that the Soviet state would not match until the 1960s,[30] and it was clear to all that the days of Russia's peasant communes were numbered. Then, during the winter of 1917–1918, Lenin's vaguely stated Decree on Land gave them a new and unlooked-for lease on life.

By attempting to force Stolypin's newly created class of independent farmers back into traditional peasant villages, Russia's rejuvenated communes undercut more than a decade of progress toward modernizing agriculture. At the same time, they worked against the Bolsheviks' desperate efforts to seize surplus grain from Russia's villages during the spring and summer of 1918. The "toiling peasantry" thus proved far less biddable than urban-oriented Bolshevik theorists had expected when they began to put the rigid mobilization measures of War Communism into effect during the summer of 1918. Even when organized into those 130,000 committees of the poor that blanketed Russia's countryside by the end of 1918, poor peasants proved reluctant to seize the grain of their communal brethren, and they continued to hinder Bolshevik efforts to mobilize the human and material resources of the Russian countryside until the Civil War's end.[31]

In addition to millions of recalcitrant peasants, other sections of the population and economy commanded the Bolsheviks' attention as Russia entered what Lenin (quoting Marx) referred to as "the period of the expropriation of the expropriators,"[32] which heralded the transition from capitalism to socialism. First and foremost, the Bolsheviks set nationalization of Russia's banks as one of their chief goals because, as Lenin warned at one point, for any revolutionary government to try to govern without doing so would be "like trying to snatch at odd kopeks [while] closing one's eyes to millions of rubles."[33] Yet, despite Lenin's confident prediction that it was "merely a question of breaking the resistance of an insignificant minority" before "a single State Bank, the biggest of the big, with branches in every rural district [and] in every factory" could be established,[34] Russia's banks at first posed problems that Russia's proletarian revolutionaries found particularly awkward to overcome. Banks in Petrograd opened and shut their doors unpredictably, permitted or refused withdrawals as they saw fit, and refused to honor drafts signed by Russia's new people's commissars or by representatives of those factories in which workers had seized control.[35] When failed attempts at negotiations, compromises, and informal agreements left them without even the cash needed to meet day-to-day government expenses and factory payrolls, the Bolsheviks resorted to force. "The iron hand that destroys also creates," Lenin told the Sovnarkom on December 14.[36] The Bolsheviks, he insisted, must adopt "extraordinary revolutionary measures" in order to "normalize the country's economic life immediately and comprehensively."[37]

Even as Lenin spoke, Red Guards and loyal Bolshevik sailors occupied Russia's banks. The day before, after several days of careful preparation, Nikolai Podvoiskii, now the full-fledged people's commissar for war, had ordered his forces to take control of all bank vaults and arrest all bank officers. "We must tear the entire machinery of banking from the hands of plunderers, marauders, and speculators," he explained in a secret memorandum. "We must drive out these saboteurs and replace them with honest servants of the people."[38] Within twenty-four hours, Podvoiskii's units had seized all the major banks in Petrograd and Moscow. "We acted quite simply," Lenin reported to the Third All-Russian Congress of Soviets a month later. "In the morning, the banks were occupied and in the evening the Central Executive Committee issued a decree [stating]: 'The banks are declared national property.' "[39]

When bank employees greeted the government's nationalization decrees by going on strike, the Bolsheviks responded with still sterner measures. Two weeks after seizing the banks, the Sovnarkom prohibited all transactions in stocks and bonds and suspended the payment of interest and dividends as a first step toward canceling the foreign loans that the Russian government had contracted before October 25, 1917. Withdrawals from personal bank accounts could not exceed 600 rubles a month, a figure that the Bolsheviks reduced to 500 rubles in February, and then raised to 750 in April. Government representatives registered the contents of every deposit box in Russia's banks and confiscated all gold, platinum, silver, and precious gems they found in private hands.[40] "Gold will cease to have power," one decree promised.[41] The exact opposite occurred. As all traditional hedges against inflation disappeared from legal exchange, its price soared on the black market. By the spring of 1922, the price of a 10 ruble tsarist gold piece reached 24 million paper rubles.[42]

Far more complicated than nationalizing banks, the Bolsheviks' attempts to nationalize industry added substantially to Russia's economic crisis. At the root of the difficulty stood Lenin himself, for at no time before late October 1917 had he encouraged his comrades to look far enough into the future to see the time when they might wield power themselves. "We have not yet won power," he had reminded them at the beginning of October. "Socialism has not yet been achieved, and we have not achieved even the beginning of the world socialist revolution." It therefore would be "inexpedient," "premature," and "even harmful," he cautioned the fiery Nikolai Bukharin's young Bolshevik extremists, "to inject into the [Party's economic] program an overdose of detail."[43] Even as Kerenskii's government entered its final days, the Bolsheviks continued to debate the prospects of power, not its uses. By late October 1917, they still had not formulated a concrete program for Russia's economic transformation from capitalism to socialism that went much beyond the April Theses, in which Lenin had called upon Russians to repudiate the war, confiscate the lands held by church, state, and landlords, abolish the police, the army, and the bureaucracy, and transfer all power to the soviets of workers' and soldiers' deputies.[44] How to take control of Russia's industry thus remained at best a question that consigned the methods and timing of nationalization to the realm of Marxist theory.

While Lenin and the Bolsheviks had concentrated upon political questions during the summer and fall of 1917, Russia's factory workers had demanded higher wages and an eight-hour day.[45] As spring had turned into summer, and as Russia's economic crisis had deepened, proletarian factory committees in Petrograd had called upon the city's workers to save the nation from disaster by taking control of their workplaces. "Those who stand at the workers' benches must save revolutionary Russia," they insisted.[46] "It is up to the workers to demonstrate initiative," another worker added, "where the industrialist-enterprisers do not."[47] Echoing Lenin's vaguely stated call for "real, not fictitious [workers'] control,"[48] the First Petrograd Conference of Factory and Mill Committees therefore had concluded at the beginning of June 1917 that "the path of escape from disaster lies only in the establishment of effective workers' control over the production of [manufactured] goods."[49]

Despite later claims that the factory committees comprised "one of the brightest pages of the revolutionary workers' movement" in 1917, and that "workers' control became the best school of economic administration for many thousands of those who stood in the workers' vanguard,"[50] neither became the panacea that their defenders envisioned. Certainly, a number of factory committees struggled valiantly to protect the workers against the worsening economic conditions that gripped Russia especially during the fall of 1917.[51] But supported as they were by armed Red Guards units, which some called "the bulwark of the revolutionary working class,"[52] factory and mill committees sometimes proved more anxious to take part in "the expropriation of the expropriators" than to oversee the revolutionary transformation of Russia's industries. In the coal mines of the Donbas, workers extorted large sums of "back pay" from fearful employers. Elsewhere, some demanded exorbitant raises and cash bonuses, while others simply took over factories, sold their stocks and machinery, and walked away with the cash collected from the sale. There was at least one report of workers ordering the directors of a factory to fill several large sacks with "war profits of the past three years" or be put into the sacks and thrown into a nearby river.[53]

Lapses into extortion and outright banditry did not blind Lenin to the value that Bolshevik-dominated factory committees might have as platforms for launching political action during the fall of 1917. "If we are speaking of a proletarian state," he wrote at the beginning of October, "then workers' control *can* become a countrywide, all-embracing, omnipresent, most precise, and most conscientious *accounting* of the production and distribution of goods." Yet, as the months after the February Revolution already had shown, men and women who had spent their lives at looms and lathes could not be transformed into managers easily, even in a proletarian state. Without the help of specialists skilled in management and technology, Russia's factories would founder, and such men could be found only among the industrialists of the old regime. "We must *compel the capitalists to work* within the framework of the new state organization," Lenin insisted. "We must . . . employ them *in the service of the new state.*"

Lenin therefore called for "countrywide, all-embracing workers' control over the capitalists" in order to assure that these men serve the people with the same energy that they had dedicated to their private interests before the Revolution. "We shall place them under comprehensive workers' control," he promised in his pamphlet *Can the Bolsheviks Retain State Power?* "We shall achieve the complete and absolute operation of the rule, 'He who does not work, neither shall he eat.' "[54] Lenin thus envisioned workers' control as an instrument for overseeing the financial and commercial activities of Russia's industries, not as a means by which workers could take over management. Factory committees must now become instruments for extending government authority, not for defending the workers' interests against the government. In a proletarian state, government and workers would be one and the same.

The Sovnarkom extended workers' rights beyond Lenin's proposals and opened the way for factory committees to continue their intervention in the management of Russia's industries when it approved the Decree on Workers' Control on November 27, 1917.[55] Yet the Bolsheviks' deep belief in centralized economic planning condemned any form of workers' control that functioned outside their government to a brief existence. Complaining that strengthening factory committees "dissipates control over production instead of concentrating it," Solomon Lozovskii, an elegant and articulate Bolshevik trade union organizer whose diplomatic and political skills would enable him to emerge unscathed from the purges that later claimed so many of the men who stood with Lenin in 1917, warned of the chaos that workers' control would create. On reflection, even Vladimir Miliutin, the thirty-three-year-old author of the decree, hurried to excuse it as the unfortunate product of a moment when "life overtook us."[56] Workers' continued meddling in factory management, and their persistent hostility to those industrialists to whom the Bolsheviks turned to manage the factories in their proletarian state, posed political and ideological dilemmas that the Sovnarkom preferred not to face. Lenin therefore had little difficulty in winning its support for centralizing the direction of Russia's industries in the Supreme Council of National Economy, which, he soon assured the Third All-Russian Congress of Soviets in mid-January, "will make it possible for us to begin work to build up a new socialist economy."[57]

Established by the Sovnarkom on December 1, 1917, the Supreme Council of National Economy became the Bolsheviks' chief instrument for bringing Russia's industries under government control. "The historical moment has arrived," Lenin wrote soon after it came into being, "when theory is being transformed into practice, vitalized by practice, corrected by practice, tested by practice [and] when the words of Marx, 'Every step of real movement is more important than a dozen programs,' become particularly true."[58] But reality failed to support his claims. As in the Bolsheviks' first efforts to nationalize the land and banks in Russia, disorganization and confusion of purpose dogged the early steps that the Supreme Council of National Economy made toward nationalization.

Contrary to the claims made by Lenin and scores of later Soviet commentators, the nationalization of Russia's industries followed no clear and certain plan before mid-1918. Certainly, the nationalization decrees issued by the Supreme Council of National Economy reflected little coherent planning, and in only about one case in four did they even implement policy decisions initiated by the council itself. Far more often, the Supreme Council worked to prevent factories from being shut down by anti-Bolshevik managers or to offset crudely conceived local seizures that threatened important factories and mines with inept management by homegrown Bolsheviks.[59] Taken together, the nationalization decrees issued by the Supreme Council during the first six months of 1918 thus proved to be a far cry from the "Red Guard assaults against capital" of which so many Soviet commentators liked to speak in Stalin's time.[60] They had little in common with the process that Marx and Engels had envisioned when they had predicted (in the *Communist Manifesto*) that "the proletariat will use its political power to gradually deprive the bourgeoisie of its entire capital [and] centralize all means of production in the hands of the state, that is, the proletariat."[61] At best, the Supreme Council's first attempts to nationalize Russia's industries reflected the Bolsheviks' overwhelming concern for self-defense and survival. Men and women thrown out of work when industrialists locked their factory gates, workers deprived of essential goods, food, and services by factory shutdowns and factories crippled by shortages of raw materials and fuel all added confusion to efforts by the Supreme Council to formulate broad policies and apply them consistently.

The Bolsheviks' cherished dream of building socialism had little to do with the decision by the Supreme Council of National Economy to announce the immediate nationalization of all heavy industry and joint-stock companies on June 28, 1918. Despite later Soviet claims that "the dictatorship of the proletariat thus gained the opportunity to carry through to a victorious conclusion the armed struggle against the foreign and domestic forces of counterrevolution,"[62] the Supreme Council's hastily prepared decision proved to be nothing more than an effort to sidestep the provisions of the Brest-Litovsk Treaty that required the Soviet government to pay direct compensation to German investors whose industries were nationalized after July 1, 1918.[63] Nonetheless, the decree marked a step toward more effective nationalization, even though it took the better part of two years to bring individual industrial complexes and groups of industries under state control. By 1920 the Bolsheviks thus had established a permanent grip upon their nation's industry, although the vagaries of the process and the disruptions inflicted by the Civil War had exacted such a terrible price that the industrial output of Central Russia, the Red heart of the Bolsheviks' new state, had fallen to a mere eighteen percent of what it had been on the eve of the Great War.[64]

The unsettled conditions in which factory workers lived and worked after the October Revolution reflected the disorganization of the Bolsheviks' efforts to nationalize their nation's economic life. Unemployment drained workers from Russia's cities so rapidly that Petrograd lost nearly three-quarters of its industrial labor force before the end of 1918, while Moscow lost two workers out of every five who had been in its factories when Nicholas II was driven from the throne. A similar exodus swept other cities in Central Russia.[65] As epidemics combined with shortages of fuel, housing, and food to cloud their vision of the future, Russian proletarians dared not look beyond the present. "We have reached the direst period in our revolution," Lenin told the Fifth All-Russian Congress of Soviets in the summer of 1918. "There never has been a more difficult period in workers' and peasants' Russia."[66] Less than a month before, Gorkii had published a six-paragraph story about a horse that had collapsed in one of Moscow's streets from hunger and overwork. As he described the "big, dirt-stained tears" that flowed from the dying beast's "thin, convulsively moving eyelids," Gorkii commented matter-of-factly: "We will all soon die for lack of food. People too."[67]

As peasants and workers proceeded with "the expropriation of the expropriators" in Russia's cities and villages, bitter doctrinal disputes divided Bolsheviks, Mensheviks, and Socialist Revolutionaries. Should both large and small industries be nationalized, and how quickly? Should Russia's future be determined by the Constituent Assembly that liberals and revolutionaries had dreamed of for decades, and to the supposed wisdom of which they had referred countless complex problems throughout 1917? Or had the October Revolution transformed the Constituent Assembly, as Lenin insisted when he announced its dissolution, into "a bourgeois and counterrevolutionary" instrument[68] that threatened the very foundations of Russia's new proletarian socialist order?

When the Constituent Assembly met for its single day-long meeting in January 1918, Mensheviks and so-called Right Socialist Revolutionaries had stood on one side and the Bolsheviks on the other. "Between us everything is over," one of Moscow's leading Bolsheviks exclaimed as he faced his proletarian socialist rivals in the refurbished assembly chamber of the Taurida Palace. "We are carrying the October Revolution against the bourgeoisie to its culmination. We and you are on different sides of the barricades."[69] Yet even among the Bolsheviks disagreements burst forth. That same month the Fourth Conference of Factory and Mill Committees in Petrograd called for immediate nationalization of "all means of production, factories, and workshops," while the First Trade Union Congress insisted at the same time that "the financial exhaustion of the country dictates a definite gradualism" in doing so.[70] Clearly, men and women dedicated to the cause of revolution found it easier to agree on principles than on the practical methods for putting them into practice.

Such disagreements reflected persistent theoretical conflicts in the ranks of Russia's revolutionaries. Most longstanding and bitter was the cleavage between the Mensheviks and the Bolsheviks that had festered ever since the embryonic Russian Social Democratic Labor Party had split in 1903. Then Lenin had insisted that only "a strong organization of professional revolutionaries" could give the Party the strength and discipline it needed to merge "*into a single whole* the spontaneous destructive force of the masses and the conscious destructive power of the revolutionaries' organization."[71] By contrast, with a dedication that had matched Lenin's own, Martov had insisted that the Party must require no more than moral commitment to revolution from its members and ought not to demand their unswerving dedication to its realization. Party organization and decision making must remain democratic, Martov had warned, and it must not follow the rigidly centralized model that Lenin favored. Guided by Lenin's precepts, the Bolsheviks had seized power in October 1917, while their Menshevik rivals had continued to argue that the laws of history forbade them to take power because Russia's "bourgeois revolution" had not yet run its course.

More broadly based than the Bolsheviks, the Mensheviks had attracted more supporters than the Bolsheviks throughout 1917, but the Socialist Revolutionaries had outnumbered them both. Large, loosely organized, and without the fixed dedication to ideology of their Bolshevik and Menshevik rivals, Russia's Socialist Revolutionary Party had sprung from neopopulist roots that had little consistency other than a longstanding dedication to the abolition of private landownership. "A conglomerate of discordant elements contending for possession of a label that commanded the good will of rural Russia," in the words of one of their leading chroniclers,[72] the Socialist Revolutionaries had drawn their main support from Russia's tens of peasant millions, not her hundreds of proletarian thousands, and that fact alone had convinced Lenin to incorporate their agrarian program into his Decree on Land.

Led by Viktor Chernov, whose talent with a pen far exceeded his ability to sway revolutionary crowds, the Socialist Revolutionaries had never unified their ranks enough to take full advantage of their huge following. In 1917, one of them later wrote, they had functioned not as "a single party but [as] a jumble of feuding political groups which could make up an entire parliament."[73] Perpetually on the brink of schism, their left, right, and center factions had intensified their feuds as the Provisional Government struggled through the summer and early fall. Then, as Kerenskii's government tottered toward its final collapse, the party tilted sharply leftward. Urged on by Mariia Spiridonova, a dedicated terrorist whose passion for peasant revolution had survived a decade in Siberian prisons, the Left Socialist Revolutionaries had called for a general armistice, workers' control of industry, and land for the peasants. Distrust of the Bolshevik-dominated soviets of workers' and soldiers' deputies had led these Left SRs to insist that peasants have a voice in government equal to that of the workers, but they had shared enough in common with the Bolsheviks in those days to join them in a stormy alliance until their differences drove them to a final break in the summer of 1918.[74]

Nowhere did their conflicting visions of Russia's revolutionary present and future divide Bolsheviks, Mensheviks, and Socialist Revolutionaries more explosively than at the tumultuous Second All-Russian Congress of Soviets that assembled at Smolnyi on the evening of October 25, 1917. "The Revolution had taught the art of filling space," Trotskii later wrote as he described how the throng in search of Russia's future had crowded into Smolnyi's great hall. Although he had long since grown accustomed to addressing revolutionary crowds in Russia's capital, he was surprised to see how overwhelmingly proletarian the assembly had become in the four months that had passed since the First All-Russian Congress of Soviets had met in June. "A gray color prevailed uninterruptedly, in costumes and in faces," Trotskii remembered. "The plebian nation had for the first time sent up an honest representation made in its own image and not retouched." Such men and women of the people cared much less about the fine points of party programs than they did about land, peace, and bread, and they had little patience with any who did not share their view. Trotskii could not forget how their heavy and cracked hands, with wrists reddened from too much cold and fingers yellowed from smoking too many cigarettes, had thrust up among "bristling bayonets" when they had voted against the moderation urged by Martov's Mensheviks and the right-wing Socialist Revolutionaries.[75] Their coats torn, their elbows frayed, these men and women of the people—"crude and ignorant folk whose devotion to the revolution was spite and despair, while their 'socialism' was hunger and an unendurable longing for rest," in the words of the Menshevik diarist Nikolai Sukhanov[76]—voted that evening to change Russia's course forever.

As passionate as any Left SR or Bolshevik in his dedication to Russia's revolution, America's John Reed remembered how Trotskii had turned upon those who had proposed compromise with Kerenskii's shattered government that night, "letting out his rich voice in cool contempt," while his "pale, cruel face" measured the impact of his words upon his audience.[77] "You are pathetic bankrupts," he had stated with unconcealed disdain. "Go where you belong from now on: into the trashbin of history"[78] The Bolsheviks' rivals had no defense against such arrogance. "I didn't believe in the victory, the success, the 'rightfulness,' or the historic mission of the Bolshevik regime," Sukhanov confessed as he watched the Bolsheviks celebrate their victory that evening. "I watched this celebration with a heavy heart."[79]

Yet their triumph in the Second All-Russian Congress of Soviets did not assure the Bolsheviks and their Left SR allies of unchallenged authority in the new workers' state they hoped to bring into being. During the next several months, many socialists dedicated to the ideals of peasant revolution, popular freedom, and social justice hurried to Russia's borderlands to join the armies of Denikin, the Czechoslovak Legion, and the forces of the Komuch government in Siberia rather than acquiesce in the Bolsheviks' crude seizure of power, while others remained in Petrograd and Moscow to challenge the Bolsheviks' proletarian dictatorship more directly.[80] Chernov, whose unyielding insistence upon the impossible dream of party unity had paralyzed the Socialist Revolutionaries throughout 1917, stood prominently among them.

National elections for Russia's Constituent Assembly in mid-November 1917 gave Chernov his first opportunity to challenge the policies of the Sovnarkom. So long awaited by Russia's revolutionaries and so long postponed by the Provisional Government, the elections once again showed the Socialist Revolutionary Party's wide appeal, as SRs of various leanings and colorations won more than half of the forty million votes cast that month. Yet, if read another way, the elections of November 1917 showed that political power had shifted decisively away from the Chernov's feuding SRs. Not only had the Bolsheviks received nearly ten million of the votes cast in the Constituent Assembly elections, but their strength had become extremely concentrated and well placed. Decisive majorities in Moscow, Petrograd, and other industrial centers gave Lenin and his lieutenants control of the garrisons and Red Guards in all the key areas of Central Russia. Beyond that, although the SRs outpolled them by some two hundred thousand votes (slightly less than five percent of the total votes cast) among Russia's army and navy units, the Bolsheviks scored their most decisive victories among the soldiers and sailors who were in the best positions to influence political events in Moscow and Petrograd. Soldiers assigned to the northern front voted two to one for the Bolsheviks over the SRs. On the western front they preferred Bolsheviks to SRs by a margin of almost four to one.[81]

The naive failure of Chernov and his allies to perceive the threat posed by the Bolsheviks' strategically placed power base prevented them from claiming the fruits of their election victory at the Constituent Assembly, which, as a confrontation between purveyors of ideals and brokers of power, proved an unequal contest from the moment its delegates assembled on the afternoon of January 5, 1918. The SR Party, one commentator remarked, "lost its nerve at the moment it was due to launch its decisive battle,"[82] and nothing proved that more dramatically than its members' failure to act decisively. Under the chairmanship of Iakov Sverdlov, a Bolshevik whose imposing presence commanded more respect among men twice his age than his youthful thirty-two years might otherwise have merited, the SRs elected Chernov the assembly's chairman. Rambling, evasive, and inept, the vague formulas and flowery rhetoric in Chernov's opening speech revealed countless flaws in the SRs' armor, into which the brilliant young Bolshevik orator Nikolai Bukharin thrust his verbal rapier with consummate skill when it came his turn to reply. "Savage, logical," speaking in a "voice which plunged and struck," according to John Reed's account,[83] Bukharin heaped scorn upon Chernov and his SRs. "Is what you want a miserable little bourgeois republic?" he asked with unconcealed contempt. Did Chernov propose to take centuries to win socialism for Russia? "In the name of the great Soviet republic of labor," Bukharin concluded, "we [would] declare war to the death on such a government!"[84]

While drunken workers, Red Guards, and Bolshevik sailors in the galleries hooted, cursed, and amused themselves by aiming their rifles in Chernov's direction, the SRs stubbornly pressed on with what the Bolsheviks knew—and many others feared—would be little more than a legislative charade. To cheers from the galleries, the Bolsheviks announced their withdrawal. Some hours later, to more cheers from the onlookers, the Left SRs did the same. Then, at four o'clock in the morning, the Bolshevik and Left SR guards demanded that Chernov bring the session to a close. Hurriedly, Chernov presented a flurry of legislative acts for the approval of those who still remained. Then, as the galleries chanted, "That's enough! That's enough!" each phrase punctuated by the ominous clicks of rifle bolts being slammed shut, Chernov announced that Russia's Constituent Assembly would reconvene that afternoon.[85] The Bolsheviks decreed otherwise. Explaining that the Constituent Assembly "could only serve as a screen for the struggle of the counterrevolutionaries to overthrow Soviet power,"[86] they announced its dissolution several hours before the delegates returned. To the armed men who closed the entrances to the Taurida Palace on orders from the Sovnarkom, the "higher form of democracy" to which Lenin had referred in *Pravda* a few days earlier could be described in the most simple terms. "We will not," one of them stated flatly, "exchange our rifles for a ballot."[87] Led by Spiridonova, who would always offer her followers more inspiration than leadership, many of those Left SRs who had joined the Bolsheviks in walking out of the Constituent Assembly concurred with such sentiments. "The Constituent Assembly has died," they announced. "Long live the soviets!"[88]

Unwilling to follow Spiridonova, Chernov and his allies insisted that "the Constituent Assembly is not dead," but there was more bravado than belief in their promise that "at the call of its president, on the day set by him, the Constituent Assembly will gather to continue its work."[89] A future as painful as any endured by their earlier monarchist and liberal opponents awaited many SRs as they began their wanderings to Siberia and beyond. At first their dream of a Russian republic flickered along the Volga, as the early successes of the Komuch government offered them a brief moment of hope. A few months later the dream revived further to the east in Ufa, only to be snuffed out by the rise of Admiral

Kolchak's authoritarian government in November 1918. Kolchak drove Chernov's SRs further toward the historical trashbin to which Trotskii had consigned them. Although the Socialist Revolutionary Party had been the beacon toward which millions of Russians had turned for guidance during the heady days of 1917, it remained only a will-o'-the-wisp flickering across Siberia's vastness a year later.

The Bolsheviks' Menshevik opponents fared no better than Chernov's SRs. The elections to the Constituent Assembly showed all too clearly that the Mensheviks' failure to heed the demands of Russia's proletarians had reduced their strength to a fraction of its former dimensions. Not counting the votes cast in the faraway Caucasus region, the Mensheviks won less than a million votes in November 1917. Denied any significant role in the Constituent Assembly, and unable to compel the Bolsheviks to moderate their policies, the party of Plekhanov, Martov, Tseretelli, and a score of other luminaries fell beneath the darkening shadow of Bolshevik absolutism. Briefly they regained some of their strength in the spring of 1918 and then, in response to tightening Bolshevik repression, became as impotent as their one-time Socialist Revolutionary rivals.[90]

While Left and Right SRs stubbornly held to their principles, a number of Mensheviks abandoned theirs. Although the more resolute among them joined the Socialist Revolutionaries in Siberia's various White governments or made their way into exile after being expelled from the All-Russian Central Executive Committee in June 1918, those who remained in Russia's Red heart purchased political survival at the terrible price of acknowledging that "the [Bolshevik] revolution of October 1917 had been historically necessary" and the Constituent Assembly counterrevolutionary.[91] In return, the Bolsheviks briefly allowed them to publish a journal in Moscow. "We are quite willing to legalize you, Menshevik gentlemen," Lenin told them at the end of 1918, "[but] we shall reserve State power . . . *for ourselves alone*."[92] The Mensheviks' future in the Soviet state would be uncertain at best. As Lenin called for "a relentless war against Menshevism," he emphasized that, although he considered it "more sensible to come to an understanding with petty bourgeois democrats," they must expect no concession. "It is a mistake to think we shall surrender a hundredth or even a thousandth part of the position we have won," he warned. "We shan't budge an inch."[93]

Before spring came in 1918, the Left SRs remained the only non-Bolshevik political force in Russia's government. Convinced that the October Revolution had tied the fate of the Revolution to the fate of Bolshevism, they had abandoned their comrades on the right and agreed to a *mariage de convenance* with their adversaries. Yet Spiridonova and her passionate followers found little romance in their union with Lenin's cold and calculating Bolsheviks. Divorce was all but certain from the moment they began their courtship, for the Left SRs' lonely position as the Bolsheviks' only adversaries never induced them to moderate their views. Two issues split them apart almost immediately: Lenin's insistence that Russia accept the ruinous terms that Germany imposed at the Brest-Litovsk peace negotiations and the Bolsheviks' cold-blooded determination to inject the poison of class conflict into the veins of the peasant society upon which the Left SRs still hoped to build socialism in Russia.

In January 1918, the Austro-German proposals at Brest-Litovsk to deprive Lenin's government of raw materials, vital industrial centers, and some of Russia's best agricultural lands outraged Bolshevik and Left SR alike. A mere fifteen members of the Bolshevik Central Committee supported Lenin's call for peace with Germany at any price, while sixteen supported Trotskii's proposal that Russia withdraw from the war but reject the Germans' peace terms, and thirty-two sided with Nikolai Bukharin's Left Communists, those Bolshevik "Young Turks" who preferred to fight a "revolutionary war" against Germany rather than accept her peace terms.[94] Like Bukharin's Left Communists, Spiridonova's Left SRs much preferred a revolutionary war, a "holy war" of Russia's proletarians against the bourgeoisie of Europe, to signing what Trotskii once called a peace written "with the sword on the flesh of living nations."[95]

For a brief moment, opposition to Lenin's call for peace at any price threatened his leadership. "If there were five hundred courageous men in Petrograd, we would put you in prison," one of Bukharin's allies exclaimed to Lenin at one point. Lenin's reply showed his confidence in the forces he commanded. "If you will calculate the probabilities," he replied icily, "you will see that it is much more likely that I will send you [to jail] than you [will send] me."[96] Most importantly, Lenin still commanded the loyalty of the Cheka. Emotionally drawn by Bukharin's call for a revolutionary war, Dzerzhinskii nonetheless followed his head not his heart and warned his angry colleagues that even the worst peace imaginable must be thought preferable to "a war to be fought simultaneously against German imperialism, the Russian bourgeoisie, and the section of the proletariat headed by Lenin."[97] Although he thought Lenin's policy "fatal for the Revolution," even Bukharin drew back from pressing his Left Communists' opposition to the point of rupture. Was it really possible to "declare war on Lenin and the Bolshevik Party?" he asked his comrades at one point. "No," he concluded. "Don't let us deceive ourselves."[98]

After bitter debate, and a disastrous experiment with Trotskii's formula of "No War, No Peace" that cost more territory than would otherwise have been lost, the Bolsheviks signed the treaty they so despised. Although the Left SRs had little choice but acquiesce, they carried the rancor of their dispute over into other debates in the coming weeks. Confident in the creative power of the masses, still certain that the Revolution would create its own institutions, and dedicated to those millions of peasants who lived from the fruits of their own labor, the Left SRs resolutely opposed the Bolsheviks' decision to bring class warfare to the Russian countryside. As Lenin and his allies moved to unite the poorest of the peasants against all who stood above them on the village economic ladder, they found themselves locked on a collision course with the Left SRs. The Fifth All-Russian Congress of Soviets became their final battleground.

On July 4, 1918, the Fifth All-Russian Congress of Soviets convened in Moscow's Bolshoi Theater, its shining white and gold interior still reminiscent of the not-so-long-ago days when dashing tsarist officers had accompanied bejeweled ladies to the operas of Rimskii-Korsakov and the richly choreographed ballets of Tchaikowsky. In those days, the Bolshoi had seen the great Chaliapin, his basso profundo reverberating through the highest balconies, give his unforgettable operatic rendering of Boris Godunov, the tsar who had been destroyed by an earlier time of troubles, when Russia had stood at the brink of collapse as she did now. From the glittering imperial box, now crowded by favored newspaper reporters and foreign guests, Nicholas and Aleksandra once had watched Glinka's *Life for the Tsar*, in which a loyal peasant sacrificed his life to save Moscow from foreign enemies. Now prisoners of the Bolsheviks in the faraway Siberian town of Ekaterinburg, Russia's fallen autocrats had less than a fortnight to live before the bullets of a Bolshevik firing squad would cut them down.

On the Bolshoi's great stage, where the great ballerinas Pavlova, Karsavina, and Kschessinska had danced the dance of the dying swan, the members of the All-Russian Central Executive Committee now sat in serried rows. Both Mephistopheles and Lucifer of the Russian Revolution, Trotskii was prominent among them, his striking features contrasting sharply to the modest, schoolmasterly appearance of Lenin. Few disputed Trotskii's genius as polemicist, orator, revolutionary tactician, military commander, and diplomat, although many among the Left SRs thoroughly despised his impassioned brilliance. Probably none hated him more than Spiridonova, who, at thirty-two, now stood as undisputed leader of the Left SRs. An assassin at the age of twenty, victim of brutal beatings and Cossack rapes during her years of penal servitude in Siberia, Spiridonova presented to the world a simple appearance that belied her iron will and inner torment. To the British diplomat Robert Bruce Lockhart, she looked "for all the world like Olga, the schoolmistress in Chekhov's *Three Sisters*." Yet Olga's eyes had never burned with the pain and passion of Spiridonova's. "The earnest, almost fanatical, expression in her eyes" forced Lockhart to conclude that "her sufferings have affected her mind."[99] Sharply divided in their commitments to Trotskii and Lenin or to Spiridonova, the men and women of the All-Russian Central Executive Committee sternly awaited the confrontation they knew must come. As if an omen of things to come, the sets from one of the most dramatic scenes of Mussorgskii's *Boris Godunov* stood behind them.

Her revolutionary dedication already legendary in a milieu filled with revolutionary legends, Spiridonova came forward on the stage of the Bolshoi on the second day of the congress to curse Lenin for "betraying the peasants."[100] Her hysterical passion stirring her fellow Left SRs into a frenzy, this woman of noble birth who had dedicated her short life to Russia's masses condemned "the dictatorship of abstract theories, the dictatorship of individuals in love with their theories," and warned for one last time that the Bolsheviks' grain-requisitioning detachments and the committees of the poor they had formed to carry class warfare into each of Russia's villages would "kill all the good feeling which the peasant has for the soviets."[101] As Spiridonova's anger rose, Lockhart's friend and colleague, the French military attaché Captain Jacques Sadoul, heard Lenin's mocking laughter from the stage behind her. A moment later, he knew how deeply it had stung her when he heard

Spiridonova exclaim that, if Lenin, Trotskii, and their allies on the Sovnarkom did not end their "treason" against the Russian people, she would "take up again the revolver and the hand grenade" as she had done in tsarist times.[102]

"Pandemonium," Lockhart remembered, greeted Spiridonova's final words. Not the tall, broad-shouldered, black-bearded Sverdlov, who presided over the assembly, not even Trotskii, whose words so often bewitched crowds and bent them to his will, could calm the uproar. Only Lenin, whose "expansive and sincere" laughter, Sadoul noted, gave "the impression of extraordinary strength,"[103] could master the throng that cheered and cursed in the theater before them. As he did so often when he was preparing to speak in public, Lenin stepped forward, "his hands thrust deep into his trouser pockets."[104] Writing at different times, in different places, and from very different points of view, Lockhart, Sadoul, and Konstantin Paustovskii all marveled at the way in which this short, excessively ordinary-looking man shaped the passions of the crowd. "He did not give a speech but spoke lightly, as if chatting with a few of his friends rather than with an audience in a huge auditorium," Paustovskii remembered. It seemed to him that, at any moment, Lenin might begin to talk about "gathering mushrooms or fishing, or about the need to make scientific weather forecasts, so natural were his voice and movements."[105] Lockhart, who thought Lenin's "self-confidence almost irritating," was surprised that he spoke "with strangely little gesticulation . . . as if he were addressing a Sunday School meeting," but was impressed at how quickly "the sheer personality of the man and the overwhelming superiority of his dialectics conquer[ed] his audience."[106] "For the present, the essence of socialism is to obtain bread," Lenin told his listeners. "[Only when we] take possession of the surplus grain and divide it among the toiling population . . . will we be in a position to take care of the toilers and poorest peasants. . . . Only a union of the city workers with the village poor who do not speculate," he concluded, "can save the Revolution."[107]

Yet Lenin's spell could not last beyond his moments at the rostrum. Perhaps angered even more by what Lockhart remembered as "the overwhelming superiority of his dialectics," Lenin's Left SR enemies unleashed torrents of abusive rebuttals as they condemned the Bolsheviks' "stupid and criminal measures" that had brought "make-believe socialism" to Russia.[108] To Sadoul the Left SRs seemed courageous, but he thought their remarks "disordered, demagogic, clumsy, unjust, enlarged by passion, but not convincing."[109] Bitter at the conflicts that had set them upon separate paths, the wounds opened by the day's debates untended and festering, the Bolsheviks and Left SRs therefore carried raw hostility in their hearts as they left the Bolshoi Theater that night. Although Sverdlov had announced that the congress would reassemble the following afternoon, few thought that their differences could be resolved by debate or that they even had any common ground left upon which to stand.

Fanatical, sentimental, and romantic, the Left SRs had not come to the Fifth All-Russian Congress of Soviets merely to trade accusations with their rivals. As the Bolsheviks soon learned, they had come prepared to stake their lives on one last desperate gamble in the streets of Moscow. "The stage revolution of yesterday," Lockhart later explained, "had been transferred to the streets and to the barricades,"[110] although few of the onlookers who had returned to the Bolshoi on the afternoon of July 6 to watch the verbal battle continue between Spiridonova and Lenin knew it at the time. Like Lockhart, Paustovskii at first was surprised to find that the Bolsheviks had failed to appear as expected and wondered why the Left SRs had assembled in unexpectedly large numbers. As the SRs began to press toward the stage, Paustovskii understood the reason for their excitement when Spiridonova, dressed in black, ran forward, her heels clicking sharply upon the boards beneath them. His reporter's eye always alert for details, Paustovskii noted that she wore a scarlet carnation pinned to her breast and held "a small steel Browning pistol in her hand." Suddenly, she raised her weapon high above her head. "Long live the revolt!" she shouted to an audience that readily took up her cry. "And that," Paustovskii concluded, "is how we reporters learned about the beginning of the revolt of the Left SRs in Moscow."[111]

Earlier that afternoon, two Left SR assassins carrying papers bearing the forged signature of Dzerzhinskii himself had entered the German Embassy and killed the German ambassador Count Wilhelm von Mirbach. Fearful that Germany might retaliate by ordering her armies to march deeper into Russian territory, Dzerzhinskii had rushed to arrest the assassins, only to be taken prisoner himself. With the chief of the Cheka as their hostage, and supported by several thousand soldiers and sailors who sympathized with their views, the Left SRs had seized Moscow's central telegraph office, one of the keys to communicating with the rest of

Russia. That had marked the high point of their success. Suffering from all the confusion inherent in their fanatical romanticism, the Left SRs had made no move against the Kremlin and had failed even to seize the Bolshoi Theater. As Spiridonova had issued her challenge from the center of the Bolshoi's stage, Paustovskii remembered that "all the Left SRs pulled revolvers from beneath their jackets and from their pockets," only to become victims of the Bolsheviks' ability to anticipate the unexpected. "At that moment," Paustovskii reported, "the calm, hard-edged voice of the commandant of the Kremlin spoke from the gallery: 'Gentlemen, Left SRs! If you attempt to leave the theater or to use your weapons, we shall open fire from the upper galleries. I advise you to sit down quietly and await a decision about your fate.' "[112] Quickly, the Bolsheviks restored order in Moscow. The Left SRs' failure had destroyed the last opposition to their power.

It remained only for the Bolsheviks to create the legal framework for their new world. While the Left SRs had fought their last bitter battles against the Brest-Litovsk Treaty and had raged against the decision to unleash class warfare in Russia's villages, a quieter but no less decisive battle had been fought in government meeting rooms in Moscow. There, a special committee that pitted Left SRs led by the jurist Mikhail Reisner against the imposing Bolshevik troika of Sverdlov, Bukharin, and Stalin, labored to draft a constitution for the workers' state that the October Revolution had brought into being. During the spring and early summer of 1918, these men had worked to prepare what might best be described as a "political prospectus"[113] for Russia's transition to socialism. They had clashed on three issues, each, perhaps, more vital to the future of the Russian Soviet Federative Socialist Republic than their conflicts over Brest-Litovsk and the peasantry. Should the government be weak or strong? Should its authority be dispersed or rigidly centralized? Should federalism bind diverse regions together loosely, or should they be welded firmly into a single republic? On all three propositions, the Left SRs defended the first alternative, while the Bolsheviks stood firmly for the latter. In each case, the stern realism of the Bolsheviks triumphed over the SRs' hopeful idealism.

The draft constitution that the Fifth All-Russian Congress of Soviets approved on July 10, 1918, represented a Bolshevik victory of unprecedented dimensions, for it made certain that Bolshevik power would dominate Russia from the smallest village assembly to the national parliament. The constitution of the Russian Soviet Federative Socialist Republic, the state formation that would oversee "the expropriation of the expropriators," thus was to be an institutional expression of the dictatorship of the proletariat, or, in the Bolshevik phrase, "the autocracy of the people."[114] Outraged at the Bolsheviks' rigidity, the Left SRs opened a campaign of assassinations like that which they had waged in their two-decades-long battle against the autocracy of the Romanovs. When the Bolsheviks responded in kind and in full measure by unleashing a reign of terror of their own in the summer of 1918, a new and more brutal phase of Russia's civil strife began. "The bourgeoisie are prepared to commit the most heinous crimes,"[115] Lenin had warned his followers soon after their October victory. Now the Bolsheviks added to that number all socialists who would not accept their vision of a powerful and stern centralized government that would rule sternly while they awaited the "withering away" of the state that Marx and Engels had promised. In reply to the Bolsheviks' challenge, Left SR terrorists unsheathed the weapons they had used to such terrible effect during the days of the Romanovs. None would be safe from their bombs and bullets that summer and fall. Soon they counted even Lenin among their victims.

CHAPTER FOUR

First Days of Terror

On August 26, 1879, fifteen young men and women met secretly in a forest near the St. Petersburg suburb of Lesnoi. As they slipped back into the city at different times and by different routes later that evening, all understood that they had been part of a momentous event that would transform Russia's revolutionary movement. That day, they had agreed that Tsar Alexander II should be assassinated. The "Will of the People," they had announced, demanded it, and the people's will must be served. Their first efforts to carry out their terrible verdict failed. Eighteen months later, the young terrorists of the People's Will Party killed Alexander II by shattering his lower body with a hand grenade made of metal shards packed around two vials of nitroglycerine. Four men and one woman paid for that crime on the gallows, and several more spent long years in prison. Yet none of them ever believed that terrorism should become an end in itself or that it should be used for personal revenge. "Terrorism for its own sake was never . . . [our] goal," a woman who plotted Alexander's death wrote after the Revolution of 1905 had freed her from the dungeons of the Schlüsselberg Fortress. "It was a means of protection, of self-defense." It was also a vital instrument, she insisted, for bringing about a national uprising which, the young terrorists hoped, would begin the revolutionary transformation of Russia.[1]

From the moment that the stalwart young revolutionaries of

the People's Will made their decision in Lesnoi forest, terrorism became a part of Russia's political landscape, and it continued to cast its fearsome, yet strangely compelling, shadow across the land until 1917. Although new generations took the places of those who fell in the battle against autocracy, their conviction that terrorism could never serve personal ends remained remarkably constant during the thirty-six years that separated Alexander II's murder from the Romanovs' overthrow. Always, a code of honor that demanded great personal sacrifice guided Russia's romantic young terrorists. "Almost always the terrorist combined his deed with the voluntary sacrifice of his own life and freedom," Mariia Spiridonova once explained. "I believe that only thus was it possible to justify the terrorist act."[2] Such a code had guided Lenin's elder brother Aleksandr, who had died on the gallows in 1887 for his attempt to kill Alexander III, and it had guided those who followed him at the beginning of the twentieth century.

By 1917, Russia's terrorists could count among their victims more than a score of generals and provincial governors (including the governors-general of Moscow and Finland), one minister of public instruction, two ministers of internal affairs, and a grand duke.[3] Yet terrorism, used as a weapon by angry and desperate revolutionaries against a government whose forces threatened to crush them at any moment was not the same thing as terror. "Terror [was] a *system* of violence, dispensed from above," I.N. Steinberg, the Left Socialist Revolutionary who served briefly as the Bolsheviks' minister of justice, explained later. "[It was] a planned and quasi-legal program to intimidate and terrify a people into submission."[4]

Such systematic terror as Steinberg described had its origins in the experience of revolutionary France, when, in the words of one of its great chroniclers, "a shadow . . . fell over the minds of the people of France, eclipsing the sentiments of sympathy and humanity, obscuring the principles of liberty and justice."[5] Those were the very principles for which the French had overthrown their king in 1789, and the ones they had struggled to defend through a succession of political, economic, and military crises during the five years that followed. Yet, as the armies of Europe's monarchs pressed against their borders, the time came when the French set aside their defense of liberty, equality, and fraternity in the name of national security. Beginning on September 5, 1793, they launched a Reign of Terror that claimed the lives of one out of every six hundred citizens of

France.[6] When the Terror finally subsided into the "Thermidorian reaction" following the execution of Robespierre nearly a year later, it had claimed the lives of some forty thousand French men and women, most of whom came not from the hated nobles and merchants but from the lower classes. [7]

Like France in 1789, Russia's revolutionary experience in 1917 had at first been free of terror and dedicated to the quest for liberty, justice, and equality. As in France during the Revolution's first months, peasants had wrought havoc in the countryside, and city mobs had done serious damage, but terror, deliberately imposed from above, was even more foreign to Russia's revolution in 1917 than it had been to France's in 1789. Men and women only recently freed from tsarist jails and Siberian exile struggled to forgive in order to forget and develop legitimate political processes to accommodate those who disagreed with their government's course. Along with hundreds of others, Ekaterina Breshko-Breshkovskaia, affectionately known as "the Little Grandmother of the Russian Revolution," who had first set foot in a tsarist prison forty-three years earlier; Fania Kaplan, the anarchist from western Russia who had spent more than a third of her life at convict labor in Siberia, some three years of which had passed in terrifying temporary blindness; Feliks Dzerzhinskii, the scion of lesser Polish aristocrats and longtime ally of Lenin, whose term of hard labor had just been extended for another six years when the Revolution freed him; Boris Savinkov, the terrorist who had fled abroad to escape a death sentence after he had helped to assassinate a grand duke and a minister of internal affairs and who once had been described by someone who knew him well as "a soul choked in blood,"[8] all had emerged from dungeons, Siberia's frozen wastes, or foreign exile to speak out for freedom in Petrograd that spring.

Caught up in their newly won political freedoms, many revolutionary Russians thus remained remarkably tolerant of political dissent. Men and women long would remember how, in March 1917, Kerenskii had marched, "like the flaming torch of revolutionary justice," through angry crowds of armed soldiers to save fallen tsarist ministers. "Pallid and with an outstretched arm," one observer wrote, he had pleaded with the mob to "keep the Revolution undefiled by shameful bloodshed,"[9] and Petrograd's enraged masses had heeded his words, just as they had heeded Trotskii during the tumultuous July Days when he had called upon them to free Chernov.[10]

Between February and October, Russians had allowed the Revolution to follow its turbulent course rather than use force to bring their ebullient countrymen under control. There had been such a reluctance to soil the Revolution with blood in those days that, in the spring of 1917, the Petrograd Soviet had abolished the death sentence and only with the greatest reluctance had restored the authority to execute deserters to Russia's front-line generals. Although such grossly corrupt tsarist statesmen as Aleksei Khvostov and Boris Stürmer had been called to account before a supreme investigating commission, they had suffered no punishment beyond imprisonment for their crimes during 1917. Given the reluctance of newly freed revolutionaries and terrorists to rule their countrymen by force, all of the imperial family, and every one of the tsarist ministers (except for those who died of natural causes), still remained alive when the Bolsheviks seized power on October 25.

The October Revolution changed Russia's mood and policy as the Bolsheviks began to rage against "the vileness . . . of the bourgeoisie and of its crowned and uncrowned hangmen" abroad, who threatened to "drown the workers' and peasants' revolution in blood." Now, "criminal plunderers," "saboteurs," "degraded elements," "wolves, jackals, and mad dogs," "lackeys of the moneybags," and "lickspittles of the exploiters" seemed to lurk in every corner of the land, and the Bolsheviks called for a "merciless suppression," a "war to the death," against those "henchmen of the bourgeoisie" who threatened Russia from within.[11] "What will the Revolution offer that is new?" Gorkii asked from the offices of *Novaia zhizn* as the Bolsheviks entered their second month in power. "How will it change the bestial Russian way of life?"[12]

Gorkii had not long to wait for his answer. Less than a week before, Trotskii had warned that "in no more than a month's time, terror will assume very violent forms,"[13] and, on the same day as *Novaia zhizn* had published Gorkii's column, Lenin had begun to make clear what Trotskii meant. "The bourgeoisie, the landowners, and all the rich classes are making desperate efforts to undermine the Revolution," he warned his colleagues on the Sovnarkom. "[They are] prepared to commit the most heinous crimes [and] . . . have even gone so far as to sabotage food distribution, thereby menacing millions of people with famine."[14] Certain, as he had said on the day after the Bolsheviks took power, that it was "an inadmissible weakness" to even think of accomplishing a revolution "without shooting,"[15] Lenin was prepared to go to any lengths to defend the new order that he and the Bolsheviks had brought into being. "The international imperialist bourgeoisie have slaughtered ten million and maimed twenty million in 'their' war to decide whether British or German vultures are to rule the world," he explained in an open letter to the workers of America some months later. "If *our* war, the war of the oppressed and exploited against the oppressors and the exploiters, results in half a million or a million casualties in all countries, the bourgeoisie will say that the former casualties are justified, while the latter are criminal." Terror, Lenin concluded, "was just and legitimate when the bourgeoisie [in France and England] resorted to it for their own benefit against feudalism [but] . . . became monstrous and criminal when the workers and poor peasants dared to use it against the bourgeoisie!"[16]

In those days, Trotskii remembered, Lenin "emphasized the absolute necessity of terror" and warned that "only unusually strong measures could save the Revolution."[17] "Do you think we can be victors without the most severe revolutionary terror?" he exclaimed when Commissar of Justice Steinberg objected to having the statement, "enemy agents, profiteers, marauders, holligans, counterrevolutionary agitators, and German spies are to be shot on the spot," appear in a proclamation that the Sovnarkom approved at the beginning of 1918. "If we are not ready to shoot a saboteur and White Guardist," Lenin asked his comrades on the Sovnarkom at one point, "what sort of revolution is that?"[18] "We can't expect to get anywhere," he told the assembled delegates of the Presidium of the Petrograd Soviet, "unless we resort to terrorism."[19]

None agreed with Lenin more emphatically than Feliks Edmundovich Dzerzhinskii, who pronounced the October Revolution in "clear and present danger" even as it scored its first triumphs. "Standing like a monk in soldier's clothing," according to one account, Dzerzhinskii told his comrades on the Sovnarkom at the beginning of December that they must have "an organization for taking revenge in the name of the Revolution"[20] against any who would seize it from them. Without hesitation, the Sovnarkom agreed. That very day, December 7, 1917, they established the All-Russian Extraordinary Commission to Combat Counterrevolution and Sabotage—the VChK, or Cheka—and named Dzerzhinskii its chief. Dzerzhinskii quickly proved to be the "staunch Jacobin" Lenin had urged his comrades on the Sovnarkom to find.[21] "Terror is an absolute necessity during times of revolution," he explained a few months later. "We terrorize the enemies of the

Soviet government in order to stop crime at its inception."[22] With the grim gallows humor with which they had long been accustomed to comment upon their government's policies, Russians already had begun to point out that the initials VChK stood not only for "Vserossiiskaia Chrezvychainaia Komissiia" (the All-Russian Extraordinary Commission), but also for "Vsiakomu cheloveku Kaput!" (Death to every man!).[23]

Few were more suited to command the Cheka than Dzerzhinskii. Tall and thin, his aquiline nose and almond eyes framed by high-set cheekbones and a Vandyke beard whose sharply sculpted point mirrored a hairline that receded sharply at his temples, "Iron Feliks" bore a disconcerting resemblance to those devout Spanish grandees who had served the Inquisition three hundred years before. His perpetually raised eyebrows gave him a look of permanent disbelief, and high-necked uniforms that encased his neck like the collar of a priest accentuated his inquisitorial image. "The most remarkable thing about him was his eyes," the British diplomat Lockhart remembered some years later. "They blazed with a steady fire of fanaticism. They never twitched. His eyelids seemed paralyzed."[24] Others shared Lockhart's opinion. Steinberg, who fought a losing battle against Dzerzhinskii's growing power in the spring of 1918, remembered that "a dry flame of fanaticism gleamed" behind his glasses. "We don't want justice," Dzerzhinskii replied to Steinberg's repeated complaints. "We want to settle accounts."

"An unquenchable hatred of his class enemies," Steinberg recalled, seared Dzerzhinskii's soul and drove him onward.[25] Yet he was not one who sought power for general gain or even personal comfort. "Iron Feliks" lived a life of such austerity that he once reprimanded a subordinate who brought him bacon and potatoes during Russia's terrible days of hunger, and his legendary capacity for work at all hours and under any conditions left none in doubt about his dedication to the revolutionary cause. "Sleep and food were for him an unpleasant necessity," one of his Cheka associates recalled. "He had absolutely no personal life whatsoever."[26] Eighteen hours a day, seven days a week, he carried on his struggle, as he ate and slept in his office and remained separated until 1919 from the wife and son he had not seen since his arrest in 1912. "I am in the front line of battle," he wrote to them in the spring of 1918. "My thought induces me to be without pity, and there is in me an iron determination to follow my thought to the end."[27] Not even his own crumbling health slowed Dzerzhinskii's frenzied pace. "Something needs to be done about Feliks Edmundovich," a worried subordinate told one of the Central Committee's secretaries. "He is coughing up blood and refuses to hear about taking any rest."[28] Dzerzhinskii saw himself as the moral guardian of those values around which the Bolsheviks hoped to shape their brave new world, and he differed little in that respect from Count Benkendorf, head of Russia's security police during the time of Tsar Nicholas I, or Joseph Fouchet, the dedicated chief of police who had helped Napoleon shape the First Empire. Dzerzhinskii's devotion to the battle against the Bolsheviks' enemies thus stemmed not from a fascination with power or from a perverse love of inflicting pain and suffering, as was the case with too many who served under him. His was a moral mission that, even under the most adverse circumstances, obliged him to remind his subordinates that their first task must always be to better Russia's future. "Concern for our children's welfare," he once told one of his deputies, "is one of the best ways to wipe out counterrevolution."[29]

Nearly a third of an adult life spent in the prisons of Nicholas II had forged in Dzerzhinskii an iron will that never yielded to adversity. He knew all too well the dungeons of Warsaw's Citadel and the cells of Moscow's notorious Butyrki Prison, and his years in tsarist jails had prepared him for the task he now faced. "When I weigh in my mind and heart what prison has given me and what it has deprived me of," he once confessed to his prison diary, "I know for certain that I should curse neither my fate nor my long years behind bars."[30] To every situation, Dzerzhinskii brought a seasoned prisoner's patience and a flint-hard revolutionary spirit. "One learns patience in prison," he told a British sculptor when she apologized for having kept him so long at a sitting,[31] and it was his endless patience and stubborn determination that allowed him to unravel the tangled plots and counter-plots that threatened the Revolution he had sworn to defend.

In the moments of freedom that had punctuated his six arrests in tsarist times, Dzerzhinskii had founded two radical newspapers, rebuilt the Polish Social Democratic Party, and led mass demonstrations, industrial strikes, and prison riots. For a decade before the Revolution he had worked closely with Lenin, and during the October Revolution he had led the assault against Petrograd's post and telegraph offices that had given the Bolsheviks control over communications between the capital and the rest of Russia. Immediately afterward, Dzerzhinskii had taken charge of security at the Bolsheviks' revolutionary headquarters at Smolnyi and, from there, had moved on to preside over the Cheka in its first offices at No. 2 Gorokhovaia Street.[32] In those days, Iron Feliks had carried the records of the Cheka in his briefcase and could safely leave its entire cash resources of a thousand rubles in an assistant's desk drawer. By the end of 1917, he still did not have a typist and continued to write out arrest orders in longhand. When he finally acquired a secretary, she still had to do double duty as an investigator.[33]

New Year's Day 1918 witnessed the first assassination attempt against Lenin, when a would-be assassin fired four shots into his automobile as it passed a crowd. From that moment, Dzerzhinskii began to transform the Cheka into the instrument of swift punishment and certain death that earned it the name of the Revolution's "avenging sword." Just three months after it had moved into the former headquarters of the Anchor and Lloyd's Insurance Companies on Moscow's Lubianka Square, the Cheka had forty-three district and provincial branches in operation. It employed more than a thousand men and women in its Lubianka offices alone, and another thousand had been enlisted in the elite Combat Detachment that served as its military arm. By mid-1918 the Cheka also had control of Russia's frontier areas and was about to establish special units at important railroad and river traffic centers.[34] "There is no sphere in our life," an officer in charge of training its agents wrote, "where the Cheka does not have its eagle eye."[35]

As Lenin found in Dzerzhinskii a man who shared his willingness to defend the Revolution by any means and at any cost, the Cheka gained the power of life and death over Russians. Fearful that the Russians were "too soft," and "not capable of applying the harsh measures of revolutionary terror" he thought necessary,[36] Lenin continued to insist that there must be a "war to the death against the rich and their hangers-on," in which "any display of weakness, hesitation, or sentimentality . . . would be an immense crime."[37] Never in modern Russia's history had any leader called for the death penalty so frequently and so openly as Lenin did in those days:

LET THEM SHOOT ON THE SPOT EVERY TENTH MAN GUILTY OF IDLENESS. [*Late December*]

WE CAN'T EXPECT TO GET ANYWHERE UNLESS WE RESORT TO

TERRORISM: SPECULATORS MUST BE SHOT ON THE SPOT. [*Mid-January 1918*]

ENEMY AGENTS, PROFITEERS, MARAUDERS, HOOLIGANS, COUNTERREVOLUTIONARY AGITATORS, AND GERMAN SPIES ARE TO BE SHOT ON THE SPOT. [*Late February*][38]

"Why do we bother with a Commissariat of Justice?" stormed Steinberg when Lenin criticized his opposition to the Cheka's summary executions. "Let's call it frankly the *Commissariat for Social Extermination* and be done with it!" His face brightening at the thought, Lenin considered Steinberg's remark. "Well put!" he reportedly exclaimed. "That's exactly what it should be."[39]

Dzerzhinskii supported Lenin's views as emphatically as Steinberg opposed them. As with Lenin, a cold hatred for the exploiters of Russia's workers consumed him to such an extent that not long before the Bolshevik Revolution he had suggested to a comrade that it might be possible to alter the "correlation of political and social forces" that determined the nation's constitution "through the subjection or extermination of some classes of society."[40] Sparing "neither brother nor friend," as he once told a correspondent from Gorkii's *Novaia zhizn*, Dzerzhinskii allowed nothing and no one to stand in the way of victory in his battle against the Bolsheviks' enemies.

"Only saints and scoundrels," Dzerzhinskii once said, could serve in Russia's secret police.[41] In fact, there were never even a handful of saints in the Cheka, and to this day the motives of some of Dzerzhinskii's cruelest and closest associates remain completely open to question. None who entered his command shared his rigid asceticism or his unswerving dedication to Lenin's revolutionary principles, nor did they share his exalted belief in the Cheka's revolutionary mission. Dzerzhinskii's deputies took pleasure from the terror they inflicted, while their chief carried deep within him a sense that his work in the cause of the Revolution had stained his soul. "I have spilt so much blood that I no longer have any right to live," he reportedly lamented as he and other Bolshevik leaders greeted the New Year at the Kremlin in 1919. "You must shoot me now."[42]

Perhaps aware that some who did not share his fervid revolutionary commitment might have second thoughts about killing for purely ideological reasons, Dzerzhinskii added subtly blended national hatreds to their incentives. Even in the Cheka's highest ranks, non-Russians outnumbered Russians by a margin of three to one. To the Ukraine, where the native population had assembled a long and sorry record of violent anti-Semitism, Dzerzhinskii sent Jewish Chekists in such numbers that more than seven out of every ten in the Cheka's headquarters in Kiev were Jews. Likewise, he sent Armenians to Georgia and, in Russia itself, relied heavily upon a brutal corps of Latvians who, according to some estimates, made up more than three-quarters of the staff at Lubianka.[43]

Neither of Dzerzhinskii's closest lieutenants was a Russian, although both had been born within the Russian Empire. Iakov Peters and Martyn Latsis had begun as farm laborers in Latvia, and each had been active in the revolutionary movement for more than a decade before 1917. Both figured prominently in the October Revolution, and both entered the Cheka before Dzerzhinskii moved its offices to Moscow in March 1918.[44] No one set down the principles that guided them more candidly than Latsis. "The Cheka," he remarked, "does not judge the enemy, but smites him. . . . The first question one ought to put to a prisoner should be: To what class does he belong? What are his origins? What is his upbringing, education, origins and profession? [The answers to] these questions ought to determine the fate of the accused. This is the implication and meaning of Red Terror." One of Latsis's supporters spoke even more bluntly. "What purpose is served by all these questions of origins and education?" he asked at one point. "One needs only to go into the kitchen [of the accused] and look into his soup pot. If there is meat in it, then he is an enemy of the people. Stand him up against a wall!"[45]

Russians' readiness to stand their enemies "up against a wall" in 1918 emphasized the deepening brutality of their Civil War. All too quickly, Red and White terror erased those legitimate means of expressing dissent that Russians had enjoyed between the revolutions of February and October. Along Russia's frontiers, White military leaders killed their enemies with reckless abandon and wielded absolute authority over the civilian governments that depended upon their protection. In Russia's Red center, the Bolsheviks took firmer control that spring. "It would be extremely stupid and absurdly utopian to assume that the transition from capitalism to socialism is possible without coercion and without dictatorship," Lenin wrote as he explained that "there is absolutely *no* contradiction in principle between Soviet (that is, socialist) democracy and the exercise of dictatorial powers by individuals." Russians must learn discipline and obedience. "*Unquestioning subordination* to a single will," he concluded, "is absolutely necessary. . . . We must learn to combine the 'public meeting' democracy of the working people—turbulent, surging, overflowing its banks like a spring flood—with *iron* discipline while at work, with *unquestioning obedience* to the will of a single person, the Soviet leader."[46]

Especially those uncompromising enemies of despotism who once had fought tsarist repression with terrorism responded angrily to the Bolsheviks' tightening dictatorship. As Russia began her second revolutionary year, Fania Kaplan, Irina Kakhovskaia, and Mariia Spiridonova, whose dedication to liberty had been tested in some of Siberia's most terrible prisons before the Revolution, turned against those whose arrogance threatened their new-won freedom. Convinced that the Bolsheviks intended to use the "breathing space" that had been bought so dearly at Brest-Litovsk to crush all opposition to their power in Russia, Spiridonova and her comrades among the Left SRs rededicated themselves to renewing the struggle against imperialism that the Bolsheviks had set aside. Although they insisted that it was "both practical and expedient to organize a series of terrorist attacks against the leading representatives of German imperialism," they knew from the beginning that the Germans were not to be their only targets. "In view of the fact that [the Bolsheviks] may take aggressive counteraction against our party," Spiridonova warned, "we are determined, if necessary, to resort to an armed defense of the positions we have occupied."[47]

The Left SRs planned to begin their terrorist campaign with an attack against Germany's recently arrived ambassador, Count Wilhelm von Mirbach, when the Fifth All-Russian Congress of Soviets assembled in Moscow's Bolshoi Theater early in July. Although Spiridonova later claimed full responsibility, the key figure in the attack was Iakov Bliumkin, a twenty-year-old former errand boy who, in the early days of the Revolution, had commanded the Socialist Revolutionary Iron Volunteers of Odessa. Well connected in Bolshevik and Left SR circles, and a frequent visitor to Moscow's literary cafes, Bliumkin proved unusually adept at taking advantage of the conflicting loyalties that reigned in revolutionary Moscow. As head of the counterespionage section of the Cheka that Dzerzhinskii and Latsis had organized to spy upon the German Embassy the moment that diplomatic relations between

Russia and Germany had been restored, he had ready access to every scrap of information about the German Embassy and its personnel that could be found in the files of the Soviet intelligence services. He therefore knew the habits and character of his prey in detail, and he had an accurate floor plan of the building in which he would launch his attack.[48] Thus able to draw directly upon all the resources of the Cheka, the Left SRs had every hope of success.

On the morning of July 6, a Saturday, Bliumkin dressed in black and went to Lubianka, where he typed on one of the Cheka's official message forms: "The All-Russian Extraordinary Commission to Combat Counterrevolution empowers its member Iakov Bliumkin and the representative of the Revolutionary Tribunal Nikolai Andreev to enter immediately into discussions with the German ambassador to Russia, Count Wilhelm Mirbach, upon a matter of direct personal interest." He then forged Dzerzhinskii's signature, affixed the proper seals, and calmly requisitioned an official car. Not long before three o'clock that afternoon, he and Andreev entered the newly opened German Embassy, later remembered by a British diplomat as "a magnificent private house" near the center of town, insisted upon speaking directly with Mirbach, and, a few minutes later, shot him. Wounded, Mirbach tried to flee, but his killers brought him down with another shot that entered his head at the rear and emerged between his eyes. For good measure, they threw a hand grenade behind them and fled, with Bliumkin being wounded and breaking his leg in the process.[49] They took refuge in the Pokrovskii Barracks, home of the Cheka Combat Detachment whose Left SR sympathies made it a key instrument in the uprising against the Bolsheviks that Spiridonova and her colleagues were about to begin.[50]

News of Mirbach's assassination filled the Bolsheviks with consternation. Fearful that the Germans might renew their war against Russia, Lenin immediately ordered the tightest security precautions to prevent any further incidents, while Dzerzhinskii rushed off to learn the details of the crime from the Germans. From the German Embassy he raced to the Pokrovskii Barracks to demand that the Combat Detachment's commander surrender Bliumkin. A dedicated Left SR himself, the commander refused and, with the help of several other members of the Left SR Central Committee, placed Dzerzhinskii under arrest. Before eight o'clock that evening, the Left SRs had seized Moscow's central telegraph office and had even arrested Latsis at Lubianka. With two of Moscow's three leading Cheka officials in their custody, the Left SRs could well afford to exult; some hours earlier, Spiridonova already had hurried to the Bolshoi Theater to announce her party's triumph to the All-Russian Congress of Soviets.

The tide, however, had begun to turn. The moment Spiridonova uttered her first challenge at the Bolshoi, the Bolsheviks placed all of the Left SRs at the congress under arrest. Not long afterward, Peters recaptured Lubianka with the support of loyal Latvian guards who had rallied behind him as a fellow countryman. Then, early on the morning of July 7, the Latvians' commander, Colonel Vatsetis, led his entire division against the rebels after promising Lenin that he would have Moscow under control by midday. With artillery and armored cars to support them, the Latvians made short work of the rebels as their cannoneers began to fire directly into the Left SR headquarters. Not long after midday they had taken more than four hundred rebels into custody and Moscow was quiet, just as Vatsetis had promised. "Taking into account [her] particular former services to the revolution,"[51] the Bolsheviks eventually sentenced Spiridonova to a year in prison and granted her an immediate amnesty, but other Left SR leaders fared far worse. Before nightfall, Dzerzhinskii had executed thirteen in the cellars of Lubianka.[52] Bliumkin made good his escape; he would reappear in the Ukraine, where he launched new terrorist attacks against the Germans and their Ukrainian sympathizers.[53]

Even before the Left SRs launched their July uprising, other plots against the Bolsheviks' tightening dictatorship had begun to take shape. Perhaps none was more complex than that shaped by Boris Savinkov, the son of a tsarist prosecutor, whose terrorist career reached back into the beginning of the twentieth century. At one time a protégé of Breshko-Breshkovskaia, Savinkov had turned to terrorism in 1904, when he had helped to kill Minister of Internal Affairs Viacheslav Plehve and Grand Duke Sergei Aleksandrovich. After a long exile in France, whence he had fled to escape a death sentence, and during which he had fought in the First World War for nearly three years as a French volunteer, Savinkov had returned to Russia to seek his fortune in his homeland's revolutionary flood. His passion for conspiracy soon enmeshed him in a tangle of sordid schemes that elevated him to the post of deputy war minister in Kerenskii's government but also led the Socialist Revolutionaries to expel him from their ranks. He had fought first against the Bolsheviks with the Cossack forces that General Krasnov led to the outskirts of Petrograd at the end of October 1917. December found him trying to work his way into the confidence of Kornilov and Alekseev in Novocherkassk, and in January he arrived in Moscow, where he established the Union for Defense of the Motherland and Liberty with their blessings.

A man whose expression was as bland as his soul was black, Savinkov moved easily in Russia's political chaos, making and reshaping alliances for his personal aggrandizement. In Moscow, he proclaimed that the Union for the Defense of the Motherland and Liberty should make no distinctions as to party or politics, and that its members need only share a sincere patriotism, a commitment to overthrow the Bolsheviks, and a pledge to reenter the war against Germany on the side of the Western allies. Anxious to spread his organization across Russia as a base from which to launch a broad assault against the Bolsheviks, Savinkov especially sought out former tsarist army officers. By the end of May he had enlisted over five thousand and claimed to have solemn promises of French aid.[54] At that moment, the Cheka came upon his trail. Although the Cheka arrested a hundred of its members soon afterward, the union's center, Latsis later admitted in his official report, "survived and continued to work at a faster pace."[55] Just more than a month later, it launched three revolts within three days.

Although no evidence ever has been found to link the two events, men from Savinkov's union attacked Iaroslavl, a city of a hundred thousand inhabitants situated on the upper Volga River some two hundred and fifty kilometers to the northeast of Moscow, on the very day that Bliumkin shot Mirbach. Before dawn on July 6, a hundred ill-armed union fighters broke into the city from the south and east. "Our entire stock of weapons numbered twelve revolvers," their commander later wrote,[56] but soon after daylight his force had driven their enemies from all but the western edge of the city. "The inhabitants rejoiced as if it were a holiday, and from early morning great crowds of people besieged our staff, wanting to join our detachments as volunteers," one White officer reported. His comrades took some comfort from the studied neutrality of Iaroslavl's factory workers and drew more encouragement from the support that some of the city's railroad workers seemed about to give.[57]

The next morning the revolt spread about a hundred kilometers to the northwest to Rybinsk. Once the center of Russia's prerevolutionary caviar industry, Rybinsk sheltered great stores of artillery ammunition that the Reds intended to use against the Czech Legion as it marched toward the Volga from Siberia. This time one of the union's members warned the Reds in advance and the attack failed, but the union continued its revolt the next day, July 8, in the small thousand-year-old town of Murom, where the Reds had established an army headquarters. There, Whites infiltrated the town at night, seized the arsenal and other key points, and arrested the entire Red headquarters staff. Hurriedly, they posted notices calling the people of Murom to arms against the Bolsheviks. "Down with the Soviet of People's Commissars!" they proclaimed. "Only by overthrowing them can we have bread, peace, and liberty! Long live unity and order in Russia!"[58] The next day the clergy held a thanksgiving service, and the local merchants showered the union men with food and supplies. They did so without the sympathy of Murom's proletarians. Soon, peasants from nearby villages joined the workers of Murom and drove out the Whites, leaving the Reds in control once again.[59] When a Bolshevik court investigated the Murom uprising some seven months later, the summary justice meted out by the Cheka already had exterminated most of those who had supported Savinkov's union.[60]

While the Reds crushed the union's forces in Murom and Rybinsk, the battle for Iaroslavl went on. During the first hours of fighting, the Whites killed the city's three senior Bolshevik officers, abolished all organs of Soviet power, and annulled all Soviet laws and decrees.[61] In a desperate attempt to win mass support, they announced that the entire region was aflame with revolt and that Moscow itself was encircled by an ever-tightening ring of anti-Bolshevik forces.[62] As the fighting went on, they exchanged their Russian rifles and ammunition for Japanese ones in order to save the Russian ammunition for their few machine guns. Yet their efforts did nothing more than give Iaroslavl a fortnight's respite before the Bolsheviks brought up heavy artillery and prepared a full-scale assault. "It is recommended to all to whom life is precious that they evacuate the city within twenty-four hours," the Bolshevik "Extraordinary Staff of the Iaroslavl Front" announced on July 20. "Our heavy guns will rain the most pitiless hurricane fire of high explosives and chemical shells upon the city [and] all who have not fled will perish beneath the rubble along with the rebels, traitors, and enemies of the revolution of the workers and poor peasants."[63] Two days later the ancient city of wood and stone that dated back to the time of Prince Iaroslav the Wise, whose Church of the Transfiguration had been built at the time of Paris's Notre Dame, and whose beautiful Church of John the Baptist had boasted no fewer than fifteen magnificent gilded domes, lay in ruins. "Nothing remained of the city that once had been so rich in architectural monuments," one eyewitness reported. "Everything was in ruins except for a small piece of the center and the part of the city around the railroad station."[64] Neither the French nor British aid that Savinkov had been promised had come in time.

The Reds now fell upon Iaroslavl in a fury. Although the official proclamation of Red Terror still lay six weeks in the future, the violence of the Bolsheviks' reprisals gave Russians a foretaste of the brutality that was soon to come. "Comrades of Iaroslavl!" the city's Red victors proclaimed. "How many hundreds of vermin and parasites would you exterminate as payment for the precious lives of our three friends [the three senior Bolsheviks killed at the beginning of the fighting]? Priests, officers, bankers, industrialists, monks, merchants—it's all the same. Neither cassock, nor uniform, nor diploma can give them protection. No mercy to the White Guardists! Remember what the Fifth All-Russian Congress of Soviets announced: 'Soviet Russia must reply to all criminal enemies of the people with mass terror against the bourgeoisie.' "[65]

In the city's main theater, the Reds found 57 Whites in hiding and shot them all before nightfall. A few days later they chose 350 more victims at random and killed them as well.[66] Convinced that their enemies would only try to escape and continue their anti-Bolshevik activity if revolutionary courts sent them to prison, the Cheka simply killed them whenever they could be found.[67] "It is essential not merely to destroy the active forces of the enemy but also to demonstrate that anyone raising the sword against the existing order will perish by the sword," Latsis wrote two days after the Bolsheviks had retaken Iaroslavl. "The meaning of civil war," he concluded, "[is] kill that you may not be killed."[68] By July, the Cheka no longer even saw public execution as a deterrent and moved its shootings from town squares into jail cellars. "Here there is a dance of life and death, a moment of truly bloody battle," Dzerzhinskii wrote to his wife from Moscow.[69] The killing of the Civil War had begun its awful crescendo.

Nowhere did Dzerzhinskii's dance of life and death play itself out in a more macabre fashion than in Ekaterinburg, a provincial town some two thousand kilometers east of Petrograd and Moscow, in which Russia's fallen sovereigns had been held prisoners since the middle of May. Ever since their arrest by Russia's first Provisional Government in March 1917, the Romanovs had faced an uncertain fate. At first, England's Ambassador Sir George Buchanan had informed Russia's new leaders that his King and government would offer them asylum and, in principle, the Provisional Government had agreed to his proposal.[70] "Our captivity at Tsarskoe Selo," wrote Pierre Gilliard, the tutor who had taught the imperial children for more than a decade, "did not seem likely to last long,"[71] and in March 1917 circumstances seemed to support his opinion. Indeed, it had seemed extremely unlikely that Nicholas, Aleksandra, their five children, and loyal servants would not be able to reach the safety of the Finnish frontier, just a few hours away by railroad, or take the newly built rail line that ran from Petrozavodsk to Murmansk, whence they could leave Russia by sea.

But the Romanovs' days of captivity stretched into weeks and months, and Gilliard's hope proved unfounded. The German government gave the necessary assurances that it would allow a ship carrying the Romanovs safe passage to England, but the British withdrew their offer of asylum, evidently out of fear that support for Russia's fallen rulers would stir unrest in England "at a critical point in the war."[72] Yet even this unexpected turn of events at first gave little cause for concern. Kept under guard in a wing of Tsarskoe Selo's Alexander Palace, the Romanovs' continued presence posed no serious problem for the Provisional Government that spring. Then, as Russian public opinion began the leftward march that would open the way for the Bolshevik victory in October, Kerenskii began to fear that he might find it difficult to keep the revolution unstained by the blood of his former sovereigns.[73] Among Kerenskii's rivals on the left, Lenin had never concealed his conviction that the Romanovs must be killed. "If, in such a cultured country as England, which had never known a Mongol yoke, bureaucratic oppression, or the tyranny of a military caste, it was necessary to behead one crowned brigand in order to teach kings to be 'constitutional' monarchs," he had written in 1911, "then, in Russia, it is necessary to behead at least one hundred Romanovs."[74]

Fearful for his prisoners' safety should they remain in the vicinity of Petrograd, and unable to set them free without outraging Russia's proletarians, Kerenskii had made plans to move them to Tobolsk, once Russia's gateway to Siberia's rich fur lands, but, in 1917, a sleepy town of twenty thousand people. Perched on the high right bank of the Irtysh River, Tobolsk lay two hundred miles from any railhead and some four days' journey by river steamer from the Siberian center of Omsk. "My choice fell upon Tobolsk," Kerenskii explained, "because it was a truly isolated place . . . and, in the winter, was almost entirely cut off from the outside world."[75]

When Kerenskii sent his captives to Tobolsk at the beginning of August 1917, he took particular care to conceal their departure from the Petrograd Soviet of Workers' and Soldiers' Deputies. "We made all the preparations for their departure in the greatest secrecy," he later wrote. "Only five or six people in all of Petrograd knew about it."[76] A special train bearing signs that falsely identified its occupants as members of the "Japanese Red Cross Mission" carried the Romanovs to the Siberian fur-trading center of Tiumen, from which a small river steamer took them on to Tobolsk.[77] It was an ironic touch, but one of which he was probably unaware, that Kerenskii guaranteed the safety of Nicholas and his family during their journey by placing them under the protection of those very Japanese to whom Russia's fallen Tsar habitually applied the word *makaki*—"little short-tailed monkeys."[78]

Along with several close friends, the Romanovs had traveled to Tobolsk with several freight cars of baggage, six chambermaids, two valets, ten footmen, three cooks, four assistant cooks, a clerk, a nurse, a doctor, a barber, a butler, a wine steward, and two pet spaniels,[79] and their lives were far from unpleasant during the winter of 1917–1918. Tucked away in Kerenskii's well-chosen Siberian retreat, they had remained insulated from the Bolshevik Revolution and untouched by its growing violence. Their first contact with Russia's new regime had not come until February 25, 1918, when the commander of their guards received orders to place them on "soldier's rations" and to limit each prisoner's expenses to an average of six hundred rubles a month.[80] Sadly, Nicholas and Aleksandra had decided they must send ten of their servants away and give up butter and coffee, but their daily menu still included grouse, wild duck, and veal, a far cry from the fare that prisoners usually endured.[81] Only in late April had their lives changed significantly for the worse, when the authorities in Moscow had ordered them moved from Tobolsk, where monarchist sympathies had remained strong, to Ekaterinburg, where the fiercely loyal Bolshevik Regional Soviet of the Urals held sway. By mid-May, Nicholas, Aleksandra, all their children, and their remaining handful of loyal servants had been confined in "the House of Special

Designation," the former home of a family of prosperous merchants by the name of Ipatiev.[82]

A large stone building that served as a lumpy crown for the highest of the low hills upon which Ekaterinburg had been built, the House of Special Designation had windows that had been whitewashed on both sides so that no one could look in or out. A high wooden fence of rough-sawn boards hammered together in the lopsided, uncaring manner of Russia's provinces surrounded the entire building and yard, all of which was guarded by an intricate network of sentry posts and machine gun emplacements. Dedicated Bolshevik workers, their hearts hardened by long years of privation and revolutionary struggle, now replaced Kerenskii's benevolent guards, and their commander made no effort to conceal the hatred he bore for his captives. According to some reports, these guards sketched pictures of Aleksandra engaged in sexual acts with Rasputin upon the walls of the single toilet that they shared with their eleven prisoners, and they insisted upon pointing them out to the young grand duchesses at every opportunity. Their meals now limited to black bread and tea, supplemented by rough fare sent in from a nearby workers' eating house, the Romanovs began to know fear, brutality, and deprivation of prison for the first time.[83]

As they had so many times in the past, Nicholas, Aleksandra, and their children took refuge in their unshakable faith in God's mercy. They met for prayers every morning before a makeshift altar covered with the delicate lace bedspread that once had adorned the Empress's chaise longue at Tsarskoe Selo. When their captors interrupted their meditations by roaring out revolutionary songs and obscene ballads, Aleksandra and her daughters responded by singing hymns.[84] Olga, the eldest, who had just turned twenty-two, shared her mother's fervent piety and wrote a number of hymns during their long captivity. "Grant us, Heavenly Father, patience, in these dark days of strife and gloom, to bear our people's persecution," one of them began. "On the threshold of the grave, breathe, O Lord, thy love into our hearts."[85] As the Romanovs' guards drank and shouted curses at "Nicholas the bloodsucker" in the rooms below, the grave was closer than any of them knew. As June turned into July, Russia's fallen rulers had less than three weeks to live.[86]

At the beginning of July, a new jailer entered the Romanovs' lives. Born in the Siberian village of Kainsk, to which his father had been exiled as a common criminal, Iakov Mikhailovich Iurovskii was a Jew of little education who had converted to Lutheranism during a year in which he had wandered through Germany and Central Europe. One of his brothers remembered him as a man who "liked to oppress people," and his sister-in-law thought him both a "despot" and an "exploiter." Despite his longstanding revolutionary sympathies, Iurovskii had built prosperous businesses during the twilight of Imperial Russia, first as a watchmaker and then, after the tsarist authorities exiled him to Ekaterinburg, as a portrait photographer.[87] A dedicated Bolshevik since the Revolution's beginnings, Iurovskii became a member of the Ural Regional Soviet and a trusted figure in the Cheka after Lenin's October victory. With the fearsome power of the Cheka behind him, he immediately brought order to the chaos that he found in the House of Special Designation when he took command on July 4, 1918. For a brief moment, the Romanovs took hope from his appearance. "The door to the shed containing our baggage has been sealed," Nicholas wrote with satisfaction in his diary four days after Iurovskii had taken command. "If only that had been done a month ago!"[88]

Iurovskii's first concern, however, was not to protect his prisoners' baggage but to prevent their escape. As the Czechoslovak Legion and its White allies advanced against Ekaterinburg at the beginning of July, Iurovskii's guards began to intercept secret messages that carried promises of liberation and restoration. "The hour of liberation is at hand, and the days of the usurpers are numbered," one such message began. Another was signed: "Someone who is ready to give his life for you—a Russian officer."[89] Fearful that the Whites might rescue his captives, Iurovskii reinforced their guards and ordered metal gratings installed over the windows in the room Nicholas shared with Aleksandra and Aleksei. "We like this type less and less," Nicholas wrote in his diary at that point. "We have no news whatever from outside."[90]

Fears that the Romanovs would escape plagued others besides Iurovskii. Earlier that month, with the Whites' advance heightening their sense of urgency, the Regional Soviet of the Urals had voted unanimously for the Romanovs' execution. Before carrying out the sentence, they sent Filipp Goloshchëkin, who had been an unemployed dental school graduate from Riga before he became regional party secretary and military commissar of the Urals, to obtain approval from Sverdlov and the All-Russian Executive Committee in Moscow. Goloshchëkin returned with instructions to stage a public trial of the Romanovs in which Trotskii would serve as the government's chief prosecutor.[91] Trotskii later claimed that he had wanted the trial to be broadcast to the entire nation by radio (a preposterous scheme because electricity had not yet been brought to most of Russia's countryside) but that Lenin had warned that there might not be enough time to arrange it because of the speed with which the Whites were advancing.[92] At about that point, the Ural Regional Soviet received word that the Czechs and the Whites menaced Ekaterinburg on two sides and that the city probably could not be held for more than a few days.[93] Lest their captives be liberated, the Regional Soviet decided—and it seems that higher authorities in Moscow approved—to carry out the execution without waiting for the formality of a staged trial. As one of Lenin's confidants reportedly explained to Trotskii a few days afterward: "Il'ich [that is, Lenin] believed that we shouldn't leave the Whites a live banner to rally around."[94]

At about seven o'clock on the evening of July 16, Iurovskii ordered Pavel Medvedev, commander of the Cheka guards who was on duty that night, to bring all of the pistols that could be found to his office.* Evidently apprehensive that the sharp crash of rifle fire would attract too much attention from people living in the vicinity of the House of Special Designation, Iurovskii had decided to use handguns to kill his prisoners because their duller reports would not carry as far. In the meantime, Petr Voikov, regional commissar for supply in Ekaterinburg, arranged for nearly two hundreds gallons of gasoline to be delivered to the abandoned Four Brothers Mine, some nine kilometers north of Ekaterinburg. Later in the day, he ordered a local chemical warehouse to send fifty gallons of sulphuric acid "without delay or excuses" to the same location.[96] As the center of Russia's platinum industry, Eka-

*Not long afterward, Medvedev returned with twelve 7.62 mm. Nagant revolvers, the standard sidearm of Russia's army during the World War I era. From other sources, Iurovskii obtained at least one 9 mm. Browning pistol, an American Colt .45 semi-automatic pistol, and two other weapons, whose bullets later could be identified only as having been fired from "a three-line [approximately .32 caliber] automatic pistol of American manufacture," and "a four-line [approximately .44 caliber] revolver," perhaps one of the weapons that the New England weapons-maker Smith and Wesson had manufactured for the Russian army in the 1870s and 1880s. Iurovskii and his colleague Voikov carried 7.65 mm. Mauser pistols, which they preferred to the Nagant revolvers.[95]

terinburg habitually stored quantities of sulphuric acid to leech out pure platinum from the ore surrounding it, but Voikov's order evidently created such a shortage that when Robert Wilton, special correspondent of *The Times*, tried to order a platinum ring when he visited Ekaterinburg to report on Admiral Kolchak's White government in 1919, he was told that the ring could not be made because there had been no sulphuric acid in the city "since the previous year."[97]

While Iurovskii and Voikov made their preparations, Nicholas, Aleksandra, their children, and servants ate a meager evening meal, chatted, and read before going to bed just before midnight as usual. At approximately 2 A.M.—the darkest hour of the night because the daylight-saving time that the Bolsheviks had introduced that summer was two hours ahead of standard time—Voikov arrived to say that all was ready. Medvedev later claimed that Iurovskii went to awaken the prisoners after Voikov arrived, while a number of eyewitnesses, as well as Medvedev's wife, insisted that Iurovskii had assigned that task to Medvedev. In any case, it seems quite certain that whoever awakened the Romanovs told them that they were to be moved to a different location because the Whites were about to attack Ekaterinburg. Hurriedly, the prisoners dressed, Nicholas and Aleksei in military field shirts and forage caps, Aleksandra and her daughters in ordinary dresses. Then Nicholas led the way, carrying Aleksei, who was still recovering from the effects of a massive hemophilic hemorrhage. Behind him came Aleksandra, the four grand duchesses, their family doctor Evgenii Botkin, their valet Aleksei Trupp, the cook Ivan Kharitonov, and the housemaid Anna Demidova, who, like two of the grand duchesses, carried pillows. When they reached the bottom of the stairs from their cramped second-floor lodgings, Iurovskii motioned them into a room that stood adjacent to a sealed storeroom, where he told them to wait until the cars that had been ordered to transport them arrived.

Some fifteen by seventeen feet in dimensions, the semibasement room into which Iurovskii ordered the Romanovs was barren of furniture. Boldly striped wallpaper covered its plaster, and large double doors filled about a third of the east and west walls. The room had but a single window, at shoulder height, on the south wall. Nicholas asked for chairs for Aleksei, Aleksandra, and himself, and Iurovskii obligingly sent one of his men to bring them. According to eyewitnesses, Aleksandra sat in one of the chairs near the southeast corner of the room, her back to the east wall, the darkened window on her left. Almost in the center of the room, Nicholas and Aleksei sat on the remaining chairs. Behind Aleksandra stood the Grand Duchesses Olga, Tatiana, and Mariia. Anastasiia, her favorite pet dog Dzhemmi in her arms, stood off to her mother's right and near to the east wall, along with Demidova, Trupp, and Kharitonov. The grand duchesses had used their pillows to cushion their mother's and brother's chairs, while Demidova held her larger pillow in arms that she most probably kept crossed in front of her in typical peasant fashion. Sleepily, they waited. During sixteen months of captivity, they had grown used to strange instructions and, most of all, to delays. Nothing seemed out of the ordinary, and Iurovskii's explanation seemed entirely plausible. In fact, they could hear the rumble of the Whites' artillery in the distance.

Whatever hopes for liberation the sound of their rescuers' guns may have stirred in the Romanovs soon were shattered. Precisely as planned, the four-ton Fiat truck that Voikov had ordered arrived, and its driver began to race the engine as he had been told. In the entrance hall that stood just beyond the west wall of the room in which the Romanovs waited, Iurovskii made a final check with a detachment of ten Cheka guards to make certain that each man knew which prisoner he was to shoot. A glance at his watch told him it was 2:45 A.M. Then, with a final reminder to his men that he reserved the execution of Nicholas and Aleksei for himself, Iurovskii led them into the room where the Romanovs waited, still groggy from their sudden awakening. "Nicholas Aleksandrovich," he announced, "by order of the Regional Soviet of the Urals, you are to be shot, along with all your family."

Nicholas barely had time to leap to his feet and utter "*Chto?*— "What?"— before Iurovskii shot him in the head, turned slightly, and fired two shots at Aleksei. Aleksandra and one of her daughters managed to cross themselves before the bullets from their killers' revolvers tore into their chests, shattering at least two of the many large precious stones that they had carried concealed in heavily padded brassieres ever since they had left Tsarskoe Selo. The rest, including Demidova, who tried to protect herself with her heavy pillow, fell in a second barrage. Then, in the heavy silence that followed, Aleksei moaned. Iurovskii stepped over and fired two more shots into his head. All were dead except for Anastasiia, who cried out more from fear than pain since she seems to have been only slightly wounded. One of the Cheka guards picked up a rifle, drove its bayonet into her several times, and then reversed his hold on the weapon so as to shatter Dzhemmi's skull with its butt. By that time, Medvedev later testified, there were "many wounds" in the victims' bodies. "Their blood flowed in streams," he remembered. It lay in puddles, "thick, like livers," on the floor.[98]

Iurovskii now moved quickly to complete his task. As dawn was breaking, he ordered his Cheka guards to load the bodies of Russia's fallen sovereigns, their children, and servants into the Fiat truck that stood waiting behind the House of Special Designation and ordered its driver to take them to the Four Brothers Mine. So that peasants from any of the small villages that nestled in the nearby woodlands would not interrupt his men at their work, Iurovskii posted guards and closed the nearby road for two days and nights. As best we can determine, the Cheka men spent those two days in the grisly tasks of cutting the corpses apart, burning them in gasoline fires, and trying to dissolve the few larger bones that remained in sulphuric acid. While his men worked, Iurovskii apparently sat on a nearby pine stump and ate some of the hard-boiled eggs he had ordered the women who supplied food to the inmates at the House of Special Designation to bring him the day before. He had even had the foresight to have had the eggs carefully packed in a basket. Their work done, Iurovskii's men gathered up the remains, shoveled them into the bottom of a nearby mine shaft, and covered them with nearly two feet of dirt. When they returned to Ekaterinburg, only the charred earth held a hint of what they had done. Criminal pathologists later found the soil beneath their fires had become saturated with melted human fat that had hardened like tallow once it had cooled.[99]

As the Whites crashed through the Bolshevik defenses around Ekaterinburg on July 25, a detachment of monarchist officers raced to the House of Special Designation to free their Emperor. They found the building deserted and clothing and personal effects of the imperial family strewn everywhere, but no clues to the prisoners' whereabouts. Pierre Gilliard, who had been separated from the Romanovs some weeks before and had come to Ekaterinburg with the Whites, found where Aleksandra had penciled a swastika, her favorite good luck symbol, on one of the window frames, and discovered another that had been drawn in similar fashion on the wallpaper over her bed. Elsewhere in the house, the Whites found more than sixty of the family's small icons, including several that bore inscriptions from Rasputin. More thorough investigations yielded conclusive evidence that great quantities of blood had been scrubbed from the floor and walls of one of the semi-basement rooms, and a careful examination of the room's floor and walls produced no fewer than twenty-two bullets. Yet the final pieces of the puzzle did not begin to fall into place until early the next year, when the Whites took Pavel Medvedev prisoner in Perm. Only then did investigators hear the first eyewitness account of the killings that had occurred in the early morning hours of July 17, and still more months passed before they learned the fate of the Romanovs' bodies.[100] Nikolai Sokolov, the criminal investigator assigned by Admiral Kolchak to unearth the details of the Romanovs' execution, concluded that the Bolsheviks had "subordinated moral principle to crime."[101] The Bolsheviks thought otherwise. "The execution of the Tsar's family was needed not only to frighten, horrify, and dishearten the enemy, but also in order to shake up our own ranks, to show them that there was no turning back, that ahead lay either complete victory or complete ruin," Trotskii explained later. "*This* Lenin sensed very well."[102]

More lay behind the execution of the Romanovs than the Bolsheviks' attempt to "frighten, horrify, and dishearten" their opponents; more, even, than an effort to destroy figureheads around whom the Whites might rally. The cold-blooded killing of women, children, and servants flowed all too easily from a current of brutality that cut deeply through Russian life in those days as the law of the gun became the law of the land. The desperate and never ending battle for food, the class warfare that the Bolsheviks fostered in town and countryside, and the political opposition that struggled not to admit its growing impotence against the organizational strength of the Bolshevik Party, the Cheka, and the Red Army, all contributed to a deepening sense that absolutes now must reign in Russia. As peasants fought to defend their food supplies against grain-requisitioning detachments from the Commissariat of Food Supply, Bolshevik authorities reported seventy-three major revolts in July and August alone.[103] All were suppressed with ferocious brutality. Lenin ordered his subordinates to "*instantly* introduce mass terror" wherever they encountered opposition.[104]

All across the lands that had once been the Russian Empire, violence begat greater violence during the summer of 1918. In the southwest, the commander of Germany's army of occupation, Field Marshal Hermann von Eichhorn, instituted a reign of terror that left a bloody trail of mass shootings and hangings across the grain-fields of the Ukraine, and the peasants replied with partisan attacks that cost the Germans close to nineteen thousand casualties. Vowing that Eichhorn must be brought to account for having "sown [the Ukraine] with gallows and corpses,"[105] Irina Kakhovskaia, Spiridonova's longtime companion in tsarist Siberian prisons, and Boris Donskoi, a Krondstadt sailor, killed Eichhorn on July 30.[106] To the south and east, White forces instituted mass executions as they pressed in upon Russia's Red center, and the Bolsheviks replied in kind. Even Petrograd, the cradle of Russia's revolution, became a terrorist battleground that summer. In June, an assassin killed Moisei Volodarskii, a Jewish trade unionist from Philadelphia who had become commissar for press, agitation, and propaganda in Petrograd and the surrounding region. Then, on August 30, Leonid Kannegiser, a youthful poet-turned-assassin, killed Moisei Uritskii, head of Petrograd's Cheka. Ironically, Uritskii, the son of devoutly Orthodox Jews from the Ukraine, had been one of the few Bolsheviks who had opposed Lenin's and Latsis's summons to terror, for he feared that it only would deepen the hatred that had begun to consume the Russians.[107]

Although he always had stood closer to Trotskii, Bukharin, and Zinoviev than to Lenin, Uritskii was assured by the circumstances of his death of a place in the Bolshevik pantheon of revolutionary heroes. No sooner had word of his murder reached the Kremlin than Lenin ordered Dzerzhinskii to Petrograd to interrogate Kannegiser. Fearful that Kannegiser was part of a larger revolutionary conspiracy, Dzerzhinskii went immediately but returned even more quickly to Moscow when he learned, on his arrival in Petrograd, that another assassin had shot Lenin. With every reason to suspect that a much larger conspiracy was afoot, the Cheka proceeded to leave no stone unturned in its effort to learn how great the danger really was.[108]

Just hours after Dzerzhinskii's departure for Petrograd on August 30, Lenin had gone to Moscow's Mikhelson Works, where he had spoken about "the dictatorship of the proletariat and the dictatorship of the bourgeoisie" to a meeting of workers at its hand grenade assembly plant. "Wherever 'democrats' are in power, you have real, barefaced robbery," with the bourgeoisie endeavoring to delude the masses with empty promises of equality and fraternity, he warned them. Factory workers therefore must join in the struggle to make a workers' government a reality in which "all who work have the right to enjoy the benefits of life." Their commitment could not be half-hearted. In the battle against the "predatory bourgeoisie," who had condemned "millions of workers" to "unrelieved destitution" under the guise of parliamentary democracy, "victory or death" could be the only alternatives. As Lenin spoke, a plainly dressed, excessively ordinary-looking woman, distinguished only by the nervous manner in which she chain-smoked cigarettes, sat near the platform and seemed to hang upon every word that was spoken. When Lenin left the hall at about seven-thirty that evening, so did she. As he walked toward his waiting automobile, the same woman reappeared, stepped from the crowd, and fired three times. One of the bullets struck Lenin in the chest, another passed through his left arm and lodged in his neck.[109]

Such terrible uncertainty reigned in those days that Stepan Gil, who had served as Lenin's chauffeur ever since the October Revolution, dared not take him directly to a hospital for fear that he might fall into the hands of a physician loyal to the Left SRs. He therefore drove the wounded Bolshevik leader at breakneck speed to the Kremlin, where Lenin insisted upon trying to climb the three flights of stairs that led to his apartment. Gil then called Vladimir Bonch-Bruevich, secretary of the Sovnarkom and one of Lenin's oldest friends, who lived in a building nearby. With typical Bolshevik discipline, Bonch-Bruevich first put Red Army units on alert and reinforced the Kremlin guard in case the attacks that had felled Lenin and Uritskii proved to be part of a larger plot to overthrow the government. He then rushed to Lenin's apartment, carrying whatever first aid supplies his physician wife kept at home. "Vladimir Ilich lay on his right side on a bed that stood near the window and groaned faintly," Bonch-Bruevich remembered as he wrote about those terrible minutes a few years later. "My chest hurts. My chest hurts a great deal," Lenin told his friend. "Your heart's not involved," Bonch-Bruevich assured him. "I can see the wounds. They're in your arm." Once he had calmed Lenin, Bonch-Bruevich called his wife at her clinic and asked her to summon other physicians whose medical skill and political loyalty she could trust. Bonch-Bruevich seemed not to know how to stop the bleeding; he tried to give Lenin first aid, although it seemed that he did little more than paint the bullet wounds with iodine. By the time his wife arrived with surgeons from her clinic to give Lenin serious medical attention, Lenin had fainted from pain and loss of blood.[110]

Meanwhile, Cheka agents searched for the young woman who

had fled from the Mikhelson Works after the shooting. A few blocks away, they found her leaning against a tree and breathing heavily. "She had the look of someone who had just eluded her pursuers," her captors later reported, and she was quickly taken into custody.[111] At Cheka headquarters, she confessed that she was Fania Kaplan, daughter of a Jewish schoolteacher from western Russia, whose parents had emigrated to America in 1911. Now aged twenty-eight, she had spent nearly eleven years in Siberian penal servitude, where she had met Spiridonova, who had convinced her to reject anarchism in favor of the peasant-centered principles of the Socialist Revolutionary Party.[112] Some expected that Kaplan's long record of dedicated service to the Revolution would lighten her sentence, but her fate was sealed from the moment of her arrest. After several days and nights in the Cheka's interrogation chambers, she was taken into an out-of-the-way courtyard and shot—at 4 P.M. on September 3—by the commandant of the Kremlin. "Red Terror is not an empty phrase," her executioner told himself as he struggled to overcome his scruples about shooting a woman. "There can be no mercy for enemies of the Revolution!"[113] "The living spirit has abandoned the Revolution," Spiridonova lamented bitterly from the Kremlin cell to which she had been confined at the beginning of July for her part in the failed Left SR uprising. "How much better it would be for Lenin to live in insecurity if only that living spirit were preserved!"[114]

Not since October 1917 had a single day's events so altered the Revolution's course as Kannegiser's murder of Uritskii and Kaplan's attack against Lenin. Kaplan's interrogation at Lubianka had hardly begun when the Red Terror fell upon Russia in all its fury.[115] "The bullet was directed not only against Comrade Lenin but also against the working class as a whole," Dzerzhinskii's brutal Latvian deputy Iakov Peters warned, as he urged Russia's proletarians to take stern measures to defend themselves. "Let the enemies of the working class remember that anyone caught in possession of arms without the required permission . . . will immediately be shot," he announced on August 31. "Anyone daring to agitate against the Soviet government will immediately be arrested and placed in a concentration camp." The Cheka, Peters promised, would "reply to the criminal designs of the enemies of the working class with mass terror." All enemies of the working class, Peters promised, "will be destroyed and crushed by the heavy hammer of the revolutionary proletariat."[116]

The next day, the official newspaper of the newly formed Red Army took up the cry for bloodshed and revenge. "We will kill our enemies in scores of hundreds," *Krasnaia gazeta* proclaimed. "Let them be thousands, let them drown themselves in their own blood. For the blood of Lenin and Uritskii . . . let there be floods of blood of the bourgeoisie—more blood, as much as possible."[117] "From now on the hymn of the working class will be a hymn of hate and revenge," *Pravda* added that same day. "The counterrevolution, this vicious mad dog, must be destroyed once and for all!"[118] Four days later, People's Commissar for Internal Affairs Grigorii Petrovskii published a formal circular that stated the government's views and gave directions to its agents. Condemning the "unusually mild measures of repression" that the Reds had employed up to that point, Petrovskii called for an immediate "end to this state of affairs." Mass terror must follow in the wake of the events of August 30. "The least opposition, the least movement among the White Guards, should be met with wholesale executions," and all of the government's resources must be directed toward making certain that there was "no hesitation or indecision whatever in carrying out mass terror."[119] Should there be any doubt that Petrovskii spoke for a united government, the Sovnarkom published a resolution the same day with the ominous warning that "the Soviet of People's Commissars . . . finds that under present circumstances it is necessary to safeguard its rear by means of terror." This meant, most simply, "shooting all persons associated with White Guard organizations, plots, and conspiracies."[120]

Less than a week after Kaplan's attack against Lenin, the Petrograd Cheka shot 512 hostages, among them several prominent tsarist officials, including the corrupt one-time Minister of Internal Affairs Aleksei Khvostov (in whom Aleksandra had placed great faith) and the notoriously reactionary minister of justice in 1914–1915, Ivan Shcheglovitov.[121] Taking seriously their leaders' promise that "for every drop of blood shed by our leaders in their fight for the ideals of socialism, the proletariat will drown the bourgeoisie in their own blood,"[122] the revolutionary sailors of Kronstadt killed four hundred hostages in a single night.[123] During those days, no prisoner was safe and everyone lived in fear. "Those of us who were lying in Butyrki Prison at that terrible time . . . will never forget the soul-racking experience," one former prisoner wrote. "Especially heart-rending was the nightly necessity of hearing, and sometimes of seeing, prisoners removed for execution."

Many were killed by chance. Some were killed even after they had been declared innocent of any wrongdoing. "Owing to the great mass of condemned," the people's prosecutor told one distraught father, "your son has been shot in error."[124]

People began to say that the much vaunted breathing space, or *peredyshka*, that Lenin claimed to have won for the Revolution at Brest-Litovsk was turning into a *zadyshka*, a death by strangulation.[125] Throughout the fall of 1918, the killings soared as the Red Terror spread into Russia's provinces. "We are resorting to Red Terror as a vaccine to inoculate the bourgeoisie," the Cheka in the town of Morshansk explained, while its counterpart in Torzhok promised that "for every head and life of our leaders, hundreds of heads of the bourgeoisie and their helpers will fall."[126] In Perm, the Cheka shot thirty-six hostages "in reply to the assassination of Uritskii and the attempt on the life of Lenin," while in Penza the Cheka announced that "for the murder . . . of one comrade . . . the Whites paid with 152 lives" and promised that "severer measures will be taken against the Whites in the future."[127] "There was not a single locality where shootings 'because of Lenin' failed to be carried out," the historian Sergei Melgunov reported after spending part of 1918 in a Cheka prison.[128] "The Cheka does not pardon," Latsis announced at one point. "It destroys all who are caught . . . on the other side of the barricade."[129] "As far as the bourgeoisie are concerned," he added elsewhere, "the tactics of mass extermination must be introduced."[130]

Latsis once estimated that the Cheka had shot more than eight thousand people in the twenty provinces of Central Russia before the end of July 1919,[131] but by all accounts that figure was a gross underestimate. Even as late as 1981, the author of what must be regarded as the definitive history of the Cheka to date could make no accurate estimate of the number of the victims.[132] Appalled at the Bolsheviks' brutality, the representatives of foreign governments expressed their "deep indignation against the regime of terror established in Petrograd, Moscow, and other cities." In reply, Russia's new Commissar of Foreign Affairs Georgii Chicherin promised "merciless war" against the bourgeoisie at home and abroad. "In Russia, violence is employed only for the sake of the sacred interests of liberation of the masses," he announced loftily. "We most vigorously decline the interest of the neutral capitalist powers in favor of the Russian bourgeoisie."[133]

The Bolsheviks now dealt in death as never before. Besides

treason, desertion, mutiny, espionage, and counterrevolutionary activity, Russians faced execution for looting, robbery, drunkenness, insubordination, issuing false exemptions from military service, prostitution, and, "with a view to combating prostitution," for having syphilis.[134] "The threat of death hung in the air at every moment," one survivor remembered. "The thought of death became so commonplace . . . that the very word *death* ceased to be fearsome."[135] Never had a modern society killed its people so readily and for so many different reasons. People began to speak of the "bloodlust of Bolshevism," while the Bolsheviks insisted that they were only responding to White Terror.[136] In vain did Gorkii warn that "physical violence will always be an incontestable proof of moral impotence," that "punishment by death does not make people better than they are," and that "killing proves nothing, except that the killer is stupid."[137] Gorkii's was not a voice that the Russians wanted to hear, for they had begun to live by other principles and abide by other rules. "In civil war, there are no courts of law for the enemy," Latsis wrote. "If you do not kill, you will be killed."[138]

The Russian masses, Gorkii once had insisted, were "cruel beasts . . . deformed by cynical violence, hideously cruel and, at the same time, incomprehensibly kind-hearted."[139] Convinced that violence, cruelty, and discipline were needed to harden the Revolution, Lenin worried that Russia's proletarians would prove too "tender-hearted." "It's a bowl of mush we have, not a dictatorship," he had lamented to Trotskii not long before Kaplan's bullets struck him down. "Russians are too kind," "Russians are lazybones, softies."[140] In the fall of 1918, Russia's Bolshevik leaders looked for a hardened revolutionary force to emerge from the crucible of violence and class warfare that the Red Terror had brought into being. "The Revolution suffered an inward change," Trotskii later wrote. "Its 'good nature' gave way. The party steel received its last tempering." At last, the Bolsheviks began to bring the Russian revolutionary spirit, so volatile and so voluble in 1917, under stern control. "In the autumn [of 1918] the great revolution really occurred," Trotskii explained. "Of the pallid weakness that the spring months had shown there was no longer a trace. Something had taken its place, it had grown stronger."[141]

Nowhere was this new sense of discipline and strength of purpose more evident than in the infant Red Army that Trotskii forged from the undisciplined masses that had fled before the

Whites' advance that summer. On September 10 his forces retook the great Volga river city of Kazan and pressed on against Simbirsk and the capital of the Komuch government in Samara. The disasters of the spring and summer of 1918—the Brest-Litovsk Treaty, the German occupation of the Ukraine, the White victories in the South and East, the uprising of the Left SRs, and the terrorist assaults against Mirbach, Uritskii, and Lenin—all seemed behind the Bolsheviks now, and the pendulum began to move in the other direction. "The Volga was cleared," Trotskii wrote as he looked back upon those days. "The Revolution was strong in men."[142] The tide in the Bolsheviks' struggle against their domestic enemies seemed to be turning that fall. Yet the shift proved to be neither rapid nor decisive, as a new array of hostile forces formed against Russia's proletarian rulers. Already invaded by their nation's enemies, the Bolsheviks now faced intervention by Russia's former allies. Well before they celebrated the first anniversary of their revolutionary victory, Lenin and his comrades saw armed men wearing the uniforms of England, France, Japan, the United States, and several other Western nations take up positions upon Russian soil.

CHAPTER FIVE

The Allies Intervene

Rarely have statesmen woven stubborn misconceptions and false assumptions into a more tangled skein of diplomatic misunderstandings than did the Bolsheviks and Russia's former allies during the months after the October Revolution. From the moment the imperial government had fallen at the beginning of March 1917, senior Allied diplomats had dismissed Lenin and his followers as the lunatic fringe of the Russian Revolution, and they had looked on in angry confusion as the political strength of these "anarchists" and "extreme socialists" had grown at the expense of more sober, less volatile men. Always, the Bolsheviks stirred deep resentment among Petrograd's diplomatic community. Sworn to end the "imperialist war" that had cost the lives of so many proletarians, the Bolsheviks opposed the Allies at every turn and condemned equally the "imperialists" of Germany, Austria, Britain, France, and the United States. America's ambassador David Francis, who once described Lenin as "a man with the brain of a sage and the heart of a monster," condemned the Bolsheviks as "inhuman brutes" and disdained them as men who "[should have] been shot as traitors."[1] Britain's Sir George Buchanan spoke of them coldly as men who "could pull down, but . . . could not build up" and at one point stated flatly that "Bolshevism was at the root of all the evils from which Russia was suffering."[2]

In a similar fashion, the Bolsheviks made no secret of their hatred for those "class enemies" and "imperialist robbers" who, they claimed, had driven the working men and women of Europe into a war that had shed oceans of proletarian blood under the guise of national defense. The "bloody history of bloody imperialism," Lenin insisted, was drawing to an end. "The corpse of capitalism is decaying and disintegrating in our midst, polluting the air and poisoning our lives, enmeshing that which is new, fresh, young, and virile in thousands of threads and bonds of that which is old, moribund, and decaying," he wrote in 1918. "The hatred these watchdogs of imperialism express for the Bolsheviks, and the sympathy of the class-conscious workers of the world," he continued, "convince us more than ever of the justice of our cause." Against the "German imperialist vultures" and the "Anglo-French and American imperialist sharks," the workers of the world would stand firm and eventually triumph. "We are invincible," Lenin insisted, "because the world proletarian revolution is invincible."[3]

In an atmosphere so clouded by ideological rhetoric, the senior Allied diplomats in Petrograd proved singularly ill suited to deal with Russia's new masters. Maurice Paléologue, the wartime French ambassador whose knowledge of Russia and the Russians exceeded that of any senior diplomat in Europe, had been recalled to Paris in May 1917. Broken in health and, for a time, uncertain in spirit, Britain's Sir George Buchanan, whose sober presence had graced the Russian scene throughout the war, had followed him to the West a few months later. Those who took their places in Petrograd could never fill the void they left behind, for the diplomats who represented the Allied governments in Russia in 1918 never managed to set aside their moral outrage at what they considered to be the Bolsheviks' betrayal of the Allied cause. Disdain and condescension filled every report they wrote and clouded every judgment they made. Unable to regard the Bolsheviks as equals, they insisted that their governments treat them as men of little consequence.

As dean of Petrograd's diplomatic corps after Buchanan's departure at the beginning of 1918, America's ambassador David Francis continued to be as uncompromising in his hatred for the Bolsheviks as he was unschooled in the complexities of the Russian land and people. A prominent and influential Democrat who had served as mayor of St. Louis, governor of Missouri, and, briefly (1896-1897), secretary of the interior in the administration of

Grover Cleveland, Francis had enjoyed a long and successful career in business and banking and had refused an ambassadorial appointment to Buenos Aires two years before he had accepted one to Russia. Habitually referred to as "the Governor" by his associates in America's Petrograd Embassy, he never became "the Ambassador,"[4] and he never succeeded in taking the proper measure of the Russians.

Too coarsely homespun for the tastes of his more elegant European colleagues, Francis thought and acted in the unvarnished manner of America's Midwest. He retained the parochial outlook of late nineteenth-century mid-America, narrow in its dimensions, but unshakable in its certainty. Courage, honesty, and stern self-discipline—but certainly not modesty—were the virtues that once led him to write: "I don't acknowledge that I have any apetite [sic] which I cannot control."[5] Francis liked good cigars, good whiskey, and a good game of cards, but his taste did not extend to fine wines, subtly seasoned dishes, and elegant entertainment. Ruggedly individualistic, unashamed of his ignorance, yet confident of his ability to meet whatever challenge he faced, he neither hid his opinions nor apologized for them. "In order to meet without quailing the heavy responsibilities and the unknown problems which lay before me," he wrote with unabashed immodesty of his thoughts on arriving in Russia in the spring of 1916, "I needed all the self-confidence born of my experience."[6]

Francis could never project that aura of sage judgment that had so distinguished Paléologue and Buchanan. Paléologue's successor, the former French Minister of War Joseph Noulens, remembered Francis only as a man who "spoke French badly and exhibited a poor acquaintance with diplomatic practice and the principles of international law."[7] Britain's diplomatic representative, Robert Bruce Lockhart, simply dismissed him as "a charming old gentleman of nearly eighty" (Francis was, in fact, sixty-seven) who was "strangely ill-fitted"[8] for the tasks with which history and his government had entrusted him. From his uninformed perspective, Francis perceived the Bolsheviks only in the crudest terms, and always against a backdrop of starkly painted blacks and whites from which all shadings of gray had been erased. "One could wish for Francis's own sake," concluded a more generous and far more distinguished American ambassador to the Soviet Union, "that he had been withdrawn betimes to the quiet old age he deserved, and that the post had either been given to a younger man of superior education and foreign experience or left in the hands of a career chargé d'affaires."[9]

While Francis and his colleagues among the senior Allied diplomats urgently counseled their governments not to recognize the Bolsheviks, some of the most dynamic men of their staffs urged the opposite course. Colonel Raymond Robins of the American Red Cross, Captain Jacques Sadoul of the French military mission, and England's Lockhart all served as unofficial liaisons between their chiefs and the new Soviet Commissariat for Foreign Affairs, and in the course of their work each came to regard Trotskii with great respect and to share his view that the Allies must not drive Bolshevik Russia into the arms of Germany. Although Russia could no longer continue as a full partner in the war, they reasoned, keeping the Bolsheviks in the Allied camp could at least deny the Germans the natural resources and raw materials they so desperately needed to extract from Russia. Less likely—but still within the realm of possibility, they argued—German pressure against the Bolsheviks might convince them to allow the Allies to send men, weapons, and supplies into Russia to reopen Europe's eastern front against the Germans. When the Germans renewed their offensive against Russia in February 1918, that improbability suddenly seemed quite possible.

As Lenin and Trotskii continued to rail against the moral and political failings of the American, British, and French "imperialists," Robins, Sadoul, and Lockhart perceived a current of sense and substance beneath their raucous revolutionary rhetoric. Certain that Trotskii hoped to establish a workable relationship with the governments of Russia's former Allies, all three agreed that their governments ought not to stand aloof from the Bolsheviks. "We persist in denying that the world turns. That is to say, we continue to insist that the Bolshevik government does not exist," Sadoul exclaimed angrily at one point.[10] To his superiors' oft-expressed fears that Trotskii was in the pay of Germany, Robins, who never minced words and thought Trotskii "a four kind son of a bitch, but the greatest Jew since Christ," bluntly remarked: "If the German General Staff bought Trotskii, they bought a lemon."[11]

Although Lockhart, Sadoul, and Robins urged their governments to take Trotskii and Lenin seriously, none of them was well suited for arguing such a case effectively with statesmen and officials too long accustomed to the glacial workings of official diplomacy. A lawyer whose socialist ideals had brought him to the attention of France's Minister of Munitions Albert Thomas, Sadoul never managed to regularize his position within his country's Russian Embassy, where Noulens, perhaps even more than Francis, was sensitive about his prerogatives and prestige. As a socialist, Sadoul sympathized with many of the Bolsheviks' ideals and was sensitive to their views. Seventy years later, the account of his experiences that he set down in a series of letters to Thomas remains a key source about life in Russia's capitals during the first months of Bolshevik rule. Sadoul knew more about what was happening in the Bolsheviks' Commissariat for Foreign Affairs than anyone else in the French Embassy, but his contempt for the policies of his superiors, and his obvious disdain for working through regular diplomatic channels, made him at best a less than consistently effective spokesman for Russia's new leaders.

Similar in personality to Sadoul, though by no means an advocate of his politics, Robins had mined coal in Kentucky, panned gold in Alaska, and supported Theodore Roosevelt's Bull Moose Party before he had become one of the founders of the Progressive Party and chaired its 1916 convention in Chicago. Like Sadoul, he admired Trotskii and moved freely in high Bolshevik circles, thanks in large part to the efforts of an impetuous and unlikely sidekick by the name of Alexander Gumberg. A son of Russian Jews who had fled the persecutions of anti-Semitic tsarist Russia to seek their fortunes in the polyglot melting pot of New York City's Lower East Side, Gumberg had collaborated with Trotskii on New York's Russian Socialist newspaper *Novyi mir* (New World), had followed him back to Petrograd in 1917, and had been well received. With Gumberg at his side as "fixer" and translator, Robins therefore moved confidently through Russia's revolutionary maelstrom. Idealism, romanticism, and a robust confidence in his own abilities heightened Robins's abiding faith in human progress. He commanded loyalty, and he gave it without reservation. "I am not built on that principle," he told a group of senators who suggested that he disavow his association with that "little Jew" Gumberg in 1919. "That little Jew went through fire with me," he told his inquisitors angrily. "I am with him to the end of the road."[12]

Unlike Sadoul and Robins, Lockhart did not bear the burden of an ambassador who did not support his views, for Britain did not name a replacement for Buchanan for more than a decade. More cosmopolitan and far better educated, Lockhart was burdened neither by Sadoul's ideological baggage nor by Robins's romantic idealism. Yet he too came under the spell of Trotskii's powerful personality and described him as "a revolutionary with the temperament of an artist and with undoubted physical courage." But there was a cynical twist in Lockhart's measure of men that was conspicuously absent from the judgments of Sadoul and Robins. "He strikes me as a man who would willingly die fighting for Russia," he wrote of Trotskii, "provided there was a big enough audience to see him do it."[13]

With Robins, Sadoul, and Lockhart, and with the governments for whom they spoke unofficially, Trotskii met conciliation with conciliation and matched insult to insult. On occasion he answered their proposals with bitter invective, yet there were times when he seemed willing to go much further than they expected. Robins was flabbergasted in January 1918, when Trotskii responded to the Allies' complaints about raw materials being smuggled into Germany by suggesting that the Allies themselves take responsibility for policing Russia's western borders. "Send your officers, American officers, Allied officers, any officers you please," Trotskii reportedly told Robins at one interview. "I will give them full authority to enforce the embargo against goods into Germany all along our whole front."[14] In that case it was Robins's superiors who barred the way to cooperation. According to the account Robins gave to an inquisitive journalist a year or so later, "the Allied and American governments, rather than admit the existence of Trotskii, let the Germans do all the grabbing of Russian raw materials on the Russian frontier."[15] Yet the men who argued so passionately for the Allies to support the Bolsheviks remained as unbalanced in their views as their superiors. Robins, Lockhart, and Sadoul never understood the depths of the Bolsheviks' ideological hatred for the governments they represented, and they failed to perceive how completely that hatred limited the possibilities for meaningful alliance with the capitalist nations of the West.

Nothing expressed that growing rift more dramatically than the Allies' decision to relocate their embassies in the provincial town of Vologda when the Bolsheviks moved Russia's capital to Moscow. A sleepy provincial town of some forty thousand, Vologda had been founded in 1147, the year in which the first mention of Moscow appeared in Russia's ancient chronicles. Situated some 560 kilometers to the east of Petrograd, it was widely known for the fine lace produced by its women, but claimed no other distinction aside from a church that Ivan the Terrible had ordered built on the model of the Kremlin's famous Cathedral of the Assumption. Thus set far to the side of history's mainstream, Vologda had nothing to recommend it as a center for Allied diplomacy except that it stood at the point where the Moscow–Arkhangelsk railroad intersected the Trans-Siberian Railway. Should the Germans advance further into Russia, or should it prove necessary to flee with the Bolsheviks, Allied diplomats thus could escape from Vologda by sea in the north or by rail across Siberia to Vladivostok in the Far East. Should their governments intervene in Russia in force, Vologda could serve as a center from which to coordinate Allied advances from Siberia and North Russia against the Bolsheviks.[16] Proud that he had led the way to Vologda, and with a touch of that arrogant condescension that darkened so many of his dealings with the Russians, Ambassador Francis announced at a dinner given by Vologda's mayor soon after his arrival that the city had become "the diplomatic capital of Russia." Francis later noted with some satisfaction that "the Russians present seemed very pleased" that their town should receive that distinction.[17] Lenin, Trotskii, and the negotiators on every side of the table at Brest-Litovsk thought otherwise.

If the Allied ambassadors found Vologda's location appealing because it straddled two major escape routes and had the potential to serve as a center from which to coordinate intervention from Siberia and North Russia, they found its links with Moscow considerably less satisfactory. Reliable information sifted through very slowly from the Bolsheviks' new capital, but the most outlandish rumors made their way there with amazing speed. Unable to separate their hopes from the real situation they faced, the Vologda diplomats proved all too willing to believe the worst about Russia's new leaders. "Vologda," Lockhart remembered, "lived on the wildest anti-Bolshevik rumors." Isolated, uncertain, and widely suspicious, the chief Allied diplomats therefore found it impossible to gauge accurately the course of events in Moscow. The remarks Ambassador Francis delivered to the people of Vologda when the Americans celebrated July 4, 1918, spoke amply of the chasm that separated their self-delusion from reality. "My country and all of the Allies consider the Russian people still in the struggle," he told his listeners with patronizing self-importance. The Americans, he assured Vologda's citizens, did not wish "to dictate to the Russian people or to interfere in the internal affairs of Russia." The United

States and the Americans wanted only for "the Russian people to have the right to dispose of themselves."

That right, Francis's remarks made clear, did not extend to letting the Russians abandon the war that had destroyed their dynasty, ruined their economy, and claimed the lives of millions of their people. Certain that every patriotic Russian "who loves his country and looks with pride upon her greatness" would want to continue the war rather than "submit tamely to [Russia's] . . . dismemberment and humiliation," Francis urged his listeners to renew the struggle against Germany. Russians should take heart from America's promise that she would "never consent to Germany making Russia a German province," he explained. The U.S. government now insisted "that all branches of the Slav race should be completely freed from German and Austrian rule," he announced proudly. "What an inspiration," he exclaimed in conclusion, "this should be to the Russians!"[18]

The Vologda ambassadors' misunderstandings of Russian events had taken them far afield indeed. "It was as if these foreign ambassadors were trying to advise their governments on an English cabinet crisis from a village in the Hebrides," Lockhart later wrote.[19] General Romei, the Italian military attaché who had gone to Moscow with Lockhart rather than to Vologda with his country's ambassador, described the fiasco much more bluntly. "If we had put all the Allied representatives there in a caldron and stirred them up," he once remarked, "not one drop of common sense would have come out of the boiling."[20]

While Francis and the other Vologda ambassadors failed to take proper measure of the Bolsheviks and the political situation in Russia, those Allied representatives who had gone to Moscow grossly oversimplified the case for establishing relations with Russia's new rulers. Sadoul, Lockhart, and, especially, Robins accepted far too uncritically some of the statements made by Lenin and Trotskii during the confusing weeks that surrounded the ratification of the Brest-Litovsk Treaty by a special Congress of Soviets in mid-March. In particular, they took some of those remarks to mean that, like the Allies, the Bolsheviks held the Germans in particular contempt. They therefore failed to understand that the Bolsheviks despised all "imperialists" equally, and that they made no real distinction between the motives and principles that guided Allies, Germans, or Austrians.

True, there was a brief opportunity for a temporary alliance, for the Bolsheviks would join any "imperialists" in any action that might strengthen the Revolution's chances for survival. But in any such alliance, Trotskii and Lenin told Robins, "the internal and foreign policies of the Soviet government will continue to be directed in accord with the principles of international socialism and that the Soviet government retains its complete independence of all nonsocialist governments."[21] No one on the Allied side fully understood the significance that the Bolsheviks attached to that caveat. Nor did any understand that, when Lenin pronounced himself "in favor of taking potatoes and weapons from the bandits of Anglo-French Imperialism," he indeed regarded them as bandits and fully expected to deal with them as such at some point.[22]

At neither Vologda nor Moscow did Allied diplomats sense the absolute certainty with which Lenin anticipated Allied armed intervention in Russia. "The Russian Socialist Soviet Republic," he warned, "still remains a lone island in the stormy sea of imperialist robbery." So long as the Great War in the West continued to split the world's imperialists into two hostile camps, Russia might be spared their combined assaults. But Lenin urged his countrymen not to take false comfort from the Allies' continued battles with Austria and Germany, for he was certain that the conflicts that presently shielded Russia must inevitably shift to an alliance against her. "This position can change in a few days," he warned. "The American bourgeoisie, now at loggerheads with Japan, can tomorrow come to terms with her because the Japanese bourgeoisie are just as likely tomorrow to come to terms with the German bourgeoisie. Their basic interests are the same."[23] The main thrust of the Bolsheviks' diplomacy with the Allies, Lenin insisted, must be to buy time. "In considering the tasks of the foreign policy of Soviet power at the present moment," he wrote, "the greatest caution, discretion, and restraint must be observed." Until Russia could defend herself against foreign attack, the Bolsheviks must "manoeuver, withdraw, bide our time, and continue our preparations with all our might."[24]

Judged by the standards employed by their probable foreign adversaries, the Bolsheviks at the time of the Brest-Litovsk peace treaty commanded only one battleworthy force: the Latvian Rifle Division that guarded the Kremlin and suppressed the Left SR uprising at the beginning of July. Motley collections of Red Guards might win scattered battles against disorganized domestic foes, but they could not defend Russia's Bolshevik government against the foreign "imperialist" attack that Lenin thought inevitable. Nor could the early Red Army formations with their heavy leavening of common criminals bent upon plunder be expected to do any better. Ready to flee at the approach of any hostile force, such Red Army units distinguished themselves by their brutality to civilians and their cowardice in battle. "The general opinion of all commanders," one telegram from the Ukrainian front read, "is that it would be better to send units of better quality even if they were only one-tenth as large."[25]

When Trotskii became commissar for war and president of the Supreme War Council in the middle of March, Soviet Russia had no real army in the field, no officer and noncommissioned officer corps to train one, and no means for mustering recruits. Brest-Litovsk had cost thousands of factories, hundreds of thousands of square miles of Russia's richest and most densely populated lands, and vast stores of natural wealth. Her industry and transport, the two sinews of modern warfare, lay in such shambles that, by October 1918, all the lands under Bolshevik control contained no more than twenty-one thousand kilometers of railroads.[26] These were hard facts, and "facts," as Lenin once said, "are stubborn things."[27] But the most difficult obstacle that Trotskii faced during the spring of 1918 was one for which the Bolsheviks themselves—and perhaps he most of all—had to shoulder the blame. From the moment revolution had broken out, the Bolsheviks had focused much of their propaganda effort upon convincing Russia's common soldiers to abandon the Great War. In his speeches to the assembled multitudes at Petrograd's vast Cirque Moderne, at Party meetings, at the Soviet of Workers' and Soldiers' Deputies, and at Smolnyi, Trotskii had hammered home his message with all his dazzling oratorical skill. Together with the war-weariness that consumed Russia's fighting men, Bolshevik propaganda had destroyed the army's will to fight well before fall had begun to turn into winter. If Soviet Russia hoped to defend herself in 1918, Trotskii needed to repair the damage wrought by the antiwar propaganda with which the Bolsheviks had so thoroughly poisoned the army's organism the year before.

To do so, he had to attack the two most fundamental documents that Russia's soldiers had brought forth from the revolutionary crucible of 1917: Order No. 1, which had placed military discipline and command decisions in the hands of elected committees of soldiers' representatives, and Order No. 8, the Declaration of Soldiers' Rights that had bestowed upon Russia's soldiers full personal and political rights, including even the right to engage in antiwar activity.[28] Discipline had to be restored and decision making removed from the hands of those ubiquitous, chaotic soldiers' committees that debated orders to attack at length every time they arrived at front-line positions. Without the full support of the Party, such an undertaking would prove fatal; even with it, Trotskii's task promised to be very difficult.

Proclaiming that "the question about forming an army is at this moment a matter of life and death,"[29] Trotskii took up his duties with the blunt announcement that only "work, discipline, and order will save the Soviet Republic."[30] The danger was great, the time left to act very short. "The Soviet Republic must have an army that can fight battles and win," he insisted. Therefore, the Revolution must pass from its first, destructive, phase to a second one in which workers, peasants, and soldiers all would work toward constructive ends. This would require stern discipline and stubborn dedication. Trotskii therefore demanded that, "in these threatening days, every honest citizen must be both a worker and a soldier."[31] Every one of Soviet Russia's defenders must swear, "before the toiling classes of Russia and the entire world," that, as a "soldier of the Army of Workers and Peasants," he or she would "conscientiously study military science" and spare "neither strength nor life in the struggle for the Russian Soviet Republic, for the cause of socialism, and for the brotherhood of peoples."[32]

With his brilliance at organization and his genius for leading men, Trotskii understood that Russia's embryonic Red Army could not develop without a large corps of officers trained in the technology of modern warfare. Because few Bolsheviks had the training or experience to lead armies in battle, Soviet Russia therefore must turn to the officers who once had served the Tsar. The Red Army officer corps, Trotskii insisted, had no choice but to take in men who once had stood upon those very pinnacles of power that the Bolsheviks had sworn to destroy. "Just as our factories need engineers, and just as our farms required trained agronomists," he explained, "so military specialists are vital for matters of defense."[33] "It is essential for us to have a real military force, one that is properly organized according to scientific military principles," he announced elsewhere. "The active and systematic participation of military specialists in all aspects of this task therefore is a matter of vital importance."[34]

Many Bolsheviks heard Trotskii's words with outrage, and even Lenin at first refrained from fully approving his plan. If the Red Army must enlist tsarist officers, some of Trotskii's comrades argued, then they must simply be used—and used up—"like lemons."[35] Former tsarist officers therefore had every reason to fear the consequences of service in Trotskii's new army. Yet, even without Lenin's open support, Trotskii boldly gave them firm assurances. To those who feared being "squeezed and thrown away like a lemon,"[36] Trotskii replied: "Those former [tsarist] generals who work conscientiously under the present difficult and unfavorable circumstances, will, despite their conservative outlook, deserve incomparably more respect from the working class than those pseudo-socialists who pursue intrigue in various out-of-the-way corners."[37]

By demanding that Russia's victorious revolutionaries make a place for the men who once had defended the old order, Trotskii extended the scope of his revolutionary vision beyond that of most men. Perhaps no other Bolshevik understood as well as he that revenge directed for too long against the elites of the old order would yield dangerous returns the young Soviet state could not afford. To push Russia into the abyss of barbarism would only make her climb back up the ladder of civilization more arduous, and Trotskii therefore hoped to halt the revolutionary excesses before they inflicted greater damage.[38] Still, he remained remarkably sensitive to the dilemmas that the sudden revolutionary transformation of 1917 had posed for ordinary Russians. "The colossal shock of the revolution awakened the human personality in the most downtrodden, persecuted, illiterate peasant," he explained to a group of cadets at the ceremonies opening Moscow's new Military Academy that fall. Although initially expressed in rude, violent, and destructive ways, this "awakened personality" held the key to the future and therefore must be cherished. Now it only needed to be fitted into the framework of the broader socialist community to become the force for progress and accomplishment that Russia so desperately needed.[39] Among other things, Trotskii hoped that such "awakened personalities" could rise to positions of command in the Red Army and that the army's special schools for training "Red commanders" would produce a new generation of proletarian officers and NCOs to lead it.[40]

"Red commander" schools could not provide even a tenth of the officers that the Soviet government required during Russia's

Civil War. In addition to noncommissioned officers and expert technicians, the Red Army needed more than fifty thousand officers before the end of 1918, and, in two more years, those requirements rose nearly tenfold. Seven out of every ten who filled those positions had served in the army of Nicholas II,[41] and the Bolsheviks had very legitimate fears that they would betray their commands to the Whites. Certain that only the lives of families and friends could provide security against betrayal, Trotskii took hostages with cold determination and methodical cruelty. He did not begin to do so until the end of September, when the events of that summer and early fall had shown that neither concentration camps nor executions could ensure the loyalty of men forced to serve a regime they held in contempt. "Let the deserters know that they are betraying their own families: their fathers, mothers, sisters, brothers, wives, and children," Trotskii announced as former tsarist officers continued to slip away to the Whites. "I am ordering the staffs of all armies of the Republic . . . to communicate by telegraph . . . a list of all officers who have gone over to the enemy camp, together with all necessary information about their families." He concluded his brief decree with orders that "the necessary measures [be taken] for the detention of the families of all deserters and traitors."[42]

So that such men might be discovered before they fled to the enemy, Trotskii placed loyal Bolshevik commissars at the side of every former tsarist officer to report upon his actions. Flanked on the left and right by commissars with revolvers drawn, Trotskii announced, such officers would serve as he required them to.[43] Certain that the Bolsheviks would avenge themselves upon their families and friends for any failure or betrayal on their part, such officers began to serve Russia's new rulers better than they had intended. "If we had not compelled them to serve us, "Lenin later confessed. "we would never have been able to build an army."[44] His enemies agreed. "The Soviet authorities," General Denikin wrote with reluctant admiration, "can take pride in the skill with which they enslaved the will and thought of the Russian general officer corps, and the officer corps more generally, by making them unwilling, but obedient, instruments of its growing strength."[45]

To supply the Red Army with weapons and ammunition proved even more difficult than to provide it with officers. One of the ironies of Russia's wartime failure had been that her soldiers' will to fight had collapsed—destroyed partially by the inhumanity of the trenches, where soldiers had waited for their comrades to be killed so they could take up their weapons—just as Russia's supplies of arms and ammunition began to equal those of her adversaries. Generous shipments of weapons by Russia's allies had played an important part in establishing their equality, but it also reflected the soaring production of Russia's own industries, which had begun to meet the demands of wartime production for the first time toward the end of 1916. Guns, bullets, and shells had not been in short supply during Kerenskii's offensive in the summer of 1917. In some battles, Russian artillery had outnumbered the enemy's heavy guns by a margin of more than five to one.[46] The Russian soldiers who had marched away from the war that fall therefore had been well armed indeed. When they marched back to their villages in February and March 1918, Russia's demobilized armies left behind two and a half million rifles, well over a billion bullets, nearly twelve thousand cannon, and more than twenty-eight million shells.[47]

Unused to the complexities of military supply, desperately short of freight cars and locomotives, and still clinging to the naive belief that their infant socialist state would not require a regular standing army because the Revolution was about to spread into the countries of their enemies, the Bolsheviks at first had not tried to save the weapons that Russia's war-weary soldiers had left behind. German soldiers advancing into the Ukraine seized great quantities of Russian guns and ammunition, and many more fell into the hands of the Whites. Trotskii's effort to establish orderly collection points and inventories came too late. By the end of 1918, the Bolsheviks had managed to save only a tenth of the cannons and rifles, a quarter of the bullets, and less than a fifth of the artillery shells that Russia's collapsing armies had abandoned nine months earlier. Able to salvage less than a twentieth of the weapons needed to arm their new Red Army from the wartime arsenals of Russia's old regime, the Bolsheviks had to manufacture the balance just when their nation's industrial production fell to a small fraction of its former output, and when large-scale efforts to move weapons factories from Petrograd to less exposed cities in the interior made arms production especially difficult.[48]

Attacks by Russia's former allies heightened the urgency of Trotskii's effort to rebuild Russia's shattered armies. At first, Allied intervention in Russia had been limited to a company of Royal Marines that the British had sent ashore at Murmansk at the beginning of March and a handful of Japanese and British troops that had disembarked from warships in Vladivostok harbor a month later. The arrival of the first British troops therefore had coincided with the last stages of the Brest-Litovsk peace negotiations, and the Bolsheviks had reacted quite moderately to the Royal Marines' landing in North Russia. Still uncertain about the Germans' intentions, Trotskii had ordered the Murmansk Soviet to "accept any and all assistance from the Allied missions and use every means to obstruct the advance of the [German] plunderers,"[49] and the Royal Marines had fought on the side of the Bolsheviks in several small engagements against the German-supported forces that anti-Bolshevik Finns sent against them.[50] Beginning in April, partly as a consequence of Britain's participation in the Vladivostok landings, and partly because of subtle changes in the Bolsheviks' relations with Germany, tension had mounted on both sides. As the Bolsheviks drew back from any further common action with the British, the British prepared to intervene at Murmansk on a much larger scale.[51]

Once described by a fellow officer as "one of the most confirmed optimists it has ever been my fortune to meet," and a man who had "no great liking for a study of detail and the trammels of red-tape,"[52] England's Major-General F.C. Poole stubbornly pushed his government toward intervention in North Russia that spring. Hopeful that intervention could reopen Europe's eastern front and secure valuable railway and timber concessions for the British, Poole had, in early April, won the support of Lord Robert Cecil, Britain's undersecretary of state for foreign affairs, for a plan to occupy Murmansk. By the middle of the month, Cecil had convinced the cabinet to order the Admiralty to make the necessary preparations.[53] Now committed to intervention, a course which their American allies still firmly opposed in principle, the British sought an invitation from Lenin's government, hoping, even into late April, that Lockhart could win Trotskii's support by arguing that Allied troops could help to forestall further German incursion into Russian territory.[54]

Although Trotskii and Lenin had toyed with the idea of accepting aid from the Allies in order to lessen German pressure against their western frontier and the Ukraine in February and March, they concluded that a modest rapprochement with Germany might offer more attractive prospects in May.[55] For that reason, in a major "Report on Foreign Policy" to a joint session of the All-Russian Central Executive Committee and the Moscow Soviet, Lenin bluntly condemned the landings at Murmansk. "The British landed their military forces at Murmansk, and we were unable to prevent this by armed force," he said in reference to additional detachments of Royal Marines that had been put ashore at the beginning of the month to engage a force of several hundred Finnish Whites. "Consequently, we are presented with demands almost in the nature of an ultimatum: If you cannot protect your neutrality, we shall wage war on your territory."[56] The Bolsheviks now wanted no Allied forces camped within their borders. While such forces remained in Russia, Commissar for Foreign Affairs Chicherin insisted a week later, the Soviet government would "not join them as allies, and [would] . . . protest against their actions on [Russian] territory."[57]

The Bolsheviks were not the only ones whose attitudes toward Allied intervention in North Russia underwent critical changes during the late spring of 1918. Firm in his belief that the United States ought not to interfere in Russia's internal affairs, America's President Woodrow Wilson had opposed intervention of any sort. Urged on by his Secretary of State Robert Lansing and his British allies, Wilson began to shift that position, and by the beginning of June, Lansing could report to Britain's ambassador that the United States was "entirely willing to send troops to Murmansk."[58] Wilson's shift did not mean that he or his government had abandoned caution. "Every foreign invasion that has gone deep into Russia has been swallowed up," America's vice-consul at Arkhangelsk wisely warned his superiors in one of the rare statements of common sense to come from an American diplomat in Russia at the time. "[If we intervene] we shall have sold our birthright in Russia for a mess of pottage."[59] The British thought differently. While President Wilson, his secretary of war, his military representative to the Allied Supreme War Council at Versailles, and the Army's chief of staff now viewed intervention in terms of limited operations to protect the large stores of Allied weapons and war supplies that had been stockpiled at Murmansk before the Brest-Litovsk peace, General Poole and his allies had begun to think in terms of offensive military action to establish a firm foothold in North Russia.[60]

Although Poole became the key figure in launching the Allied landings in North Russia, his military experience had failed to prepare him for the complex diplomatic role that task required. His well-meant optimism in no way matched the gravity of the situation he faced, and his jovial condescension proved ill suited for dealing with Russians whose education, military experience, and sophistication exceeded his own. "He treated [the two chief representatives of the anti-Bolshevik forces in the North] . . . rather as a house-master might treat a couple of his prefects, giving them to understand that they must realize their responsibilities . . . yet determined none the less that no action taken by them should run contrary to his own preconcerted plans," General Maynard remembered. Poole thought the special diplomatic envoy the Bolsheviks sent from Moscow to be "quite a good old bird,"[61] and during the weeks after his arrival in North Russia on May 24, he put together an outrageously distorted estimate of the forces he faced. The Bolsheviks, he concluded, could offer no serious resistance. At the same time, he estimated that at least fifteen thousand Finnish Whites (there were, in fact, no more than a few hundred) already had begun to advance against his positions.[62]

Such wildly inflated estimates reflected Poole's gross inability to take accurate stock of the Allies' position. Yet his judgment of the situation was not so blatantly one-sided as his misreading of the enemy forces arrayed against him might lead one to think. Poole clearly perceived that the presence of troops wearing the uniforms of governments who refused to recognize them as Russia's rulers must offend the Bolsheviks, and he urged his superiors to grant the Bolsheviks the diplomatic recognition that the Allies had withheld since October. "We shall be obliged to recognize them as the *de facto* government, which policy I have always advocated," Poole wrote in a report to Britain's Director of Military Intelligence.[63] Otherwise, the Bolsheviks must consider any Allied efforts to defend the Murmansk Region against the Finnish Whites and their German allies a hostile act.

Composed of Royal Marines, U.S. sailors, Serbian infantry, and a handful of French artillerymen, Poole's force numbered less than two thousand, but it was supported by Allied warships and posed a particularly serious dilemma for Aleksei Mikhailovich Iurev, chairman of the Murmansk Regional Soviet, who had to answer to his superiors in Moscow for the manner in which he dealt with it. Once described as "a colorful figure, tall, with dangling limbs, a long horse-like face, and constantly smoking a large underslung South African pipe,"[64] Iurev had made his way as an oiler and ship's fireman since the age of fourteen and had been practicing that trade when he arrived in Murmansk in November 1917. Instinctively dedicated to a primitive sort of political anarchism, he neither understood the "scientific" Marxism of the Bolsheviks nor shared the views of those who held him responsible for dealing with the Allies' landings. "The Allies will not leave Murmansk," he reported to the Sovnarkom after several meetings with Poole. "The advantage of superior forces is, indisputably, on their side."

Iurev did not dispute the Allies' "imperialist" purposes, but unlike his superiors, he thought that their presence could be used to practical advantage. The Allies, he explained in a telegram to Moscow, could be counted upon to "defend the region against the Germans and the Finns, give all aid possible to the local population and to any who fight against the Germans, [and] support the authority of the Regional Soviet." Sympathetic to the Bolsheviks, but not prepared to recognize them as the absolute masters of North Russia, Iurev and his comrades at Murmansk therefore recommended that Lenin's government attempt to reap whatever advantages could be gotten from the Allies' presence. No other course seemed reasonable or, for that matter, possible. "It is impossible," he concluded bluntly, "to force the Allies to leave."[65]

In Moscow, Lenin, Trotskii, and Commissar for Foreign Affairs Chicherin insisted that it must be otherwise. "The English landing must be considered a hostile act," Lenin and Trotskii telegraphed to Iurev in response to the landing of a second force under Britain's General Maynard at the end of June. "Any assistance, direct or indirect, to the invading hirelings must be regarded as treason." With a grand flourish, Lenin and Trotskii ordered Iurev and the Murmansk Regional Soviet to administer "a decisive rebuff" to the "hirelings" of the British, French, and American capitalists, but they spoke only vaguely about how that could be done.[66] Warning that "we will all go to hell" if they failed to come to terms with Poole's and Maynard's forces, Iurev fired off a series of angry telegrams to Lenin and Trotskii. "It is impossible to . . . retrieve one's losses with phrases,"[67] he announced stubbornly. "I ask [you] to give precise instructions on what it is necessary to do. Playing with phrases cannot help."[68] Outraged by Iurev's bold insubordination, Lenin and Trotskii declared him "an enemy of the people" on July 1. That night, Chicherin made one final effort to bring the Murmansk Regional Soviet chairman to heel with vague assurances that "the Soviet army will do its duty to the very end," and that "we shall fight with all our power against any imperialist invasion." Iurev remained unmoved and insisted that the Bolsheviks must support their grand rhetoric with shipments of food, arms, and men if they expected him to resist the Allied landings.

> "You constantly utter beautiful phrases but not once have you told how to go about realizing them," he told Chicherin bitterly. "The Germans are strangling us and you go on hoping that they will become magnanimous. If you know a way out of our condition please tell it to us and the toiling people will follow you."
>
> "Your duty," Chicherin replied," is to protest against the invasion, make no agreements with the imperialist plunderers, . . . and to defend Soviet Russia."
>
> "Can you supply the region with the food which we are now lacking and send us a force sufficient to carry out your instructions?" Iurev asked stubbornly. "If not, there is no need of lecturing us."[69]
>
> "Tell the admirals who put you up to this that, in the event of an armed intervention into the territory of revolutionary Russia, they will encounter a popular uprising," Chicherin replied in an insulting insinuation that Iurev no longer remained his own master.
>
> "If you persist in thinking of me in this way," Iurev retorted, "then I can say that I have the impression that Count Mirbach is standing behind *your* back and suggesting these thoughts to you."[70]

Clearly the break could not be repaired. Three days later, the Bolsheviks cut the telegraph lines and blew up the key railroad bridges that connected Murmansk and North Russia with Petrograd and Moscow.[71] In reply, Iurev and the Murmansk Regional Soviet concluded an agreement for "the defense of the Murmansk Region against the powers of the German coalition" with the British, American, and French military representatives on July 6.

As they had done on previous occasions, the Allies hurried to deny any territorial ambitions in North Russia. "The sole reason for concluding this Agreement," they stated, "is to save the Murmansk Region in its integrity for the great undivided Russia."[72] Some among the Allies did not share their governments' high sense of moral purpose, and Poole viewed the break between the Russians at Murmansk and Moscow in decidedly practical terms. "The break of Iurev and his comrades with Moscow," he wrote to the War

Office, "has put the rope around their own necks and if they show signs of faltering I shall be there to stiffen them."[73] A week later, he added: "Now that they have broken with Moscow they realize their dependence on us for everything so they will become more and more pliable."[74]

Combined with the Allied Supreme War Council's decision to send several more battalions to Murmansk and Arkhangelsk,[75] the agreement signed with the Murmansk Regional Soviet on July 6 opened the way for full-scale Allied intervention in North Russia. It would have been difficult enough to fight a limited defensive campaign, but General Poole's plan to occupy Arkhangelsk with five thousand Allied troops and to launch a major offensive into the interior once he had augmented that force with a hundred thousand anti-Bolshevik Russians approached the realm of pure fantasy. To this day it remains anyone's guess how Poole expected to recruit that number of anti-Bolsheviks from a region whose population numbered approximately a half million, nor is it clear how he planned to feed a population that had been cut off from its traditional sources of food supplies in Russia's hinterland,[76] but that was the plan that the Allied Supreme War Council at Versailles approved at the urging of England's first lord of the admiralty.[77] By mid-July, the Allies had committed themselves to wage a full-fledged offensive campaign in some of the roughest terrain and most inhospitable climate to be found anywhere in the Western world.

The beginnings of the Allies' intervention in Arkhangelsk coincided with the flight of their ambassadors from Vologda, where, during the late spring and early summer, the dead calm of Russian provincial life had surrounded them. The placidity of the provinces, the glacial slowness of the provinces, and the boredom of the provinces all had been lamented by Russia's greatest writers from Pushkin to Chekhov, and none had ever disputed the truth of their descriptions. As a rule, thoughtful and ambitious Russians fled the provinces to make their way in their nation's capital cities, yet it was precisely those qualities of provincial life that the Russians sought to escape that had insulated the Allied ambassadors at Vologda from the Revolution's growing turmoil. Outrageous rumors had come in profusion to Vologda, and those had disturbed its tranquility from time to time. But judging from Francis's accounts of endless card games played with his fellow diplomats and his report of their efforts to lay out a crude golf course, the life of Vologda's diplomats had been none too distressing during the months when the Bolsheviks had made peace with the Germans and the Allied forces had prepared the first stages of their intervention.[78]

Upon this unsuspecting, peaceful scene of senior Allied diplomats playing golf under the walls of the local monastery, reports of the Left SRs' uprising, subsequent outbreaks in Iaroslavl, Murom, and Rybinsk, news of the assassination of Count Mirbach, and Poole's announcement that he intended to occupy Arkhangelsk within the next two or three weeks all burst with fearsome suddenness during the second week of July. Fearful that they might be taken hostages by the Bolsheviks, Allied diplomats decided to move to Arkhangelsk. "I had held a special train on the Vologda tracks for five months," Francis later explained.[79] On July 23 he decided to use it, only to have Chicherin forbid its departure. When Chicherin released the ambassadors' train after nearly two days of negotiations, Francis led the Vologda diplomatic corps northward shortly before dawn on July 25. They arrived in Arkhangelsk the next day and left by steamer for the British-held port of Kandalaksha two days later. Within a week, Poole's forces entered Arkhangelsk to establish an anti-Bolshevik government sworn to restore all "liberties and institutions of true popular government" to Russia,[80] under the presidency of Nikolai Chaikovskii, a distinguished veteran of Russia's revolutionary movement and a moderate socialist. Like the Provisional Government of Autonomous Siberia in Omsk and the forces of Komuch in Samara and Ufa, Chaikovskii's Supreme Administration of the North claimed to derive its authority from the fallen Constituent Assembly.[81]

In a jagged arc that stretched some fifteen hundred miles southeastward from Murmansk above the Arctic Circle, to Ufa in western Siberia, and then to Samara, Simbirsk, and Kazan on the Volga, men united against the Bolsheviks by the dream of a freely elected Russian Constituent Assembly had spread their forces across Russia's North and East by mid-August 1918. They had done so with the direct support of those Allies who had vowed repeatedly that "the domestic policy of Russia is a matter for Russia alone," and that, "whatever Government the Russians desire to have, the Russians ought to have, and it is not for us to interfere in any way in that matter."[82] Now, those same statesmen took a different view. "To re-establish order in Russia will be a herculean task," England's Lord Robert Cecil told the War Cabinet in September. "No half-baked constitutionalism could possibly succeed in it. The only possible way out seems to be a provisional military Government."[83] Not without reason did Lenin speak with bitterness against those "imperialists" whose "systematic policy," he claimed, was designed "to throttle Soviet Russia so as to again drag Russia into the ring of imperialist wars."[84]

The intervention Lenin feared was not to be confined to North Russia, and Trotskii's fledgling Red Army soon had to face foreign troops in Siberia as well. On July 6, America's President Wilson suddenly announced at a special meeting attended by his closest advisers that the United States would send arms, ammunition, supplies, and seven thousand troops to Vladivostok in support of the Czechoslovak Legion, whose valiant soldiers had continued to fight their way back and forth along the Trans-Siberian Railway. At the same time, Wilson insisted, America had no intention "to interfere in the internal affairs of Russia" and would "guarantee" that her troops would "not impair the political or territorial sovereignty of Russia."[85] "Military action," he wrote in a famous *aide-mémoire* that went out over Secretary of State Lansing's signature on July 17, would be "admissible in Russia . . . only to help the Czecho-Slovaks consolidate their forces and get into successful co-operation with their Slavic kinsmen and to steady any efforts at self-government or self-defense in which the Russians themselves may be willing to accept assistance." This, he stated firmly, "is in the interest of what the Russian people themselves desire."[86]

President Wilson's change of heart opened the way for massive Allied intervention in Siberia. Vladivostok, Imperial Russia's "Mistress of the East," upon whose main street stood a monument bearing words: "Where once the Russian flag has been raised, it must never be lowered,"[87] became the gateway through which a new wave of Allied men and weapons flowed into Russia. Beginning on August 3, with eight hundred men of Britain's Middlesex Regiment, the city played host to the French (a contingent of five hundred colonial troops, which arrived on August 9), the Japanese Twelfth Division (August 11), and the Americans (August 16), followed by men wearing the uniforms of Poland, Czechoslovakia, China, Serbia, Canada, and Italy. Some of these comprised only token forces; others counted as formidable armies. By the middle of September, the U.S. forces under the command of Major-General William S. Graves numbered more than eight thousand men. Two weeks later, the number of Japanese fighting men in Siberia's Maritime Provinces reached seventy-three thousand.[88] Together with some sixty thousand soldiers of the Czechoslovak Legion[89] and various White units, the anti-Bolshevik forces in Siberia in the fall of 1918 outnumbered those in any other area of Russia several times over.

As in North Russia, the Allies proved more willing to dispatch troops to Siberia than to define the scope and duration of their involvement. Initially, the French and British concentrated upon organizing and arming Czech and Russian forces to fight against the Bolsheviks in an effort to reopen Europe's eastern front against Central Powers. The large military missions they sent to Siberia for that purpose quickly became embroiled in the quagmire of Russian revolutionary politics, and the fact that no firmly established anti-Bolshevik government comparable to Chaikovskii's Supreme Administration of the North or Denikin's government in the South had appeared in eastern Siberia by the fall of 1918 further complicated their efforts. The French and British at first had looked to the anti-Bolshevik forces further west—to the Czechoslovak Legion, to the armies of the Komuch government in Samara, and to the forces of the Provisional Government of Autonomous Siberia in Omsk—to support their plans, and General Poole had planned to advance southeastward from Arkhangelsk to link up with the Czechs. That had been impractical once the Czechs made it clear that they had no intention of seeking a northwest passage out of Siberia.[90] As Poole's countrymen entered Siberia from the Far East, they therefore looked to other anti-Bolsheviks for support. "Unite with us in defense of your liberties!" they urged. "Our one desire is to see Russia strong and free and then to retire and watch the Russian people work out its destinies in accordance with the freely expressed wishes of the people."[91]

Because their limited armed forces in Siberia obliged the French and British to rely upon intrigue to strengthen their position, their meddling quickly enflamed an already volatile situation. With their sympathies ranging from monarchist to socialist, the Komuch government, the Provisional Government of Autonomous Siberia, and the Czechoslovak Legion all remained suspicious of each other's political programs, and Siberia soon was awash with rumors and intrigue. "There are rumors about revolutions in the purely Mexican style," a prominent White commander wrote in his diary in mid-October, as General Knox, head of Britain's military mission in Siberia, came and went with messages from the warring factions. "It's an absolute farce," he continued. That fall, Siberia seemed like "Mexico in the midst of snow and frost."[92] As ready to intrigue among themselves as they were to fight Bolsheviks or Germans, these groups of Whites quickly fell victim to the Allies' meddling. Before winter came in 1918, the Czechs ceased to take any active part in the Civil War, while the Omsk Directorate superseded the Komuch government and the Provisional Government of Autonomous Siberia, only to be replaced a few weeks later by the government of the military strongman Admiral Aleksandr Kolchak. With relief, as 1918 drew to a close, the chief statesmen of those nations whose soldiers had shed so much blood to make the world safe for democracy welcomed Kolchak's dictatorship in Siberia. After a brief reminder to his colleagues in Britain's cabinet that "a permanent military despotism in Russia would be a very serious menace to the peace of the world," Britain's Under-Secretary of State for Foreign Affairs Lord Robert Cecil nonetheless argued that, in Siberia, Britain must "aim at securing military chiefs whom we can trust" and make her support "indispensable" to them in order to guarantee their loyalty.[93]

By contrast with the British and French, the Japanese and the Americans had come to Siberia to broaden their foothold in the Far East. But the presence of nearly ten thousand Americans, and seven times as many Japanese, produced tensions fully as volatile in Siberia's Far East as the meddling of Britain and France had produced in the regions further to the west. In May, Lenin had predicted that Japan and America must inevitably come to a "desperate clash" in the Pacific lands of the Far East,[94] and as their armies vied for control of Siberia's far-flung railways in the sparsely settled regions east of Lake Baikal, they came perilously close to making that prediction come true. On balance, the specter of strengthened Japanese influence in Siberia concerned some of America's leading statesmen considerably more than the prospect of Bolshevik control in Russia. "I do not know that I rightly understand Bolshevikism [sic]," Secretary of War Newton Baker wrote that November. "So much of it as I do understand I don't like, but I have a feeling that, if the Russians do like it, they are entitled to have it." On the other hand, Baker deeply feared the Japanese. "The difficulty of securing Japanese withdrawal is growing every hour," he warned General Graves. "I dread to think how we should all feel if we are rudely awakened some day to a realization that Japan has gone in under our wing and so completely mastered the country that she cannot be either induced out or forced out."[95]

No American faced the Japanese more directly in those months than Major-General William S. Graves, the American commander who found himself "pitch-forked into the melee at Vladivostok," to quote his own picturesque description, without any precise "information as to the military, political, social, economic, or financial situation in Russia."[96] Until July 1918, Graves had known nothing about Siberia, Russia, or the Japanese. After spending most of the First World War at the War Department as secretary of the General Staff, he had finally gotten a long hoped-for field command—the Eighth Division, which was waiting to be shipped to France from its base at Camp Fremont, California—in mid-July, only to receive two weeks later secret orders to take part of the division, along with the Twenty-seventh and Thirty-first Infantry Regiments from the Philippines to Vladivostok. Far less prepared for the delicately balanced diplomatic situation that awaited him than his Japanese counterparts, and with no more precise instructions than Wilson's ambiguously worded and somewhat contradictory *aide-mémoire* that Secretary of State Lansing had issued on July 17, Graves fought an unevenly matched battle against Japanese influence in Siberia. That America's interests did not suffer more than they did was a tribute to his tenacity, personal integrity, and raw courage.

Strengthened by Allied support, the Czechoslovak Legion, the armies of the Komuch government, and the forces of the Provisional Government of Autonomous Siberia drove the Bolsheviks in disordered retreat all along Russia's frontiers. As Bolshevik power crumbled in Ekaterinburg, Ufa, Samara, Simbirsk, and Kazan, Lenin's claim that "our Republic of Soviets is *invincible*," seemed improbable, if not absurdly fanciful.[97] By late August 1918, when Soviet Russia had shrunk to the size of the medieval Muscovite state over which Ivan the Terrible had begun to rule in 1547, even Trotskii began to have doubts about the future. "At times, one had the feeling that everything was slipping away and falling to pieces," he recalled. "One wondered if a country so exhausted, so ravaged, and so desperate, had enough life left in it to support a new regime and preserve its independence." For a moment, it seemed that the Bolsheviks' enemies would coordinate a gigantic assault against them. "More and more, the front of the Civil War was taking the shape of a noose that seemed to be closing tighter and tighter around Moscow," Trotskii wrote. "The soil itself seemed to be infected with panic," he concluded. "Everything was crumbling. There was nothing to hold on to. The situation seemed hopeless."[98]

Trotskii could spur men in times of crisis to find deep within themselves those hidden well-springs of strength and determination that few men realize they possess. To shore up the Bolsheviks' crumbling defenses along the Volga, he readied a special train that arrived at the front just as the fleeing soldiers of the Red Army reached Sviiazhsk, some fifteen miles to the west of Kazan. Like so many of the tens of thousands of nondescript small towns that dot Russia's landscape, Sviiazhsk claimed no distinction whatsoever, and its one brief moment in history had come when Ivan the Terrible had presided over its founding during the course of his long siege against Kazan in the early 1550s. Yet it was to be at Sviiazhsk that the course of Russia's Civil War shifted decisively. During August 1918, Sviiazhsk became the Valmy of the Russian Revolution, the point where the Bolsheviks, like the armies of revolutionary France in 1792, first halted the advance of armies that marched to restore the old order, which had crumbled so readily at the first onslaught of revolution.

The train Trotskii took to Sviiazhsk included a printing press, a telegraph apparatus, a radio station capable of receiving messages from Moscow and Western Europe, its own electrical generating system, a library, a mobile Russian bathhouse, and a garage that held several automobiles and a large reserve of gasoline.[99] With artful sensitivity, Trotoskii produced boots for the barefooted, tobacco, medicines, watches, food, even field glasses and machine guns, to raise the morale of Red Army fighting men at critical points along the front. "Tens, even hundreds, of times," he later wrote, "[the train's resources] served as that one shovelful of coal needed at a particular moment to keep the fire from dying out."[100] By direct wire from his train, he ordered weapons, ammunition, and supplies from Moscow and then arranged for their delivery under some of the worst conditions that ever confronted a military commander.

Perhaps no account better captured the psychological brilliance of Trotskii's accomplishment at Sviiazhsk than that left by Larissa Reisner, the beautiful twenty-two-year-old wife of the dedicated commander of the Bolsheviks' Volga River flotilla who headed its intelligence section in 1918.[101] Trotskii once described Reisner, who died of typhus before she reached thirty, as "an Olympian goddess who combined a subtle, ironical wit with the courage of a warrior,"[102] and she spoke of him as "an organizing genius." During the terrible days when the infant Red Army faced defeat at

Sviiazhsk in August 1918, Larissa Reisner wrote, Trotskii "beat back the current to fight against the weariness of four years of war, and against the stormy waters of the revolution itself, which, over the whole country, was sweeping aside the old hated discipline like so much flotsam. . . . At Trotskii's side," she remembered, "we could die in battle with the last cartridge gone, oblivious to our wounds, for Trotskii incarnated the holy demagoguery of battle. . . . This," she concluded, "is what we used to whisper among ourselves on those nights of a quick-freezing autumn, lying jumbled in our heaps over the station floor [at Sviiazhsk]."[103] Reisner's comrades were few, for armies at Kazan counted in the hundreds, not the tens of thousands as in the First World War. Neither side had more than three thousand men when Kazan fell to the Whites in August, nor were the numbers substantially different when the Reds recaptured it in September.[104]

Most of all, Trotskii brought discipline to the Bolsheviks' shattered forces at Sviiazhsk. "An army cannot be built without repression," he once wrote. "The commander will always find it necessary to place the soldier between the possibility that death lies ahead and the certainty that it lies behind." Trotskii therefore brought to Sviiazhsk the stern belief that only the harshest measures could bring the tattered Red Army back to life. Vowing that "all cowards, self-seekers, and traitors will not escape the bullet," he moved quickly to prove that he meant what he said. When a regiment abandoned its position, he promptly executed its commissar and commander, and then proceeded to shoot randomly selected soldiers from its ranks. "A red-hot iron," he explained with grim satisfaction, "has been applied to a festering wound."[105]

Brutal treatments sometimes yield remarkable cures, and Trotskii's "red-hot iron" produced striking results. During the month after his special train arrived at Sviiazhsk, he regrouped the Red Army. Gunboats to bombard Kazan from the river and airplanes capable of carrying 1,600-kilogram bombs made striking additions to his forces that strengthened morale.[106] Reisner remembered how fresh artillery made its way to Sviiazhsk across sabotaged railways, and others recalled the decisive impact made by the handful of dedicated young fighters Trotskii summoned from Moscow.[107] At the same time, Trotskii assembled a group of officers from whose ranks arose a number of brilliant Red Army commanders, and these would form the core of its command staff in the battle to retake Kazan.

Mikhail Tukhachevskii, a twenty-five-year-old nobleman from the western Russian province of Smolensk, ranked high among them. Behind his bland expression and slightly protruding, heavily lidded eyes lay a brilliant mind that was particularly adept at military planning and organization. Destined to become a marshal of the Soviet Union at the age of forty-two, just two years before he was shot in Stalin's purge in 1937–1938,[108] Tukhachevskii rose to command the First Red Army on the Volga within six months after he joined the Bolsheviks. On September 12, two days after Red forces took Kazan, he breached the Volga at Simbirsk by hurling his forces across a kilometer-long bridge in the face of heavy enemy gunfire.[109] Tukhachevskii thus solidified the Reds' hold on the Volga's eastern bank and opened the way to capture the capital of the Komuch government at Samara a month later. By that time, army communiqués from the Volga front reported "masses of deserters"—sometimes as many as two hundred in a single day—fleeing from the Komuch army to join the Red forces.[110]

Yet, Tukhachevskii's experience in 1918 did not match his daring, and Trotskii therefore placed the Bolsheviks' Volga High Command in other hands. To lead the assault against the armies of Komuch, Trotskii turned to Ioakim Vatsetis, a man of proven accomplishment, whose dedication had been tested during some of the Bolsheviks' most desperate moments. Bald at the age of forty-five, his heavy jowls flowing into a thick neck that always seemed too large for his high-standing military collar and endowed him with a look somewhat akin to Mussolini, Vatsetis "was not much to look at" in the opinion of some of his contemporaries. "Short, so fat that he seemed as wide as he was tall," this son of a wretchedly poor Latvian farm laborer suffered an ailment that made his eyes appear perpetually inflamed, but he had nonetheless risen to the rank of colonel in the armies of Nicholas II through bravery, talent, and an appropriate measure of good luck. A man whose only vices were his love of abundant food and drink, Vatsetis had joined the Bolsheviks immediately after their October victory in 1917 and had commanded the Latvian Rifle Division that had crushed the July uprising of the Left SRs in Moscow. Now, as commander of the Bolsheviks' eastern front, his first duty was to carry out Trotskii's harsh commands and prepare the fledgling Red Army to take the offensive.[111] He did so with a stubborn singlemindedness that Trotskii much admired. "Vatsetis was enterprising, energetic, and resourceful," Trotskii later wrote. "He never lost himself in the chaos of the revolution, but cheerfully wallowed through . . . appealing, exhorting, and giving orders."[112]

Vatsetis had been among the last to leave Kazan when it had fallen to the Whites. Now, with Trotskii's help, he made ready to fight his way back. "The taking of Kazan means merciless revenge against the enemies of the revolution," Trotskii told the soldiers of the Fifth Red Army. "[It] means rest and rewards for all brave and staunch defenders of the revolution." At the same time he assured Kazan's defenders that "the Soviet government is making war only upon the rich, the usurpers, and the imperialists," and he appealed to all workers and peasants among them to join the Red Army that was mobilizing at Sviiazhsk. "To all workers we extend a fraternal hand," he announced. "Each of you who comes over to our side voluntarily will receive a full pardon and a fraternal welcome." To the "enemies of working people, the landlords, the capitalists, the officers and their Czechoslovak mercenaries," Trotskii promised death. "Those peasants and workers, who have sold themselves to the White Guards and voluntarily do not throw down their weapons," he decreed, "will be shot, along with those dear sons of the bourgeoisie, officers, and landlords." The "counterrevolutionary bandits of Kazan, Simbirsk, and Samara," he warned, would be wise to remember the pitiless manner in which the Red Terror had been waged in Iaroslavl after it had been retaken. "Bourgeois conspirators, foreign agents-provocateurs, and White guards officers," he concluded, "will be exterminated without exception." The workers and peasants must know where their duty lay in the battle against such enemies. "Do not allow the enemy to move a step further!" he exhorted. "Tear Kazan from his hands!" "Drown him in the Volga!" "Forward to Kazan!"[113]

Supported by gunfire from Raskolnikov's river flotilla, Vatsetis launched the Fifth Red Army's final assault against Kazan at half past three on the morning of September 10. As his men stormed its walls from the north, south, and west, the city's defenses collapsed, and by early afternoon the Reds once again held sway.[114] "September 10 is to be a red letter day in the annals of the socialist revolution," Trotskii announced that afternoon. "Units of the Fifth Army had torn Kazan from the grip of the White Guards and Czechoslovaks. This is a turning point," he exulted. "The advance of the bourgeois armies had been stopped at last."[115] The next day, *Pravda* spread the news across the Bolsheviks' domains. "The taking of Kazan is the first truly major victory of the Red Army," it rejoiced. "The Red Army has learned how to fight."[116] Trotskii could not let the victory at Kazan pass without one final oratorical flourish: "Why are we fighting under the walls of Kazan? Why are we fighting on the Volga and in the Urals?" he asked a huge crowd that had gathered at the Kazan Theater on the day after the Reds' victory. "We are fighting," he answered, "to settle the question of whether the homes, palaces, cities, sun, and heavens will belong to the people who live by their labor, to the workers, peasants, and the poor, or whether they will belong to the bourgeoisie and the landlords."[117]

Trotskii could well afford a moment's jubilation as the Red Army moved on to take Simbirsk and Samara that fall. "The lowest ebb of the revolution—the moment of the fall of Kazan—now was behind us," he explained later. The revolution was on the move once again.[118] Yet, simply to be marching forward did not guarantee victory in the year ahead. As the Red Army stormed into Samara to drive the Komuch government into exile several hundred miles to the east in Ufa, Germany's struggle on Europe's western front collapsed, leaving the Allies free to dedicate greater resources to the support of the Whites. "The year 1918 was coming to an end after having swept across Russia like a wild whirlwind," Aleksei Tolstoi wrote at the end of his great Civil War novel *1918*. "But all of this only marked the beginning of the great struggle, only a deployment of forces before the critical events of the year 1919."[119]

At every point where Red confronted White, the Allies increased their commitments to the Bolsheviks' enemies in terms of money, weapons, supplies, and men so that the new year brought new defeats to the Bolsheviks before it brought them new victories. In the South, Denikin drew new strength from French and English weapons, supplies, and fighting units. In North Russia, Britain and the United States deepened their commitment to intervention and tightened their defenses, while, in Siberia, the stern government of a military strongman—the dictatorship of Admiral Kolchak—provided the focus for political and military action that the governments of Japan, the United States, Britain, and France had sought in vain ever since the Bolshevik victory in October 1917. At the same time, Germany's defeat in the West decisively altered the balance of forces in those areas of Eastern Europe where Russian and German had come into conflict. In the Ukraine, a resurgence of Ukrainian nationalism accompanied the departure of the German armies and the fall of Hetman Skoropadsky's puppet government to produce a more brutal and bitter conflict between the Bolsheviks, the armies of Denikin, the nationalist guerrilla forces of Simon Petliura, and the peasant partisans of the anarchist Nestor Makhno. To the north, in the newly independent Baltic states of Latvia and Estonia, a new threat arose in the person of General Nikolai Iudenich, whose British-supported troops soon threatened Petrograd itself. As the tide again turned against the Bolsheviks, the summer and fall of 1919 would see them lose much of the ground they had gained the year before. Enemy forces came closer to Petrograd and Moscow in the fall of 1919 than at any other time in the Civil War.

Left, THE COSSACK ATAMAN SEMENOV
P. N. Vrangel Collection, Hoover Institution Archives

Below left, ADMIRAL ALEKSANDR KOLCHAK
Ivan Serebrennikov Collection, Hoover Institution Archives

Below, THE COSSACK ATAMAN KALMYKOV
James Whitehead Collection, Hoover Institution Archives

Right, General Count Petr Wrangel
P. N. Vrangel Collection, Hoover Institution Archives

Below, Stalin in 1917
The Bettmann Archive, Inc.

Top left, Trotskii and his staff in Red Square

Bottom left, Trotskii as Commissar of War

Below, Trotskii addressing a crowd in Red Square in Moscow

All photos: The Bettmann Archive, Inc.

Right, Lenin
The Bettmann Archive, Inc.

Top left,
General Nikolai Iudenich

Bottom left,
General Mai-Maevskii

Below,
General Anton Ivanovich Denikin
Three photos: Library of Congress

Above, Russians being mobilized to fight the Poles in 1920

Top right, An execution of Partisans in Siberia
Ivan Serebrennikov Collection, Hoover Institution Archives

Bottom right, Red Guards in Vladivostok
Two photos: The Bettmann Archive, Inc.

Above, SOLDIERS OF THE CZECH LEGION IN ACTION
Library of Congress

Top right, AN ARMORED TRAIN IN SIBERIA
Charles O'Brien Collection, Hoover Institution Archives

Bottom right, A MOBILE MACHINEGUN UNIT JOINING KOLCHAK'S RETREAT
The Bettmann Archive, Inc.

Below, A CZECH ARMORED TRAIN
James Whitehead Collection, Hoover Institution Archives

Above, An early Soviet photomontage dramatizing the slaughter of the Eastern Front in World War I.
Library of Congress

Top left, U.S. Army and Navy forces in Vladivostok
U.S. Signal Corps Photo, Rodney Searle Sprigg Collection, Hoover Institution Archives

Bottom left,
U.S. Army forces in North Russia
Roger Lewis Collection, Hoover Institution Archives

Above, Tearing down a house in Petrograd for fuel
B. F. Sokolov Collection, Hoover Institution Archives

Right, A market in a ravine at Nizhnii-Novgorod
Library of Congress

Famine Victims
Samara.

Above, REFUGEES DURING THE CIVIL WAR
The Bettmann Archive, Inc.

Top left, FAMINE VICTIMS
ARA Collection, Hoover Institution Archives

Bottom left, FAMINE VICTIMS ARRESTED FOR CANNIBALISM
ARA Photo from the Charles L. Hall Collection, Hoover Institution Archives

Below, A COMMITTEE OF THE POOR DIVIDES UP THE LAND IN A RUSSIAN VILLAGE
The Bettmann Archive, Inc.

Part Two

1919

CHAPTER SIX

Denikin and the Cossacks

VATSETIS'S STORMING of Kazan on September 10, 1918, began to transform the Russian Civil War from a conflict of small, disordered units into a war of more substantial armies fighting along fronts laid out according to standard military principles. During the next year, Reds and Whites each put approximately half a million men into their front lines and supported them with several thousand machine guns and hundreds of cannon.[1] Now certain that volunteers could never provide the quantities of men needed for their war effort, and no longer obliged to take the protests of the Left SRs into account, the Bolsheviks turned to conscription to fulfill Lenin's call for an armed force of three million men.[2] Although three out of every five men drafted eventually deserted, reliable official estimates placed the strength of the Red Army at two million men in mid-1919 and three million by the end of the year. At the end of 1920, its numbers exceeded five million. Such forces could never become as overwhelming as their numbers made them appear because Trotskii's Red Army suffered from a chronically bloated rear that kept as many as nine out of every ten men in uniform out of the battle line.[3] Still, during 1919, the Red Army changed decisively and permanently from a motley assortment of unruly workers, ill-trained peasants, Austro-Hungarian prisoners of war, and migrant Chinese and Korean laborers into a sternly disciplined military force with a well-established chain of command.

Unable to match the Reds' manpower, the Whites nonetheless developed substantial resources of their own during the year after their defeat at Kazan. Allied troops held most of the front-line positions along the Murmansk-Arkhangelsk front, while at least two hundred thousand more helped the Whites to compensate for their shortage of rear-echelon reserves in the Ukraine, the Caucasus, and the rail centers of Siberia. Because Imperial Russia had developed few armaments industries in her border areas, the Whites had to depend upon foreign sources for their weapons. On all fronts, the Allies supplied them with weapons, ammunition, and vital lines of credit, especially after the Central Powers surrendered in November 1918. Just between March and September of the following year, the Allies sent Denikin's Volunteer Army nearly a thousand field guns, more than a quarter million rifles, over seven thousand machine guns, a hundred tanks, nearly two hundred airplanes, several million shells, and several hundred million rifle cartridges. According to Denikin's own estimates, half of those weapons and material came from the British. The Allies sent similar shipments to other fronts at about the same time. At one point, the United States sent over a quarter million rifles, nearly two thousand machine guns, and four hundred pieces of artillery to the White forces in Siberia.[4]

Neither profligate nor indiscriminate in their aid, the Allies were at times surprisingly openhanded in view of the difficulties involved in shipping armaments and ammunition over supply lines that stretched nearly halfway around the globe. Such distances alone made it inevitable that the Whites at times would suffer shortages, and at those moments, they stood only too ready to condemn the Allies for refusing to give them blank checks to draw upon the arsenals of Western Europe and America. General Iudenich, who began his advance against Petrograd in mid-1919 with an army of less than twenty thousand men, lamented that the Allies had supplied him with "only" fifty thousand rifles and ninety million cartridges. Some of his artillery units had as many as five thousand shells per gun in reserve—considerably more than the Germans had set aside for the massive artillery bombardments they had unleashed against the Russians in 1915—but he thought that number insufficient. Although it was by no means clear how he could have kept them in proper repair or even have supplied them with gasoline if the British had agreed to send them, Iudenich thought it miserly indeed that the Allies refused his request for more than two hundred planes, fifteen tanks, and fifteen armored cars before he began his advance.[5]

While the Whites in 1919 had to rely upon supply lines that stretched from Odessa and Sevastopol to Marseilles and Newcastle, and even lengthier combinations of sea lanes and rail lines that stretched from Seattle and San Francisco into Siberia, the Reds enjoyed the comparative luxury of more compact lines of communication and supply within their constricted domains. Trotskii's Red Armies also had the advantage of marching to a single, insistent drummer and sharing a common sense of purpose. As the lands under their control shrank, as they bore the scourge of famine and epidemics, and as their White foes pressed more persistently toward Moscow, the Reds had their backs to the wall and pulled together accordingly. "Politics," Lenin once said, drawing upon the study he had made of Clausewitz's writings in 1915, "is the reason, and war is only the tool, not the other way around."[6] Neither he, nor Trotskii, nor Stalin, nor anyone else who held a high position in the Bolshevik government during the Civil War ever lost sight of that maxim. The Reds therefore kept their political goal of uniting the lands of the former Russian Empire under a single Bolshevik government first and foremost in mind, and that gave a clear focus to their military actions. Whenever they advanced—or any time they held advancing White armies at bay—the beleaguered Reds could claim victory. For the Whites, victory could come only through continued advance. Moscow must be taken. No matter what else they accomplished, if they failed to take Moscow they would have to admit defeat.

While the Reds pursued their course with singleminded stubbornness, the Whites allowed politics to divide them continually and irreparably. In retrospect, they spoke of a "White idea" that had united them in a common cause "as simple as the heart of a true patriot, as strong as his will, and as intense as his devotion to the Motherland," an idea that summoned men to sacrifice their personal interests in the name of the common good.[7] But at no time during the fighting of the years 1918–1921 did such beliefs actually unite the Whites. From the very beginning, the nationalist strivings of Ukrainians, Estonians, Lithuanians, Finns, Poles, and a dozen other ethnic and national groups cut deep and unbridgeable chasms between them and the Russians, who were themselves bitterly split by political commitments to monarchy, democracy, republicanism, and several forms of socialism. Fearful of dividing their followers, very few White leaders offered any clear sense of direction to the many Russians who struggled to find a way through the treacherous currents that swirled around them. Following Alekseev's early example, such men concealed their vision of Russia's future and spoke only of the present. "What right have we, a small group of people, to decide the fate of our nation without the knowledge and consent of the Russian people." Denikin asked an assembly in the Kuban. "I place the happiness of our Motherland above all else," he added at another point. "I am working for the liberation of Russia. The form of its government is a question of secondary importance."[8]

Strained denials that they preferred any form of government to any other, and continued promises that a Constituent Assembly would decide such vital questions as land reform after the war's end, set White leaders dramatically apart from those Bolsheviks who presented every crisis as a challenge that Russia's masses must meet if they hoped to open the way to a better future and be worthy of it when it came. "The Soviet Republic is surrounded by enemies," Lenin told Russia's workers after the Czechs had seized the Trans-Siberian Railway and the Whites had taken Kazan in August 1918. Lenin bluntly portrayed the gravity of the crisis his listeners faced, but he never left any doubt that proletarian justice, right, and socialism could prevail. "A rising spirit will ensure victory," he promised. "The triumph of the world workers' revolution is not far off."[9] Trotskii spoke in the same vein. "[These are] extremely difficult days and weeks for our young Soviet Republic," he told a mass meeting in Moscow as the crises of 1918 deepened. Russia faced hunger and disease. She had endured the losses of Brest-Litovsk only to see the Germans move into the Ukraine and the Czechoslovak Legion seize Siberia. But even from these losses, Trotskii drew words of encouragement. "Although we are still weak," he told his listeners, "the course of events has raised us up to an immense height. The Russian working class is at this moment the only working class in the entire world which does not suffer political oppression. Yes, things are bad for us right now," he concluded, "but the Russian working class has been the first to draw itself up to its full height and say: 'This is where I begin to learn how to steer the ship of state.' "[10]

While Lenin and Trotskii spoke of triumph in defeat, the

Whites spoke in gloomy tones, even in victory. In Murmansk, in Arkhangelsk, in Ekaterinburg, and along the Volga during the summer of 1918, White leaders emphasized only the uncertain future that lay ahead when they announced their victories. "Great difficulties stand in the way of regenerating Russia," they insisted, for there was "terrible ruin," and rehabilitation would demand "incredible effort."[11] "We are a sick people," they maintained. "We have become weak and spiritually impoverished."[12] Even after his triumphant armies had battered their way more than eight hundred miles into the heart of Red Russia and stood less than a hundred miles from the great Tula armories and just more than two hundred miles away from Moscow in the fall of 1919, Denikin told Odessa's workers that "our state has been demolished, ravaged, and destroyed," and that "to rebuild everything anew will be a colossal task." He then returned to the theme that Russia must have a powerful, united army to destroy Bolshevism and open the way for a Constituent Assembly to decide the people's fate.[13] Always, he spoke as a general, as an "honest but stubborn soldier," one of his fellow officers remembered. "[He was] completely lacking in the flexibility and crafty wisdom so essential for a diplomat."[14] Of all the White regimes that rose and fell in those days, only the Komuch government dared proclaim that "the land has irrevocably become the property of the people" and promise that it would "not permit any attempt to return it into the hands of the landlords."[15] Elsewhere, the Whites insisted that the masses must be ready to sacrifice their lives in battle against the Reds while they waited in uncertainty for an as yet unelected Constituent Assembly to shape their future.

Perhaps nowhere did political dissension, nationalist strivings, and economic conflict persevere more stubbornly among the Whites than in the relationships between Denikin's Volunteer Army and Krasnov's Cossacks. As happened too frequently among the Whites, Denikin and Krasnov had pursued different courses against Bolshevism after their hostile meeting in Manycheskaia at the end of May 1918. Certain that he could not drive the Bolsheviks from the lands of the Don without German aid, Krasnov continued to seek favor with the German occupation army in the Ukraine during the summer and fall. Yet, despite the weapons and ammunition the Germans could offer, he remained aloof from them in the arena of international politics, just as he did from the Allies. "Remember," he told one Cossack audience, "that neither Germans, nor English, nor Japanese can save Russia. Not even Russia herself can save Russia. Russia will be saved by her Cossacks."[16] For several months, it seemed that Krasnov spoke the truth. Able to triple the number of Cossacks under his command between mid-May and mid-July, he quickly drove the Reds from the Don lands and began to move against Tsaritsyn, the great industrial city on the Volga whose petroleum storage tanks, armaments works, and railroad repair shops had served the Reds as a citadel and communications center ever since their first victories.[17] To seize Tsaritsyn meant to take control of the railroads in Russia's Southeast and to gain access to the output of some of the greatest armaments works outside of Petrograd, Moscow, and Tula. For that reason, the Reds defended it with all the resources they could muster. Tsaritsyn became the "Red Verdun," draining Red and White alike in a series of bloody battles that stretched from early fall 1918 into the summer of the next year.

Two men of no previous military experience, both of them little known outside inner Bolshevik Party circles, led the defense of Tsaritsyn in a manner that won them permanent places in the Reds' Civil War pantheon. The son of a poor railroad worker from South Russia, Kliment Voroshilov had joined the Party in the year Lenin had split with the Mensheviks, and he had been a loyal Bolshevik from that day forth. A metalworker by trade, he had served the Bolsheviks as a labor organizer in the Donbas, in the oil center of Baku, in Petrograd, and in Tsaritsyn. Because he had spent much of the First World War in prison and Siberian exile, Voroshilov had never fired a shot in anger or faced enemy bullets before the October Revolution. A passionate defender of the new world that the Bolsheviks hoped to create, this man whom some called the "locksmith of Lugansk"[18] proved to be utterly fearless under fire as he led the Donbas miners against the German armies that invaded the Ukraine in the spring of 1918. When his Fifth Red Ukrainian Army could stand no longer against the Germans, Voroshilov fell back from Kharkov to Tsaritsyn, some four hundred miles to the east, where he added regiments of Tsaritsyn factory workers to his Donbas miners and turned to meet the attack of Krasnov and his Cossacks.[19] Supported by Semën Budënnyi, the thirty-five-year-old tsarist sergeant-major who had risen to lead the Red Cavalry in the South, Voroshilov launched a bitter attack against those former tsarist officers to whom Trotskii had given positions of responsibility in the Red Army. In that he received the whole-hearted support of Iosif Vissarionovich Stalin, the Bolshevik commissar of nationalities, whom Lenin had sent to the lower Volga that summer to oversee the collection of grain from the region's stubborn and hostile peasants.

A swarthy, pockmarked man who stood somewhat short of five and a half feet in height and whose left arm had been slightly withered from a near-fatal childhood bout with blood poisoning, Stalin had a genius for organization that surpassed that of Trotskii and rivaled that of Lenin. Born in the humblest of circumstances in the ancient Georgian mountain village of Gori, he had begun adolescence as a seminarian and had ended it as a full-blown revolutionary wanted by the police. Later, he had changed his name from Dzhugashvili to Stalin—the man of steel—and his revolutionary career, filled with imprisonments, daring escapes, and escapades that included bank robberies, convinced others that his revolutionary pseudonym was well deserved. In 1917, the February Revolution had found him in Turukhansk, a remote prison colony above the Arctic Circle where the brutal climate made escape impossible. Nonetheless, Stalin reached revolutionary Petrograd a full three weeks before Lenin and some two months ahead of Trotskii. He supported Lenin at every turn. Instinctively, he opposed Trotskii whenever possible. Still, his early arrival in Petrograd and the influential position he held on the editorial boards of several Bolshevik newspapers and in the Party's Central Committee failed to make Stalin a prominent public figure that year. Throughout 1917 he remained a gray shadow, always working behind the scenes, but never stepping into the forefront of Russia's revolutionary turmoil. Although few outside the Party's inner circles knew him, he had carved out for himself a powerful position in the Party's central apparatus by the time the Bolsheviks seized power in October.[20]

As commissar of nationalities, Stalin exercised a decisive influence upon some of the Civil War's most important events. At Tsaritsyn he quickly became involved in the "military opposition" of Voroshilov and Budënnyi against Trotskii's former tsarist officers and encouraged outright insubordination against such despised "bourgeois" figures. Raging against Trotskii, whom he continued to criticize at every opportunity, Stalin seized control of Tsaritsyn's defense effort not long after Lenin sent him to speed up grain shipments from the surrounding region. "I must have military powers," he wrote Lenin in mid-July. "[I] will remove those army commanders and commissars who are ruining things. That's what the interests of the cause bid me to do."[21] Thus Stalin began his career as a dictator, yet his first effort followed a rocky course. Grandly and arrogantly, he promised the capture of Baku, of the North Caucasus, and even of Turkestan. When none of these victories came to pass and Tsaritsyn still remained in danger, Trotskii pressed for Stalin's removal. "I insist categorically on Stalin's recall," he telegraphed to Lenin at the beginning of October. "We have a colossal superiority of forces, but there is utter anarchy at the top. I can put a stop to it in twenty-four hours, provided I have your firm and clear-cut support."[22] The next day, Vatsetis added his plea to Trotskii's. "Stalin's activities," he telegraphed to Lenin, "undermine all my plans."[23] In mid-October, Lenin approved the course Trotskii and Vatsetis demanded, but the fruits of victory must have tasted sour to Trotskii when he learned that Stalin had returned to Moscow to sit upon the newly formed Soviet of Workers' and Peasants' Defense as Lenin's deputy. In the meantime, the struggle for Tsaritsyn continued.

On three separate occasions—in October and December 1918, and again in January 1919—Krasnov's Cossacks surrounded Tsaritsyn, and each time the Red Army broke free. On the first occasion they were saved from disaster only by the sudden appearance of Dmitrii Zhloba's Steel Division, whose commander had defied the orders of his superiors in the North Caucasus in order to march to Tsaritsyn's defense. Concealing their movements by forced night marches, Zhloba's fifteen thousand men covered eight hundred kilometers in sixteen days. On the seventeenth, they broke through Krasnov's unguarded rear.[24] For the next month, Reds and Whites remained evenly balanced. Then, in December and January, the sheer weight of numbers began to tilt the balance in favor of the Reds, who by early 1919 outnumbered and outgunned their enemies by a margin of three to one.[25] In contrast to the previous spring, the quality of these increased forces now proved to be decisively better than many of the units Krasnov commanded. "Not more than half were fit for combat," Krasnov wrote of one corps that arrived from Kiev to reinforce his Cossacks. "The remainder were priests, nurses, miscellaneous females, officers of counter-intelligence services, policemen, aged colonels who had been signed up as commanders of nonexistent infantry regiments, artillery divisions, and cavalry squadrons, and, finally, various 'personalities,' all of them with a more or less colorful past, who were in search of positions as governors, vice-governors, and mayors."[26] Before the end of January, the Red Army pushed Krasnov's forces back along a wide front. With his German supporters now defeated in the West and no longer able to supply him with arms and weapons, and with the Allies intervening in the South in support of Denikin, Krasnov merged his forces with Denikin's Volunteer Army and resigned in the middle of February.[27]

Although Krasnov remained first and foremost a Cossack in his political vision and war aims, Denikin thought in broader, all-Russian, terms. For Denikin, the principles that dictated the destruction of Bolshevism were simple truths. He believed in Freedom and in Justice, but he insisted that these could flourish only if men and nations lived by the Law. Most of all, he believed in a "united, great, and indivisible Russia," in which all nationalities and classes would live in harmony.[28] "It matters not whether you stand on the Left or the Right," he pleaded at one point. "Love our tormented Motherland and help us save her."[29] Any questions about what form of government should follow a White victory, he insisted, faded into insignificance when compared with the desperate need for Russia's liberation from the yoke of Bolshevism. He therefore called upon all men and women who loved freedom and justice to set aside their political and social differences and to dedicate themselves to "a fight to the death against Bolshevism."[30]

The simple truths of Freedom, God, and Country that seemed so self-evident to Denikin were not so to others. All through the towns and cities of Russia's southern lands, men bitterly debated whether the Volunteer Army should stand for monarchy or democracy, and few seemed willing to set the issue aside until the battle for liberation had been won. To such men Denikin replied that "in all good conscience I consider it equally possible to serve Russia honestly under a monarchy or a republic," but that any statement of preference for one or the other could only weaken the struggle against Bolshevism. "Why raise the monarchist flag?" he asked when some of his senior officers urged that the Volunteer Army's High Command declare itself in favor of a restoration. "In order to divide us immediately into two camps and start an internecine struggle?" For the present, the battle for Russia's liberation must take precedence. "I shall not fight for any particular form of government," Denikin announced simply. "I am fighting only for Russia."[31] The greatest irony of all was that this singleminded dedication to the principle left the destiny of the land he sought to liberate in the hands of the very politicians he scorned the most.

While Denikin's armies marched against the Reds, Constitutional Democrats, monarchists, moderate socialists, and more radical Socialist Revolutionaries—all those who had failed so miserably to gauge the nation's pulse in 1917—intrigued in his rear. While Denikin called for unity of purpose, these men sowed the seeds of discord and then lamented the bitter cup those seeds brought forth.

Intent upon establishing a safe southern base from which the Volunteer Army could operate, Denikin had launched his second campaign into the Kuban just as Krasnov had begun to concentrate his forces against the Reds at Tsaritsyn at the beginning of June. Less than nine thousand men, supported by twenty-one field guns and two armored cars, marched with him. Outnumbered nine to one by the Reds, and outgunned by an even greater margin, Denikin and his chief commanders nonetheless advanced with greater confidence than they had a few months before.[32] In February the Volunteer Army had been little more than a band of tattered refugees fleeing before the columns of triumphant Red Guards. Now, as they faced Red forces among whom Trotskii's stern discipline had not yet taken hold, they advanced toward clearly conceived strategic objectives. Intent upon severing rail connections between Moscow, Tsaritsyn, and the main centers of the Caucasus, Denikin's generals concentrated upon key rail junctions that promised to yield priceless reserves of weapons and ammunition. In less than a month, Denikin's forces had stormed the rail centers of Torgovaia, Velikokniazheskaia, Tikhoretskaia, and Kushchevka, and were poised once again to assault Ekaterinodar. By the beginning of July they had severed the Reds' link with Kuban and had increased their arsenal by more than fifty field guns, three armored trains, and great stores of small arms and ammunition.[33]

Denikin paid a high price for these victories, despite the ease with which his forces routed the Reds in the early days of the Second Kuban Campaign. Most costly of all, the Second Kuban Campaign cost the life of General Markov, the officer with whom Denikin had shared life on the battlefield since the first days of the Great War. Together the two men had led the famed Iron Brigade to victory on Russia's southwestern front in 1915 and 1916. Together they had taken command of that front when Kornilov had become Russia's supreme commander in the summer of 1917, and together they had shared a cell at Bykhov prison in the weeks after the "Kornilov Revolt." Denikin's second in command throughout the Great War, Markov had prided himself on being a fighting general and served the Whites as a front-line commander. A man of gallantry and a dedicated monarchist from his first day to his last, Markov had given the First Kuban Campaign the name of the Icy March and had fought his way through enemy fire repeatedly during the early days of the Civil War. On one occasion he had personally led his men in a daring attack against a Bolshevik armored train and had emerged unscathed and laughing at the ease of his victory. In mid-June, the next to the last shell fired by another retreating armored train at an out-of-the-way railroad station took Markov's life.[34] To Denikin, the loss of his closest friend was a shattering blow. Many others among the Volunteers thought it the worst disaster since the death of Kornilov, for Markov had possessed a genius for winning men's hearts that had drawn his soldiers to him. His death left a "great void" in the army, Denikin later wrote. "How many times, when we were searching for a real man among the frightening array of nonentities," he remembered, "we . . . would say sorrowfully: 'If only Markov were still alive.' "[35]

Without Markov, Denikin leaned increasingly upon Romanovskii, another close personal friend and long-time comrade. "Ivan Pavlovich [Romanovskii] is the only man alive in whom I have absolute trust and from whom I have no secrets," he told the Volunteer Army's chaplain some months after Markov's death. "I can tell him things that I would not even tell my wife."[36] To others, however, Romanovskii seemed unworthy of such trust. Once the quartermaster general of Russia's armies under the fallen Provisional Government, Romanovskii had the outward appearance of an eternal staff officer. Yet behind the bland features that seemed so much more like those of a bureaucrat than a general lay courage as great as Markov's, although of a cooler, more measured sort. "I have never seen anyone so cool as Ivan Pavlovich," one of his fellow generals remarked. "If a grenade were to explode at his feet, he would not even blink an eye."[37] Markov's fiery daring had drawn men to him, while Romanovskii's icy calm formed a barrier between him and comrades who thought him arrogant and cold. Except for Denikin, who had absolute faith in his integrity, almost none among the White officers trusted him, and few could sense his political views. Markov's personality had helped to offset Denikin's own lack of personal magnetism; Romanovskii's only accentuated it. Men called him the "evil genius of the Volunteer Army."[38]

Eventually, Denikin's loyal defense of the man whose great virtues others never recognized cost him the support of his own army's High Command.[39]

Knowing that Markov's black, cross-marked banner would never again wave above a battlefield, Denikin ordered the final storming of Ekaterinodar just before the middle of August and entered the city with his victorious troops on the 16th. No longer were Denikin's soldiers nomads, for the Volunteer Army had at last secured a geographical base and a political center. Ten days later, units of the Volunteer Army went on to capture the port of Novorossiisk to gain an important outlet to the sea. Quickly, Ekaterinodar replaced Kiev as the political capital of White Russia. From this new center of White power, Denikin proceeded to shape the Volunteer Army into the largest and best-led force that the Red Armies faced during the fall, winter, and spring of 1918–1919. His first task was to replace the army's terrible losses, which, he estimated, totaled nearly thirty thousand men, even though its ranks had never held more than ten thousand at any one time.[40]

Such replacements could not be expected to come from volunteers. "The bloody, mortally exhausted face of the ordinary Russian," Denikin once confessed, "stared out from between the lines of communiques that joyfully announced victories" to remind him that common folk had grown tired of fighting.[41] Like Trotskii, he understood that the masses of Russia would no longer go to battle willingly, and like the Bolsheviks, he turned to conscription to increase his forces. Within a month after the fall of Ekaterinodar, Denikin had close to forty thousand men, supported by nearly a hundred cannon and more than two hundred and fifty machine guns, under his command.[42] That spring, the Volunteer Army had barely survived its Icy March. Now it had become a significant military force able to fight campaigns spread out along several hundred kilometers of front. No longer dependent upon men who had consented to support his cause for a few weeks or months, Denikin now began to think in more grandiose terms. "The Volunteer Army has not ended its crusade," he wrote soon after he entered Ekaterinodar. "Desecrated by Soviet Power, Russia awaits her deliverance."[43] Intent upon that mission, Denikin prepared to march against Moscow.

If victory brought Denikin a new sense of confidence, it also brought new problems, most of which lay in the political arena, where he suffered the greatest disabilities. Even as he liberated

Ekaterinodar, he had to contend with advocates of Kuban regionalism who rejected his call to march against the Bolsheviks in Russia proper and demanded that the Kuban become a sovereign state with an independent foreign policy and its own armed forces.[44] Always the blunt soldier and staunch Russian patriot, Denikin was quick to challenge the Kuban politicians' self-interested particularism. "It is time to cast aside disputes, intrigues, and regionalism," he pleaded. "Russia must be liberated. It will not profit you to do otherwise for your own well-being will become a plaything in the hands of domestic and foreign enemies of Russia and the Russian people." The Volunteer Army, he promised, would "recognize, now and in the future, the widest possible autonomy for all the component parts of the Russian state, with the most solicitous attention being paid to the ancient traditions of the Cossacks," but Bolshevism could never be conquered by separate and independent forces. "There must be a united Russian Army, with a united front and a united command," he insisted. Russia must be "united and undivided."[45]

The Kuban leaders insisted that it could not be so. For the next year, this juxtaposition of opposites caused bitter conflict in the South. Denikin spoke of the "strange today" in which the Kuban flag waved over the palace of the Kuban Cossacks' chief and looked forward to the "joyous, happy tomorrow" when the "tri-colored Russian national flag" would replace it.[46] At one point he even considered using the crack Kornilov regiment to disperse those Kuban politicians who argued that their government should separate from the Volunteer Army.[47] Intended to forestall dissension by postponing discussions on all questions about liberated Russia's future, Denikin's insistence upon unity until the Bolsheviks had been defeated eventually proved more divisive than unifying.

Even those who supported Denikin's call for a "great, united, and undivided Russia" were by no means at one in their political views. Nor did their visions of Russia's future agree. The most powerful and best-organized nonrevolutionary political party before 1917, the Kadets hoped to play a major role in Denikin's Russia, but even they found it difficult to agree on a program of political action. After the October Revolution, many Kadets had made their way to Kiev, where Miliukov had allied his party with the Germans. Many of his colleagues found that alliance, designed "to seek a base of support and real power in the midst of chaos and disorder to resurrect the fallen Russian state,"[48] impossible to accept and turned away from Miliukov and Kiev to Denikin and the dying Alekseev in the Kuban. Certain that the precepts of Russian Constitutional Democracy would supply the fundamental principles upon which post-Bolshevik Russia would be based, a number of prominent Kadets hurried to Ekaterinodar, where, despite Miliukov's objections, they agreed to support Denikin as supreme leader of the Volunteer Army and the territorial administration it represented.[49]

The key in leading the Kadets into an alliance with Denikin and the Volunteer Army in the fall of 1918 was Nikolai Astrov, a forty-nine-year-old Moscow lawyer whom the uncertainties of war and revolution had turned into a prominent politician. Although a number of Kadets argued that any movement against the Bolsheviks must begin by building regional bases of support "from below," and although Miliukov continued to dream of a return to monarchy in Russia, Astrov and his Moscow allies firmly opposed both courses on the grounds that either would hopelessly fragment any attempt at unity. True to his Kadet heritage, Astrov emphasized legality and legalism. While Denikin and his fellow generals called for victory over Bolshevism and the creation of a "great, united, and indivisible Russia," Astrov and his Kadet comrades spoke about a constitution and the need for carefully worded administrative regulations.

Typical of civilians everywhere, Astrov's Kadets found military rule disturbing. "It was necessary," Astrov later explained, "to force the agents of military authority into some new way of thinking, to prevent the continuation of methods whereby military authority ran roughshod over local populations and social organs."[50] He and the Kadets therefore thought first of protecting personal rights and private property, neither of which had much meaning for those masses to whom the Bolsheviks appealed directly with slogans and crude proclamations.[51] Dedicated to the quest for unity and order, Astrov and his Kadet comrades could neither compete with the Bolsheviks for the loyalty of Russia's masses nor moderate the arbitrary authority that Denikin's commanders wielded over civilians. Helpless, they looked on while the reactionary General Dragomirov began the persecutions of Jews that would turn into full-fledged pogroms the next spring and the sadistic General Pokrovskii hanged socialists *en masse* in the courtyard outside his window "to improve the appetite."[52]

A growing toleration for conservative and reactionary views

among some of Denikin's generals increased the tension in those areas of Russia's southern borderlands where regionalists, moderates, and socialists struggled to clarify their relationship to the advancing forces of the Volunteer Army during the fall and winter of 1918–1919. As their victories increased, Denikin's generals called more loudly for the liberation of a "united and indivisible" Russia and became less tolerant of any who spoke for separatism or regionalism. In vain did the Cossack Ataman Krasnov plead for more modest regional goals. "It is still too early to speak of the future of Russia as a whole," he wrote to one of Denikin's deputies in October. "We cannot start to divide the hide of the bear before he has been killed. It will be difficult—almost impossible, in fact—for any of us to kill this bear on his own," he concluded. "We must unite."[53] Yet the firm unity that Denikin and his supporters demanded in the fall of 1918 could not coexist with movements for national autonomy and independence. As fall turned into winter that year, the anti-Bolshevik forces in South Russia stood sharply divided.

In the Don, the Ukraine, and the Crimea, Krasnov, Skoropadsky, and General Suleiman Sulkevich, a Lithuanian Muslim who had commanded a special Muslim corps for the Germans in Romania and whom the Germans had installed as ruler of the Crimea in the spring of 1918, all had based their separatist regimes upon German support. Although Krasnov had made his peace with the Germans only after considerable soul-searching—and only on the condition that he remain free to pursue his own course against the Bolsheviks—Skoropadsky and Sulkevich had been German puppets from the beginning.[54] Both had enjoyed the support of fugitive Whites from Moscow and Petrograd as Miliukov had called upon his Kadets to support a pro-German policy in Kiev, and as other Kadets had taken the same position in the Crimea. "Insofar as we have become cultured Europeans it is only thanks to the Germans," one of them explained. "Our science, our technology, and philosophy [all] are fruits of German cultural influence. Even economically we are tied to Germany and not to England or France."[55] Throughout the spring and summer of 1918, all three regimes had supplied the Germans with badly needed foodstuffs in return for weapons, and Sulkevich and Skoropadsky had depended heavily upon German occupation forces to defend their unpopular governments. So long as the Germans held their own in the West, the situation could be expected to continue, but any shift in the balance of force promised to change political relationships in the East.

By early fall it had become clear to anti-Bolshevik forces all across South Russia that Germany was losing the war in the West and that the days of German occupation in the East were numbered. Skoropadsky and Sulkevich both hurried to seek broader support for their regimes, the former among White Russian officers who had taken refuge in Kiev, and the latter by currying favor with a number of influential Kadets who had been seeking to build popular support "from below" for a regional Crimean government.[56] Neither succeeded. In the Crimea, a coalition of Kadets overthrew Sulkevich in mid-November, and in December the forces of Petliura's Directory forced Skoropadsky to flee the Ukraine disguised as a wounded German officer.[57]

Germany's defeat and the collapse of Skoropadsky's and Sulkevich's governments by no means united the Whites in South Russia, for the more liberal regimes that replaced them proved to be even more staunchly separatist and more rigidly opposed to Denikin's program of a "united and indivisible" Russia. Ten days after the Allies signed an armistice in the West, an array of anti-Bolshevik politicians, including Miliukov, former tsarist Minister of Agriculture Aleksandr Krivoshein, Baron Aleksandr Meller-Zakomelskii, known both for his brutal suppression of mutinies during the Revolution of 1905 and for his key role in forming the Progressive Bloc in 1915, and some twenty others assembled in Jassy, the temporary capital of Romania, to form a united front against the Bolsheviks. As the Jassy delegates spoke at length with Allied representatives, each emphasized his narrow personal interests or those of the group he represented as the key to defeating the Bolsheviks. Yet their common hatred of Bolshevism was not strong enough to let them set aside their differences, even with the possibility of Allied aid looming large upon the horizon. Clearly sensing how divided Russia's anti-Bolshevik forces really were, some of the Allies began to have second thoughts about intervention.

In the words of its leading student, the Jassy Conference would become a "fiasco" for the White movement.[58] Supported by Miliukov, a number of politicians at Jassy called for a temporary dictatorship under Russia's former Supreme Commander Grand Duke Nikolai Nikolaevich, while others argued for a dictatorship under Denikin, a directorate, and several other alternative, but unrealistic, schemes. Reflecting their chief's hatred for Denikin, Krasnov's representatives insisted that the Don Cossacks could not be subordinated to the Volunteer Army so long as Denikin retained command. Dictatorship, democracy, republicanism, separatism, regionalism, and the dream of all-Russian unity each had its champions among men who arrogantly believed that they alone knew the path the Whites must follow. Once again, the intellectual rigidity and contentious personalities of the men who sought alternatives to Bolshevism prevented them from uniting against the Red menace that threatened them all.[59]

Germany's precipitous retreat from Eastern Europe and the Allies' decision to intervene in South Russia thus magnified the political problems Denikin faced at the end of 1918. He had to plead the Whites' case with those Allied representatives who came to Ekaterinodar at precisely the moment when other Whites sought to undermine his status with the Allies at Jassy and, after its occupation by the French in mid-December, at the great Black Sea port city of Odessa.

As the Allied landings and shipments of weapons and supplies made clear, the French and British had long since agreed upon their respective zones of activity in Russia's southern lands. Based upon the Anglo-French convention of December 23, 1917, the British took responsibility for the lands between the Don and Volga rivers, the Transcaucasus, and Central Asia, while the French concentrated upon the territory that had been occupied by the Austro-German armies to the west of the Don after the Peace of Brest-Litovsk. The British therefore took it upon themselves to supply the Volunteer Army and to occupy Baku and Batum, while the French attended to the Ukraine, where they increased their initial 2,400-man force to more than 60,000 before the end of February. For the British, the choice of alliances was between the all-Russian Denikin and the Cossack separatist Krasnov; for the French it was between Denikin, whose Volunteer Army began to extend its influence north and west from the Kuban, and the Ukrainian nationalist forces of Petliura.[60] The British more readily, and the French more reluctantly, both chose Denikin.

Shipments of Allied weapons and munitions, and the prospect of even greater Allied aid to come, strengthened Denikin's authority as the chief commander of anti-Bolshevik forces in South Russia. At the same time, the collapse of German authority brought Krasnov's downfall in the Don lands. Despite his protracted efforts to postpone the inevitable, he had no choice but subordinate his forces to Denikin once he no longer could depend upon German weapons to arm his soldiers. Named Commander-in-Chief of the

Armed Forces of South Russia at the end of December 1918, Denikin gained undisputed control at the beginning of February, when Krasnov resigned as Ataman of the Don Cossacks. By early March 1919, his northern front, defended by over forty thousand troops, stretched more than seven hundred and fifty kilometers from Mariupol in the west to a point approximately one hundred kilometers southeast of the Tsaritsyn–Ekaterinodar railroad in the east. Although the Red Army continued to outnumber his forces, Denikin had the advantage of better officers and superior cavalry. "The superiority of his cavalry in the first period of the struggle," Trotskii once said, "proved to be a great asset for Denikin and allowed him to deal us a series of very heavy blows."[61] Reinforced by the first Allied shipments of munitions and weapons, these two assets made it possible for Denikin to inflict serious damage upon the Reds in the early months of 1919.

Nonetheless, the first months of the new year were not a time of uninterrupted success for Denikin's army. Early January 1919 had seen the Volunteer Army establish undisputed control of the North Caucasus and its key cities of Novorossiisk, Ekaterinodar, and Stavropol.[62] Yet, the same month also brought Krasnov's final retreat from Tsaritsyn in a defeat that shattered the Don Cossacks and drove their leader from office. This left Denikin to defend the Don lands against Red forces that stood poised to advance from Tsaritsyn in the northeast and from the eastern Ukraine to the northwest, where new Bolshevik units had moved into the vacuum left by the Germans' departure. All along their front, Denikin's men faced three-to-one odds.[63] This overwhelming numerical superiority allowed the Bolsheviks to pose an awesome threat despite their shortage of cavalry and first-rate commanders.

The man who did the most to halt the Reds' advance in March and April 1919 was General Vladimir Zenonovich Mai-Maevskii, the man whom Denikin had placed in command of the Volunteer Army's left flank when he assumed supreme command in February and whose twelve thousand men had to face General Kozhevnikov's newly formed and well-equipped Thirteenth Red Army in the Donbas. Grossly overweight, his small piglike eyes accentuated by oval steel-rimmed glasses that sat above flabby cheeks, fleshy jowls, and a triple chin, Mai-Maevskii looked every inch the dedicated drunkard that he was. His pear-shaped body encased in a uniform that exaggerated its decidedly unmilitary proportions, no one could have imagined that he did anything but dedicate himself to the vodka and women whose presence in his headquarters perpetually outraged some of his military superiors. "If he had not worn a uniform, you would have taken him for a comedian from a little provincial theater," General Wrangel later wrote. "He knew how to make himself pleasant, and success had not robbed him of his hearty manner. But his conduct at his headquarters in Rostov roused the indignation of every honest man."[64] Despite his unmilitary bearing and the orgies that made his headquarters notorious, few in Denikin's command better deserved the accolade of fighting general than this man whose stomach protruded so far that he never saw his own boots on parade. He commanded intense loyalty from his men, who respected his great courage, overlooked his faults, and nicknamed him "Kutuzov," after the general who had commanded Russia's armies during the defeat of Napoleon in 1812.[65]

If the weather had been against the Whites on the Icy March, it took Mai-Maevskii's side in the late winter and early spring of 1919. The first thaws in the spring turned roads into rivers of mud and fields into oozing seas that held the boots of men and the hooves of horses in a stubborn grip. As mud sucked the wheels of guns and wagons down to their axles, the Reds suffered immense communication and supply problems, while Mai-Maevskii, who had a dense and well-developed rail network at his back, found it comparatively easy to move against them. Taking full advantage of this rare occasion when his forces enjoyed a tactical edge, Mai-Maevskii held the Reds at bay until the roads and fields dried toward the middle of May. Then the Volunteer Army, now officially named the Armed Forces of South Russia to signify that Denikin had incorporated the Don Cossack Army of General Sidorin and the Caucasian forces of General Wrangel into his command, moved to the offensive.[66]

This proved to be a propitious moment. In the East, the Siberian armies of Admiral Kolchak had seized Ufa and once again threatened Kazan and the Volga; at the same time, the Cossacks in the northernmost section of the Don Territory rose against the Bolsheviks. As the Bolsheviks struggled to contend with these crises, Denikin launched his armies northward in a massive triple thrust designed to converge on Moscow. Within a fortnight, a line of victories marked his entire front. On his left, the stiff, lean General Kutepov, once commander of the elite tsarist Preobrazhenskii Guards, and destined to be kidnapped in Paris by Bolshevik agents a decade later, took Belgorod on June 23. Two days later,

Mai-Maevskii's forces broke through to the vital Ukrainian industrial center of Kharkov, and on June 30, General A.G. Skhuro seized Ekaterinoslav. In Denikin's center, Sidorin's Don Cossacks drove back the Eighth and Ninth Red Armies. Most dramatically of all, the Caucasus Army of General Wrangel stormed into Tsaritsyn, the "Red Verdun" on Denikin's right that the Bolsheviks had sworn never to surrender, on the evening of June 30.

No commander among the advancing Whites projected a conqueror's image better than Baron Petr Nikolaevich Wrangel, the forty-year-old aristocrat whose towering self-esteem more than matched his remarkable height. A man of extreme vanity, Wrangel cut an imposing figure at a time when combat and disease had all but emptied the White ranks of charismatic leaders. The daring Kornilov and the dashing Markov were dead, their only legacy being the elite divisions that bore their names, and the commanders who had taken their places could hardly rule men's hearts in the way they once had done. A World War I guerrilla chieftain-turned-general, Shkuro was scarcely more than a glorified bandit. Mai-Maevskii, whose bravery won him his men's respect, was a drunkard whose unmilitary bearing accentuated his inability to remain sober. General Pokrovskii's love of mass hangings clearly marked him as a sadist, and General Slashchev was a morphine addict who stood all too often on the brink of madness. Honest, forthright, and incorruptible, Denikin had none of the personal magnetism that even these men of flawed character possessed. In 1919, only Wrangel combined will, talent, and an unshakable belief in his ability to save Russia with an aura of genuine charisma.

Disdainful of those "spurred and laced" officers whose "unconquerable aversion to the endless whining of bullets and the bursting of shells" kept them far to the rear,[67] Wrangel began his career as a fighting lieutenant and ended as a fighting commander-in-chief. Well over six feet tall, his booming voice proclaiming his leadership over the men around him, Wrangel came from a family of Baltic barons whose various branches had served the sovereigns of Prussia, Sweden, and Russia with distinction. A graduate of Russia's prestigious General Staff Academy, he perpetually shunned the staff positions to which his education entitled him in favor of field commands. Always he commanded Cossacks. Denikin thought him the best cavalry commander in the South and gave him a brigade the moment he offered his services. Dedicated in his service to God, Tsar, and Russia, Wrangel despised the Bolsheviks to the deepest depths of his soul, and mercy to such enemies was never numbered among his virtues. When several thousand Bolshevik prisoners were brought before him in October 1918, he shot nearly four hundred of them on the spot and then offered the rest the choice "to atone for their crime and prove their loyalty to their country" or face the same fate.[68] Able to speak well of democracy and republics if the situation required, Wrangel always remained a monarchist at heart. From his first day to his last, an observer once wrote, he remained "an officer of the cavalry regiment of His Imperial Majesty."[69]

In command of the Caucasus Army, Wrangel celebrated the arrival of spring with a resounding victory at Velikokniazheskaia, a key railway junction located at the point between Ekaterinodar and Tsaritsyn where the Novorossiisk-Tsaritsyn Railway crossed the Manych River. There, his Kuban Cossack cavalrymen shattered the Tenth Red Army and came away from four days of fighting in the middle of May with fifty-five cannon, more than a hundred machine guns, and fifteen thousand prisoners. At Velikokniazheskaia, Wrangel promised Denikin that he would be at Tsaritsyn's gates in three weeks, even though his men still had to cross two hundred miles of steppe and salt marshes, where food proved to be scarce and water rarer still. With newly arrived British tanks and armored cars to open a way through Tsaritsyn's barbed wire defenses, Wrangel carried the Red Verdun after another four days of heavy fighting at the end of June in one of the greatest White victories of the Civil War. Two armored trains (one named for Lenin and the other for Trotskii), 131 locomotives, ten thousand trucks, including more than two thousand that had been loaded with munitions, seventy cannon, and three hundred machine guns comprised the war materiel that fell to the Whites that day. Together with forty thousand prisoners, "it was," Wrangel later wrote, "an immense amount of spoil."[70]

With Ekaterinoslav, Kharkov, and Tsaritsyn in his hands, Denikin turned his eyes toward Moscow. On July 3, after he had attended a solemn high mass in Tsaritsyn's cathedral, Denikin reviewed Wrangel's victorious troops. "Tsaritsyn has been taken, and we are now on the march into the heart of Russia," he told the men who stood at attention before him. With rare elation, he announced: *"Today I have ordered our armed forces to advance against Moscow."*[71] Described in more detail in what became known as his "Moscow Directive," Denikin's plan was for Wrangel to march north against

Saratov and Penza and then to turn westward, first against Nizhnii-Novgorod and then against Moscow. In the meantime, Sidorin's Don Cossacks were to march against Moscow by way of Voronezh and Riazan, while Mai-Maevskii's Volunteer Army would attack Kursk, Orël, and Tula, after sending units against Kiev to protect his exposed western flank, before launching assaults against Moscow from the southwest.[72] Denikin began to believe that victory was within sight and that an advance along a broad front, the goal for which commanders had strived in vain throughout the First World War, could be accomplished. Wrangel thought just the reverse. "The advance on Moscow," he wrote, "was nothing more nor less than a death sentence for the Armies of Southern Russia."[73]

When Denikin issued his "Moscow Directive," his armies occupied a front that extended some eight hundred miles in a great, meandering arc from Ekaterinoslav in the west through Kharkov in the north to Tsaritsyn in the east. Although his front-line forces now exceeded a hundred thousand, and roughly equaled the numbers of their Red opponents, the length of his front obliged Denikin to stretch his forces dangerously thin.[74] Beyond that, he had allowed himself no time to consolidate the newly liberated lands from which he would draw reinforcements and supplies in his rear. Not even the Kuban, let alone the Don Territory and the lands that lay to its north and east, could be counted upon for unqualified support. Some of them—especially such cities as Rostov, Tsaritsyn, and Kharkov, whose large concentrations of factory work forces sympathized with the Bolsheviks—could be expected to support the Reds whenever an opportunity presented itself.

Yet proletarians who sympathized with the Reds was one of the least of the problems that plagued Denikin's rear. Former tsarist bureaucrats, whose standards of integrity had never been high, and former tsarist officers, whose loose living and hard drinking left them perpetually short of cash, created a fertile and fetid atmosphere in which corruption flourished. Shortages of every kind plagued the Whites' Russia, just as they did the Bolsheviks' domains, and the money and supplies sent that summer by the Allies provided great opportunities for speculation and theft. "I did not, during the whole of my service with the Army in Russia, ever see a nurse in a British uniform, but I have seen girls, who were emphatically not nurses, walking the streets of Novorossiisk wearing regulation British hospital skirts and stockings," wrote John Hodgson, a British war correspondent sent to report about life in

Denikin's Russia. "I saw and talked to young ladies of good social standing . . . who were wearing costumes made of British officers' serge," he added, as he wrote of men at the front who went into battle "wearing practically nothing but a print shirt and a patched pair of trousers." Almost every minor bureaucrat in South Russia seemed to have a new, crisply creased British summer uniform. "It is impossible to believe," Hodgson reported, "that we sent out clothing for the benefit of lawyers and petty civil officials."[75]

Complaints about the brutal behavior of drunken officers and soldiers who terrorized civilians and fired their weapons indiscriminately in city streets filled the newspapers of Denikin's Russia that summer.[76] In Rostov, soldiers took food, wine, and wealth from unarmed civilians at gunpoint, and one White general openly sold protection to the city's gambling dens. Violence became a way of life as the Whites failed utterly to bring a rule of law to the lands they governed. Surprisingly, they now called these areas "occupied territory," not "liberated lands," and treated the men and women of what once had been their homeland as conquered enemies.[77] "The fundamental bases of civil liberties are violated throughout the territory occupied by the Volunteer Army," a South Russian trade union congress complained that summer as its members reported illegal arrests, robbery, and murder by Denikin's civil and military officials.[78] Eventually, the people of South Russia came to prefer predictable and orderly exploitation at the hands of the Reds rather than face the capricious and uncontrolled rapacity of the Whites. When that moment came, all hope for the White cause collapsed.

Denikin took no part in such corruption and remained poor while others grew rich. "My last pair of trousers has come apart and my summer tunic is too short to cover them,"[79] he replied simply when one of his aides asked why he continued to wear a winter overcoat that summer. To set an example, Denikin turned back half of his pay to the Volunteer Army's treasury, and General Lukomskii accepted a salary that barely provided food for himself and his wife.[80] Yet men such as these were tiny islands in the midst of a swollen sea of corruption. Helplessly, Denikin looked on as officers in whom he had placed his trust stole, swindled, took bribes, and peddled influence. "From the lowest to the highest, the Russian people has fallen so low that I cannot foretell when it will be able to rise from the mire," he lamented in a letter to his wife that spring.[81] Yet unlike Wrangel, who readily ordered men shot or hanged for theft and drunkenness,[82] Denikin remained reluctant to order the brutal punishments needed to curb the greed of Russia's would-be liberators and always drew back from doing so.

Nor would the majority of his senior officers, most of whom declined to follow Wrangel's example, take stern measures. Dedicated to drunkenness and debauchery, Mai-Maevskii could be counted upon to turn a blind eye and a deaf ear to such goings-on. General Shkuro, who readily condoned banditry, scarcely could be expected to put an end to the black market any more than could Generals Pokrovskii and Slashchev, both of whom permitted widespread looting. All of them encouraged pogroms against the large population of Jews in South Russia and allowed their officers and men to rob and rape freely. "Depravity has reached the point of absolute shamelessness," wrote Father Georgii Shavelskii, the chaplain of Denikin's armies. "Thievery, speculation, corruption, and outright shamelessness have rotted the army's spirit. A pillaging army is not an army," he concluded sadly. "It is nothing but a gang of thieves."[83] Too late, Denikin realized his mistake. "We should have started at the top [in our efforts to wipe out corruption]," he wrote in his memoirs. "Instead of that, [we] went after the rank and file."[84]

Transferred to the military sphere, such massive corruption quickly proved destructive. While Denikin's desperate commanders tried to break through Red fortifications with infantry, British tanks sat on the dock at Novorossiisk. Although Hodgson found "it was always possible for a local profiteer to bribe railway officials and obtain freight cars . . . on a colossal scale," it proved impossible to find trains or trucks to move the tanks inland. "One night," Hodgson noted sadly, "a typical Black Sea storm caused one of the tanks to slip its moorings, and the whole consignment [of ten] slid quietly to the bottom of the harbor." Nor was that an isolated instance. While men dying from typhus and dysentery lay on rotting, lice-infested sacks, Hodgson watched the equipment for an entire two hundred-bed British hospital disappear at wharfside. "Beds, blankets, sheets, mattresses, and pillows disappeared as if by magic," he reported. "They found their way to the houses of staff officers and members of the Kuban Government."[85]

Denikin's decision to advance while these problems plagued his rear was not so much a product of wishful thinking as his critics have insisted for there were solid arguments to be made in support of his plan. Certainly the momentum that he had won by his rapid advances that spring and summer would have have been lost had he waited to consolidate his position as General Wrangel urged him to do. Furthermore, if it was not to be overwhelmed by the mass army that Trotskii had begun to create, the Volunteer Army had to increase its numbers, and that could be done only if Denikin advanced into Russia's more densely populated center. Denikin therefore had to take the limited opportunity that Fate presented in mid-1919. He had no choice but to make the most of it.

Denikin's victories stirred a bitter debate within the Red High Command about whether to continue its victorious advance against Kolchak's armies in Siberia or to strengthen the sagging southern front against Denikin. More cautious now that he had become commander-in-chief of the Red armed forces than when he commanded the Bolsheviks' Siberian front, Vatsetis urged that the Reds halt their advance at the Urals and use the coming winter to assemble the reserves needed to launch a final, crushing blow against Kolchak in the spring of 1920. Certain that the chief threat now lay in the South, Trotskii shared Vatsetis's opinion, but Sergi Kamenev, a thirty-eight-year-old former tsarist colonel who had replaced Vatsetis on the Siberian front, took a different view. Convinced that Vatsetis and Trotskii had overestimated Kolchak's reserves, Kamenev argued that Kolchak could be crushed that winter if the Red Army continued its pursuit. Even if the high command diverted several of his divisions from the eastern front to strengthen its forces in the South, Kamenev insisted that the fighting must continue in the East.[86] To end the debate, Vatsetis replaced Kamenev with General Samoilov, a former tsarist officer who had commanded the Tenth Army before the Revolution. Yet Samoilov brought neither sound strategy nor common sense to his new command. When he changed the direction of his main attack five times in ten days, even Trotskii had to agree to Kamenev's reinstatement.[87]

The conflict between Vatsetis and Kamenev masked a far more sinister and deadly rivalry. The feud between Stalin and Trotskii that had raged so openly during the siege of Tsaritsyn in the summer and fall of 1918 had by no means ended when Wrangel had stormed the city. As each rival watched for openings to attack the other, Stalin quickly displayed the virtuosity at Party in-fighting that would make him Lenin's successor in less than a decade. When Kamenev proved correct in his estimate of Kolchak's forces, Stalin therefore moved quickly against Vatsetis and, on July 3, 1919, convinced the Bolsheviks' Central Committee to name Kamenev as a replacement for Trotskii's hand-picked commander-in-chief. At the same time, Vatsetis and three of Trotskii's close friends on the key Revolutionary War Council were removed and replaced by Kamenev and three other reliable allies.[88] As commissar for war, Trotskii remained the council's chairman, but Stalin's allies could outvote him by a margin of two to one.

This new balance of forces on the Revolutionary War Council produced a decisive shift in the Bolsheviks' strategy. As carefully chosen units under Tukhachevskii and the brilliant peasant cavalryman Vasilii Bliukher drove Kolchak's forces from western Siberia and seized the key city of Zlatoust with its large armory,[89] the Red High Command shifted the bulk of its forces to the South, where the powerful Ninth and Tenth Red Armies formed the core of Kamenev's assault forces. Then, with troops from the eastern front strengthening his force as he marched along the Volga toward Tsaritsyn, Kamenev planned to continue his attack southwestward through the Don Valley against Novocherkassk and Rostov. Judged on purely military grounds, it was a sound plan. The recapture of Tsaritsyn would prevent Denikin from linking his forces with the Whites in Siberia, and Red control of the Tsaritsyn-Novocherkassk-Rostov line would make it impossible for him to receive the Allied supplies that were pouring into Novocherkassk by separating the Kuban from the Don lands.

Immediately, Trotskii attacked Kamenev's plan. While Kamenev, the graduate of the Imperial General Staff Academy, thought first of strategy, Trotskii, the revolutionary tactician, thought more in terms of the political and social revolution he had so carefully shaped. "If it had not been a time of civil war," he later wrote, Kamenev's plan "would have been perfectly correct." As it was, however, a Red assault against the Don lands would only "drive everyone capable of bearing arms [in that region] into the ranks of the White army."[90] From Tsaritsyn to Rostov, Trotskii warned, Red armies would be operating in hostile territory, for the Cossacks had shown themselves unsympathetic to the Bolsheviks in the past and now would join firmly with Denikin in defense of their homes and lands. He therefore argued that the main blow against Denikin must be centered upon the Donbas and aimed toward Kharkov and Ekaterinoslav further to the west. Although it would be more difficult to move troops from the eastern front to the Donbas than to the Volga, such a campaign would have the great advantage of fighting in areas that had heavy concentrations of industrial workers, who resented their recent "liberation" by the Whites and remained sympathetic to the Bolsheviks. The advantages of operating in territory inhabited by a friendly population, with a dense network of roads and railways to bring in reinforcements, ammunition, and weapons, Trotskii insisted, would more than offset the difficulties of attacking Denikin's stronger center rather than his weaker flank.[91]

Two days after they had relieved Vatsetis, the Bolshevik Central Committee voted to follow Kamenev's strategy in the South. Certain that "the error of the plan was clear beyond any doubt,"[92] Trotskii offered to resign as commissar of war and to leave the Central Committee and the Revolutionary War Council. At that point, Lenin intervened. Anxious to keep Trotskii's services, and fearful that any open discord between the man who had led the October uprising in Petrograd and forged the Red Army would produce great disquiet, he insisted that Trotskii's resignation could not be accepted. To show his personal confidence, he issued a blanket endorsement "without reservation" of any order that his commissar of war might issue.[93] Supported by an extremely prestigious statement of Lenin's confidence, Trotskii retained his posts, but he nonetheless bore the burden of supporting a strategy against Denikin that he thought wrong-headed, short-sighted, and extremely dangerous.

Time soon proved Trotskii correct and justified his apprehensions to the fullest. In mid-August, some fifty thousand troops of the elite Eighth and Ninth Red Armies struck at Tsaritsyn, while General Selivachev, who once had served under Denikin on Russia's southwest front in 1917, led forty thousand less experienced troops against the main force that Denikin had sent from Kharkov and the Donbas toward Moscow.[94] With the disputes in their high command not yet resolved, the Reds proved no match for the Whites, and Selivachev's advance quickly turned into a retreat. "What is going on?" Lenin wrote angrily to the Revolutionary War Council. "We outnumbered the enemy four to one. What is happening? How did we let such chances slip through our fingers?"[95]

When, after six weeks of hard fighting, Wrangel finally halted the Red advance against Tsaritsyn, it became clear that Kamenev's strategy was in danger of failing.[96] In early September, the Whites reached Kursk. Ten days later, on September 17, Shkuro's cavalry took Voronezh, and at the end of the month, Denikin's First Army Corps stormed Orël. A hundred miles to the northeast lay the great

Tula armory, for two centuries the largest producer of rifles for Russia's army. One hundred and twenty miles directly north of Tula stood Moscow, which now seemed very much in danger.

As the Reds struggled to launch a counteroffensive against Denikin, the cavalry of the Don Cossack General Mamontov wrought havoc in their rear. Recruited from among those Cossack communities which had suffered especially at the hands of the Bolsheviks, Mamontov's eight thousand cavalrymen broke through the Reds' front on August 10 and began a lightning campaign that caught their opponents completely off guard. Moving swiftly across the monotonous flatness of Russia's black-earth region, long famed for the richness of its soil and the fullness of its crops, Mamontov's Cossack cavalrymen were in the provincial capital of Tambov within a week. From there they moved north by northwest to Ranenburg, and then, when their Red pursuers increased in number, they turned south by southwest and burned and looted their way to Voronezh, once headquarters of the Fifth Imperial Army Corps, which stood near the confluence of the Voronezh and Don rivers. On September 19, forty days and five hundred miles after they had begun their foray, they burst through the Reds' front once again and joined General Shkuro's Kuban Cossack cavalry some fifty miles south of Voronezh.[97]

Mamontov's raid planted kernels of apprehension in the hearts of many Bolshevik commanders. Yet cavalry such as his could not be relied upon consistently, because it served itself before it served any larger goals. Himself insubordinate too often, Mamontov undercut much of the tactical advantage that could have been derived from his raid on Bolshevik supply lines by ranging over too large an area rather than concentrating on the rear of the powerful Eighth and Ninth Red Armies, which were pressing so hard against Wrangel's defenses at Tsaritsyn. Too much dedicated to plundering enemy towns and cities, and too little subjected to proper discipline, his raging cavalrymen eventually inflicted nearly as much damage upon the Whites as they did the Reds. "An army taught by the example of its leaders to loot and drink," Wrangel remarked angrily," could not restore Russia."[98] Indeed, Mamontov's cavalrymen's brutal pillaging caused many Russians who might otherwise have supported the White cause to turn against it, for the Cossacks drew few distinctions between Bolshevik property and that of peasants, workers, merchants, or nobles.

Despite its long-range failings, Mamontov's raid still counted as another in Denikin's string of impressive victories. Now the great southern ports of Novorossiisk, Odessa, and Nikolaev lay to his rear. So did the important industrial and trading centers of Kharkov, Kursk, Rostov, and Tsaritsyn. With about forty million people, roughly equal in population to modern France, Denikin's domain was more than three times its size, with nearly three quarters of a million square miles of territory. By the end of September 1919, his advance units stood slightly more than two hundred miles south of Moscow, and there was good reason for the Reds to fear further White victories that fall. As Denikin made ready to continue his advance against Tula, the British-supported White armies of General Nikolai Iudenich were approaching Petrograd in the North, so that both Red capitals were threatened simultaneously. The tone of Bolshevik directives therefore became increasingly strident and bitter. Soviet power would remain "to avenge the deaths of working men and women" long after the Whites had gone, Trotskii wrote threateningly at one point. All provincial "counterrevolutionary vermin" who were inclined to support the Whites, he warned, should keep that in mind.[99] Everything must be thrown into the battle to save Bolshevism. "Every reserve of revolutionary energy that our Party possesses must be used in the struggle against Denikin," a circular from the Central Committee announced at the end of September. "Denikin must be destroyed, and will be destroyed, by a new upsurge of our proletarian-communists' revolutionary will."[100]

At the end of September, few Whites saw anything beyond desperate posturing in such proclamations. For a moment, even Denikin had visions of reaching Moscow before winter. "Do not worry," he told the Kadet leader Nikolai Astrov at one point. "I will drink tea in your house in Moscow."[101] Yet, as Denikin's armies scored their most dramatic triumphs, the terrible uncertainties that plagued his rear began to take a toll. Far too quickly, his subordinates had established too many institutions in the newly liberated territories that seemed dangerously reminiscent of the regime that had been overthrown in 1917. "They kept saying that it was terrible under the Bolsheviks, that it was impossible to live under a Soviet regime," one observer wrote, "but they never made clear precisely what political and social structure they proposed to set up in place of the Soviet one."[102] "Old officials, old landlords, old policemen were apt to follow in the wake" of Denikin's victorious armies, another commentator added,[103] and their authority was too readily and too often defended by Cossack whips, just as it had been in the days of the old regime. Men and women of wealth and rank looked for the rebirth of the world from which they had been driven in 1917 in the South of Russia. "Look! Look!" one Kadet happily greeted a friend as he arrived in Ekaterinodar after Denikin's government had been established there. "There are our gendarmes, yes, indeed our old, prerevolutionary gendarmes!"[104]

Such obvious delight at seeing again those who represented the long-discredited institutions of the old order left too many with the fear that a White victory would herald a triumph of reaction and a return of the old regime. In September 1919, these fears kindled the flames of revolt in the rear areas of Denikin's armies. Preferring the uncertainty of the Bolsheviks' brave new world to the possibility of returning to the crumbling edifices of Old Russia, the peasants and workers began to shift their support from the Whites to the Reds. First on Denikin's left flank, and then in his rear, the peasant partisans of the anarchist leader Nestor Makhno seized large segments of the Ukraine. Other peasants launched other revolts in Denikin's rear, and the mountain tribesmen of Daghestan rose in insurrection. Even as he took Orël at the end of September, Denikin had to shift desperately needed reserves from his front to defend the security of his exploding rear areas as he and his generals turned to make war upon the very peasants they had sworn to save from the abuses of Bolshevism.[105]

At that moment, the Reds' new strength made itself felt all along Denikin's front. Between September 1 and November 15, the Red high command had increased its combat forces on the southern and southwestern fronts by more than a hundred thousand men.[106] That they supplied those fronts with more than 4,400 machine guns and nearly 1,000 pieces of artillery showed that the Soviet weapons industry had begun to play a part in the conflict.[107] Perhaps most important of all, the Reds finally matched the Whites' superior cavalry. During 1918 and part of 1919, Trotskii had opposed any thought of forming cavalry on the Red side because he saw it as an outdated weapon of an aristocratic old order that was in the process of withering away. Although his front commanders had called repeatedly for mounted troops, he had remained adamant until Mamontov's raid changed his mind. Then, suddenly fearful that cavalry had "become the most powerful means for defense and attack in the hands of the most conservative and decaying classes," Trotskii insisted, in September 1919, that Russia's workers and peasants "must tear this weapon from their hands and make it their own. . . . A powerful cavalry is vital for the Soviet Republic," he concluded. "Red cavalrymen—forward! Proletarians to horse!"[108]

Others—especially Voroshilov and Stalin, the defenders of Tsaritsyn against Krasnov's Cossacks in the fall and winter of 1918—had understood the role that cavalry forces must play in the warfare of the Russian steppes long before Trotskii began to do so. Trotskii's ideological strictures to the contrary, the Bolsheviks set out to increase the cavalry forces at Tsaritsyn toward the end of 1918. To do so, they turned to Semën Mikhailovich Budënnyi, the son of a poor Cossack sharecropper who knew horses and horsemen as few other proletarian fighting men did at the time. Budënnyi had been drafted into the tsarist army in 1903 and had shown a natural talent for leadership. After the Russo-Japanese War he had been appointed to the Imperial Cavalry Riding School in St. Petersburg, had graduated first in his class and had entered the First World War as a sergeant-major in the elite Imperial Dragoons. Always, Budënnyi cast an imposing shadow. Tall and big boned, his mustaches swirling upward dramatically in a pair of impressive handlebars, he had a well-deserved reputation for bravery and had won all the decorations for valor that the Imperial Army could bestow.

Budënnyi began his career as a Red Army commander just a few weeks after the October Revolution. During the next year, he led increasingly larger cavalry forces against the Whites, first in the Don lands and then at Tsaritsyn, where he formed a close alliance with Stalin and Voroshilov as men who believed in the new proletarian style of warfare that stressed mobility. With their support, Budënnyi shaped his forces into the First Red Cavalry Corps, which became the First Red Cavalry Army at the end of 1919. Astride the best mounts that could be found on what remained of the imperial stud farms, and denied the freedom to loot what their White counterparts enjoyed, Budënnyi's horsemen soon proved more than a match for Mamontov's Cossacks. On October 24, they decisively defeated the vaunted White cavalry at Voronezh. Within a month, Budënnyi's First Cavalry Corps had driven a wedge between Denikin's right and his center. By early January 1920, Red cavalrymen cantered through the streets of Rostov-on-the-Don, the scene of the first White victory, in December 1917.[109]

Budënnyi's first triumphs coincided with a major shift in the Reds' strategy. During late September and early October, Denikin's victories at Orël and Voronezh had thoroughly discredited Kamenev's grand strategy in the eyes of the Soviet high command, and Trotskii had won their consent to split the cumbersome wedge that Kamenev had aimed at Tsaritsyn into two more mobile groups, each capable of striking against Denikin's main force in the vicinity of Orël and Kursk while they continued to apply pressure against Wrangel's defenses around Tsaritsyn. Now, Denikin's elite Kornilov and Markov divisions faced the Reds' best forces, not their weakest units, and with his few reserves tied down by Makhno's peasant partisan forces in the Ukraine, Denikin had nothing with which to shift the balance.

Once Budënnyi's victory at Voronezh had opened the way for the Reds to cross the Don and split the Don and Volunteer armies, Denikin had no choice but retreat. As the towns and cities that the Whites had occupied so recently fell again to the Reds, Denikin struggled desperately to salvage the fortunes of his cause. Commanders who had failed to unite in victory now grew more acrimonious in defeat. When Denikin replaced Mai-Maevsksii with Wrangel, and Wrangel sanctimoniously removed both Mamontov and Shkuro, the Cossacks' morale collapsed. By the end of the year, Mamontov's once seemingly invincible cavalry refused even to face Budënnyi's forces. Bitterly disheartened, Denikin removed Wrangel from command just a fortnight after he had appointed him.[110] By that time, the Reds had advanced more than seven hundred kilometers against Denikin's best forces. Although at some points more than three hundred kilometers from their front headquarters, they continued to press on. Only at the end of February 1920 did their offensive come to a halt as Denikin's crumbling armies finally held firm on the banks of the Kuban River. Surrounded by conspiracies and intrigues, Denikin tried to rebuild his crumbling defenses while his commanders feuded more rancorously than ever. "I am sick at heart," he wrote to his wife as he complained of the "power which has oppressed me like a heavy yoke and tied me like a slave to a cart too heavy to pull."[111] He had just more than a month left before he would lose his command. On April 3, 1920, he left Russia forever after his army's senior officers had chosen General Wrangel to command in his stead. "I am spiritually broken and I am physically ill," he had told his new chief-of-staff a few days before he left on a quarter-century's journey that took him to Constantinople, London, Budapest, and Paris before he reached Ann Arbor, Michigan, in 1947. "The army has lost faith in its leader and I have lost faith in the army."[112]

Denikin and the Cossacks had represented White Russia's best hope in 1919, but it had not been the only one. Earlier that year, events in Siberia had given rise to equally great hopes and expectations, as Admiral Aleksandr Kolchak's stern dictatorship had welded together those unlikely allies that had formed feuding White governments in Omsk, Samara, and Ufa earlier in 1918. Ranging across the entire political spectrum, from radical socialists who sang the "Internationale" at political meetings to reactionary former tsarist officers who roared out the lines of "God Save the Tsar" in the cafes of Omsk, Siberian political life had been a morass of intrigue and violence during the year after the Bolsheviks had taken power. Kolchak had changed that in an instant. On the night of November 17–18, 1918, a number of officers and Cossacks of the Omsk garrison, probably with the approval of their superiors, had arrested several prominent Socialist Revolutionary politicians and installed Kolchak as supreme ruler. Summoning the Siberians "to unity, to struggle with Bolshevism, to labor, and to sacrifices,"[113] Kolchak then launched a campaign against the Bolsheviks that took his armies nearly to the banks of the Volga in the spring of 1919 and threatened the Reds from the East at about the same time as Denikin was beginning his advance from the Kuban. Indeed, the rise and fall of the Arctic explorer-turned-dictator, whose great personal integrity contrasted so dramatically with the corrupt self-seeking of his associates, comprised one of the most striking episodes in the history of the Russian Civil War.

CHAPTER SEVEN

Siberia's Supreme Ruler

While the Cossacks' long heritage as Russia's defenders drew some of the Bolsheviks' most prominent enemies toward the southern borderlands in 1918 and 1919, the vast spaces of Siberia stirred visions of freedom on a grand scale in the minds of many others. A place where nature and history had juxtaposed striking opposites, Siberia encompassed some of the world's most sparsely populated lands with its greatest accumulation of natural resources. A frozen white sea in winter, when it endured the most extreme cold of any inhabited region on earth, Siberia became a mass of flowers in summer. More than a quarter of the world's timber grew within its boundaries, and for at least three hundred years it had been Europe's richest storehouse of rare furs. Its mines yielded great supplies of gold, silver, and platinum; its diamonds, rubies, and emeralds ranked among the finest in the world.

Vast quantities of oil, coal, zinc, manganese, lead, copper, natural gas, and every mineral known to man still lay buried beneath Siberia's frozen surface at the beginning of Russia's Civil War. Her mighty rivers were among the world's most powerful, the potential source of billions upon billions of kilowatts once they were harnessed. No lake on the Eurasian continent came close to equaling the expanse of Siberia's Lake Baikal, and none in the world surpassed its depth of more than six thousand feet. Men always had been awed by Siberia, but in 1918 they had just begun to learn the extent of her wealth and potential. "The greater part of Siberia's mineral wealth is as yet lying waste, and is scarcely even known," a government source had noted in 1900.[1] Even on the eve of the First World War, shortages of capital and labor still prevented many of Siberia's known gold deposits from being mined.

Siberia's great distances, and the fact that much of its territory lay at latitudes well to the north of New York and Chicago, meant that time and space took on different dimensions within her boundaries. Daylight at midnight in summer became darkness at noon in the winter, and men counted distances not in single miles but in scores and hundreds. People who had not journeyed through Siberia could not imagine its vastness. In an effort to impart that sense to his readers, George Kennan, the American scholar and journalist who traveled across Siberia just before the Trans-Siberian Railway was built at the end of the nineteenth century, explained that, if a map of Siberia were drawn according to the scale used in Britain's famous ordinance survey maps, it would require a sheet of paper nearly a half-mile in width. If all of the continental United States were set down in the center of Siberia, Kennan pointed out, there would be so much room left over that Alaska and all of Europe (excluding European Russia) could be fitted in and still leave enough space to accommodate France and Great Britain a second time.[2]

To add to its many contrasts, history had made Siberia a land of great freedom and heavy servitude at one and the same time. Its more than five million square miles of land had remained untouched by the yoke of serfdom that had held millions of men and women in European Russia in bondage for centuries until the Emancipation of 1861 had set them free. From the seventeenth century until the nineteenth, Siberia had been the home of semi-nomadic natives, hunters, and Russian trappers who recognized no master but the tsar and ranged freely across the vastness of Eurasia to gather the pelts of the elusive ermine, sable, lynx, fox, marten, and otter. Later, miners and a few settlers had joined them. Combined with a goodly number of men and women dedicated to turning a fast ruble, these rough and ready folk had made nineteenth-century Siberia into a version of America's Wild West magnified by at least a factor of ten and set against an Oriental backdrop that made it all the more exotic and complex.

In this land of great cold and great natural wealth, hard drinking and hard living took a heavy toll. Vodka was Siberia's universal currency, its universal entertainment, its universal plague, and the basis upon which a number of eminent and respectable men built great fortunes. Gennadii Iudin, the Siberian bibliophile whose great library forms an important part of the Library of Congress's Slavonic Collection, parlayed a handful of rubles into a fortune worth millions by building a distillery in Krasnoiarsk. By the time of the Russo-Japanese War, Kharbin, the "Aladdin City" that the Russians built at the end of the 1890s on a land concession obtained from the Chinese in Manchuria, had a distillery that produced three million gallons of vodka a year,[3] and there were dozens more whose output was equally large. As in all boom-town cultures, Siberians generally preferred to dispense vice and vodka than to foster learning. In the late 1880s, Kennan discovered from official sources that Siberia had at least thirty taverns for every school.[4]

If Siberia knew more freedom than other parts of Russia, it also served as the tsars' greatest prison. To Siberia's mines and places of exile Russia's rulers sent more than a million men and women before the Revolution, with the number of new victims rising well beyond ten thousand a year during the last decades of the nineteenth century.[5] Hundreds of thousands of men and women found guilty of crimes ranging from murder to vagrancy dug gold and silver for the tsar's treasury from Siberia's mines during the century before 1917. Over a hundred thousand more braved winter storms, raging rivers, perpetual hunger, and incessant fevers to build the Trans-Siberian Railway that, at the beginning of the twentieth century, finally made it possible to travel from one end of the Russian Empire to the other by modern transportation.[6] Men and women condemned to suffer the bonds of penal servitude aged quickly and died young. Too often they perished by their own hands rather than face years of physical abuse, psychological torment, malnutrition, and disease.

Many of the men and women sent to Siberia thus found life hard beyond belief, and such revolutionaries as the Menshevik leader Martov, who contracted tuberculosis of the throat in the years during which he was condemned to live at the edge of the Arctic Circle, bore the scars of Siberian suffering to their graves. Yet others among the exiles found a surprising amount of freedom in the vast lands that stretched from the Ural Mountains to the Pacific. In the late 1850s, careless tsarist authorities had allowed the revolutionary anarchist Mikhail Bakunin to travel so freely in Siberia that he eventually journeyed two thousand miles down the

Amur River to its mouth and boarded a ship for Yokohama to complete his escape.[7] George Kennan found Aleksandr Kropotkin, younger brother of the well-known anarchist, living in "a rather spacious log house" with "a good working library of two or three hundred volumes," even though he had been exiled to Siberia for "political untrustworthiness."[8] Even at the end of the century, Lenin still found it possible during the three years he spent in Siberian exile to find the leisure and research materials needed to write *The Development of Capitalism in Russia*, a book long praised for its detailed statistical examination of Russia's agricultural development after the abolition of serfdom.

During the two decades that separated Lenin's exile from the Bolsheviks' seizure of power in October 1917, the completion of the Trans-Siberian Railway transformed some of Siberia's towns and cities, the largest of which numbered less than fifty thousand in 1890, into a string of boom towns that stretched from Cheliabinsk, in the eastern foothills of the Urals, to Vladivostok more than four thousand miles to the east. Omsk, site of the infamous prison where Dostoevskii labored for four years and headquarters of the Fourth Siberian Imperial Army Corps; Novo-Nikolaevsk, a favorite gathering point for big game hunters in search of the elusive wapiti and ibex; Krasnoiarsk, the site of Iudin's distillery and home of the Railway Technical School built to train engineers for Siberia's railways; and Irkutsk, the "Paris of Siberia," which stood 3,384 miles east of Moscow and boasted two professional theater companies, which its citizens subsidized to the tune of nearly a hundred thousand rubles a year,[9] all soared to more than eighty thousand inhabitants before 1914. Beyond Lake Baikal, Chita, famous as the place where two of Russia's most prominent princesses had joined husbands exiled for their part in the abortive Decembrist uprising of 1825, now served as the gateway from which travelers either continued their journeys on the Chinese-Eastern Railway through Kharbin to Vladivostok or boarded a river steamer at Sretensk for a fifteen hundred–mile journey downstream to Khabarovsk, where they began another five hundred–mile rail journey to Vladivostok. These, and a number of other centers set astride the Trans-Siberian's spur lines, grew at an unprecedented rate during the new century's first decade. The populations of Ekaterinburg, one of western Siberia's key mining centers, and Tomsk, home of Siberia's only university, more than quadrupled between 1895 and 1914, and smaller cities grew even faster. Founded less than a quarter century earlier, Kharbin saw its population approach a hundred thousand by the beginning of the First World War.

All things about Siberia—its climate, natural resources, daily life, and conditions of development—differed from those found anywhere else in Russia, and these made the Revolution and Civil War different there as well. Although revolution came quickly to Siberia along the railroads, it did not touch those towns and hamlets that lay beyond the railroads' reach until weeks and months later. The Civil War followed a similar course. In other parts of Russia fighting spread out along broad fronts connected by major urban centers in late 1918 and 1919, as the armies of Denikin pressed north from the Kuban and those of Iudenich marched against Petrograd from Estonia's Baltic coast. As a result of Siberia's vastness, warfare centered more directly upon the railroads as armored trains plied the region's few rail lines to bombard railheads and vital industrial centers. Carrying their own fuel, weapons, troops, and food, these land-bound battleships became fighting machines unto themselves. The *Destroyer*, an armored train used by the Cossack guerrilla Grigorii Semenov in the Transbaikal region, carried a contingent of fifty-seven men and officers, protected its ten machineguns with half-inch armored plate backed by eighteen inches of reinforced concrete, and carried two three-inch guns and two one-pounder cannon,[10] while the *Orlik*, the famed "Eaglet" built by civil engineers who fought as part of the Czech Legion, had guns mounted in armored turrets similar to those used in heavy battleships.

Using the railways, the Bolsheviks had established Soviet power in all of the major towns and cities between Cheliabinsk and Khabarovsk by February 1918. Thus, as the Bolsheviks' *Chronicle of the Civil War in Siberia* triumphantly recorded, Omsk, Tomsk, Irkutsk, Ekaterinburg, Chita, and Blagoveshchensk all had placed themselves under the authority of the Soviet of People's Commissars before the October Revolution celebrated its four-month anniversary.[11] Yet by the time local soviets took control of Vladivostok in May, the Bolsheviks' hold had begun to slip further to the west. As units of the Czech Legion moved triumphantly back and forth along the Trans-Siberian that spring and summer, Bolshevik power centers fell like ninepins. The Czechs took Novo-Nikolaevsk, Cheliabinsk, and Tomsk before the end of May. Omsk fell on June 7, Vladivostok before the end of the month, and Irkutsk in mid-July. Well before the end of September, all the remaining centers of Soviet power in Siberia had been destroyed.[12]

The Czech Legion was only in part responsible for the Reds' rapid collapse in the lands east of the Urals during the summer of 1918. Between the Volga and the Pacific, no less than nineteen governments, some directed by sober men to promote the general welfare and others used chiefly to advance the self-interest of corrupt, self-serving leaders, arose to oppose the Bolsheviks.[13] Most prominent among the former, the government of Komuch in Samara and the Provisional Government of Autonomous Siberia in Omsk, vied to establish their claims as the Constituent Assembly's legitimate heirs since both had been formed by men and women whom the Bolsheviks had driven from Petrograd's Constituent Assembly chamber in January 1918. Each mistrusted the other, and neither could establish hegemony in Siberia on its own. Nor could either become a focal point for Siberia's anti-Bolshevik forces. Until late 1918, Siberia's Whites remained fragmented, disunited, and working at cross-purposes, despite the efforts of responsible Russians and their anxious allies to unite them.

None proved more persistent in urging such unity upon the warring Russians that summer and fall than the French and the Czechs. At two conferences at Cheliabinsk, first in mid-July and again in late August, both tried in vain to establish some sense of common interest among the contentious Russian Whites but failed to accomplish anything beyond emphasizing the conflicts that separated them. "*A struggle for power* between Samara and Omsk had become inevitable," one member of the Provisional Government of Autonomous Siberia wrote even before the second Cheliabinsk conference opened.[14] By August, as petty politicians squabbled more over precedence than principles, the two governments actually became embroiled in a tariff war over freight shipments (including weapons and other war materiel) that passed across the Urals.[15] "That this would make it possible for the Red Army to destroy its enemies bit by bit," one White general wrote sadly, "evidently never occurred to them."[16]

If squabbling politicians seemed unable to see the forest for the trees, the men in command of Siberia's military forces saw the need for unity more clearly. "The army and its officers are awaiting an all-Russian government," one observer reported. Supported by the Allies, who wanted a single stable White government to replace

Siberia's confusing array of petty political centers working at cross-purposes, senior military officers began to insist that politicians cut short their "senseless chatter" and concentrate upon supporting their efforts to beat back new Red attacks.[17] As the Siberian summer neared its end, politicians and soldiers agreed to debate the question of unification once more at Ufa, the capital of Bashkiria and the last city before the railroad from Moscow crossed the Urals and connected with the Trans-Siberian.

Founded during the reign of Ivan the Terrible as an outpost from which to collect tribute and impose the power of Moscow upon the warlike Bashkirs, Ufa in 1918 preserved little of its military beginnings. Described by Baedeker a few years earlier as "prettily situated" in the European foothills of the time-worn Ural Mountains at the confluence of the Belaia and Ufa rivers, Ufa was irreparably scarred by the soul-chilling boredom of Russia's provinces. It suffered from the "not particularly lively character of a provincial town," one observer wrote in a masterful understatement, even though its population of slightly more than a hundred thousand had more than doubled since the beginning of the century.[18] Because life in Ufa moved at the turgid pace that had stirred the scorn of every major Russian urban writer since Aleksandr Pushkin, the descent of more than a hundred and fifty delegates representing fourteen different Siberian "governments" and nine political parties and groups upon its Grand Siberian Hotel at the beginning of September created a particular stir. Flags, placards bearing political slogans, and huge crowds milling in the streets were not a part of everyday life in any Siberian city, and particularly not in Ufa.[19]

Although the Siberian Whites had failed repeatedly to unite, the Ufa delegates all spoke of unity as their chief concern. As he called the conference to order at its opening session on the evening of September 8, Nikolai Avksentiev, Russia's minister of internal affairs in August 1917 and president of the Council of the Republic on the eve of Kerenskii's fall, called upon the delegates to "take a solemn . . . oath not to leave this place . . . without establishing a unified Russian state." Russia could no longer afford the luxury of fragmented political allegiances. The time had come, he insisted, "to create at last, out of all the scattered fragments . . . of our land, one mighty, free, independent Russian state." Treason had "built its nest at the very heart of Russia," he warned. Only a "strong government inspired with the ideal of Russia's freedom and independence" could "repel the enemy trampling under foot the Russian people, its liberty and state."[20] As Avksentiev spoke, events added substance and urgency to his words. Already, Trotskii had begun to assemble assault units on the middle Volga for the attack that would return Kazan to Bolshevik hands two days later.

The fall of Kazan on September 10, and young General Tukhachevskii's success in breaching the Volga at Simbirsk two days afterward, put the Komuch government in serious danger and put its rivals on notice that the time left for settling differences had grown very short. As their representatives debated the form that a unified government should take, one Siberian government after another relinquished its claims in favor of a single source of authority. On September 23, the Ufa State Conference proudly announced that "the Supreme Authority throughout the entire Russian state has been entrusted to the Provisional All-Russian Government," which would be composed of an elected Directorate of five people.[21] Both socialists and nonsocialists had a place. Among the former, Avksentiev, the moderate socialist Nikolai Chaikovskii (who at that moment presided over the Supreme Administration of the North at Arkhangelsk), and Petr Vologodskii, a Socialist Revolutionary attorney from Tomsk who had led the Provisional Government of Autonomous Siberia that spring and summer as the chairman of its Council of Ministers, were the conference's first choices, while Nikolai Astrov (who was far away in Denikin's newly captured Ekaterinodar), and General Vasilii Boldyrev, who had risen from a poor peasant family to command Russia's Fifth Army on the eve of the October Revolution, represented Russia's liberals and moderates.[22] Boldyrev became commander-in-chief of the Directorate's armed forces.

Clearly the Directorate could hardly claim to be all-Russian, given the existence of Chaikovskii's Supreme Administration of the North and Denikin's government in the South.[23] That proved to be all the more the case when both Chaikovskii and Astrov refused the posts the Ufa Conference offered them. The Ufa Conference therefore replaced Astrov and Chaikovskii with Vladimir Zenzinov, a Socialist Revolutionary who had served on the Executive Committee of the Petrograd Soviet in 1917, and Vladimir Vinogradov, a Moscow-educated Kadet attorney who had lived much of his life in Siberia and had been elected to the Third and Fourth Dumas as a delegate from Astrakhan.[24] Together, in General Boldyrev's words, these men "took shelter in the Grand Siberian Hotel in a city thick with intrigue and hostility"[25] to proclaim that, "in the name of saving our homeland from final ruin," and at the "unanimous request of representatives of all classes and sections of the population," the All-Russian Provisional Government would establish "a united, independent, free, and great Russian State."[26] As Trotskii's revived Red Armies pressed eastward past Kazan and Simbirsk toward Samara, it was clear that the Bolsheviks thought otherwise. So did a number of Socialist Revolutionaries who angrily repudiated the meeting at Ufa as a "Walpurgis Night"—a night of witches and sorcerers.[27] At the other end of the political spectrum, the conservatives in the Provisional Government of Autonomous Siberia and elsewhere continued to demand a dictatorship to unify Siberia's diverse political forces. The Ufa State Conference's effort to create unity out of Siberia's chaos had failed even before it had a chance to begin.

Although obvious in retrospect, that failure was not immediately apparent to Avksentiev and his colleagues, and the disdain of both Left and Right did not prevent them from trying to establish a government at Omsk during October. As they labored to organize a stable Council of Ministers, the thick cloud of intrigue that had enveloped Omsk since the day of their arrival grew darker and more ominous. Plots and counterplots simmered in out-of-the-way corners, back rooms, government offices, and military headquarters as conservatives and socialists laid plans to rid themselves of each other. "There's murder in the streets," General Boldyrev wrote in his diary in late October, as knives, pistols, and garrotes began to claim their prey.[28] The authorities frequently could not determine whether the victims had fallen at the hands of bandits or political assassins because both flourished so abundantly in the atmosphere of treachery, violence, and disdain for the law that pervaded Omsk that fall.

More and more clearly, a strong government led by a resolute leader seemed to be the only solution to the problems that the Omsk authorities faced. Yet even ineffective efforts to bring order out of chaos stirred other fears, especially among men who owed their prime allegiance to the Left. "Repression and the general political situation in Siberia frighten me greatly," Zenzinov confided to his diary in mid-October. With characteristic exaggeration, he added, "military cliques reign supreme everywhere."[29] The military had not yet become supreme, but soon it would be. A fortnight later, Zenzinov's apprehension had deepened appreciably. "We live, as it were, on a volcano, which is ready to erupt at any moment," he and Avksentiev wrote in a joint letter to some of their Socialist Revolutionary comrades. "Every morning we sit and expect that they will come to arrest us."[30] In vain, the Directorate sought a middle path and proclaimed their "profound belief" that "every part and nationality of the great Russian state . . . [would] unite in a single mighty whole, under the resolute guidance of the all-Russian supreme authority, to lead our tormented fatherland out of the abyss of disintegration."[31] They had delayed too long. Events of Russia's Civil War were moving quickly to push them to one side as men and women left too long in uncertainty began to look for a leader resolute enough to respond effectively to the advancing Red Armies.

Ironically, as October neared its end, the Czechoslovak Legion became the only military force willing to defend the Directorate, yet its soldiers did so only at the cost of abandoning the front they had held against the Bolsheviks for five months. "The way to Ufa is almost entirely open," a worried Boldyrev noted in his diary on October 15. "The first Czechoslovak Division has abandoned the front." A fortnight later he reported that all the Czechs had gone to the rear to reestablish order. Yet even as the Czechs urged decisive action, the Directorate refused to use its last weapon of self-defense effectively. "Everyone is afraid that we are not resolute enough to hold power," Boldyrev confessed at the beginning of November. "This disturbs the advocates of stern authority immensely."[32] It disturbed the Czechs even more. Still sympathetic to socialist ideals, they remained ready for one moment more to support men such as Zenzinov and Avksentiev against the rising wave of sentiment in favor of a Siberian "dictatorship." "Within two days," one Czech officer told Avksentiev and Zenzinov, "we can clear Omsk of all the reactionary scoundrels."[33] The Directorate thought that too high a price to pay for safety. "The Directorate," General Boldyrev insisted proudly, "does not shoot people and does not put them in prison."[34]

In disgust, the Czechs abandoned the struggle. As the armies of Germany and Austria prepared to capitulate in the West, and as Masaryk announced Czechoslovak independence in Prague on October 28, they had no reason to continue their battle in the East. "They had decided," one observer explained, "that they had fought enough for Russia and that it was time to go home to a free

Czechoslovakia."[35] Without the Czechs, the Directorate had no defense against Siberia's rising call for a strong government. Just as the officers of the Volunteer Army had named Denikin a "dictator" to unify the ranks of the Whites in South Russia at the time of Alekseev's death, so did Siberia's Whites seek to replace rampant unfettered democracy with military dictatorship. They did so with a great deal more urgency than had the Whites in the South. As October moved into November, few doubted that the time that remained for action had grown very short.

Even as the Directorate finally formed a government at the end of October, more resolute men had begun to lay plans for its overthrow. "It is very disappointing," England's General Knox wrote in a document he signed with Boldyrev at that time, "that Russia's leaders have for so long failed to come to an agreement about the composition of a Provisional Government. We have the right to insist," he concluded, "that all personal and political interests be set aside and that an authoritative government be formed which would place no obstacles in the way of establishing an army for the salvation of Russia."[36] General Boldyrev knew that Knox already had found his candidate for the dictatorship he hoped would come in the wake of the Directorate's fall. "In political and military circles, the preference for a dictatorship grows stronger and stronger," he noted in his diary at the end of October. "Most likely, this idea will be tied in some way to Kolchak."[37]

Aleksandr Vasilevich Kolchak, the man upon whom Russia's military men and allies had begun to focus their hopes in the fall of 1918, had turned forty-four on November 4, the day the Directorate named him its minister of war and navy. Tall and dark, with piercing black eyes, a well-shaped aristocratic nose and an elegantly cleft chin, he looked every inch the hero whom rumor and legend proclaimed him to be. A proud Russian patriot and a man whose old-fashioned code of honor surrounded him with an aura of integrity in a milieu known for its corruption and self-interest, Kolchak had dedicated himself to following in the footsteps of his naval officer father from the moment he entered St. Petersburg's Naval Academy. Famed as a Polar explorer and a friend of Britain's Admiral Jellicoe, he had a well-deserved reputation as one of the best officers in a navy whose history included few accomplishments and fewer victories. In October 1917, the Bolshevik seizure of power had found him at sea, en route to Russia's Far Eastern lands after a series of inconclusive diplomatic discussions in the United States, and he began his anti-Bolshevik career in Japan before he ever returned to Russia. For the next year, Kolchak moved between Japan and the Russian Asiatic mainland, at times attempting to organize White units in Manchuria and, at others, seeking a position in the British armed forces.[38]

During August 1918, Kolchak met several times in Japan with General Sir Alfred Knox, England's military attaché to Russia throughout the First World War and the anti-Soviet head of the military mission the British sent to Russia after the Bolsheviks took power. Any government that hoped to stand against the Bolsheviks, Kolchak told Knox, "must lean on an armed force." Without an army and the will to use it, he insisted, any anti-Bolshevik government in Siberia would "be a fiction" and be destined to fall victim to "anyone else who has an armed force at his disposal."[39] Kolchak and Knox therefore agreed that only a military dictatorship could oppose the Bolsheviks in Siberia. Somewhat more than a month later, the two men traveled from Vladivostok to Omsk in Knox's special train. Knox already had reported to Britain's director of military intelligence before they left Vladivostok that Kolchak was "the best Russian for our purpose in the Far East."[40]

Kolchak's views about power and the obligation to use it mirrored the opinions that Under-Secretary of State for Foreign Affairs Lord Robert Cecil had expressed to his colleagues in the British Cabinet at the beginning of September 1918. Certain that "half-baked constitutionalism" could never restore order in Russia, Lord Cecil had concluded that only "a provisional military Government" could hope to succeed in that "herculean task." Yet, if what he had gone on to call "military dictatorship" offered a solution to the immediate problem of Bolshevism, Cecil feared its long-term consequences. "A permanent military despotism in Russia," he had warned his colleagues, "would be a very serious menace to the peace of the world." Cecil therefore had concluded that the British must "aim at securing military chiefs whom we can trust . . . [while] making ourselves indispensable to them" so as to make it more difficult for them to slip out of control.[41] Both Cecil and Knox wanted someone to head a White government in Siberia who would crush dissent and do their bidding. It was, Knox stated bluntly a few weeks later, "a matter of indifference of what complexion the Government may be so long as it is strong and just and willing and able to defend the new Russian army from internationalist and other harmful propaganda."[42]

Exactly how—or whether—the British advanced Kolchak's candidacy probably never will be known. Certainly the claim made by Colonel John Ward, commander of a small British detachment in Omsk, that "my machine guns commanded every street leading to the Russian military headquarters"[43] to make it impossible for sympathetic Czech units to come to the rescue of Kolchak's opponents adds substance to the view that the British played an important part in Kolchak's *coup d'état*, and Zenzinov's report that Knox once recommended that Chernov, the Socialist Revolutionaries' founder and most respected leader, ought to be shot strengthens that image.[44] But other evidence points in the opposite direction. Without doubt, Knox and Kolchak had become friends, and as a friend, the English general enjoyed considerable influence. Yet Knox on occasion tried to slow the march of events, not hasten it. Early in November he evidently warned Kolchak that any attempt to overthrow the Directorate "would at present be fatal."[45] He then left Omsk and did not return for nearly a month. When the coup that overthrew the Directorate occurred, Knox was in Vladivostok, more than three and a half thousand miles to the east.[46]

While Knox appears to have remained cautious, others in Siberia had grown very impatient. Although the Socialist Revolutionaries had preserved a more effective organization east of the Urals than elsewhere in Russia, Siberia nonetheless remained a stronghold of conservative opinion in which thousands of former tsarist army officers found support among thousands more anti-Bolshevik politicians and relatively prosperous peasants.[47] In addition to Siberia's many avowed monarchists, the Kadets played a prominent role in White politics that winter. Even more than those of their comrades who had followed Miliukov and Astrov to the South, the Siberian Kadets placed their faith in authoritarian principles, called for "firm statesmanlike authority" and "businesslike administration," and put their hope for the future in a strong dictatorship.[48] "The time of charming myths and illusions has passed," a Kadet speaker had announced to "stormy applause" in Omsk that summer. "Public opinion has come to the conclusion that, in a country . . . where the passions of civil war are raging, there must inevitably be established a firm one-man authority capable of saving the state."[49] Now disdainful of democracy and openly hostile to socialism, the Kadets had little confidence in the socialist-dominated Directorate. Neither did the Cossacks and former tsarist officers who filled the cafes and assembly halls of

Omsk as winter returned in full force. By mid-November, few among them were not willing to see the Directorate overthrown. Knox and his British comrades therefore needed to do little more than lend a sympathetic ear, and there is little to indicate that they did more than that before the coup broke out. Certainly, no hard evidence has yet come to light to support the repeated French claim that the British brought Kolchak to power in an effort to prevent them from strengthening their influence in Siberia that winter.[50]

Although murky questions about who stood behind the plots and conspiracies that fouled the Omsk air in mid-November must remain unanswered, the sequence of events of the *coup d'état* that overthrew the Directorate on the night of November 17, 1918, is clear enough. After dinner that evening, Avksentiev and Zenzinov went to a private meeting at the apartment of Deputy Minister of Internal Affairs Evgenii Rogovskii, who, like them, belonged to the Socialist Revolutionary Party. Around midnight, a group of Cossack officers stormed into the apartment, arrested Avksentiev, Zenzinov, Rogovskii, and a member of the Socialist Revolutionaries' Central Committee and dragged them into the street, where "about three hundred men," according to Avksentiev's account, surrounded them, loaded them into a truck, and took them to an army headquarters on the outskirts of Omsk.[51] Long before the sun rose on the morning of November 18, three leading socialist members of the Directorate and its Council of Ministers thus found themselves under heavy guard by officers who thought their political views dangerous if not outright seditious.

Word of the arrests spread quickly. Premier Vologodskii received word almost immediately and called an emergency meeting of the new government. "The Directorate has been arrested!" his secretary announced as he made the calls. "There's to be an emergency meeting of the Council of Ministers immediately."[52] Kolchak, who had just returned from a tour of front-line positions, was among the first to appear when the ministers began to assemble sometime before six that morning.[53] Without much discussion about how to secure the release of Avksentiev, Zenzinov, and their comrades or punish the men who so flagrantly had violated the law by placing them under arrest, the Kadet attorney Vinogradov, in addition to Vologodskii, the only member of the Directorate still at liberty in Omsk, posed the question: "Will we have a dictatorship?"[54] Briefly the council considered the question and, among the ministers appointed by the Directorate, all but one voted to replace the government that had put them in power with a dictator. "I lived through some minutes of extreme agitation," one member later wrote. "Who could be dictator? After our theoretical discussions about the form of governmental power, we had to face this fateful question."[55] It appears that Kolchak and the army's chief of staff both proposed General Boldyrev, the commander-in-chief, who at that moment was seven hundred miles to the west in Ufa. Yet Boldyrev was at best a man of regional reputation whose name commanded little recognition outside of Siberia. Only Kolchak, the friend of British generals and admirals, renowned Polar explorer, and resolute naval commander, who, rumor had it, had been ruthless in crushing socialist agitation when he had commanded the Black Sea Fleet in 1917, had the prestige to become a credible dictator. When the council members voted that morning, all but one cast his ballot for Kolchak.[56]

Daylight still had not yet lightened the leaden Siberian winter sky on the morning of November 18, 1918, when Aleksandr Kolchak became supreme ruler and commander-in-chief of all the land and naval forces of Russia. "Taking up the cross of this authority under the extremely difficult conditions of civil war," he telegraphed to all parts of Siberia, "I shall follow neither the path of reaction nor the fatal course of partisan politics. My main objective will be to organize an effective army [and] to triumph over Bolshevism."[57]

Kolchak's terms would not be easy, and he did not promise the glorious future that Lenin and Trotskii perpetually held before their audiences. "Fellow citizens," he concluded as he took up the reins of power offered to him by the crumbling Directorate. "I summon you . . . to hard work and to suffering."[58] All in the same day, he ordered the Socialist Revolutionary ministers freed, arranged to have them escorted safely out of Russia, appointed a special court to investigate the circumstances of their illegal arrest, and promoted three of the officers who had broken into Rogovskii's apartment on the night of November 17. Two of them were promoted to the rank of colonel; their leader received the rank of major general.[59] Kolchak might well speak of the time when "the people will freely choose the form of government they desire."[60] In the meantime, socialists would find life very difficult under his regime.

Kolchak had no illusions about the dimensions of the crisis that faced him when he took power in Omsk. "Russia is broken into parts, her economy is in shambles, [and] she has no army," he announced at a meeting to which he had summoned the editors of several Siberian newspapers. "They call me a dictator," he went on. "Well, let it be so." After reminding his listeners that the Roman Senate had named dictators to guide the republic in times of crisis, he assured them that he viewed his appointment as supreme ruler in similar terms. "I am firmly convinced," he told them, "that a government can function and develop in our times only on the basis of firm democratic foundations," and Bolshevism, he warned, betrayed those precepts. Everything must be dedicated to a "merciless, implacable struggle against the Bolsheviks," he insisted, and the army must be restored immediately for that purpose. Like Denikin, Kolchak saw the army as the key to Russia's future. "If the intelligentsia is the brain of a nation," he concluded, "its army is the source of its strength and its fortress." Only a strong army could defeat the Bolsheviks, unite Russia, and make it possible to summon the National Assembly that would shape Russia's future. Certain that only a "madman" would try to carry out such a program alone, Kolchak called Siberia's citizens to join him in the "resurrection of Russia."[61]

It was one thing to speak of strong armed forces, a united people, legality, and order, but it was another thing entirely to create them out of the chaos that reigned in Siberia at the end of 1918. To shape the lands east of the Urals into a unified realm, Kolchak had to bring together pillaging bands of peasants and Cossacks who recognized no authority beyond their own; establish some grounds for common action between the feuding Japanese, Americans, and British intervention forces, all of whom had come to Siberia mainly to undercut each other's influence; and, at the same time, organize viable institutions of government. He could not control Siberia unless he held the Trans-Siberian Railway firmly, and none of the forces he commanded at the end of November 1918 held much of the Trans-Siberian east of Omsk. The Czech Legion held some sections, the Japanese held others, and the Americans held others still. Those sections not held by one of those three remained the domain of the two Cossack chieftains Semenov and Kalmykov, both of whom already had earned wide notoriety for their barbarity in a war that saw atrocities committed by both sides all too often. As Kolchak took power in Omsk, armed forces other than his own controlled thirty-five hundred miles of the military lifeline upon which he depended. From the first, he would be dependent upon others for his survival.

Kolchak drew his main support from the British, the armorers and the financiers of his government. In him they found the military strongman they had sought in Kornilov, Kaledin, and Krasnov. Here at last was a commander who spoke of legality, order, freedom, and firm democratic foundations and did not consign capitalists to the purgatory of world revolution. Perhaps best of all, he had come to power with the firm promise to "undertake to pay in full . . . all legitimate financial obligations of the [tsarist] government."[62] Kolchak, Knox reported, was "honest, patriotic, and capable."[63] The Americans recognized his patriotism, but doubted his dedication to democratic ideals and freedom despite the urgings of their consul general at Irkutsk to lend him "friendly sympathy and assistance" in his efforts to "restore law and order."[64] Unmoved by such pleadings, General William Graves, commander of more than eight thousand American soldiers strung out along the Trans-Siberia Railway, reported repeatedly on the brutality of Kolchak's regime. Others supported his view. "I must report," America's ambassador to Japan wrote to his superiors in the State Department in mid-1919, "that the Kolchak government has failed to command the confidence of anybody in Siberia except a small discredited group of reactionaries, monarchists, and former military officials."[65] Still searching for a policy in Siberia, the Americans withheld recognition of Kolchak's government but sent arms, ammunition, and loans while its diplomats and politicians debated the Supreme Ruler's commitment to democracy.

An "effective fighting force" and "victory over Bolshevism," Kolchak had said when the Directorate collapsed, were to be his first concerns as supreme ruler.[66] He had at his command the crumbling armies that had fought so well for the Komuch government that summer, the armed forces of the fallen Omsk Directorate, and a number of independent Cossack units, some of which operated perilously close to the line that separated partisan warfare from brigandage. These numbered less than half of the anti-Red forces in Siberia at that time, but the others recognized Kolchak's authority only nominally or not at all. Supported by Japanese gold and weapons, the Cossack and peasant bandit forces of the self-styled atamans Grigorii Semenov and Ivan Kalmykov now fought their own campaigns for their own purposes in Siberia. Kolchak could count upon them only in those rare instances when their aims coincided with his. Far more often, they threatened his supply lines and siphoned off desperately needed war materiel as it passed along the Trans-Siberian Railway through the territory under their control.

Siberia also held close to a hundred thousand Allied troops, whose arrival in the summer and early fall of 1918 their governments had justified on the grounds that they would help the Czech Legion reopen the eastern front against Germany and Austria. The armistice signed on November 11 had eliminated that justification for intervention, but none of the Allied governments had dared openly commit their forces in Russia to fight against the Bolsheviks, although they obviously had been sent for that purpose. With the exception of units of the English Hampshire Regiment that had been in Omsk at the time of Kolchak's *coup d'état*, the Allied forces were spread along the two thousand miles of eastern Siberian railroads that stretched from Lake Baikal to Vladivostok. At various times during the next eighteen months, parts of these forces would be called upon to fight against the Reds, against Kolchak, against Semenov and Kalmykov, and against each other.

Beyond these forces in late 1918, Siberia held a horde of ex-tsarist officers who had remained aloof from the Siberian White armies of 1918 because they opposed the presence of socialists in the governments they defended. Certain that socialists would have no place in Kolchak's government, these men now flocked to Omsk to join his forces and brought with them all of the most objectionable characteristics of the old tsarist army. More concerned, as one American diplomat remarked, with "the reconquest of former grafts" than with fairness, justice, or the public welfare,[67] too many of these men dedicated themselves to mindless discipline and the corrupt pursuit of personal advantage. The worst excesses of tsarism and none of its virtues thus appeared in Kolchak's Siberia as these former tsarist officers interpreted the supreme ruler's order to wipe out Bolsheviks in a particularly broad and brutal fashion. "In Siberia," America's General Graves wrote in disgust, "the word Bolshevik meant a human being who did not . . . give encouragement to the restoration to power of representatives of Autocracy in Russia."[68]

To draw together those forces who would serve him, and to woo those who remained neutral or uncommitted, Kolchak appealed to civic virtue. "All officers, all soldiers, and all military support personnel must stand aloof from any form of politics," he announced less than a week after he took power in Omsk. "I insist," he went on, that "officers and soldiers exclude all political discussions and party conflicts from their midst."[69] Like Denikin, Kolchak believed that the army must be the government's instrument and defender, not its moral arbiter or the creator of its policies. "Without an army there is no independence, no freedom, not even a state," he once wrote. The Siberian army, "a new, young army," held the key to "life or death, well-being or misery." Only its victories could free Russia from Bolshevism and the threat of "shameful slavery."[70]

Yet, to talk of victory in Omsk at the end of 1918 seemed nearly as absurd as it had been for Lenin to speak of victory in Moscow a few months before. Kolchak's rise to power as Siberia's supreme ruler had so incensed most of the Czech Legion's leaders that they had withdrawn their units from the conflict. Now concerned only to return to their newly independent homeland, the well-trained Czech and Slovak soldiers whose stubborn courage had played such a part in the White victories during the summer of 1918 turned their backs on the fighting. The soldiers who filled Kolchak's armies in their place needed boots, uniforms, weapons, ammunition, and training in how to use them. Dependent upon supply lines that stretched more than halfway around the globe from England, France, and the west coast of the United States, Kolchak's armies received war materiel only in fits and starts. Always they remained at the mercy of the Allies' uncertain commitments, the vagaries of Trans-Siberian Railway schedules, and the good will of Semenov and Kalmykov, who, on more than one occasion, appropriated large Allied shipments for themselves. "There's too much intrigue, too many power struggles, too much personal ambition and greed," one of the few honest officials in Kolchak's administration lamented to his diary.[71] Staff and support groups served themselves generously to the clothing and boots that reached Kolchak's western front before they sent them on to men in the field. On occasion, senior staff officers went so far as to divert entire trains and sell their contents on the black market. With their men clothed in rags and shod only in bark shoes as they fought through snowdrifts, desperate commanders at the front began to take supplies from each other at gunpoint in the spring of 1919.[72]

Kolchak had come to power preaching "victory over Bolshevism" at a time when Trotskii's new Red Army was marching from victory to victory on its eastern front. Led by the indefatigable twenty-five-year-old idolizer of Napoleon and one-time imperial page Mikhail Tukhachevskii, the First Red Army had stormed into the Komuch government's former capital at Samara on October 8, less than a month after it had smashed across the Volga at Simbirsk. Supported by the Fourth and Fifth Red Armies on his right and left flanks, Tukhachevskii then had pressed on to take both Orenburg and Ufa before the end of the year. By the beginning of 1919, his armies stood in the western foothills of the southern Urals.

Further to Tukhachevskii's north, the Second Red Army had crossed the Volga above Kazan to march against Izhevsk, home of the Izhevsk Armament Works and nerve center of the best-known and most enduring working-class rebellion against the Bolsheviks during the entire Civil War. Early that August, Izhevsk had burst into revolt, and its citizens had formed the Izhevsk People's Army, which, within a month, had seized eight thousand square miles of territory with a population of nearly a million. The capture of Izhevsk by the Second Red Army after nearly a month of fighting on November 7 had crushed the revolt, but it left the Third Red Army on the extreme left flank of the front without support when the Reds had encountered heavy White opposition between Perm and Ekaterinburg.[73] While the Second, Fifth, First, and Fourth Red Armies had advanced during the last weeks of 1918, the Third Army therefore had stumbled and then collapsed as its soldiers retreated two hundred miles in twenty days. "The morale and efficiency of the army were deplorable owing to the weariness of the units, the result of six months of continuous fighting without relief," Stalin and Dzerzhinskii concluded when they investigated the disaster.[74]

As the soldiers of the Third Red Army struggled through deep snow and temperatures that stood at thirty-five degrees below zero, their morale broke. The commanders of the Third Army's engineers and transport groups and many other senior officers defected to the Whites, causing Stalin and Dzerzhinskii to lash out once again at Trotskii's policy of recruiting former tsarist officers into the Red Army. On the day before Christmas, the battle-weary soldiers of the Third Red Army, some of whom begged their comrades to shoot them to spare them from going on, finally gave up Perm, center of the Ural mining industry and home of the Motovilikha Artillery Works.[75] As the Whites stormed into the city, they captured a treasure trove of spoils. Reluctantly, the Reds admitted that their losses included at least 43,000 tons of coal, 1.2 million tons of ore, nearly 350,000 tons of smelted and manufactured metals, 297 locomotives, 3,000 freight cars, 250 machine guns, 20,000 rifles, 10,000 shells, 10 million rifle cartridges, and nearly 20,000 men.[76]

As heavy blizzards and paralyzing cold made further offensives impossible at the beginning of 1919, Reds and Whites regrouped their forces. Perhaps encouraged by the unexpected fall of Perm, probably enticed by the will-o'-the-wisp of linking his forces with the Anglo-American force in North Russia and launching a joint assault against Moscow, and certainly too envious of Denikin's growing success in the South to consider forcing his advance in that direction, Kolchak positioned nearly half of his 112,000 troops to face the Second and Third Red Armies in the northern Perm-Viatka sector of his front more than six hundred miles north and west of Denikin's forces.[77]

Anxious not to lose the momentum he had gained with the capture of Perm, Kolchak hurried to resume his offensive even though heavy snow still clogged the mountain passes that connected his front and rear. On March 6, he attacked the Fifth Red Army, and within a week the Whites had retaken Ufa, split the Bolsheviks' eastern front at the point where the Fifth and Second Red Armies joined, and broadened their advance to cover a front that stretched nearly seven hundred miles from the deep forests of the northern Urals to the Orenburg steppes. By the middle of April, the Whites had driven a wedge more than a hundred miles wide between the Fifth and Second Red Armies and had regained nearly two hundred thousand square miles of territory with a population of more than five million. Their advance units stood less than sixty miles from Samara, less than seventy from Simbirsk, and a mere fifty-six miles from Kazan.[78] At one point, ski detachments from some of Kolchak's northernmost positions met reconnaissance forces from the Russo-Allied forces in North Russia.[79] It was the closest Kolchak's forces ever came to linking up with any other White front.

For the Reds, Kolchak's victories represented an unlooked-for and shocking setback. At first Lenin minimized the danger. "Victory will be ours," he promised at the end of March. "The Red Army is invincible because it has united millions of working peasants with the workers, who . . . become steeled after slight reverses and are more and more boldly marching against the enemy."[80] The enemies the Red Army faced in Siberia, he told a plenary meeting of the Moscow Soviet a few days later, were "the forces of a decrepit, dying, hopelessly sick old man—international capitalism."

Nonetheless, he dared not conceal from his listeners that Kolchak's "gangs of volunteer White Guards" were "of imposing dimensions" and were receiving "vast quantities of arms and munitions" from England and the United States.[81] "Kolchak's victories on the eastern front are creating an extremely grave danger for the Soviet Republic," he reported to the Bolsheviks' Central Committee a week after. "Our efforts must be exerted to the utmost to smash Kolchak."[82]

So serious did Lenin think the danger that he dared not rely only upon exhortation, political propaganda, and coercion to assemble the reserves needed to shore up the Bolsheviks' crumbling defenses in the foothills of the Urals. "It must be made clear to every mobilized man," he insisted, "that his immediate departure for the front will mean an improvement in his food situation."[83] At the front, he promised Petrograd's hungry proletarians, "soldier workers . . . will obtain food for themselves and will be able to send food parcels to their families."[84] "We need methods that are new, decisive, and revolutionary," he insisted to his comrades on the Bolsheviks' Central Committee. "By giving each [volunteer] the right to send two twenty-pound parcels of food home each month, and by allowing these parcels to be sent free of charge, we shall, at the same time, improve the food situation of our starving capitals and northern provinces."[85]

As always, Lenin and the Central Committee relied upon dedicated Communists to instill courage in their less resolute comrades in the most dangerous areas of the front. Petrograd sent a special battalion of elite workers, and the Executive Committee of Penza province sent a Communist shock regiment. The West Russian city of Vitebsk assigned one union member in five to the struggle against Kolchak, and Novgorod assigned one out of every two. Bolshevik party organizations in Moscow, Vologda, Kaluga, and Nizhnii-Novgorod sent at least one member in ten and sometimes as many as one in four.[86] In April, nearly a thousand dedicated Communists joined the battered Third Red Army in the defensive positions it had taken up a hundred miles to the west of Perm, while specially chosen men from twenty-two provinces converged on assembly points at Viatka, Kazan, Simbirsk, and Samara to march to the aid of their beleaguered comrades at the front.[87]

Before the end of May, some twenty thousand Bolshevik party members and another sixty thousand elite workers had been sent to the East. The newly organized Komsomol, the Communist Youth

League, sent three thousand of its best members, while the Central Committee arranged for ten to twenty thousand peasants who had proved their dedication to the Bolshevik cause to be sent from each county.[88] "Peasants!" a special newspaper published by a propaganda train named *October Revolution* exclaimed. "It is now your turn to defend what the Revolution has won for you. Kolchak is coming to take away your lands and to make you slaves of the landlords and village police chiefs again. Poor peasants to arms! Everyone into the battle against Kolchak!"[89] At the same time, "Papa" Kalinin, the peasant who had risen to become president of the Bolsheviks' All-Russian Executive Committee, added his own special summons. "Let us strengthen the fraternal union between the workers and peasants!" he urged. "Smash the evil band of landlords and capitalists!"[90]

Determined Communist fighters alone could not defeat Kolchak's White armies. The scathing report that Stalin and Dzerzhinskii had submitted to the Bolsheviks' Central Committee at the end of January about the Third Army's collapse had admittedly been shaped partly as an attack against Trotskii and Vatsetis, but it also had contained some hard and painful conclusions that had to be taken seriously. Entire regiments and battalions had deserted under fire, and others had melted away as they marched to relieve battered front-line units. At least two regiments of the Third Red Army had attacked their comrades in the rear. One entire brigade had been ordered into battle before many of its men had learned how to use their rifles. A key bridge had not been destroyed when the army retreated from Perm, no evacuation plan had been prepared, and little had been done to protect the railroads in the army's rear against sabotage.[91] More generally, some of the problems that had afflicted the Third Army affected the entire eastern front. "The practice of fighting without reserves must be stopped," Stalin and Dzerzhinskii warned. "[Otherwise] disaster will be inevitable." Yet reserves could not be deployed without better communications and a more effective chain of command. "An army cannot operate as a self-contained and absolutely autonomous unit," Stalin and Dzerzhinskii emphasized. "It is necessary to establish . . . a system of strictly centralized control of the operations of various armies."[92]

Their conclusions proved by Kolchak's continued successes, Stalin's and Dzerzhinskii's stern warnings brought new commanders to the front and sent others to the rear. None proved more vital to the success of the coming campaign than Mikhail Vasilevich

Frunze, the thirty-three-year-old Bolshevik millworker whose first battle experience had come when he had led a brigade of Moscow workers and soldiers against the forces of the Provisional Government in October 1917. As the Civil War had spread across Russia, Frunze had displayed a talent for organization and a flair for succeeding at difficult tasks. At first he had worked in the rear of the Red Army to organize new units and supply ones already in the field. Yet Frunze was not a man to be satisfied with rear-echelon service. For the better part of a year, his pleas for a front-line command fell on deaf ears. Then, on the day after Stalin and Dzerzhinskii submitted their report to Lenin and the Central Committee, Frunze received command of the disgruntled and rebellious Fourth Red Army near Orsk, some three hundred miles south and east of Ufa. The mutinous men of the Fourth Army quickly learned that their young commander, who wore his beard neatly trimmed and his cavalry forage cap set at the jaunty angle favored by enlisted men of the time, had a will of iron and a heart of steel. Charged with anchoring the right flank of the eastern front, Frunze quickly instituted a strict regime that enabled him to hold the army together even as Kolchak's Cossacks forced it to retreat toward Orenburg and Uralsk.[93]

Kolchak's victories in March and April 1919 proved less decisive than they appeared at first, and the Reds soon began to profit from the tactical, strategic, and logistical problems that Siberia's supreme ruler could not put to rest. As had been the case with Denikin, disorder caused by corrupt subordinates and large numbers of proletarians sympathetic to the Bolsheviks in his newly occupied lands forced Kolchak to fight his battles in 1919 with his rear areas in turmoil. Omsk itself had a large and volatile contingent of workers, most of whom found employment in the railway workshops of Kulomzino, a proletarian suburb that had grown up across the river from the main part of the city, and Perm had its nearby Motovilikha Works, which for two centuries had produced cannon for the Russian army. These employed thousands of men and women who shared the Bolsheviks' vision of Russia's future. So did many more workshops in the smaller manufacturing centers that Kolchak's troops occupied as they moved across the Urals into European Russia.

The bitterness that Kolchak's corrupt officials stirred among workers who feared a future in which they would be ruled by a government that bore disturbing similarities to the tsarist regime surfaced very quickly. Anxious to crush all socialists of whatever stamp, Kolchak had decreed strict censorship for all newspapers and journals the day he took power, and he had moved quickly to organize a large counterintelligence service. Nonetheless, the Bolsheviks had kept a small core of conspirators within Omsk itself, and on December 22, these had led the railroad workers of Kulomzino in revolt. With seventy-two firearms (fifty of which were single-shot Berdan rifles left over from the Russo-Turkish War of 1877), three hand grenades, and four sabers among them, their midnight uprising had little hope of success, especially since Kolchak's counterintelligence almost certainly knew their plans beforehand. Still, the Bolshevik rebels seized the city prison and freed more than a hundred political prisoners before the government forces crushed them with heavy gunfire.[94]

One could hardly expect Kolchak's officers to be any less brutal in crushing the Omsk uprising than the Bolsheviks had been in dealing with the revolt of the Left Socialist Revolutionaries in Moscow and Iaroslavl the previous summer, and the figure of nearly five hundred men and women killed in the fighting and executed by firing squads seems scarcely out of the ordinary in the atmosphere of deepening vengeance that marked Russia's Civil War. Far more shocking were fifteen executions carried out on the bank of the Irtysh River soon after the revolt had been crushed. Most of these victims had been prisoners whom the Bolsheviks had driven forcibly from Omsk Prison, and as members of the Constituent Assembly who believed in legality and despised the Bolsheviks as thoroughly as did Kolchak's men, they had returned to prison of their own free will. Their faith in White justice had cost them their lives. On the very night they had returned, one of Kolchak's lieutenants had taken them to a field court-martial, and when it had refused to convict them without evidence, he had shot them all. Nil Fomin, a gentle man of high and generous principles who had played a key role in overthrowing the Bolsheviks in a number of Siberian cities that spring and summer, had been among them.[95]

Kolchak later complained that such senseless acts of violence had been part of an effort to discredit him in the eyes of those Allied representatives at Omsk who were trying to convince their governments to support him. Yet such brutality could not help but be a part of any struggle in which men fought for ideologies and killed to eradicate visions of the future that did not coincide with their own. Prisoners reported seeing people "who were literally covered with wounds and their flesh torn by flogging with iron rods"[96] before they met their deaths in ways that shocked men dedicated to legality, justice, and the preservation of human life. "We are returning to the prehistoric period in human history," one newspaper lamented in defiance of Kolchak's censorship decrees. "We are verging on the death of human civilization and its culture . . . for which so many generations of our more worthy ancestors have labored."[97]

Such mindless brutality did violence to the human spirit, yet it paled next to the tortures that the vicious renegade Cossack chieftains Semenov and Kalmykov inflicted upon their victims in the wild Siberian regions to the east of Lake Baikal. Twenty-seven at the time of the Bolshevik Revolution, Semenov had grown up in Russia's Transbaikal lands. The son of a prosperous Cossack father and a Buriat mother, he had entered the army in 1911 and had become a junior officer before the Great War. General Wrangel, who first met him when he took command of the Nerchinsk Cossacks on the Transcaucasus front during the winter of 1916, thought him "an exemplary soldier, especially courageous when under the eye of his superior,"[98] an observation that was not particularly difficult to make since Semenov wore the coveted St. George's Cross for extraordinary valor. Like so many able men of obscure origin, Semenov's fortunes had soared after the February Revolution. Kerenskii had sent him to the Far East to recruit a Mongolian division, and when the Bolsheviks had seized power, Semenov had turned those troops against them. Until the Czech Legion had taken up arms against the Bolsheviks, his had been the only significant anti-Bolshevik force in Siberia. With Japanese support, he had turned the lands immediately east of Lake Baikal into a private fiefdom, with its capital at Chita.[99]

As other anti-Bolshevik forces had taken shape in Siberia during the second half of 1918, the British, French, and Americans had turned away from Semenov to leaders they thought more honorable and reliable. Especially America's General Graves scorned Semenov as "a murderer, robber, and a most dissolute scoundrel [who] . . . could not have existed one week in Siberia if he had not had the protection of Japan."[100] With Japanese gold, weapons, and ammunition, Semenov wielded undisputed power in the Trans-Baikal region throughout Kolchak's reign. There, he instituted a regime of terror and coercion that enabled him to confiscate the wealth of men and women who lived under his authority and steal anything that passed through his domains along the Trans-Siberian

Railway. General Graves reported that his robberies included a half-million dollars' worth of furs that belonged to a company in New York City.[101] At one point, he even demanded fifteen thousand rifles from the Americans as a price for allowing another thirty-five thousand to reach Kolchak's forces.[102] Innocent men and women dangled by the scores from telegraph poles in the vicinity of his capital,[103] and his men machine-gunned freight cars full of victims at execution fields along the railway. "The bodies had been placed into two ditches," an appalled American soldier reported after he had visited the scene of one such mass murder. "In one ditch the bodies were entirely covered; in the other ditch many arms or legs were left uncovered."[104] Not surprisingly, being a Bolshevik or aiding the Bolsheviks was more than enough reason for a capital sentence in Semenov's domains. Yet Semenov executed most of his victims either to satisfy a whim or on the far more nebulous charge of being guilty of having "hindered mobilization."[105]

Semenov owed a portion of his success to the wit, wisdom, and tactical genius of Baron Roman Ungern-Sternberg, perhaps the most bizarre of his lieutenants and certainly one of the most cruel. Once described by General Wrangel as "the type that is invaluable in wartime and impossible in times of peace," Ungern-Sternberg, like Semenov, had been a squadron commander in the Nerchinsk Cossacks under Wrangel's command, and also like Semenov, he wore the St. George's Cross. Physically, mentally, and morally, he was a tangle of contradictions. Wrangel thought him "fair and puny-looking" but quickly discovered that he had "an iron constitution and ruthless energy." Although appalled by the baron's personal uncleanliness and lack of military bearing, Wrangel also remembered him as a man having the "shyness of a savage." Not a professional soldier, Ungern-Sternberg was a hunter and a killer of men. "War was his natural element," Wrangel concluded. "He was not an officer, but a hero out of one of Mayne Reid's novels."[106]

Wrangel's estimate, formed from remembrances of times before the Revolution unleashed men's capricious madness, supplies only a partial measure of the man upon whom Semenov relied to extend his power into the far-flung lands of Mongolia that lay to the south of the Trans-Siberian Railway. The accounts of those who knew Ungern-Sternberg during the Civil War paint a terrifying picture of a man grown used to killing and, perhaps, unhinged by having held too long the power of life and death over others. Baron

Budberg once called him a "specialist in floggings and shootings,"[107] and by his orders, men and women suffered death by beating, hanging, beheading, disemboweling, and countless other tortures that transformed them from living human beings into what one witness called a "formless bloody mass."[108] Ungern-Sternberg's staff physician described one of his written orders as "the product of the diseased brain of a pervert and a megalomaniac affected with a thirst for human blood" and recalled how he "suddenly shrieked in falsetto" when he wanted to add emphasis to his remarks. His fixed gaze made men feel as if he wanted "to leap into [their] souls." In Ungern-Sternberg's presence, this man who had dedicated himself to the preservation of life wrote, "I felt that my life was hanging by a hair."[109]

With Ungern-Sternberg, Semenov controlled nearly a quarter million square miles of lands between Lake Baikal and the point where the Shilka River flows into the Amur. Further to the east, the sadistic bandit Ivan Kalmykov, who also was supported by the Japanese, ruled from Khabarovsk, a dreary, chilly, eastern Siberian provincial town where the average annual temperature stood just one degree above freezing. Not yet thirty, with snakelike eyes that flicked from face to face, and curls that spilled over his forehead from beneath a tight-fitting karakul cap, Kalmykov had fought with Semenov and Ungern-Sternberg in the ranks of the Nerchinsk Cossacks during the First World War and owed his position as ataman of the Ussuri Cossacks to having murdered the legitimate candidate for the position in the fall of 1918.[110] No one ever thought him trustworthy, and General Graves once called him "the worst scoundrel I ever saw or heard of."[111] According to one report, Kalmykov ordered the summary execution of his entire "Military Juridical Department" because he disliked some of the sentences they imposed.[112] He was, in the words of Baron Budberg, who lived some months under Kalmykov's regime before he became a high-ranking official at Kolchak's supreme headquarters, "a fully qualified war criminal."[113] Early in 1919, men who lacked Kalmykov's stomach for senseless killings mutinied against him and sought sanctuary at General Graves' headquarters.[114] After that, only men who shared Kalmykov's perverted pleasure in the killing of innocents remained under his command.

Kalmykov, Semenov, and Ungern-Sternberg were only the most notorious of an appallingly unprincipled group of men who violated the laws of God, man, and nature with impunity in Russia's Far East during the dark days of 1918 and 1919. "[He] devotes himself exclusively to drinking and disorderly conduct," one War Ministry report said of Ataman I. N. Krasilnikov, the Cossack officer whose men had played a key role in Kolchak's rise to power but refused all orders to fight against the Red Army on the Ural front in 1919. "[His] soldiers violate women, carry out arbitrary searches for the purpose of robbery," the report continued. "The whole population is eager for Bolshevism. The situation is critical."[115] At the other end of Kolchak's domains, General Sergei Rozanov, a tsarist army officer who first joined the Bolsheviks and then defected to the Whites to become Kolchak's plenipotentiary in the Far East, took hostages by the hundreds and killed them by the dozens. General Pavel Ivanov-Rinov rivaled Rozanov's cruelty and surpassed his graft to such a degree that, according to reliable sources, he spent two hundred thousand rubles on two banquets in Vladivostok while the ragged men in his command starved.[116]

Together, these men produced what Russians called the *atamanshchina*, the reign of terror by robber princes and false Cossack chieftains supported by Japanese guns and Japanese gold that so effectively destroyed the stability of Kolchak's rear when the Reds renewed their advance in the spring of 1919. "The influence of *atamanshchina* is spreading wider and wider and becoming more and more dangerous," Baron Budberg wrote at the end of March. "They wanted to create a force to shatter Bolshevism," he lamented, "but ended up only helping the Bolsheviks by giving them a priceless opportunity to prove that their repeated warnings that the 'Hydra of counterrevolution has raised its bloody head' were based on facts."[117] A month later, Budberg added: "[*atamanshchina*] is helping Bolshevism more than all the preachings and propaganda of comrades Lenin and Trotskii put together."[118] Sadly he confided to his diary what he feared must be the end result: "*Finis Rossiae!*"[119]

Nor was arbitrariness, corruption, and unfettered cruelty limited to those areas where the *atamanshchina* held sway. "All over Siberia . . . there is an orgy of arrest without charges; of execution without even the pretense of trial; and confiscation without color of authority," America's Ambassador Roland Morris reported. "Fear—panic fear has seized everyone. Men suspect each other and live in constant terror that some spy or enemy will cry 'Bolshevik' and condemn them to instant death."[120] To General Graves it seemed that the word "Bolshevik" applied to "everyone who did not support Kolchak and the autocratic class surrounding him. . . . The political meaning of the word 'Bolshevik,' as used in Siberia," Graves concluded, "took in all the representatives of such [elected] Zemstvo organizations [of local self-government] as were opposed to the ideas of Kolchak."[121] In fact, Kolchak found it difficult to tolerate any sort of opposition and reacted very badly to it. "He pounded the table with his fist, flung everything onto the floor, seized a penknife, and angrily slashed the arm of his chair," Georgii Gins, deputy minister of education and executive secretary of the government, wrote of Kolchak during a meeting he had with several ministers who had asked to discuss improvements in the government's nearly immobile transportation system. "Leave me in peace!" Gins remembered him shouting. "I forbid you to bring up such questions. Today I am going to the Council of Ministers and will order that . . . there will be *ab-so-lute-ly* no reforms."[122]

Kolchak's unstable personality, his inability to choose subordinates, and his utter inexperience with land warfare aggravated the problems caused by the turmoil in his rear. Under pressure, he lost his temper too often, turned against men who spoke the truth too openly, and exhibited all those mean characteristics of a man whom Fate has burdened with responsibilities beyond his limited abilities. Almost daily from his office in Kolchak's War Ministry, Baron Budberg poured forth laments about the "utter disorganization," the "kaleidoscopic change in moods and decisions," "the professional illiteracy" of the army's high command, and the "childish temper and conceit" of Kolchak and his councillors. "Many have already taken refuge in alcohol and cocaine," Budberg noted as he spoke of "our inability to organize a real army and put talented and knowledgeable people in responsible positions." Corruption, moral decay, intrigues, and gross self-interest had thoroughly saturated Kolchak's Russia even before it had been fully created. "The poison of *atamanshchina* and the sweetness of living beyond the law has penetrated too deeply everywhere," Budberg concluded sadly. "In all likelihood, it will devour us and then will perish in its own stench."[123]

The stench was everywhere. "The sharp, acrid, heavily charged atmosphere of political struggle, of party and personal interests, of greed [and] speculation by politicians, merchants, and contractors, has enshrouded [us] in a stinking fog," Budberg wrote.[124] Like Budberg, other sensible men sensed the danger that

Kolchak's reactionary advisers posed to the vision of a free Russia. "The general political situation is confusing, disturbing, and unstable," the Kadet Nikolai Ustrialov wrote. "The darkest, most mindless sort of military reaction is developing. It's like living on top of a volcano all the time. Few have any real hope of defeating the Bolsheviks."[125] Yet, for Ustrialov, the prospect of victory seemed scarcely more comforting. "This is not the new Russia, this is not the future . . . and there's nothing to celebrate in its triumph," he confided to his diary. "This is not the avant-garde of a renovated system of government," he concluded at the beginning of February. "It is the rear-guard of a past that is slipping into eternity."[126]

Certain that Kolchak's government represented their best hope, Imperial Russia's fallen lords, landlords, bankers, politicians, and high officials had converged on Omsk in 1919 in hopes of regaining what the revolutions of 1917 had taken from them. They had come with their wives, their children, and their mistresses to live as best they could in a city whose population had risen nearly sixfold above its normal hundred thousand in a few weeks. Men and women used to large mansions and luxurious apartments now lived in single rooms, yet they all sensed a dramatic improvement over life in the Russia from which they had fled. "We live well here," Ustrialov wrote as he compared life in Omsk with the "Moscow chaos" of the previous year. "The geese are extremely fat. Every day a milkmaid brings a jug of milk, and there's as much sugar as anyone could want."[127] Yet such plenty proved to be a cruel and passing illusion at best. As hordes of hopeful men and women poured into Omsk, prices soared. In the space of a few months, the cost of flour rose by a fifth, salt by a quarter, and sugar and oil by a sixth. The price of bread and meat both doubled and that of tea tripled.[128] Victimized by rampant speculation at home and the depredations of Semenov and Kalmykov to the east, the economy of Kolchak's Russia began to crumble.

This proved to be but one of many signs that heralded the fall of Siberia's supreme ruler. Despite Trotskii's misgivings, the Red high command in April had given Frunze a force that included the Turkestan Army and the First, Fourth, and Fifth Red Armies. "Almost everywhere our forces were falling back," Frunze later wrote as he recalled the conditions under which he took up his new command. "We needed not only a colossal will but a clear and certain belief that only by going over to the attack could our situation be changed for the better."[129] Supported by factories that more than doubled their production of rifles, machine guns, shells, and bullets between April and July,[130] Frunze assembled his forces near Buzuluk, a rail depot about halfway between Samara and Orenburg. After promising his men that "with firm faith in the rightness of its cause, the Red Army will achieve miracles,"[131] he launched an attack toward Buguruslan and Bugulma to the northeast. "Soldiers of the Red Army!" Frunze's general order of April 10 proclaimed. "Forward to the final decisive battle against the hireling of capitalism Kolchak! Forward to a joyful and shining future for working people!"[132] Aiming his attack with unerring precision, Frunze struck Kolchak's advancing armies in the flank and the rear to begin some of the most bloody fighting of the entire Civil War.

Frunze's first victories opened the way for the Red Army to begin a general offensive against Kolchak's forces on April 28. Urged on by Frunze's general orders, and reinforced by men sent from local Bolshevik organizations all across Russia, the Reds began an advance against the Whites that made heroes by the dozens and earned some of the leading Soviet World War II commanders their spurs. Vasilii Chuikov, who later commanded at Stalingrad, launched the Soviet assault against Warsaw, and opened the attack against Berlin in the final days of World War II, commanded the Fortieth Red Infantry in those days, and Dmitrii Karbyshev, one of Brusilov's brilliant young strategists in 1916 who became a Hero of the Soviet Union in 1946, fortified several key centers in Russia's Trans-Volga provinces. Within a fortnight, Frunze's advance seemed so certain that *Pravda* had begun to describe it as "methodical."[133] By the middle of the month, Frunze's forces had forced Kolchak's front lines back a hundred miles, and not even the bitter disputes between Trotskii, Stalin, and their factions in the Red High Command that changed the commander-in-chief of the eastern front three times in as many weeks could halt his advance. "Our first step is to take Ufa," Frunze announced to the men of the Turkestan Red Army. "Our last will be [to see] all of Siberia freed from Kolchak!"[134] "The initiative has shifted into the hands of the Reds," Baron Budberg wrote from Kolchak's War Ministry in Omsk. "Our offensive has played itself out."[135] "It has become necessary to ask," he confided to his diary a week later, "if we shall be able to hold the Urals."[136]

As Frunze's forces pushed eastward, Kolchak's defenses began to crumble. Perhaps fearful of another unexpected reversal, and certainly impatient to cross the Urals quickly, Lenin urged his commanders to be vigilant. "Exert all forces to the utmost," he telegraphed to the men at the eastern front headquarters. "You are responsible for seeing to it that your units do not begin to break apart and that they don't lose courage."[137] With the taste of victory ever fresh in their mouths, and supported by the Second and Third Red Armies to the North, Frunze's men continued their advance, while Kolchak desperately shifted commanders, placing his confidence first in the arrogant, inept Czech General Rudolf Gaida, then in the sober but timid former tsarist staff officer Mikhail Diterikhs, and then in the stupid and cocksure Dmitrii Lebedev. None could stem Frunze's assault upon the Urals. By the beginning of June, Frunze's divisions were approaching Ufa, where Kolchak's commanders had begun their offensive six months before. On June 8, Frunze himself suffered a concussion when a White shell exploded nearby. His adjutant remembered how the elite White shock battalions of General Kappel—all of them men who had won the Cross of St. George during the First World War—had advanced the next morning "with fixed bayonets, silent, holding their fire" in their last effort to stem the Red advance at Ufa. "With the skull and crossbones insignia mounted on their caps, sleeves, and epaulettes," he wrote, "they made a terrifying impression" as they attacked through a field of rye.[138] When the Reds' machine guns cut Kappel's battalions apart, others took their places until more than three thousand of Russia's bravest and best soldiers lay dead before the Red positions. That night, the men of the Twenty-fifth Rifle Division, whose legendary commander Vasilii Chapaev had been wounded in the struggle, occupied Ufa. Further to the north, the Second Red Army had taken Izhevsk two days before, and within a fortnight, the workers in the weapons factories of Izhevsk had begun to produce five hundred rifles a day for the Red Army.[139]

Frunze's victory at Ufa posed a critical question for the Red high command. Certain that Kolchak had greater reserves behind the Urals, Trotskii and Vatsetis wanted to concentrate upon destroying Denikin's forces in the South and wait until spring before they pursued Kolchak further. Stalin's faction, and particularly Kamenev as commander of the eastern front, insisted that the Urals could be breached and Kolchak's defenses shattered before winter.[140] Kamenev's position particularly appealed to Lenin. "Mobilize three quarters of the members of the Party and the workers' unions," he telegraphed to eastern front headquarters the day Ufa fell. "Now we must work in a truly revolutionary fashion."[141] Now in command of the Fifth Red Army, Tukhachevskii by that time already had completed his plans for breaching the Urals and moving into the western Siberian plain. By the end of the month, the mountains had been crossed, their eastern foothills taken, and the Fifth Army stood poised to assault Zlatoust.[142] Once that key center fell on July 13, the way to Cheliabinsk and Omsk lay open. Kolchak's future had become very uncertain. "It is estimated," General Graves reported, "that on July 1, outside the office holding and military class, the Omsk Government had less than 1% of followers."[143] Baron Budberg stated the matter even more bluntly. "Once the Urals were lost," he wrote in his diary, "the central government needed to be not at Omsk but Irkutsk [some 1,500 miles further east], on the frontier between eastern and western Siberia."[144]

The Reds' victories in May and June raised tensions in Kolchak's government to a fever pitch. Men became more selfish and violent, less willing to compromise, and desperate to find a scapegoat. Kolchak supporters launched a pogrom against the Jews in Ekaterinburg in July that claimed some two thousand casualties, which, in view of the city's comparatively small Jewish population, counted as an appalling massacre.[145] In Omsk, the Kadet Ustrialov, who had come from Moscow to serve in Kolchak's government, wrote that "people are packing suitcases, and the 'poor' openly rejoice and wait for the Bolsheviks to arrive." With a fatalism that had become typical of all too many in Kolchak's Russia, Ustrialov dismissed what he called "the empiricism of savages" and concluded that one could live only for the moment. "One lives a tense and intense life," he wrote. The summer heat, the "dusty, airless streets of Omsk," all seemed to close in on the dying Kolchak government. "Will we have to flee again?" Ustrialov asked. "Why? Where? Isn't it all pointless?"[146] Even the cold, businesslike Budberg admitted the strain. "[After a meeting of the Council of Ministers] I came home feeling as mean as the devil," he confessed to his diary in mid-July. "Can one really call this a government?" he asked himself. "Can one really call this clique of second-rate citizens who have fastened themselves onto Omsk a government?"[147]

That summer, the cities of western Siberia fell like dominoes before the Red Army's advance. White soldiers surrendered by the thousands. Others fled even before they saw the enemy. As they advanced, the Reds gathered priceless rolling stock, weapons, and supplies. At the important rail terminal of Cheliabinsk, "the gateway to the granary of Russia," as some called it, Tukhachevskii's Fifth Red Army took 15,000 prisoners and seized more than 3,500 freight cars and nearly three dozen locomotives.[148] "You ordered us to take the Urals before winter," Tukhachevskii's soldiers wrote to Lenin on August 9. "The Urals are ours. We are now moving into Siberia."[149] "The front has completely collapsed," Budberg admitted as he surveyed the damage from Kolchak's War Ministry. By the middle of August, the Whites had fewer than fifteen thousand men still in the field, a mere fifth of the force they had commanded at the beginning of May. Divisions had shrunk to less than a thousand men, and some regiments had no more than a hundred. "It is impossible to attack because we have no infantry," Budberg explained. "In the government there is moral rot, dissension, and intrigues by men ruled only by ambition and egotism. In the countryside there is rebellion and anarchy. In society, panic, crude self-interest, bribery, and every sort of loathsome behavior reign supreme."[150] In vain did Kolchak call for a "holy war" against the Reds, woo Siberia's Cossacks and peasants with promises of greater democracy, and warn his followers that "no one, except yourselves, will defend or save you."[151] Not even the bitter cold of Siberia's approaching winter could freeze the triumphant Red tide that surged toward the East.

If sin has a price, the corruption and gross self-interest of the men who governed Kolchak's Russia proved costly indeed. In no other theater of the Civil War did the masses support the Reds more energetically than in Siberia during 1919. All across the four thousand miles that separated Cheliabinsk from Vladivostok, peasants long accustomed to thinking and acting more independently than their European Russian brethren, workers who saw no advantage in the return of Imperial Russia's world of industrial exploitation, and others to whom Kolchak's privilege-ridden Russia offered no vision of a better future took to the woods and hills that stretched along the Trans-Siberian Railway to attack supply trains and harass small detachments of White regulars as they moved through the countryside. Some carried rifles, pistols, sabers, even a hand grenade or two, but others had no better weapons than pitchforks or axes. Some partisan regiments could arm only every third or fourth man with a rifle. In one, there was one rifle for every fifteen. Particularly in western Siberia, where many peasants had experience smelting and casting iron, partisan blacksmiths produced crude homemade cannon in desperate attempts to match the Whites' superior weapons. Yet given their location, hundreds—even thousands—of miles behind Kolchak's front lines, Siberia's partisan units inevitably suffered desperate shortages of weapons and ammunition that no amount of ingenuity could offset.[152]

In some cases, Siberia's partisans formed special units that fought throughout the entire year against Kolchak. In the Transbaikal region south of Nerchinsk, the Forest Commune was one such force. Further to the west, the Peasant Red Army of Western Siberia, which at one time claimed a strength of more than fifteen thousand, was another. Where they were not strong enough to fight as combat units in the field, the partisans spread their secret organizations through Siberia's villages and used them to organize peasant uprisings. One group of Red partisans in central Siberia claimed to have organizations in more than five hundred peasant villages and did considerable damage to a force of twelve thousand that Kolchak sent against them in the summer of 1919. Further to the west, in the region south of Cheliabinsk, another uprising put more than twenty-five thousand peasants into the field before Kolchak's regular forces crushed it in April 1919. "Their hatred is terrible to behold," one White officer reported to his superiors. "Even women and twelve-year-old children are fighting against us."[153]

Red Army soldiers flushed with four months of uninterrupted victories at his front and tight-lipped partisans and raging peasants in his rear, Kolchak faced a desperate situation as the first anniversary of his November coup drew near. Before the middle of August, the Reds had taken Uralsk, Orenburg, Ekaterinburg, and Cheliabinsk. As summer turned to fall, they moved more quickly and covered most of the five hundred miles that separated Cheliabinsk from Omsk by late October. "The unloading—that is, the evacuation—of Omsk has been announced," Ustrialov wrote at the end of October. "At the front things are bad, 'catastrophic,' in fact. The fall of Omsk, evidently, is inevitable." Ustrialov spoke of mass panic, of people so desperate to flee that they went on foot when there were no trains. He felt fortunate to be leaving in a heated freight car. "If we actually reach Irkutsk," he asked, "what lies ahead? A reprieve? Will it be for a year, a week, or one night?" While he waited to leave Omsk, Ustrialov surveyed the ruins of the White movement. "Everywhere they are fleeing," he wrote in his diary. "Iudenich has been beaten [at Petrograd], Denikin is in retreat. The counterrevolution has been smashed. Hail revolution," he added in Latin. "We who are about to die salute you!"[154] One well-informed White journalist later reported that, when Kolchak's Council of Ministers left Omsk on November 10, they had to bribe senior railway officials before their train was allowed to leave.[155] "State authority in Omsk," General Budberg added from the hospital bed to which he had been evacuated because of a liver infection, "has become a ghostly mirage."[156] Four days later, on November 14, the Reds occupied Omsk and found that the Whites had abandoned three armored trains, two hundred locomotives, three thousand railroad cars, and a half million artillery shells, along with more than forty thousand prisoners of war, including a thousand officers.[157]

They did not capture Kolchak, for he had left Omsk on November 12 with the last of the imperial gold reserve that the Komuch forces had seized at Kazan more than a year before. His ministers had made the 1,534-mile journey from Omsk to Irkutsk without great difficulty, but Kolchak now found that his delay of forty-eight hours had cost him dearly. Shuttled back and forth and shunted onto sidings by sullen railroad workers at every station, his train moved at a painful pace. Two weeks passed, then three, then four. Slowly, Kolchak and his entourage moved toward Irkutsk, their route perpetually blocked by disabled trains and by Czech legionnaires, who used the opportunity to settle scores with a White leader whose politics and person they despised. At times, advance Bolshevik units captured trains that followed in Kolchak's wake. As his journey passed into its second month, their front line moved more rapidly than his train. Briefly, Kolchak considered fleeing into Mongolia rather than trying to rejoin his senior statesmen in Irkutsk, but events overwhelmed him. At one point he gave his personal guard the choice between going with him or joining the Bolsheviks. Almost to a man, the men in whose loyalty he had believed absolutely repaid his trust by joining the Bolsheviks. Even some of his officers suggested that he ought to place himself under the protection of the Allies because they could flee into Mongolia more easily without him. By early January, Kolchak had been reduced to traveling in a single second-class Pullman car that flew the flags of England, the United States, France, Japan, and Czechoslovakia.[158]

While Kolchak struggled to rejoin his government at Irkutsk, the last vestiges of his authority crumbled. The Czech General

Gaida, an Austrian army deserter who had begun his military career as a hospital orderly and had risen to become the commander of Kolchak's northern armies as they had advanced westward beyond Perm at the beginning of the year, staged a revolt against Kolchak's authority in Vladivostok on November 17 that was put down only at the cost of many Russian lives.[159] Then, on Christmas Eve, revolt burst out in Irkutsk itself with a coalition of vengeful Mensheviks and Socialist Revolutionaries seeking to oust Kolchak from power. Less than a fortnight later, on January 5, they took control, announcing the formation of a government called the Political Center, which proclaimed an immediate peace with the Bolsheviks. The same day, in a gesture that was as futile as it was meaningless, Kolchak had transferred his title of supreme ruler to General Denikin, who was in full retreat himself.[160]

The final act in the drama of Kolchak's personal tragedy opened at 9:55 in the evening of January 15,[161] when the Czechs turned him over to representatives of the Political Center in Irkutsk. Although the Political Center itself was made up mainly of Mensheviks and Socialist Revolutionaries, large contingents of Red Guards filled the city's streets, making it clear that a transfer of power to the Bolsheviks must soon be accomplished. That time came more quickly than most observers expected, for the Political Center abdicated in favor of the Bolsheviks only six days later. On January 21, 1920, Kolchak thus passed into Bolshevik hands. An Extraordinary Investigating Commission, formed before the Bolsheviks took power and therefore including a majority of Mensheviks and Socialist Revolutionaries, interviewed him that day and continued their interrogation over nine lengthy sessions, the last of which ended on the afternoon of February 6. On several occasions, Lenin sent telegrams ordering that "Kolchak not be executed" so that he could be brought to trial,[162] but circumstances dictated otherwise. Early in February, remnants of those shattered White armies that had been driven aside by the Reds' rapid advance began to fight their way toward Irkutsk in a final effort to rescue Siberia's fallen supreme ruler. Fearful that Kolchak might escape, local Bolsheviks under the direction of the Irkutsk Cheka shot him on the morning of February 7, 1920, and cast his body into a hole cut in the ice of the Angara River.

Chaos enveloped eastern Siberia in 1920 as the men who had been responsible for the *atamanshchina* slipped totally out of control. The history of the Civil War in the Far East during 1920 thus would become the story of the Bolsheviks' struggle to subjugate the guerrilla bandits commanded by Semenov, Kalmykov, and a dozen lesser leaders, to reestablish dependable transportation along the Trans-Siberian Railway, and to develop the instruments for an orderly exploitation of Siberia's resources. Their effort would be complicated by the presence of large Japanese occupation forces, which remained for more than two years after the Americans and other Allies departed, mainly because the Japanese surrendered their dreams of empire in Siberia's easternmost regions only with the greatest reluctance. Red Army soldiers thus faced the Japanese and those of Semenov's, Kalmykov's, and Kolchak's forces that had taken sanctuary among them throughout 1920 and 1921. Even as late as 1921, the Japanese supplied Siberia's last White forces with twelve thousand rifles, fifty machine guns, and over three hundred thousand cartridges. The Reds did not regain Khabarovsk until mid-February 1922 and did not retake Vladivostok until the end of October.[163] Thus, the last efforts to stem the Red advance into Siberia were supported by the Japanese alone, for the Western Allies had long since departed.

The departure of the Americans and their European allies from Siberia in the spring of 1920 indicated their realization that their greatest hope for victory over the Bolsheviks had collapsed. With Kolchak's defeat, the Allies' bright vision of a massive White assault against Red Moscow and Petrograd had dimmed to a distant, fading glimmer. Their hope in 1919 had been broader than Kolchak's Siberian dictatorship, broader even than Kolchak's and Denikin's dictatorships combined. At one time in 1919, the Allies had envisioned nothing less than a great three-pronged assault against Moscow and Petrograd, which involved the armies of Denikin from the South, those of Kolchak from the East, and an attack from North Russia and the Baltic by the combined Anglo-Russo-American forces on the Arkhangelsk-Murmansk front and the White armies of General Nikolai Iudenich in Estonia. Each assault had come tantalizingly close to its mark. Denikin had reached Orël. Kolchak had stood scarcely more than fifty miles from the Volga, the last great barrier separating his armies from Moscow. But if Kolchak and Denikin had come close, Iudenich, about whom the Allies had been the least certain, came the closest. Just as Denikin reached Orël in mid-October 1919, the armies that Iudenich had formed from repatriated prisoners of war reached Tsarskoe Selo, the summer palace of Catherine the Great, a mere fifteen miles to the south of Petrograd.

"Is it a bad thing for us or a good thing that the Germans should equip a corps of Russians collected from their Russian prisoners and use them to attack the Bolsheviks?" Winston Churchill had asked Lord Balfour in August. For a brief moment, as the Reds' Petrograd front seemed about to collapse, it had seemed that he had his answer.[164]

CHAPTER EIGHT

The Petrograd Front

IN THE LANDS of North Russia and the Baltic, the last half of 1918 produced dramatic changes that left Petrograd, once the well-guarded capital of Imperial Russia, dangerously exposed to attack. In less than six months, five new independent states emerged in the Baltic lands that once had been part of the Russian Empire, beginning with Poland in the west, and including Lithuania, Latvia, Estonia, and Finland further east. Half a millennium of antagonism and conflict made it certain that all of these states would be anti-Russian. Looked at from the other side, the same historical experience meant that the Bolsheviks must inevitably deny these states their newly won independence. Further to the north, in the area centered around the White Sea ports of Murmansk and Arkhangelsk that British and American campaign chronicles spoke of as North Russia, the forces of Finland, the Allies, the White Russians, and the Bolsheviks clashed in further conflict. Here, no new states appeared, yet the antagonism between the Bolsheviks and the traditionally more independent peoples of the region offered little prospect for a peaceful settlement, especially as the Allies began to concentrate troops in that area during the late summer and fall. Looked at on a map, the new Baltic states and North Russia took the shape of a half-opened fan. Petrograd, home of Russia's shipbuilding and armaments industry, its imperial capital for two centuries, and a key gateway to Russia's interior, stood at its pivot.

From the moment they had signed the Treaty of Brest-Litovsk, the Bolsheviks had faced the certainty that any renewed offensive by the Germans could sweep to Petrograd in a matter of days. Yet Germany's collapse in the fall of 1918 did nothing to lessen the danger. The frontier of newly independent Estonia stood a mere hundred miles from Petrograd's suburbs, and thanks to German efforts during the summer of 1918, Estonia's large, staunchly anti-Bolshevik army was well trained and well armed. To make matters worse, Finland's German-supported White government had crushed the last sparks of Red Finn resistance several months before the armistice in the West. With more than seventy thousand men and women being put on trial for alleged Communist sympathies that fall and winter, the White Finns in no way lagged behind the Estonians in demonstrating their hatred for the Reds.[1] Similar situations developed in Latvia, Lithuania, and North Russia. At any moment, a well-supported, well-timed attack along any one of the handful of key railroads that once had connected the capital of the Russian Empire with its Baltic and northern lands thus could bring enemies to the city's gates. Should the tangled skein of political strivings and nationalist dreams that kept Poles, Finns, Estonians, Latvians, Lithuanians, and anti-Bolshevik Russians apart ever be unraveled sufficiently for them to act in concert, Petrograd's defenses almost certainly would fall.

Although this danger loomed large in the fall, the armistice of November 11, 1918, which allowed the Allies to think of shifting reserves of men, weapons, and materiel to support the anti-Bolshevik forces in the Baltic and North Russia, made it larger still. None who ruled England or America shared the Bolsheviks' dream of a better proletarian world, and few did so in France. There was no shortage of statesmen in those days who hoped to bring down what Winston Churchill once called "the foul baboonery of Bolshevism."[2] Even as the guns of the Great War's last bitter battles had crashed out along Europe's blood-soaked western front, England, the United States, France, and even Serbia had sent troops to North Russia, and England had moved her fleet into the Finnish Gulf to threaten Petrograd's defenses at the Bolsheviks' naval base at Kronstadt. Months before the guns fell silent on the western front, the Allies thus had taken the first steps in a campaign that could have returned the Whites to Petrograd. In military terms, it required only that they enlarge their commitment after November 1918 to succeed.

As long as they had faced the armies of Imperial Germany in the West, the Allied governments had claimed that the troops they landed in North Russia had been sent to defend those vital White Sea ports through which they had supplied the faltering armies of Russia until late 1917 and where immense stockpiles of Allied war supplies still remained. The purpose of such troops, President Wilson's *aide-mémoire* of July 17 had stated, was to guard Allied stores, "which subsequently may be needed by Russian forces," at Murmansk and Arkhangelsk and to render "such aid as may be acceptable to the Russians in the organization of their own self-defense."[3] Germany's defeat rendered such statements of purpose meaningless. Unless Allied policymakers were prepared to apply them to the Bolsheviks, "every argument which had led to intervention," as Winston Churchill later lamented, "had disappeared."[4] Wilson's *aide-mémoire* had stated emphatically that American troops must not "take part in organized intervention" against the Bolsheviks, and Britain's Foreign Secretary Lord Balfour had spoken even more bluntly about the domestic political liabilities that intervention against the Bolsheviks would entail. "This country," he wrote a fortnight after the armistice with Germany, "would certainly refuse to see its forces . . . dissipated over the huge expanse of Russia in order to carry out political reforms in a State which is no longer a belligerent Ally."[5]

Political factors thus heavily outweighed purely military considerations in the Allies' efforts to confront Bolshevism in North Russia and the Baltic, although those were the areas in which it was easiest to strengthen their forces and supply them. "Our armies were melting fast," Churchill later wrote. "The British people would not supply the men or the money for any large military establishment elsewhere than on the Rhine [and] it was highly questionable whether any troops raised under compulsion for the war against Germany would consent to fight anybody else in any circumstances."[6] Hopeful that fate might yet shape their policy for them by allowing Russia's Whites to shatter Trotskii's new Red Army, the Allies thus struggled to support anti-Bolshevik forces in Russia yet not anger their own people by large-scale intervention. "No alternative is open at the present than to use such troops as we possess to the best advantage . . . and, in the case of the Baltic provinces, to protect as far as we can the nascent nationalities by the help of our Fleet," Lord Balfour wrote. "Such a policy must necessarily seem halting and imperfect," he confessed apologetically, "but it is all that we can accomplish or ought in existing circumstances to attempt."[7]

The Allied governments thus directed their commanders on the Petrograd front to use their men and weapons "to the best advantage," but gave them no clear guidance about how to do so. For all of them it was, as the American secretary of war had warned General Graves a few months earlier, like "walking on eggs loaded with dynamite."[8] Yet it was scarcely better for the Reds, who had chosen a policy of restraint in North Russia and the Baltic in order to concentrate their limited resources in the South and East, where the danger seemed greatest. In the Baltic lands, the volatile forces of nationalism too long suppressed threatened to explode in ways that the Reds dared not think about while, in North Russia, Allied commanders planned military victories their governments dared not allow them to claim.

Although Petrograd remained secure in the days after the Great War's end, the Bolsheviks knew only too well that some commander or government might at any moment try to claim the military victory that dangled so tantalizingly just out of reach. The greatest threat seemed to be from North Russia, where the Allies had increased their forces rapidly between July and October 1918. There, the danger came not from the sober and cautious General Sir Charles Maynard, who remained content to employ the fifteen thousand troops under his command to defend the vital port facilities at Murmansk and the key Murmansk–Petrograd railroad, but from General Poole, his arrogant and reckless counterpart in Arkhangelsk. Although he had told America's Ambassador Francis that he could do little beyond "playing a game of bluff" against the Reds with the sixteen thousand men he commanded, Poole chafed to open an offensive.[9] Recklessly, he sent strike forces from Arkhangelsk toward Vologda in the south and Kotlas in the southwest, where they risked being isolated deep in the hinterland of North Russia.

The danger from Poole was not limited to his rash forays into the Russian hinterland. Unable to challenge the Bolsheviks effectively, he turned to meddle in the affairs of Nikolai Chaikovskii's Supreme Administration of the North to an extent that no independent government could tolerate. During just one week in August, Poole decreed which flags could and could not be flown over government buildings, appointed an Allied military governor for Arkhangelsk over the objections of the Russians, and even threatened all city residents who spread rumors that might "cause alarm or confusion among troops or civilians friendly to the Allies" with execution.[10] Chaikovskii protested angrily and repeatedly. By the beginning of September, his conflict with Poole had grown so heated that one Allied diplomat described it as "an open struggle."[11] Poole made it no secret that he thought Chaikovskii and his government of moderate socialists "totally incapable" in military matters, "hopeless" as allies, and "not far removed from Bolsheviks" in their politics.[12] There is some evidence that Poole and his military intelligence staff even supported an ill-fated attempt by the conservative commander-in-chief of the White forces in Arkhangelsk to overthrow Chaikovskii's government at the beginning of September.[13]

Such condescension and arrogance irritated Poole's more sensible countrymen and outraged many of his allies. Only the violently antisocialist French Ambassador Joseph Noulens dared to speak of the British commander's "loyalty and good sense" and commend his insensitive appointment of a French colonel as governor-general of Arkhangelsk as "a gesture of inter-allied friendship." Never one to conceal his low opinion of his nation's Russian allies, Noulens thought that the senior Allied diplomats at Arkhangelsk should be "officious and benevolent guides" for Chaikovskii's Russians, who, because of "being placed for the first time at the head of affairs," needed "supervision and control."[14] Neither the British nor the Americans shared that view. Britain's commissioner in North Russia warned repeatedly that Chaikovskii's Supreme Administration "must appear to have real authority" if it hoped to win support among the Russians.[15] And, although certainly no defender of left-wing politicians, America's Ambassador Francis found Poole's crude actions offensive enough to complain that "British soldiers have been colonizers for so long that they did not know how to respect the feelings of socialists."[16] Half a world away in Washington, D.C., Francis's superiors took an even sterner view. Unless Poole became "more considerate of the civil authorities in North Russia," an angry President Wilson told the British government at that point, America would withdraw her forces from North Russia.[17]

Since more than half Poole's force were Americans, President

Wilson's protests bore weight. American and British diplomats sternly counseled Poole to rescind the most arrogant expressions of what one British diplomat bluntly referred to as the "occupation" regime he had imposed upon the Russians. Then, while Poole looked on with grudging and surly acquiescence, American and British diplomats asked Chaikovskii to appoint a Russian governor-general with full authority in Arkhangelsk. Such changes could be accomplished readily enough, but the damage Poole had done to White Russian self-esteem could not be so easily repaired. By mid-September, few in London or Washington doubted that Poole must be replaced. After calling him to London for consultations at the end of the month, the British government never allowed him to return to North Russia.

Acting Brigadier-General William Edmund Ironside, D.S.O., C.M.G., K.C.B., and holder of the Croix de Guerre and Legion of Honor at the age of thirty-eight, officially replaced Poole a month later. Square-jawed and square-shouldered, his heavy brows knit in a perpetual frown, "Tiny" Ironside stood six feet four inches tall and weighed over two hundred and fifty pounds. A sandy-haired, blue-eyed Scot who had made his life in the British army as his father had before him, he had fought for England in South Africa and in France and had spent most of the years between the two conflicts on the British General Staff. During the summer of 1918, he had commanded England's Ninety-ninth Infantry Brigade in France and had left the trenches of the western front in September confessing that he could "hardly bear the thought" of leaving the fighting behind. Ironside cared much for the army and not one whit for politics. He had no interest in the endless succession of schemes hatched by squabbling Russians and disheartened Allied ambassadors, all of them bored by the isolation they endured in faraway Arkhangelsk. Ironside's chief concerns were the welfare of his men and the difficult tactical position in which they would find themselves once ice closed navigation in the White Sea. "We were a tiny army of not very first-class troops, sitting on the edge of Russia's vast territory," he later wrote. "No one could tell what the outcome of this struggle would be, but we were inextricably mixed up in it for at least six months."[18]

By his own account a man whose heart "was always in the command of men,"[19] Ironside was every inch a soldier's soldier. "He typifies all that we mean by the perfect British soldier," one war correspondent wrote after spending the winter of 1918–1919 with him in North Russia. "He exudes a personality that submerges everything and everybody round him."[20] Ironside so thoroughly captivated America's Ambassador Francis at their first dinner meeting that the dean of the Allied diplomats in Arkhangelsk hurried to list the new commander's virtues in a lengthy cabled dispatch to his superiors at the Department of State. Perhaps equating this British artilleryman's toughness with the legendary invulnerability of America's first full-fledged warship, and misreporting his name accordingly, Francis reported that "General Ironsides . . . is descended direct from the last Saxon king of England, was dismissed from St. Andrew's School when he was ten and one-half years old because he whipped the teacher, . . . [and] speaks six languages with equal fluency—English, French, Russian, German, Italian, Swedish." With the admiration typical of a man who spoke no foreign language passably, Francis added that the new Allied commander could "converse, although not fluently, in eleven other languages," and explained that, at the beginning of the Great War, "he was the first British officer to land in France."[21]

Although his report somewhat exaggerated Ironside's linguistic and command achievements, Francis's enthusiasm was typical of the men with whom Ironside dealt in North Russia. Yet the replacement of a blustering commander by a more popular and efficient one could do little to lessen the difficulties the Allies faced in the North. Ironside might well confide in a nasty aside to his diary that Poole had suffered from "the valour of ignorance" during his months at Arkhangelsk, but he soon learned that the commanders of the anti-Bolshevik Russian forces were even worse. Without "sufficient military or administrative knowledge," they were "hopeless dreamers"[22] who, Ironside quickly determined, "had done exactly nothing during the two and a half months they had been in office." Although convinced that "volunteering was totally alien to the Russian mind," these men firmly rejected conscription as an alternative. "They rather haughtily told me," Ironside reported in amazement, "that conscription was undemocratic."[23]

If those Russians who might have been incorporated into the Allied forces in North Russia were of poor quality, Ironside quickly discovered that many of the Allied troops under his command were not much better. "Our troops were uniformly bad," he later wrote, "and two of the Allied contingents could hardly defend themselves."[24] Certain that Poole's widely dispersed forces could not even be properly supplied during the winter, let alone stand against a Red offensive, Ironside decided to retreat from the advanced positions that the Allies had taken up in August in order to consolidate his forces closer to Arkhangelsk. "It was impossible for a small force such as that in Archangel to push its way far into Russia without a definite objective," he later explained. Until the Allies made larger commitments in North Russia or coordinated their operations with the Whites in Siberia, Ironside wisely concluded that "no blow delivered by us [against the Bolsheviks] would be sufficient in itself."[25] Merely defending Arkhangelsk, which, by November, had "become like a hive of bees upset by an unwonted hammering from without,"[26] would be no easy task with the forces at hand. Only the fact that the Red Army faced far more serious dangers on other fronts and sent less than first-rate commanders to North Russia gave Ironside any grounds for optimism. "The Bolsheviks were badly led," he reported later, "and failed utterly in the task of turning us out of Archangel, which should have been an easy one."[27]

As the Armistice approached in November 1918, neither Ironside nor any of the Allied ambassadors who clustered around his headquarters received any clear instructions about their governments' policy toward the Bolsheviks. Among the lonely men in North Russia, the hope of uniting with the White armies in Siberia for a joint offensive against Petrograd and Moscow remained, but it faded as they learned more about the barriers of terrain, climate, and distance that separated them.[28] Too often and for too long, the Allies in the North knew nothing of what was happening in the East. In the meantime, Ironside had to prepare for a winter in hostile territory. To his amazement, he found that the ambassadors of his allies "thought there would be a tacit cease-fire as soon as the Germans were out of the struggle . . . [and] did not think that we should have a strenuous time during the winter."[29] Events quickly proved that Ironside had good reason to fear otherwise. "On the very afternoon of Armistice Day," he wrote, "all the vain hopes of a peaceful evacuation or a quiet winter campaign, which so many people had cherished, disappeared in a flash" as the Reds launched one of their few heavy assaults against the Allied forces that still held positions some distance up the Dvina River from Arkhangelsk.[30]

With no clear objective for his troops yet set by Allied planners in London, Paris, and Washington, Ironside pulled his forces back toward Arkhangelsk in November 1918. "The force found itself with the worst possible position that a Regular force, small in number, can find itself in," he explained in one of his reports. "Exposed to an irregular but numberless enemy, it had no clear objective except that it must remain upon the defensive."[31] To make matters worse, it became fully as difficult to keep men in the fighting line once the Great War had ended as Lord Balfour had predicted. "The announcement of an Armistice, the horrors of a long winter, and the moral effect of the port of Arkhangelsk being closed to navigation for eight months," Ironside reported, "had a bad effect upon the weaker members of the Command."[32] Fighting general that he was, Ironside prescribed large doses of rigorous training combined with raids against weak enemy positions "as a means . . . for maintaining the offensive spirit in the men" and as a remedy for crumbling morale. Yet the Russians under his command would have no part of such undertakings and took refuge in grandiose plans for large-scale offensives against uncertain objectives. "An offensive is the Russian cure for all ills of ill discipline," Ironside explained to his superiors at one point, "and they generally insist that it must be immediate, which means ill-prepared." Unable to take the offensive, and unwilling to hone their fighting skills with operations fought on a lesser scale, the Russians at Arkhangelsk grew even more discontented than the Allies. "Inaction is fatal to Russian troops," Ironside warned. "They are more like children than anything else [and] they must be kept employed."[33]

In Murmansk, some five hundred miles by sea to the north and west of Arkhangelsk, General Maynard faced similar difficulties. His first task in the summer of 1918 had been to defend the newly built Murmansk-Petrograd Railway against the very real threat of attacks by the Germans and their White Finn allies, and he therefore had been obliged to establish fortified bases at such far-flung points as Pechenga to his north and Kandalaksha, Kem, and Soroka along the railroad to the south. As winter approached, these had to be supplied despite a shortage of food and funds brought on by the War Office's inclination to give first priority to Arkhangelsk, where the chief Allied diplomats had taken up residence.

To make matters worse, the Red Finns, who had been more than willing to fight with Maynard against the Germans, had no desire to take up arms against the Bolsheviks. "The [Red Finn] Legion had been useless to me since the Armistice," Maynard confessed. "Finland was calling them, and to Finland they meant to return." Yet the Finnish Whites, now triumphantly in power in their homeland, insisted that the Red Finns must be included among those tens of thousands who were being brought to trial for Red sympathies. Throughout the winter and into the spring and summer of 1919, Maynard sought repatriation for his disgruntled fighters. "They are a pig-headed lot of revolutionaries, and . . . they will refuse to submit much longer to being pariahs and outcasts from their country," he warned his superiors. "Every effort must be made to compel the Finnish government to allow my Finn warriors to return to their country as peaceful citizens."[34] Only at the end of August 1919, after a special British mission had pleaded their cause in Helsinki for more than a month, did the government of Finland's Regent Mannerheim finally allow the Red Finns who had fought against the Germans in North Russia during the summer and fall of 1918 to return.[35]

Problems of supply, disease, subzero cold, and, perhaps most of all, boredom and lack of purpose weighed heavily upon the Allied command in North Russia during the winter of 1918–1919. As howling winds dumped some six feet of snow upon Arkhangelsk soon after 1919 began, and with the temperature regularly at thirty degrees below zero Fahrenheit, Ironside's forces faced problems for which even the most diligent efforts and the best intentions had not prepared them. "Water cooled machine guns could only be used in heated blockhouses, and non-freezing mixture [i.e. anti-freeze] made little difference in the open," one ordnance expert reported. Transport officers complained that "boiling water poured into radiators would often become cold before engines could be started" and that even nonfreezing oils froze quickly.[36] Artillery officers found that shell fuses failed to detonate and that the unpredictable effects of subzero temperatures on cordite charges reduced the range of their guns by as much as ten percent. "The effect of extreme cold on the behaviour of cordite is very marked," one of them wrote. "The nitro-glycerine [brought to] the surface of the cordite [by the subzero temperatures] being somewhat sensitive," he added in a masterpiece of understatement, "there may be an element of danger in storage at such low temperatures."[37]

To the problem of cold, the Russians' ignorance of the most basic rules of sanitation added the ravages of disease that winter. "At Archangel, the river is constantly polluted and contains an unduly high percentage of sewage organisms," one British doctor reported. "If the precautions advised are not put into constant use," he warned, "all the elements necessary for the development of a water borne epidemic on a large scale are present." Disease raged in cycles that winter, and a flood of refugees into Arkhangelsk made the danger worse. Just as a severe cholera epidemic began to subside during the fall of 1918, the Spanish influenza—the dreaded *ispanka*—struck, and Arkhangelsk reported some ten thousand cases before the disease ran its course. Other diseases followed in sequence as the months progressed. Unable to overcome the primitive conditions of Russian life and the gross carelessness of the Russians when it came to sanitation, Allied military doctors faced an epidemic of typhoid in addition to onslaughts of scurvy, diarrhea, and smallpox before the winter reached its end.[38]

Disease, inaction, loneliness, and the ravages of Arctic cold and darkness all took their toll upon the morale of the Allies and their Russian comrades that winter. Everywhere, and at every opportunity, the Bolsheviks spread propaganda among the defenders of Arkhangelsk and Murmansk that lowered their morale further. "British soldiers!" one such leaflet proclaimed. "Stop fighting us!" Now that an armistice had been signed and the fighting had ended in Europe, handbills nailed to trees and scattered along city streets asked: "Why don't you return home?" "What are you fighting for?"[39] Not surprisingly, the Russian Whites were the first to give way. "There was not one of them who showed any white-hot patriotism to win through, such as the Bolshevik leaders seemed to possess in so large a measure," Ironside later wrote. "They seemed to me to be just timid bureaucrats."[40] On December 11, the First Arkhangelsk Infantry Regiment mutinied when the new Russian commander-in-chief ordered two of its units to take up positions on the so-called railway front, some fifty miles down the Arkhangelsk–Vologda railroad. To the dismay of President Chaikovskii, thirteen of its leaders had to be shot on the spot.[41]

For the time being, the Allied units proved more reliable, but the interminable darkness of the Arctic winter took its toll upon them and at the end of February 1919, British and French units mutinied.[42] "We won't make an attact [sic] on you," one American company announced in a propaganda broadside they addressed to the Reds. "If you wait 2-½ months we will be out of Russia." Everywhere the Americans resented being commanded by the British and being ordered to hold most of the front-line positions. "The majority of the people here are in simpothy [*sic*] with the Bolo [i.e. Bolsheviks]," one American sergeant wrote in his diary. "I don't blame them in fact I am 9/10 Bolo myself."[43] Although he minimized the danger in his reports, none sensed the collapse of the Allied soldiers' morale more clearly than Ironside himself. "We were drawing terribly near to the end of our tether as an efficient fighting force," he later confessed. "Boredom amongst those who were not fighting, combined with the numbing effect of the cold and darkness, had brought . . . [our men] to a state of exasperation with which it was very difficult to deal."[44]

Then, as they moved against Kolchak's forces further east, the Bolsheviks intensified their attacks in the North. After an American unit manning its forward defenses suffered eighty-five percent casualties, the Allies surrendered the key North Russian town of Shenkursk at the end of January and abandoned all hope for a union with Kolchak's forces. A motley assortment of British, Canadian, Serbian, Karelian, and Russian troops operating as part of Maynard's force turned the balance briefly in the Allies' favor when they captured Segezha, a key railhead on the Murmansk–Petrograd line, in mid-February. But Red attacks against Bolshie Ozerki and Obozerskaia a month later wiped out their gains and all but severed the fragile route that linked Arkhangelsk and Murmansk by land some two months before the spring thaw reopened the sea lanes between the two ports.[45] By then, both the American and British governments had announced their decision to withdraw their forces from North Russia.

In large measure due to the opposition of England's newly appointed secretary of state for war Winston Churchill, the Allied withdrawal moved more slowly than anyone had imagined. At a meeting of the Allied Supreme War Council in mid-February, Churchill insisted that North Russia ought not to be evacuated and that the Allies ought to send "volunteers, technical experts, arms, munitions, tanks, [and] aeroplanes" to support the Whites.[46] An ardent interventionist, Churchill urged the Allies to "consider the possibilities of joint military action [against the Bolsheviks] by the Associated Powers acting in conjunction with the independent border States and pro-Ally Governments in Russia."[47] It would be like "pulling out the linch-pin from the whole machine," he warned at one point, to abandon the Whites in their struggle against the Bolsheviks.[48]

Yet Churchill's stubborn eloquence did no more than delay the day when, as he once remarked, the Allies would "leave everyone in Russia to stew in their own juices."[49] In the meantime, it became the task of General Evgenii Miller, formerly governor-general of Arkhangelsk, commander-in-chief of the armed forces of the Supreme Administration of the North, administrator of foreign affairs, and now head of the anti-Bolsheviks in North Russia, to establish a government and an army that could carry on the struggle.[50] An officer who once had served as chief of staff to the dashing General Gurko in the armies of Nicholas II, Miller still wore the long mustache of a tsarist cavalryman. Tall and still slender despite his fifty-one years, Miller looked less than his age, spoke French and German fluently, and made a good first impression. One British diplomat remembered him as "a courteous gentleman of middle age with whom it is easy to do business, but . . . not a man to inspire enthusiasm or go outside the bounds of customary bureaucratic procedure."[51] Some of his subordinates condemned him as a "rear-echelon general" who appeared at the front "only when there was absolutely no fighting,"[52] while others praised his "extreme thoughtfulness and seriousness."[53] General Maynard later spoke of Miller's apparently unshakable dedication to the White cause. "He never wavered," Maynard wrote, "in his conviction that Russia would breast successfully the cataclysmal flood now threatening to engulf her."[54]

Whatever his failings and virtues, Miller doubled the number of Russians under arms to nearly six thousand by the end of January 1919. A month later, that figure had doubled again, and by the end of April, according to Ironside's estimates, Miller commanded a force of sixteen thousand men.[55] Yet the men under his command had come less willingly than any who served Denikin or Kolchak. Too many Russians in North Russia stood perpetually on the brink of mutiny, and throughout the late winter and spring of 1919, they stepped repeatedly into the precipice of open revolt. Desertion became so frequent that, when Miller's second-in-command announced in late spring that anyone who sympathized with the Bolsheviks was free to apply for permission to join them, almost six thousand men and women did so within a fortnight. At the end of April, a battalion of the Third North Russian Rifle Regiment went over to the Reds *en masse*, and a few days later the entire Eighth Russian Rifle Regiment followed its example. Although order returned in June, July brought a wave of mutinies that spread across the entire North Russian front from Lake Onega to the Dvina River.[56] Every White officer slept with a rifle and extra ammunition in those days. "Hardly a single reliable unit remained among Miller's forces," one Soviet commentator wrote. Continued defections in the late summer and early fall provided more evidence to support that claim.[57]

Disaffection among Miller's troops mirrored the disaffection with the White cause in North Russia more generally, for the aristocratic and conservative Miller commanded much less popular support than had Chaikovskii. While he told Ironside that "the Tsar had been his master, and he would always remain faithful to his memory, but it was for the people of Russia to decide whether there would be a Tsar once more,"[58] the hard truth was that Miller's government included only one socialist, a man whose abrasive manner left him unable to exert any decisive influence inside the government or command public support outside it. Concerned moderates warned to no avail of the growing "enmity between government and population." Miller remained the elegant tsarist officer, still clad in his imperial uniform and shining gold epaulets, both of which stirred unpleasant memories in the minds of common Russians. Miller therefore presided over a divided government and a divided populace. "With your departure, the moral weight of the Northern Government became considerably reduced," one of Chaikovskii's friends wrote to him that spring. "The mass of the people is turning back to Bolshevism."[59]

None proved more hostile to Miller's conservative regime than the Socialist Revolutionary workers of Arkhangelsk and Murmansk when word reached them in February that several of their more prominent comrades in Moscow had made their peace with the Bolsheviks to form a united front against the forces of "counterrevolution." Already angry because Miller had forbidden labor protest on pain of heavy fines and prison sentences, the factory workers of North Russia turned upon his government as they celebrated the second anniversary of the February Revolution. "Soviet authority," one fiery speaker claimed at a meeting of over a thousand factory workers, "is the only natural protector of the interests of the working class." The time soon would come, he promised, when soldiers would "walk hand in hand with the workers in the protection of their interests."[60] Already inclined to view proletarians with suspicion, Miller's government shot more than forty pro-Bolshevik workers between March 24 and April 6.[61] In Murmansk, Maynard's men fortified their barracks and slept with bayonets fixed on loaded rifles.[62]

With the workers of North Russia and their allies temporarily weakened by the reprisals of late March and early April, Miller took more power into his hands, "naturally and logically" in the view of some, more guilefully in the opinion of others.[63] Certainly his recognition of Kolchak's authority as head of the Provisional All-Russian National Government at the end of April made Miller's actual power even greater for Kolchak had hurried to bestow upon him "independence in regard to concrete practical measures necessitated by extraordinary circumstances."[64] When, on July 12, the Provisional Government of North Russia voted its own dissolution, Miller's authority as Kolchak's governor-general and commander-in-chief of all anti-Bolshevik Russian forces on the northern front became absolute. As with Denikin in the South and Kolchak in the East, the Whites in North Russia had transformed their brief and fragile experiment with democracy into a dictatorship. When the last Allied forces of the Western democracies left North Russia in mid-October 1919, they left behind a military dictatorship which, unlike the dictatorship of Lenin, which its leaders had condemned with such self-righteous indignation, had no support among the masses it ruled.

Still, the Allied withdrawal from North Russia at the end of September did not sound the immediate death knell of Miller's regime. For a brief moment in the fall of 1919, Miller's army of fifty thousand men knew hope, elation, and even success.[65] "We are in Russia once again!" an officer was heard to exclaim as he greeted a comrade on September 27, the day after the Allies left Arkhangelsk. "How do you like the *Russian* city of Arkhangelsk?"[66] At first, Miller's forces drove the Bolsheviks back. Then, at the beginning of 1920, his armies and government began to crumble, leaving everyone in North Russia certain of the Reds' triumph. "One sensed a change in the attitude of the soldiers [and] . . . a recognition of the hopelessness of further struggle took possession of them," Miller explained a few years later. "Speaking of their desire to spare their families further ruin, and with tears in their eyes, as if to beg forgiveness for their behavior, they parted from their officers and scattered to their villages."[67]

Now aware that Kolchak had been executed and that Denikin's triumphant advance against Tula and Moscow had turned into a retreat, Miller formed his last government on February 14, 1920. Called the "Government of Salvation" by some, the "Government of Evacuation," by others, and the "Government of Stupidity"[68] by those who realized how completely the sands of time had run out for the anti-Bolshevik forces in North Russia, this government collapsed in less than a week. Advised on February 14 that some of his key forces could hold for not more than two or three days,[69] Miller announced that the situation, "though serious, was not particularly threatening."[70] Two days later, on the night of February 18, he, his government, and a large number of staff officers quietly boarded the icebreaker *Minin* that had anchored at Arkhangelsk's Cathedral Quay. Before noon the next day, February 19, the fifty-ninth anniversary of the emancipation of the Russian serfs, which had been designed to place Russia upon the path to peaceful modernization, they fled to Norway.[71] Two days later, Bolshevik workers and Red Army units occupied Arkhangelsk and Murmansk to establish Soviet power in North Russia.

During the months of Miller's final struggles, the workers and soldiers of Petrograd had turned back an even more serious attack that had come in the form of a sudden advance by the armies of General Iudenich through Russia's Baltic coastal regions. At the beginning of 1919, few White politicians and generals, and even fewer of their allies among the statesmen of the West, had taken Iudenich's small Northwestern White Army very seriously. Yet Iudenich had taken advantage of the Reds' preoccupation with Denikin and Kolchak to begin a mad dash that carried him from Estonia's eastern frontier in September to the outskirts of Petrograd in October. Like the German armies in 1941, Iudenich's soldiers looked down into Red Petrograd from the Pulkovo Heights. "There was the dome of St. Isaac's and the gilt spire of the Admiralty," one of them later wrote. "One could even see trains pulling out of the Nicholas Station."[72] So confident were Iudenich's forces on that day that one of his generals is said to have dismissed a fellow officer's offer of fieldglasses with the remark that he would be walking down Petrograd's main street the next day in any case.[73]

When he appeared in Estonia in mid-1919 to lead the Northwestern White Army, General of the Infantry Nikolai Nikolaevich Iudenich was fifty-six years old but looked considerably older. Squint-eyed, pudgy, and short, his luxuriant drooping mustache contrasting sharply with his balding head, he in no way looked like the officer who had led the imperial army of the Caucasus to victory against the Turks at Erzerum and Trapezond less than three years before. One statesman was so put off by his appearance that he described him as "physically slack and entirely lacking in those inspiring qualities which a political and military leader of his standing should possess."[74] Others thought his behavior even more suspicious than his looks, for Iudenich's actions during the revolutionary year of 1917 had contrasted as sharply with his principles as his physical appearance did with his war record. A proud nobleman from the Belorussian province of Minsk who had been trained to serve his tsar, his country, and his class, he had found it difficult to find his bearings in Russia's revolutionary turmoil in 1917. Skeptically, perhaps even somewhat cynically, he had toyed with democracy after Nicholas II's abdication and had risen to command the Caucasus front for the Provisional Government. Yet, this effort to serve democratic Russia had been half-hearted at best. Iudenich the self-conscious aristocratic imperial servitor could never become Iudenich the unpretentious servant of the people.

After the Bolshevik Revolution, Iudenich rejected what he considered to be the false precepts of the proletarian state and went briefly into retirement. Suddenly, he turned against Russia's new masters with a vengeance. His monarchist principles invigorated by his brief flirtation with democracy, he gave rein to all the pride and prejudice of the tsarist officer class. When he fled from Soviet Russia to newly independent Finland in the fall of 1918, it was rumored that he refused to call upon Marshal Mannerheim because Mannerheim's rank had been inferior to his own in the old imperial army and thus, in Iudenich's view, obligated Finland's newly chosen regent to call upon him first.[75] If true, this was but one more example of Iudenich's many stubborn refusals to accommodate his Old Regime principles to the realities of life and politics in the modern world. Like Kolchak, unwilling to concede Finland's separation from Russia, Iudenich made no alliance with Mannerheim's Finland against the Bolsheviks and sought a base of operations in Estonia instead.[76] The fledgling Northwestern White Army, born of the Germans' desperation and the Whites' hatred for the Reds, became the weapon he would wield against the Bolsheviks.

Some months before Iudenich came upon the scene, the Northwestern White Army had had its beginnings in the events that had followed closely upon the heels of the Allied victory over the Central Powers. In the Baltic, the collapse of Imperial Germany had opened the way for a new Red assault against those newly independent states that German guns and German diplomacy had brought into being. Proclaiming that "the counterrevolutionary partition wall between the revolutionary West and Socialist Russia will in the end be swept away," the Bolsheviks' Commissar of Nationalities Stalin promised in mid-November 1918 that "revolution and Soviet governments" would come to Russia's Baltic lands in "the very near future." As the Bolsheviks organized Latvian, Lithuanian, and Estonian peoples' armies on Soviet territory to liberate the workers of their homelands, Stalin confidently vowed that "proletarian revolution, awe-inspiring and mighty, is on the march through the world," and that the "petty kinglets" of Estonia, Latvia, and Lithuania would "be no exception."[77]

Riga, the capital and main seaport of Latvia, fell to the Reds at the beginning of January 1919, and pro-Bolshevik forces entered Lithuania's capital of Vilna soon afterward. Only in Estonia, the smallest of the three Baltic republics, did the Reds fail to make headway, in no small measure thanks to the intervention of the Finns, who joined with the Estonians and the small anti-Bolshevik Northwestern White Army to keep the Estonian capital of Reval out of Bolshevik hands.[78] "My attitude on the Estonian struggle for freedom could not be other than positive," Marshal Mannerheim explained some years later. "Apart from the humanitarian aspect of the matter, it was obviously in Finland's interests to have the southern shores of the Gulf of Finland held by a friendly Power."[79]

The Finns' rapid withdrawal from Estonia after its territory had been cleared of Reds at the end of February 1919 meant that Estonia's armed forces and the Northwestern White Army were the only anti-Bolshevik forces that remained in Russia's former Baltic lands. Created at the ancient Russian city of Pskov just prior to the Germans' evacuation in late October 1918, the Northwestern White Army had been shaped around some six thousand men, a quarter of them tsarist officers. Its beginnings at Pskov, a once-proud ancient Russian city now transformed by the Revolution's turmoil into an oozing moral sore whose corrupt drainage contaminated German, White Russian, and Soviet citizens alike, had not helped the Northwestern White Army to prosper. "Entire hordes of speculators did business in those days," one observer explained. "Speculation had become Pskov's way of life."[80] Red and White alike moved freely back and forth across the frontier, as venal border guards and corrupt officials stood aside to let them pass. Most traded in goods; some trafficked in military and political secrets and sold their information to whoever paid the highest price.[81] At Pskov, only men with money flourished. When the Germans' lavish promises of more than a hundred million rubles, sixty thousand rifles, nearly six hundred machine guns, and twenty-five million cartridges in aid failed to materialize, the Whites suffered accordingly.[82] In November 1918, three-quarters of the soldiers in the Northwestern White Army had no overcoats, half had no boots, the infantry had no bayonets, and the artillery had no horses to move its guns.[83]

Poorly armed, badly clothed, and ineptly led, the Northwestern White Army had entered the field as the Germans withdrew from Russia, and its first military action had been a precipitous flight into Estonia at the end of November 1918. Conflicts between some three dozen squabbling tsarist generals, all of whom demanded commands commensurate with their former rank, created tensions that threatened to destroy the army even before it could face the Reds in battle, and it fell to Gerneral Aleksandr Rodzianko, a former Imperial Guards officer who combined first-rate horsemanship with distinctly second-rate strategy and tactics, to keep these self-serving generals in balance. An officer who once claimed that he was "not a politician" and whose memoirs insisted that, as an army commander, he had dealt with political questions "only insofar as they were directly tied to military activity," Rodzianko nonetheless bettered the relationship between the Northwestern White Army and the Estonians sufficiently for the two forces to launch a brief joint offensive that gave the Northwestern White Army its first base on Russian territory by driving the Bolsheviks from Pskov and Iamburg at the end of May.[84]

Rodzianko's first victories brought a population of half a million under the authority of Iudenich's government-in-exile in Helsinki.[85] Yet the Whites did not rule well, as subordinates over whom Rodzianko lost control launched a reign of terror against the Reds who had opposed them and the Jews who had not.[86] Perhaps most notorious among White Army commanders, General Bulak-Balakhovich, the self-styled "ataman of peasant and partisan legions," committed extortion, robbery, and murder among the people of Pskov and Gdov for the better part of two months. Bulak-Balakhovich called upon the Red Army soldiers to defect and killed them when they did. "You know me," he announced. "I am the servant of the people. I am the sword of the people's justice."[87] Bulak-Balakhovich hanged Reds from Pskov's lampposts and threatened its Jews with pogroms unless they paid huge ransoms, which some claimed he used to settle his gambling debts.[88] In one of his most memorable outrages, he was reported to have ordered Pskov's entire Cheka to execute themselves. "I have no bullets to spare," he reportedly told his victims. "And I have no one to hang you because all my men are busy with other things. I'll give you half an hour," he concluded. "You'll have to hang yourselves." They did so. In one case, according to an onlooker, the rope broke and the victim fell to the ground. When he tried to escape, one of Bulak-Balakhovich's officers ran him down, seized the rope that dangled from his neck, dragged him to the river's edge, and drowned him.[89]

With men like Bulak-Balakhovich, Rodzianko worked to build the Northwestern Army while Iudenich negotiated for Allied support and Allied weapons from his headquarters in Helsinki.[90] Still heavily influenced by the strategies of the First World War, rather than thinking in terms of the more mobile tactics that the Civil War had called into being, they requested weapons, ammunition, and supplies that vastly exceeded the needs of the mobile, fast-moving campaign they needed to fight. Three thousand machine guns, more than two hundred field guns (including several of the massive eleven-inch howitzers that had been used to demolish the complex entrenchments of the western front in 1918), some two hundred airplanes, nearly fifty tanks and armored cars, and clothing and weapons for close to fifty thousand men comprised Iudenich's estimates of his minimal needs at a time when the Northwestern White Army still had less than ten thousand men.[91] At the same time, he made overtures to the Swedes (from whom he eventually received thirty-five million kroner)[92] and even opened negotiations with Mannerheim in the hope of convincing him to commit Finland's large army to support his assault against Petrograd.[93]

More fearful of an attack by the Finns than by the Northwestern White Army, the Bolsheviks already had begun to mobilize the workers of Petrograd for the city's defense a month before Iudenich and Mannerheim began their negotiations, and on May 17, Lenin had sent Stalin to take charge of the city's defenses. "Soviet Russia cannot give up Petrograd even for the briefest moment," the Central Committee announced. "The significance of this city, which first raised the banner of rebellion against the bourgeoisie, is too great."[94]

Calling upon all workers between the ages of eighteen and forty to fight for "Red Petrograd," Stalin began to shape Petrograd's defenses. Men trained in factory yards, in parks, and anywhere else where field guns could be unlimbered and infantry could mount mock attacks. Before the end of May, he promised Lenin that he could "defend Petrograd with credit against any attack from the sea,"[95] yet on June 9 he called urgently for reinforcements. "To save Piter," he telegraphed Lenin that night, "it is essential that we be sent, without wasting a single moment, three strong regiments."[96] The only hostile fire that Petrograd's defenders had faced since Stalin's arrival had been a desultory exchange between several Finnish ships and the Soviet destroyer *Gavriil* in the vicinity of Krasnaia Gorka, one of the fortresses that guarded the approaches to Petrograd some fifteen miles to the west of the city's main naval defenses at Kronstadt.[97] It was impressive testimony to Stalin's powers of persuasion that Lenin nonetheless urged eastern front headquarters to divert men to Petrograd's defense and that, on June 10, the Bolshevik Central Committee designated the Petrograd front to be the one in the greatest danger.

The danger lay within Stalin's own defenses, not beyond them. For two centuries the guns of the great naval bastion of Kronstadt had protected the anchorage of Russia's Baltic Fleet and had barred the way upriver to Petrograd. Now, as Stalin strengthened Petrograd's defenses, they provided the screen behind which the Red Baltic Fleet took refuge from the British squadron that had moved into the Gulf of Finland. Yet, just as Stalin became certain of Petrograd's naval defenses, an attack came from precisely that sector. On June 13, the garrisons at Krasnaia Gorka and its sister fort Seraia Loshad turned their heavy guns against the Red sailors at Kronstadt. Stalin struck decisively without wasting a moment. That evening he ordered two battleships from the Red Fleet to bombard the rebels' positions. The next day he added planes and more ships to the bombardment and sent eight hundred Kronstadt sailors to retake the forts.[98] Despite the intervention of a British torpedo boat, which sank one of the Soviet cruisers, the rebellion at Krasnaia Gorka collapsed two days later. Fifty miles to the west in Iamburg, Rodzianko had looked on and done nothing. Later he blamed the British navy for the rebels' defeat. It was "very possible" that the British had not been more energetic, he later wrote in an absurd effort to excuse his own failings, because the rebels already had informed them they would not join the British navy and would continue to fight only as part of the Northwestern White Army.[99]

With Krasnaia Gorka and Seraia Loshad restored to the Reds, Stalin launched a new wave of terror. That the rebels would be killed was a forgone conclusion, but Stalin also executed nearly seventy officers at Kronstadt for their supposed sympathy for the rebels.[100] "We have unearthed a big conspiracy in the Kronstadt area," he reported proudly to Lenin two days after Krasnaia Gorka fell. "The aim of the conspiracy was to seize possession of the fortress, take control of the fleet, open fire on the rear of our troops, and clear the road to Petrograd for Rodzianko." Although Stalin announced that "the relevant documents" that outlined the conspiracy and made it clear how the British had financed it "have fallen into our hands," such materials have yet to come to light. Within a fortnight, Stalin returned to Moscow to claim credit for his "defense" of Petrograd, although the city never faced any serious threat at any time in the summer of 1919 because the Whites were too weak and too disunited to mount an attack.[101]

While Stalin had prepared Petrograd's defenses, the Whites had passed the summer of 1919 in political squabbles. Convinced that the Northwestern White Army could not reach Petrograd without Finnish support, Iudenich agreed to recognize Finland's complete independence in any postwar settlement, but Kolchak, whom Iudenich had recognized as Russia's supreme ruler in May, stubbornly refused.[102] Anxious to turn the Northwestern White Army into a force that could fight its way across the hundred-odd miles that separated them from Petrograd on its own, Iudenich transferred his headquarters from Helsinki to Narva on Estonia's eastern frontier at the end of July. Despite the victories Rodzianko had won in May, he faced a difficult task. "The Northwest army was absolutely unready for such a serious undertaking as seizing the capital, one of the main strongholds of Bolshevism," one of his associates wrote. "[It] remained weak in numbers and was completely unequipped for military action, especially in the fall climate."[103] Like Stalin, Iudenich ordered the conscription of all men between the ages of nineteen and forty-five; unlike Stalin's, his effort produced very disappointing results. Despite some claims that the Northwestern White Army had grown to thirty-five, or even fifty, thousand before summer's end,[104] the fact was that Iudenich's forces stood at less than a quarter of that figure at the end of August.[105]

While the Whites struggled to get their bearings, the reinforcements that the Reds had sent to the Petrograd front at Stalin's urging came into play. Taking full advantage of a bitter dispute over strategy that had developed between Iudenich, who insisted that Iamburg and the crossings over the Luga River be held at all costs, and Rodzianko, who argued that the Whites should withdraw toward Pskov, the Seventh Red Army retook Iamburg on

August 5.[106] Three days later, the Bolsheviks promised that the Red Army would respect Estonia's independence and would not enter Estonian territory so long as the Estonians would evacuate Pskov and withdraw behind their frontiers. "Rumors of the Bolsheviks' peace proposals rapidly spread through the Estonian forces," one of Iudenich's close advisers remembered. "The soldiers began to ask their superiors more and more urgently: 'Why do we keep on fighting?' "[107] At that point, Iudenich moved decisively to make a bad situation much worse. In contrast to the Bolshevik peace offer, he asked that the entire Estonian army of twenty-five thousand men be placed under his command in return for a very reluctant and qualified recognition of Estonian independence.[108] For a moment, an Estonian peace with the Bolsheviks, which would have left Iudenich no land base from which to operate, seemed very likely.

Blunt British interference saved Iudenich. Acting on instructions from General Sir Hubert Gough, chief of the Allied military mission in the Baltic, England's Brigadier-General Frank G. Marsh summoned the Russians and Estonians to the British Consulate for an urgent meeting on the evening of August 10. "The situation of the Northwestern White Army is bad," Marsh told the Russians. "To be more precise, it is catastrophic. Extreme measures are needed . . . and I am relying upon the patriotism of everyone here to make this final effort work. The Allies," Marsh continued, "consider it absolutely necessary to form a government in the Northwest Region, and it is necessary for that to be done before we leave this room." The Russians, he stated, must stop arguing and form a government that would give full recognition to Estonian independence. "It is now 6:15," Marsh announced flatly. "I am giving you until 7:00 because, at that time, the Estonian government will arrive for negotiations with the government you have formed. If you don't do this, then the Allies will abandon you to your own devices."[109] With that, he turned on his heel and left the room.

Three plenipotentiaries who spoke for the Government of the Northwest Russian Region emerged from the room at Marsh's appointed hour. Yet the agreement they signed with the Estonians four days later did not produce the result that the British envoys had expected. When the Estonians demanded full recognition by the Allies, the British Foreign Office angrily announced that Marsh and Gough had overstepped their authority and "acted with a precipitancy, a levity, and a lack of responsibilty for which it is difficult to find a parallel."[110] Not only the British disdained what Lord Curzon once described as "the Ruritanian experiment which General Gough and his Merry Men have been making in Estonia."[111] When Kolchak's representatives in London and Paris announced that their government would never recognize Estonian independence, Iudenich hurried to complain that General Marsh had forced him to accept a government made up of "men of doubtful character" under circumstances that he had found "deeply humiliating." The recognition of Estonian independence that had emerged from Marsh's forced deliberations, Iudenich now insisted, was "utterly worthless."[112]

Even as Iudenich, Kolchak, the Estonians, and the Allies traded accusations, the Whites in Russia's Northwest received some dramatic assistance. Ready to act against the Bolsheviks should Britain's statesmen call upon them to do so, Rear-Admiral Sir Walter Cowan's squadron had been in the eastern waters of the Baltic and the Finnish Gulf for several months when, on the night after the Bolsheviks had crushed the rebellion at Krasnaia Gorka, a torpedo boat commanded by Lieutenant Augustus Agar had sunk the Red cruiser *Oleg* with a single well-launched torpedo. Far from criticizing the deliberate sinking of a warship belonging to a nation with whom they were not officially at war, the British Admiralty had awarded Agar the Victoria Cross. In mid-August, the Bolsheviks heard from Cowan and Agar again, this time behind the supposedly impregnable defenses at Kronstadt itself, when Cowan sent Agar's and seven other torpedo boats to destroy the battleships of the Red Baltic Fleet. Supported by RAF biplanes, which diverted the Bolsheviks' attention with a rare night bombing attack launched from a small landing strip hacked out of the Finnish forest near Koivisto, Agar and his Finnish smuggler navigators sank the battleships *Andrei Pervozvannyi* and *Petropavlovsk* in less than half an hour. "When England strikes, it strikes hard," Mannerheim remarked when he heard of the attack.[113] For Iudenich, Agar's success meant that his troops need not fear bombardments from the heavy twelve-inch guns of the *Petropavlovsk* and the *Andrei Pervozvannyi* should the Northwestern White Army advance along the Baltic coast toward Petrograd.

Other events soon dampened the Whites' elation about the British attack at Kronstadt. When the Reds stormed into Pskov on September 8, their victory deprived the Northwestern Army of its last base of operations on Russian soil and left it at the mercy of those very Estonians whose independence and national aspirations Iudenich, in a shocking lack of foresight, had rejected as "utterly worthless" not more than a fortnight before. Knowing that if the Estonians now took up the Bolsheviks' still-standing offer of peace the situation of the Northwestern White Army would become hopeless, Iudenich realized that he could not delay his long-planned advance against Petrograd. Still desperately short of men, he explored an alliance with General Count Rüdiger von der Goltz, the German officer who had helped the Finns to drive the Reds from Helsinki in April 1918.[114] Von der Goltz had arrived at the beginning of 1919 in the Latvian port of Libau, where, despite several defeats at the hands of the Latvians and Estonians, and in open violation of General Gough's direct orders to return to Germany,[115] he had organized the so-called Army of Western Russia, whose numbers roughly equaled Iudenich's Northwestern White Army. Dedicated to the personal glorification of von der Goltz and the reestablishment of German influence in the Baltic lands, the Army of Western Russia quickly became notorious for its brutal treatment of Latvians, Estonians, and Bolsheviks. Called by some the "vanguard of Nazism," the *Freikorps* units under von der Goltz's command instituted what one British diplomat called "a veritable reign of terror" that claimed the lives of some three thousand Latvians in Riga alone.[116]

In carving his bloody path, von der Goltz was supported by Colonel Prince Bermondt-Avalov, perhaps the most flamboyant figure to surface in the Baltic lands at that time, and certainly one of the most outrageous. Few knew much about him except that, some months earlier, he had appeared in Skoropadsky's Ukraine, where he had claimed to represent Denikin, that he had gone to Germany at the time of Skoropadsky's fall and then had appeared in the Baltic lands a few weeks after the 1918 armistice. Bermondt-Avalov possessed a lavish supply of jewels and perfume, both of which he used to excess, and was said to relieve his suppressed anger by emptying his pistol into the ceiling of his quarters.[117] Although his claims to military prowess were completely open to question, he had men to command and Iudenich therefore tried to convince him and von der Goltz to join his march against Petrograd. Other loyalties and other plans ruled both men in a way that worked to Iudenich's extreme disadvantage when the Northwestern White Army began its advance in October. At that moment, Bermondt-Avalov and von der Goltz turned their forces against Riga and forced Admiral Cowan to divert his squadron to defend the Latvians' capital.[118] Even more damaging to the Whites' cause, Iudenich's brief flirtation with these two adventurers convinced the Estonians to reopen peace negotiations with the Bolsheviks for fear that the Northwestern White Army and the Army of Western Russia might join against them. Certain that a Soviet–Estonian peace would deny him the use of Estonian territory, Iudenich therefore hurried to reestablish his army on Russian soil even though he still commanded many fewer troops than he thought necessary to take the offensive.

As he began his march against Petrograd, Iudenich knew that it would require vast quantities of food and supplies to transform Russia's former capital into a base for his Government of the Northwest Russian Region. "It is a city still in a state of siege," one White intelligence source had reported just a week before Cowan's raid on Kronstadt. A half-pound of bread and a bowl of watery soup "into which bits of poor quality fish have been crumbled" comprised the basic ration for adult Petrograders that summer. In June, a pound of bread had cost 130 rubles on the black market.[119] By fall, the price of white bread had nearly tripled, potatoes stood at 75 rubles a pound, and a pound of butter had soared to 1,500 rubles.[120] Certain that feeding Petrograd's population would be a matter of great urgency if the Whites captured the city, Iudenich's staff had given serious attention to how they would secure and transport the necessary provisions. "By reason of the refugees from Bolshevist districts coming in for bread," they predicted, Petrograd's population would increase by more than half within a month. If they kept to their plan of setting each adult's weekly ration at seven pounds of bread, two pounds of meat, and a half pound of barley, dried peas, rice, or grits, in addition to a quarter pound each of salt, sugar, and condensed milk, the Whites would need nearly four thousand tons of supplies during the first week alone.[121] Should Iudenich take Petrograd, he would have to depend absolutely upon his Allies to feed the people under his control.

Iudenich began his offensive against Petrograd at the beginning of October, often a season of gray weather, rain, mud, and fog in the Baltic lands of Eastern Europe.[122] This time he faced not the dour Stalin, whose merciless repression drove men to battle out of fear, but Trotskii, the revolutionary orator of unmatched brilliance, whose fiery words inspired men and women to face great danger and perform greater feats in the name of the Revolution. Trotskii sent men and women to Petrograd's defenses with their hearts seared by his revolutionary passion and comforted by his abiding belief in the new world the Bolsheviks were building. "Happy is he," Trotskii once exclaimed, "who in his mind and heart feels the electrical current of our great epoch!"[123] At Petrograd, Trotskii gave its starving men and women a new belief in themselves and a certainty that a place in the revolutionary pantheon awaited each who did his duty. By contrast, the flat rhetoric of Iudenich and Rodzianko, both of whom continued to quarrel bitterly about who should command in the field, offered very little to stir the hearts of the men who marched with them.[124] The "ultimate purpose" of their campaign, they announced in the prolix language of commanders who knew nothing of the dreams of the men they led, must be the "implantation of order and legality" in Russia.[125] Former prisoners of war just returning from Germany, local peasants, and a few workers marched with them, but they did so reluctantly. Even Iudenich's first victories did not stem the rising tide of desertions that began on the very day his army left Narva.

Despite the squabbling in their high command, the soldiers of the Northwestern White Army opened their offensive on September 28 with a series of astounding victories. Within a week, the forces on Iudenich's right flank took the key town of Luga and cut rail connections between Pskov and Petrograd. Further to the north, the main White assault force stormed into Iamburg on October 11. Ahead lay two main rail lines that intersected near Gatchina, just twenty-nine miles southwest of Petrograd. By either route, Petrograd stood less than eighty miles away. Knowing that his only hope for success lay in a lightning thrust that would carry him into Petrograd before his fragile army melted away, Iudenich attacked directly along these two lines. Five days later, the first units of the Northwestern Army reached Gatchina and, on October 20, went on to storm the Pulkovo Heights, within rifle range of Petrograd's suburbs.[126] Now certain that Denikin had taken Orël, White newspapers printed banner headlines which announced that "Victory Is Near," and "Tomorrow Will Bring Victory."[127] Lenin even began to talk of abandoning Petrograd. "There remained only one thing to do in his opinion," Trotskii remembered. "Abandon Petrograd and shorten the front."[128] Meanwhile, White commanders vied to reach the city. So confident of victory was the commanding general of Iudenich's Third Infantry Division that he ignored orders to cut the Moscow–Petrograd railway at Tosno, some twenty-five miles east of Gatchina, and turned his troops north toward Petrograd in the hope of being the first to enter.[129]

Everyone had reckoned without Trotskii. Protesting vehemently against any plan to abandon the "cradle of the Revolution," Trotskii insisted that the Bolsheviks must "hold Petrograd at any cost" and hurried north from Moscow on the night of October 16, just hours after Iudenich's troops had moved through Gatchina.[130] His mind working as he went, he dictated his thoughts about the crisis he would face when his train arrived in Petrograd the next morning. "Petrograd is not Iamburg. Nor is it Luga," he reminded himself. "There are tens of thousands of Communists, a large garrison, and huge, almost inexhaustible resources for building engineering and artillery defenses." To him, the possibilities for Petrograd's defense seemed almost without limit. "Once having broken into this gigantic city, the White Guards would find themselves in the midst of a stone labyrinth," he wrote as he drafted what was to be his battle plan should Iudenich enter the city. "Every house will become an enigma, a threat, or a mortal danger," he wrote. "Whence should [the Whites] expect the next blow? From a window? From a loft? From a cellar? From behind a corner? From everywhere!" Trotskii exclaimed with satisfaction. "All that is needed are a few thousand people who have firmly resolved not to surrender Petrograd."[131] It was a seductive picture, one calculated to give hope to men and women who had thought none remained.

As always, those around him—including even Lenin—drew strength from Trotskii's unshakable revolutionary confidence. "I enclose a proclamation which the Council of Defense asked me to write," Lenin wrote to him the next day. "I worked too quickly and it turned out badly. It would be better," the chairman of the Sovnarkom concluded, "if you wrote your own [proclamation] and put my signature beneath it."[132] But Trotskii needed more than the freedom to sign Lenin's name if he hoped to bar Iudenich's path, for the situation he faced when he arrived in Petrograd on the morning of October 17 could hardly have been worse. "I found a state of extreme confusion," he remembered. "The situation called for exceptional measures. The enemy was at the very gates."[133] Two days later Trotskii stood before the Petrograd Soviet of Workers', Peasants', and Soldiers' Deputies, over which he had presided during the heady revolutionary days of 1905 and 1917. "I will make no secret of the fact that I have come here with a soul filled with alarm," he told them. "Perhaps no other city on earth has lived through what Petrograd has endured." Yet, despite what Petrograd had suffered, she must suffer again. Their city, he told Petrograd's hungry people, was "a revolutionary barometer of the Red Soviet Republic," and its loss would be a catastrophe, a "mortal danger," for all of Bolshevik Russia. This, he insisted, could not, must not, happen. "Red Petrograd," Trotskii concluded with one of his dazzling oratorical flourishes, "must remain what it has always been—the torch of the Revolution, the iron rock upon which we will build the church of the future."[134]

"The inward rallying had begun," one of Petrograd's leading Bolsheviks later wrote. "Everybody began to realize that only one road was left—forward. All avenues of retreat had been cut."[135] Trotskii remembered how Petrograd's proletarians, "their faces pale from malnutrition, clad in rags and tatters, their shoes worn through and often not even matching," had marched resolutely to their city's defense two years before when the White forces of Krasnov had threatened their revolution from the same point. "We won't surrender Piter, will we, comrades?" Trotskii recalled them asking each other. "No, we won't!" Always the superb revolutionary street tactician, Trotskii sensed the workers' change of mood the moment it began. "A new spirit," he later wrote, "began to blow from the workers' districts to the barracks, to the units in the rear guard, and to the army in the field."[136] As Iudenich's forces at Pulkovo prepared their final assault, this legion of workers transformed Petrograd into the labyrinthine fortress Trotskii had envisoned during his lonely night journey from Moscow a few days before. A sudden stroke of good fortune eased his task. Thanks to the blatant insubordination of one of Iudenich's key commanders, the Third White Infantry Division had rushed toward Petrograd without breaking the Reds' hold on the key rail junction at Tosno. This made it possible to send arms, ammunition, supplies, and reinforcements to Petrograd's defenders from Moscow, no matter how much pressure the Whites might exert from Pulkovo and the west.

As quickly as it had risen, the tide of victory that had swept Iudenich's forces into Petrograd's suburbs ebbed. "Iudenich's advance has come to a halt," Trotskii rejoiced on the evening of October 21. "Not only have we stopped the advance but we have struck a powerful blow against the enemy."[137] That night, the Reds drove the Whites from Pulkovo and retook Tsarskoe Selo and Pavlovsk two days later. On November 7, the second anniversary of the Bolshevik Revolution and his fortieth birthday, Trotskii stood before the Bolshevik Central Committee to report his victory. "In the battle for Petrograd, Soviet power showed that it stands on its feet firmly and indestructibly," he announced. "For that reason the Petrograd battle will have great . . . significance in the weeks and months ahead." Perhaps more confident than at any time since the October Revolution, Trotskii looked forward with an optimism rarely seen in the centers of Bolshevik power. "I believe that, with an army such as ours," he concluded, "the third year of Soviet power will be the year that sees the complete destruction of our enemies and a firm peace."[138]

In the Northwest, Iudenich's forces faced certain catastrophe. Their movements now closely coordinated, the Seventh and Fifteenth Red Armies attacked the Northwestern White Army simultaneously from the east and south. Collecting massive reinforcements from their rear areas as they advanced, the Reds retook Gatchina on October 27. Four days later, they drove the Whites from Luga, and on November 7, they celebrated the second anniversary of the Revolution by linking forces to the south and east of Iamburg. The Seventh Red Army alone now outnumbered Iudenich's forces by three to one. A week later, Iamburg fell and the victorious Reds drove the Northwestern Army to the edge of the Estonian frontier, where thousands of White refugees, their hopes shattered, already huddled in misery and want.[139] "Every village, every house and every shelter of any sort were literally overflowing with miserable, hungry, freezing people," one observer later wrote. "There was not a single sheltered corner where the retreating soldiers could warm themselves and rest. The fighting men therefore had to live without shelter during days and nights when the temperature was ten to eighteen degrees below zero."[140]

All too easily reminded of Iudenich's stubborn reluctance to recognize their independence, and in no mood to jeopardize their peace negotiations with Lenin's government by appearing to shelter its enemies, the Estonians heeded Trotskii's warning that "an independent Estonia cannot continue to serve as a kennel for the pet dogs of counterrevolution"[141] and refused to allow either refugees or soldiers from the Northwestern White Army to cross the frontier to the shelter of Narva. After urgent pleas from Iudenich and several members of his crumbling government, they relented and permitted the Whites to enter Estonia in small groups, provided that they had surrendered their weapons and did not wear their uniforms. "All those who served in the *former* Northwestern Army must not wear their uniforms [on Estonian soil]," they insisted. "In accordance with international law the soldiers of a foreign State, and particularly an army that *no longer exists* does not have the right to enter the borders of another State in uniform."[142] With no refuge for its soldiers and no haven for itself, the government that the Northwestern White Army supported therefore came to an end on December 5.

When Iudenich left the comfort of Reval's Hotel Commerce to flee Estonia under British protection a month later, he left more than ten thousand defeated soldiers and twice that number of refugees behind to be ravaged by hunger, cold, and disease.[143] First by the hundreds, and then by the thousands, hungry, ill-clothed, and wretchedly housed soldiers fell before the onslaught of a terrible epidemic of spotted typhus. "Now they are beginning to talk and write about the Golgotha of the Northwestern Army," one of them wrote. "But, in my opinion, Golgotha is far too mild an expression to describe all the torment that these soldiers and officers must endure. . . . You undoubtedly recall the pictures portraying the retreating French forces [of Napoleon] in 1812," he continued. "Hungry, emaciated, shivering from the cold, raving from madness, these people are portrayed as being wrapped in blankets, shawls, women's jackets, and God knows what other rags. I must tell you that I have seen many soldiers here who are dressed only slightly better than that."[144]

A few of Iudenich's soldiers tried to reach the forces of Denikin and Wrangel in South Russia, but most made their peace with the Reds or searched for ways to rebuild their lives in some other country. With them they carried shattered hopes and a tragic sense of an opportunity too easily lost. Unwittingly, one of them wrote a bitter epitaph to their failure in a letter to a friend. "The entire Northwestern Army," he concluded, "was a huge misunderstanding, but, unfortunately, an immensely sad and extremely bitter misunderstanding."[145] Nowhere else had the Whites tried to build a force on the soil of another country to fight the Reds, and nowhere else had they labored so energetically to enlist other national armies in their struggle. The Government of the Northwest Russian Region, so briefly established and so utterly dependent upon resources outside its control, had been insignificant in terms of the territory it had held and the population it had tried to govern, but it had been a danger nonetheless because it had threatened Petrograd, the "cradle of the Revolution," itself.

Paradoxically, Iudenich's greatest triumph had given Trotskii one of his finest hours and had made the Bolsheviks stronger still. But the Civil War's most decisive battles had been—and would continue to be—fought elsewhere. Some already had been waged in the vastness of Siberia, where, by a quirk of fate, the Reds made their triumphal entry into Kolchak's capital of Omsk on the same day as they took Iamburg. Other battles continued in the South, where, to add irony to irony, the Red Armies turned back Denikin's effort to advance beyond Orël on the same day as Trotskii's forces drove Iudenich's men from the Pulkovo Heights. There therefore was more than mere optimism behind Trotskii's remark to his comrades on the Central Committee that 1920 would bring an end to the struggle between Red and White. By the end of 1919, the Bolsheviks held more territory more firmly than at any time since the October Revolution.

With the governments and armies of Kolchak and Iudenich gone, and those of Denikin and Miller in full retreat, the Whites thus entered 1920 far weaker than they had been a year before. Yet strength still remained in the Bolsheviks' opponents. Perhaps nowhere was that more evident than in the Ukraine, where the fighting of 1919 would be far less conclusive than on the other fronts of the Civil War. There, a volatile mixture of peasant anarchism and proletarian class hatred combined with outraged nationalism and virulent anti-Semitism to explode into the bloodiest and most vicious conflict of the Russian Civil War. In the Ukraine, where men and women dreamed as passionately of national independence as they did in Finland or the Baltic states, the ferment of social upheaval, religious bigotry, and class warfare proceeded to turn dreams into nightmares.

CHAPTER NINE

The Ukraine in Ferment

No region of the Russian Empire witnessed more violence, more destruction, and more unvarnished cruelty of man to man during Russia's Civil War than the Ukraine. Elsewhere in the former empire's borderlands White forces had established territorial bases, marched against Moscow, and then, when their effort failed, retreated to the safety of the frontier once again. In almost every case, non-Russian nationalist aspirations had complicated the Whites' efforts as emergent peoples seeking independence had interposed themselves between them and the Reds. Iudenich had fallen afoul of the Estonians' and Finns' demands for national states in the Baltic. Denikin had struggled to come to grips with dreams of independence cherished by Georgians and the peoples of the Kuban, the Crimea, and Armenia. The Allied commanders in North Russia had confronted the nationalist aspirations of the Finns and Karelians, and Kolchak had faced a host of demands from a plethora of nationalities in Siberia. From the beginning, the Whites had insisted that nationalist dreams must be set aside until a freely elected Constituent Assembly could decide the fate of those non-Russian men and women who once had languished under Russia's fallen tsars. Surprisingly, they had their way. Only Iudenich had suffered any serious direct repercussions from his reluctance to recognize the nationalist aspirations of the people upon whose territory he had built the Northwestern White Army.

The situation in the Ukraine, where men and women proud of their past and anxious to embark upon a non-Russian future refused to place victory over Bolshevism ahead of their long-held dreams of independence, proved to be far more volatile and complex. Its lands repeatedly torn by German occupation, Bolshevik expansionism, Ukrainian nationalism, peasant anarchism, and Polish invasion, the Ukraine became a battleground over which armies fought without respite between the fall of 1917 and the summer of 1920. In the rich lands that once had been the Russian Empire's fertile southwest granary, Reds fought against Whites, peasants fought against landlords and townsfolk, Ukrainians fought against Germans, Russians, and Poles, and anarchists fought against all efforts to impose any sort of state order upon them. Kiev, the capital of the Ukraine for more than a millennium, changed hands no less than sixteen times in thirty-six months.[1] "These were convulsive, violent times," Konstantin Paustovskii wrote in his recollections of the months he spent in Kiev during 1918 and 1919. "It was impossible to grasp what was going on. . . . Every regime hurried to publish as many declarations and decrees as possible, hoping that at least a few of them might filter down into the realm of real life and stick to it in some fashion."[2]

The dreams of national freedom that sustained the men and women of the Ukraine during these troubled times stretched back a thousand years to those long-ago days when the founding of Moscow as a remote frontier outpost lay more than a century in the future and medieval Kiev stood among the most vibrant cities of the Western world. Located at the point where the "Great Amber Road" from the Baltic to Constantinople intersected with the trade routes that carried the spices and treasures of the Orient to the West, Kiev of the eleventh and twelth centuries drew upon the rich heritage of the Near and Middle East, integrated it with her Slavic past, and seasoned the resulting mixture with European borrowings. Richly ornamented brick palaces and great stone cathedrals, the largest of which covered more than fourteen thousand square feet, adorned its center, and libraries, schools, and hospitals made the lives of its citizens richer and more comfortable than those of their counterparts in the West. With its ruling Riurikid dynasty linked to almost every important royal family of Christian Europe by ties of marriage and its people mentioned repeatedly and with respect in such early Western epics as the *Chanson de Roland* and the *Niebelungenlied*, Kiev thus enjoyed well-merited international acclaim.

But the importance of Kiev to the medieval West reached far beyond the realms of trade and politics. As the eastern outpost of the Christian world, Kiev stood as a bastion against the onslaught of the less civilized peoples of the Asian steppe. Some historians have claimed that the cultural accomplishments of the High Middle Ages might not have been possible had it not been for Kiev's readiness to defend Europe's eastern gateway against the hordes that eventually overwhelmed her.[3] Yet the city whose brilliance had so thoroughly illuminated Europe's eastern frontier during the eleventh and twelfth centuries crumbled as quickly as it had arisen. Torn apart by internecine conflicts and shattered by attacks from Asia's Mongol hordes, Kiev retained only the merest shreds of her former glory by the middle of the thirteenth century. As the political centers of Eastern Europe shifted elsewhere, the history of Kiev and its people became linked to that of other nations. First in league with the Grand Duchy of Lithuania, then under the suzerainty of Poland, and, finally, as a part of the Russian Empire, Kiev and its Ukrainian people lived beneath the authority of foreign rulers. Not even the great seventeenth-century wars of Bogdan Khmelnitsky, the greatest of the Ukrainian Cossack chieftains, could establish an independent Ukrainian state. Not until 1917, when Kiev's National Rada defied Russia's Provisional Government and proclaimed a republic, did the Ukraine seriously try to claim its independence.

Perhaps because of long centuries spent in dreaming of the day when they would become free, the Ukrainians who struggled to shape a national state in the midst of Russia's revolutionary turmoil wasted little love upon their neighbors. Branded as "age-long enemies" and "bloodsuckers of the people,"[4] Russians stirred particular anger among those Ukrainian patriots whose ancestors had borne the weight of the Russian yoke for too long. Yet there were some who did not share these xenophobic sentiments. Some Ukrainian nationalists looked to the Germans and the Austrians for support in establishing an independent Ukraine, and a few rich lords in 1917 even dared to envision a future in which their land would remain allied with the Russians in a loose union of autonomous states under the aegis of a democratic Russian federation.[5] Only for the despised *zhidy*, the Jews, did Ukrainians reserve almost unanimous hatred. Long the object of persecution in the Ukraine, the Jews had seen some two hundred thousand of their ancestors butchered in the seventeenth century by Khmelnitsky's Cossacks in what one noted historian has called "the greatest single massacre of Jews prior to Hitler."[6] Now identified not only as "Christ killers" and "bloodsuckers" but as agents of those Bolsheviks who would replace "the landlords' yoke" with "Jewish slavery,"[7] the Ukrainian Jews soon became the victims of a new and vicious wave of anti-Semitism as the collapse of effective government made such virulent hatreds a part of everyday life in the Ukraine between 1917 and 1921.

Taking advantage of the weakness of the Provisional Government, the National Rada, which had begun to meet as a Ukrainian national assembly in Kiev soon after Russia's February Revolution, moved steadily toward independence in 1917. As its leaders summoned the people of the Ukraine to "a decisive struggle against . . . disorder and anarchy"[8] after the Bolsheviks' victory, the Rada proclaimed a Ukrainian People's Republic would rule until a freely elected Ukrainian Constituent Assembly should "form a government for the whole of the territory of the Ukrainian Republic."[9] Yet independence could not be won so easily. Although Stalin as commissar of nationalities continued to insist that "there can be no conflict between the Ukrainians and Russian peoples [because], . . . in the struggle against the landlords and capitalists they are all brothers and comrades," no Ukrainian could forget his promise that "fratricidal bloodshed of the peoples" would result if the Ukraine remained aloof from Russia's new government of people's commissars.[10] To Russians, Stalin stated his views even more bluntly. "The Soviet of People's Commissars will not hesitate to wage a determined fight against the Rada," he told the assembled All-Russian Central Executive Committee in mid-December.[11] "The Rada, or rather its General Secretariat, is a government of traitors to socialism who call themselves socialists in order to deceive the masses," he added in an article that appeared in *Pravda* the next day. Only a "Rada of the soviets of workers, soldiers, and peasants of the Ukraine," he concluded, could "protect the interests of the Ukrainian people [against] . . . the landlords and capitalists."[12]

Quickly, the Bolsheviks moved to buttress Stalin's warnings with deeds. Supported by some of the Red Guard troops that had marched with Antonov-Ovseenko against the White forces of Alekseev and Kaledin, a handful of fugitive Ukrainian Bolsheviks proclaimed a Soviet government in the northeastern Ukrainian industrial city of Kharkov at the end of December. From there, Antonov's Socialist Revolutionary chief of staff, the former tsarist captain Mikhail Muravev, marched against the uncertain and unorganized forces of the Rada to the southwest. Muravev captured Poltava at the cost of a single casualty on January 19 and began to shell Kiev with his heavy artillery nine days later.[13] Bitter fighting followed the bombardment as Kiev's defenders fought from building to building. "After a five-day battle in the streets of Kiev, I have taken control of the city," Muravev reported to Antonov on February 9, 1918.[14] "A Soviet of Workers' and Peasants' Deputies and a Military-Revolutionary Committee is working energetically," he told Lenin by direct wire a few days later. "Soviet power in the Ukraine is growing stronger."[15]

Yet Muravev's victory proved to be less complete than he thought. On the day before Kiev fell, the ministers of the Rada had escaped to Zhitomir, a provincial capital some fifty miles to the west, where they quickly showed that they still had winning cards to play. Using their vast reserves of grain to entice recognition from the Bolsheviks' hungry enemies, they opened separate negotiations with the Germans and Austrians at Brest-Litovsk, where, at two o'clock on the morning of February 9, some ten hours before Kiev's defenses collapsed, they signed a separate peace with the Central Powers, to whom they immediately appealed for aid against "the enemy of our liberty who has invaded our native land in order to subjugate the Ukrainian people with fire and sword."[16] Anxious to protect the grain supplies and raw materials of the Ukraine, the Germans did not need a second invitation. In less than ten days, Austro-German units were on the march, moving quickly along key rail lines, supported by heavy guns hastily mounted on railroad flatcars.[17] On March 2, just three weeks after Muravev had taken Kiev, they drove the Bolsheviks from the city.

As Muravev's Red Guards fled in panic, the Rada returned to Kiev in triumph to proclaim that the Germans had come "for a limited period of time as friends and supporters to help us at a difficult moment of our life." These new forces, they promised, had "no intention either of altering our laws and regulations or limiting the independence and sovereignty of our Republic."[18] In their delight at being rid of the Bolsheviks, one of their leaders confessed ruefully, the Rada's ministers had forgotten the wise

Ukrainian proverb which warned men and women too ready to rely upon others that "you must sing the tune of the person on whose wagon you ride."[19]

The Germans' tune, the Ukrainians soon found, had but a single theme. With the city folk of Austria and Germany desperately short of food, the German chief of staff in the Ukraine wrote, it must be the first task of their armies in the East "to extract . . . grain and other foodstuffs—the more the better!"[20] Therefore, while the Rada settled itself in Kiev, the Germans continued their march southeastward to Kharkov, Kherson, and Ekaterinoslav. By the end of May, the vast coalfields of the Donbas and the rich grainfields of the Ukraine both lay under their control,[21] but they found it far more difficult to exploit these new resources than they had imagined. Concerned to win the masses' support with radical land distribution programs and economic reforms, the Rada failed to restore the processes of local government that the Bolshevik invasion had destroyed, with the result that the Germans found it extremely difficult to collect grain from the surly Ukrainian peasants. "It is very doubtful whether this government, composed as it is exclusively of left opportunists, will be able to establish firm authority," one senior German officer telegraphed from Kiev the week after his forces entered the city. Many Germans, not a few Ukrainian lords, and a sizable number of wealthy peasants shared that view.[22]

As spring planting neared, Germany's ambassador Baron Adolf Mumm von Schwarzenstein began to refer to the Rada as a "pseudo-government"[23] and worried about its ability to ensure that the desperately needed new crops of wheat and rye would be planted. "Permanent collaboration with these men, who, because of their socialist theories, cease to comprehend the real state of affairs, is impossible," he told his superiors in Berlin in mid-April. "A change in governments," he added three days later, "would not in itself be unfortunate."[24] Mumm had no objection if, "insofar as it is possible, a Ukrainian government should be preserved," but insisted that any government which replaced the Rada "must not hinder the military and economic undertakings of the German authorities."[25] More fearful of the Rada's radical economic reform programs than of cooperation with the Germans, a number of Ukrainian lords proved ready to pay the Germans' price to establish the puppet government that Mumm envisioned. General Pavlo Skoropadsky, graduate of the Imperial Russian Corps of Pages, aide-de-camp to Nicholas II, and one of the wealthiest men in the Ukraine, stood at their head.

Like his father before him, Skoropadsky had spent his adult life in the service of Russia's tsars and had neither the native pride nor the regional prejudice needed to become a Ukrainian national leader. He and Field Marshal Hermann von Eichhorn, commander-in-chief of the Austro-German forces in the Ukraine, had married nieces of Count Durnovo, a notoriously reactionary Russian minister of internal affairs, and close family ties bound them still. No longer able to serve the Russians, Skoropadsky therefore chose not to serve the Rada but the Germans. On April 29, 1918, just one week before his forty-sixth birthday, he led a *coup d'état* against the men who had ruled so ineptly in the name of the Ukrainian people. "Disorder and anarchy reign throughout the country . . . [and] the once prosperous Ukraine is now threatened by the approaching phantom of starvation," he announced as he took power.[26] "Only a firm authority can reestablish order," he told the Landowners' League Congress that conferred the ancient title of hetman upon him that day. "I pray to God to grant me the strength to save the Ukraine."[27] Skoropadsky, who spoke no Ukrainian, was to be a dictator dedicated to the old world of imperial privilege that the Revolution had swept away. For him, there could be few concessions to the new egalitarian order. "My Fatherland," he said firmly at one point, "cannot become the [testing] ground for socialistic experiments."[28] His was a government, the Ukrainian National Political Union complained, composed of men "Ukrainian by blood but Muscovite in spirit."[29]

Protected by von Eichhorn's armies, Skoropadsky's conservative regime produced a rapid and surprising economic recovery. "The Hetman's revolution was carried out under the slogan of the restoration of landed property and freedom of trade," one knowledgeable observer wrote,[30] and this produced substantial improvement in industrial and commercial circles, not to mention the agriculture of the Ukraine's great lords. Attracted by its apparent stability and prosperity, men and women who once had been part of Russia's upper and middle classes flooded into Kiev from the Bolsheviks' domains. No longer fearful of being cursed as *burzhui*, as part of the bourgeoisie, they sought to forget the shattered lives they had left behind. Theaters, restaurants, and cafes overflowed with elegant men and women. Speculators and black marketeers plied their trade in luxury goods sold at exorbitant prices, and prostitutes reveled in a steadily increasing clientele.[31] "Life in Kiev in those days reminded one of a feast in time of plague," Paustovskii remembered. "Gambling dens and houses of prostitution sprang up overnight. They sold cocaine openly on the Bessarabka, where teen-aged whores offered themselves for sale."[32]

Not all the Russian refugees who came to Kiev in the summer of 1918 reveled in cafes, black markets, and whorehouses. Among those who fled the grim, gray world of the Bolsheviks came influential members of the Constitutional Democratic Party, the Kadets, who had played such a key role in Russian affairs in the weeks after the February Revolution. Now stripped of their power, but still hoping to find a base from which to mount a new assault against the men who had driven them from office, some of Russia's fugitive Kadets gave Skoropadsky their support. Now willing to set the bitterness of the Great War aside in order to reach an accommodation with Germany, which one of them went so far as to describe as "a true friend and ally of democratic Russia," no fewer than seven Kadets appeared in Skoropadsky's first cabinet. "Our history shows," one of them announced with self-righteous self-justification, "that Russia's interests have always been tied more closely to Germany than to England."[33] Although they still refused to accept the possibility of a fully independent Ukraine and argued that their support of Skoropadsky's government stemmed simply from "a realistic evaluation of the present circumstances," they followed what they called the "tactics of accommodation," in the hope of winning German support in their efforts to rid Russia of the Bolsheviks. Once freed of the Bolsheviks, a unified Russia could accept certain "priority" relationships between Germany and the Ukraine, Kadet leader and one-time Russian Foreign Minister Miliukov told the Germans, but these should be "as few as possible."[34]

If the Kadets found it possible to accommodate themselves to Skoropadsky's regime, Ukrainian nationalists, workers, and peasants did not. Volodimir Vinnichenko, the Ukrainian nationalist leader whose memoirs recounted his people's Civil War struggles in immense detail, called Skoropadsky "a Russian general of Little Russian origin" and condemned him as "a sentimental degenerate." Others cursed Skoropadsky's rigid censorship, which closed some of the most influential socialist and nationalist newspapers in the Ukraine, his uncompromising defense of private property, and his unyielding insistence upon meeting the Germans' demands as he called upon the Ukrainians to dedicate themselves to "work instead of politics."[35] Few doubted Skoropadsky's readiness to set German demands ahead of Ukrainian freedoms. "The tragedy of the Hetman's government," one observer concluded, "was that . . . above him was a more powerful, mailed fist on which everything in reality depended."[36]

Tension rose all across the Ukraine as nationalists, revolutionaries, peasants, and workers turned against Skoropadsky's regime. So many German and Austrian soldiers died at the hands of Ukrainian partisans during the summer and fall of 1918 that the German High Command considered fining Skoropadsky's government from 50,000 rubles for the death of each private to 200,000 rubles for the death of a general.[37] Mysterious explosions in German ammunition dumps in Kiev claimed several hundred lives at once, and at the end of July, Russian terrorists assassinated Skoropadsky's brother-in-law Field Marshal von Eichhorn himself.[38] Briefly, Skoropadsky considered an accommodation with the Ukrainian nationalists but found that impossible unless he made greater social and political concessions than he or the Germans could allow.

"In general, the Germans toyed with the Ukraine like a cat plays with a mouse, first tightening its grip and then allowing its victim to run free and savor the illusion of freedom, all the while watching to make certain that its prey didn't escape its clutches," one Ukrainian remembered bitterly.[39] That fall, German demands for Ukrainian food and Ukrainian raw materials increased. By November, nearly a million tons of foodstuffs, over thirteen thousand tons of hemp, a million hides and skins, and close to five thousand tons of tobacco had been shipped from the Ukraine to Germany, Austria, and Hungary. As if that were not enough, Skoropadsky agreed to send more than a third of the Ukraine's total grain harvest to the Central Powers the following year.[40] Angry railroad workers, who had welcomed the Germans so enthusiastically in March, organized strikes against them in July. Quite probably, only their defeat by the Western Allies and the Armistice of November 11, 1918, prevented the Germans from imposing a much sterner regime upon the Ukraine before the end of the year.

Germany's defeat shattered the base upon which Skoropadsky had built his regime. Without German protection his government had little hope of standing against the Ukrainian nationalist forces that Vinnichenko and the office worker-turned-publicist-turned-soldier Simon Petliura had begun to mobilize for an insurrection. For a few desperate weeks, Skoropadsky pleaded with the Allies to become his new protectors and even called for the Ukraine to become a part of a federated all-Russian state ruled by the Whites. "The Ukraine must take the lead in the matter of the establishment of an all-Russian federation," he insisted as he appointed a new cabinet composed mainly of Russian monarchists in mid-November. "I hereby commission the newly formed cabinet to undertake the execution of this great historic task in the very near future."[41] Without winning the Allies or the Whites to his cause, his effort infuriated his nationalist enemies and cost him the support of those Ukrainian conservatives who had presided over his rise to power. Despite Ataman Krasnov's grandiose statement that "now again, as a millennium ago, the eyes of all the better people of Russia are upon Kiev,"[42] the Cossacks of the Don made no move to help Skoropadsky, and Denikin's armies remained occupied elsewhere.

Once Skoropadsky had committed himself to a pro-Russian course, his enemies moved quickly. "They declared war directly upon the hetman as a traitor to the Ukraine," one of Kiev's citizens later wrote.[43] Now heading a rival government, Vinnichenko and Petliura drove Skoropadsky from office in less than a month. "The heroic efforts of the armed toiling men and women of the Ukraine have swept the destructive landlord-monarchist authority of the Hetman's government from the face of the land," they announced as they returned to Kiev. Triumphantly, their newly formed Directory invited "the toiling intelligentsia to take a decisive stand on the side of the working classes and to apply all its strength, knowledge, and talent to the task of creating a new, just, and healthy life for everyone."[44]

Determined to be as nationalist and democratic as Skoropadsky's government had been aristocratic and dictatorial, the Directory launched a broad campaign of Ukrainization and proletarianization. Boldly, it annulled all laws of the Hetman's government that had been "directed against the interests of the toiling classes," promised land to the peasants, especially those who had fought against Skoropadsky, declared that "the so-called ruling classes, the classes of the landed and industrial bourgeoisie . . . responsible for the ruin of the national economy . . . can have no voice in the government," and bestowed the right to rule solely upon "the toiling people of an independent Ukrainian People's Republic."[45] No one proved more dedicated to the Ukrainian past than Petliura himself, the insurance company bookkeeper who had taken up the sword in the name of workers' rights and Ukrainian national independence. Variously called a bandit, the Ukrainian Garibaldi, and the "savior of European civilization from Great Russian imperialism,"[46] Petliura, like Stalin, had spent his adolescent years studying for the priesthood before he began to champion the causes of socialism and Ukrainian nationalism. Thirty-nine when he rose to share power with Vinnichenko in the Directory, he was a man of action, albeit a pompous and pretentious one, who, Paustovskii remembered, appealed especially to maidservants, governesses, and retired Ukrainian generals.

Because the Ukrainians had yet to develop a clear sense of national identity and national interest, the Directory's efforts to emphasize a "Ukrainian" past as the key to a "Ukrainian" future often proved more comic than serious. "Everything was rebuilt to look like the Ukraine in the olden days," Paustovskii wrote of his days in Kiev. "It was hard to tell if something serious was going on or if the city was merely acting out a play with characters dressed up like old-time Ukrainian peasant rebels."[47] One resident thought that Kiev resembled "a gigantic sign painter's workshop," as men with paintbrushes and ladders paraded through the streets changing Russian signs into Ukrainian ones.[48] Nothing seemed fixed and nothing seemed permanent, as men and women struggled to shape their lives according to information, the accuracy of which no one believed. "Rumors took on an elemental, almost cosmic quality under Petliura," Paustovskii wrote. Some of these seemed so dazzling in their falsity that the amazed young Russian writer kept a list of them, remembering especially the rumor that the great actress Vera Kholodnaia had proclaimed herself empress of the Ukraine and had gathered an army to enforce her claim. "It was a monumental collection of lies," he concluded, a true chronicle of "the irrepressible fantasies of helplessly confused people."[49]

Too much about Petliura's regime seemed artificial and contrived. Despite its ringing proclamations and its efforts to awaken a joyful awareness of the past in the people of Kiev by dressing soldiers and tradesfolk in Ukrainian national costumes, a sense of deepening desperation gripped Ukrainians. As the Directory failed to replace the strict regulations of Skoropadsky and the Germans with any firm controls of its own, prices soared out of control. Paustovskii remembered how some of Kiev's enterprising citizens set out to offset rampant inflation with a flood of counterfeit money. "There was not a single print shop in Kiev where typesetters and lithographers were not happily producing Petliura money," he wrote in his remembrances of those days. "Many enterprising citizens even made counterfeit money at home with the help of little brushes and cheap watercolors."[50] As the value of money plummeted, white bread sold for three hundred rubles a pound, the same weight of sugar cost more than twice that amount, and a pound of lard sold for even more.[51] That winter, shortages of fuel oil and coal halted trains and shut down factories. "The country was drifting into a cosmic, impenetrable fog," Paustovskii thought. "The same empty streets with the same people turning green from cold and hunger scurrying along them," now seemed to have become a permanent part of life in the Ukraine.[52]

To make matters worse, people began to fight their own private wars. Without any effective central government, local chiefs established petty tyrannies in Kharkov, Poltava, Ekaterinoslav, Chernobyl, Radomysl, and Chernigov, and these neither enforced the policies of the Directory nor even agreed with them. Although their visions of the future varied widely—at one time or another they condemned such diverse groups as the Chinese, the Russians, the *zhidy*, and the Latvians—all of these local regimes despised outside authority and hated the Jews. Dominated by crude self-interest, the atamans of the Ukraine thus remained at odds with the Directory, the Bolsheviks, and each other. "Physical force," Vinnichenko lamented later, "remained in the hands of elements that either did not understand the revolution or were outright counterrevolutionary and even anti-Ukrainian." The result was chaos. "It was this complete lack of control, the autocratic behavior of civil and military authorities," Vinnichenko concluded, "that proved to be both a conscious and unconscious counterrevolution for us."[53]

Its economy in shambles, its political authority ineffective and without popular support, the Directory faced a new attack by the Bolsheviks. Anxious to take advantage of the breakdown of authority that had accompanied Germany's defeat, Trotskii had been so quick to order the Red Army into the Ukraine that, before the middle of January, Bolshevik forces had taken the key Ukrainian cities of Kharkov and Chernigov and turned toward Kiev.[54] As the Reds closed their siege around the city, Petliura's agents spread one final rumor, which, by its magnificently outrageous falseness, symbolized the absurdity of the Directory's flailing attempts to govern. A deadly violet ray supplied by a "friend of a free Ukraine," Kiev's fearful citizens were told, was soon to be used against the Bolsheviks by Petliura's forces, and it was imperative that all civilians remain in their cellars to avoid unnecessary casualties. Paustovskii recalled how, "on the night of the violet ray, the city was deathly quiet," as the people of Kiev waited below ground to learn the results. The next morning, they emerged to find that Petliura and his men had fled, having used the city's deserted streets to speed their escape.[55] More than a hundred miles to the west, on a small strip of Galician territory that Ukrainian peasants had salvaged from the debris of the crumbling Austro-Hungarian Empire, Petliura found a refuge. There, he began to rebuild the shattered forces with which he would return to Kiev a few months later.

In the meantime, the Red Army took command of Kiev on February 5, 1919. This time, one resident reported, the Bolsheviks came "without massacres and without executions"[56] to a city where some people had begun to think that even a stern Bolshevik government might be preferable to "the loathesome Ukrainian anarchy" they had endured under the Rada and Petliura. "It would be better to have one devil who is firmly seated," a young woman wrote in her diary. "These eternal changes of government can drive you out of your mind." Hers was a theme that many men and women found appealing in the chaos of 1919, but civil strife had not yet scarred people's lives deeply enough at the beginning of the year to compel the individualistic men and women of the Ukraine to accept the Bolsheviks' rigid egalitarianism. Too much was taken and not enough given that spring. Like the Germans, the Bolsheviks saw the Ukraine as a source of desperately needed food, and Lenin therefore placed some of his most trusted lieutenants in command. New and bitter conflicts between Russians and Ukrainians broke out almost immediately, and as in those parts of Russia that came under their control in 1918 and 1919, the Bolsheviks turned to Red Terror and the Cheka to impose their will. Always anxious to use national and racial hatreds to advantage, Dzerzhinskii placed Jews in seven of the Cheka's ten top positions and saw to it that Jews made up nearly eighty percent of the rank-and-file Cheka agents in the Ukraine.[57] The victims of centuries of anti-Semitic abuse, the Jews of the Ukraine now had a chance to take revenge upon their long-time persecutors as the Cheka began to claim its victims.

Led by Nikifor Grigorev—captain in the tsarist army, supporter of Skoropadsky, ally of Petliura, and Bolshevik general by the age of thirty-five—and strengthened by the defection of several key atamans from Petliura's army, the Bolsheviks moved decisively from Kiev toward the Black Sea ports of Nikolaev and Odessa as spring approached. Dedicated to drinking and fighting, Grigorev served and betrayed all causes equally as grandiose dreams of the Revolution filled his mind with glorious visions of self-aggrandizement. Vowing to destroy his enemies "like flies, with a single wave of my hand,"[58] he saw himself at times as an Ukrainian Lenin and, at others, as an Ukrainian Napoleon. "[Some men] await me as they do God himself," he proclaimed. "[Others] have announced that I am their star of salvation."[59] A man of startling contradictions, Grigorev swore allegiance to the Bolsheviks and cursed the "Communist-*zhidy*" in the same breath.[60] Complex, choleric, always mercuric, he fought for every side in the struggles that surged across the Ukraine until Nestor Makhno, an even more colorful and charismatic rebel chieftain, had him assassinated in July.[61]

Grigorev seized large stores of weapons and ammunition at Tiraspol and Nikolaev before he turned toward Odessa, where disagreements between the Russian Whites and the occupying French expeditionary force soon made it possible for his weaker armies to triumph.[62] French fighting men disdained the Whites as "barbarians and villains," as "traitors" whose "treachery" in 1917 had allowed Germany to concentrate most of her dwindling resources against the western front. "You must not stand on ceremony with these people," the French commander Franchet d'Esperey told his officers about the Whites at one point. "Shoot them without further ado if anything occurs, commencing with the moujiks [the peasants] and ending with their highest representatives."[63] None under d'Esperey's command disputed that view. "Having kept his head at Verdun and . . . the Marne," one French officer remarked, "no French soldier would agree to losing it on the Russian fields."[64] To Denikin's outrage, the French command therefore pitted anti-Bolshevik factions against each other and denied the Russians any part in planning the city's defense. At the beginning of March they even refused to allow forces loyal to Denikin to defend the large military supply depots at Tiraspol and Nikolaev against Grigorev's advancing armies.[65]

When he approached Odessa, Grigorev thus found the French bitterly at odds with the Russians and still in search of a policy against the Bolsheviks. Unwilling to commit themselves to an open and unlimited struggle against Lenin's government, and ever responsive to domestic political pressures that demanded their withdrawal, the Allies agreed to evacuate Odessa at the end of March. Without evacuation plans, and without enough ships, forty thousand troops and thirty thousand civilians tried to flee the city during the first five days of April. Complaining that the Russian Volunteer Army "merits a thousand times the scorn that all have heaped upon it," the French thus brought an end to what one of their senior officers described as "the complete failure of a ridiculous adventure."[66] A barrage of self-congratulatory telegrams flooded into Moscow as the Bolsheviks took command of the vast military stores that the French had left behind. "Long Live the World Socialist Revolution," they proclaimed. "Long Live Red Odessa!"[67]

Although Grigorev's Reds had taken Odessa, they could not hold the Ukraine. As part of the campaign that took Denikin's Volunteer Army to Orël and beyond, General Mai-Maevskii's forces drove the Reds from Kharkov and Ekaterinoslav at the end of June and then moved on to take Kiev at the end of August in order to secure Denikin's left flank when his armies turned toward Moscow. At the same time, the armies of Petliura's Ukrainian People's Republic began to march against Kiev from Galicia, while a population starved by shortages and tortured by the atrocities of the Cheka anxiously awaited them. "For the past week I have alternated between hope and despair," a young woman wrote in her diary as she spoke of her hopes for the Reds' defeat. Then, at seven o'clock on the evening of August 30, 1919, she penned the first joyous words she had written in nearly six months. "They are leaving!" she exclaimed as the Bolsheviks, unable to stand against assaults from two directions at once, began their retreat. "They are leaving! They are leaving!"[68]

Delighted to be freed of the Bolsheviks' oppression, the men and women of Kiev greeted Petliura's Ukrainian forces when they entered the city the next morning. A few hours later, some of Mai-Maevskii's units under General Bredov entered the city from the east. Briefly the two forces clashed in the city's center until the Kievans' delight at the Bolsheviks' defeat overwhelmed all other hostilities. "There was a general sense of unity reminiscent of the first days of the Revolution," one of them wrote. "Bolshevik power, the Cheka, and the executions now seemed like some sort of evil dream that had been forever buried."[69] For a few days, the people of Kiev remained united in celebrating their liberation and in mourning the men and women whose lives had been cut short by Cheka executioners. Then, as quickly as it had formed, that unity broke apart.

Nothing summed up the irreconcilable differences that separated the Volunteer Army from the forces of the Ukrainian People's Republic more forcefully than the statement that the Russian monarchist Vasilii Shulgin published in the first issue of the resurrected conservative Russian newspaper *Kievlianin* (The Citizen of Kiev). "The Southwest Region," Shulgin wrote, "is Russian, Russian, Russian." Never again must the forces of the Volunteer Army surrender it "either to the Ukrainian traitors [of Petliura] or to Jewish executioners [of the Cheka]."[70] His was a view that Denikin shared wholeheartedly. In the Ukrainians' efforts to realize their dream of independence, Denikin saw nothing more than a traitorous attempt by "past associates of the Germans" to subvert Russian unity.[71] Opposed by Denikin and not supported by the Allies, Petliura's movement fell apart. Ravaged by typhus, his forces shrank to less than two thousand men before the end of October. By the end of the year, Petliura and the champions of Ukrainian nationalism had no options left but an ill-fated alliance with the Poles. In the meantime, Denikin imposed a regime marked by a stubborn rejection of all Ukrainian nationalist hopes and a vicious hatred for all Jews. As the pogroms of 1919 burst upon the Jews of the Ukraine with incredible ferocity, the enemies of Bolshevism committed some of the most brutal acts of persecution in the modern history of the Western world.

The Ukraine had been a land of pogroms ever since the Cossack legions of Khmelnitsky had butchered some two hundred thousand Jews and wiped out more than seven hundred Jewish settlements in the mid-seventeenth century. Less than a hundred years later, Ukrainian peasant rebels had murdered another fifty thousand, and the Jews of Russia's West and Southwest had endured new outbreaks of anti-Semitic hatred during the years that followed.[72] As the nineteenth century drew to a close, pogroms had become a regular feature of life in those provinces that encompassed the infamous Pale of Settlement, where Russia's autocrats had confined their Empire's unfortunate Jews since the time of Catherine the Great. The summer and fall after the assassination of Alexander II in 1881 had seen a particularly violent wave of such outbreaks, and although their fury had burned itself out before the winter's first snows, pogroms had continued sporadically for the next two decades. In Moscow, dedicated anti-Semites referred to the Jewish High Holy Days as the "*zhid*-hunting season" and celebrated Passover 1891 with a pogrom that eventually drove twenty thousand

Jews from their homes.[73] At the beginning of the twentieth century, no Jew could pass a crowd of lower-class Ukrainians or Russians without fear of hearing the terrible cry "*Bei zhidov!*"—"Smash the Jews!"

In 1903, a new wave of violence had burst upon the Jews of Russia's Southwest. This time the violence had centered in Kishinev, the capital of Bessarabia, where on Easter Sunday mobs of artisans, workers, petty tradesmen, and minor bureaucrats had murdered nearly fifty Jews, injured more than six hundred, and looted some thirteen hundred homes and shops before the authorities had summoned troops to halt the carnage.[74] Thanks to the investigations of Michael Davitt, a native of Ireland who wrote for the Hearst newspapers in America, and to the writings of Vladimir Korolenko, the renowned Russian populist writer who refused to contain his outrage at what he had seen, Russians and Europeans no longer could turn a blind eye to the plight of Russia's Jews after the events in Kishinev. "I have before me a record of thirteen girls and women of ages ranging from seventeen to forty-eight, who were assaulted by from two to twenty men and in many cases left for dead," Davitt wrote as he went on to tell the tale of a woman blinded by spikes before her tormenters killed her by driving them past her eyes and into her brain.[75] Both Davitt and Korolenko wrote of Mottel Greenspoon, the Jewish glazier who had been castrated and trampled to death when he tried to defend sixteen Jewish women and girls who were being raped by a mob that had just been blessed by the Bishop of Kishinev. Angrily, Korolenko asked how many people in Russia still could claim to have any humanitarian feelings in the face of such "barbaric bitterness."[76] In reply, the Russian authorities blamed the Jews. The Emperor himself, Russia's minister of war confided to his diary a week later, had told him that "the Jews needed to be taught a lesson because they had been putting on airs and leading the revolutionary movement."[77] Father Ioann of Kronstadt, a priest renowned for his piety, had proclaimed that "the Jews themselves were the cause of those disorders, the wounds inflicted, and the murders committed."[78]

The revolutionary events of 1905, which had freed Russians from the worst abuses of their centuries-old autocracy, also had included nearly seven hundred pogroms against the Jews, more than eight out of every ten of which had occurred in the Ukraine or nearby Bessarabia.[79] Although the new constitutional government that the Russians had won during the Revolution of 1905 claimed to defend their rights, Russia's Jews still had remained spectral citizens, with mere shadows of civil rights. Then, the First World War had heaped new abuse upon them. Ready to defend Tsar and Country despite centuries of mistreatment by both, the Jews had stepped forward to take their places alongside their Christian tormenters in an army that proclaimed them unfit to wear the Cross of St. George and whose censors dedicated themselves to obliterating references to Jewish bravery from the Russian press. The Jews remained the "real enemy," Russia's leading anti-Semites proclaimed. One statesman went so far as to insist that "the evil influence of the Jews is undeniable," as he condemned those European and American financiers who insisted that better treatment of the Jews must be a precondition for new war loans for the Russian government.[80]

As Jews fought and died for Russia in 1914 and 1915, their country's leading right-wing newspapers cursed them as traitors. "No pardon for the Jew!" one of them proclaimed. "The blood of the sons of Holy Russia, which they betray each day, cries out for vengeance!"[81] Senior officers warned army quartermasters not to buy food from Jewish merchants because products of Jewish manufacture "have things put in them that can make people very sick."[82] As the victorious armies of Germany fought their way into Russia's western provinces in 1915, Russian commanders herded Jews into boxcars by the tens of thousands and shipped them eastward to be abandoned in the empire's interior. "It is always necessary to have a scapegoat in reserve," France's ambassador remarked sadly. "So infamous a calumny could only have been given birth in a despotic country."[83]

The masses of the Russian Empire harbored such intense hatred for the Jews that the despotism of the tsarist government actually served to hold anti-Semitism in check. Nowhere was this more evident than in the Ukraine, where the indignities suffered by the Jews between 1881 and 1917 paled into insignificance during the Civil War. As the last vestiges of effective government crumbled into uncontrolled turbulence in 1919, the one and a half million Jews of the Ukraine became the victims of the most vicious anti-Semitic attacks to sweep their land since the days of Khmelnitsky. Estimates of the numbers killed ran as high as one Jew out of every thirteen.[84] Hundreds of thousands were left homeless, and tens of thousands more became the victims of serious injuries or disease. Many Jewish women contracted venereal infections when they were raped by men from areas of the Russian Empire in which syphilis had reached epidemic proportions.[85] Others had their beauty destroyed forever by beatings and tortures administered by peasants and soldiers who took pleasure in doing so. In some cases, pogromists spared the lives of particularly beautiful women; in others, they killed them for that very reason.[86]

The pogroms of 1919 began in Volynsk, in the northwestern corner of the Ukraine, into which some of Petliura's atamans had begun to concentrate their forces as they retreated from the Bolshevik advance against Kiev. Although the Cossacks and Ukrainian peasants who waged these first battles against the Jews often spared their lives in return for huge ransoms, they nonetheless subjected them to numerous and gross indignities. During the pogrom that swept through Ovruch during the first half of January, the Cossack Ataman Kozyr-Zyrka took special pleasure in forcing Jews to dance naked while they sang religious songs.[87] Always, Ukrainians' identification of the Jews with the Bolsheviks played a central part in the violence, and nowhere more so than in Proskurov, sometimes described as "the most lively town in the province of Podolsk," where Jews made up nearly half of its fifty thousand citizens. Enraged by a Bolshevik attempt to seize the city, Petliurist forces killed one Jew out of every fifteen and then went on to nearby Felshtin, where they killed one in three.[88] When the rivers thawed and navigation reopened, some of the anti-Bolshevik Ukrainian forces shifted their methods of execution from shooting to drowning and took particular pleasure in throwing Jews overboard from the steamers that plied the Dnepr River between Kiev and Chernobyl.[89]

As late winter turned into spring, the pogroms spread and the violence deepened. When Ataman Grigorev broke with the Bolsheviks at the beginning of May, he summoned all Ukrainians "capable of bearing arms to mobilize within three days" and called upon the "tormented people of the Ukraine," the "holy toilers," the "people of God," to a battle to the death against the Bolsheviks and the Jews.[90] Quickly, anti-Semitism and anti-Bolshevism took on religious dimensions. "Jew-Communists," Ukrainians insisted on a number of occasions, had "changed our holy houses of God into stables."[91] Acting directly on the anti-Semitic exhortations in Grigorev's "Universal" decree of May 7, 1919, Ukrainian soldiers butchered some four hundred Jews out of a population of thirty-five thousand in the district of Uman and wounded hundreds more. "It should be noted," a Russian Red Cross report noted in an appendix, "that the pogromists committed special atrocities when they were drunk—when they became absolute beasts." At those times, Cossacks cut off the ears, noses, and breasts of women and tortured men with equal brutality. "Special attention is called to the numerous cases of the killing of entire families," the Red Cross report continued. Eyewitnesses reported that, as one old man lay writhing in agony from a gunshot wound, some of the Christian children of Uman began to stone him to death.[92]

After the slaughter at Uman, Grigorev's forces ordered the district's surviving Jews to collect all the corpses and to bury them in mass graves. "When the Jews, among whom were many fathers, mothers, wives, brothers, sisters, and children of the dead, were digging the graves and weeping," witnesses later testified, "[Grigorev's rebels] made fun of them." At one point, the soldiers forbade the women to weep, and as the Jews began to pile their dead in the graves, their Christian tormenters began to sing obscene songs. Still full of hatred, the peasants of Uman proclaimed their determination to "starve the *zhidy* to death," and even Christian women who looked like Jews found it difficult to buy food in those days. "Everywhere Jews were plundered and killed," the Red Cross report concluded. "The picture of the pogroms and massacres was of the same sort almost everywhere: looting, beating, killing on an enormous scale [and] violation of women."[93] Sadly, the Red Cross report did not exaggerate. During the second half of May, more than fifty pogroms occurred in the provinces of Kiev, Kherson, and Poltava, where Grigorev's authority was the strongest.[94]

Not Grigorev's limited and poorly disciplined forces but only a more efficiently organized army that operated over a wider area could accomplish mass killings, and this became possible only when Denikin's forces arrived in mid-1919. That summer and fall, anti-Semitic venom fairly dripped from some of the public pronouncements of Denikin's generals. "The hour is near when we can begin to breathe easily and be freed from that diabolical hand that chains us in slavery, destroying our faith and our church," one of them proclaimed as he promised that "the diabolical force that lives in the hearts of Jew-Communists will be destroyed."[95] An agent in the Azbuka, Denikin's counterintelligence service, spoke openly of the need to render harmless the "Jewish microbe,"[96] while Osvag, the propaganda agency of Denikin's government, blamed the Jews for lost battles (special Jewish detachments, it claimed, ambushed Volunteer Army units),[97] inflation (the Jews supposedly hoarded food and scarce goods to drive up prices), and Bolshevism. "That little Jew Leiba Bronshtein [known to the world as Trotskii]," one monarchist pamphlet announced angrily, "[now] sits in the Tsar's place in Moscow."[98]

To Osvag's pamphleteers and their allies, Trotskii was only one Jew among many who had betrayed Russia in the name of class warfare. The Jews' dedication to Bolshevism, and their willingness to "incite the classes against each other according to the recipe of the 'great master Karl Marx,'" the conservative Russian publicist Vasilii Shulgin insisted, were "well-known" facts. Shulgin had no doubt that the Jews merited the misery brought by the pogroms, and he had no hesitation about spreading false reports that Jewish snipers fired repeatedly at Volunteer Army soldiers in the streets of Kiev. When a special investigation proved that none of his charges had a grain of truth, Shulgin made no effort to retract his accusations. "The fate [of the Jews] will depend upon the course they follow," he wrote in one of his most famous articles. "Is it really possible that the torture of fear [brought on by the pogroms] will not show [the Jews] the right way?"[99] Even the Kadets, who once had opposed Shulgin's conservative monarchist opinions, now supported similar views. Anti-Semitism could serve as "a creative force" for "national reunification," one of the leading Kadet newspapers explained. At a time of waning popular support for the White cause, anti-Semitism might become a vehicle for increasing peasant support for the struggle against Bolshevism.[100]

Although Denikin himself never approved of pogroms, he spoke out against them with caution, for there was dissension enough in the White camp without taking its officers to task for their blatant anti-Semitism, especially since he believed that the masses had good reason to hate the Jews.[101] Unwilling to punish officers whose paranoid delusions about the Jewish threat made them obsessed with seeking out and eradicating "Jew-Communists," Denikin allowed the pogroms to continue as the Whites searched frantically for common ground upon which to construct a social base of support for their regime among the bitterly anti-Semitic people of the Ukraine. No longer spontaneous outpourings of racial and religious hatred, pogroms now became coldly calculated incidents of wholesale rape, extreme brutality, and unprecedented destruction. In a single day at the end of August in the Jewish settlement of Kremenchug, the Whites raped 350 women, including pregnant women, women who had just given birth, and even women who were dying.[102]

Then, as the Reds began to challenge the Volunteer Army more effectively from the north and east that fall, the pogroms turned into orgies of mass butchery.[103] At the end of September, a five-day pogrom destroyed two hundred buildings and slaughtered nearly two thousand Jews in Fastov, a town that Baedeker had described before the Great War as "prettily situated" along the route of the Moscow–Kiev railroad. After the pogrom, the Jewish quarter of Fastov lay in utter ruins, its synagogue strewn with the bodies of murdered men, women, children, and old people. "The flourishing town of Fastov," the *Kievan Echo* reported, "has been transformed into a graveyard."[104] A few days later, the Jews of Kiev suffered a similar fate. Inflamed by articles in Shulgin's *Kievlianin* and its companion in anti-Semitism, *Vechernie ogni* (Evening Lights), Denikin's men threw defenseless Jews from the upper stories of buildings, killed others with bayonets and sabers, and drowned still others in the river. "Gigantic five- and six-story buildings begin to shriek from top to bottom," Shulgin wrote as he described how Kiev's Jews, "seized with mortal anguish," screamed "with inhuman voices" as the "men with bayonets" worked their way through the city's streets.[105] As fall turned into winter in 1919, no end to the violence seemed in sight.

All across the Ukraine, anti-Semitism poisoned the minds of men. Officers of high principles, good education, and deeply ingrained personal scruples began to rob, rape, and murder as a matter of course. Almost no one spoke in the Jews' defense, and comparatively few even gave them food or shelter. In the Ukraine, there were few indeed who dared to repeat Gorkii's bold statement that anti-Semitism was "a disgrace to Russian culture" and that "the Jews, as the old, strong leaven of humanity, have always exalted its spirit, bringing restless noble ideals into the world."[106] As one observer wrote, men preferred "to remain silent, and to wash their hands."[107] Certain that they faced extermination if the Whites remained, the Jews of the Ukraine turned to the Bolsheviks, who shot pogromists and outlawed anti-Semitic writings. From time to time, sporadic pogroms occurred in areas held by the Reds to be sure, but when compared with the tens of thousands of murders by the Whites, the few hundred pogrom deaths that Jews suffered in Bolshevik-held territory left few among them in doubt that Lenin's regime offered better chances for survival. It therefore was no accident that entire Jewish settlements began to follow Red Army units when they retreated rather than face the tender mercies of Denikin's soldiers.[108]

The breakdown of all governmental authority that accompanied the anti-Semitic violence of 1919 in the Ukraine was attributable only in part to the ebb and flow of the fighting. Beneath the mantle of nationalism that covered the Ukraine during the Civil War flourished a deep streak of peasant anarchism that disdained all authority imposed from above. Primitive in their outlook, passionate in their hatred of Russians, Jews, and cities, the men and women of rural Ukraine therefore took up arms in a cause of their own making while Red fought against White and Petliura's nationalist forces fought against Denikin's Volunteer Army. Led by men who had risen from their midst and who shared their way of life and their beliefs, the Ukrainian peasants set out in 1918–1919 to fight for their own vision of the future by destroying railroads, cutting telegraph and telephone lines, and waging war against any who disputed their right to do so.

Born the youngest son of a poor stableman in 1889, and raised by his mother in the southeastern Ukrainian town of Guliai Pole after his father's sudden death, Nestor Ivanovich Makhno best exemplified the peasant anarchism of the Ukraine. A tender of cattle and sheep at seven, farmhand at twelve, and factory worker at sixteen, Makhno learned his hatred for authority on the farms of rich German Mennonite peasants around Guliai Pole and acquired his rudimentary knowledge of history, political economy, and anarchist theory in Moscow's Butyrki Prison, where he had been sent to serve a life sentence at the age of eighteen for killing a Russian policeman. Arrogant, unrepentant, and stubbornly uncompromising in his disdain for authority, Makhno spent much of his time at Butyrki in chains or in solitary confinement. Then, after nearly nine years, the amnesty proclaimed by Russia's first Provisional Government released him at the beginning of March 1917.[109] Proclaiming himself "a revolutionary first and an anarchist second,"[110] Makhno left prison with a clear sense of mission. "I felt certain that I could accomplish something useful," he later wrote. "Freedom, equality, and solidarity [now] would be the principles that would guide men and human society. . . . This was the thought that had obsessed me during my long years in prison."[111]

Makhno drew men to him despite his short stature and relative youth. He had studied the anarchist writings of Bakunin, whose condemnation of cities and large-scale industries fit so well with the anti-urban, anti-industrial feelings of the Ukrainian peasants, and his program was precisely the sort that struck responsive chords in peasant hearts. All instruments of authority, all political parties, and all ruling classes, whether they governed in the name of tsar and nobles, the bourgeoisie, or the proletariat, must be abolished so that people could live and act "justly and like brothers and work for the good of everyone."[112] Certain of the "peasantry's kinship with the ideas of anarchism,"[113] and equally certain that "a powerful revolutionary force" flourished in "toiling peasant" hearts,[114] Makhno urged the common folk of Guliai Pole to organize a peasant union to defend their freedom and protect the lands that the new revolutionary order would bestow upon them. "We shall work together to destroy slavery," he promised them at one point, "so that we may set ourselves and our brothers on the road to the new order."[115]

Quickly, Makhno's peasant union spread its influence. As the instruments of state authority crumbled in the Ukraine, Makhno formed a Committee for the Defense of the Revolution, which began to expropriate the property of landowners, industrialists, prosperous shopkeepers, and rich peasants in and around Guliai Pole. "We are disarming the entire bourgeoisie of this region and abolishing its right to land, factories, plants, printing shops, theaters, coliseums, moviehouses, and other types of public enterprises—in short, all forms of the people's wealth," its leaders had announced in August 1917.[116] Armed to the teeth and dressed in wildly outlandish clothing gathered from the closets of lords and the shelves of tradesmen, the Guliai Pole peasants resembled their boisterous Cossack forebears of the Zaporozhian Sich as they cursed and caroused the long summer nights away. Guliai Pole, one eyewitness wrote, looked for all the world "like a painting by Repin: exotic, gaudy, and unusual."[117]

Yet Makhno was more than a twentieth-century Taras Bulba ready to fight for God and the Cossack brotherhood against all enemies. Behind the raucous celebrations that filled the towns around Guliai Pole in the summer and fall of 1918 lay a deep belief in an egalitarian revolutionary order that spurred men to stake their lives on its defense. Makhno's was not to be the "Paper Revolution" of the Bolsheviks, which he spoke of with such disdain,[118] nor was it to be the restoration of elite privilege at the expense of the masses planned by the Whites. His was to be a struggle for "liberty and a stateless communist society" in which "slavery will vanish and state authority will have no place,"[119] and where, as he once announced to a congress of peasants, "the land belongs to nobody and it can be used only by those who care about it and cultivate it."[120] Not the red flag of Soviet Social Democracy, but the black banner of anarchism waved above Makhno's armies. On both sides it bore the same inscription, worked in silver: "Liberty or Death!" and "Land for the Peasants and Factories for the Workers!"[121]

Makhno pledged his allegiance to no man or party. "The Makhno Army does not represent any authority," he insisted. "It will not subject anyone to any obligation whatsoever."[122] With this force, sometimes as small as a few hundred, at other times as large as thirty thousand,[123] Makhno fought the Austro-German armies of occupation and the forces of Skoropadsky and Petliura. Most of all, he fought the armies of Denikin and the Bolsheviks. With the latter, he made temporary alliances. With the former, he decreed a fight to the death from the very first, for Denikin's advance promised to destroy the dreams of men who measured their freedom by the breadth of the Ukrainian steppes. Ukrainian nationalism, Denikin continued to insist, was an "unthinkable" device created by the Germans before the Great War to undermine Russia's strength. His armies therefore were marching "to recover for the Russian people their lost unity," and his advance therefore threatened a restoration of the landlords, the officials, and the government that Makhno's followers so thoroughly hated.[124] Most of all, a White victory promised the destruction of a free Ukraine. "Your wager on an independent Ukraine is lost," Denikin announced bluntly at a dinner given in his honor by the authorities of Ekaterinoslav soon after his forces had occupied that southeast Ukrainian city. "Long live a unified and undivided Russia!"[125]

Neither Fate nor the Ukrainians allowed Denikin to claim victory so easily. While his Whites faced the Reds in the north and the remnants of Petliura's armies in the west, Makhno's Revolutionary Partisan Army of the Ukraine wrought havoc in their rear. Early in October, Makhno took Berdiansk, an important port on the Sea of Azov, where he destroyed vital reserves of some sixty thousand heavy artillery shells just as Denikin launched his final assault against Orël.[126] Within a fortnight, his fast-moving columns cut the supply lines that connected Denikin's advancing columns with the Black Sea ports upon which they depended for weapons, ammunition, and supplies and seized a half-dozen other critical points, including the key center of Ekaterinoslav.[127] Always strengthening its fighting resources while depriving Denikin's men of theirs, the Revolutionary Partisan Army of the Ukraine seized guns, cannon, and cartridges from the Whites. "Conditions behind the lines were more chaotic than ever," an American pilot who had joined the Whites later wrote. "Makhno was looting trains and depots with impunity, and White officialdom was losing what little control over the civilian population it had."[128] Reluctantly, Denikin withdrew key units from his front and sent them to parry Makhno's attacks only to realize, too late, how costly that decision had been. Makhno's peasant partisans, he confessed later, "destroyed our rear and the front at the most critical period." Others agreed. "There is no doubt," a *Le Temps* correspondent reported from Moscow, "that Denikin's defeat is explained more by the uprisings of the peasants who brandished Makhno's black flag than by the success of Trotskii's regular army."[129]

The year 1919 thus ended in the Ukraine as it had begun, with the Reds struggling to extend their control from the major cities into the countryside. Yet, for those Ukrainian nationalists who had entered the year with high hopes for independence, the situation was much worse at the end of 1919 than at the beginning. Once Trotskii's Red Army had crushed Iudenich and Kolchak and driven Denikin's forces back upon their bases in the Crimea and the Kuban, it turned upon Makhno's partisan forces with a vengeance. The Red Army took Kharkov and Kiev at the end of December, and in mid-January 1920, after a typhus epidemic had decimated his forces, a reestablished Central Committee of the Ukrainian Communist Party declared Makhno an outlaw. Yet the Bolsheviks could not free themselves from Makhno's grasp so easily, and it became one of the supreme ironies of the Russian Civil War that his attacks against the rear of the Red Army made it possible for the resurrected White armies—the despised *zolotopogonniki* (officers with gold epaulettes)—to return briefly to the southern Ukraine in 1920.

Despite such momentary victories by their enemies, the Reds had become far stronger than any of their opponents by the time that the Civil War entered its third year. The key to their strength at the end of 1919 lay in the Sovnarkom's genius for mobilizing the people and resources under its control for war in a manner that neither Makhno nor Petliura could match. Responding to Lenin's exhortation (set down in a circular letter to all party organizations at the beginning of July) that the "Soviet Republic . . . must become *a single military camp*" in which, as "a fortress besieged by world capital," the Soviet government had the "duty to mobilize the whole population for the war," the Bolsheviks had struggled to dedicate every man, every woman, every ruble, every mouthful of food, and every weapon to their war effort. "We would be fools or criminals," Lenin had insisted then, "if we [did not] . . . *suspend or reduce everything* that is not absolutely indispensable [to the war effort]."[130] Supported by the Red Terror of Dzerzhinskii's Cheka and by the growing force of the Red Army, the Bolsheviks had begun to bring their resources to bear in a manner that the Whites could not. Iron discipline had been the key to their success. "Work, Discipline, and Order will save the Soviet Republic," Trotskii had promised when he had addressed the Moscow Soviet at the end of March 1918.[131] As 1919 came to an end, it seemed that his promise might be fulfilled. Once weak and erratic, the Red heart of Russia had begun to beat with a new, powerful pulse.

CHAPTER TEN

In the Red Heart of Russia

In October 1917, the Bolsheviks had set out to build a brave new world in which the toiling men and women of Russia would stand at the center of their nation's politics, economy, society, and culture. As they had struggled to blaze a trail toward the proletarian utopia of their dreams, in which Russians would look beyond crass self-interest to build a life based upon equality and social justice for all, every step had taken them across new ground. Bravely—perhaps even foolishly—they had faced the Revolution's first grave crises with a sense that, "even if we are conquered, we [will] have done great things."[1] At Lenin's urging, they had ended Russia's war with Germany and Austria. They had struggled to bring food to Russia's starving city folk, and they had given their lives in battle against the forces of counterrevolution. Always, their inexperience and idealism had combined with traditional Russian inefficiency to make every effort fall short of their hopes. Hunger, war, and pestilence had persisted through their first year as new and deepening crises had demanded continual reappraisals of Bolshevik theory and perpetual adjustments in Bolshevik practice. Again and again, the Bolsheviks had stood at the brink of defeat only to be drawn back from the precipice's edge at the last and final moment by Lenin's genius for striking the proper balance between concession, conciliation, and coercion.

Repeatedly, Lenin urged the Bolsheviks to accommodate their

ideals of 1917 to the harder realities of 1918. "It would be extremely stupid and absurdly utopian to assume that the transition from capitalism to socialism is possible without coercion and without dictatorship," he had told the Bolsheviks' Central Committee at the end of April 1918. "We must learn to combine the 'public meeting' democracy of the working people—turbulent, surging, overflowing its banks like a spring flood—with *iron* discipline while at work, with *unquestioning obedience* to the will of a single person, the Soviet leader."[2] Yet, even the shock of their first encounters with the hard realities of Russian life did not dim the Bolsheviks' memories of those first desperate months when they and their comrades, still few in number but full of ideas, had moved toward the future with breathless optimism. "It was, in the end, a wonderful time," Aleksandra Kollontai wrote as she recalled her days as commissar of public welfare. "We were hungry and had many sleepless nights. There were many difficulties, misfortunes, and chances of defeat. The feeling that helped us was that all we produced, even if it was no more than a decree, would come to be a historical example and help others move ahead."[3]

Few struggled more valiantly to set an historical example during the first days of the Revolution than Kollontai herself. One of the anarchists whom the U.S. government deported to the Soviet Union in 1919 remembered her as "a tall and stately woman, every inch the *grande dame* rather than the fiery revolutionist," who appeared "remarkably young and radiant" despite her forty-seven years.[4] France's Jacques Sadoul spoke of her elegance, her "light, soft hair," her "long and supple body," and her "profound and gentle blue eyes,"[5] and very few who met her did not fall under the spell of her cool, aristocratic charm. The daughter of a tsarist general whose genealogy reached back to a prince who had ruled the principality of Pskov in the thirteenth century, Kollontai had dedicated her adult life to the Bolsheviks and the working women of Russia. Always elegantly dressed, her well-tended beauty contrasting sharply with the work-worn women whose cause she championed, she became what the American journalist Louise Bryant once called "the only articulate voice of the new order for women" among men who paid lip service to the equality of women but did little to put it into practice.[6]

Kollontai insisted that "the self-preservation of the individual"—women as well as men—must be of paramount importance in the Bolsheviks' new world.[7] "We are used to evaluating a woman not as a personality with individual qualities and failings irrespective of her physical and emotional experience, but only as an appendage of a man," she once wrote. "Only a change in the economic role of woman, and her independent involvement in production, can and will bring about the weakening of these mistaken and hypocritical ideas."[8] No longer could a woman's self-worth be defined in terms of the experience of love. Lives built around visions of passionate kisses, starry nights, and moonlit waves must be set aside in favor of more meaningful accomplishments. The Communist "new woman" must serve "the social idea, science, [and] creativity," Kollontai explained.[9] "The 'wifie,' the shadow of the husband," must become the "woman as human being."[10]

In the Bolsheviks' new world, Kollontai insisted, every woman must become "a human being possessing a characteristic value, with her own individuality," and thus become capable of breaking "the rusted fetters of her sex."[11] Women therefore must be freed from the "blind alley" in which the act of giving themselves in love condemned them to lives of perpetual childbearing and never-ending servile labor.[12] Liberation from the dual marriage-imposed servitudes of kitchen and nursery thus lay at the center of Kollontai's campaign. "The separation of the kitchen from marriage," she wrote, would be a "great reform, no less important than the separation of Church from State."[13] In a similar fashion, she insisted that maternity, the natural right of every woman, must remain "sacred." Every mother, she wrote, must rest secure in the knowledge "that, once she fulfills her natural function [in giving birth] . . . the collective will love and attend to her and her child."[14] Society therefore must provide nurseries and kindergartens in which children, one of its most precious resources, could be raised "in a hygenic, morally pure atmosphere,"[15] leaving their mothers free to work "for the benefit of the large family-society."[16] Only when society liberated women from the burdens of child care and left them free to realize their full potential as citizens would motherhood "no longer [be] a cross" and women be free to enjoy "the great happiness of being a mother" to the fullest.[17] "The task which we have now set for ourselves," one of Kollontai's female comrades told a conference of working women in 1919, "is principally to train the mother as citizen and to set the working mother free from the care of her child."[18]

Kollontai believed that the Communist society that could free women from the fetters of child care and the kitchen, also could create a new sexual morality that could liberate them from the disabilities that romantic love in a capitalist world had imposed upon their lives. "Up to now," she wrote, "the main content of a woman's life was directed upon the experience of love," and this had forced her into unequal relationships with men, who traditionally had centered their lives elsewhere. Thus, while a man found his main fulfillment outside of love, a woman found it only within love's framework as the loyal, loving wife who remained at home to wait for her man to enter, and reenter, her life. Now, Kollontai insisted, women must become equal to men in their dedication to self, personality, and independence. "Activity, resistance, determination, toughness, that is to say, characteristics which hitherto were viewed as the hallmark and privilege of men" must become part of the life of the New Woman. "A significant transformation had to be effected in the psychic image of woman," Kollontai continued. "Her mental life had to develop itself strongly [and] she had to gather a rich store of intellectual values so that she would not be bankrupt at the moment she ceased to pay her tribute to the man." In the life of the New Woman, work would become "more important, more valuable, holier than all the joys of the heart [and] all the delights of passion."[19]

This did not mean the New Woman must be condemned to a life without love in the Communist society Kollontai hoped to shape. Nor did her vision of sexual liberation substitute mindlessly practiced sex for the deeper joys of love. Although its form and substance would be transformed, Kollontai promised that Eros would "occupy a worthy place" in a society where a "love collective" would be the goal of male and female proletarians seeking the ultimate in human love experience. Ties between men and women would become less selfish, less possessive, and more lofty, with "more such threads connecting soul to soul, heart to heart, and mind to mind."[20] In Kollontai's world of a "transformed Eros," one expert concluded, "the sexual code of communism would allow for manifold varieties of marital and nonmarital love and sex combinations, and all 'loving hearts' would be supported and nourished spiritually in the 'love collective.' "[21]

Especially in the West, Kollontai's contemporaries often depicted her as an apostle of uncontrolled sexual promiscuity, whose doctrines stemmed from an insatiable desire to share her body with men. Yet, to lead a life of crude sexual promiscuity and liberate the women of Bolshevik Russia to follow that example was never Kollontai's aim, and her behavior always remained much more that of a puritanical revolutionary than of a revolutionary libertine. Two love affairs and two marriages comprised the entirety of her known love life, a record that is neither shocking nor even unusual in the context of her times.[22] She had broken away from her first marriage not to be free to give herself to other men indiscriminately but to give deeper meaning to her life. "The happy life of a housewife and spouse became for me a 'cage,' " she once confessed. "Love, marriage, family, all were secondary, transient matters. . . . I had to break with the man of my choice, otherwise . . . I would have exposed myself to the danger of losing my selfhood."[23] Stubbornly, Kollontai worked during the Civil War to bring that half of Russia's adult population, which previously had been confined to kitchen, nursery, and Church, into the mainstream of Communist society so that the talents of women could be used for the benefit of all. The woman as citizen, she insisted, must replace the woman as sex object, mother, cook, laundress, and all-purpose servant.

It proved much easier to envision a society of liberated women than to create one. In October 1917, not even Kollontai herself had set down a clear plan for bringing the New Woman into being, and none of her revolutionary mentors—not Marx, Engels, Bebel, or even Lenin—had spoken with authority about such thorny sexual questions as prostitution, free love, marriage, adultery, divorce, and abortion. Most took the position that marriage and prostitution represented the obverse and reverse of the same bourgeois sexual coin, and that, as Lenin wrote on the eve of the Great War, "as long as wage slavery exists, prostitution must inevitably continue."[24] Contraception and abortion, Lenin insisted, as he called for "the unconditional annulment of all laws against abortions," must be available for all,[25] but he always seemed more anxious to free women to bear children in Bolshevik Russia than to encourage them to have abortions as proof of their liberation. Like Kollontai, he and other Bolsheviks shared Bebel's view that "a woman who gives birth to children renders at least the same service to the commonwealth as the man who defends his country,"[26] and therefore hoped to encourage childbearing by liberating women from its burdens rather than free them from the social responsibility to produce a new generation of socialist workers. "Motherhood," Kollontai emphasized at one point, "must be safeguarded . . . in order to guarantee a steady stream of fit workers for the Workers' Republic in the future."[27]

The Bolsheviks thus remained quite conservative in their views about family and childbirth. Divorce, they had long since agreed, must become the right of all women, but, as Lenin remarked on the eve of the Revolution, although "one cannot be a democrat and socialist without demanding full freedom of divorce . . . it should not be difficult to realize that recognition of the *freedom* to leave one's husband is not an *invitation* to all wives to do so."[28]

All such statements represented compromise, and none of them offered much in the way of directions for transforming the "enslaved" capitalist woman of past and present into the liberated New Woman of the socialist future. Bolsheviks simply assumed that, once they were freed from the economic exploitation of capitalism, women would see their lot dramatically improved.[29] Just the introduction of electricity into proletarian homes (something that stood high on the Bolsheviks' list of priorities), Lenin wrote in 1913, would "relieve millions of 'domestic slaves' of the need to spend three-fourths of their lives in smelly kitchens."[30]

Thus the Bolsheviks embarked upon their revolutionary course in October 1917 with no blueprints in hand for creating the world of female freedom and equality that they had portrayed in their speeches and writings. "We were so few in number that we could all sit on the same sofa," Kollontai later wrote.[31] Their inexperience was amazing, their idealism more so, and "magnificent illusions," Kollontai remembered, gripped them all.[32] Named commissar of public welfare, the only woman on the Sovnarkom, Kollontai worked to aid the war wounded, reorganized orphanages into government children's homes, established hostels for street urchins, and presided over the abolition of all laws that subordinated Russia's women to men. Wives no longer had to follow their husbands, and the government promised women equal pay for equal work and removed all restrictions on divorce.[33] Still intoxicated by the heady atmosphere of newly won power, Kollontai set out to plan a nationwide system of free public health services. Proudly, she established a Central Office for Maternity and Infant Welfare and Homes for Maternity and Infant Care which she envisioned as the beginnings of a comprehensive, nationwide, state-supported system of prenatal care for the women of Russia.[34] "At last," she announced triumphantly, "the working class can build, with its own hands, forms of child care that will not deprive a child of its mother or a mother of her child."[35]

It was one thing to issue decrees, but quite another to put them into effect. There were no funds to build the centers for prenatal and child care that Kollontai envisioned, no way to aid the legions of men whose minds and bodies had been shattered by war, and no resources even to feed the hungry children of Russian working women. Civil War and famine transformed Kollontai's dream of a nationwide network of nurseries and child care centers into what even sympathetic observers described as a "bleak succession of infants' homes . . . full of yellow ghosts of babies with restless, empty hands" tended by half-starved doctors and nurses.[36] Desperate to find shelter for the mobs of armless, legless, and sightless veterans who thronged Petrograd, she issued orders to transform the city's Aleksandr Nevskii Monastery into a home for war-wounded, only to have the monks marshal Petrograd's masses against her. Kollontai, the believer in nonviolence, had to watch armed sailors she had summoned to the scene kill monks and workers in her presence.[37]

Obliged to suffer Lenin's rebuke for her impetuousness and lack of political skill,[38] Kollontai began to understand the vast chasm that separated her ideals from reality in Russia. After years of exile, she no longer knew the Russian proletariat, she confessed to Sadoul, who by that time considered her "a good comrade."[39] Russia's inert, superstitious masses, she lamented, trailed far behind their comrades in the West. "I sometimes had the feeling that to be a commissar seemed to be a burden beyond one's strength," she wrote some years later. "But here it was. This was the Revolution. We were building a new world." Sternly, she stiffened her resolve with the admonition: "You need more courage, Kollontai!"[40] How much courage became clear less than two weeks after her battle with the monks. Anxious to better the lives of Petrograd's working women, Kollontai had tried to transform a tsarist foundling home into a model prenatal center, which she pretentiously called the Palace of Motherhood, over the bitter protests of the upper-class women who had run it before the Revolution. She paid no heed to their mounting protests. Then, one night at the end of January, this showplace for Kollontai's ideas burned under extremely suspicious circumstances. By morning, nothing remained but the huge sign, "Palace of Motherhood," that still hung over the door.[41]

Before the Revolution was three months old, the reality of Old Russia had forced Kollontai to compromise her principles too many times. For the woman whom Sadoul once called the "Red Madonna" and the "Vestal of the Revolution,"[42] the militant wave that had carried the Bolsheviks to victory in 1917 had reached its crest. As the euphoria of the Revolution's first days faded, Kollontai sensed how illusory her expectations had been, and she faced the fearsome knowledge that illusions could—and would—crumble. Her romance and marriage with people's commissar of the navy, the "jolly, self-confident giant" Pavel Dybenko,[43] whom she passionately defended before the Sovnarkom when he was accused of treason that spring, and Lenin's cutting remark that he "wouldn't bet on the reliability [and] endurance in struggle of those women who confuse their personal romances with politics,"[44] weakened her position at just the time when it seemed to her that Bolshevik policies had begun to threaten the Revolution's survival. Certain that Lenin's call to accept the Brest-Litovsk Treaty represented a humiliating betrayal of the ideals of the October Revolution, Kollontai resigned her post as commissar of public welfare in March 1918. As she traveled to Tsaritsyn, Kazan, and the textile mills of Orekhovo to plead the Revolution's cause, the Civil War quickly sucked her into its maelstrom.

As the Civil War measured the Bolsheviks' ideologies and illusions against the raw reality of Russian life, Kollontai's extreme views and passionate expectations proved very fragile. Other women whose idealism had been better tempered by reality before the Revolution proved more suited to command the movement Kollontai had championed. Certainly Inessa Armand, born Elisabeth d'Herbenville, the daughter of Parisian music hall performers, who had been raised by a family of wealthy French emigré industrialists in Moscow,[45] was one such woman. Well-educated, sensitive, and beautiful (she was described by the biographer of Lenin's wife as "an exceptional being who combined beauty with intelligence, femininity with energy, [and] practical sense with revolutionary ardor"),[46] she married the second son of her benefactors, the Armands, bore him five children in seven years, and then left him to have an affair with his younger brother.

Resolved to become a "human being" rather than a "female," Madame Armand, now using the name Inessa, became a full-fledged revolutionary before she turned thirty. She took part in the Moscow armed uprising of December 1905, was arrested, put in prison, and sent to Siberia. At the age of thirty-six, she escaped to the West and worked closely with Lenin and his wife Nadezhda Krupskaia, a staunch advocate of women's education and author of *The Woman Worker*, one of the first revolutionary Russian pamphlets about women.[47] Although less committed than Kollontai or Inessa to a separate movement for women's rights, Krupskaia nonetheless saw the value of concentrated work among working-class women if for no other reason than to prevent the Mensheviks from taking the lead.[48] With Krupskaia's support, the Bolsheviks therefore began to publish *Rabotnitsa* (Working Woman), a special newspaper for women workers, although Krupskaia continued to insist that the Party's chief concern must be to unite women and men in "the common cause," not create a special organization (as Kollontai and Inessa urged) to act as an advocate for women within the Party.[49]

Inessa's close association with Lenin and Krupskaia before the Great War gave her a clearer sense of the Bolsheviks' limited commitment to women's liberation after the October Revolution. Rightly sensing that Kollontai's efforts as commissar of public welfare to establish a semi-autonomous women's department within the Party continued to be viewed as unacceptably feminist and separatist, Inessa moved more cautiously. Always more attuned to subtly expressed nuances of political opposition than her comrade, she first organized several small conferences of Moscow working women in the spring of 1918.[50] Only in mid-November, after a year of preparation, did she summon the First All-Russian Congress of Working Women and Peasants, the first of its kind ever to convene on such a scale in Russia. Now moving more boldly than she had in the spring, Inessa vowed to win the women of Russia to the side of Soviet power by freeing them from the slavery of kitchen and nursery, abolishing the double standard of morality, and making it possible, as Kollontai once had said, to establish a system "in which the participation of women in the productive life of society will not contradict their natural and also socially necessary task of bearing children."[51]

For women who had cowered behind Muslim veils in the Trans-Volga and Central Asia, borne the beatings and the grinding labor of domestic slavery in Russia's villages, and suffered lives of such want in city factories that prostitution remained their only alternative to starvation, the First All-Russian Congress of Working Women and Peasants was perhaps the most revolutionary event of Russia's first two revolutionary years. Worn, tired, but hopeful, these women descended upon the Kremlin's Hall of Unions in a gray-brown wave of lumpy padded jackets, greasy sheepskins, tattered army overcoats, and shapeless felt boots, the monotony of which was broken only by an occasional red kerchief or embroidered blouse. Nearly four times the three hundred delegates Inessa and Kollontai had expected came to listen, learn, and demand. Unused to politics, unaccustomed, even, to the world outside their villages and factories, many of these women were not yet able to comprehend the full meaning of Inessa's call for liberation. But they understood what it meant to outlaw the word *baba*, the condescending, demeaning term that working men and peasants applied to any women between the age of sixteen and eighty.[52] And they knew enough to cheer ecstatically when Lenin appeared to tell them that "the success of the Revolution depends upon how much the women take part in it" and that the Soviet government was "doing everything in its power to enable women to carry on independent proletarian socialist work."[53] They vowed to continue the struggle, to shape Soviet Woman in a new image, and to "give Communist society a new member"[54] in the form of tens of millions of female workers dedicated to bettering the society in which they lived and worked as free women.

Far more subtly than Kollontai, Inessa used the First All-Russian Congress of Working Women and Peasants to apply pressure upon the Bolshevik leaders to establish what became known as the Zhenotdel, the Women's Section of the Central Committee Secretariat, to press for the complete liberation of all Russian women. "If the emancipation of women is unthinkable without communism," she once wrote, "then communism is unthinkable without the full emancipation of women."[55] Like the Party itself, Zhenotdel had regional, provincial, and local subsections that communicated with a central Moscow office near the Kremlin that some party wags hastened to dub "Baba Central."[56]

Although some Bolsheviks did not take Zhenotdel seriously, Inessa and Kollontai hoped it could recruit mass female support against some of the most difficult social problems the Bolsheviks inherited from the fallen tsarist regime. Damned by the Bolsheviks as the curse of all capitalist societies, a war against prostitution became one of their first crusades. In Russia as elsewhere, the coming of the Industrial Revolution had heralded a surge in prostitution and an epidemic of venereal disease. Prostitution was at first confined to houses of officially registered whores, the opening of which traditionally received blessings from the local priest,[57] but it had burst the bonds of state regulation very quickly. As more men sought work in Russia's factories, the demand for prostitutes' services soared, and as the labor force in Russia's industrial centers came to include large numbers of women who received anywhere from a tenth to a third of the wages of their male counterparts, the number of women in desperate economic need grew at a similar pace. "Under such hopeless economic conditions," one commentator remarked a few years after the Revolution, "it is no wonder that many a woman who was paid for her sex instead of her work fell victim to prostitution merely to keep body and soul together."[58] Aside from cigarette makers, who were far and away the worst paid of any female workers in Russia, servant girls and seamstresses were the most frequent victims. If arrested, registration and receipt of the dreaded "yellow card" of a whore effectively closed virtually all avenues of escape for such women. "In most cases," an investigator reported to an Anti-Syphilis Congress that met in St. Petersburg at the turn of the century, "the yellow certificate forms an absolute bar to the admission of a woman to working life."[59]

Most women who traded in sex on the eve of the Russian Revolution did not carry the "yellow card" and practiced the whore's trade to supplement earnings too meager for survival. In contrast to the wretched wages earned by Russia's female workers, a few prostitutes reportedly earned fifteen times as much as the best-paid male factory hands, and almost any whore could expect to take in at least as much in a month as some of the best-paid skilled machinists. For hungry women with sick and starving children, the economic benefits of prostitution proved all but irresistible. Not counting the bored, well-bred ladies who pursued the whore's trade as a form of amusement, approximately one Petrograd woman in thirty was a prostitute at the beginning of 1917. Such women rendered sexual services in hotel rooms, workers' dormitories, bathhouses, public gardens, and back alleys.[60] This, Kollontai lamented in a speech to a Zhenotdel conference, was the "sinister legacy of our bourgeois capitalist past," which drove the victims of "poverty, hunger, deprivation, and glaring social inequalities" to sell their bodies instead of (or in addition to) their labor.[61]

After Inessa Armand died of cholera and Kollontai replaced her as head of Zhenotdel toward the end of 1920, Bolshevik policy focused not upon the act of prostitution but upon its violation of Communist workers' discipline. "The workers' collective condemns the prostitute," Kollontai insisted, "not because she gives her body to many men but because, like the legal wife who stays at home, she does no useful work for society. . . . The best way to fight prostitution," she concluded, "is to raise the political consciousness of the broad masses of women and to draw them into the revolutionary struggle to build communism." Kollontai maintained that prostitution could not be done away with by government regulations and pious statements of Communist ethics. "Our productive apparatus is still in a state of collapse, and the dislocation of the national economy continues," she told a Zhenotdel conference the year after she replaced Inessa. "These and other economic and social conditions lead women to prostitute their bodies. To struggle against prostitution chiefly means to struggle against these conditions."[62] Nothing could have stated the dilemma more clearly. The battle against prostitution would not be won quickly, precisely because the struggle against the economic and social conditions that sustained it was destined to be long and difficult.

As much as the women of Zhenotdel condemned it, the act of prostitution expressed a woman's effort to better her lot. Yet there were others in Russia who had not even that prospect before them. Especially during the Civil War, Zhenotdel concentrated much of its attention upon the least enlightened and most desperately oppressed of Russia's women, the millions upon millions of peasants who had neither political consciousness nor a vision of a better future. If the life of a peasant man was hard in Russia at the time of the Revolution, the life of a peasant woman was harder still, for women bore burdens far in excess of those shouldered by their men. In a society where poverty dictated the home production of life's necessities, all of the domestic chores were theirs, in addition to heavy labor in the fields. At harvest time, men stood upright as they wielded scythes, while women bent to the ground to work only with sickles.

Women's never-ending domestic labors were punctuated by frequent births and only slightly fewer deaths, for in some parts of Russia as many as seven infants out of every ten died at birth or did not live beyond their first year. "The peasant woman dragged through life," one sympathetic observer reported, "working as hard as the men in the fields, having and losing her babies, cooking and carrying water, washing the clothes in the river, making the fires, spinning and weaving through the winter months, milking the cows, and for all this getting nothing but abuse and beatings from her husband."[63] For a lifetime, the work and the abuse continued, with no respite and no reward. "A chicken is not a bird," an old Russian proverb stated bluntly, "and a peasant woman is not a human being." It must be the task of Zhenotdel, Inessa and Kollontai insisted, to draw such women out of their huts and project their horizons beyond the villages in which so many of their kind traditionally had been born, lived, and died. Quite rightly, they sensed that some of these poor women would grasp the essence of Communism—stated in terms of labor-saving machines, cooperative nurseries, bakeries, laundries, and kitchens—more readily than their men, who could be counted upon to cling to their old ways and their land.[64]

If Kollontai had been the Bolshevik champion of women's liberation, Anatolii Lunacharskii, the "poet of revolution," who called himself "an intellectual among Bolsheviks and a Bolshevik among intellectuals,"[65] became the commander-in-chief of their first campaigns to educate Russia's masses. At forty-two, "a slight, student-like figure with the sensitive face of an artist," in John Reed's remembrance,[66] Lunacharskii had dedicated much of his life to elaborating the emotional and ethical dimensions of Marxism in order to counterbalance its rational and scientific aspects. Proclaiming that "without enthusiasm nothing great can be accomplished by man,"[67] he brought to Bolshevik inner circles a generosity of spirit unmatched by any of his comrades. Sometimes the target of Lenin's anger because his commitment to aesthetics and ethics carried him beyond the limits of Bolshevik orthodoxy, Lunacharskii nonetheless remained a man who commanded Lenin's respect. "He is drawn to the future with his whole being," Lenin once said. "That is why there is such joy and laughter in him. And he is ready to give that joy and laughter to everyone."[68] Others shared that view. "To us, the prerevolutionary intelligentsia, he seemed to be the incarnation of the most charming qualities of Soviet power from the very first days of its existence," the critic and translator Kornei Chukovskii concluded some years later. "It is difficult to imagine any other person who could have been so marvelously equipped for the historical role he had to play."[69]

As Bolshevik Russia's first commissar of enlightenment, Lunacharskii served as the patron of arts and letters among an intelligentsia that was largely hostile to Bolshevism, and he waged the first battles in a campaign to stamp out illiteracy among Russia's masses. Stubbornly certain that "the people themselves, consciously or unconsciously, must evolve their own culture," he insisted that the educational system of Bolshevik Russia must rest firmly upon popular initiative. "All school affairs must be handed over to the organs of local self-government," he announced on his third day in office. "Workers', soldiers', and peasants' cultural-educational organizations must achieve full autonomy."[70] Yet, unlike some of his more radical proletarian comrades, Lunacharskii valued Russia's past cultural achievements and thought that proletarian education, art, and culture could not develop apart from the broader tradition. "The independence of proletarian creativity," he insisted "presupposes an acquaintance with all the fruits of preceding cultures."[71]

So fearful was Lunacharskii that the cultural monuments of Russia's past would not be preserved for the proletariat to build upon that he reportedly left a meeting of the Sovnarkom in tears at the news that Bolsheviks had bombarded St. Basil's Cathedral and the Kremlin during their battle for Moscow in November 1917. That very afternoon, he resigned from the Sovnarkom in protest against the "bestial ferocity" of the Red Guards, only to return to the government a few hours later when he learned that the first reports of damage had been exaggerated. Still, he insisted that even the modest damage done during the Reds' final assault against the Kremlin was "a horrible, irreparable misfortune" and pleaded for Russia's angry proletarians to spare their nation's art treasures. "I beg you, comrades, to give me your support," he concluded as he announced his return to Lenin's government. "Preserve for yourselves and your descendants the beauty of our land."[72]

Like his more politically astute comrades on the Sovnarkom, Lunacharskii found it difficult to take control of his commissariat because of stubborn opposition from tsarist and Provisional Government officials who continued to insist that the Bolsheviks had seized power illegally. Only in mid-November, after he had worked out of a small office in the Winter Palace for nearly a month, did Lunacharskii force the issue over the objections of his irate predecessor, the Countess Panina, who, as the Provisional Government's deputy minister of education, protested his arrival by removing nearly a hundred thousand rubles from the teachers' pension fund.[73] To show their support for the countess, most of the ministry's senior officials denounced the Bolsheviks as the "destroyers of the glorious February Revolution," left their offices, and never returned. "I tried to find new officials to replace the old ones," Lunacharskii later wrote, "but qualified people did not come our way. . . . I thought that perhaps some of the liberal and radical teachers [from the Provisional Government's State Education Committee] would agree to work with us, but that didn't work out either."[74] That many of Russia's writers, artists, journalists, and teachers stood against the new regime made Lunacharskii's task more difficult, especially since most Bolsheviks preferred more exciting political assignments than he had to offer. Fighting the Whites, building the new order, struggling against counterrevolutionary plots, and combatting sabotage all proved more attractive to the average Bolshevik than did developing programs for mass education and selecting toys for workers' and peasants' kindergartens.

As in Zhenotdel, women provided many of the recruits for the Commissariat of Enlightenment as Lunacharskii's search for politically reliable officials who could help to shape proletarian culture and foster mass education brought him to the wives and relatives of many leading Bolsheviks. Natalia Trotskaia, Olga Kameneva (Kamenev's wife and Trotskii's sister), Vera Bonch-Bruevich, Ludmila and Vera Menzhinskaia (whose brother succeeded Dzerzhinskii), and Zlata Lilina (Zinoviev's wife) all took positions in Lunacharskii's commissariat, and so did Lenin's sister Anna Elizarova. Nadezhda Krupskaia played an especially important part in Lunacharskii's work. Unlike most Bolsheviks, she came from a family that sympathized with Russia's revolutionary movement, and her father had been obliged to resign from the imperial artillery for that reason. As an adolescent, Nadezhda (whose name means "hope" in Russian) had set out to become a schoolteacher. In her early twenties she had refocused that ambition upon teaching Marxism to the workers of St. Petersburg, had been arrested, and after a stay in prison, had married Lenin in 1898. She had spent the next two decades working with Lenin in Siberia, Geneva, London, and Krakow before she had accompanied him triumphantly back to Russia in April 1917. Although the author of the first Russian work about women and problems they faced as the overworked, underpaid underclass of Russia's proletariat, Krupskaia always remained more dedicated to the cause of education than to that of women. Well-read about the theory and practice of education and a dedicated teacher of the masses, Krupskaia had much to offer Lunacharskii when, at Lenin's suggestion, he added her to his administrative cabinet at the beginning of November 1917.[75]

Like Lunacharskii, Krupskaia at first believed that Russia's masses should shape their own educational destiny. "Let us not be afraid of the people," she insisted boldly. "Our job is to help the people *in fact* to take their fate into their own hands."[76] Yet Russia's teachers proved to be among the most stubborn early opponents of the Bolsheviks' regime, and they opposed their program so strenuously that, by mid-1919, Krupskaia had begun to urge the commissariat to exercise *"more authority, not fearing to intervene,* in dealing with the educational authorities in the provinces."[77] Lunacharskii agreed. After speaking out against people who preferred "to continue in the role of political matadors rather than the role of teachers," and warning that "the people's power, represented by the dictatorship of the proletariat, [would] not be kind" to those who opposed his programs, he dissolved the teachers' unions around which the Bolsheviks' opponents had organized their opposition. "Better educationalists," he insisted confidently, would "come from the people."[78]

The Bolsheviks' massive campaign against illiteracy gave Lunacharskii grounds for that seemingly utopian belief. "To overcome illiteracy is not a political task," Lenin once said. "It is a condition without which one cannot even talk about politics." In an illiterate society, a government could not communicate with its people, and there could be no hope of enlisting their support. "The illiterate person," Lenin insisted, "stands outside of politics. First it is necessary to teach him his ABCs. Without it, there are only rumors, fairy tales, and prejudices, but not politics."[79] Certain that they must do better to bring the masses into direct contact with their government than their predecessors had done, the Bolsheviks had declared war upon illiteracy in Russia as soon as they took power. They had found thousands of enthusiastic men and women from all walks of life to help launch their campaign. From Moscow to Tashkent, from the lonely provinces of the Far North to the bustling trade centers of the Volga, dedicated men and women came forward to offer their knowledge to the people, to teach the adult men and women of Russia to read and write. "We know that across the great expanse of the Russian land there are those corners where people have not yet heard the voice of a person who can read and write," two young nurses wrote to Lunacharskii's commissariat at the end of 1917. "That's where we want to go."[80] The immensity of the task that lay ahead was overwhelming. There were provinces where the number of illiterates stood well above a quarter million, and villages where not a single woman could read or write.[81] A new "movement to the people," far more massive than the revolutionary one that the tsarist government had suppressed in the 1870's, had to be brought into being. "Is it not utopian," Krupskaia asked rhetorically, "to think of liquidating illiteracy quickly in our illiterate Russia . . . where the female rural population is almost universally illiterate and where half of the peasant men cannot sign their names?"[82]

In fact, the campaign against illiteracy proved to be one of the Bolsheviks' most successful undertakings. All across Russia, posters proclaimed: "Down with Illiteracy!" "Literacy Is the Sword that Can Conquer the Forces of Ignorance!"[83] In Red Army units, illiteracy squads worked in barracks, on the march, and even during lulls in the fighting to teach soldiers to read and write. "Two days of study, then a week in battle," Red soldiers sang as they marched. "Two days with pencils, a week with bayonets."[84] Because the Bolsheviks wanted to shape an entire socialist society and "raise the consciousness of all Soviet people,"[85] Krupskaia insisted that Russia's illiterates be taught from specially prepared primers that emphasized Communist morality and exhorted teachers and students to work for the collective. "He who once was nothing now will become everything," one primer promised. "We are building a new world without tyrants or slaves." "The defense of the Revolution is the duty of all toilers," another book of ABCs for adults taught its readers. "Communists are the defenders of the workers' interests all around the globe."[86] Dedication produced dramatic success. Within two years, more than six out of every ten people over the age of eight in Russia could read and write, at least haltingly. Yet, no amount of dedication could eradicate illiteracy overnight, or even in a few years. At the end of the Civil War, more than fifty million Soviet citizens still could not read and write.[87]

No matter how desperately needed, education could not remain the sole focus of Lunacharskii's work as commissar of enlightenment. The entire surging, amorphous literary and artistic world of Russia required his attention no less than did the task of educating Russia's masses, and because so many of Russia's writers, actors, dancers, musicians, and artists remained hostile to the Bolsheviks after the October Revolution, Lunacharskii knew that he must woo them and win them if Lenin's government was not to face the opposition of the nation's most articulate citizens. His close ties to prerevolutionary Russia's artistic world and his own accomplishments as poet, literary critic, and champion of art and religion against Plekhanov's supremely rationalist version of Marxism[88] made him especially well suited for that task. "There was nothing monolithic in his world view," one of his deputies remembered.

"He was excited by Levitan and Tatlin, Picasso and the Wanderers, the circus and Tchaikovsky."[89] As an artist, Lunacharskii therefore could tolerate extreme diversity in culture, while, as a Bolshevik, he would defend rigid discipline in politics. As commissar of enlightenment it became his task to find a common ground on which Russia's turbulent and undisciplined artists could stand with the Bolsheviks' supremely disciplined leaders and revolutionary strategists.

Never had Russia's arts been more diverse than in 1917, for the Revolution had come at a time when her writers, painters, and poets were midway through a series of daring experiments, the outcome of which no one yet could imagine. Bolshevik Moscow teemed with literary movements and artistic credos, all celebrating their liberation by the Revolution. Especially in a score of back alley and subterranean cafés, art and poetry came together in a resounding cacophony of new shapes and sounds as artists and writers tested their new freedom. Every credo had a movement, and every movement had its literary café—some called them "poetry inns"[90]—where young men and women cursed the past, ignored the present, and cheered the future before noisy audiences that, the young poet Ilia Ehrenburg remembered, "stared at us with curiosity, like visitors looking at monkeys in the zoo."[91] The "Tenth Muse," "Three-Leaved Clover," "Domino," "Pittoresque," "Red Cockerel," "Pegasus' Trough," "The Poets' Cafe," and "The Forge"— which provided forums for Futurists, Cubists, Suprematists, Imaginists, Expressionists, Presentists, Accidentists, Anarchists, and an untranslatable group called the Nichevoki (the Nothing-ists)—all flared brightly and then passed quickly into oblivion. Everything seemed so new that even the most recent past seemed far away. To Arthur Ransome, biographer of Poe and Oscar Wilde, who had come to see Russia's new world at first hand, "a gulf seemed to have passed" between past and present, and the plays of Chekhov that audiences had thought so full of meaning on the eve of the Great War, now seemed very remote.[92]

The distance seemed particularly great between the raging young revolutionary artists of Civil War Moscow and the artists of Russia's turn-of-the-century avant-garde, who, a scant decade before, had shaped an apocalyptic vision that looked for the cleansing flames of war and revolution to transform a world that had grown too comfortable and too complacent. Among them, the *enfants ter-*

ribles Andrei Belyi and Aleksandr Blok had pursued the fleeting image of Sophia, the Beautiful Lady, through whom, the philosopher Vladimir Solovev had promised, men would one day unite flesh and spirit in a mystical and erotic union. For artists such as these, who lived in a world that had drawn its inspiration from the West and had dared the laws of God or man to restrain their art, the contrast between Europe and Russia had grown more striking as the cataclysm of the Great War approached. "You are sober, we are drunk; you are rational, we are frenzied; you are just, we are lawless," one of them had proclaimed. "For you, politics is knowledge, for us it is a religion."[93] As they had reveled in these stark contrasts, the men and women of Russia's prewar avant-garde had turned to the East to search for a new faith that would unite them with the people.

Fearful of the future, but fascinated by their apocalyptic vision, these "children of Russia's dreadful years,"[94] as Blok once had called them, had found a temple for their new faith at Viacheslav Ivanov's famous Petersburg "Tower"—the rooftop apartment overlooking the Taurida Gardens—from which all boundaries of time and space had been erased by thick carpets and boarded up windows. There, Belyi remembered, day and night blended soundlessly into one to create a "brilliant but insane life [that] destroyed the very foundations of time." Yet the time and space that "Viacheslav the Magnificent" had sought to exclude from the "capriciously interlaced corridors, rooms, and doorless anterooms" of his Tower[95] could not be banished from an outside world in which accelerating time and contracting space had forever altered the ways of men and politics. Life had slipped out of focus. As the Great War had approached in 1914, Russia's avant-garde had exchanged the elegance of Ivanov's Tower for the primitive rawness of "The Stray Dog," a cellar cabaret on Petrograd's Mikhailovskaia Square, where the stench of sweat, cheap tobacco, and urine from a perpetually malfunctioning toilet replaced the delicate scents of Ivanov's incense. Flickering ever so faintly in the distance, the flame of revolution had beckoned Russia's avant-garde poets and artists in those days. Like moths drawn to a burning candle, they had awaited its cleansing fires with morbid fascination, not knowing how thoroughly the approaching revolutionary holocaust would consume them.

Revolution had brought liberation, but it also had erased the points of reference from which Russia's turn-of-the-century avant-garde writers and artists had taken their bearings. As they looked at revolutionary Moscow in stunned bewilderment, these men and women suddenly found themselves middle-aged and hopelessly adrift in the new Bolshevik world of proletarian life and culture. Georgii Chulkov, the poet who once had promised that his vision of mystical anarchism would transcend the "antinomy of freedom and necessity" by means of Eros,[96] now looked like "a large, sickly bird," willing only to recite the poetry of the mid-nineteenth-century archconservative Tiutchev.[97] Once the sex-driven lion of literary Moscow, the Decadent poet Konstantin Balmont, who had proclaimed, "I experienced my first passionate thought about women at five,"[98] now cursed Moscow's proletarian cowards and tried to make his way onto the city's teeming tramcars by shouting, "Make way, you dogs! Make way for the child of the Sun!"[99]

Like Chulkov and Balmont, so Viacheslav Ivanov, the man who had stood beyond the future's brink a scant half-decade before, now seemed as far removed from the present as the heroes of Chekhov's plays. "Time had made a leap forward, leaving behind the eccentric of Zubovskii Boulevard with his nineteenth-century clothes, his maenads, his Isolde, his Oriental roses and his psalms," Ehrenburg concluded, as his reverence for Ivanov's accomplishments struggled against his pity that Ivanov's "heart was not burning but slowly freezing."[100] "Doesn't it make you happy to feel free of everything that once seemed eternal and unshakable?" one of Ivanov's aging contemporaries asked as the winter of 1918–1919 drew to an end.[101] Still unable to sort out his own feelings about the turmoil that surged around him, Ehrenburg could not answer. Too much still seemed unfamiliar and unclear. "The sphinx set riddles for people which they could not solve and the sphinx devoured them," he wrote many years later. "Art beckoned, but I still thought about the riddles of the sphinx."[102]

Everything and everyone connected with art in Moscow came together at the Poets' Cafe, which the energetic Futurist artist-poet David Burliuk had opened with Maiakovskii and the poet Vasilii Kamenskii in an abandoned back alley commercial laundry with funds provided by the famous Moscow confectioner Dmitrii Filipov.[103] Beginning with the black door that bore its name scrawled in irregular red letters, the Poets' Cafe stood as a monument to the revolutionary turmoil that surged around Russia's artists. Burliuk and his Cubist friends had smeared the walls with black paint, over which they had emblazoned an array of swollen female torsos and many-legged horses' rumps, among which they had interspersed green, yellow, and red stripes and detached eyes. "I love to watch children dying," a line from one of Maiakovskii's prerevolutionary poems had been scrawled across one wall. They had painted the wall behind the stage a vivid orange.

The cafe's patrons—artists, poets, journalists, Red Army soldiers and sailors laden with weapons and hand grenades, and a strange assortment of speculators, whom the management disparagingly referred to as "bourgeoisie who hadn't had their throats cut yet"—sat on stools arranged around crude tables covered with gray homespun cloths. Iakov Bliumkin, the soon-to-be-assassin of the German ambassador Mirbach, could be seen there, his solicitous attention reminiscent of a benevolent godfather. In the days before Dzerzhinskii destroyed them and their nearby headquarters, Moscow's anarchists, dressed in black, with automatic pistols and daggers bristling from bandoliers that bore the slogan "Death to Capital!" lounged along the cafe's walls between street battles with the police or other gangs. The city was hungry in those days and growing hungrier. Yet food and excitement always could be found at the Poets' Cafe. "At the Poets' Cafe," Ehrenburg remembered, "I often saw a Mauser [automatic pistol] beside a plate of cakes on a table."[104]

On some evenings, slogans ruled the Poets' Cafe. Once the slogan was "Down with All Kings." Another time, it was "A Stage for All." Heavily made up, his lorgnette delicately raised, Burliuk sometimes would mount the stage to declaim: "I am fond of pregnant men." Urged on by Burliuk and Maiakovskii, artists sitting in the audience performed: opera singers whose voices were too powerful for the long narrow room, dancers not dressed to dance, and popular singers whose voices seemed flat and one-dimensional without their accompanists. Still finding his way and not yet part of the Soviet cultural establishment, the young composer Sergei Prokofiev sometimes played his latest works. The poet-singer Aristarkh Klimov, accompanied by several girls from the all-girl commune over which he reigned in Petrovskii Park, sang romantic ballads. Sometimes, the "King of Clowns" Vladimir Durov presided. Night after night, week after week, the parade of performers to the cafe's stage never ceased. Once, even Lunacharskii gave a speech in which he criticized Futurism, praised Maiakovskii's talent, but condemned his never-ending self-promotion.

No matter what the occasion, events and performances at the Poets' Cafe turned around Maiakovskii, irrepressible, irresponsible, and determined to enjoy a full measure of fame in his lifetime. At times silent and brooding, at others, stormy, rude and disdainful, yet often generous and charming, Maiakovskii remained the Futurist among Futurists. He had abandoned the vivid yellow- and black-striped tunic that had been his badge of office before and during the war. Now, he wore a worker's cap tilted back on his head set off by a red scarf tied in a large knot at his neck. Often, as he listened to the cafe's poetry and music, Maiakovskii sketched the performers and gave his drawings away. Sometimes he would autograph his books with his favorite inscription: "For Internal Use Only."[105] On several occasions, Maiakovskii read from "Man," his newest poem. "You must sit quietly," he would begin, his hands stuffed into his trouser pockets, a cigarette dangling from his mouth. "As quiet as buttercups."[106]

Before the Poets' Cafe closed and they went to the provinces in the spring of 1918, Moscow's artists celebrated May Day by decorating the city with Futurist and Suprematist paintings. According to Bonch-Bruevich's report, the idea of decorating Moscow "in such a way as to give it an entirely different appearance from any other city in Europe" had come from Lenin himself, who had suggested mounting key slogans from Marx and Engels on prominent buildings.[107] Turned over to Lunacharskii, the project of "decorating" the capital quickly got out of hand, and Moscow's revolutionary artists went to work with their brushes on the rows of vendors' booths and long board fences to produce something very different from what Lenin had in mind. "Demented squares battled with rhomboids on the peeling facades of colonnaded Empire villas," Ehrenburg later wrote. "Faces with triangles for eyes popped up everywhere." Unable to comprehend what meaning the artists had intended, one old woman was heard to lament that "they want us to worship the devil," as she looked at a Cubist painting with a large fish eye in its center.[108] Then, on the eve of the May Day celebrations, some of Moscow's artists painted the trees along the Kremlin wall in vivid shades of violet, brick red, blue, and crimson. Cursing the "decadentism" that had produced such work, Lenin ordered a massive cleanup, only to find that Moscow's revolutionary artists had worked with paints that no amount of scrubbing would remove.[109] Nearly a year later, some of the paintings still remained for visitors to comment upon. Arthur Ransome saw them in February 1918, pronounced them "delightful," and thought that something about their primitive brilliance fit especially well with the atmosphere of Moscow at that time. "They seemed less like Futurist paintings," he wrote, "than like some traditional survival, linking new Moscow with the Middle Ages."[110]

Although Lunacharskii shared some of Lenin's distaste for abstract art, he remained more willing to tolerate the excesses of Russia's volatile young Futurists because they, as revolutionary artists, sympathized with the Revolution and supported the Bolsheviks at a time when most other writers and artists would not. "It is better to make a mistake by giving the people something which will never gain their sympathy," he warned at the end of 1918, "than to hide a work that may bear fruit in the future under a bush on the grounds that it does not suit somebody's taste just now."[111] Even as conservatives demanded that the Commissariat of Enlightenment restrain Russia's exploding arts, Lunacharskii stubbornly held his ground. "I say that there must be freedom in the cultural field," he insisted two years later. "I consider that one of my functions [as commissar of enlightenment] . . . is the defense of the rights of free culture against Red sycophancy."[112]

In Petrograd, a number of Futurists employed in the Department of Literature and Art at the Commissariat for Enlightenment tried Lunacharskii's patience even further when they began to publish an explosive small weekly paper entitled *Iskusstvo kommuny* (Art of the Commune), at the end of 1918. In its pages the artists Natan Altman, Iurii Annenkov, Kazimir Malevich, and Marc Chagall, joined with Maiakovskii and a pleiad of poets and writers to publish an astonishing array of revolutionary statements that looked only to the future, demanded the eradication of the past, and recognized no authority beyond themselves. "There is no beauty without struggle," the first issue of *Iskusstvo kommuny* proclaimed. "There are no masterpieces without violence."[113] Art, they insisted, must know no limits, recognize no authority, and break out of every traditional constraint. "What we need is not a dead cathedral of art, where dead masterpieces can languish, but a living factory of the human spirit," Maiakovskii exclaimed. "We need raw art, raw words, raw deeds," he concluded. "Art ought not to be collected in lifeless cathedral-museums. It should be everywhere—on the streets, in streetcars, in factories, in workshops, and in workers' apartments."[114]

Iskusstvo kommuny summoned Russia's artists of the Left to join the battle against tradition and the classics and demanded the immediate consignment of the nation's entire artistic past to history's trashbin. "I must confess that I am embarrassed," Lunacharskii wrote after he looked over the first issues. "I am painfully shocked," he added in a rough draft that he did not publish. "And [I] blush for Maiakovskii."[115] Maiakovskii dismissed all criticism and pleas for moderation with scorn. Once, he had urged his countrymen to "throw Pushkin, Dostoevskii, and Tolstoi overboard from the steamer of modernity."[116] Now he demanded to know "why Pushkin and the other generals of the classics have not yet been attacked." The time had come "for bullets to begin to ricochet against museum walls," he insisted.[117] "The streets are our brushes," he announced in his "Order of the Day to the Army of Art." "And city squares—our palettes."[118] The revolution in art must continue, and it must not slacken pace. "Form into columns!" Maiakovskii ordered at the beginning of "Left March." "Left! Left! Left!" As his famous poem moved toward its conclusion, its urgency deepened. "Who there moved his right?" he demanded. "Left! Left! Left!"[119] Maiakovskii had decided that poets and artists could not march alone. When he returned to Moscow in the spring of 1919, he dedicated himself anew to the people of Russia and began to speak not to dozens but for millions. "150,000,000 are the authors of this poem," he insisted, as he began to write "One Hundred and Fifty Million." "150,000,000 speak with my lips."[120]

In Moscow, Maiakovskii went to work for ROSTA, the Russian Telegraph Agency, where his friend, the graphic artist Mikhail Cheremnykh, had conceived the idea of spreading political commentary and educational propaganda among the masses by placing large sheets of captioned cartoons in shop windows. As perfected by Cheremnykh and Maiakovskii, ROSTA "Windows of Satire" translated political messages into easily remembered two-liners illustrated by cartoon figures that dramatized the main points for men and women who still found it difficult to puzzle out the letters.[121] Often made with stencils that could be cut rapidly and reproduced on any surface, ROSTA windows made it possible to send powerful political messages quickly to semiliterate men and women and, at the same time, to conserve paper, which, by 1919, had become one of the most scarce resources in Bolshevik Russia. Convinced that the failure of the Romanovs and their Provisional Government successors to communicate with Russia's workers and peasants had been a key factor in their downfall in 1917, the Bolsheviks had searched for effective ways to explain their aims to the masses and enlist their support. For the first time, a government on Russian soil had thought it worthwhile to build a base of political support among the masses.

As the popularity of ROSTA Windows of Satire spread to towns and cities across Russia, Maiakovskii and his friends worked at a frenzied pace, usually on the floor of a shabby room not far from where the Poets' Cafe had been the year before. A *burzhuika*, one of those legendary small portable stoves that burned the smallest scraps of wood and paper to provide minimal quantities of heat in Russia's fuel-starved cities, smoked ineffectively in one corner. Maiakovskii and his friends used it mainly to keep their glue, inks, and paints from freezing. "Our hands swollen with cold, we wore fur hats and felt boots while we worked," Cheremnykh remembered. Maiakovskii also wore his overcoat and gloves.[122] Maiakovskii wrote most of the the two-line captions in those days, while Cheremnykh and Lilia Brik, Maiakovskii's long-time mistress and the wife of one of his best friends, did most of the illustrations and cut stencils. Sometimes they worked for days and nights without sleep in a never-ending race to convert the latest news bulletins into cartoons and captions. "It would often happen," Maiakovskii remembered, that we would receive word by telegraph of a victory at the front and, within forty minutes—an hour at most—colorful posters about it would be hanging in the streets."[123] Sometimes, the cartoons and captions would be stenciled directly onto fences, building walls, and sidewalks if paper could not be found. Within a year, ROSTA had nearly fifty workrooms in other cities with some of the greatest Russian artists and satirists working at the tasks that Cheremnykh, Maiakovskii, and Lilia Brik had begun.

Although ROSTA's Windows of Satire communicated with the tens of millions of toilers as the Red Army pushed back the forces of Kolchak, Denikin, and Iudenich in 1919, they were by no means the Bolsheviks' most dramatic effort. Emblazoned with slogans and heroic paintings of peasants, soldiers, and workers striving to build a new world of social justice and proletarian solidarity, propaganda trains bearing such names as *Lenin*, *October Revolution*, *Red Banner*, *Red Cossack*, and *Red East* carried the gospel of communism across Bolshevik Russia in 1919 and 1920. Each train carried autos to transport speakers to villages beyond the railroad's reach, a printing press, huge quantities of books, brochures, and pamphlets written in simple language, and an assortment of specially prepared films that brought Russia's new leaders to the people.[124] At the same time, these moving propaganda centers brought provincial Russia closer to the Bolsheviks. Together with *Red Star*, a large riverboat that towed a floating movie theater capable of holding up to eight hundred people, these trains allowed Bolsheviks who had spent their adult lives in cities and foreign exile to see at first hand the land they had come to rule.

Even though Nicholas II had ruled Russia for twenty years longer than the Bolsheviks, thanks to the work of propaganda trains and riverboats, peasants knew far better by the end of the Civil War what Lenin looked like, what his voice sounded like, and what he hoped to accomplish. The impact of that experience upon the lives of men and women for whom the technology of the industrial age still remained a distant mystery must have been staggering. At the very least, it gave them a sense of participation in the political life of Russia, and when the leading Bolsheviks traveled on propaganda trains and riverboats themselves, that sense must have deepened appreciably. Certainly, a number of influential Bolsheviks rode the propaganda trains for that reason. Lunacharskii spent several weeks aboard propaganda trains in order to see at first hand the problems his commissariat faced, and so did the Civil War commissars of justice, public health, and internal affairs. In order to see how rural teachers lived and worked, Krupskaia spent several months on the *Red Star* as it worked its way along the Volga and Kama rivers under the watchful eye of Viacheslav Molotov, the young party activist who became Stalin's faithful henchman and commissar of foreign affairs.[125]

The Bolsheviks insisted that complaints and petitions must be heard and attended to during such journeys to strengthen the masses' belief that their new leaders listened and acted in their interests.[126] Yet it proved very difficult for city-bred Bolsheviks to assure suspicious peasants that workers and peasants were equal partners in Russia's new order. To do so became the task of Mikhail Kalinin, president of the Central Executive Committee and affectionately known to the masses as "Papa." Born a peasant in the central Russian province of Tver, Kalinin at forty-four used his peasant origins to further the Bolsheviks' cause as he rode the *October Revolution* propaganda train across Central Russia, the Ukraine, and western Siberia in 1919 and 1920. "I want to know how things are going, comrades," he would tell his listeners, the whiteness of his beard and his potatolike nose making him appear older and less sophisticated than he was. As the peasants reeled off their complaints, he would answer them simply, but with a firmness that left no doubt that he and his comrades intended to pursue the course they had set. Yes, he knew that life for the peasants was hard and that Bolshevik agents had taken their grain, horses, and cattle. But, he would point out, such requisitions were caused by events over which the Bolsheviks had no control. Once the Bolsheviks drove the Whites from the grain fields of the Kuban, Ukraine, and western Siberia, Kalinin promised his listeners, such requisitions would end. In the meantime, he urged them to remember that, "at each step of a new life, especially the first one, it is only natural to have misunderstandings and problems. It is impossible," he counseled them in his best village elder fashion, "to move to the next step without them."

In the meantime, Kalinin insisted, he wanted to know if the authorities had dealt fairly with his listeners. Had they paid for the cattle and grain they had taken? If not, had the peasants kept their receipts? If so, he would personally see to it that they received payment immediately. Were the local authorities just? Were they honest or did they steal? Were they sober or did they get drunk too often? All these things, Kalinin explained, were of direct concern to the Bolsheviks. "We want to regulate life in such a manner that there will be complete justice for all," he assured his listeners. "The law must work for all of us," he insisted, "not the other way around." Then, after he had dealt with those complaints that could be settled quickly, Kalinin would ask: "Well, comrades, have we fixed things up?" Yes, they would assure him, that had been done.[127] "Well, comrades," he would conclude as he made ready to leave, "I wish you peace, harmony, and a good harvest." Over and over Kalinin repeated the same ritual with the same results. His dedication kept him in the countryside for nearly nine months in 1919, for no other senior Bolshevik had his gift for speaking to Russia's peasants. "Comrade Kalinin embodies the essence of our workers' and peasants' Russia," Frunze once announced to a mass meeting in Orenburg. The fact that Kalinin, a peasant and "one of the most simple men imaginable," had come to be president of the Central Executive Committee of Bolshevik Russia, Frunze explained, showed clear proof of "the great transformation that the working class and peasants of Russia have accomplished."[128]

While Kalinin's rise allowed the Bolsheviks to claim that a lowly peasant had bridged the chasm that had separated Russia's masses from the pinnacle of political power before the Revolution, his simple verbal magic could not so easily or quickly close the gap that traditionally had separated town from country. For the better part of two centuries, Russia's Europeanized rulers, upper classes, and city folk had lived in a world apart from those millions of peasants who had tilled the soil as they had in the Middle Ages. Until well past the middle of the nineteenth century, such men and women knew virtually nothing of peasant life, and even those writers and artists who had tried to paint peasants—or write about them—had produced idealized accounts at best. Educated Russians remained appallingly unaware of the want and misery in which most rural folk lived, just as they remained ignorant about the peasants' dreams, hopes, and aspirations. How peasants hoped to structure their lives should they have the opportunity to live in the best of all possible worlds continued to be a question about which the Russian intelligentsia knew almost nothing. Comforting images of rural lives lived simply but well, in which buxom peasant women kneaded dough, spun flax, and nursed infants, while their strong, vigorous husbands cut wood and reaped grain, prevailed. In a society based upon serf labor, educated Russians dared not challenge that view or look beneath the veneer of peasant life they witnessed during their infrequent summer visits to their estates in the country. Few wanted to know the truth. It would have been too fearsome to admit that every serf was a potential enemy who might at any time plunge a dagger into the throats of those who thought themselves such benevolent masters. They therefore continued to cling to their illusions and found even the challenges posed by so modest an abolitionist tract as the *Hunting Sketches* that Ivan Turgenev published in 1852 disquieting.

Just how ignorant educated Russians were about peasant life became strikingly clear after the emancipation of the serfs in 1861. In the mid-1870s, several thousand young men and women from urban, educated Russia plumbed the depths of rural want and village misery when they went into the countryside to preach the gospel of socialism to the peasants and came away with their preconceptions shattered and their illusions dashed. "Until that point, I had never seen the true ugliness of peasant life at first hand," the terrorist leader Vera Figner remembered. "Under those horrible impressions that I drew from seeing the material side of the people's daily life, those three months [in the village] were for me a terrible experience."[129] Only among the peasants did Russia's radical young men and women begin to sense the extent of the gap, yet the experience of the 1870s gave the city-bred revolutionaries of Russia no understanding about how to bridge it. Russia's revolutionaries of the late nineteenth century therefore tried to urbanize their dealings with the peasants and build the first foundations of a proletarian revolutionary movement among those rural folk who came to Russia's growing industrial centers in search of new and better lives.

Lenin and his Bolsheviks had entered 1917 with only the most crudely formulated agrarian program, and after the October Revolution they had borrowed much of their plans for bringing the Revolution to Russia's countryside from their Socialist Revolutionary rivals. Not unlike those tsarist champions of Russian modernization who, in the 1880s and 1890s, had squeezed the surplus capital needed to finance Russia's industrial development from the peasantry, they drew too heavily upon the resources of the countryside to rebuild Russia's war-torn cities. In 1891, that sort of program had produced the greatest famine of the nineteenth century in the Russian countryside. Now, as the Bolsheviks began to focus their reconstruction efforts upon Russia's cities and factory workers at the expense of her peasants and countryside, their urban-centered policies threatened to produce some of the same negative results as had the economic programs of their late nineteenth-century tsarist predecessors.

That the Bolsheviks could begin to think of reconstruction at the end of 1919 indicated the extent of their victories during that year. The armies of Kolchak and Iudenich had been driven from the field. Denikin's forces were being pushed back toward their bases in the Crimea, and only the invading armies of newly independent Poland still seemed to pose a serious danger. Yet the Bolsheviks had won their battles only by draining every resource and straining every fiber of their national economy to the utmost. Certain that if they did not win today they would not live to face the problems of tomorrow, they had lived only in the present, and long-term dangers of short-term solutions could not concern them. With no thought for tomorrow, desperately needed urban housing had been torn down for fuel, and factories that did not produce military goods had been stripped to meet the perpetual emergencies of wartime supply in a nation whose industrial capacity had all but collapsed. Only as the Civil War's urgency receded at the end of 1919 and they faced the full extent of Russia's domestic crises did the Bolsheviks begin to realize how dearly the victories of 1919 had been bought. Bolshevik Russia, Viktor Shklovskii concluded then, had "ruined whole factories to make boots out of [machine] fan belts."[130]

For more than two years, Russians had consumed more than they had produced, as their leaders drained every resource to keep their armies in the field and their ship of state afloat. The struggles of 1920 thus would center less upon defeating the White armies and more upon economic survival, as the domestic crises created by war and revolution deepened. "We were living on our last reserves," Shklovskii remembered. "Our hardships kept piling on; we wore them like clothing."[131] In the struggle to survive, men and women became just another resource to be used and expended by the state as circumstances demanded, for the dictatorship of the proletariat—acting in the name of the "people's will"—began to shape Russians' lives in cruel and brutal ways. "A country outside the law—that is what Russia is turning into," one bitter citizen wrote. Russia, he concluded with disgust, was becoming a "dungocracy" ruled by rigid and insensitive "boorocrats."[132]

Part Three

1920

CHAPTER ELEVEN

The Struggle to Survive

DURING THE FIRST two years of Russia's Civil War, the Bolsheviks' survival had hinged upon transforming the Red Guards units they had led into the streets of Petrograd in October 1917 into the sternly disciplined Red Army forces that defeated Denikin, Kolchak, and Iudenich. That single task had required all their energy and had consumed all their resources. "All institutions must be adapted to the war and placed on a military footing," Lenin had insisted during the dark days when Denikin had opened his offensive against Moscow. Workers and peasants must understand that "probably the most critical moment for the socialist revolution" was upon them. They must "pull themselves together like soldiers and concentrate . . . directly on the tasks of the war." Everything that was not "absolutely indispensable" had to be set aside. "[It is] our right and our duty," Lenin had announced firmly, "to mobilize the whole population for war to a man."[1]

During the summer and fall of 1919, the slogan "All out for the Fight Against Denikin!" had been the rallying cry that the Reds had carried into battle. Featured in ROSTA windows all across Russia and spread across the headlines of *Pravda*, it told Russians that Bolshevik promises of a new world of social justice and prosperity must be postponed and that more sacrifices still must be made. That year, nearly two million Russians had been drafted into a Red Army that now lived by discipline as stern as any known in the tsarist forces.[2] Although some senior commanders protested against the "bloody discipline" that imposed thousands of capital sentences and carried out hundreds of executions during those difficult days,[3] the Bolsheviks insisted that Trotskii's principle of applying "a red-hot iron to the festering wound" of cowardice and disobedience in their ranks could not be relaxed. "Offenses that may be condoned in a uneducated, unenlightened man," Trotskii said in the summer of 1919, "cannot be excused in a member of the Party that stands at the head of the working classes of the world."[4] Little of the free wheeling, grass-roots democracy of the elected soldiers' committees of 1917 remained in Trotskii's forces, nor did the Red Army of late 1919 bear more than a foggy resemblance to those Red Guards who had brought the Bolsheviks to power. The day was soon to come when junior Red Army officers would have to request permission to speak or even light a cigarette in the presence of a superior.[5]

When the two and a half million–man Red Army of 1919 more than doubled in 1920, it suffered critical shortages of weapons, ammunition, and clothing.[6] At its best, Bolshevik Russia's armaments industry could manufacture only about fifty thousand rifles a month during the Civil War. Even when combined with the output of small arms repair shops, this provided the Red Army with only enough rifles to arm one out of every two of its soldiers by the end of 1920. Other industries did no better. Crippled by shortages of fuel, raw materials, and skilled labor, Soviet factories produced scarcely enough overcoats, shirts, trousers, and boots to supply half of the army's needs during the last year of the Civil War.[7] Red Army men thus wore uniforms patched together from tsarist leftovers and foreign military clothing captured from the Whites while they carried an assortment of weapons every bit as mixed as any that their tsarist predecessors had taken into battle.[8] Nonetheless, by anyone's standard, the five and a quarter million–man Red Army of late 1920 stood as a monument to the Bolsheviks' singlemindedness. Undeniably, they had proved their ability to extract greater sacrifices from the people they ruled than any other government in Russia's modern history.

While the Red Army grew strong by draining an entire nation's resources during 1919 and 1920, Russia's city folk lived from hand to mouth. As the administrative and supply networks that once had provided them with food, fuel, repair services, medical care, and public utilities crumbled, only scattered shards of the once-rich civic life that had flourished in Russia's cities before the Revolution remained. Since all effective city cleaning services had ceased at the beginning of the Revolution three years before, a report that appeared in *Pravda* calculated, seventeen cartloads of refuse and human waste had accumulated for every house in Moscow.[9] Waste filled courtyards, back alleys, abandoned apartments, and even main streets. There was a report that, after a group of soldiers had gutted the first floor of one Moscow house, they had moved to the second floor, cut a hole in the floor, locked the apartment below, and used the hole as a toilet for the entire winter of 1919–1920.[10] Conditions were worse, perhaps, in Petrograd, where grass and even wild flowers had begun to grow in once-busy streets.[11] "Sanitary conditions are simply not to be described in the language of decency," one Petrograd professor wrote as he tried to describe the effects of the spring thaw on wastewater pipes that had frozen and burst that winter.[12] Not constrained by such delicacy, the anti-Bolshevik historian and Moscow University professor Iurii Gote spoke more bluntly. "Everything is strewn with shit and pissed upon such as it never was under the old order," he wrote in his diary at the beginning of 1920. "The reformers of Russian life," he concluded bitterly, "should have in the first place taught people how to use the latrines."[13] As he looked back on those days a few years later, the literary critic Viktor Shklovskii took a more charitable view of his countrymen's faults. "It wasn't so much swinishness," he explained, "as the use of things from a new point of view."[14]

Life became geared to necessity, not choice, as Moscow and Petrograd fought a losing battle to remain respectable as Russia's past and present capital cities. "Everything had its own time," Shklovskii remembered. "Girls with thick braids surrendered themselves at five-thirty in the afternoon because the streetcars stopped running at six." Shklovskii had a friend who wrote a learned book about the similarities between the Malayan and Japanese languages in a tiny shelter he had erected in the middle of his old lodgings out of four chairs, a tarpaulin, and some rugs, which he warmed with his breath and an electric light during those times when there was electricity.[15] Men and women began to measure success by the possession of life's necessities, not its luxuries. "Nina is busy with preparations for the winter—the most elementary and unexpected, such as drying turnips," Gote wrote in an account about how his severely diabetic wife spent some of the last days of her life in the late fall of 1919. "All these are matters of life and death," he added, "arising from the contemporary situation."[16]

"Everyday life—was prehistoric, the everyday life of the cave age," Ilia Ehrenburg remembered. To obtain a few potatoes, a piece of fat, a bit of soap, or a desperately needed article of clothing all counted as triumphant accomplishments. With the production of consumer goods still at a virtual standstill, everything in civilian Russia began to move through a perpetual recycling process that reshaped frivolous castoffs into everyday necessities. Green hats made from felt that once had covered billiard tables, dresses sewn from velvet curtains torn from palace windows, and bearskin rugs converted into overcoats became the height of fashion as people struggled to preserve some shred of the lives they had known before. "That is when I realized what a pair of trousers means to a man of thirty," Ehrenburg confessed. To get his trousers at one of the Bolsheviks' supply centers, Ehrenburg had to choose between them and a desperately needed overcoat and then, to get the overcoat, he had to sell a fortnight's bread ration on the black market.[17] No one had enough, everyone was in need, and the quantity of goods available to meet basic human needs seemed to have become rigidly fixed. "Everything was as bare and open as a watch with its back off," Shklovskii remembered.[18] "Our dominant impression of things Russian," reported H.G. Wells, who visited Petrograd and Moscow in the fall of 1920, "is an impression of a vast irreparable breakdown."[19] With the bitter humor that so often sustained them in times of crisis, the Russians shared Wells's conclusion. "Petrograd is paradise," one of them remarked cynically to a British journalist that fall. "Here men eat apples and go naked."[20]

There was very little food, fewer goods, and almost no services in Russia's cities during the winter of 1919–1920. Stores and shops had long since given way to Soviet ration centers that passed out carelessly assembled meager portions of frost-bitten potatoes, rotten fish, and coarse bread. What meat there was usually came from horses that had died of hunger and overwork. One of the first sights that greeted the British journalist Arthur Ransome when he arrived in Moscow in 1919 was a flock of starving crows that followed a sledge of emaciated horse carcasses, "tearing greedily at the meat" despite the driver's efforts to drive them off.[21] Often, by the time such meat reached distribution centers, it was slimy and rotten, "almost runny," Shklovskii remembered.[22] Everyone craved fats and sugar. "Our dreams were always full of eating, especially eating pounds of butter and other fats," the Petrograd sociologist Pitirim Sorokin confessed,[23] while Shklovskii never forgot "how hard it was to get a few pieces of sugar home without eating them." Shklovskii especially savored the fond memory of an occasion when the ration center had given out small pieces of beef. "What a fantastic taste it had!" he exclaimed. "It was like the first time you slept with a woman. Something entirely new."[24]

People with official meal tickets ate in communal dining rooms. As a privileged foreigner, Ransome had one meal a day of "very good soup, together with a second course of a scrap of meat or fish" at Moscow's National Hotel.[25] At the Hotel Metropole three long blocks away, Ilia Ehrenburg found only "thin soup, millet gruel, or frozen potatoes," even though it had taken a note from the deputy commissar of foreign affairs to put him on the daily dinner list.[26] Assigned to even more modest facilities, Gote complained of "indescribable filth and portraits of the god Marx and his disciples" that dominated the scene at the Moscow University dining room.[27] Sorokin remembered that his Petrograd colleagues, "standing in line with dishes and spoons, which everyone had to bring from home, were like the beggars' line at church doors in former times." One of the scientists in their group, he explained, calculated that "we wasted more strength in walking and in waiting there [at the dining room] than we received in vitamins and calories from the food." Still, Sorokin and his friends made their way to the university dining room every day from points spread out across the city. "The words 'dinner,' and 'I have dined,' " he wrote, "had a pleasant sound and gave a sort of impression that we still were getting something to eat," he wrote. Afterward, Sorokin and his friends took their leave with the words, "Goodbye, I hope you will be alive tomorrow," and went their separate ways. "As the days went by," he remembered sadly, "fewer and fewer of us were left to say it."[28]

Desperate citizens of the Bolsheviks' new order supplemented their starvation rations with purchases on the black market. In Moscow, this meant slipping into nearby peasant villages or visiting the Sukharevka, once described by a visiting journalist as "a crowded study in need and greed,"[29] where anything could be had for a price. "Here gathered proletarian and aristocrat, Communist and bourgeois, peasant and intellectual," the deported American anarchist Emma Goldman wrote. "Here they were bound by the common desire to sell and buy."[30] Rare Bokhara rugs, precious antiques, and priceless Chinese vases shared pride of place with such tsarist leftovers as silk underwear and French cosmetics, although such prosaic items as butter, eggs, and flour attracted larger crowds and commanded exorbitant prices. Gote traded "a felt jacket for potatoes [and] shoes for butter. We sold a lady's cloak," he added, "and with the money bought flour." Prices rose higher that fall. "Flour costs six or seven thousand rubles [for a *pud*, or thirty-six pounds]," Gote wrote in mid-November. "We spent 1,000 rubles yesterday buying 10 eggs and 4 pounds of soap." Fear crept into his diary entries as winter deepened. "The matter of hunger is becoming so urgent," he wrote at the end of 1919, "that you think that no matter how many things you sell there still won't be enough money." Prices seemed to rise according to some fearsome law of mathematics that could not be brought under control. "Millet costs 9,500–10,000 rubles a *pud*," Gote reported in mid-January 1920. "Flour has risen to 13–15,000 rubles," he added six weeks later, "millet to 16–17,000."[31]

Even Lenin admitted that the people of Moscow could not survive without the black market. "It was found this spring and summer," he reported to a conference of factory committees and trade unions in mid-1919, that "the urban worker obtained about half of his food from the Commissariat of Food Supply and had to buy the rest on the open market, at Sukharevka." In vain, Lenin condemned "food profiteering" as "sheer plunder" and "the most infamous corruption."[32] "The Bolsheviks want to clamp down on Sukharevka," Gote wrote, "but then a Sukharevka would spring up on every corner and crossing."[33] People without goods to trade for food turned to other mediums of exchange. Young Soviet office girls exchanged sex with high officials for flour, sugar, and silk stockings.[34] Other women had to settle for less. When she arrived in Petrograd at the beginning of 1920, Emma Goldman found crowds of women selling their bodies for "a pound of bread, a piece of soap or chocolate." Only Red Army soldiers, who received extra rations, could pay their price. "It was too ghastly, too incredible to be real," Goldman wrote. "Yet there they were—those shivering creatures for sale and their buyers, the Red defenders of the Revolution."[35]

As the winter of 1919–1920 continued, the situation grew worse. "The problem of food supplies overshadows everything else except the problem of heating," Gote confided to his diary. "This is the life style of Eskimos." Everyone and everything began to freeze. Families and friends huddled with strangers for warmth around the tiny, smoking iron stoves called *burzhuiki*. "The secret [of using a *burzhuika*] was to stoke it with splinters cut as thin as straw," Konstantin Paustovskii once explained. "This produced a fierce, though short-lived flame [to heat food or water] and used up only the smallest amount of fuel."[36] Even a *burzhuika* could be heated only for brief moments with the scraps of fuel at hand. "Our brains are beginning to rattle in our skulls from the cold," Gote wrote as he watched the temperature inside his Moscow apartment fall to three degrees below freezing. At work it was no better. "It is now below zero inside the building [of the Rumiantsev Museum]," he added on the fifty-ninth anniversary of the emancipation of Russia's serfs. "Ink is freezing, hands grow numb."[37]

In Petrograd, bone-chilling dampness made the cold worse. In normal times, this produced the unusual frost that coated cold stone and turned the granite pillars of St. Isaac's Cathedral into ethereal silver-pink shafts. In the winter of 1919–1920, such frost began to coat the outer walls of uninhabited buildings with a silvery coating that was broken only by the city's rare heated rooms. These, Shklovskii wrote, "showed up from the street as occasional dark patches on the silver."[38] As a general cry arose that patients were freezing to death, the Bolshevik commissar for health decreed that city hospitals had first claim to any firewood that reached Petrograd and Moscow.[39] "Everything was now divided into two categories: combustible and noncombustible," Shklovskii explained as he recalled how people came to his apartment to get warm because its temperature sometimes rose as high as forty-five degrees.[40] "The most valuable present one could give or receive," the ever observant sociologist Sorokin remembered some years later, "was a piece of firewood."[41]

More imprisoned by tradition than they cared to admit, the Bolsheviks tried to solve the crises of daily life by creating more of those instruments of bureaucracy that had plagued life in Imperial Russia. "Institutions, commissions, committees, councils, and collectives are sprouting like mushrooms," one high-ranking army officer reported after he fled to Finland,[42] but, far more than in the old days, a lack of direction and purpose marred their function. "Institutions and ideas, thrown into a common heap, rage in primitive passion and wildly seek to disentangle themselves," the Jewish Russo-American anarchist Alexander Berkman wrote as he observed the chaos of Soviet offices in Moscow.[43] Despite a severe paper shortage, Russia's new Bolshevik bureaucracy produced an avalanche of papers and documents. "I felt in the whirl of a huge machine, its wheels unceasingly . . . grinding out slips of paper, endless paper for the guidance of the millions of Russia," Berkman wrote after a visit to the Bolsheviks' Central Committee headquarters.[44] All of this had a direct impact upon Russians' daily lives because all of the agencies and slips of paper "for the guidance of the millions" caused more waiting and created even longer delays. Ehrenburg waited in line all day merely to obtain the coupon that entitled him to begin his search through Moscow's supply centers for a pair of trousers.[45] "Our existence was filled with queues," Sorokin remembered. "The real scientific definition of Communism, based on experience," he once wrote, "is queues, endless queues."[46]

Responsibility for providing the goods and services that had been supplied by private enterprise before the Revolution now fell into the hands of petty Soviet bureaucrats. People had to apply to the proper government office for a plumber, for house repairs, for train tickets, for meal tickets, for clothing vouchers, for firewood, even for coffins and burial permissions. Every new Bolshevik official could demand bribes and favors because each controlled some permission or paper that people needed to conduct their lives. "People communicated perfectly by means of hints or even without saying anything at all," one official on the Central Timber Committee later wrote as he described bureaucrats who spent hundreds of thousands of rubles on cards and liquor. "An atmosphere of utter corruption reigns in government offices," he continued. "Those Communists and semi-Communists who occupy the most responsible posts are particularly expert practitioners of this art."[47] Some saw in this proliferation of corruption and bureaucratic interference a cynical attempt to discourage people from laying claim to scarce goods and services. "All kinds of red tape were especially introduced," Shklovskii concluded as he recalled the endless lines of people waiting to receive rations of food and firewood, "so that people would give up and go away."[48]

Although the new Bolshevik bureaucracy had obvious links with Russia's fallen past, it displayed a meanness not known in former times. Perpetually fearful of offending their superiors in their anxiety to carve places for themselves in the new order, Russia's new bureaucrats became boorish, brutish, and cruel to those who stood beneath them in the hierarchy of daily life. Every apartment house had a bureaucracy that allocated space and assigned public chores, and every workplace, whether factory, library, or laboratory, had a similar organization responsible to the "collective," of which all workers were a part. Although he once had remarked that "an intelligentsia that has by its own efforts brought things to the point where it has to saw wood itself . . . is good for nothing else," Gote joined readily in the labors of his collective. "We live like everyone else here, and participate in the common work," he wrote of a few days spent in the country in 1920. "My responsibilities include carrying water and firewood and watering the garden."[49] Strong, young, and "accustomed to do manual work" himself, Sorokin nonetheless found the compulsory labor required of university professors in Petrograd by despotic Bolshevik bureaucrats in the winter of 1919–1920 painful to behold. "Covered with mud and blood, in their threadbare clothing," middle-aged and elderly men and their wives, "who had never in their lives done other than intellectual work," now had to move wood and trash for the betterment of what some of them had begun to call the "Russian Surely Fantastic Soviet Republic" instead of the Russian Soviet Federative Socialist Republic, its proper designation.[50] As Bolshevik influence peddlers and bureaucrats reached into the most personal and private corners of Russians' daily lives to settle scores for real or imagined injuries suffered in days past, they stirred outrage that became all the more bitter because it had to remain impotent.

Unable to bear such insult and injury, men and women sought refuge in death. "Suicides are becoming more frequent every day," information compiled by White military intelligence about conditions in Petrograd reported in mid-summer 1919.[51] Everyone seemed to know cases that allowed them to put several human faces on that generalization. "Mrs. D.'s beautiful daughter, Vera, threw herself out of the fifth-story window of our apartment," Sorokin wrote in his journal. "Vera was like a flower that could not live in this soil of cruelty and bestiality." Starting in early 1920, Sorokin's notes became a litany of death: "Professor Khvostov hanged himself." "Yesterday Professor Inostransev took potassium cyanide." "Professor Rosenblatt has just put an end to his life." "Professors Rozin, Diakonov, two Volkovs, Viliev, Kapustin, Pokrovskii, Batushkov, Kulisher, Ostrogorskii, Karpinskii, Arseniev, one after another have died and others are dying."[52] Accounts left by others confirm Sorokin's reports. "Professor V.M. Khvostov has hanged himself, apparently as a result of an acute attack of melancholy," Gote wrote in his diary on February 14, 1920. "Death, cold and hungry, is everywhere," he added five days later. "Reports of deaths are pouring down like rain."[53]

While suicide liberated some, other sorts of death claimed others. For all Russians, death was as near as the nearest typhus-bearing louse, as the disease that had taken such a toll during the first two years of the Civil War continued its deadly rampage. People starved and froze to death. They died from cholera, from colds that turned into pneumonia, and because lifesaving operations could not be performed. During the winter of 1919–1920, Russians died from any disease that required medical treatment because there was almost no medicine. "Gentlemen, I beg you not to die so rapidly," Petrograd University's rector pleaded with grim gallows humor. "In dying you find relief for yourselves, but you cause us a great deal of trouble [for] you know how difficult it is for us to get coffins for you."[54] All across Russia, shortages of coffins combined with the studied unconcern of Russia's new Bolshevik bureaucrats to add to the grief of men and women who lost loved ones that winter. When Gote's wife slipped into a diabetic coma and died in a sanatorium outside of Moscow at the end of 1919, her coffin had to be fashioned out of the rough remains of a broken garden fence. Grateful to those who had sacrificed fuel so that his wife could be decently buried, Gote placed the coffin on a small horse-drawn sledge, which he drove himself to the graveyard at Moscow's Virgins' Convent thirty miles away. He drove all one night to avoid the police. "The moon was shining and the whole sky was sown with stars," he told his diary. "Her last ride was in this magical setting." Like so many Russians, even those who greeted the Revolution with great hopes, Gote now saw only emptiness ahead. "The Revolution has devoured everything that was most dear to me," he wrote on the last night of 1919. "There is nothing ahead," he added a few days later, "but terrible loneliness and fear of hunger."[55]

Life in other Russian cities was no easier than in Moscow and Petrograd. In Kharkov, Emma Goldman found "lines of emaciated and crippled figures, men and women, waiting for their turn to receive . . . their pittance in the form of rations" in the corridor outside the offices of the Commissariat of Social Welfare.[56] Things seemed even worse in Odessa. "Everywhere, numerous employees deliberately wasted their time while thousands of applicants spent days and weeks in the corridors and offices without receiving the least attention," Goldman wrote as she recalled her disgust at the studied indifference of Russia's new bureaucrats to human suffering. "Everyone," she added, "was busy with something other than the work entrusted to him."[57] Berkman found the same thing in Kiev. Like Goldman, he was appalled at the callous cruelty of petty Bolshevik officials who passed their days gossiping while long lines of "worn, tired people, looking hungry and apathetic" jammed the corridors outside their offices.[58] Few were willing to help; few even seemed to care as officials insulated themselves from the people they were supposed to serve by a curtain of mean-spirited unconcern. "The ordinary work in the government offices of Russia is shockingly done," H.G. Wells wrote as he compared the Russia he had known in 1914 with that which he saw in 1920. "The slackness and inaccuracy are indescribable."[59]

Even in cities closer to the source of supply, food seemed no more plentiful than in Moscow and Petrograd. In Kharkov, the heart of the Ukrainian breadlands, Berkman found that a pound loaf of bread cost a third of a worker's monthly salary on the black market. "The Soviet salary of twenty of the most noted Russian professors," he reported, "equals—according to the present purchasing power of the ruble—the amount allowed by the old regime budget for the support of the watchdog at government institutions."[60] Further to the south, at the once bustling port city of Odessa, Konstantin Paustovskii found only starvation rations. "Day after day, we consumed two or three spoonfuls of coarse barley gruel flavored with a green, vaseline-like substance," he wrote of his meals in Odessa during those days. "The bread had one remarkable quality," he added. "The crust was quite separate from the inside . . . [and] the space between the two was filled with . . . a sour, slightly fermented liquid." Paustovskii remembered how he and his friends suffered from finger joints swollen from malnutrition and cold and how the swellings broke open and bled.[61] Everywhere it seemed to be the same. H.G. Wells may not have been far off the mark when he wrote that "ruin is the primary Russian fact of the present time."[62] Bolshevik officials thought the same thing. "The workers of the towns and of some of the villages choke in the throes of hunger," a gloomy report from the Central Committee for Labor Conscription announced in *Pravda* early in 1920. "The railroads barely crawl. The houses are crumbling. The towns are full of refuse. Epidemics spread and death strikes to the right and to the left. Industry is ruined."[63]

The continuing failure of Bolshevik Russia's railroads to recover from the Civil War's devastation underlay all the other domestic crises of 1919–1920. Only about one in five of Russia's seventy thousand kilometers of track remained undamaged by the end of 1919. The Civil War's fighting had destroyed close to three thousand bridges and only two out of every five of Russia's sixteen thousand wartime locomotives remained in working condition. Most of these had been manufactured before 1900, and some had been in service since 1870. Many still consumed enormous quantities of wood, the fuel most needed to heat Russia's freezing cities. Bolshevik planners therefore had to burn wood to transport wood at a time when the supply available to railroads had fallen to a third of what it had been on the eve of the Revolution. The supply of rails for repairing Russia's war-damaged lines at the beginning of 1920 amounted to a mere eighth of the amount needed. There were so few parts to repair worn-out locomotives that less than half of the railroad engines that had to be taken into depots for repairs in 1919 returned to service by the end of the year. Desperate mechanics cannibalized those in the worst condition to keep others running for a while longer and, in the process, turned Russia's rail sidings into vast graveyards for dead locomotives and broken freight cars. Even then, locomotive repair shops in Bolshevik Russia could put fewer than ten engines a day back into service.[64] Statesmen began to fear that a catastrophe could not be averted. "However badly the tsarist ministers may have managed, however destructive the imperialist war may have been," Lenin's chief railway expert stated at a meeting of economic experts that winter, "in the last account, it is the Revolution and the Civil War that have destroyed our railroads."[65]

Other sectors of Russian industry broke apart in a similar fashion. Turkestan, Russia's only source of raw cotton before the Revolution, had established a Soviet Republic in the spring of 1918, but the violently anti-Bolshevik Orenburg Cossacks had kept it—and the desperately needed supplies of cotton fiber it produced—cut off from Bolshevik Russia's mills for two years.[66] Able to manufacture no more than a twentieth of the cotton thread they had spun before the First World War, Russia's cotton mills came to a virtual standstill.[67] Nor could the production of linen or wool be expanded to take the place of cotton. As hungry Russians killed their sheep for meat rather than feed them scarce grain, the production of raw wool plummeted and as the Baltic countries of Estonia, Latvia, and Lithuania proclaimed their independence, Bolshevik Russia lost one of its major sources of flax.[68] So long as the

Allied blockade continued, the men and women of Lenin's Russia had to do without new cloth.

The Bolsheviks also had to do without oil from Baku until the end of 1919, and without iron and coal from the Ukraine until 1920. Russia's production of coal in 1920 scarcely reached a quarter of what it had been in 1913, while oil production stood at slightly more than a third. Russia's mills and factories faced the winter of 1919–1920 with only a tenth of the fuel they needed. By the spring of 1920, the fuel shortage had become so severe that Lenin ordered textile workers into nearby bogs to dig peat for Russia's idle electric generators.[69] With too few raw materials and too little fuel, iron production in 1920 fell to about a fortieth of the prewar figure. Steel stood at a sixtieth and copper production stopped altogether. Russia produced less than a fifteenth of her prewar output of sugar, and her factories now turned out only a fiftieth part of the axes, scythes, and sickles.[70] "Men are plowing with burnt staves instead of plowshares," Arthur Ransome reported in 1920.[71] In the countryside, one could buy ten eggs (which sold for three hundred rubles in Moscow) for a small box of matches. Salt had become so scarce that, in some places, peasants would sell their produce for nothing else. In the cities, workers had no food, clothing, or fuel. In the countryside, the peasants had no matches, boots, salt, or tools.[72] "Such a decline in the productive forces . . . of an enormous society of a hundred million," a leading Soviet economist wrote a few years later, "is unprecedented in human history."[73]

Absenteeism rose in an appalling crescendo. Factory workers saw their revolutionary victory as an emancipation from the discipline of the workplace, and their productivity fell to a mere fifth of what it had been six years before. Absenteeism at the Kolomenskii Metalworks rose above forty percent at the beginning of 1920. The average worker missed more than four days on the job every month, and some railway workers failed to report for work as often as every other day. Although they pleaded illness, most men and women spent their illegitimate absences searching for food for themselves and their families.[74] "Anarchy in production, or, as Professor Grinevitskii has said, 'the revolutionary disintegration of industry,' " Nikolai Bukharin stated flatly in 1920, "is an historically inevitable stage [in our development]."[75] As if to emphasize that point, the Bolsheviks deprived workers of their last incentive to be productive by leveling wages just when the real prices of food and consumer goods soared to fourteen times their prewar levels. An average worker's wages in mid-1920 would buy slightly less than a fiftieth of what they had bought at the beginning of the First World War.[76]

A moving sea of people intent upon finding food spread across Russia. "Like maddened ants they cover every inch of space," Alexander Berkman wrote of the crowds that rode the train he took to the South that summer. Even gunfire could not stem the desperate crowds of men, women, and children who tried to flee Russia's towns and cities as nearly three out of every five Petrograders and two of every five Muscovites fled into the countryside. "Death from a bullet," Berkman concluded sadly, "is no more terrible to them than starvation."[77] So many men and women had fled Russia's cities by the end of 1920 that her industrial labor force numbered only a third of the number needed to produce economic recovery.[78] Chronic unemployment had been a key factor in driving Russian workers into the revolutionary movement before the First World War. Now, a shortage of factory workers threatened to make economic recovery impossible.

For a society being built on the principle that its revolutionary industrial proletarians would show its conservative peasants the way to a better future, the flight of Russia's factory workers raised troublesome problems, for it returned factory workers to a world many Bolsheviks knew to be hostile to socialism. Young Nikolai Bukharin first began to worry about "the disintegration of the proletariat as a class" in March 1918,[79] and although he had extolled the political consciousness of Russia's workers as "an inexhaustible reservoir of organizational energy"[80] during the Civil War, he renewed his warnings in 1920. The "petty bourgeois" character of the peasant society to which Russia's factory workers had returned between 1918 and 1920, Bukharin insisted at the Bolsheviks' Tenth Party Congress, had cooled their revolutionary ardor and had deadened their class consciousness. This "gangrenous" infection of workers, Bukharin warned his comrades, constituted "the greatest danger of the present moment." The "peasantization" of the proletariat now threatened to obliterate the workers' sense of themselves as a revolutionary force.[81]

As unskilled and semi-skilled peasants replaced those dedicated Communist workers who had fallen in the battles against Kolchak, Iudenich, and Denikin, Russia's proletariat threatened to fall victim to a variety of "petty bourgeois" ailments.[82] Just as

Trotskii had called for dedicated Communists to stiffen the backbone of Bolshevik Russia's collapsing armies in 1918 and 1919, so he and his comrades now tried to use examples of proletarian behavior "worthy of emulation" to spur reluctant workers to greater effort. Communist *subbotniki*, days of voluntary unpaid labor when Bolshevik workers put their backs to the tasks that needed to be done most urgently, became one means to that end. The first to do so were two hundred workers on the Moscow-Kazan Railway who, after vowing that "Communists must not grudge their health and life for the gains of the Revolution," worked a thousand hours without pay on Saturday, May 10, 1919. "The enthusiasm and team spirit displayed during work were extraordinary," a reporter wrote in *Pravda*. "At the sight of this collective effort," he continued, "one's conviction was strengthened that the victory of the working class was unshakable." As the Moscow-Kazan Railway workers, "with the light of joy in their eyes," joined in singing the "Internationale," the *Pravda* account concluded ecstatically, "it seemed as if the triumphant strains of the triumphant anthem . . . would spread through the whole of working-class Russia and shake up the weary and the slack."[83]

Stirred by the attention their comrades on the Moscow-Kazan Railway received, other workers vowed to continue such *subbotniki* "until complete victory over Kolchak has been achieved."[84] Reports of *subbotniki* poured in, some of them claiming to have raised productivity by more than a thousand percent.[85] *Subbotniki* marked "the *actual* beginning of *Communism*," Lenin explained in a special pamphlet entitled *A Great Beginning*. "If in starving Moscow, in the summer of 1919, the starving workers . . . could start this great work," even greater things would be achieved once the Civil War had been won. Lenin saw in *subbotniki* a possible key to unlocking the enigma of the peasantry. "It is precisely proletarian work such as that put into Communist *subbotniki* that will win the complete respect and love of the peasants for the proletarian state," he insisted. "Such work and such work alone," he concluded, "will completely convince the peasant that we are right, that Communism is right, make him our devoted ally, and, hence, will lead to the complete elimination of our food difficulties."[86]

All too typically, the Bolsheviks' passion for organization and control led them to institutionalize *subbotniki* in an effort to make them a part of daily life in their new society. "Our *subbotniki* are still weak, and each . . . reveals a host of defects in arrangement, organization, and discipline," Lenin wrote as he urged the Bolsheviks to organize this "new discipline of work in common" on a larger and larger scale. "We shall work for years and decades practicing *subbotniki*, developing them, spreading them, improving them and converting them into a habit," Lenin promised. "[That way] we shall achieve the victory of Communist labor." By the time the Bolsheviks celebrated May Day 1920 with an all-Russian *subbotnik* in which nearly a half-million workers took part in Moscow alone, what once had been voluntary labor by dedicated Communist workers had been transformed into an arduous new burden for all. [87] "[The *subbotniki*] drain my energies completely," an exhausted woman complained to Emma Goldman in Petrograd in the fall of 1920. "[At first] we all felt inspired, especially when we saw our leading comrades take pick and shovel and pitch in. But this is all a matter of the past. The *subbotniki* have become gray and spiritless, beneath an obligation imposed without regard to inclination, physical fitness, or the amount of other work one has to do."[88]

The institutionalization of *subbotniki* reflected Bolshevik leaders' efforts to conscript Russia's able-bodied citizens into a national army of labor to rebuild their nation's shattered economic life. They had first spoken of such a mobilization at the end of 1918, when they had announced that the "militarization of labor is the consequence of the wartime mobilization of industry and is its logical conclusion."[89] A few months later, they had restated their position at the Eighth Party Congress by calling for "a universal mobilization of everyone fit for work," but they had preferred only to state their principle of universal labor mobilization rather than implement it.[90] Even when Trotskii urged them to apply the methods that had defeated Iudenich, Denikin, and Kolchak to "the extreme breakdown of productive forces and economic chaos"[91] that confronted Russia at the end of 1919, his comrades on the Central Committee hesitated to take so radical a step. Unpopular though it was, Trotskii continued to call for mobilization of Russia's workers. Mines and factories must be put back into operation, railroads brought back into service, and fields brought back under cultivation. "Our economic situation," he stated bluntly in a speech to Bolshevik trade union leaders in mid-January 1920, "is a hundred times worse than our military situation was at its very worst."[92] He therefore urged that Russia's civilian workers be subjected to the military discipline that had enabled the Red Army to defeat the Whites on several fronts at once. Few besides Lenin supported that extreme position. Out of thirty-six Bolshevik trade union leaders who heard Lenin speak in favor of Trotskii's proposals, only two voted for them.[93] Too ready to be rid of the wartime discipline, other Bolsheviks condemned such proposals as a return to *arakcheevshchina*, the tyrannical rule of General Arakcheev, who had served as Alexander I's confidant a century before.

With Lenin's support, Trotskii already had begun to test his plans for massive labor mobilizations elsewhere. On January 15, 1920, he transformed the Third Red Army, then serving in the Urals against the remnants of Kolchak's forces, into the First Revolutionary Army of Labor. Within a fortnight, he formed the Second Revolutionary Army of Labor to rebuild the Moscow-Kazan Railway and organized the Ukrainian Labor Army for reconstruction work in the mines of the Donbas. Somewhat later, he sent units of the Fourth Red Army to build a railway for transporting oil from Turkestan and assigned parts of the Seventh Red Army to dig peat around Petrograd.[94] As his legendary train sped from Moscow toward the Urals at the beginning of February 1920, Trotskii announced that these forces would lead the fight against hunger and cold. "Bread for the Starving!" he proclaimed grandly. "Fuel for the Freezing! These are our slogans now."[95] He insisted that commanders and commissars must bear the same responsibility for their men's behavior as they did in battle and that "deserters from the labor front" must be punished as deserters from the Red Army.[96] "A deserter from labor," Trotskii announced in one of his orders, "is as contemptible and despicable as a deserter from the battlefield."[97]

Trotskii's plans to mobilize the talents and labor of every Russian for the tasks of economic reconstruction seemed more compelling on paper than in practice. It was one thing to allocate complex tasks to labor regiments and divisions according to their training and abilities, but it was something very different to translate those plans into actual men, women, equipment, raw materials, and food and put them to work in a certain place at a specific time. Soldiers who had fought willingly against the Whites saw little reason to work in distant parts of Bolshevik Russia when their own untilled fields beckoned them home, and Trotskii's assurances that the work of the labor armies was "not slave labor but high service to the socialist fatherland" could not convince them that building railroads and digging coal for the Bolsheviks should take precedence over seeing their families.[98] Only the severest restraints kept unwilling men in the Urals, the Transcaucasus, and the Ukraine when they wanted to be elsewhere, but compulsion could not make them into efficient working forces.

Despite his glowing pronouncements, inefficiency and gross waste of scarce resources characterized the work of Trotskii's labor armies. Although they proved to be far more than the "empty bureaucratic fantasy" that some of their enemies claimed them to be,[99] Trotskii still found it extremely difficult to apply military organization and discipline to recalcitrant civilian work forces. As if to insulate himself from the human nature that defied his best efforts, he took refuge in a flurry of blueprints for even more ambitious schemes. "He displayed astounding originality and inventiveness," his leading biographer concluded, "but his imagination worked feverishly in a vacuum and his ideas were out of joint with reality."[100] For a moment Trotskii became so isolated from reality that, when his private train derailed in the Urals during a February blizzard, a full day passed before anyone noticed its absence. The collapse of Russia's economic life had become so complete by the beginning of 1920 that nobody paid any serious attention to the whereabouts of the commissar of war and president of the Supreme War Council.[101]

To allocate scarce resources and labor in a society in such dire straits as Civil War Russia required precise and careful organization, and it was in organization that the Bolsheviks had always excelled in comparison to other revolutionaries. While other arrogant, impractical, and improbable revolutionaries had squabbled over interpretations and principles and had split repeatedly into weakened factions during the decade between the revolutions of 1905 and 1917, the Bolsheviks' organizational ability had kept them more closely united. It had been that same emphasis upon organization that had enabled them to seize power in October 1917. Although many able Bolsheviks fell during the first two years of the Civil War, it proved to be the measure of Lenin's organizational genius that their party always could renew itself from those seemingly endless wellsprings of proletarian consciousness that flowed among factory workers and poor peasants. Bolshevik Party membership therefore grew steadily to more than a quarter of a million at the beginning of 1919, and then almost doubled before the Ninth Party Congress met in March 1920.

By then, Bolshevik men and women dominated every level of government and authority throughout the Soviet Republic to give the Party an unassailable monopoly of power.[102] Cemented by common hopes, aspirations, and beliefs, and directed by stern directives from above, the Communist Party provided what may have been the single greatest source of psychological stability in a society where many traditional points of reference had disappeared. As Lenin and Trotskii called upon *zakalënnye bolsheviki*—hardened Bolsheviks—to accomplish tasks that seemed all but impossible, their many victories in 1919 showed that their confidence had not been misplaced. "[Only] because tens, hundreds, thousands and, in the last account, millions marched as one man when the Central Committee gave the order," Lenin later said, "were we in a position to conquer."[103]

As they battled against the Whites, hardened Bolsheviks also fought to take full control of Russia. "The Communist Party has set winning decisive influence and complete leadership in all organizations of the working classes as its goal," the Eighth Party Congress announced in March 1919. "In particular, the Communist Party aims to gain control over . . . the Soviets and to win the full implementation of its program."[104] Thus began the "Year of the Party," in which the Communist Party worked to eradicate the last vestiges of non-Bolshevik groups in the Russian labor movement and win unchallenged authority in Russia's trade unions, cooperatives, and soviets, where the masses had first expressed their power in 1917. Yet the Party went further in its efforts to dominate Russia. As the soviets and trade unions came under its control, it took on so much responsibility for Russia's government that more than half of all Party members took positions in her civilian or military administration.[105] By 1920, the bureaucracy that ruled Russia had become Bolshevik to its very core.

The bureaucracy through which the Bolsheviks controlled Russia and the Russians had more than its share of dark and seamy qualities. As the intensity of the fighting diminished toward the end of 1919, the number of men and women who supported the Bolsheviks to feather their personal nests began to increase. Everyone had stories to tell about the greed and insensitivity of "radish Communists," whose Red exterior masked a White core, and who lived comfortably while others froze and starved. Arrayed in the contraband finery of the empire's fallen aristocrats, they became the new tyrants of Russia's towns and cities. Deeply imbedded in the tightly woven administrative fabric of Bolshevik Russia, such men and women survived repeated attempts to purge the Party of what

Lenin once called "the offal of the old capitalist system."[106] Bureaucratism became the curse of the Party and Soviet Russia. "You can throw out the Tsar, throw out the landowners, throw out the capitalists," Lenin remarked at one point. "But you cannot 'throw out' bureaucracy in a peasant country, you cannot 'wipe it off the face of the earth.' You can only *reduce* it by slow and stubborn effort."[107] "We shall be fighting the evils of bureaucracy," he warned, "for many years to come."[108]

Even as Lenin spoke, Bolshevik bureaucrats spread an avalanche of regulations, restrictions, forms, and permissions across Russia that made the most simple things difficult. Everything had its controls and counter-controls. Everywhere plans were drafted, proposed, discussed, and, on the basis of extensive suggestions for improvements and revisions, redrafted, resubmitted, and discussed all over again as Bolshevik bureaucrats prepared elaborate proposals to build schools, hospitals, and modern housing when Russia's workers had not yet even begun to produce medicines, hospital equipment, electricity, or even building materials. Perhaps nothing expressed better the chasm that separated such bureaucrats from the people they ruled than the "unified economic plan" that Trotskii presented to the Ninth Party Congress at the end of March 1920. "First and foremost must come the improvement of transportation, shipment, and storage of essential grain reserves, fuel, and raw materials," he explained. Then, Russia's economic reconstruction would proceed by firm and logical steps: "production of machines for transportation and for the production of fuel, raw materials, and grain; intensified development and production of machines to produce consumer goods; intensified production of consumer goods themselves." Such flat, factual statements took no notice of the barriers that loomed ahead. "The realization of this proposed plan," Trotskii concluded, "will be made possible not by means of the separate, one-time, heroic efforts of the advanced elements of the working class, but by dogged, systematic, and well-planned labor that draws into its sphere ever increasing numbers of the toiling masses."[109]

The same ruthless energy that had served him so well in building the Red Army led Trotskii to ignore the stubborn skepticism of Russia's civilians. Russians desperately needed to put the ruin and deprivation of war behind them, and it was unlikely that they would produce the huge quantities of raw materials, grain, fuel, and machines needed to complete the first three stages of the "unified economic plan" in return for nothing more than the Bolsheviks' oft-repeated promises that their labor would make a better life possible. More detailed plans only muddied further the already turgid waters in which Russian men and women searched to find the shape of things to come. "One of the sins of the economic organizations of Soviet Russia," one observer wrote sadly, "is not that there are no plans but that there are too many of them."[110]

Unworkable plans drawn up according to unrealistic estimates based on unavailable resources could do little to repair Russia's economic devastation. Nor could they create that sense of civic responsibility that builds political consensus and frees governments from the need to rule by force. Many Russians shared no common vision with their new leaders and had yet to develop any sense of loyalty to the Bolsheviks' government. The Bolsheviks' extensive propaganda and educational campaigns had made certain that, even in distant villages, most people had heard of Lenin and Trotskii, and, of course, they knew the story of Mikhail Kalinin, the peasant who had risen to become president of the Russian Soviet Republic. But very few Russians knew much about the principles that underlay their new government or the men who served it. In a survey taken in one of the provinces that lay along the Volga River, not one person could identify Georgii Chicherin, Trotskii's successor as commissar of foreign affairs. Another survey showed that many Russians did not know what words such as "project," "memorandum," and "intrigue" meant. Some thought that a diplomatic note had something to do with music.[111] Rather than admit that the real enemies they faced were an acute lack of civic responsibility among the people they ruled, the Bolsheviks proclaimed "bungling," "shirking," and "sabotage" to be the reason for their inability to mobilize the working men and women of Russia in the cause of economic reconstruction. To deal with such spectral foes required a massive invasion of Russians' daily lives. For the first time in their modern history, the men and women of Russia became responsible not only for what they said and did, but for what they thought.

Now openly acknowledged by the Bolsheviks' Central Committee as an instrument for "fulfilling the will of the Party and the proletariat,"[112] Dzerzhinskii's Cheka became the Bolsheviks' chief defense against their inability to mobilize Russians to rebuild their nation's economic life. Although its brutality against the Whites continued unabated in those areas where Bolsheviks still vied for control, the Cheka now became an instrument to coerce a nation as it began to search for "enemies of the people" among peasants, Red Army soldiers, workers, bureaucrats, and even loyal Bolsheviks. "The form of our struggle against our enemies must change," Dzerzhinskii told the Central Executive Committee in February 1919 as he argued (very prematurely, it turned out) that the battle against the Whites had been won. "They now are trying to worm their way into our Soviet institutions so that, once they have infiltrated our ranks, they can sabotage our work." Nothing could have expressed more clearly the Bolsheviks' increasingly paranoid response to the crises that surrounded them. "We know that we have enemies in almost all our institutions," Dzerzhinskii concluded, "but we cannot smash our institutions. We have to dig out clues and try to catch them."[113] Its resources now focused upon government offices, trade unions, factories, villages, and party headquarters, the Cheka declared war against the Russians. "In this struggle, the organs of the Cheka must become an instrument for realizing the centralized will of the proletariat," Lenin told the Fourth Conference of Provincial Chekas a year later. He therefore insisted that the Cheka must become "a weapon for creating the sort of discipline that we have been able to establish in the Red Army [in society as a whole]."[114]

Dzerzhinskii shared all the fears of internal enemies that plagued Lenin and his comrades. Power had not softened him physically or morally, for he had continued to live a thoroughly ascetic life, even when others had begun to enjoy the comforts that their newly won positions made possible. Although he had exercised the power of life and death over men under the most trying conditions, Dzerzhinskii still remained true to his once-stated ideal that a Chekist always must have "a cool head, a warm heart, and clean hands."[115] His features sharpened by age and the burdens of office, Dzerzhinskii now resembled the Grand Inquisitor more than ever. When his appointment as commissar of internal affairs in March 1919 enabled him to combine the personnel of the Cheka with the much larger institutional and financial resources of one of Soviet Russia's most important commissariats, he shaped the two into an institution of uniquely pervasive coercive abilities. Eventually, the Cheka became reorganized as the GPU, the acronym for *Gosudarstvennoe politicheskoe upravlenie* (State Political Administration), which, popular gallows humor bitterly remarked, really stood for the phrase "*Gospodi, pomilui umershikh*," or "Lord, have mercy upon the dead."[116] With a clear mandate to act as the Party's special instrument to rout out sedition and sabotage wherever it might threaten the Bolsheviks' efforts to move ahead with Russia's economic reconstruction,[117] Dzerzhinskii's Cheka became in every sense the avenging sword of the Revolution.

As the Cheka expanded its work beyond those Civil War fronts where it faced enemies in open battle, it took control of Russia's railways, waterways, frontiers, cities, large towns, factories, and government offices. Everywhere, it searched for "White Guardists," "saboteurs," and "shirkers" who might be trying to undermine Russia from within. Far distant were the days when Dzerzhinskii had carried the Cheka's entire files around Petrograd in a briefcase. Now the Cheka's dossiers about real, suspected, and imagined enemies numbered in the tens of thousands. How a person's parents and grandparents had been employed, where and how they had lived, and whom they had entertained in their homes all became important, as things written or said in days long past returned to haunt innocent Russians. Inheritor of the tsarist belief that it was in man's nature to do evil, the Cheka lived with the frustrating conviction that most crimes inevitably would go undiscovered and unpunished. Its agents always tried to uncover new crimes in the course of every inquiry. "One should never . . . confront [a suspect] . . . with material evidence convicting him of guilt at the beginning of an interrogation," the Cheka instructed its interrogators. "It is important to ascertain first other participants in the case and the possibility of other as yet undisclosed crimes."[118]

As they violated the minds and bodies of their victims, the Cheka's inquisitors abandoned every moral principle that guided the behavior of civilized men and women. Usually, prisoners were questioned late at night after they had been kept without sleep and fed starvation rations for long periods. Hunger and disease were part of everyday life in Cheka prisons, but so were physical and psychological tortures. Rapes of female prisoners by Cheka guards and interrogators were so commonplace that they occasioned comment from superiors only if performed in some particularly brutal or perverted fashion. Threats against relatives, whippings, and beatings (during which interrogators sometimes gouged out one of the victim's eyes) were everyday methods of extracting confessions, but each Cheka headquarters evidently developed certain specialities. The Cheka in Voronezh rolled its prisoners around inside a barrel into which nails had been driven, while the Cheka in Kharkov used scalping as a preferred form of torture. In Armavir, the Cheka used a "death wreath" that applied increasing pressure to a prisoner's skull; at Tsaritsyn, they separated prisoners' joints by sawing through their bones; and, in Omsk, they poured molten sealing wax on prisoners' faces, arms, and necks. In Kiev, Chekists installed rats in pieces of pipe that had been closed at one end, placed the open end against prisoners' stomachs, and then heated the pipes until the rats, maddened by the heat, tried to escape by gnawing their way into the prisoners' intestines.[119]

Like the sword of Damocles, the threat of death hung over every prisoner of the Cheka, not only because interrogators terrorized prisoners with mock executions,[120] but because real executions occurred very often. Estimates of men and women killed by Cheka executioners between 1918 and the end of the Civil War in 1921 vary wildly from a few thousand (Dzerzhinskii's lieutenant Martyn Latsis set the total for this period at 12,733)[121] into the hundreds of thousands, and one estimate set the number of Cheka victims for the somewhat longer period between the October Revolution and Lenin's death at the astronomical figure of one and three-quarters million.[122] Although they do not take into account those killed when the Cheka suppressed hundreds of insurrections against Soviet authority, the best estimates set the probable number of executions at about a hundred thousand,[123] or about seven times the number killed by the tsarist government during the entire century before the Revolution. That staggering statistic becomes even more appalling if we remember that it does not include those who died in Cheka prisons from disease, hunger, or beatings. To this day, it remains impossible to do more than guess at the number of men, women, and children whose lives were snuffed out by the Cheka between 1918 and 1921.

If any estimate of the Cheka's victims must remain an uncertain conjecture, the methods by which they met their deaths are far better known. Chekist executioners sometimes crucified their victims in Ekaterinoslav and Kiev. In Odessa, they favored chaining White officers to planks and pushing them slowly into furnaces or boiling water. The Sevastopol Cheka preferred mass hangings. In other places, the Cheka beheaded its victims by twisting their necks until their heads could be torn off. Some executioners had their victims stoned to death. Denikin's investigators discovered corpses whose lungs, throats, and mouths had been packed with earth. Other victims died after being chopped apart with axes. Still others were skinned alive. Severing arms and legs, disemboweling, blinding, cutting off tongues, ears, and noses, and various sorts of sexual mutilation often prolonged victims' agonies before the executions.[124]

Most commonly, an executioner fired a single bullet into the base of his victim's skull. When larger numbers of prisoners needed to be killed quickly, as in cases where sudden advances by White forces threatened their liberation, Cheka firing squads and machine-gunners did the killing. As the armies of General Denikin advanced toward Kiev, more than four hundred Cheka prisoners met their deaths in that fashion on the night of August 26, 1919. In Kharkov, the Cheka killed seventy-nine in a single night, and there were reports that some two thousand died in Ekaterinodar during one twenty-four-hour period in August 1920.[125] "The whole of it was coated with blood—blood ankle deep . . . and horribly mixed with human brains, chips of skull-bone, wisps of hair, and the like," investigators from Denikin's forces reported after they visited the main Cheka "slaughterhouse" in Kiev. "A conspicuous object," their report concluded, "was the wooden block upon which the victims had to lay their heads for the purpose of being brained with a crowbar, with, in the floor beside it, a traphole filled to the brim with human brain-matter from the shattering of the skulls."[126]

The largest numbers of killings occurred in the Crimea, where the Cheka unleashed a wave of atrocities that claimed close to fifty thousand victims when Wrangel's White armies fled in November 1920. Reputedly based on the testimony of eyewitnesses, some accounts claimed that close to thirty thousand people died in Balaklava and Sevastopol alone. In the words of one report, the main streets of Sevastopol became "richly garnished with wind-swayed corpses" as the Cheka proceeded to hang suspected Whites wherever they found them. In the seaport city of Feodosia, ancient wells that had been dug by thirteenth-century Genoese traders became burial pits, and when the wells could hold no more, the Cheka marched its prisoners into the countryside to dig mass graves before they were shot. At nearby Kerch, at the entrance to the Sea of Azov, the Cheka organized "trips to the Kuban," during which they took large numbers of victims out to sea and drowned them while the frantic wives and mothers of the victims looked on.[127]

At times, women did the killing. Rozalia Zalkind, one of the most notorious Cheka executioners, had smuggled the revolutionary newspaper *Iskra* (Spark) into Russia from Westen Europe as a young woman and had been a dedicated Bolshevik since the beginning of the century. The daughter of a wealthy Jewish merchant from Kiev, she had deployed armored streetcars during the Moscow uprising of December 1905, in what has been called "a rehearsal in miniature of the days when, as a leading political commissar in the Civil War, she would assist in disposing of armored trains and divisions of men."[128] Known to friend and foe alike as Zemliachka, she served as a commissar in the Eighth and Thirteenth Red Armies during the Civil War and became legendary for her cruelty. In her forties when the Civil War began, Zemliachka dressed in the stereotypical leather garb of a Bolshevik commissar and killed with a vengeance. "We need pitiless, unceasing struggle against the snakes who are hiding in secret," she announced in *Krasnyi Krym* (Red Crimea), the newspaper that the Bolsheviks began to publish when they drove Wrangel's forces from Simferopol. "We must annihilate them, sweep them out with an iron broom from everywhere." Together with the Hungarian Bolshevik Bela Kun, Zemliachka spread a reign of terror across the Crimea that, she promised, would enable the "worker-titans" of Russia to "bear peace to the whole world through a sea of precious blood." Others spoke similar words. "With the punishing, merciless sword of Red Terror," one of her associates promised, "we shall go over all the Crimea and clear it of all the hangmen, enslavers, and tormentors of the working class."[129] At the beginning of 1921, Zemliachka received the Order of the Red Banner for her "tireless, selfless, and energetic organizational and political work," which, her superiors announced, had "helped to bring about the final victory of the Red Army."[130]

Forced labor camps and prisons awaited those who escaped death at the hands of the Cheka inquisitors. The People's Commissariat of Justice operated 267 prisons, which in October 1920 contained slightly more than fourteen thousand men and women imprisoned by the Cheka in addition to another thirty-four thousand who had been sentenced by revolutionary tribunals and regular Soviet courts. Perhaps the most notorious of these were Butyrki, the tsarist prison to which Dzerzhinskii and many of his Bolshevik comrades had been condemned in the days before the Revolution, and the Cheka prisons on Bolshaia Lubianka, the street behind present-day Dzerzhinskii Square. Well into the 1920s, the Russian emigré press overflowed with complaints of prison bread rations that came to as little as an eighth of a pound a day, and of soup made from spoiled and rotted ingredients. Supplemented by "unpeeled potatoes," the prison soup ration "consisted of putrid chunks of horse head, some scraps of horsehair and hide, some rags, and morsels of a sort of jellylike substance, all floating about together in a dark-colored, evil-smelling liquid," one woman wrote as she recalled how her fellow prisoners at Viatka prison "threw themselves with a perfect animal avidity" upon it.[131] Survivors from Soviet prisons spoke repeatedly of toilet facilities that overflowed with human excrement, which, according to one official British report was "piled up to such an extent that the prisoners were unable to sit down when using them."[132] Other former prisoners complained about food prepared without salt, about temperatures in cells that stood just a few degrees above freezing, and, in at least one case, that "only cold water was issued [for washing] and that but once a day."[133]

All of Russia was starving in those days, and the Cheka can hardly be condemned because its prison rations were no better than what ordinary Russians had to eat. Nor can it be blamed for toilets that functioned no better than those many Russians found in the apartments of Moscow and Petrograd. The soup at Viatka prison seems to have been scarcely worse than the "insufferable" concoction that Alexander Berkman bought in a central Moscow street market, and its "jellylike substance" calls to mind the vaseline-like material that flavored the few spoonfuls of barley gruel that comprised Paustovskii's daily ration in Odessa at about the same time.[134] What was not part of life on the outside, and what made prison life more justifiably terrifying under the Bolshevik regime, was the capricious brutality of the guards, the immensely crowded conditions, and prison officials' frequent refusal to separate prisoners suffering from such deadly contagious diseases as typhus, influenza, and cholera from healthy inmates. General Denikin's investigators reported that, in one of Tsaritsyn's jails, a cell measuring slightly over two hundred square feet held forty prisoners and that one only a bit larger had held more than a hundred.[135] "More than one witness has likened the prison of the Extraordinary Commission [i.e. the Cheka prison on Bolshaia Lubianka] to the Black Hole of Calcutta," an official British report, based in part on the testimony of British citizens who had spent time in Cheka prisons, added a year later. "People were huddled together so closely that there was no room to lie or even sit down."[136] Infectious diseases spread with lightning speed under such conditions, and there can be no doubt that Cheka jailors' refusal to observe even the simplest quarantine rules killed many prisoners.

Although crowding was less severe, life in Cheka concentration and forced labor camps was no less brutal than in its prisons. At first, forced labor camps had been organized for workers who failed to adapt themselves to the rules of the Soviet workplace, and since their main purpose was to "reeducate" such workers and return them to society, their regimen had not been severe. That changed very quickly when the camps became detention centers for prisoners of war and Cheka prisoners. In late 1920, Dzerzhinskii's Commissariat of Internal Affairs operated eighty-four such camps, which held slightly more than twenty-five thousand civilians, about half of whom had been sent there by the Cheka, in addition to Civil War prisoners. Almost three-quarters of all prisoners listed as having committed such anti-Soviet crimes as counterrevolutionary activity, speculation, or desertion were workers and peasants, precisely the men and women who were supposed to be the Bolsheviks' closest allies.[137] Within a decade, these forced labor camps evolved into the massive slave labor network of the Stalin era, with all the inhumanity that Stalin's system entailed.

Even the Stalin slave labor camps at their worst did not rival the brutality of the Cheka's concentration camps during the Civil War era. Designed to isolate and punish the Bolsheviks' "class enemies," these camps still remain shrouded in mystery. Anxious to preserve security and to draw a curtain of silence around them, the Cheka located many such camps behind the thick and sturdy walls of the ancient monasteries that once had defended the Russian countryside, especially in the Far North. Near Kholmogory, some forty miles upstream from Arkhangelsk on the Dvina River, the Cheka built one of its first and most notorious camps late in 1919. Once described as a "camp of death," where many prisoners were executed and where the rest "perished, slowly and surely, of ill treatment and neglect,"[138] the Kholmogory camp eventually evolved into a broad network of concentration camps known as SLON, the Russian acronym for *Severnye lageria osobogo naznacheniia*, or Northern Camps of Special Purpose. SLON (*slon* also is the Russian word for elephant) absorbed thousands of prisoners, of whom very few survived. Its northernmost camp was on the shores of the Arctic Ocean in an ancient monastery at Pertominsk, some seventy miles north of Arkhangelsk. Commanded for some time by a sadist who shot prisoners for entertainment, Pertominsk's death rate at one point rose so sharply that a commission of inquiry relieved its commandant, although the practices that had caused the prisoners' deaths (indiscriminate shootings, disease, and torture) continued unabated.[139] In fact, they soon increased as the Cheka embarked upon a campaign to exterminate tens of thousands who had been shipped north for that purpose. A favorite method of execution at Pertominsk and Kholmogory was to load prisoners onto a barge, tow it out to sea, and then drown all on board by sinking the overloaded vessel with gunfire.

Toward the end of the Civil War, the ancient Solovetskii monastery became the center of the SLON network. Founded in 1429 by Saints Hermann and Sabbatius on Solovetskii Island at the point where the White Sea flows into the Gulf of Onega, this was one of Old Russia's greatest fortress monasteries and one of its richest. Isolated from the mainland by ice floes between October and June, the monastery also had a dark side to its history, for Russia's rulers had incarcerated some of their most stubborn political foes within its walls ever since the time of Ivan the Terrible. Colloquially called Solovki, it became the Cheka's chief concentration camp for "hostile class elements," incorrigible criminals, anarchists, and non-Bolshevik socialists.[140] It was the Cheka's intent that few prisoners at Solovki should survive very long. "The sooner we get rid of them," Dzerzhinskii once said of these prisoners, "the sooner we will reach socialism." He therefore called for "a struggle the final result of which must be that not one counterrevolutionary survives."[141] Whenever they judged that flogging, starvation, disease, and overwork did not claim the lives of their prisoners quickly enough, the Cheka jailers turned to shootings and mass drownings. "These repeated massacres," one expert concluded, "make estimates of the concentration camp population at this time meaningless."[142]

In carrying out tortures and executions, the Cheka saw itself as the self-righteous builder of the new world that the Bolsheviks had promised. "For us there do not, and cannot, exist the old systems of morality and 'humanity' invented by the bourgeoisie for the purpose of oppressing and exploiting the 'lower classes,' " the weekly newspaper of the Ukrainian Cheka explained. "To us all is permitted, for we are the first in the world to raise the sword . . . in the name of freeing all from bondage. . . . Only the complete and final death of that [old] world," it insisted, "will save us from the return of the old jackals."[143] Even low-ranking Chekists justified their behavior in such terms. "After all," one of them told an acquaintance in Odessa as he described how he had killed two of his bourgeois victims, "I have only done my duty as a revolutionary."[144] Lenin himself condoned the Cheka's lawlessness and provided a moral justification for it. "Is there such a thing as Communist morality?" he once asked. "Of course there is," he told a group of young Communists in the fall of 1920. "[Communist] morality is what serves to destroy the old exploiting society and to unite all the working people around the proletariat, which is building up a new Communist society. Communist morality," Lenin concluded, " is that which . . . unites the working people against all exploitation."[145] The destruction of class enemies therefore became a morally and socially responsible act. "A good Communist," Lenin told the Ninth Party Congress, "is at the same time a good Chekist."[146]

Even after Russia's aristocracy, bourgeoisie, and so-called rich peasants had been thoroughly destroyed, the numbers of prison and concentration camp inmates continued to rise. Solovki had about three hundred inmates at the end of the Civil War, but in less than a decade its population rose to half a million. Unable to reconcile the rigid precepts of party discipline with the individual initiative that Russia's economic reconstruction required, the Bolsheviks deepened their repression against the masses. Yet Bolshevik coercion did not go unchallenged. The year 1920 saw anti-Bolshevik uprisings spread from the Ukraine to Siberia. Some fifty thousand insurgents marched with the peasant rebel leader Antonov in Central Russia's turbulent Tambov province that fall, and rebels in western Siberia's Tiumen province rose in even greater numbers.[147] By the beginning of 1921, the Cheka reported no fewer than 118 revolts in various parts of Russia.[148] Just to crush Antonov's revolt in Tambov required nearly forty thousand Red Army troops.[149]

The peculiarity of such revolts, a Soviet historian once wrote, "was that, as a consequence of the increasing dissatisfaction of the peasants at this time, middle and poor peasants took part."[150] Few among the Bolsheviks failed to sense the extent of the danger. "[Relations] between the working class and the peasants," Lenin told the Tenth Party Congress in March 1921, "are not what we had believed them to be." Quickly, he warned his listeners that the explosive tensions between town and country during 1920 were "a far greater danger than all the Denikins, Kolchaks, and Iudeniches put together."[151] To offset that danger the Cheka destroyed entire villages, rounded up their inhabitants, and shipped them to concentration camps during the next several months. According to the ubiquitous Order No. 171 of June 11, 1921, the oldest worker in any household found to have a hidden weapon was to be shot, the eldest breadwinner of any family that gave shelter to a "bandit" (or a "bandit's" family) was to be shot, and so were hostages taken from all settlements in which hidden weapons were discovered. The Bolsheviks insisted that all such measures, in addition to burning homes and entire villages, were "to be carried out mercilessly."[152] A number of Chekists earned the Order of the Red Banner for their dedicated efforts to carry out those measures.[153]

Unrest among angry workers and peasants because of nationwide crises in transportation, agriculture, industry, and fuel production were not the only dangers that the Bolsheviks faced in 1920. In April, General Baron Petr Wrangel formed the tattered remnants of Denikin's Armed Forces of South Russia into a new army and, from within the natural fortress of the Crimean peninsula, launched a new assault against the Bolsheviks. The armed forces of newly independent Poland opened a campaign against Russia at the end of the same month. Led by Marshal Jozef Piłsudski, who dreamed of a Greater Poland that would reach from the Baltic to the Black Sea, the Polish army brushed aside the Red forces defending the approaches of Zhitomir and took the city in a single day. Piłsudski's distrust of all Russians, Red and White, had led him to refuse a joint campaign with Denikin the previous fall. Now, his armies sped across the hundred and fifty miles of Ukrainian plain that separated the Polish frontier from Kiev and took the city in less than two weeks. Before the middle of May, the Soviet government found itself dangerously threatened by a major foreign war. In battle against Poland, the anvil upon which so many Russian dreams had been shattered in the past, the struggling Soviet state now received its final tempering.

CHAPTER TWELVE

"Give Us Warsaw!"

FOR ALMOST A THOUSAND YEARS, East and West had clashed at the Russo–Polish frontier. In the Middle Ages, Roman Catholic Poland had stood as the eastern outpost of Western civilization facing Orthodox Russia, heir to the polyglot autocratic heritage of Byzantium and the Mongol East. Like her Western neighbors, Poland had reveled in the cultural brilliance of the Renaissance before the painful turmoil of the Reformation's religious wars had come upon her. Poland, too, had built great universities then, beginning in the fourteenth century with the University of Krakow, where printing had flourished a scant two decades after Gutenberg had printed his first Bible. Copernicus, the first proud bearer of Polish science to the centers of Europe, had studied at Krakow, and so had many of the great scholars who followed in his footsteps. Poland had given the music of Chopin to the West, the science of Madame Curie (née Maria Skłodowska), and the poetry of Adam Mickiewicz. The Polish nobleman Tadeusz Kościuszko had fought for America's freedom in her revolutionary war against England. A century earlier, Poland's King Jan Sobieski had stemmed the infidel's advance into Europe by his victory over the Ottoman Turks before the walls of Vienna.

Poland's contributions to Western culture stemmed from deeply set, well-nourished roots. Like much of the west, a long tradition of self-government in Poland's towns and cities had instilled a strong sense of civic responsibility in its citizens as the modern age began. Constitutional government, in which the people limited the power of their kings and obliged them to rule within the law, therefore had been a longstanding part of Poland's experience. From the councils of Poland's princes and the local diets of her gentry in the thirteenth and fourteenth centuries had come the Sejm, the great assembly that had legislated for the Polish nation three hundred years later. Poles cherished the law and respected the rights of men before it. Before it was destroyed by invading Russian armies, none other than England's Edmund Burke had lauded the Polish Constitution of 1791 as one of the greatest any nation ever had received.

Like their European brethren, the Poles believed that the borders they shared with Russia marked a vast historical and cultural abyss that divided Europe from Asia. Russia's Christianity had come from Byzantium, not Rome, and her early churchmen had been renowned for their asceticism, not their learning. The pursuit of knowledge thus had been much less a part of life in medieval Russia than in Poland. Nor had self-government and constitutional monarchy figured in Russia's experience, for the dual heritage of Byzantine autocracy and Mongol despotism had encouraged her tsars to remain above the law and to rule outside it as God's special representatives. "In the [Orthodox] Christian world, autocracy is the highest level of power," the nineteenth-century Russian poet Vasilii Zhukovskii had explained. "It is the last link between the power of man and the power of God."[1] Many Russians took pride in their government and lauded the virtues of autocracy. "A state without an absolute ruler," one of them wrote in 1847, "is like an orchestra without a conductor."[2] Others even insisted that "the Emperor is not only the representative of God—he is the embodiment of the creative power itself."[3] Regrettably, such exalted visions of the emperor's benevolent power never could be transformed into reality. At best, Russia's rulers treated their people as benevolent conquerors might treat vanquished foes.

Although her eighteenth-century autocrats and aristocrats had become Europeanized, Russia's very different historical experience had continued to keep East and West apart. "The East is not the West," one Russian writer had proclaimed in the 1850s. "We have a different temperament, a different character, different blood, a different physiognomy, a different outlook, a different cast of mind, different beliefs, hopes, desires. . . . [We have] different conditions, a different history," he concluded. "Everything is different."[4] Indeed it was. To the Marquis de Custine, the French apostle of monarchy whom a visit to Russia in 1839 transformed into an avowed "partisan of constitutions," Russia was a "prison without leisure." Any European who had "well examined" Russia, de Custine concluded after he returned to France, "will be content to live anywhere else."[5] Certainly none held that view more ardently than the Poles, whose state had slipped from the maps of Europe after the Third Partition of 1795, in which Russia had taken a leading part. Poland, her great national poet of freedom Mickiewicz concluded, was "the embodiment of the idea totally opposite to that of Russia."[6] At the Russo–Polish frontier, Poland stood for freedom against slavery, for law against tyranny, and for Western civilization against the barbarism of Asia.

Much of historic Poland, including its capital at Warsaw and its eastern Lithuanian borderlands, became a part of the Russian Empire during the nineteenth century. Briefly, the Emperor Alexander I had championed a resurrected Poland endowed with a liberal constitution and united to Russia by dynastic ties at the Congress of Vienna in 1814. Yet the hostility of the Russians and the Poles' demands for the return of their Lithuanian borderlands soon ended the ill-fated experiment of a tsar who ruled as an autocrat in one realm but hoped to pass for a constitutional monarch in another. In November 1830, the so-called Congress Kingdom of Poland exploded in a revolt that cost the Poles their constitution and all that remained of their independence. The Polish Charter of 1815 joined Russia's other trophies in the Kremlin Armory, and Alexander's successor, Nicholas I, proceeded to rule Poland as an autocrat. Nicholas built a citadel in the midst of Warsaw, garrisoned it with Russian troops, and vowed to turn its guns upon the city at the first hint of new trouble. Nor could the next generation of Poles reverse their fathers' failure to free their nation from the Russian yoke. The Polish Revolution of 1863 ended even more disastrously than its predecessor. Beginning in the 1860s, uncompromising Russification made Poland an integral part of the tsar's domains until the armies of Imperial Germany drove the Russians out in 1915.

Russia's defeats in 1915 did not bring independence to the Poles. Although the Allies spoke out loudly in the cause of Polish independence, the Germans still ruled in Warsaw, and they hoped to shape Poland into a buffer between Germany and Russia after the war. "Russia must not for the second time advance her armies to the undefended frontier of East and West Prussia," Germany's Chancellor Bethmann-Hollweg announced in April 1916. "Neither should she once again establish a gate for invasion against undefended Germany on the Vistula."[7] When the Germans began to speak of recreating a Polish kingdom in November 1916, they therefore had serious limitations in mind. "Poland cannot pursue a foreign policy of her own," Bethmann-Hollweg and Austria's Foreign Minister Baron von Burian agreed. "Poland can only be allowed to conclude treaties with other States in so far as the contents of those treaties are not in conflict with the limitations imposed by the . . . Central Powers."[8] Germany insisted that she must remain free to take Eastern Europe's Baltic lands for herself, and her statesmen urged Poland to look for compensation elsewhere. "Your hopes, Poles, should be directed toward Galicia and the Ukraine," a close adviser to the governor-general of German-occupied Poland once said. "We will help you in that."[9] Yet, as national consciousness and national pride began to rise among the peoples of Eastern Europe in 1917, the possibilities for such compensation grew dim. "The Kaiser takes the view," one of Emperor Wilhelm's friends wrote, "that whatever may be the solution of the Polish question, it will always be wrong. . . . This question cannot be solved," he concluded. "One has only to choose a 'modus' which may be least bad."[10]

No German could understand just how closely Poles linked their destiny to the lands the Kaiser intended to claim. Ever since the marriage of Poland's young Queen Jadwiga to the Grand Duke Jagiełło of Lithuania in 1386, Poland's union with Lithuania had been the key to her greatness. For three hundred years, a great Polish-Lithuanian state had stretched from the Baltic to the Black Sea to fill the seven hundred-mile-wide strip of rich forest and farmlands that spread from west to east between the Oder and Dnepr rivers. This was historic Poland, and its heart lay as much in Lithuania as in the lands around Warsaw. "Lithuania, my homeland, you are health," Mickiewicz had written in the opening lines of *Pan Tadeusz*. "One only realizes how precious you are after you have been lost." Almost a hundred years later, as German armies replaced the Russians in Lithuania, Mickiewicz's agony still burned in the depths of every Polish soul. "Germans have today replaced the Russians in Poland," General Józef Piłsudski announced. "We must resist the Germans."[11]

The year 1915 was not the time to do so, nor was 1916. Piłsudski and his Polish Legions therefore fought on the side of the

Germans for the better part of two years, and they played an important part in halting Brusilov's Russian offensive in the summer of 1916. Then, in the space of six weeks, the balance of world affairs shifted. Revolution broke out in Russia, and on April 2, 1917, America entered the war in Europe. Although the German occupation authorities now allowed the Poles more control over their schools and courts, they still were in no mood to give them free rein at home or abroad. The armies of Germany had just stopped France's Nivelle Offensive and had taken over four hundred thousand British lives at Passchendaele. German submarines claimed more than a half million tons of Allied shipping every month that summer, and German armies stood triumphant everywhere in the East. When Piłsudski moved to put distance between himself and the Germans as a prelude to greater Polish resistance, he quickly found himself in a cell of the fortress at Magdeburg.

As Russia's broken armies fell apart like so many pieces of wet mud in 1917, Germany remained free to move her Polish pawn as she saw fit. With her triumphant armies spread from the English Channel to the shores of Russia's Lake Peipus and the eastern Baltic, Germany stood as the arbiter of Europe's eastern lands, and it seemed inevitable that she would determine the fate of the millions of Eastern European men and women who once had been ruled by the tsars of Russia. She did not do so to the Poles' advantage. Even when Lenin's government had been brought to its knees and forced to sign the brutal peace at Brest-Litovsk, Germany's General von Hoffmann allowed the Bolsheviks to keep portions of those rich Lithuanian borderlands that the Poles still claimed as their own. But the future whose course had seemed so certain in mid-1918 again shifted dramatically before the end of the year. A scant eight months after the Treaty of Brest-Litovsk, the German armies crumbled in the West.

Germany's defeat threw all of Eastern Europe into turmoil. Peace brought nearly a dozen new states into being, all newly independent from their fallen Russian, Austrian, German, and Turkish masters, and each intent upon realizing its broadest "historic" frontiers. To the south and east, Romanian faced Hungarian and South Slav faced Italian. In Eastern Europe's borderlands, Ukrainians, Latvians, Lithuanians, and Estonians faced Russians. Reds fought Whites in the Baltic lands, in Finland, and in the Ukraine. German, Hungarian, and Slovak Reds fought in Munich, Berlin, Budapest, and Košice to spread the world revolution whose triumph Lenin and Trotskii continued to promise from Moscow. At the very center of Eastern Europe's conflicts stood the Poles, ready to fight Czechs, Germans, Slovaks, Russians, and Ukrainians and, if necessary, Estonians, Lithuanians, and Latvians. "The War of the Giants has ended," Winston Churchill remarked to Lloyd George on the night the Armistice was signed. "The quarrels of the pygmies have begun."[12]

The pygmies thought of themselves as giants nonetheless, and none more so than Józef Piłsudski, who entered Warsaw on the day of the western Armistice to become Poland's chief of state and commander-in-chief of its armies. Just short of fifty-one, Piłsudski wore his steel-gray hair closely cropped in the style of a Prussian officer and his mustache long and drooping in the manner of the ancient Cossacks. His deepset eyes of hard blue-gray bored through men's defenses and probed the souls that lay beneath. Britain's Viscount d'Abernon thought him "so striking as to be almost theatrical," spoke admiringly of his immense courage, and, more reluctantly, of his passion for intrigue.[13] None knew Piłsudski's inner thoughts or plans, for he kept much to himself, yet no one ever doubted his love for Poland or his dedication to the cause of her freedom. Those were the fires that burned within him and stirred the passions of the Poles he led. Long-oppressed men and women, worn by hunger and tormented by war, suddenly stood proud and tall. Nothing seemed too difficult or too daring. Crowds of "thin and anemic" people who, England's Sir Esme Howard remembered, had sunken cheeks and "great hollow eyes" came alive in the winter of 1918–1919. To Howard they seemed like "a people raised unexpectedly and almost miraculously like Lazarus from the dead."[14] Reborn, the Poles turned to claim their place in the sun. Certain that their time had come, they set out to restore the Greater Poland of olden times.

Piłsudski's heart lay in the Polish-Lithuanian borderlands, especially in his native city of Wilno. "One of the most lovely things in my life has been Wilno," he once wrote. "All that is beautiful in my spirit has been touched by Wilno."[15] Wilno was "a better Poland, a Lithuanian Poland," one of Piłsudski's contemporary biographers explained, "and Lithuanians were for him the salt of the Polish earth."[16] "I am never really happy except there," he once confessed to a British diplomat at a dinner in honor of the Inter-Allied Mission in Warsaw. "[Even] when I was a fugitive proscribed by the Russian police I never could let a year go by without seeing my homeland."[17] In the shadow of Wilno's ruined castle, monument to Lithuania's medieval greatness, Piłsudski had attended the Russian gymnasium, the symbol of the tsarist yoke that had come in the wake of the Polish Revolution of 1863. At that "accursed Russian school,"[18] Piłsudski remembered, he had learned to hate the Russians and to love Poland in the manner of the great poets Mickiewicz and Juliusz Słowacki, who had grown to manhood in the same place. Like them, he dreamed of a Greater Poland. To them he owed his romantic vision of Poland's Lithuanian past and his hope for her glorious future.

Love of country, dreams of her future, and hatred for all things Russian sustained Piłsudski during the five years he spent as a political prisoner in Siberia between 1887 and 1892. When he returned to Wilno, it was to continue his work against the tsarist government on behalf of a free Greater Poland, whose boundaries were determined by his romantic vision of the Polish-Lithuanian state that had flourished in the fourteenth to seventeenth centuries. For almost a decade (1896–1905) he lived in exile in London. He spent the year after the Revolution of 1905 feigning madness in a Russian insane asylum in order to avoid harsher punishment, then escaped, and in 1908 organized a train robbery near Wilno that captured almost a quarter million rubles for the cause of Poland's revolutionaries. His life between 1887 and 1914 thus had some of the hallmarks that had distinguished the early revolutionary careers of Lenin, Stalin, and Trotskii, although he possessed neither the theoretical genius of Lenin nor the oratorical brilliance of Trotskii. Piłsudski the radical journalist, train robber, and revolutionary street tactician won no broad following among Poles before the outbreak of the First World War, and Roman Dmowski, his archrival, who urged Poland's conservative National Democratic Party to follow a pro-Entente, pro-Russian course, continued to be more popular. Dmowski's pro-Allied sentiments kept him out of Poland during the war, while Piłsudski's willingness to work with the Germans allowed him to remain in his homeland. Germany's defeat in November 1918 therefore found him able to reach Warsaw quickly, while Dmowskii and his other political adversaries languished in Paris and London. As leader of those Polish Legions that had fought against the Russians from 1915 to 1918, Piłsudski took command of Poland. Warsaw's beautiful Belwederska Palace became his headquarters.[19]

Piłsudski's beginnings as Poland's chief of state were not destined to be peaceful. As the Germans withdrew from Oberkommando-Ostfront, the area that stretched fifteen hundred miles southward from the Baltic to separate the infant Polish state from its year-old Bolshevik rival, Polish and Bolshevik units moved into the vacuum. When sixty-two officers and men from the Polish Wilno Detachment took eighty Red Army soldiers prisoner on February 14, 1919, in a brief engagement at Bereza Kartuska, an inconsequential point some fifty miles southwest of Baranowicze, the Polish-Soviet war, whose beginnings Soviet historians traditionally date from Piłsudski's attack against Zhitomir and Kiev nearly fifteen months later, had begun.[20] During the 440 days that separated the skirmish at Bereza Kartuska from the clash at Zhitomir, the fighting flared, sputtered, and flared again in an incoherent staccato of dashes along railways and defenses at riverbanks and railheads as Russian and Pole each tried to impose some form upon hundreds of spasmodic conflicts that began and broke off according to no apparent pattern or plan.

This was no repetition of the monster sledgehammer artillery assaults with which Germany's generals had battered their way forward during the campaigns of 1915 and 1916. With small units spread thinly across vast areas, the battles of 1919 matched man against man and pitted both sides against nature. From early fall to late spring, storms roared in from the east to freeze men and beasts in a single night, only to be countered by storms from the West that, in the same span of time, thawed frozen rivers and marshes into morasses of raging melt-water and mud. Drawn by the false lure of campaigns unhindered by great natural obstacles, some of the world's greatest captains had pitted themselves and their men against this land of sparse settlements and great distances in years past. Against the adversaries of climate and space, Sweden's Charles XII had suffered defeat in 1709. Napoleon had failed similarly in 1812, and, in the years 1941–1943, the massive formations of Hitler's Wehrmacht would meet the same fate. Here, in 1919, Russian confronted Pole at crossroads, on forest trails, and in hedgerows on what each thought to be his native soil in battles that had no real beginning or end and brought neither victory nor defeat.

As the Poles once again made ready to defend the culture of Europe at the Russo–Polish frontier, the great chasm that had separated Russian from Pole for centuries still yawned. Again, Polish ideas of liberty faced Muscovite absolutism, now called the dictatorship of the proletariat. Poland stood for Catholicism, patriotism, and dedication to the political and social principles of the bourgeois and aristocratic West. Soviet Russia stood against private property, for nationalization of private enterprises, eradication of aristocracy, and destruction of the bourgeoisie. The Bolsheviks dreamed of a world that lay much further in the future than any among them imagined. The Poles fought to resurrect a past that had long since passed irrevocably into history. Neither side was ready for war in February 1919, but each insisted that the borderlands of Eastern Europe could not belong to the other.

More quickly than the Poles, the Bolsheviks moved into the borderlands almost as soon as the Allies had signed their armistice in the West. "The process of liberation of the Western [border] regions goes forward," Stalin reported as commissar of nationalities on December 22, 1918. "In Lithuania, the revolutionary conflagration is growing. Wilno is already in the hands of the Soviet of Workers' and Landless Peasants' Deputies," he concluded with satisfaction. "Things are moving."[21] Soviet socialist republics appeared in Lithuania and Belorussia before the end of 1918 and combined into the Soviet Socialist Republic of Lithuania-Belorussia two months later. Although the Bolsheviks vowed to support these fragile governments, which had little popular support and even less authority, they could not do very much as long as the much stronger armies of Denikin, Kolchak, and Iudenich continued to challenge them on other fronts. When the Poles launched their first attacks in February 1919, the entire Bolshevik force on the western front numbered forty-six thousand men, a scant tenth of the army the Red high command had sent against Kolchak.[22] Only the Poles' extreme military weakness at the beginning of 1919 made it possible for the Bolsheviks to assume that they could avoid any serious confrontation in the western borderlands for the time being.

At that point, the Poles faced armed threats on several frontiers. Poland's army numbered less than two hundred thousand at the beginning of April, and it had to be divided between Silesia, East Prussia, Eastern Galicia, and the Russo–Polish borderlands, where enemies challenged Poland's territorial claims. Not until General Józef Haller brought fifty thousand Poles from France, General Lucjan Żeligowski marched his Polish division from Odessa to Lwów, and ten thousand survivors of Colonel Rumsza's Polish Siberian Brigade landed at Gdansk after sailing three-quarters of the way around the world from Vladivostok in the summer of 1919, did Poland's army become a formidable force.

Until then, General Iwaszkiewicz's Lithuanian-Belorussian Division, supported by such volunteer units as the Samoobrona forces of Wilno, Minsk, and Grodno, had to defend Poland's eastern lands against the Russians with weapons gathered from every First World War front. Supported by field guns that came from England, France, Austria, Russia, and Italy, Polish units carried rifles made in Japan, England, France, Germany, America, and Russia. Some of these weapons had been made before the Russo-Turkish War of 1877–1878, and no two types fired the same ammunition. That men trained to use one type of rifle had to carry another into battle could not be the concern of Poland's handful of desperate ordnance officers. It required all their ingenuity just to match ammunition to rifles at the front.[23] Nor were shortages of men, weapons, and ammunition the only problems Poland's leaders faced. During their occupation of Eastern Europe, the Germans had converted many of the region's wide-gauge rail lines to the standard European track, while those under Russian control to the east remained laid out in the four-inch-wider Russian gauge. Trains set to accommodate one gauge could not run on the other. For a time, the railroads themselves barred east-west movement in the Russo-Polish borderlands.[24]

All these difficulties did not prevent the Poles from greeting spring in 1919 with a well-planned assault against Wilno, the only major city on the Russo–Polish front. This was the city closest to Piłsudski's heart, the source of the romantic patriotism that nourished his dreams of a restored Greater Poland, and he therefore commanded the campaign against the Reds himself. On April 21, after two days of hard fighting in which the workers of Wilno turned upon the Reds, Piłsudski led his forces into the city in triumph.[25] During the previous twenty-six months, the people of Wilno had lived under eight regimes, whose political views had ranged from the stern conservative monarchism of tsarist Russia and Wilhelmian Germany to the unfettered political and social radicalism of the Lithuanian-Belorussian Socialist Republic. Now they had been freed by one of their native sons. The liberator he always had longed to be, Piłsudski spoke to the people of Wilno in a manner that stirred memories of those long-ago Jagiełłonian days when the Grand Duchy of Lithuania and Poland had been joined. "The Polish Army brings Liberty and Freedom to you all," he proclaimed. "In this land which God seemed to have forsaken, liberty must reign," Piłsudski continued, his quaintly archaic sentiments seeming strangely out of place when cast amid the cynicism of postwar Europe. Wilno's and Lithuania's, "state of perpetual subjection" to foreign conquerors "must be removed once and for all," he insisted. The "nationality problems and religious affairs" of Lithuania must be settled in a manner determined by the Lithuanians themselves.[26]

Lenin saw Wilno as a key to Russia's western borderlands and ordered its recapture immediately "so as not to give the Whites a chance to bring up more forces and strengthen their position."[27] Yet this was more than his commissars and commanders in Lithuania could accomplish. Red forces had just been driven out of Estonia and Latvia, Kolchak's legions had marched to within seventy miles of the Volga, and Denikin's Army of South Russia was advancing in the Donbas and against Tsaritsyn. In retreat along the Baltic coast, forced to fight major campaigns in the south and east simultaneously, and obliged to defend the recent occupation of the Ukraine, the Soviet high command had no resources left to fight in the west. When the Poles renewed their attack in July, they had no choice but surrender their next line of defenses at Minsk, Równo, Luniniec, and Lwów. With his armies at the Dvina and Berezina rivers by the end of August, Piłsudski had virtually regained the eastern limits of the ancient Polish-Lithuanian commonwealth, but he had failed to reach an understanding with those Lithuanian nationalists who refused to see union with Poland as the key to their future greatness. Nor could he move much further into Russia with the very limited resources at Poland's command. Pressed by enemies on Poland's other frontiers, in desperate need of every resource required to make war or enjoy peace, and fearful that the Entente might bestow Poland's newly occupied territories upon the Whites should Denikin or Kolchak reach Moscow, Piłsudski tried to preserve Poland's new frontiers by negotiating with the Bolsheviks.[28]

Although shaped by different events and aspirations, the view from the Soviet side was no more optimistic than from Piłsudski's. The Bolsheviks continued to think of Poland as their bridge to the West, the Red causeway that could link revolution in Russia to revolution in Germany. "The path of the world conflagration passes over the corpse of Poland," Tukhachevskii once remarked, and few Bolsheviks were prepared to abandon their dream of world revolution so quickly.[29] But as Denikin advanced against Orël in October, Iudenich took Gatchina and turned toward the Revolution's Red cradle in Petrograd, and the Russians faced their third winter without food and fuel, the Bolsheviks were in no position to open a road to Germany. In an effort "to sacrifice," as Lenin said, "space in order to gain time," Russia's Commissar for Foreign Affairs Georgii Chicherin addressed peace proposals to Finland, Latvia, Estonia, and Lithuania. On October 11, 1919, just three days before Denikin's army broke through the Red defenses at Orël, Julian Marchlewski, the Polish Communist whose contacts with the Spartakists in Germany and the Bolsheviks in Russia made him a personification of the Red bridge between East and West, met with Piłsudski's representatives at the remote Mikaszewicze railway station, in Polish-held territory, some sixty miles east of Pinsk.[30]

Briefly, peace seemed possible, as each side made appropriate concessions. When joint action with the Whites might well have shattered the Bolsheviks' southern front, the Poles refused to support Denikin's advance against Moscow. "Poland is not the gendarme of Europe and does not want to be," Piłsudski instructed his representatives to tell the Bolsheviks at Mikaszewicze."Poland wants to, and will, look solely and exclusively after her own interests."[31] At the same time, Lenin's negotiators accepted most of Piłsudski's conditions for a ceasefire, and peace seemed close enough for Lenin to announce publicly that "we can see that the Polish offensive on the western front is coming to an end."[32] When the Red Army launched its first successful counterattacks against Denikin, there was even some talk (which Lenin quickly squelched) of using Polish guerrilla units to blow up trains, bridges, and ammunition dumps in Denikin's rear.[33]

Despite these encouraging signs, the Poles trusted neither Reds nor Whites enough to allow the ceasefire to develop into peace if an end to the fighting would require them to reduce their forces in the borderlands.[34] Any powerful Russian state threatened Piłsudski's dream of an Eastern European confederation centered upon a Greater Poland, and he insisted that Poland therefore must preserve her eastern defenses. "Irrespective of what her government will be, Russia is terribly imperialistic," Piłsudski told a group of French journalists as he explained that a Russia ruled by Kolchak or Denikin would threaten Poland fully as much as one ruled by Lenin. The Poles could only hope that the Russian Civil War would exhaust victor and vanquished alike and leave a strong Poland triumphant in the borderlands. Confident that the Bolsheviks sought peace only as a temporary expedient, the Poles rejected any thought of more than a ceasefire. Peace negotiations therefore broke up in mid-December.[35] Both delegations vowed to revive discussions later, but neither ever returned to Mikaszewicze.

Some three weeks before their representatives reached Mikaszewicze in October, the Poles had sent urgent requests for weapons and supplies to the Allies. From the French, who had been their major suppliers of arms and equipment, they requested 150,000 rifles, 400 machine guns, well over a 100 million rounds of rifle ammunition, and more than a million artillery shells to supplement the weapons and supplies ordered earlier that year.[36] A fortnight later, the first wintry blasts struck the tattered and torn Polish army in the field. As reports of sentries standing guard without overcoats and marching in freezing mud and slush without boots flooded in, Poland's Prime Minister Ignacy Paderewski, the world famous pianist who had turned to politics in his twilight years, begged help from the British. "We are determined to hold our own against the barbarian Bolshevist forces," Paderewski insisted, "[but,] unassisted, we cannot any longer oppose the enemy." Poland's soldiers needed at least three hundred thousand uniforms and pairs of boots within a fortnight. If Poland's defenses were not to crumble, England must supply them as well as the locomotives and freightcars to transport them to Warsaw. "If such assistance is not granted immediately," Paderewski concluded, "the entire line of our Bolshevist front may break down at any moment."[37]

Britain's Secretary for War Winston Churchill could not at that point convince his cabinet to support the Poles against the Bolsheviks. France proved somewhat less reluctant and so did the United States. From French reserves in Salonika, American war supplies left behind in France, and captured German and Austrian weapons stockpiled in Italy and Germany, Poland received rifles, ammunition, uniforms, and aircraft before the year's end.[38] But this was marginal aid at best. France's loan of nearly four hundred million francs in September 1919 equaled the cost of keeping Poland's army in the field for less than two weeks. Uncertain about the true state of affairs in Poland, the Allies had concluded that Paderewski had overstated the danger and had modified their response accordingly. At the meeting of the Allied Supreme War Council that discussed France's loan to the Poles, Lloyd George claimed that there were not more than eighty thousand Red troops on Poland's eastern frontier. According to his estimate, they faced a quarter million Poles.[39]

Although the Allies worked with grossly exaggerated estimates of troop strength on both sides, the balance that Lloyd George had seen in the Poles' favor began to shift at the beginning of 1920. Now freed from the triple burden of fighting simultaneously in the Baltic, Siberia, and South Russia, the Bolsheviks turned their attention to their western front. "We must direct all our attention to preparing and strengthening the western front," Lenin insisted when he ordered that men and materiel be transferred from Siberia and the Urals to the Polish frontier with all speed at the end of February. "It is necessary," he concluded, "to announce the slogan: 'Make Ready for War with Poland.' "[40] Perhaps remembering Trotskii's vow that "when we have finished with Denikin, we shall throw the full weight of our reserves onto the Polish front" in order to deprive the Poles of what he once had called their "temporary, marauders' victory,"[41] willing hands did Lenin's bidding.

By the time the spring floods dried, 65,000 combat troops, with 3,208 machine guns and 665 cannon, had moved into position on the Soviet side of Russia's western front. These did not take into account rear echelon and support troops, which outnumbered the Red Army's combat forces by margins of eight or nine to one.[42] Like their Polish foes, these Bolshevik units went to war with Allied weapons, only theirs had come not as reluctant Allied gifts but as spoils of war taken from the shattered forces of Kolchak, Iudenich, and Denikin. The Poles thus fought Allied-made tanks, artillery, and airplanes with limited quantities of weapons of the same sort. If the Allies had been reluctant to arm the Poles as fully as their vast reserves permitted in 1919, they unwittingly had armed the Bolsheviks much more generously.

As the spring sun warmed the plains of Eastern Europe in 1920, a war that contrasted sharply with the experience of Europe's great captains took shape on the Russo–Polish frontier. None of the grand strategies of the Great War's campaigns had any meaning here, nor did the tactical lessons that commanders had learned so painfully in Europe's trenches. In Europe's far-flung eastern borderlands, men did not fight shoulder to shoulder, packed into miles of sodden trenches, to win a few hundred yards of shell-torn, blood-soaked ground. The Russo–Polish War of 1920 became a mobile war of sudden decisions and unpredictable outcomes. Here, cavalrymen paid a final tribute to the tactics of a bygone era at the same time as they experimented with strategies that younger commanders would apply with brutal effect in battles that ranged from the English Channel to the Volga a scant generation later.

Perhaps more than the Bolsheviks, the Poles could not tolerate a war without movement. "A passive defense with badly trained soldiers, insufficient strength, and inadequate equipment would inevitably have caused the breaking of the front," General Władysław Sikorski later explained. Passivity, Sikorski insisted, was "one of the worst blunders a commander can commit, as only an offensive is able to bring about a decision."[43] Piłsudski therefore favored what he called a "*stratégie de plein air*," a strategy of open spaces,[44] in which, as one Polish general later explained, "swiftness of movement, suddenness of concentration, [and] tactics of surprise" became the keys to victory.[45] For that reason, the Poles disdained a new flurry of Soviet peace notes that spring and countered the Bolshevik buildup with plans for an attack. "What [the Bolsheviks] . . . desire is a peace extracted by fists," Piłsudski told a French newspaper correspondent. "I know that the Bolsheviks are concentrating big forces on our front," he concluded. "They are making a mistake."[46] To attack under such circumstances was to Piłsudski's taste and in his nature. "One is tempted to liken him to a rhinoceros—indestructible, myopic, unpredictable," a historian once wrote. "Having once been provoked, there was always the possibility that he would charge again."[47]

Piłsudski had men, weapons, and machines ready for war in the spring of 1920, but he hoped to come to terms with Lithuania before he attacked the Russians. When he had occupied Wilno during the Easter holidays of 1919, he had tried to moderate the impact of his army's eastward march by public statements that the Lithuanians themselves must decide whether their state would become part of a Polish-Lithuanian federation or be independent, but vehement criticism of his statements from Poland's National Democrats robbed his effort of much of its intended effect. As a rival elected Lithuanian government with clearly national aims emerged at Kaunas in the course of 1919, it became certain that any effort to recreate a Polish-Lithuanian commonwealth could succeed only at the cost of some of Piłsudski's most cherished dreams. Courted by the Bolsheviks as part of their Baltic peace offensive, viewed sympathetically by the Allies, and given de facto recognition by the British, Lithuania's infant national government at Kaunas rejected the longstanding identification of its nobility with Poland.[48] Piłsudski therefore could not look to Lithuania to support him should he attack the Red armies that were massing to his east unless he openly supported the policies of the enemies of his aristocratic Lithuanian allies.

Unable to do so, and without allies elsewhere in the East, he turned to Simon Petliura, who had taken refuge in Poland along with the last tattered shreds of his fallen Ukrainian nationalist government.

Petliura held no political power. Only a handful of men followed him, and the Bolsheviks now ruled his homeland. But he still claimed to speak for the Ukraine and offered the alliance Piłsudski needed before he marched East. The Ukraine remained Eastern Europe's richest granary, and its Donbas coalfields and Krivoi Rog iron pits held the wherewithal to build an industrial base of awesome dimensions. The Bolsheviks intended to use those resources to feed the Russians and to forge an industrial complex greater than any shaped by their tsarist predecessors. For Piłsudski, the Ukraine offered an alternative to Lithuania as a base for his long-dreamed-of confederation of Europe's eastern borderlands. The grain, iron, and coal of the Ukraine could become the raw materials from which to shape a political structure that stretched from the Black Sea to the Baltic and to erect an anti-Bolshevik barrier between Russia and Poland.[49] During the third week of April, Piłsudski's government therefore signed a series of treaties with the Ukrainian government-in-exile that recognized Petliura as the head of state in an independent Ukrainian People's Republic, granted limited territorial concessions to Poland, provided for mutual economic cooperation, and placed all Ukrainian armed forces under the authority of the Polish high command.[50]

Choosing a fortuitous moment when the desertion of one brigade and the mutiny of another had thrown the Twelfth and Fourteenth Red Armies into turmoil, the Poles attacked the Soviet forces in the northwestern Ukraine on April 25, 1920. With the Polish Fourth and Sixth Armies moving in support on its flanks, Piłsudski's Third Army Group stormed into the Soviet-held city of Zhitomir at dawn on April 26, having covered more than fifty miles in twenty-four hours. With one well-timed stroke, the Poles had split the Fourteenth and Twelfth Red Armies and swept away all opposition. Eleven days later, they marched into Kiev to "liberate" the city for the fifteenth time in three years.[51] Yet, unlike those who had come to Kiev before him, Piłsudski vowed that his was to be no conquering army. "From the moment that . . . the free [Ukrainian] nation is strong enough to settle its own fortunes," he promised, "the Polish soldier will return beyond the frontier, having fulfilled his honorable task in the struggle for the freedom of nations."[52] A few days later, the Poles crossed the Dnepr and established a ten mile-wide bridgehead on its eastern bank. For the first time in two hundred and fifty years, the Dnepr stood at the backs of Polish soldiers who looked toward Moscow. An historic road filled with danger lay ahead.

Between Kiev and Moscow lay five hundred miles of empty space into which Russian armies in years past had retreated without giving battle as they drew invaders further from their bases of supply. There lay the fateful field of Poltava, where Russia's would-be conqueror Charles XII of Sweden had met destruction at the hands of Peter the Great, and the town of Malo-Iaroslavets, where Napoleon had suffered the first great defeat of his Russian campaign. If Piłsudski remained in Kiev, he risked having his army crumble beneath the weight of those tensions that filled every corner of the Ukraine; if he advanced, he risked losing his army into the void that separated him from Moscow. His Soviet adversaries therefore encouraged him to continue his march. Less than a week after the Third Army Group took Zhitomir, the Red High Command urged that Poland's army be enticed into Russia in order "to suspend it in midair."[53]

In the meantime, the Red High Command summoned General Tukhachevskii to Smolensk to take command of the counteroffensive they intended to launch further north. Tukhachevskii had amassed a spectacular string of victories since he had offered his services to the Bolsheviks in the fall of 1917 as a young nobleman freshly escaped from a German prison camp. Brilliant, impetuous, and cruel, he looked to do the unexpected and to win fame or death before he turned thirty. His strength lay in his raw military genius, which had won him the respect of Trotskii, whose concept of "permanent revolution" was reflected in Tukhachevskii's idea of "permanent offensive." But Tukhachevskii had his weaknesses, too. Most important of all, some of his most brilliant successes had embarrassed Stalin's closest allies and had earned him Stalin's hatred.[54]

Tukhachevskii took command of Russia's western front on April 29, 1920, less than three months after turning twenty-seven. At that age, his idol Napoleon had taken command of the Italian campaign for revolutionary France, and Tukhachevskii was determined to accomplish no less than he. Dedicated to winning glory for Bolshevik Russia in its first foreign war, he soon was to have a wealth of resources such as no Red Army commander had yet enjoyed. "By the [late] spring of 1920," he later wrote, "we were in a position [after defeating Iudenich, Kolchak, and Denikin] to transfer almost all our military forces to the western front."[55] Tukhachevskii had more than men and weapons to support him. At his back he had a rising wave of Russian chauvinism, which, despite Lenin's warnings against mixing national prejudices with proletarian internationalism[56] and other leading Bolsheviks' assurances that "war with Poland is a class war, and is as far from being a national war as Heaven is from the Earth,"[57] buoyed men's spirits and drew many not yet committed to the Bolshevik cause into its ranks. The number of Communists at the front soared, and they helped to cement units of raw recruits into disciplined fighting forces. "We have obtained a new Communist order of Samurai, which—without any caste privileges—knows how to die and teaches others to die for the cause of the workers' class," Trotskii exulted as he extolled the men and women who gave their lives so readily.[58] With these forces Tukhachevskii planned to march directly against Warsaw. It was a daring plan but, as Piłsudski himself later said, "logically correct."[59]

While Tukhachevskii made his preparations at Smolensk, the First Red Cavalry Army attacked the Poles in the Ukraine. Called the Konarmiia—the Cavalry Army—by the Russians, this elite strike force proved to be unlike any other to emerge from the Civil War's conflict. Formed at the end of 1919 to offset the Whites' Cossack cavalry, it drew many of its recruits from the ranks of renegade Cossacks and bandits. Well-clad and well-armed, the Konarmiia enjoyed the best that Red quartermasters and ordnance officers had to offer. Three air squadrons provided reconnaissance for its advancing columns, and each of its four divisions had the support of an armored train. The fact that one trooper in five was a worker, often a Communist miner or metalworker from the Donbas, helped to neutralize the stormy backgrounds of the others and made the Konarmiia one of the best disciplined forces in the Red Army. The Konarmiia fought with assurance and could move with surprising speed. The first days of April had found it resting at Maikop in the Kuban after having destroyed the remnants of Denikin's shattered Army of South Russia. On May 13, thirty-nine days and 750 miles later, the troopers of the Konarmiia cantered into Uman, just 125 miles southeast of Kiev, having bloodied their sabers in an attack against the defenders of Makhno's Ukrainian partisan stronghold at Guliai Pole on the way.[60]

Credit for transforming brawling Cossacks and bandits into

dedicated Communists belonged to the chief political officer of the Konarmiia, Kliment Voroshilov, the metalworker of Lugansk who had joined the Bolsheviks in 1903, endured prison and exile during the twilight of Imperial Russia, and risen to high rank in the Red Army under the protection of Stalin. Despite Trotskii's statement that "Voroshilov always reminded one more of a small shopowner than of a proletarian,"[61] he was a brilliant organizer who built a well-deserved reputation during the early days of the Civil War for his uncanny ability to shape scraps of manpower and odds and ends of materiel into an effective fighting machine. Dedicated to producing Communists in Konarmiia squadron schools, the stolid and precise Voroshilov made the ideal political commissar for the Konarmiia, and the perfect counterbalance to its dashing, no less stubborn leader, Semën Mikhailovich Budënnyi. Under Voroshilov's tutelage, the men of the Konarmiia learned to read as they marched and used the ABCs of Communism as their primer. A sharp sense of class conflict shaped their view of the world around them and defined their relation to it. "I am a son of the arisen masses, a soldier in the toilers' ranks," they sang as they moved across the steppes of South Russia. "I am in the vanguard of the vanguard, I am your faithful knight, O freedom!"[62]

The troopers of the Konarmiia drew their inspiration from their commander Budënnyi. A cavalryman's cavalryman who, at the age of forty, had spent half his life in the saddle, Budënnyi's almond-shaped, heavily lidded eyes resembled Dzerzhinskii's but that was the only resemblance between the two. Slender and aristocratic, Dzerzhinskii overpowered men with his iron will; Budënnyi met his foes face to face, always confident that his physical strength would carry him through. He led the Konarmiia into battle like a squadron commander, always in front, always seeking to engage the enemy. To the end of his days, even after he had worn the two inch–wide stars and heavy oak leaf braid of a marshal of the Soviet Union for more than a quarter century, Budënnyi remained at heart the Cossack cavalryman who had cut his way through a hundred forays, the wild horseman of the steppes whom dedication to the Bolsheviks' cause had tamed.[63]

As they launched their first attacks on May 27, Budënnyi's troopers learned that the Poles were more stubborn adversaries than the White forces they had fought in South Russia. Wild cavalry charges across open ground had struck fear into the hearts of Denikin's men and shattered their defenses, but Polish infantry proved more steadfast and better able to hold their ground. As repeated attacks against entrenched Polish infantry ground up his forces and took the lives of several key officers, Budënnyi quickly shifted tactics, turned his cavalry into infantry, and attacked in scattered formations. On June 5, three of his divisions broke through the Polish lines. Two days later, they stormed into Zhitomir and Berdichev to liberate five thousand Red Army prisoners of war. Within six weeks, the Konarmiia had taken Piłsudski's headquarters at Równo and had crossed the river Zbruch in the direction of the great Polish industrial center of Lwów.[64] "The successes of the Cavalry Army of Budënnyi have so completely demoralized our troops in the entire theater of war," one of Piłsudski's generals reported at the end of June, "that it seems that there is nothing we can do to offset them."[65]

Behind Budënnyi's raging cavalry came the infantry of the Twelfth and Fourteenth Red Armies under the command of Aleksandr Egorov, commander-in-chief of the southwestern front, and a proletarian officer who also stood in Stalin's inner circle. A burly peasant who had been a stevedore and a blacksmith before he entered the army, Egorov, like Budënnyi, had taught himself to read as an adult. A Left Socialist Revolutionary until mid-1918, he had become a Bolshevik in the wake of the Left SRs' abortive Moscow uprising. Later that year he served with Voroshilov and Budënnyi at Tsaritsyn and, like them, had become one of Stalin's allies.[66] Now Egorov moved quickly to support Budënnyi's early successes. Together they returned Kiev, Zhitomir, and several other key cities east of the river Słucz to Russian hands and swept the Ukraine clean of Poland's armies before the middle of June. Piłsudski's effort had weakened Poland's armies, precipitated a cabinet crisis in Warsaw, failed to establish a sympathetic government in the Ukraine, and stirred anti-Polish sentiments in Russia sufficiently to broaden support for the Bolsheviks dramatically.[67]

Budënnyi's and Egorov's early victories in the Ukraine had come before Tukhachevskii was ready to open the offensive for which the Red high command had given him unqualified support. In part due to the valiant efforts of the Forty-third Regiment's young commander Vasilii Chuikov, who later would command the Red Armies at Stalingrad and Berlin, a portion of Tukhachevskii's forces had crossed the Berezina River in the middle of May. But Chuikov's valor could not offset the imperfect supply lines on the western front, and Tukhachevskii needed more time to move men and supplies into position before he could attack the Poles in force. After Chuikov's first battles, he withdrew to more defensible positions while he assembled all the resources Bolshevik Russia had to offer.

For the next six weeks, Lenin, Trotskii, and their comrades all urged Russians into the battle Tukhachevskii was preparing to begin. "The entire internal life of the country must be subordinated to wartime needs," Lenin told a meeting of workers, soldiers, and peasants that spring. "Only those people who cannot help at the front should remain here."[68] "Mobilize your best fighters to defend the cause of the socialist idea," Trotskii urged at the same meeting. "Our task is not yet finished. Forward to the western front!"[69] A few days later, he cursed the "self-interested and power-hungry Polish lords, landowners, capitalists, and exploiters of the toiling masses" as his special train carried him to Russia's western front. "Ukrainian, White Russian, Lithuanian, and Russian workers and peasants," Trotskii insisted, "must join with the Workers' and Peasants' Red Army to replenish its ranks with volunteers, maintain its supplies, and provide everything else needed so that we can smash this predatory tribe of Polish lords who are trying to rob and enslave our toiling masses."[70]

At the end of 1919, Lenin and Trotskii had summoned Russia's "*zakalënnye bolsheviki*"—hardened Bolsheviks—to the heavy tasks of peaceful reconstruction. Now, less than six months later, they called them back to war. By the thousands, dedicated Communists put down their tools and plows and turned toward the western front. A special appeal from General Brusilov summoned tsarist officers and noncoms to support the Bolshevik cause against the Poles,[71] and Trotskii transformed his abortive labor armies into real armies once again. That summer, the number of men in the Red Army soared past five million, although nine out of every ten were rear echelon support troops, some of them still without rifles. The forces assembled to fight the Poles therefore were much less overwhelming than such huge numbers indicate. Estimates of Soviet troop strength on the western front at various times in 1920 vary wildly, and not even Tukhachevskii knew for certain how many men served under his command. Probably somewhere between ninety and a hundred thousand men at the beginning of June, with perhaps another thirty to forty thousand added to the combat forces before the end of the month, comprised his fighting forces. With nearly six hundred guns to support their advance, these formed a powerful assault force with which the Poles would find it difficult to reckon.[72]

At the beginning of June, Tukhachevskii formed the Third Cavalry Corps, the Kavkor, as a powerful mobile strike force similar to Budënnyi's Konarmiia in the Southwest. For its commander, he chose Gaia Gai, the eldest son of a Persian mother and an Armenian Socialist who had taken refuge in Persia from the Russian authorities during the 1880s. Gai had lived the sort of exotic, adventurous life from which legends are made. Born in Persia, he had returned to Russia in his teens, had been a radical journalist in Georgia's capital of Tiflis, and had spent five years in jail for his revolutionary activities, all before the tsarist authorities had drafted him at the age of twenty-one in 1914. Because of his background, Gai had been assigned to the Turkish front, where repeated bravery under fire won him a battalion commander's stars, the Cross of St. George, and the Order of St. Anne. Captured by the Turks, he escaped and returned, badly wounded, to Russia on the eve of the February Revolution. Gai had become a Bolshevik before the October Revolution. During the latter part of 1918, he had become one of Tukhachevskii's most trusted commanders, first as chief of the First Red Army against Kolchak and then, at the end of 1919, as commander of a special cavalry corps on the southern front. When Tukhachevskii needed a similar mobile shock force on the western front, he thought immediately of Gai and summoned him to Smolensk.[73]

Using the drive that Budënnyi and Egorov had launched from the south to support his flank, Tukhachevskii on July 4 sent five armies crashing across the Berezina and Gaina rivers on a front that stretched some two hundred miles southward from Drissa to Bobruisk. Spread out on Tukhachevskii's right, Gai's Kavkor repeatedly rolled up the Poles' left flank in a series of daring attacks that brought them to Minsk in a week. The following day, the Bolsheviks recognized Lithuania's independence and agreed that Wilno, which Gai's forces occupied two days later, would become its capital. Despite their prime minister's cynical remark that the Russians had not given them Wilno "for our beautiful eyes or from good will,"[74] the Lithuanians supported Russia's march into Poland. With their independence fully recognized, they were in no mood to complain, and, as Tukhachevskii's armies swept past, they were in no position to do so.[75]

With Gai's Kavkor turning its left flank again, and with their armies reeling from the incessant hammering of Tukhachevskii's infantry columns, the Poles fell back upon their defenses at the Niemen and Szczara rivers. Directly in Gai's line of march stood Grodno, once a major link in the western fortress defenses of Imperial Russia and now the anchor of the Polish left. With Tukhachevskii's Fourth, Fifteenth, Third, and Sixteenth Red Armies still fifty miles to the east, Gai burst into Grodno on the morning of July 19 to fight against stiffening Polish resistance without reinforcements or infantry support. Then, as the Poles weakened their right flank to strengthen their forces at Grodno, the Third and Sixteenth Armies stormed across the Szczara while the Fourth Army advanced along the Wilno–Grodno railway line and moved into position northwest of the city. "On the morning of July 21," Gai later wrote, "the Eighth, Tenth, and Fifth divisions [of the Fourth Red Army] closed the trap upon the enemy."[76] With heavy losses, the Poles broke out of the Bolshevik encirclement to the south, but only after they had abandoned most of their artillery. With Grodno's riverfront in ruins and its railroad station in flames, Tukhachevskii's Red Armies held the third great prize of Europe's eastern borderlands.[77]

During the first three weeks of his campaign, Tukhachevskii had driven Piłsudski's forces from those eastern borderlands that no Great Power would agree to bestow upon the Poles, but the victory at Grodno drastically changed the diplomatic climate within which the Russians would have to fight if the war continued. To move forward to Brest-Litovsk, Tukhachevskii's next logical objective, meant crossing the river Bug, the so-called Curzon Line, which the Allies had agreed, on December 8, 1919, was to mark Poland's eastern frontier.[78] Three days before Tukhachevskii's forces took Wilno, England's Foreign Secretary Lord Curzon had dispatched a note to Russia's Commissar of Foreign Affairs Chicherin in which he had urged an armistice and restated the Allies' view that the Bug frontier marked Poland's eastern boundary. Evidently with almost the entire Politburo behind him,[79] Chicherin had rejected Curzon's "ultimatum" and insisted that the Russo–Polish frontier approved by the Allies had been drawn up under the influence of "counterrevolutionary Russian elements" and could not be the basis for serious negotiation. Poland must negotiate directly with Russia, Chicherin replied to the British. There could be no intermediaries.[80]

Chicherin's reply to the Allies left no doubt about Tukhachevskii's course. Brest-Litovsk should be taken in a fortnight, a directive from his headquarters stated on July 23, and Warsaw should be occupied "not later than August 12."[81] For a moment, the strain of constant advance drained the energy that had driven Tukhachevskii's columns forward. Sheer weight of numbers breached Poland's fourth line of defense at the Bug, and even Gai's Kavkor advanced without its usual reckless intensity. It took the Kavkor a full week to break through the Poles' defenses at Łomża at the end of July, and although the Sixteenth Red Army crossed the Bug at Brest-Litovsk at the beginning of August with more of the élan it had shown earlier in the campaign, it was driven back by a Polish counterattack. Polish resistance and Russian lethargy both proved transitory once the Bug had been decisively breached. As they moved westward across the lands their fallen comrades in the armies of Imperial Russia had been forced to abandon to German arms during the Great Retreat of 1915, Tukhachevskii's men took pride in their new power. Now they marched confidently to songs of certain victory: "Like lava, the Soviet soldiers/ Will sweep away all the dirt forever," they sang. "Warsaw will become Red./ And so will all the cities of the world."[82] Ostrołęka and Przasnysz, both scenes of Russian defeats in 1915, now fell to Tukhachevskii's forces. Piłsudski described the Polish lines as "a kaleidoscope of chaos" and spoke of the "heavy, monstrous, uncontainable cloud" of Red forces that hovered to the north, south, and east of Warsaw.[83]

By early August, Red armies stood only a few miles from Warsaw.[84] Delegates to the Second Comintern Congress meeting in Moscow followed Tukhachevskii's progress with increasing excitement as the Bolsheviks hung a huge map on the wall of their assembly hall and marked the Soviet positions with a thicket of tiny red flags. "The delegates every morning stood with breathless interest before this map," the congress's president Zinoviev remembered. "The best representatives of the international proletariat . . . all perfectly realized that, if the military aim of our army was achieved, it would mean an immense acceleration of the international proletarian revolution."[85] To the east of Warsaw, Red flags stood in profusion. The Polish bridge that could carry Russia's revolutionary armies into Germany's industrial heartland was being crossed more rapidly than anyone had expected. Again moving in advance of Tukhachevskii's main force, some units of the Kavkor were only two hundred miles east of Berlin and only a hundred miles south of Gdansk. "You have inflicted upon the attacking force of White Poland a shattering defeat," Trotskii rejoiced from Moscow. "Forward, men of the Red Army! Heroes, on to Warsaw!"[86]

Although the red flags moved forward day by day, victory proved to be more elusive than the Russians expected. Tukhachevskii's dash to Warsaw had cost him a third of his assault force and up to ninety percent of those "hardened Bolsheviks" whom Lenin and Trotskii had summoned to the struggle a scant four months before.[87] Gai had outrun his supply lines and had led the Kavkor so far to the west that he could no longer turn to close the right wing of Tukhachevskii's offensive around Warsaw from the north. At the same time, Budënnyi and Egorov had begun to shift their columns away from Warsaw toward Lwów. Especially Budënnyi slowed his line of march as he changed direction. The cavalry commander whose troopers had raged unchecked across the Ukraine in May and June had advanced a mere fifty-seven miles in July, while Gai covered four hundred.[88]

A complex combination of caprice, vanity, and military necessity were responsible for the positions in which the forces on Russia's western and southwestern fronts found themselves in mid-August 1920. In search of a personal triumph to counterbalance that of Tukhachevskii and his patron Trotskii, Stalin (as chief political commissar for the southwestern front) wanted to capture the important industrial center of Lwów. As a metallurgical and textile center situated in the vicinity of the Borysław-Drogobych oilfields, Lwów was a prize worth having, but it was not the equal of Warsaw, nor was it the objective toward which the Reds' offensive had been committed. For that reason, Stalin's outright refusal to transfer Budënnyi's Konarmiia and the Twelfth Red Army to Tukhachevskii when the Red high command ordered him to do so has been counted as nothing less than an act of outright insubordination.[89] "Who on earth," Lenin asked in amazement at one point, "would want to get to Warsaw by going through Lwów![90] Yet, apart from Stalin's personal vanity and his increasingly bitter rivalry with Trotskii, there were military considerations that justified the reluctance of the southwestern front commanders to support Tukhachevskii, and these have to be taken into account. On June 6, the remnants of South Russia's White armies under the command of General Baron Wrangel had burst out of their Crimean containment in a final desperate attempt to salvage their shattered hopes for a White victory. Within a week, Wrangel's forces had taken eight thousand prisoners, seized thirty guns, captured two armored trains, and reached the lower Dnepr. Three weeks later, they annihilated the First Red Cavalry Corps.[91] Contrary to all Bolshevik expectations, the exhausted Whites had become a force to be reckoned with once again.

Wrangel's front line in July stood nearer to the Donbas and the great Ukrainian industrial center of Kharkov than the forces of Budënnyi and Egorov were to Warsaw, and Russia's strategy in the South therefore had to take into account the possibility that he might strike into the rear areas of the southwestern front. "Wrangel is operating in the rear of our armies engaged against the Poles, that is, in the most dangerous place for us," Stalin warned in an interview with a *Pravda* correspondent. "It is ridiculous to talk of a 'march on Warsaw,' or, in general, of the lasting character of our successes [against the Poles]," he concluded, "so long as the Wrangel danger has not been eliminated."[92] The danger of Wrangel and the personal vanity of Stalin therefore meant that, as Tukhachevskii moved his armies into position along the Wisła for a final assault against Warsaw, the closest units on the southwestern front were nearly two hundred miles away, with no chance of advancing quickly enough to give him any support.

While their armies had been losing battle after battle to Tukhachevskii's Russians, Poland's leaders had been working feverishly to strengthen their reserves. At the beginning of July, Deputy War Minister Kazimierz Sosnkowski had told the Poles that they were living through the war's "most critical moments" and had spoken bluntly of the rigors that lay ahead. "The clock is striking midnight, the hour which will decide the fate of the war," he said. "Let everyone who does not give everything to our motherland, anyone who shows weakness in this time of trial, remember that the heavy responsibility for the fate of our nation will lie upon his conscience."[93]

As Sosnkowski had hoped, Tukhachevskii's advance welded Poland together and strengthened her will, and when Polish workers and bourgeoisie set aside those conflicts upon which the Russians had depended to erode their enemies' national unity, the class war that Lenin had envisioned never took shape. Without hesitation, Poles placed their historic hatred for Russians ahead of any "class" economic or political interests, and feelings against the Russians ran so deep that summer that, out of 24,000 Poles subjected to Communist indoctrination in Russian-held areas, a paltry 123 joined the Bolsheviks. In many areas, the Polish Socialist Party formed the workers of Poland into special battalions to fight their historic Russian foes as men all across Poland took up arms. By the time that Tukhachevskii's forces approached the suburbs of Warsaw, over a hundred and sixty thousand volunteers had joined the hundred and fifty thousand fighting men who had been drafted in July.[94]

These were not the dull, slow-to-learn, hard-to-train peasant conscripts who had filled Poland's regiments earlier that spring. Men with technical training and high intelligence now came forward to fill the gaps in Poland's defenses. Almost immediately, Trotskii sensed the change. This was not the "army of slaves, held by force, steeped in priests' lies and bourgeois deceit" of which he had spoken publicly earlier. "We have operating against us for the first time," he warned the Central Committee, "a regular army led by good technicians."[95] By the middle of August, Poland's army reached the strength of the combined forces on the Soviet western and southwestern fronts. With the balance in numbers even, the key factors now became strategy, tactics, luck, and, above all, will.

The moral imperatives that cast the Battle of Warsaw as a struggle between Communism and Christianity for the gateway to Europe caused contemporaries to exaggerate its significance. Britain's Viscount d'Abernon, who arrived in July to head the Inter-Allied Mission to Poland, called the Battle of Warsaw "the eighteenth decisive battle of the world," comparable to Marathon, Sedan, and the Marne. Certain that "the very existence of Western civilization would have been imperilled" by a Soviet victory in Poland, d'Abernon ranked Piłsudski's triumph over the Russians on a moral par with Charles Martel's victory over the Saracens at Tours more than a thousand years before. "The Battle of Tours saved our ancestors of Britain and our neighbors of Gaul from the yoke of the Koran," he concluded. "It is probable that the Battle of Warsaw preserved Central and parts of Western Europe from a more subversive danger—the fanatical tyranny of the Soviets."[96] Piłsudski himself had no such delusions. The battle, he later wrote, was a "*bijatyka*," a brawl, "where standard methods and doctrines simply . . . [did] not apply," and where the bulk of Poland's forces had to be committed to the "absurdity, both logically and strategically," of defending Warsaw while their commanders struggled to launch a counterattack from a different point altogether.[97]

Especially from Piłsudski, the situation at Warsaw demanded a willingness to do the unexpected and the will to see it through. As Tukhachevskii's armies closed in at the beginning of August,

Piłsudski therefore disposed his forces not merely to bar the approaches to Poland's capital but to launch a counteroffensive just when the Russians opened their final assault. Neither commander had a clear strategy in mind until the last moment, and although circumstances would eventually prove more favorable to the Poles than the Russians, confusion saturated both sides. While Tukhachevskii appeared to emulate the strategy of attacking Warsaw from the north and northeast that the Russian General Paskevich had followed when he had crushed the Poles in 1831, Piłsudski shifted some of his best forces to the south, away from his adversary's main thrust, to the region where the Wieprz River passed between Dęblin and Kock. From that point, he hoped to drive his "striking force" of some twenty thousand men into Tukhachevskii's rear to produce enough chaos to allow the forces defending Warsaw to open a counteroffensive. Should that effort fail, he expected to have Tukhachevskii's Sixteenth, Third, and Fifteenth Red Armies, as well as the smaller Mozyr Group that stretched between Tukhachevskii's left and Egorov's right, fall upon him with a weight that would almost certainly bring defeat. Although he had to take the risk, it was not one that any general could have relished because the success depended too much upon the actions of commanders other than himself.

It was Piłsudski's good fortune to be able to rely upon some of Poland's best commanders to defend Warsaw and shift to a counteroffensive against the Russians at the proper moment. Between August 12 and 16, generals Sikorski, Haller, Latinik, Raszewski, and Zielinski defended both the Wkra River front in the north and the vital Wisła bridgehead that centered upon the suburb of Praga to Warsaw's northeast against the raging Kavkor and the Fourth Red Army. With over a hundred and thirty thousand men, they outnumbered Tukhachevskii's force by more than a tenth, but they had to bear the full weight of the battle while Piłsudski moved his "striking force" into position. With singular dedication, the Poles fought with whatever weapons came to hand. At the Wisła bridgehead, the best-armed and best-trained Poles fought with heavy concentrations of machine guns, artillery, and even tanks, while, on the Wkra, one unit actually tried to defend a fort at Modlin with cannon from the Napoleonic wars. Yet it was on the Wkra, a hundred miles to the north of Piłsudski's position, that events made the success of his "striking force" certain. On August 15, General Sikorski first realized that his Fifth Army, with nothing more than three infantry and one cavalry divisions, faced not the Kavkor and the Fourth Red Army, but Tukhachevskii's main assault force.

What Piłsudski had not known when he moved his "striking force" into position was that Tukhachevskii had fully committed his Sixteenth, Third, and Fifteenth armies to the attack against Warsaw from the north and northeast rather than from the east and had left the Mozyr Group with less than seven thousand men to hold more than fifty miles of front that stretched between the Sixteenth Red Army on his left and the Twelfth on Egorov's right. This made the Dęblin–Kock sector the weakest point in the Russians' line, and once the Red commanders had committed themselves to attacks against Warsaw and Lwów that drew their main forces away from the Mozyr Group, it became the hardest to reinforce. Therefore, when Piłsudski launched his counterattack on the morning of August 16, his forces brushed past the Mozyr Group and drove directly into Tukhachevskii's undefended rear. By nightfall, Piłsudski had seized the heavy guns that the Russians were moving up to batter Warsaw. Then, with Tukhachevskii caught by surprise and off balance, the "striking force" struck deadly blows at the Sixteenth, Third, and Fifteenth Red Armies, while the units assigned to defend Warsaw advanced against them in a maneuver that completely cut off the Fourth Red Army and Gai's Kavkor from the rest of Tukhachevskii's force. Out of food, fodder, and cartridges, and with the entire Polish army between them and their line of retreat, Gai's Kavkor and the Fourth Red Army crossed the frontier to internment in Germany rather than face annihilation at the hands of the pursuing Poles.[98]

Although the Poles' victory shifted the balance dramatically, it did not end the war. Budënnyi's powerful Konarmiia and the Twelfth and Fourteenth Red Armies remained in action in Poland's southeast, and in late August they broke off their attack against Lwów and turned to support Tukhachevskii's retreat. At Zamość, Poland's cavalry clashed with the Konarmiia in the last great cavalry battle in Europe's history and one from which Budënnyi extricated his forces with heavy losses and only at the last possible moment. While Budënnyi fought in the south, Tukhachevskii faced the Poles along the Niemen River, where, after several days of battle, he had to leave the field to the enemy. Throughout September and into October, the Poles reclaimed their lands. Komarów, Kowel, Łuck, Równo, Swięciany, Molodeczno now saw the Russians fall back in defeat a second time. Wilno, by virtue of a fictitious "mutiny" to assuage the consciences of the Allies, fell to the Poles before the middle of October, and despite angry calls for a second war with Poland, Lenin's government sued for peace. On October 12, the Poles signed an armistice with the Russians. A week later the fighting stopped. For the first time since August 1914, all was quiet on Europe's eastern front.[99]

"Soldiers! You have made Poland strong, confident, and free," Piłsudski proclaimed as he announced the armistice. "A country which, in two years, has produced soldiers such as you, " he concluded, "can regard its future with tranquility."[100] The Russian reaction was less assuring. "In those localities which we give her according to the peace agreement," Lenin said, "Poland will maintain herself only by force." The Bolsheviks, he promised, would use the peace "for strengthening our army."[101] A time for reckoning would come later. In the meantime, the Bolsheviks would gain a desperately needed respite to deal with Russia's economic crises and Wrangel's continuing attacks in the South. "We have won," Lenin insisted elsewhere. "Anyone who examines the map will see that we have won, that we have emerged from this war with more territory than we had before it started."[102]

In fact, both sides could claim victory in the armistice of October 1920 and the peace their negotiators signed at Riga on March 18, 1921. Poland regained some of the historically "Polish" towns in Europe's eastern borderlands, including Grodno, Lwów, Równo, and, after 1923, Wilno, and moved her eastern frontier more than a hundred miles east of the Curzon Line that the Allies had established at the end of 1919. For the Russians, the claim to victory inevitably was weaker.[103] Still, as Lenin pointed out in a speech on October 15, the Russo–Polish border was fifty miles west of the line the Russians had offered to accept during their peace talks with the Poles in April.[104] Perhaps more important, peace spared the Bolsheviks from fighting a third major winter campaign and allowed them to concentrate their resources against Wrangel's army. The fighting of the Civil War now had come full circle. As the conflict died down in the West, the Red High Command turned its attention once again—and for the final time—to the South. In the Crimea, scene of Imperial Russia's only lost war before 1914, the Russian Empire breathed its last as the Bolsheviks made their final march to victory.

CHAPTER THIRTEEN

The End of the Whites

Six hundred miles south of Moscow, the narrow thread of the Perekop Isthmus suspends the Crimean Peninsula into the waters of the Black Sea. Ancient Scythian conquerors had claimed its northern and central lands early in the millennium before Christ while Greek colonists from Chersonesus and Theodosia had settled on its fertile southern shores. Seven hundred years later, Imperial Rome had claimed allegiance from the descendants of the Greeks, who had continued to flourish under Roman protection for another three hundred years. Goths, Huns, Avars, Khazars, Byzantine Greeks, and Tatars all had entered the Crimean sanctuary as conquerors in the centuries after Rome fell before medieval Venetian and Genoese traders arrived to make the Crimea the northeastern terminus of their far-flung sea lanes. After them, the Tatars, now tributaries of the Turkish sultan, had ruled the Crimea from their seat at Bakhchisarai, the legendary "Garden of the Khans," until Catherine the Great had annexed it to Russia in 1783 as a trophy from her first war against the Ottoman Empire.

The playground of tsars and nobles from the moment Catherine added it to Russia's domains, the Crimea was a geographical world apart from Moscow. Palaces, villas, and sea resorts dotted its sun-soaked southern shores, where ancient Greek ruins and Genoese fortresses stood interspersed with Muslim minarets and Russian monasteries in an exotic architectural jumble. Groves of cypresses, magnolias, mimosas, figs, olives, and pomegranates, all so unlike the vegetation of Great Russia, mixed with forests of oak, beech, black pine, and fir. Before war and revolution had shattered the Crimea's economy, nearly twenty thousand acres of vineyards had produced three and a half million gallons of wine every year. In winter, its gardens had grown the flowers that special trains had brought to the Empress Aleksandra's boudoir each week, even when there had been no trains to carry weapons, ammunition, and warm winter clothing to the men who filled the frozen trenches on Russia's western front during the second and third winters of the Great War.

In this fertile haven, so often called Russia's Riviera, the tattered soldiers of Denikin's Volunteer Army had taken refuge after their disastrous flight from the South Russian port of Novorossiisk, when, as a gray, wet dawn had broken on March 26, 1920, they had rushed headlong onto waiting ships and left horses, artillery, and more than twenty thousand of their comrades fighting and cursing on the quay.[1] In the Crimea, they joined hordes of nobles and churchmen of the Old Regime, together with the liberal politicians, writers, publicists, and lawyers of the Provisional Government. To the Crimea had come statesmen without offices, governors without provinces, lords and ladies without lands and manor houses, and financiers and industrialists with neither banks nor factories, politicians without constituencies, and generals without armies. The list of those who once had had, whom the Revolution had transformed into those who had not, seemed endless. Bitter enemies during the last days of Imperial Russia all had come together in the Crimea, their union cemented by their hatred for the Bolsheviks and their common dream of regaining their lost wealth and homeland. None believed that the Bolsheviks could be conquered after the defeats of Iudenich, Kolchak, and Denikin, yet none knew how to make peace. Destined to remain in limbo for eight months more, theirs was a cause without hope, a future without promise.

Shattered after their almost certain victory of October 1919 had turned into defeat, the Whites thus could envision no course in the spring of 1920 but to regroup their forces against the rapidly strengthening Red Armies. "As long as we have even one chance in a hundred, we ought not to lay down our arms," their chief-of-staff insisted as Denikin prepared to turn over his command to General Baron Petr Wrangel at the beginning of April. "If we had even one chance that would be true," another commander replied, "but I think the enemy has not only ninety-nine chances out of a hundred, but ninety-nine point nine."[2] Even the most optimistic of the Whites now settled for modest goals. "Russia cannot be freed by a triumphant march from the Crimea to Moscow," General Wrangel insisted as he issued his first orders as the Whites' commander-in-chief. At best, the Whites could hope to "preserve the honor of the Russian flag entrusted to the army" and "create, in no matter how tiny a corner of Russia, a form of government and way of life that will attract . . . those who now suffer under the Red yoke."[3] Although a fighting general accustomed to winning against heavy odds, Wrangel thus took command not to defeat the Reds but to negotiate the best possible terms with them.[4] "It was clear to me that the situation really was hopeless," he wrote some years later. "The cavalry had no horses, and none of the units had transport, artillery, or machine guns. The men were in rags and very bitter," he concluded. "Under these conditions, the remains of the Volunteer Army no longer constituted an effective fighting force."[5]

Although many White survivors have remembered him as being too arrogant and too ready to demand rapid solutions to complex problems, none have denied the immense force of Wrangel's will. A man who found it easy to instill in others his own stern sense of purpose, Wrangel took over Denikin's shattered armies with a determination that no other White officer could match. Passionate patriotism and icy hatred for those Bolshevik politicians who had destroyed the Russia he loved made him willing to pay any price and work with any ally against his enemies. Aristocratic to the core, he had no scruples about the strange bedfellows that politics in a democratic world brought his way. "I need men of strong character, who know how the masses live and how to shape their lives," he stated bluntly. "For me, party or political colorings are completely meaningless."[6] Wrangel therefore continued Denikin's contacts with the French, English, and the Americans, but he also turned to the Ukrainians, the Metropolitan of Kiev, and even to Makhno.[7] "Even with the devil," he once proclaimed of his willingness to seek alliances that Denikin had shunned. "But for Russia and against the Bolsheviks."[8] Bolshevik propagandists called him the Black Baron and admired his genius while they cursed his politics. "In terms of quality," one Soviet military expert wrote a few years later, "Wrangel's army was the best fighting force ever organized by the Russian and international counterrevolution in the armed struggle against the Soviet republics."[9]

Wrangel did not plan a new march against Moscow, but he had no intention of relinquishing that "tiny corner of Russia" in which he and the Whites had taken refuge. This "last strip of native soil"[10] was to become Wrangel's Crimean bastion, a haven for men and women who preferred exile to life under the Bolsheviks. Here, in a territory of less than sixteen thousand square miles, more than three-quarters of which were rough grazing lands for sheep, food and housing had to be found for some twenty-five thousand fighting men and nearly twenty times that number of war invalids and refugees who looked to them for protection.[11] To make the Crimea safe, Wrangel needed to fortify the Perekop Isthmus and bring under control the insurgent mountain forces that fought Reds and Whites with equal fury. These tasks demanded great dedication and even greater ingenuity. "We had nothing with which to re-equip the army," Wrangel remembered. "We had just enough rifles to go around, but we had almost no machine guns or artillery. Nearly all the tanks, armored cars, and airplanes had fallen into the hands of the enemy [at Novorossiisk]," he continued. "Our stock of ammunition, especially artillery shells, could only last for a very short time."[12]

Most of all, Wrangel needed food for his army and the hordes of civilians who clogged its rear. Although its orchards and vineyards had long supplied Russia with fruits and wines that her mainland fields could not produce, the Crimea grew very little grain or beef. "Completely lacking in natural resources, the tiny Crimea had been obliged to feed and support not only the army but its endlessly growing rear echelons for months," Wrangel later explained. "In peacetime, it lived at the expense of the fertile Northern Taurida [on the mainland]," he went on. "Now . . . it could feed neither its own population nor the army."[13] Separated from the Northern Taurida by the same Perekop Isthmus whose growing fortifications he intended to use to prevent the Reds from bursting into his Crimean sanctuary, Wrangel needed other sources of supply. Bread grains, meat, coal, and oil all had to be found, as well as uniforms, weapons, and ammunition. Without them, the Whites could not survive for more than a few weeks.

White leaders from Alekseev and Kornilov to Iudenich and Kolchak—and General Denikin perhaps most of all—had expected the men and women of Russia to support their cause because duty as loyal Russians demanded it. Better attuned to public opinion despite his strong monarchist views, Wrangel set out to win the masses' support by offering them a stake in his government. He therefore turned to two genuinely talented statesmen whose talents Denikin had too long ignored. One was Petr Struve, who had made Russian culture and Russian politics his lifelong concern, and who became Wrangel's foreign minister. The other was Aleksandr Krivoshein, the aging tsarist statesman who became his prime minister.

A man whose perpetually rumpled appearance contrasted sharply with Wrangel's precise elegance, Struve ably represented Wrangel in Paris and London. He had an erudition that few could match and a sense of humanity that stood above the petty political squabbles that embroiled so many Whites during those days. Convinced that the unstable international situation might combine with Soviet economic and political weaknesses to produce crises that could enable a small but stable White government to expand its geographical boundaries, Struve sensed that Wrangel's leadership might yet enable something to be salvaged for the Whites' cause. "Cautious people now say 'there is hope,' " he wrote to one of his close friends as Wrangel took command. "Until recently they used to speak in terms of utter hopelessness."[14]

After a brief infatuation with Marxism in his youth, Struve had greeted the twentieth century with the statement that "the cultural and political liberation of Russia . . . must become a national cause."[15] He had moved considerably to the right in the spectrum of liberal opinion at the time of the Revolution of 1905 and, during Russia's brief flirtation with constitutional government, had stood in the innermost circles of the Kadet Party until he had resigned from its Central Committee in 1915. Two years later, Struve's writings on economic theory had won him membership in the Russian Academy of Sciences. Although he had fled to the South to become a member of the Volunteer Army's Council immediately after the Bolsheviks' victory, he had returned to live illegally in Moscow as a member of the National Center for much of 1918, until his anti-Bolshevik publishing activities made him a marked man. Struve had wandered as a fugitive in North Russia for three months before he had escaped to Finland. After some brief dealings with Iudenich and Mannerheim in Helsinki, he had moved on to London and Paris, where he had worked with a number of prominent White diplomats before he moved to Novorossiisk to edit one of the leading newspapers in Denikin's Russia. During the winter of 1919–1920, Struve had shared a railway car with Wrangel. After both of them left South Russia at the beginning of 1920, the two men had continued to discuss Russian politics at length in the coffeehouses of Constantinople.[16]

Struve urged Wrangel to "implement a leftist policy with rightist hands"[17] in order to cement a firm union between the masses and his government. Krivoshein, a man of subtle political instincts who had been a close associate of Russia's first great prime minister Stolypin and had served as minister of agriculture during the first years of the Great War, fully shared those views. As one who had urged the government of Nicholas II to seek broader public participation, Krivoshein understood the failings of Russia's agriculture and the conditions in which her peasants lived as few others did. Like many other tsarist statesmen, the Bolshevik Revolution first had driven him to the German-occupied Ukraine and then to Paris. Unlike many of his associates, he had left the safety of Paris late in 1919 to return to South Russia, where, convinced that Denikin could no longer hold the White movement together, he had worked to oust him from his post. Wrangel thought Krivoshein "a distinguished administrator who always chose first-rate subordinates" and "a man of outstanding intelligence with an extraordinary dedication to his work."[18] Krivoshein therefore quickly found a place in Wrangel's inner circle along with Struve, whom he had known since the war years and with whom he had renewed his association on the eve of the debacle at Novorossiisk. During the winter of 1919–1920, Krivoshein had joined Struve and Wrangel frequently in Constantinople's coffeehouses. When Krivoshein returned to the Crimea the next spring, Wrangel immediately brought him into his inner circle.[19]

Just as they had insisted that decisions about the fate of the men and women who wanted to break free from Russia's borderlands must be set aside until the Civil War's end, Denikin and his advisers had made every effort to postpone land reform. By doing so they had weakened support for the Whites' cause among those millions of poor peasants whom the Bolsheviks enticed with Lenin's widely publicized program to abolish all private landholding. Convinced that Denikin's failure to support far-reaching land reforms had denied him the support of Russia's land-hungry peasants, Wrangel moved quickly to rectify his predecessor's tactical mistake. "We had to tear our enemies' principal political weapon from their hands, ignite the imagination of the army and the masses, and make a favorable impression on opinion abroad," he explained later. "The present situation would not allow us to wait any longer. This Gordian knot had to be cut."[20]

Wrangel's effort to cut the Gordian knot of land reform reflected Krivoshein's long experience as an agricultural reformer in the government of Nicholas II, but his personal flair for publicity gave it a more striking character. After he entrusted the task of a drafting land reform law to one of Krivoshein's most trusted former assistants in the Imperial Ministry of Agriculture, Wrangel hastened to publish his own views in support of the commission's work.[21] "The land should belong to those who till it, and its ownership should be based on the rights of private property," he wrote as he called for "the distribution of land at a specially established price among those who have little or none at all."[22] Wrangel would not go so far as to make a free gift of the land or give it to every person who wanted it,[23] but his effort to force concessions from Russia's reluctant aristocrats marked a major shift in the politics of the declining White movement. "I am deeply convinced," one observer wrote, "that if the Land Decree . . . published by General Wrangel on May 25, 1920, had been issued by General Denikin on May 25, 1918, the results of the Civil War would have been entirely different. If the Volunteer Army, with English tanks and cannon, but without the Land Decree and in spite of the hatred of the entire peasant mass, could have advanced as far as Orël," he added, "then with the Land Decree, which would have brought the peasant masses over to its side, it might well have reached Moscow."[24] Such words overemphasized the appeal of Wrangel's program to Russia's peasants, but they highlighted one of the Whites' most serious failings. Reluctance to concede that Old Russia could never return had made it impossible for them to build the strong social base needed to rival the growing support of Russia's masses for the Bolsheviks in 1918 and 1919.

If Wrangel's willingness to woo Russia's peasants with land reform contrasted sharply with Denikin's reluctance, so did his insistence upon law and order in his rear, where peasants still called the Volunteer Army (*Dobrarmiia* in Russian) the *Grabarmiia* (the Looting Army).[25] Wrangel had taken command in South Russia as commander-in-chief and regent with dictatorial powers, and his plan to implement a "leftist policy with rightist hands" in no way restrained his willingness to use his extraordinary authority. "We are in a besieged fortress and only a firm and unified governing power can save us," he warned.[26] "The essential task," he continued, "is the creation of a rule of law for the people of the part of South Russia which is occupied by my troops, so that the people's aspirations might be satisfied in the broadest possible manner."[27] Convinced that "one of the main reasons for the dissolution of General Denikin's army was the absence of a firm ruling structure and a sense of lawfulness,"[28] Wrangel set out to establish a police force that could put down lawlessness and build a counterintelligence service that would wipe out the Bolshevik underground that had operated so effectively in Denikin's rear. "I will let nothing stop me from carrying out my duty and will get rid of anyone who gets in my way," he stated coldly when the angry mayor of Simferopol protested the summary hanging of men found guilty of looting and desertion. "I warn you," he concluded, "that I shall not hesitate to add one more to the number [of people who have been hanged], even if that one should be you yourself."[29]

To build a state in which it would become possible for "the peasant, after having gained full ownership of the land he tills, to devote himself to peaceful labor, for the honest worker to be assured of bread in his old age, and for true freedom and law to reign in Holy Russia,"[30] Wrangel believed that stern discipline, applied in a fair and evenhanded manner, must replace the habits of tyranny and corruption that Bolshevik officials shared with their predecessors in the fallen imperial government. Life without control, he concluded, had had its day, and civic responsibility must replace gross self-interest among the Russians. Yet Wrangel also insisted that party politics, so much a part of civic life in the West, had no more place in the Crimea than did officials who filled their pockets at the people's expense. "Until the struggle [against the Bolsheviks] is over, all parties must work as one and do whatever needs to be done without any partisan spirit," he insisted. "For me," he stated flatly, "there are neither monarchists nor republicans, but only knowledgeable workers."[31]

Whatever Wrangel hoped to accomplish by orderly government and land reform in the civilian sector, he knew that the shattered army to which he had fallen heir must be rebuilt if the Whites hoped to survive the summer.[32] He needed weapons, ammunition, and equipment from the Allies, and he needed more fighting men to hold the Crimea's defenses. As sprawling staffs clogged his army's rear to the point where colonels became more prevalent there than in the fighting line,[33] Wrangel cut bloated support units, ordered recovered casualties back to the front, and ended long stays in the Crimean cities of Simferopol and Sevastopol for men who no longer required medical attention. "I gave orders that anyone who was fit to fight was not to leave his unit without a valid reason and that all the wounded who had recovered were to leave the hospital and return to the front," he wrote of his first weeks in command.[34] Convinced that it was better to be too stern than too lenient, Wrangel also enforced regulations about military courtesy and proper dress to restore discipline and strengthen his soldiers' *esprit de corps*.

One of Denikin's greatest failings as commander-in-chief of the Armed Forces of South Russia had been his inability to control plundering by his soldiers and corruption among their senior officers. Less tolerant, more stern, and more confident, Wrangel shared none of Denikin's misplaced confidence in the honor of his commanders and ordered that deserters, looters, and lawbreakers be punished relentlessly despite vigorous protests from men who represented special interests. In contrast to Denikin, who had issued a flood of draconian laws but rarely enforced them, Wrangel issued few but insisted upon death sentences for convicted offenders. As his stern measures took effect, people began to speak of "the sudden and miraculous change in the army's disposition" and the "miracle . . . that had given the army new courage and faith in itself."[35] After its long retreat and the disasters of the previous winter, the Volunteer Army, now renamed the Russian Army, began to look—and behave—like an army at war once again.

If Denikin had been unduly lenient with men who stole and plundered, he had been unreasonably harsh with those who had fought in the Red Army. Although his propaganda leaflets promised otherwise, he sent Red Army officers and men who defected to the Whites to prison or left them to languish under a heavy cloud of suspicion.[36] "We had not brought peace and pardon, but a cruel and vengeful sword," Wrangel complained of the days when Denikin had marched on Moscow. "This unwise and cruel policy . . . antagonized those who were ready to become our allies and transformed those seeking our friendship into enemies." Convinced that, as both sides had turned to conscription in 1919, the composition of their armies had changed, and that Denikin's suspicion of men who had served the Bolsheviks or the separatist cause of any non-Russian national group had far less grounds than had been the case eighteen months before, Wrangel rejected what he called Denikin's "one-sided, intransigent policy" in favor of a moderate one. Certain that men now fought not for ideas or beliefs but because they had no choice, he insisted that "their presence in either army depended in large measure on the vagaries of geographical circumstance" and treated them accordingly.

Anxious to strengthen his armed forces and convinced, as Denikin never had been, that "there were many honest Russian men in the ranks of the Red Army," Wrangel urged men to desert the Bolsheviks and join his tiny Crimean force, which, he insisted, was the "true Russian Army." This force was the legitimate heir to the military legacy of Peter the Great and Marshal Kutuzov, conqueror of Napoleon. In its ranks, loyal Russians might still carry on the traditions of the once invincible Russian army to which generations of men had given their lives so that Russia "might be happy." Wrangel called upon all men who still carried within their hearts a love of country to accept his offer of patriotic atonement. "As an old officer who has given the best years of his life to our Motherland," he concluded in one of his proclamations to the Red Armies in South Russia, "I promise you that I shall forget what is past and give you an opportunity to redeem yourselves."[37] Wrangel withdrew Denikin's insistence upon a united, indivisible Russia and made the same promise to the Ukrainians and even the Georgians, whose food supplies Denikin once had tried to interrupt. Men and women who wished to be free of Russia's control no longer needed to set their dreams aside while they fought with the Whites to destroy a common enemy.

If Wrangel's stern discipline and personal charisma restored the fighting spirit of his armed forces, his efforts in the diplomatic arena brought more mixed results. Denikin's and Kolchak's defeats had convinced the British government that the White cause was "utterly and hopelessly lost" and that the time had come to end the conflict in Russia. There was no point, Britain's Foreign Secretary Lord Curzon insisted, in "running a really grave risk with no possibly good result,"[38] especially at a time when the British government hoped to reopen Anglo–Soviet trade. Convinced that "the prolongation of the civil war in Russia is, on the whole, the most disquieting element in the European situation at present,"[39] Lord Curzon had instructed Britain's high commissioner at Constantinople on April 24, 1920, to state his government's views to Denikin in such a way as to make certain that he retained no hopes "that all is not really and finally over."[40] To ease the bitter pill, Curzon promised that England would negotiate with the Soviet government to arrange "an amnesty for the population of the Crimea in general and for the personnel of the Volunteer Army in particular" and would offer Denikin and his chief supporters "a hospitable refuge" in England. Should the Whites decide to "prolong an obviously hopeless struggle," Curzon now stated flatly, "the British Government will find itself obliged to . . . cease, from that moment, all assistance or subvention of any sort."[41]

Since he already knew that Denikin intended to resign, Britain's high commissioner communicated Curzon's instructions directly to Wrangel—to his mind the most probable successor to Denikin—at lunch aboard his flagship in Constantinople's harbor. Given the Bolsheviks' overwhelming superiority in men and weapons, Wrangel felt that "England's refusal to give us any further help took away our last hope."[42] Even though the White officers who elected him commander-in-chief on April 4 agreed that his chief task must be to "negotiate through Allied mediation the best possible terms with the Bolsheviks,"[43] Wrangel would not capitulate as Curzon demanded. Nor would he be forced into direct negotiations with his enemies. The English, he warned, must bear the burden of the negotiations and the responsibility for any settlement. "If we reject their mediation, our refusal will give them the opportunity to stand aside and wash their hands of us entirely," he explained to his senior commanders. "I will never agree to direct negotiations with the Bolsheviks," he insisted, "but I think that it is essential not to give the English a chance to pull out of the game. We must transfer the odium of the negotiations to them," he concluded, "and draw them out long enough so that we can strengthen our fortifications, put our combat forces and our rear area in order, and secure coal and oil for the fleet in the event that an evacuation becomes necessary."[44]

Wrangel thus intended to keep every option open. He demanded that the British guarantee "the safety of all those who are part of our armed forces, the population of the territories they occupy, those refugees who wish to return to Russia, and those who have fought against the Bolsheviks and now are detained in the prisons of Soviet Russia" in any agreement they might negotiate with the Bolsheviks, and warned that he could not order "those who consider it a dishonor to accept an amnesty at the hands of the enemy."[45] At the same time, he opened negotiations with the French to develop new sources for armaments and munitions. With no cash and almost no economic resources, Wrangel could offer only extremely speculative enticements, but the richness of the possible returns helped to offset the risk. To attract credits to buy munitions, Wrangel therefore offered the French access to the vast resources of South Russia: the coal of the Donbas, the oil of Baku, and the grain of the Taurida and Kuban.[46] None of them lay within his control, but he hoped to conquer them all that summer.

To win supporters for Wrangel's program in Paris, Struve began to speak of "attaching vast significance to the correlation between Russian interests and the economic interests of the Allied Powers, especially France."[47] With the help of Vladimir Burtsev (publisher of a weekly Russian newspaper in Paris and one of the few Russian socialists who had sided with the Whites from the beginning of the Civil War), Maurice Paléologue (formerly France's ambassador to Russia and presently secretary general of the French Foreign Ministry), and Eugène Petit (chief of chancery to the new French prime minister Alexandre Millerand), he launched an intensive propaganda campaign in Europe that warned against dealing with the Bolsheviks and emphasized the progressive policies of Wrangel's government.[48] The Whites in South Russia thus began to play their allies against each other for the first time. Denikin had stubbornly refused to engage in such maneuvers to better his political and military situation; Wrangel had no such compunctions.

The French made Wrangel's task easier by urging the Allies to support the border states of Eastern Europe against the Bolsheviks just as the British called for an end to the conflict and a reopening of East–West trade. As it had been since the eighteenth century, Poland remained the focus of France's interest in Eastern Europe, and Piłsudski had no intention of making peace with Lenin's government that spring. When the French hinted that they would help Wrangel as part of a broader effort to support Poland's attack against Russia, Krivoshein and Paléologue began to speak not only of joint action against the Red Army but even of subordinating troops to the Polish High Command.[49] The Russians could not have chosen a better moment to make such an approach to the French; Krivoshein held his first meeting with Paléologue on the very day that Piłsudski's armies crossed the Dnepr at Kiev.[50]

With Piłsudski's legions facing Moscow, the Bolshevik High Command had to shift the forces they had been massing against Wrangel's Crimean bastion to the Ukrainian and Polish fronts. This offered the Whites a priceless opportunity to establish defensive beachheads on the mainland and improve their food supplies. After more than two years of watching opportunities slip away from his predecessors, Wrangel now moved quickly. He had assembled every available weapon and shell within reach during his two months as supreme commander, and he therefore had considerably more resources at hand than his memoirs would have us believe. His fighting forces numbered just under thirty-two thousand infantry and cavalry, supported by more than 100 pieces of artillery, 630 machine guns, three dozen tanks and armored cars, 4 armored trains, and 24 airplanes.[51] Perhaps most important, he had taken men who had stood at the brink of defeat and restored their will to fight. "In place of the bony specter of death," he wrote later, "there now flamed a radiant vision of victory."[52]

As Piłsudski's columns advanced, Wrangel ordered his newly strengthened forces into action. "The Russian Army marches to liberate its native land from the Red vermin," he proclaimed. "Help me, Russian people! Help me to save our motherland!"[53] To delay a rupture with the British, Wrangel insisted that his forces advance "not with any aggressive intention but solely to obtain food" from the rich grain-growing Northern Taurida that lay just beyond his Crimean refuge. The British knew otherwise. "General Wrangel," the permanent under-secretary of the Foreign Office remarked crossly, "seems to be engaged in a crooked game and to be hoodwinking us in order to gain time."[54] A strong supporter of Wrangel, England's high commissioner at Constantinople openly regretted his superiors' decision to "withhold support from [Wrangel's] disciplined, organized, and efficient force."[55] Yet Wrangel's supporters among Britain's generals, admirals, and diplomats could not alter their government's stand. Should he advance into Northern Taurida, Lord Curzon warned Wrangel flatly, "His Majesty's Government will be unable to concern themselves any further with the fate of your army."[56] The break between the Whites and their British allies that Denikin had avoided at all costs had come. "British Naval forces," the Admiralty telegraphed sternly to its high commissioner at Constantinople on June 11, "are to afford no, repeat no, support to Wrangel in offence or defence."[57]

Without the British, and not yet certain of the French, who continued to promise much but deliver little, Wrangel moved forward alone and in deadly earnest at the beginning of June. For at least a fortnight, his counterintelligence staff had been sending false signals to deceive the Bolsheviks into thinking that his main attack would be a seaborne assault in the vicinity of Odessa, Novocherkassk, or Khorly, where the Whites had attempted a landing in mid-April.[58] In fact, he planned to concentrate his forces considerably further east. General Iakov Slashchëv's Second Corps of slightly more than six thousand men would open Wrangel's offensive with a landing at Kirilovka in the rear of the Thirteenth Red Army. Then, General Pisarëv would follow with an attack across the railway bridge that spanned the Sivash at Chongar, and the main White force under General Kutepov would launch a frontal assault against the Thirteenth Red Army from Perekop. Coming in the midst of a heavy summer storm at dawn on June 6, Slashchëv's landing, which included artillery and several tanks and armored cars, took his opponents so completely by surprise that his advance units reached the Sevastopol-Melitopol Railway, some twenty miles south of Melitopol, that same evening.[59] The next day, Pisarëv opened an artillery barrage and took up the attack at the Chongar Bridge, while Kutepov, supported by artillery, tanks, two armored trains, and Wrangel's small air force broke out of his fortifications at Perekop.[60]

As his commanders reported victory after victory, Wrangel looked for heroes to personify the new Russian Army he had brought into being. On the second day of the fighting, he bestowed his new medal of honor, the Order of St. Nicholas the Miracle Worker, upon a tank lieutenant, and the high command drank champagne in his honor.[61] Three days later, Slashchëv took Melitopol, the provincial capital of the Northern Taurida, while Pisarëv and Kutepov continued to drive back the weakened Thirteenth Red Army. Even the most optimistic Whites had not expected success to come so swiftly or completely. "The Reds are retreating!" one delighted officer wrote in his diary. "The gates of the Crimea have been thrown wide open!"[62] As thousands of prisoners and captured weapons poured into the Crimea during the next few weeks, it seemed as if the White movement had found new life, yet Wrangel, the dispassionate Baltic German, knew too well the extent of his success and the limits of his followers' dedication. "Russians are inclined to shift from deep depression to joyous optimism in a single moment," he wrote later. "Those who only recently had thought of the Crimea as a tomb now regarded it as an impregnable fortress."[63]

By the middle of June, Wrangel's armies held the left bank of the Dnepr from Aleshka to the vicinity of Nikopol and had established a defensive line from that point southeastward to Berdiansk on the Sea of Azov. They had doubled the territory under their control in a fortnight and had won rich stores of meat, grain, and horses. "Every success of the Wrangel rebels, no matter how small or temporary, threatens us with still greater calamities," the Bolsheviks' Central Committee reported to senior party officials. Wrangel's forces now posed a serious danger to Russia's grain, coal, and oil supplies. "We can delay no longer," they concluded. "Wrangel must be destroyed."[64] That that task would prove more difficult than the Bolsheviks wanted to believe became clear when the Red High Command ordered a counteroffensive against the Whites at the end of June. Within a week, Wrangel's troops smashed their attackers' front and cut to pieces the elite Red Cavalry led by the Donbas miner Dmitrii Zhloba. By the beginning of July, the Bolsheviks knew that they had to take the reborn White Army seriously. Yet, as the numbers of Red Army soared past five million that summer, they also must have sensed the fragility of Wrangel's early summer triumphs. Certainly, his former allies spoke of that hard and certain truth among themselves, and perhaps none did so more sadly than Winston Churchill, the most ardent defender of intervention in England's War Office. "As soon as the Bolsheviks are able to divert their main strength from Poland," he warned his colleagues in the cabinet, "they will crush him."[65] "A new figure of unusual energy and quality," Churchill wrote a few years later, Wrangel "too late had reached first place in White Russian counsels."[66]

On a number of occasions, Wrangel had criticized Denikin for his ill-planned, precipitous race toward Moscow in the summer and fall of 1919. Now, as the temptation to continue his advance into the Ukraine rose before him, he remained determined not to outrun his lines of supply. Although he could draw food supplies from the Northern Taurida, he remained critically short of men, weapons, and ammunition, and despite their victories, some of his senior commanders had proved less reliable than he had hoped. By far the worst was General Slashchëv, who always carried a caged crow into battle for good luck.[67] When Slashchëv visited his headquarters that summer, Wrangel found him "thoroughly addicted to narcotics and alcohol," a man who had crossed that fragile boundary that separates eccentricity from madness. When he returned Slashchëv's visit the following day, Wrangel found the commander of his Second Corps sprawled amid a jumble of liquor bottles. Despite the summer heat, Slashchëv wore a fantastical uniform made out of a long white Turkish robe trimmed with gold lace and fur and shared his quarters with a menagerie of tame birds. "There was a crane and a raven, a swallow, and also a starling," Wrangel noted in amazement. "They were hopping about on the table and the sofa," he added, "fluttering here and there and perching on their master's head and shoulders." Appalled, yet pitying Slashchëv's fallen state, Wrangel ordered a doctor to examine him. "His appearance left me with no doubt," he stated firmly, "that I was dealing with a man completely overcome by mental illness."[68] With strong reassurances of his personal affection, but firmly insistent that one of the Whites' best fighting generals needed medical treatment, Wrangel relieved Slashchëv of his command.

Although Wrangel had lessened his food supply problems by taking the Northern Taurida, he still required other resources to keep his army in the field. He needed foreign oil and coal to fuel his fleet, and his new French allies continued to be anything but generous in extending credits without security. In mid-July, Struve reported that Millerand had insisted that he could not even extend de facto recognition until Wrangel's government agreed "to recognize all financial obligations of previous Russian governments corresponding to the territory presently occupied."[69] Soon, the French demanded even more. Before they would extend armaments credits to Wrangel, they insisted that he open his ministries of Finance, Trade, and Industry to French agents and grant them monopolies in South Russia that included control of its customs and railroads.[70] For raw materials that he could exchange directly for weapons and supplies, Wrangel therefore again turned toward the Kuban, the scene of the Whites' Icy March in 1918 and their refuge during much of the Civil War. There, he expected to take advantage of the powerful anti-Soviet guerrilla movement that had gathered some fifteen thousand insurgents into the Caucasian foothills after the Reds had driven the Whites from Ekaterinodar that March. By adding these insurgents to his armed forces and by sweeping the Kuban free of Bolsheviks, Wrangel hoped to exchange his newly won economic base in the Northern Taurida for the much richer Kuban.[71]

Eager to return to their native fields, the Kuban Cossacks held the key to the summer campaign that Wrangel launched under the command of the Cossack General Ulagai. An officer whom Wrangel once described as "a man of exemplary courage and great military talents . . . [who] understood the art of getting out of difficult situations and knew how to take advantage of them,"[72] Ulagai stood out as one of those rare men whose integrity had remained unblemished throughout the Civil War. He could lead the often rebellious Cossacks into battle and be counted upon to prevent the looting that Wrangel so despised, but his failing was that he responded too slowly to new tactical situations and could not change strategy as the shifting sands of Civil War campaigns often required. "When he took on a task, he seemed to look for obstacles which would hinder its completion," Wrangel later wrote, "but once he made up his mind, he would carry out his decision brilliantly."[73]

Evidently Ulagai's ability to prevent the plundering that had made Denikin's army so unpopular in the Kuban and South Russia the year before overshadowed Wrangel's doubts about his faults. "I knew about his weaknesses, [especially] his lack of organizational ability," Wrangel later wrote, "[but] I was so completely occupied by political questions and the problems of commanding our troops on the northern front, that I gave little attention to how my generals . . . executed the plan [for the campaign in the Kuban]."[74] Ulagai and his commanders also had no sense about security. Unlike Slashchëv's surprise landing at Kirilovka at the beginning of June, Ulagai's plans for invading the Kuban soon became an open secret. "People are discussing the landing openly in the bazaars," one of Wrangel's worried staff officers confided to his diary a few days before Ulagai's soldiers embarked.[75] Everyone ignored the false information with which Wrangel's General Staff hoped to draw the enemy's attention away from Ulagai's landing site.[76] Red and White alike knew where and when Ulagai's landing would take place and made their plans accordingly.

Ulagai's landing at Primorsko-Akhtarskaia on August 13 brought more than four thousand horses and sixteen thousand men, about half of whom were noncombatants, to the Kuban coast.[77] Confident of victory, Ulagai had allowed a horde of support groups and refugees who wanted to return home to accompany his combat units to the Kuban, and the sea of civilians that flowed in his wake threatened more dangers than any sensible commander should have taken on. "General Ulagai's gigantic staff . . . gave the impression of a disorderly mob of people chosen at random," Wrangel wrote when he described the worries that plagued him as he watched their embarkation. "An enormous number of Kuban refugees trailed along after the troops," he added. "The crowding at the embarkation point was unbelievable . . . [and] some of the young military cadets actually fainted from lack of air."[78]

After announcing that "only a decisive advance can bring us success," and that "our base is in the Kuban, we have burned our ships,"[79] Ulagai left his host of refugees and huge reserves of arms, ammunition, and provisions at Primorsko-Akhtarskaia and seized the important railroad junction at Timoshevskaia, some fifty miles inland and only thirty miles north of Ekaterinodar. For a moment it seemed that he might press forward, seize Ekaterinodar, and link up with the partisan Army of the Regeneration of Russia that had operated in the Caucasian foothills to the southeast since the Reds had taken Ekaterinodar in March. Yet the horde of camp followers at his rear did not allow him to think only of the road ahead. Ulagai therefore hesitated at Timoshevskaia and then withdrew toward Primorsko-Akhtarskaia, hoping to strengthen his strike force with more local peasants and Cossacks before he tried to take Ekaterinodar.[80]

The days Ulagai wasted at Timoshevskaia allowed the Bolsheviks to gather their forces and seize the initiative. "People of the Don and the Kuban! If you want a peaceful life and the chance to work in peace, help the Red Army crush the White Guard bands of Wrangel the Last-Born at the water's very edge," Trotskii exclaimed as his special train raced toward the south to meet Wrangel's new threat.[81] "The Kuban has not risen to greet Wrangel!" he rejoiced three days later. "The Kuban has turned its back on this German baron."[82] On September 7, scarcely three weeks after his first landing, the Reds drove Ulagai's forces from the Kuban. Thanks to the Red Army deserters he recruited, Ulagai returned to the Crimea with more men than he had taken, but Wrangel's effort to establish a stronger, richer territorial base lay in shambles.[83] "The number of mouths that the government had to feed now came to something like two hundred and fifty or three hundred thousand, [and] the cost of feeding all these people far exceeded our resources," Wrangel remembered sadly. "Grain remained our sole export," he continued. "Our hopes for a foreign loan had become very dim, for the future of the government of South Russia seemed extremely precarious."[84]

Certain that the Bolsheviks would mass their forces against him if they made peace with the Poles, Wrangel decided to press his northern front deeper into the grain-rich Ukraine, support the Poles against their common enemy, and keep Piłsudski at war with the Red Army. "If Poland accepted the peace that the government of Lloyd George insisted upon and that was being put forth so urgently by the Bolsheviks, it would have been the end for us,"

Wrangel later explained. "Once freed from the western front, three and a half Bolshevik armies would have been able to fall upon us, and the outcome of such an attack could easily be foreseen."[85] Fearful that the Poles would accept the Bolsheviks' offer of peace once Piłsudski had driven the Red Army back from Warsaw, Wrangel planned a new offensive that would carry his armies across the Dnepr and link them up with the reluctant Poles before Soviet diplomats enticed them into an armistice.

Although the Allies had showered aid upon Denikin when he had launched his ill-fated offensive against Moscow the year before, they gave Wrangel only the most meager support for his coming campaign in the southern Ukraine. The British had become so stubborn in refusing support to the Whites that they would not even allow private businessmen to sell Wrangel's quartermasters used saddles and bridles,[86] and the French, still vociferous in their talk about aid, continued to send very little. Now garbed in a sad assortment of tattered uniforms combined with odd shirts and trousers, Wrangel's men lived from day to day, always short of food, clothing, weapons, and ammunition. "What terrible, scandalous destitution the men suffered," Wrangel lamented when he reviewed them at the beginning of September. "[Yet] they marched with firm and vigorous steps," he added proudly, "as if the regiments of Old Russia had arisen from the grave."[87] Unlike Denikin's shattered armies a few months before, these men still believed in themselves and had the will to fight.

To relieve the pressure from the Thirteenth Red Army against his northeast flank at the beginning of September, Wrangel attacked Mariupol on the Sea of Azov. As he pressed his attack to the north and east, his forces advanced into the Ukraine and approached what remained of Makhno's main base at Guliai Pole.[88] So unwilling to strike an alliance with the hated *zolotopogonshchiki* that he hanged Wrangel's emissary, Makhno negotiated a truce with the Reds and sent a brigade-strength partisan force against the Whites.[89] At first it seemed that the clever partisan leader had chosen the losing side. When White cavalry detachments raided the important rail junction of Sinelnikovo to the east of Ekaterinoslav, captured the ancient Cossack stronghold at Khortitsa, and seized the important river town of Aleksandrovsk at the beginning of October, it began to look as if Wrangel had successfully defied those who had so confidently predicted his army's demise.

Success seemed even more possible when Wrangel's forces

crossed the Dnepr on October 8, the day after his raid against Sinelnikovo, and established a bridgehead some fifteen miles deep on the right bank of the Dnepr within the first twenty-four hours. Out of the tangle of contradictory reports that poured into Moscow, Trotskii even concluded that Wrangel might now survive the winter. "[They have] much experience, great initiative, and a lot of guts," he wrote of Wrangel's forces. "The struggle for the Black Sea coast is going to take a number of weeks and, if the campaign does not require the entire winter, it will in any case last well into the winter months."[90] Trotskii's fears proved groundless, for Wrangel's success continued for only two more days. As his commanders lost their nerve against counterattacks by heavy Red reinforcements, Wrangel's exhausted armies stumbled back across the Dnepr on October 13, only to learn that the Poles had signed an armistice with the Soviets at Riga the day before.[91] "We are now alone in a struggle that will decide the fate not only of our country but of the whole of humanity," Wrangel told his soldiers. "Our brothers in the Red butchers' dungeons put their faith in you; and I, your old comrade-in-arms, trust my invincible eagles. This is not the first time that we have waged unequal warfare," he concluded. "God stands on the side of right, not might."[92]

Wrangel now mustered every man and weapon to meet the Reds' attack. Counting his reserves, he had 23,070 infantry and 11,795 cavalry, supported by just more than 200 field guns, 1,663 machine guns, 14 armored trains, 45 armored cars and tanks, and 42 planes.[93] The quality of men and machines had deteriorated since his first victories in the Northern Taurida. Armored cars, tanks, and planes had been reduced to a desperate state of disrepair by the last month of fighting, and some of his best commanders, including the brilliant cavalryman General Babiev, had been killed. Although the numbers of fighting men under Wrangel's command remained relatively constant, the heavy casualties of the summer's campaigns had forced him to replace seasoned veterans with Red Army captives, recruits, and draftees who had neither the experience nor the dedication that three years of Civil War had forged in the men whose places they had to fill. As the strategic situation became more desperate, and as the pressures of a society under siege weighed more heavily upon them, too many of Wrangel's soldiers began to think only of escape.

Inexperienced front-line troops turned their thoughts to the rear because they understood that raw self-interest had overwhelmed the spirit of self-sacrifice among the Crimea's civilians. As those vices that fed upon the misery of the unfortunate sank their roots into the decaying hopes of Russia's last Whites, only things related to survival retained any value. Trade in gold, precious stones, passports, and exit visas flourished, and the prices of food, medicines, and shelter soared. People began to know real hunger for the first time since Wrangel had taken command, and they now suffered as their Red brethren had done during the previous two winters. "We are dying of hunger," one desperate wife wrote to her husband at the front. "We have sold everything we had. I have only my body left to sell." Such letters shattered the morale of even the most hardened fighters, and men began to talk about leaving the front to shoot "all those worthless bastards in the rear."[94] As White soldiers turned their thoughts away from the enemy at the front, the moral and strategic initiative shifted to the Red High Command. Red soldiers now felt confident of victory. The genius of the commanders who led them gave them every reason to feel that way.

On September 27, Mikhail Frunze, the Bolshevik millhand-turned-general, had arrived in Kharkov to take command of the southern front. Fresh from a string of triumphs that stretched from Siberia to Turkestan, the iron-willed Frunze was not a man to accept anything short of victory. "Wrangel must be smashed, and that is what the armies of the southern front are going to accomplish," he announced in his first general order. "The victory of the workers' army, despite all the efforts of our enemies, is inevitable. So let's get down to work!"[95] By the end of October, Frunze's infantry outnumbered Wrangel's by more than four to one, his cavalry enjoyed a superiority of three to one, and the artillery a margin of better than two to one.[96] The Reds had a thousand more machine guns than did the Whites, and although the numbers of tanks, armored cars, armored trains, and planes on each side remained about equal, the Reds' were of higher quality and in much better repair. Perhaps most important of all, Frunze had better troops. As thousands of trade union activists and dedicated party members joined the fight, the portion of Frunze's soldiers who belonged to the Bolshevik Party or were candidates for membership rose to one in eight.[97]

White commanders always fought to bring more Russian territory under their control, but Frunze fought only to destroy the enemies of his Soviet government. "Our task is not the occupation of territory," he told one of his commanders, "but the destruction of the living forces of the enemy."[98] To do so, he called upon some of the Red Army's best commanders. On Frunze's orders, Budënnyi brought his Konarmiia to the South as soon as it could be released from the Polish front. Even before he arrived, Vasilii Bliukher, the poor wagonmaker whose tactical genius had won him high praise in the fighting against Kolchak, added his legendary Fifty-first Division to Frunze's forces. Seriously wounded during the Great Retreat of 1915, Bliukher had been discharged from the tsarist army some two years before the Revolution, had taken up arms for the Bolsheviks in 1918, and had performed such feats of valor that he became the first recipient of the Bolsheviks' new Order of the Red Banner. Now, against Wrangel, he was about to win still greater acclaim.

In a desperate effort to defend his grain supply, Wrangel and his generals decided to hold the Northern Taurida against the likes of Bliukher, Frunze, and Budënnyi rather than retreat into the Crimean bastion that offered more protection. "Not only would a retreat . . . into the Crimean Peninsula have condemned us to hunger and privation, but it would have been a sign of our inability to continue an active struggle," he explained later. "Once shut up in the Crimea, we would have ceased to be a danger to the Soviet Government and would have lost all interest in the eyes of the Western Powers." Yet, in fighting the Reds outside the Crimea, Wrangel risked being cut off from his fortress by the powerful forces that Frunze had positioned on his left flank at the Kakhovka bridgehead. The risks were huge, the chances for success very small. "It was a desperate gamble," Wrangel confessed, "but any other decision inevitably would have brought us immediately to the end."[99]

Before the end of October, Frunze had deployed five armies—the Fourth, Sixth, and Thirteenth Red Armies, and the First and Second Red Cavalry Armies supported by Makhno's partisan forces—in a shallow arc that stretched from Kherson at the mouth of the Dnepr on his western flank to Nogaisk on the Sea of Azov some two hundred and fifty miles to the east. Confident that he could break Wrangel's front, and hopeful that he could cut off his retreating armies before they reached the Crimea,[100] Frunze planned to attack the Whites along the eastern two-thirds of his front, while Budënnyi's Konarmiia (the First Cavalry Army), would advance toward Perekop and the Sivash from Kakhovka to cut off the Whites' escape. When the first Red units stormed forward at daybreak on October 28, the temperature had fallen to fifteen degrees below freezing.[101]

"There had not been such a frost in the Crimea for decades," Wrangel wrote when he recalled how the temperatures tormented his men that day and for more than a fortnight afterward.[102] In Moscow, Lenin called for more boots and greatcoats to be sent to Frunze's soldiers and insisted that only the "shortage of warm clothing and footwear" stood between the Red Army and victory.[103] On the other side, Wrangel's men could only stuff their shirts with straw. Their ragged uniforms had barely survived the summer. They had nothing more to protect themselves from the unexpected cold.

Wrangel's ragged soldiers gave way slowly before the great weight of the Red Army during the next week of bitter fighting, and Frunze's first assault failed to produce the triumph he had anticipated. Bliukher's and Budënnyi's forces had advanced more than seventy-five miles in less than three days in a desperate effort to reach the railroad that could cut Wrangel's line of retreat into the Crimea, but the Red units to their east had to fight for every piece of ground and moved more slowly. "I am amazed at the enormous energy of the enemy's resistance," Frunze reported to his superiors in Moscow. "There is no doubt that he fought more fiercely and stubbornly than any other army could have."[104] Wrangel's retreating army therefore won the race to the Crimea, where the desperate efforts of military cadets and headquarters units prevented Bliukher's riflemen from taking the Salkovo Pass and bursting through the first line of defenses at Perekop.[105] Yet the Whites paid dearly for their brief successes. As they battered their way through the Northern Taurida, Frunze's forces took nearly twenty thousand prisoners, a hundred field guns, a great number of machine guns, tens of thousands of shells, and millions of rifle cartridges.[106] "The army remained intact," Wrangel later reported, "but its fighting abilities were not what they had been." Nor had the food supply for which he had risked so much been saved. More than thirty-six thousand tons of grain that Wrangel's quartermasters had stockpiled from the fall harvest at railheads in Melitopol and Genichesk fell into Frunze's hands.[107]

By failing to encircle Wrangel's army before it reached the Crimea, Frunze had missed his best chance to score a decisive victory. Now obliged to storm the Whites' Crimean fortress, he added more weight to his forces and sent the aerial photographers who had joined his recently strengthened air force to chart Wrangel's line of defenses.[108] By the end of the first week in November, he had assembled 188,771 men, supported by nearly three thousand machine guns, over six hundred field guns, and twenty-three armored trains, to attack the 26,000 White regulars and 16,000 ill-armed reserves who manned the Crimea's defenses.[109]

Frunze planned his main attack against the Turkish Wall, an eighteenth-century Turkish barrier along which Wrangel had strung heavily sheltered machine gun and artillery emplacements, all with interlocking fields of fire that concentrated upon the heavy barbed wire barriers that comprised the first line of defenses at Perekop. Behind them, the Whites' remaining armored trains could move back and forth along the recently extended Sevastopol-Iushun-Armiansk branch railroad to keep the wall's approaches under fire from their heavy guns.[110] When Frunze ordered Bliukher's Fifty-first Division to lead the attack, Bliukher concentrated his riflemen so heavily that in some places he had one man for every forty-three inches of front and a machine gun to support every seventeen men. On Bliukher's left, facing the salt marshes of the Sivash and the Chongar Bridge slightly further to the east, Frunze placed Budënnyi's Konarmiia, the Fourth Red Army, and Makhno's partisans, while he held the better part of three armies in reserve.[111] According to Soviet accounts, these forces all were in a fighting mood, ready to celebrate the third anniversary of the Bolshevik Revolution on November 7 by defeating the last major White force on Russian soil.

Despite the men and weapons that Frunze had assembled for the coming battle, the sense of defeat that had overwhelmed Denikin and the Whites at Novorossiisk at the end of 1919 had not yet infected the defenders of the Crimea. Wrangel had begun to make preparations for a massive evacuation, but he had done so quietly and had gone to great lengths to mask his purpose. "The measures we had taken had calmed the anxieties that had been aroused," he later wrote. "Behind the lines all remained calm because everyone believed in the impregnability of the Perekop fortifications."[112] Wrangel's recollections did not exaggerate. The newspapers of the Crimea still spoke confidently of the defenses that guarded the Perekop Isthmus, the Chongar Bridge, and the shoreline in between. "The fortifications of the Sivash and Perekop are so strong that the Red High Command has neither the men nor the machines to breach them," the newspaper *Vremia* (The Times), promised on November 4. "All the armed forces of Sovdepia together cannot frighten the Crimea."[113] Perhaps still hoping to halt Frunze, but more intent upon buying enough time to carry out an orderly evacuation, Wrangel unified his First and Second armies under General Kutepov, the best and most durable of his remaining front-line commanders. Universally known for his vicious cruelty toward Bolsheviks and Bolshevik sympathizers, and widely suspected of taking huge bribes in return for export and import permits when he had been in charge of Novorossiisk,[114] Kutepov nonetheless held Wrangel's full confidence as a commander who "could deal with any situation, a man of great military prowess and exceptional tenacity in pursuing what he set out to accomplish."[115] Kutepov would hold the Turkish Wall if any man could. If he could not, then Wrangel would know for certain that the end had come.[116]

After giving the last of his orders for the disposition of his troops on the morning of November 7, Frunze went to Budënnyi's headquarters, where he, Budënnyi, and Voroshilov drafted a special telegram to congratulate Lenin on the third anniversary of the Bolshevik Revolution and to promise him a final victory for the occasion. "In the name of the armies of the southern front, now having made ready to deliver the final blow against the den of the mortally wounded beast, and in the name of the renowned eagles of the First Cavalry Army," they began, "greetings. Our iron-hard infantry, daring cavalry, invincible artillery [and] clear-sighted, swift airmen . . . will free this last bit of Soviet land from all enemies," they promised Lenin.[117] Perhaps more than any other unit in South Russia, Bliukher's Fifty-first Division merited those superlatives, and it was upon its frontal assault against the Turkish Wall defenses that Frunze, Voroshilov, and Budënnyi counted to break open to Wrangel's Crimean bastion. Yet the unforeseen and the unexpected aided their cause more than any amount of valor could have done. Nature, whose forces had so tormented the people of Bolshevik Russia for the past two bitter winters, this time took the Bolsheviks' side and opened for them new avenues of attack that no one had anticipated.

Perhaps only twice or thrice in a lifetime, a strong wind blows toward the Crimea from the northwest and forces the shallow waters that cover the Sivash salt flats eastward to expose the foul-smelling mud that lies beneath. On November 7, 1920, nature combined such a raging wind with temperatures so severe that, on the night of November 7–8, the Sivash's rarely exposed mud bottom froze hard enough to support men and horses. At ten o'clock that evening, while most of Bliukher's Fifty-first Division were preparing to assault Kutepov's positions along the Turkish Wall, the Fifteenth and Fifty-second Rifle Divisions along with the Fifty-First Division's One Hundred Fifty-third Rifle and Cavalry Brigades moved to take advantage of this unforeseen opportunity. Heavy fog swirled around them and obscured their approach from Wrangel's lookouts on the Lithuanian Peninsula as they advanced across the four miles of the Sivash. All too quickly the feet of the leading ranks of men and horses churned the frozen sea bottom into freezing muck, forced those who followed to slow their advance, and increased the chances for discovery. Nonetheless, the entire force reached dry land undetected just as the direction of the wind changed and the water began to rise.

As dawn broke on November 8, Frunze's mud-soaked soldiers attacked the weak forces that Wrangel had left on the Lithuanian Peninsula to guard against the improbability of an amphibious attack. What commanders on both sides had expected to be an obscure corner of the battle for the Crimea now became its key as Kutepov ordered counterattacks to support the peninsula's defenders just when Bliukher's Fifty-first Division moved forward against the Turkish Wall. All day the battle's outcome remained uncertain, and the Red and White positions seemed equally perilous. Should Bliukher's assault troops fail, it would be a simple matter for Kutepov to turn and destroy the small Red force that threatened his rear from the Lithuanian Peninsula now that the sea waters had returned to the Sivash and Frunze could neither reinforce nor recall it. On the other hand, should Bliukher's attack succeed and should the Reds advance beyond the Lithuanian Peninsula, Kutepov's main force risked encirclement by a far stronger enemy. The outcome depended upon Bliukher breaking through the defenses at the Turkish Wall and the ability of the Red forces on the Lithuanian Peninsula to hold until he could do so.

After delaying for several hours because of the thick fog, Bliukher opened his first artillery barrages against the Turkish Wall just as the units that had crossed the Sivash reached the Lithuanian Peninsula. Four hours later, his infantry moved ahead. At first, no amount of supporting fire seemed able to diminish the firestorm that Kutepov's artillery and machine gunners unleashed upon their attackers. In some of Bliukher's regiments, casualties soared to sixty percent as murderous gunfire drove back three successive waves of infantry. Only at half past three o'clock on the morning of November 9 did the Fifty-first Division's fourth assault overwhelm the wall's defenders. "A mountain fell from my shoulders," Frunze later confessed. "With the capture of Perekop the danger of the two divisions that had been cut off by the rising waters of the Sivash being destroyed slipped away."[118]

Frunze's relief marked the beginning of Wrangel's darkest hours. "General Kutepov reported that, in view of the developing situation—the enemy's penetration of our position at Perekop, and the danger of being surrounded—he had just given the order for a retreat to the next line of fortified positions," Wrangel wrote of the evening of November 9 when he received word that the Turkish Wall had fallen. "We were at the brink of disaster," he concluded. "The limits of the army's ability to resist already had been exceeded, and fortifications could stop the enemy no longer. Urgent measures were needed to rescue the army and the civilian population."[119]

In sharp contrast to Denikin's wretchedly botched withdrawal from Novorossiisk the year before, Wrangel had planned for evacuation while he had worked for victory. He therefore had sufficient reserves of coal and oil to fuel every ship over which the Whites had control, and he now moved to stretch every resource to the utmost. "The least hesitation, the slightest blunder, could ruin everything," he warned.[120] On November 11, he ordered all White ships to previously selected embarkation points: some to Evpatoriia, some to Sevastopol and Ialta, and still others to Feodosiia and Kerch. Then, while Kutepov fought rear-guard actions to slow the Reds' advance, Wrangel made the last of his preparations. All the sick and wounded, then government officials, civilians, and the entire armed forces must be evacuated before the Reds arrived. The next day, Wrangel gave his final orders. Troops were to break away from the enemy and move to the nearest ports of embarkation, leaving all heavy supplies and heavy weapons behind, while "all those who have shared with the army its journey to Calvary"—the soldiers' families, the families of civil officials, and "anyone else who might be in danger if they fell into the hands of the enemy"—were to proceed to the ports with them.[121]

It was brilliant evidence of Wrangel's ability to control troops and civilians that the evacuation took place with a minimum of panic and disorder. By midafternoon on November 14, Sevastopol had been evacuated, and having received word that the evacuation of Evpatoriia also had been accomplished, Wrangel left the quay and boarded the cruiser *General Kornilov*, which was to carry him into exile. At Ialta, the same scene was repeated at nine o'clock the next morning. The following morning it was repeated again at Feodosiia, and, a few hours later, yet again at Kerch. By four o'clock on the afternoon of November 16, 1920, the last of the Whites—145,693 men, women, and children—were aboard 126 ships en route to Constantinople. By then the rare November cold had lifted, and the southern sun warmed the ships' decks. "I felt an immense weight lift from my heart," Wrangel confessed later. Then, for him and for the masses of refugees with him, came sadness. "Farewell, my homeland!" he wrote as he recalled those last moments three years later.[122] "Farewell, Russia!" another of the passengers aboard the *General Kornilov* added in his diary.[123] As the shores of the Crimea slipped beyond the horizon, the White crusade that General Alekseev had proclaimed against the Reds on the day of Lenin's victory three years and nine days before had reached its end.

The Reds reveled in their victory. "Our triumphant Red standards are now firmly planted on the shores of the Crimea . . . [and] the last stronghold and hope of the Russian bourgeoisie and their foreign capitalist accomplices has been destroyed," Frunze announced to his troops on the day after Wrangel turned his flotilla toward Constantinople. "Long live the valiant Red Army! Long live the final worldwide victory of Communism!"[124] No less a voice than Maiakovskii's spread Frunze's news across Soviet Russia. "Glory to you, O heroes who wear the Red star," he exclaimed triumphantly. "To you, comrades—Glory, Glory, Glory!—Forever and ever!"[125]

Each in its turn, White armies in North Russia, in the Northwest, in Siberia, in the Ukraine, and in South Russia had stumbled and broken apart as the Bolsheviks had spread their control outward from Russia's Red center during 1919 and 1920. The armies of Poland had been held in check, and the remnants of Makhno's insurgent army, which now broke its temporary alliance with the Reds and left the Crimea to renew its fight against the Bolsheviks in the Ukraine, would be crushed in another few months. The Bolsheviks had fought against armies supported by the strongest nations on earth, had survived the struggle, and now wielded power in nearly all of the lands from which Russia's emperors had claimed allegiance in the days when they had held sway over a sixth of the earth's surface and the sun never had set upon their domains. Lenin had every right to claim, as he did in a speech celebrating the third anniversary of the October Revolution, that "despite the unparalleled efforts of our enemies, we have won," and that the victory he invited his comrades to celebrate was "a gigantic victory, one that previously none of us would have believed possible."[126]

Although the Bolsheviks' "second gathering of the Russian lands" was nearing an end as Wrangel's ships steamed away from their Crimean ports, some of the most glittering gems in the imperial crown had yet to be returned to Russia's new Soviet masters. Between the Black Sea and the Caspian, just to the south of the Kuban territory that had formed the heartland of Denikin's Russia, lay the Transcaucasus, the fabled lands of Georgia, Armenia, and Azerbaidjan. Thence, Jason and his Argonauts had sailed in their quest for the Golden Fleece, and there Prometheus had been chained. From the lands of Azerbaidjan, the ancient sage Zoroaster had first spoken, and out of the fusion of Persia with Azerbaidjan (called Media by the ancients) had come the empire of Cyrus the Great.[127] Further to the east, Turkestan stretched from the Caspian more than fifteen hundred miles east to China. Through its mountain passes, the Huns had traveled in their migration from the Chinese plains to Europe. The great Asian conqueror Tamerlane had taken the same route, crossing the Pass of a Thousand Stones, in which, according to legend, he had ordered each man to place a stone upon a pile from which, on his return, each would remove one so that those which remained would serve as a monument to those who had fallen in battle.[128] Its deserts and steppes cut by six great rivers along which fields of cotton, wheat, and rice flourished, Turkestan had been the last addition to Russia's domains, with some of the last conquests coming a scant quarter-century before the Revolution.

For centuries, Turkestan's key cities of Tashkent, Samarkand, Bukhara, Kokand, and Khiva had flourished as great centers of trade and culture between East and West. In the days when it was renowned as the center of Central Asia's trade, nearly five hundred mosques and centers of religious study had crowded behind the eight miles of earthen walls that surrounded Bukhara. A hundred and sixty miles to the east, Samarkand, which already had celebrated its millennium when Tamerlane had made it his capital in 1369, had entertained Alexander the Great in earlier times. There, not far from the site from which the massive sky blue dome of his tomb, the Gur-Emir, would rise one day, Tamerlane had built the Mosque of Bibi-Khanum in honor of his favorite wife.[129] Hosts to a dozen conquerors, but now only pale shadows of their former greatness, these ancient cities held the key to Bolshevik control in the vast Turkestan lands. In Tashkent and the surrounding region resided a comparative handful of Russian workers and soldiers (a bit more than ten percent of the region's population), whose political activism allowed them to dominate the region's illiterate and inarticulate Moslem majority. Samarkand, Bukhara, Khiva, and Kokand remained the focus of the traditional Moslem and anti-Russian influences that opposed Turkestan's handful of Russian Bolsheviks in their attempt to link their destiny to that of Russia.

Rich in history, these lands were even richer in natural resources, not the least of which were the world's largest oilfields at Baku and the sprawling cottonfields of Turkestan. Fought over for centuries by Russia and her neighbors, these regions held vital riches that no Russian ruler could be without, and they commanded key gateways into the Russian heartland that no responsible government dared leave unattended. It therefore had been no accident that the Bolsheviks had tried to woo the peoples of the Transcaucasus, Siberia, and Turkestan with a "Declaration of Rights to the Peoples of Russia and the Muslim Tribes of Russia and the East" before they had been in power a month, or that the Asiatic scene had remained one of Stalin's preoccupations even during the Civil War's darkest days. "Have not the inestimable natural resources . . . of the East been an 'apple of discord' between the imperialists of all countries?" he asked not long after the Bolsheviks' first anniversary had passed. "The East should not be forgotten for a single moment," he warned. "It is the task of Communism to break the age-long sleep of the oppressed peoples of the East. . . . Without this, the definite triumph of socialism, complete victory over imperialism, is unthinkable."[130]

In their most optimistic moments, men such as Stalin envisioned millions of Europeans marching beneath the banners of socialism with tens of millions of Russians. Yet even this awesome vision paled next to the prospect of hundreds of millions of Asians marching for the same cause. Stalin spoke of this in his article about "The October Revolution and the National Question" in November 1918, when he cheered the Bolsheviks for having "erected a bridge between the socialist West and the enslaved East."[131] Less than a year later, Trotskii joined him in lamenting that "we have up to now devoted too little attention to the situation in Asia" and urged that, "somewhere in the Urals or in Turkestan," the Sovnarkom should establish "a revolutionary academy, the political and military headquarters of the Asian Revolution."[132] Before such dreams could be dreamed, the incorporation of Turkestan, Azerbaidjan, Armenia, and Georgia into the Bolsheviks' domains had to be accomplished. The formation of a Turkestan Soviet Republic less than a week after the Bolsheviks seized power in Petrograd, and its brutal destruction of a Moslem effort to establish a rival government in Kokand early in 1918, marked the beginnings of that process.[133]

The history of the Civil War in Turkestan was dominated by the stubborn survival of the Turkestan Soviet Republic despite long isolation from the Red center of Soviet Russia. Some twelve hundred miles to the northwest of the republic's center in Tashkent, the Orenburg Cossacks stood astride the Tashkent-Orenburg-Moscow Railway and prevented all overland contact with Moscow at the same time as the Emirate of Bukhara, the Khanate of Khiva, and the violently anti-Bolshevik trainmen who controlled the railroad that ran from Tashkent to Krasnovodsk via Ashkhabad closed all access to the Caspian in the west.[134] Deprived of fuel and grain from Russia and abroad, the people of the Turkestan Soviet Republic starved. At times the fuel crisis became so acute that desperate trainmen burned railroad ties, cottonseed oil, and even dried fish to fuel the handful of trains needed to continue the "railway war" between Reds and Cossacks that flowed back and forth from one railhead to another.[135]

During 1919, the capture of Orenburg by the Reds in January, Kolchak's failure to retake the city that summer, the British decision to withdraw their support from the anti-Bolshevik forces at Ashkhabad and Krasnovodsk, and the Red Army's steady advance against Kolchak's crumbling armies during the last half of the year opened the way for the Fourth and First Red Armies—now called the Turkestan Army Group and commanded by Frunze—to lift the Cossack blockade of the Orenburg-Tashkent Railway. As supplies from Russia began to relieve the shortages of grain and fuel in Tashkent during the fall and winter of 1919–1920, Frunze's forces began to carry out Lenin's order for "the complete liquidation of the Ural Cossacks."[136] Only a few hundred of this once numerous and powerful Cossack host escaped their fury by trekking some eight hundred miles across the Transcaspian desert to Persia. Then Frunze turned to open the western frontier of Turkestan to the Caspian, where the armed forces of the Turkestan Soviet Republic already had taken Ashkhabad in July and had begun their advance against Krasnovodsk.

Joint efforts by the Russian and Turkestan Reds captured Krasnovodsk and Khiva in February 1920. Bukhara held out until the beginning of September, when the Red artillery finally smashed its gates and took the city by storm. The Emir of Bukhara then fled to Afghanistan to become a trader in karakul, a kind of tightly curled sheep's fleece that enjoyed great popularity as a material for well-to-do elderly women's coats in the West, while Frunze took command of the campaign against Wrangel. Although the Basmachi—guerrilla bands of Moslem bandits and rebels who opposed Russian authority—continued to fight against Turkestan's Soviet government for several more years, the region had been effectively returned to the Russian fold by the end of 1920, along with all the religious and racial tensions that it had suffered under the tsars. These would prove very difficult to overcome, and it would take years of effort by the authorities in Moscow before Turkestan's Russian minority would concede a larger role in government and party affairs to the region's Moslems.[137]

The bitter racial, religious, and national conflicts that so poisoned the early days of Soviet power in Turkestan also plagued Bolshevik efforts to restore Russian control in Azerbaidjan, Georgia, and Armenia. In Turkestan, the conflict had been primarily one of Turkic Moslems against Russians, but in the Transcaucasus it proved to be even more bitter and complex. Moslem Azerbaidjani Tatars and Christian Armenians had been foes for centuries, and the pogroms that the Moslems had waged against the Armenians in Baku during the first years of the twentieth century had been every bit as vicious as those that the Ukrainians and Russians had inflicted upon the Jews at the same time. Outside of Baku, which was by far the largest, most cosmopolitan city in the entire region, Armenians predominated in the Azerbaidjanian district of Karabakh, while Azerbaidjanis inhabited several enclaves in Armenia. In the mountainous western regions of the Transcaucasus, the Georgians despised the Azerbaidjanis only slightly less than did the Armenians, yet they and the Armenians, who inhabited the tablelands overlooked by the towering Mount Ararat to the southwest, shared little in common beside their Christianity. Historically, Georgians and Armenians had been enemies, although Armenians outnumbered Georgians in the Georgian capital of Tiflis by a considerable margin.

Economic and social tensions made religious and racial conflicts more explosive still. In Azerbaidjan, beys and khans ruled as feudal overlords over a devoutly Muslim and almost entirely illiterate peasantry. The Christian princes of Georgia ruled their peasants in similar fashion. A small commercial class had emerged by the beginning of the twentieth century in Armenia and Georgia, although in Azerbaidjan the Tatar business class numbered no more than a scant handful. Apart from a few railway workers, neither Armenia or Georgia had an industrial proletariat worthy of the name; only Baku had a working-class population of any significance. As political conflicts stirred this seething caldron of religious, racial, national, economic, and social unrest in the Transcaucasus, the tension mounted. In Armenia, the Dashnaktsutiun, sometimes called the Dashnak Party in Western accounts, championed the liberation of all Armenians from Russia and Turkey and maintained loose ties with the Russian Socialist Revolutionaries, while the Musavat Party of Azerbaidjan, made up mainly of the handful of educated and trading classes, sought closer ties with the Turks against the Russians, Armenians, and Georgians. Two hundred thousand refugees from the Turks' 1915 massacre of Armenians in Anatolia brought still another source of conflict to Armenia and Azerbaidjan on the eve of the Civil War.[138]

In Georgia, the Mensheviks played the dominant role as a national party. Although allied with their Russian namesakes, the Georgian Mensheviks followed a nationalist program designed to establish Georgian independence and strengthen Georgian authority over other nationalities living within their borders. More than their Russian counterparts, Georgia's Mensheviks disdained the Bolsheviks. "We prefer the imperialists of the West," the Georgian Menshevik leader Noi Zhordaniia once stated bluntly, "to the fanatics of the East."[139] Georgia's Mensheviks therefore signed an alliance with Germany in May 1918, which brought a German garrison to Tiflis and placed all of Georgia's raw materials, especially her manganese, at Germany's disposal for the remainder of the First World War.[140] In doing so they gained for the moment a protector against the Bolsheviks and spared themselves the fate of large parts of Armenia and Azerbaidjan, which had been overrun by the armies of Germany's Turkish ally that spring.

While the policies of Armenia and Georgia remained staunchly anti-Russian and anti-Bolshevik after the October Revolution, the workers of Baku chose a very different course. Located on the western shore of the Caspian Sea, Baku stood at the center of the world's largest oilfield, from which, on the eve of the Great War, some three thousand oil wells had pumped crude oil for all of Russia. A raging boomtown for at least four decades before the war, its population of 334,000 had risen by more than two thousand percent since the mid-1870s, and much of that increase had been skilled Russian and Armenian workers. By 1917, more than six out of every ten office workers and more than seven out of every ten skilled industrial workers in Baku were Russian or Armenian, while fully three out of every four unskilled laborers were Muslims. Many of these workers lived without women, and there was a grim grayness about their lives that nothing seemed able to erase. Outside the city's aristocratic center, oil stood in puddles and filled the air, and its vapors stained clothing, skin, and lungs. Subterranean naphtha gas bubbled up through mud volcanoes. Elsewhere it rose from fissures in the earth and, in at least one place, even rose from a spring beneath the sea.[141] "The road to hell, I thought, would be very similar," one visitor observed after she had driven through the forest of oil derricks that surrounded Baku some years before the war. "It was a picture of unremitting and hopeless gloom."[142] Nonetheless, the workers of Baku had been slow to anger and slower to become radicalized. "There is not the slightest interest in politics," one Bolshevik had complained in a letter to Lenin in the spring of 1914.[143]

Even though they had strengthened their position in Baku as the Transcaucasus had slipped from Russia's control during 1917, Baku's Bolsheviks continued to support a coalition government for several months after their comrades had seized power in Petrograd. Yet they did so uneasily. None among them had forgotten the Azerbaidjani pogroms against the Armenians in 1905, and they worried that the Turkish atrocities of 1915 against the Armenians in Anatolia might encourage their coreligionists in Baku to follow their example. Fearful that the city's Muslims might at any moment launch a nationalist counterrevolution that would submerge Russians and Armenians in its fury, Baku's Bolsheviks joined with the city's Dashnaks in three days of bloody street fighting that claimed the lives of nearly three thousand Muslims during the first part of April 1918.[144] While Georgia and Armenia declared their independence that spring, the Bolsheviks of Baku, led by Stepan Shaumian, a Georgian-born Armenian of great personal magnetism who has sometimes been called the Lenin of the Caucasus, took control of the city and drew closer to Russia.[145]

On April 25, 1918, Shaumian and his followers organized the Baku Commune, modeled upon Marx's and Lenin's visions of the Paris Commune of 1871, and began what one commentator has called a "short-lived experiment in maximalist socialist administration."[146] Just a few months past his thirty-ninth birthday, Shaumian became chairman of Baku's Soviet of People's Commissars and commissar of foreign affairs. Following his lead, Baku's Bolsheviks dedicated themselves to restoring the shipment of oil to their comrades in Moscow. At first they enjoyed such success that they increased the March export figure of 26,500 tons by almost twenty times before the end of June.[147] But Shaumian's Moscow allies could not send him in return the grain needed to relieve Baku's terrible famine, and his too hasty nationalization of the oil industry stirred bitter feelings among those foreign industrialists whose companies controlled Azerbaidjan's oil production. Starving workers and angry oil barons made poor allies at a time when Shaumian and his comrades needed support against the Musavat leaders, who had begun to raise an army against them. As the Musavat forces, supported by Turkish troops fresh from their successful invasion of Armenia, advanced against Baku, the Dashnaks abandoned the Bolsheviks. Fearful for their lives in any city in which the Turks and Azerbaidjanis ruled, the Dashnaks now demanded that the Baku Soviet seek more powerful defenders.[148]

Over the violent objections of Shaumian and his comrades, but with images of the 1905 Azerbaidjani massacres of the Armenians still fresh in their minds, the Dashnaks convinced a small majority of the Baku Soviet to seek the protection of a British expeditionary force then in North Persia under the command of General Dunsterville. As their farewell message proclaimed, the Bolsheviks' leaders—later known as the Twenty-six Baku Commissars—left Baku angrily at the end of July "with bitterness in our hearts [and] with curses on our lips."[149] Yet their hope of escaping to Soviet-held Astrakhan to the north proved illusory. While their successors at Baku struggled to halt the Turks at the city's gates, the twenty-six commissars suffered arrest and imprisonment. Eventually, their captors took them to a remote place in the desert between Krasnovodsk and Ashkhabad and shot them all on the morning of September 20.[150] By then, Dunsterville's force had left Baku in disgust, thoroughly sick of local politics and local watermelons ("an uninteresting fruit [sold] at an enormous price," in Dunsterville's opinion),[151] and the Turko-Azerbaidjani army had taken the city, which they held until the collapse of the Central Powers in November.[152]

The Allies' victory over the Central Powers meant that England replaced Germany and Turkey as the chief foreign influence not only in Azerbaidjan, from which the oil-hungry British exported more than 330 million gallons of oil and nearly a half million tons of manganese in less than a year,[153] but in Armenia and Georgia. Of the latter two, Armenia led the most precarious existence. When she declared her independence in 1918, Turkish troops held two-thirds of her territory and half of the people living in the unoccupied Armenian lands were refugees. Spared from famine only by the American Relief Administration, her economy shattered by a currency whose value fell by more than five thousand percent in eight months, Armenia's government spent more than ten times its income during its two years of independence and lived largely upon the contributions of Armenians living abroad. This crushing combination of poverty, hunger, and military weakness did not prevent Armenia's leaders from following bellicose policies toward its neighbors. In December 1918, less than a month after the armies of defeated Turkey had withdrawn from the Transcaucasus, Armenia fought Georgia for the Borchalinsk region. The next year, she fought Azerbaidjan for the Karabakh, and, the year after that, for the region of Zangezur. During her first winter of independence, Armenia ordered her troops to occupy parts of Turkish Eastern Anatolia, proclaimed the annexation of Turkish Armenia in May 1919, and went to war with Turkey to defend her claim in 1920.[154]

As in Azerbaidjan, British forces replaced those of the Central Powers in Georgia after the Allied victory. Like the Germans before them, the British interfered little in the internal affairs of the Menshevik-dominated Georgian government, which introduced a broad program of land reform, nationalized Georgia's few industries, and struggled to maintain an army with which to war against its neighbors. Such perpetual fighting destroyed any hope that Georgia, Armenia, and Azerbaidjan might combine under a single government, and this left each of them particularly vulnerable to attacks by the Red Army when the British withdrew their forces in 1919. From his stronghold in the Kuban just to the north, Denikin only made matters worse with short-sighted policies that weakened them still further. To Denikin, Menshevik Georgia and Musavat Azerbaidjan stood as avowed enemies of his belief in a "great, united, and undivided Russia." When the British withdrew, he created more unrest among these "self-made entities . . . which are openly hostile to Russian statehood"[155] by blocking food shipments to their starving people.[156]

As the armies of Denikin, Iudenich, and Kolchak crumbled, the Red High Command laid its plans to retake the Transcaucasus. Desperate to reopen the oil lines that once had flowed from Baku, they planned their first assaults against Azerbaidjan, whose government unwisely had shifted most of its armed forces to the southwest for a new campaign against Armenia during February and March 1920. Supported by armored trains, the battle-hardened Eleventh Red Army moved into position in Derbent, just beyond Azerbaidjan's undefended northern frontiers, at the beginning of April. As it did so, Bolshevik agents organized an underground force of some four thousand men to seize power when it marched against Baku. Well-planned and well-executed, the campaign ended in five days with the occupation of Baku by Red forces on April 28.

Victorious without firing more than a handful of shots, the soldiers of the Eleventh Red Army scarcely broke their cadence as they turned westward and crossed into Georgia and Armenia the following week.[157] Then, as Polish troops opened their first attacks against Kiev and Belorussia, the Eleventh Red Army halted. Until the armies of Poland and Wrangel had been dealt with, the Bolsheviks would settle for consolidating their power in Azerbaidjan and nourishing their dreams of Asian revolution through such symbolically satisfying events as the First Congress of the Peoples of the East, which they organized in Baku at the beginning of September.

Presided over by the ebullient Zinoviev, the Bolsheviks' master of rhetorical pyrotechnics, who used the opportunity to conjure up visions of eight hundred million Asians marching in "a real holy war against the British and French capitalists," the First Congress of the Peoples of the East brought some two thousand delegates, including Turks, Persians, Armenians, Chinese, and representatives of most of the Asiatic nationalities living in lands under Soviet control, together in Baku. As they basked in the memory of the triumphs won by Genghis Khan and Tamerlane and spoke of the day when the Red East would rise to build a new Communist culture, they heard John Reed, who would die just five weeks later in Moscow, deliver his final condemnation of America's capitalists and warn for one last time that "whoever believes [the] promises [of Uncle Sam] will pay in blood."[158] In practical terms, the congress accomplished little, although it is quite probable that Stalin and his close associate, the cruelly efficient Georgian revolutionary Grigorii Ordzhonikidze, used it to form the Revolutionary Committee of the Soviet Socialist Republic of Armenia, to which the Bolsheviks would demand that the Armenian government relinquish its authority at the end of November.[159]

Scarcely three weeks after the Baku Congress ended, the armies of Turkey invaded Armenia to dispute her occupation of Eastern Anatolia. After two days of fighting, they halted their offensive for a month and then moved quickly toward Armenia's capital city of Erivan. As Armenia's statesmen sued for peace, the Eleventh Red Army crossed their eastern frontier. Backed by Soviet bayonets, the Revolutionary Committee of the Socialist Republic of Armenia took power on November 29. "Long live Soviet Armenia!" Stalin proclaimed joyfully in *Pravda*. "Armenia, so long martyred and tormented, with its people condemned by the grace of the Entente and the Dashnaks to starvation [and] ruin . . . has now found salvation by proclaiming itself a Soviet land."[160] Well before Christmas 1920, the leading Dashnaks had been arrested, the Red Army of Armenia formed, and the laws that the Sovnarkom had decreed for Russia imposed upon Armenia. Compulsory food requisitions conducted in savage fashion became a part of everyday life in newly sovietized Armenia as the new year began, and before the end of January 1921, the officers of Armenia's army had been deported to Azerbaidjan or Russia.[161] Now that Azerbaidjan and Armenia had been absorbed, only Georgia, Stalin's homeland, which he now condemned as "the main base of British and French imperialist operations," remained free of Russian occupation. Georgia's turn had come. "Georgia," Stalin promised at the end of November, "is in its last gasp."[162]

Home of such brutal and uncompromising Bolsheviks as Stalin, Ordzhonikidze, and Lavrentii Beria, Georgia was, nonetheless, a traditional stronghold of Menshevism. Most of the Mensheviks in the tsarist Duma before the Revolution had come from Georgia. Several of them had played a major part in the revolutionary events of March and April 1917 in Petrograd, while such others as Akakii Chkhenkeli, Evgenii Gegechkori, and the senior statesman (born in the same year as Lenin) Noi Zhordaniia had struggled to guide the Revolution's course among the fiercely nationalistic people of their homeland. Well known in European and Russian socialist circles, they all remained Georgians first and foremost. National interest therefore always took precedence over international socialism, and the overwhelming strength of their Menshevik Party in Georgia gave them a political base such as few politicians enjoyed anywhere else. Georgia had no centers of powerful resistance to national policy as the Musavat Azerbaidjanis endured in Baku or the Dashnak Armenians faced in their Turkish, Azerbaidjani, or Georgian districts. Georgia, after 1917, was a more cohesive state than any other nation in the Transcaucasus.

Yet the Georgians' very passion for nationhood caused them difficulties. As they drove all non-Georgians from their army and civil service in 1918 and 1919, Georgians' chauvinism became as extreme as the Bolsheviks revolutionary leveling in Russia. United in a common cause, Georgia's leaders moved quickly to widen their borders at the expense of their Armenian and Azerbaidjani neighbors, and their territorial greed astounded foreign observers.[163] "The Free and Independent Social-Democratic State of Georgia will always remain in my memory as a classic example of an imperialist 'small nation,' " one British journalist wrote a year later. "Both in territory-snatching outside and bureaucratic tyranny inside, its chauvinism was beyond all bounds."[164]

Although Georgia could press her demands against crumbling Armenia and divided Azerbaidjan, she had no force capable of withstanding the Red Army. Evidently fearful of British intervention, Lenin had opposed Stalin's plan to take Georgia by force, but Stalin and his deputy Ordzhonikidze pressed ahead, reassured, it seems, by Lloyd George's statement to Russia's representative at the Anglo–Soviet trade treaty negotiations that England considered the entire Caucasus as lying within the Soviet sphere of influence.[165] When the Red Army launched its first attack against Georgia on February 17, 1921, the British did nothing. A month later, they signed the Anglo–Russian Trade Agreement, which promised to "remove forthwith all obstacles hitherto placed in the way of the resumption of trade between the United Kingdom and Russia."[166] As Turkestan, Armenia, and Azerbaidjan had done before her, Georgia faced the Red Army alone.

Advancing across the rugged Caucasus Mountains through the Darial Pass in the north, while other units moved west from Azerbaidjan, the Red Armies converged on Tiflis two days later. Outnumbered more than three to one, the Georgians held out for a week until large Red reinforcements from Baku overwhelmed their defenses. On February 25, the Red Army entered Tiflis. "The Red banner of the Soviet regime is aloft in Tiflis!" Ordzhonikidze telegraphed triumphantly to Lenin. "Long Live Soviet Georgia!"[167] Still apprehensive about the virulent anti-Russian sentiments for which the Georgians were so well known, Lenin continued to counsel caution, even in victory. "Bear in mind," he warned Ordzhonikidze a few days later, "that Georgia's domestic and international positions both require that her Communists should avoid any mechanical copying of the Russian pattern. They must skillfully work out their own flexible tactics, based on bigger concessions."[168]

During the next several years, incessant uprisings against the Soviet authorities by Georgia's hardy mountaineers proved the wisdom of Lenin's call for caution, but it did not alter the fact that, by March 1921, all of the Transcaucasus had come under Soviet control. In the mountains of the Caucasus, in the Central Russian province of Tambov, and in the faraway lands of eastern Siberia, revolts against Soviet authority would flare for several more years, but none would ever challenge Bolshevik hegemony as had those great White movements of the years 1918–1920. After more than three years of civil war, the process of "regathering the Russian lands" had come to an end. "The last of the hostile armies has been driven from our territory," Lenin told the Bolsheviks who assembled to hear him address the Tenth Congress of the Russian Communist Party on March 8, 1921. "That is our achievement!"[169]

CHAPTER FOURTEEN

Victory's Bitter Fruit

By the beginning of March 1921, the Bolsheviks reigned supreme over all but a few corners of the lands that once had been the Russian Empire. From Murmansk and Arkhangelsk in the North to Odessa, Tiflis, and Baku in the South, from Minsk in the West to Khabarovsk in the Far East, the Red flag waved proudly where Russia's imperial eagles once had soared. With outlets on four seas, Soviet Russia now welcomed ships from many corners of the globe. No longer the "fortress besieged by world capital" that Lenin had described some twenty months earlier,[1] Red Russia had moved decisively onto the international stage as a legitimate state in the eyes of her one-time adversaries. "There is a great change in Russia . . . from the wild extravagant Communism of a year or two ago, or even a few months ago," Lloyd George assured the House of Commons. "[There has been] a complete change in the attitude of the Bolshevik government to what is called capitalism, towards private enterprise, towards communal effort, towards nationalization."[2]

What Europeans regarded as a striking transformation in Soviet attitudes had begun after 1919, a year in which Lenin's Russia had suffered complete isolation from the outside world. Convinced that Bolshevism was, as Churchill once said, a "foul baboonery,"[3] and that (in the words of *The Times* of London) "the best fate that we should desire for Bolshevism is that it should commit suicide,"[4] fourteen nations had sent troops to fight on the side of the Whites that year. Yet the isolation of 1919 could not continue, for neither Soviet Russia nor her enemies had the resources to wage warfare without end. Nearly six years of fighting had exhausted Red and White alike, and all longed to return to peace and prosperity. As they shifted from the production of armaments to consumer goods, Europe's factories hungered for Russia's raw materials, and, as Lenin told the Eighth Congress of Soviets in 1919, Russia needed "to buy [from England] as soon as possible the machinery necessary for our extensive plan to rehabilitate the national economy," which had been shattered by so many years of turmoil.[5] Having failed to destroy Bolshevism, Europeans now resolved to accommodate it into the framework of international politics through peaceful means. "We have failed to restore Russia to sanity by force," Lloyd George remarked just before Denikin resigned his command in South Russia. "I believe we can save her by trade."[6]

As the British withdrawal from North and South Russia, Siberia, and the Transcaucasus signaled the Western Allies' retreat from their commitment to reshape revolutionary Russia in their own democratic image, senior Bolsheviks publicly refocused their vision of the triumph of world revolution upon a more distant time. Both sides began to speak of peace. An "Address to the Polish People" in February 1920 insisted that the Soviet government was "not striving, and cannot strive, to plant Communism by force in other countries." When Lenin spoke of prosecuting the "war for peace with extreme energy" at the Ninth Bolshevik Party Congress a month later, Soviet Russia already had made peace with Estonia and had concluded an agreement with England for the repatriation of war prisoners. "A *modus vivendi* must be found in order that our socialist states and the capitalist states may coexist peacefully and in normal relations with one another," Commissar for Foreign Affairs Chicherin insisted during the months that followed. "This is a necessity in the interest of all."[7] Trotskii stated his government's desire for accommodation in even more conciliatory terms. "Not only can we live with bourgeois governments," he told the socialist American journalist John Reed that September, "but we can work together with them within limits that are very broad."[8] "By no means do we think that history has imposed upon Russia's worker-peasant government the obligation to bring about a revolution in every country," he added in an interview with a British correspondent later that same day. "In fact, we think that the workers and peasants of Russia can be of greater service to the toilers of the world at this moment by concentrating all their efforts on work in economic and cultural matters."[9]

When the Allies lifted their economic blockade of Soviet Russia in mid-January 1920, a succession of understandings, agreements, and treaties began to shape the *modus vivendi* of which Chicherin and Trotskii had spoken. After peace with Estonia and the Anglo–Soviet repatriation agreement came an unofficial trade agreement with Sweden and peace treaties with Lithuania, Latvia, and Finland. An armistice in October 1920, followed by a formal treaty early in 1921, ended the Russo–Polish War that had postponed British and Soviet negotiators' efforts to conclude an Anglo–Soviet trade treaty the previous summer. "We have achieved tremendous successes and have won not only a breathing-space but something much more significant," Lenin told a group of Bolsheviks from Moscow province in November. "We have entered a new period in which we have won the right to our fundamental international existence in the network of capitalist states."[10] Perhaps more than any other event that year, the Anglo–Soviet Trade Treaty, which opened a new era in economic relations between Russia and the West in March 1921, and which Chicherin grandly proclaimed "a turning-point in Soviet foreign policy,"[11] gave substance to Lenin's claim.

A series of trade agreements with Germany, Italy, Austria, and a number of lesser states followed. This did not make Soviet Russia a willing or ready ally of Western nations, nor did it produce a flowering of East–West trade, as some of its architects had hoped, but it did mute the raw antagonism that had dominated East–West relations during the Civil War years, and it did shape a new era of relations among them. Sadly, Russia struck her closest alliance in this new era with Weimar Germany. During the first five years that the Anglo–Soviet treaty was in effect, Britain traded only reluctantly with the Soviet Union, to the modest tune of just more than a hundred million pounds,[12] but Germany and Russia became much closer economic partners from the moment they shocked Europe by signing the Treaty of Rapallo in the spring of 1922. Thus, one expert wrote, "the two outcasts of European society, overcoming the barrier of ideological differences, joined hands, and, in so doing, recovered their status and their self-esteem as independent members of the society."[13] Less than two decades later, history revealed the tragic consequences of that union in the alliance between Stalin and Hitler.

Despite Soviet Russia's promising diplomatic beginnings in 1920–1921, the fruit of victory at home proved more bitter than sweet. More than six years of war had devastated every area of Russian life. Only two-thirds of the land under cultivation at the beginning of the First World War was being farmed at the Civil War's end,[14] and without fertilizers, agricultural machinery, or even sufficient hand tools, that land produced a great deal less than it had before the war. The Russians in 1920 therefore reaped barely two-fifths of what they had harvested in 1916, the year before the turmoil of revolution and civil war had come upon them. To make matters worse, no rain fell in the summer of 1920 and little snow came the next winter. In the summer of 1921, average temperatures in the Middle Volga grain fields rose to the level of those in Cairo, and many of Russia's best fields yielded less than her peasants planted. Before summer ended, *Pravda* reported that famine from the drought had touched "about 25,000,000" people.[15]

Their reserves long since seized by Bolshevik grain-requisitioning detachments, Russia's peasants diluted their scant supplies of flour with acorns, weeds, bark, even clay and dried manure. A year later, more than two out of every three people in southeastern Russia were starving.[16] Then, hunger-crazed men and women ate flesh torn from rotting, once-buried animal carcasses. "One knew a starving village by its utter desolation." one observer explained. "Not a living soul could be seen in the street, which seemed to have given up its function and become merely a dividing line between rows of silent huts."[17] As in all starving societies, cannibalism made its grim appearance. Village folk spoke of eating human flesh "with a curious quietness," one representative of the American Relief Administration reported. In the western Siberian city of Orenburg, the city authorities forbade the sale of ground meat after they learned that a murderer had sold the flesh of his victim in the bazaar.[18] "I ask all honest European and American people for prompt aid," Maksim Gorkii wrote in a desperate appeal. "Give bread and medicine."[19]

Fearful of reducing the workers' daily rations after three years in which they rarely had risen above the subsistence level, Bolshevik officials had ignored the poor harvest of 1920 and had postponed the inevitable day of reckoning. Then, as grain collections fell short of their expectations, they had to reduce daily food allotments by as much as a third just when Russia's working men and women needed extra calories to face another winter of fuel shortages. "We failed to see the full danger of the crisis approaching with the spring and succumbed to the natural desire to increase the starving workers' ration," Lenin told the Tenth Party Congress in March 1921. "It was a mistake typical of all our work," he continued. "The transition from war to peace confronted us with a whole number of difficulties and problems, and we had neither the experience, the training, nor the requisite material to overcome them. This worsened, intensified, and aggravated the crisis to an extraordinary extent."[20]

Once again, workers went without food, and their hunger, combined with shortages of fuel and raw materials, had a disastrous impact upon the Bolsheviks' efforts to rebuild Russia's industry. At the beginning of February 1921, fuel and food shortages forced the authorities to close more than five dozen of Petrograd's largest plants, including the Putilov Works, whose workers had supported the Bolsheviks so energetically in 1917. Even when enough fuel and raw materials could be assembled, hunger lowered workers' productivity by as much as two-thirds of what it had been in 1913.[21] That, in turn, left town and country desperately short of manufactured goods. At one point, officials in the Commissariat of Food Supply reported that they had been unable to ship grain to Russia's cities from Siberia and the Kuban because a shortage of sewing machines had made it impossible to sew enough grainsacks.[22]

For three years, Russia's peasants and workers had surrendered their grain and labor to the Bolshevik cause. Grudgingly, they had allowed the Bolsheviks to postpone the prosperous, free, and just future that Lenin had promised in order to defeat Kolchak, Denikin, Iudenich, the Poles, Wrangel, and the Western nations that supported them. So long as the fighting had continued, they had endured the shortages, the coercion, the labor armies, and the requisitions that War Communism had imposed; but once the Whites had left the field, Russia's working folk expected relief from their burdens, especially from the hated grain requisitions. The cumbersome, unstable, wasteful, oppressive, hand-to-mouth policies of War Communism that continued as 1920 moved past its midpoint therefore deepened the Russians' discontent. Then, as the Soviet government began to demobilize the Red Army's five million soldiers, hordes of men poured back into civilian life to swell the armies of unemployed in town and country. Hungry men without work and in search of the better world the Bolsheviks had promised added another element of instability to an already volatile situation.

Men who had lived by the law of the gun during the months and years when they had fought the Whites would not readily accept platitudes piously mouthed by rear-echelon Bolshevik bureaucrats who had grown fat while they had risked their lives. Peasants who traditionally had known how to fight against government repression only with scythes and pitchforks now knew how to fight with modern weapons.

While Russia's workers, peasants, and demobilized soldiers looked for greater opportunities and wider choices to replace the coercive, militarized society that War Communism had produced, Lenin insisted that "we must not give up measures of compulsion" lest Russia slip into "the abyss of economic collapse on the brink of which we are standing."[23] In reply, an old peasant at the Eighth Congress of Soviets had vented his countrymen's anger against the double meanings with which the Bolsheviks had endowed their revolutionary promises. "The land belongs to us but the bread belongs to you," he declared bitterly. "The water belongs to us, but the fish to you; the forests are ours, but the timber is yours."[24] "We welcome Soviet power," another peasant added cynically, "but give us plows, harrows, and machines and stop seizing our grain, milk, eggs, and meat."[25] Unwilling to trade their dreams of land and freedom for more promises of a brighter, ever-distant future, the toiling men and women of Russia began to voice their protests in the centuries-old language of mass revolts. Near the western slope of the Urals, in the pine woods of Viatka province, the fires of peasant war—bitter, elemental, and cruel—flared across the Russian countryside in June 1920 for the first time since 1918.

From Viatka the revolts spread in September to Vladimir, scarcely more than a hundred miles northeast of Moscow. From there, their flames raced into the Ukraine, the Crimea, the Don territory, the Kuban, the Trans-Volga lands, and western Siberia as the peasants, supported for the first time by demobilized Red Army men, turned upon the Bolshevik grain-requisitioning detachments that came to take their crops that fall.[26] By February 1921, the Cheka reported no fewer than 118 revolts within Soviet Russia.[27] "We find ourselves in a new kind of war, a new form of war, which is summed up in the word 'banditry,' " Lenin told the Tenth Party Congress when it assembled the following month. "[This is] when tens and hundreds of thousands of demobilized soldiers, who are accustomed to the toils of war and regard it almost as their only trade, return, impoverished and ruined, and are unable to find work." This was not the time for embroidering upon the truth, and Lenin made no attempt to gloss over the danger Russia faced from the men he and Trotskii had cheered so often as the Revolution's heroes. Given the "very much worse conditions and incredible hardships in the countryside," he told the assembled party delegates bluntly, demobilization had led to "a continuation of the war, but in a new form."[28] "Tens and hundreds of thousands, and possibly even larger numbers of people . . . see no way out of this disastrous situation," he confessed in a closing speech to the congress a few days later. "The peasantry," he concluded, "have some very deep grounds for dissatisfaction."[29]

Especially in the province of Tambov, in the midst of Russia's black-soil lands some two hundred and fifty miles southeast of Moscow, the peasants had reason for complaint. Almost everyone in Tambov—927 out of every 1,000 of its 3,650,000 inhabitants—lived on the land, making it one of the most densely populated rural areas in Russia. Although the accuracy of all Civil War statistics remains in dispute, perhaps as many as ninety-three out of every hundred peasant households in Tambov worked less than fifteen acres of land in 1920. Many of these peasants still broke their land every spring with a *sokha*, a primitive wooden instrument drawn by man, woman, or beast that did little more than scratch the soil's surface. Tambov folk still planted their seed by hand, and their women still reaped with sickles and threshed with flails. According to a survey done by Kerenskii's government, only one Tambov household in seven owned such simple agricultural machines as planters or reapers.[30]

Ever since the serf emancipation of 1861, plentiful labor and rich soil had not produced abundant crops in overpopulated, land-hungry Tambov, and deep poverty remained the rule. Since the province had many more workers than could be employed on its farmlands, the draft levies of the First World War actually had come as a modest blessing in disguise, for they had taken mainly surplus workers, and Tambov's modest grain output had not declined appreciably before 1917. Fought much closer to home, the Civil War had made Tambov's longstanding economic difficulties much worse. Denikin's advance toward Moscow had laid waste to large parts of the province, and a combination of war damage and peasant resistance to grain requisitioning had shrunk precipitously the amount of land under cultivation.[31] Too many peasants struggling for too long to farm too little land with too few of the implements of modern agriculture had produced deep economic and social tension. "There was really a malignant discord here," one observer had remarked in 1914.[32] Revolution and civil war had made the discord much worse. Tambov's peasants only needed a way to focus their discontent and a means to express it. By 1920 they had both.

For centuries, bandits had lived by their wits and in defiance of the authorities in the ravines of eastern Tambov. Thickly wooded with birch, willow, and pine, these havens connected with the great forests that stretched across the middle Volga from the Urals to the Far North, and men on the run could travel through them for hundreds of miles without emerging into the open. On the eve of the Revolution, army deserters had begun to take refuge in the robbers' ravines; and during the spring of 1918, those energetic and resourceful peasants who stood to suffer the most from the depredations of the Soviet regime in the Tambov countryside joined them. They called themselves Greens, a name that probably came from the forests in which they lived. Some were well educated and had a broader view of the world around them. Others focused their concerns more narrowly upon the province or district whence they had come.[33] Although they formed alliances with the local peasants and remained hostile to Reds and Whites alike, the Greens of Tambov posed no serious threat to Bolshevik authority until after the Whites' defeat. Then, as demobilized Red Army men swelled their ranks in 1920, the Greens became the peasants' champions against the Bolsheviks.

To the extent that they had any political sympathies, the Greens of Tambov shared the views of those Left Socialist Revolutionaries who had survived the uprising of July 1918.[34] Socialist Revolutionaries had always been the most peasant-oriented of any radical party in Russia, and Tambov had been a Socialist Revolutionary stronghold since the beginning of the century. Like the peasants, the Socialist Revolutionaries disdained the culture and politics of the city, and they shared the farmers' hatred for the men from the city who seized their grain and left them to make their bread out of roots and bark. Socialist Revolutionaries naturally played an important part in organizing the Union of the Working Peasantry that swore in May 1920 to "fight the Bolsheviks to the end," and they helped to establish a wide-ranging network of representatives in Tambov's villages and hamlets. Although the Socialist Revolutionary Party officially spoke against open revolt, many of its members took up arms on the side of the Greens in 1920. Aleksandr Antonov, a colorful, ruggedly individualistic man somewhere between thirty and thirty-five years of age whose daring exploits soon cast him as a modern-day Robin Hood in the peasants' imaginations, became their leader.[35]

A childhood spent in a small town on the edge of the forest had given Antonov a close identification with rural life even though he did not come from peasant stock. After spending his teen-age years in trouble with the authorities, he had joined the Socialist Revolutionary Party, been sentenced to twelve years' penal servitude in Siberia for robbery soon after the Revolution of 1905, and returned home only after the February Revolution. Dissatisfied with the Socialist Revolutionaries' passivity during the Kerenskii era and anxious for decisive action in Russia's provinces, Antonov had shifted his loyalties to their extensive left wing, which had allied briefly with the Bolsheviks after the October Revolution. In those days, the Left SRs had made Antonov chief of the militia in his native district until the ill-fated Left SR uprising in Moscow had forced him to go into hiding in the forests. When Bolshevik grain-requisitioning detachments seized the poor harvest of Tambov's peasants that fall and spring, Antonov began to organize the Greens into a rebel force.[36]

Satisfied with minor forays against those Reds and Whites who threatened his forest sanctuary, Antonov remained in the shadows for the better part of two years. Then, as the Poles halted Tukhachevskii's armies at Warsaw and as Wrangel pushed into the Ukraine from his foothold in the Northern Taurida late in the summer of 1920, he led his forces in open rebellion against the Reds. Well-schooled in the details of Tambov's terrain, Antonov ranged at will across the southern counties of the province. With fewer than six thousand men at their command, the authorities could do little to stop him, and his partisans massacred several large Red forces that ventured beyond the safety of Tambov's larger towns.[37] As the peasants began to see Antonov as the "invincible avenger of their violated interests,"[38] they offered him shelter and supplies. That fall and winter, the flames of peasant war began to sear the Tambov countryside.

What Soviet commentators have called "black terror, blind and merciless,"[39] claimed hundreds of lives that fall. Tambov partisans nailed known and suspected Bolsheviks to trees, often by driving a single railroad spike through the victim's left arm and foot and leaving him to dangle in agony a few feet above the ground.[40] With all the brutality of those savage armies that Genghis Khan had led across their land seven hundred years before, the Greens maimed and mutilated their victims, flaying some, quartering others, and disemboweling still others. Vengeful partisans gouged out eyes, chopped off limbs, mutilated sexual organs, slashed tendons, and unraveled intestines. They often buried captured enemies alive, but took care to leave their victims' heads above ground so that peasant women could urinate on them before the village dogs closed in to gnaw the still living flesh from their faces and skulls.[41] By the end of the year, the Greens had erased Soviet power in several large counties in southern Tambov, and Lenin began to fear that the "Antonov fire"—the *antonovshchina*, as the Russians called it—might burn out of control. The "*swift and complete liquidation*" of the *antonovshchina*, Lenin told Trotskii's deputy at the Commissariat of War in mid-October, must be accomplished without delay. "The most swift (and exemplary) liquidation" of Antonov's forces, he added in a note to Dzerzhinskii a few days later, had become "absolutely essential."[42]

At the urging of Lenin and his lieutenants, Red terror came to Tambov during the winter of 1920–1921. Without the institutional strength and human resources to impose it as resolutely as they had in Russia's larger cities, the Bolsheviks at first alternated between wholesale cruelty, in which they burned entire villages suspected of supporting the Greens, and extreme leniency, in which they pardoned prisoners en masse. Then, Antonov-Ovseenko, the street fighter who had played a prominent role in Bolshevik military affairs ever since he had arrested the Provisional Government in the wee hours of October 26,1917, took charge of the campaign against Antonov's rebels. Known by the code name "Bayonet" before the Revolution, Antonov-Ovseenko could be counted upon to be resolute in his brutality. When it became clear that Antonov-Ovseenko's chief talent lay in warfare against civilians, the Bolshevik Central Committee appointed Tukhachevskii to command the military operations against Antonov at the beginning of May 1921 and left the Bayonet free to concentrate his cruelty on the forces of the Tambov Cheka.[43]

Freed from the pressures of war against the Poles and Wrangel, and with Lenin warning the Commissariat of War of the need to "drive [its commanders] forward by the mane and by the tail" to speed up the capture of Antonov,[44] the Soviet high command poured men and materiel into Tambov's rebel infested woodlands. Before the spring thaw, the Red forces in Tambov reached forty thousand. Nearly five hundred machine guns, five dozen field guns, armored cars and trains, and two squadrons of planes bolstered their strength still further, while the Green forces probably never rose above twenty thousand ill-armed men.[45] As Tukhachevskii pressed forward in the field, Antonov-Ovseenko opened a campaign of terror that held entire villages hostage for the conduct of rebel relatives, neighbors, and friends. Any weapon found concealed on a peasant's person or in his home brought death by shooting. Any family that sheltered a "bandit" or a "bandit's" family lost its property, suffered banishment, and forfeited the life of its eldest breadwinner.[46] Helpless hostages faced similar fates, and many Tambov peasants had to pay for the deeds of their neighbors with their lives, while others suffered deportation to Cheka concentration camps in the Far North.[47] "War is war," Lenin stated flatly then. "Guns are not just for decoration."[48]

As the Bolsheviks prepared to crush Antonov's Greens, they tried to separate them from their peasant supporters by abolishing grain requisitions and substituting a more modest tax in kind. This new tax, Lenin explained to a plenary meeting of the Moscow Soviet at the end of February 1921, marked an attempt to solve Russia's food shortages in a manner "satisfactory to the nonparty peasants and to the mass of the people."[49] This meant that, after the peasants turned over about a fourth of their crops to the government, they could dispose of the rest as they saw fit. "The tax in kind," Lenin wrote in a pamphlet bearing that title, "is a transition from War Communism to a regular socialist exchange of products."[50]

In fact, the tax in kind marked the beginning of a hasty retreat from the dogmatic principles of War Communism to a New Economic Policy, proclaimed in Moscow on March 21, 1921, that encouraged private enterprise in what Lenin conceded was an attempt to use "freedom of trade" and a limited return to capitalism to induce Russia's food producers to "set to work on their farms with greater confidence and with a will." Only in this way could Bolshevik Russia overcome the devastation of the Civil War and the peasants' stubborn resistance to full-fledged socialism. "The national economy must be put on its feet at all costs," Lenin insisted. "The first thing to do is to restore, consolidate, and improve peasant farming."[51] In Tambov, the Bolsheviks offered peasant rebels both the "wolf's fang" and the "fox's tail," as the saying went.[52] Those who wished to could lay down their arms and rejoin their countrymen in Tambov's villages. Those who refused this final offer of peace would be dealt with mercilessly by Antonov-Ovseenko and Tukhachevskii.

As the weight of the Soviet forces began to crush Antonov's partisans, they broke into ever smaller groups that met the Bolsheviks' advances with more terrorist killings. "Black terror" reached its lowest depths of bestiality during the summer of 1921, as the Reds smashed one partisan group after another and the Greens responded with the desperation of men who had lost all hope of victory. By the end of August, all of Antonov's lieutenants had fallen, the Union of the Working Peasantry had been smashed, and Tambov's "Antonov fire" had been quenched. Antonov, it seems, may have fled to nearby Saratov province, or he may have remained in hiding within the ravines of Tambov. Soviet sources claim that he survived the ruin of his movement for the better part of a year. Then, on July 29, 1922, *Pravda* carried a brief announcement that "on July 24, after a two-hour fire-fight between the Tambov section of the GPU [the acronym for the reorganized Cheka] and the well-known leader of the SR movement Antonov and his brother Dmitrii, both bandits were killed."[53] Some have doubted the truth of Soviet accounts about Antonov's death,[54] but it seems virtually certain that he did not emerge alive from the ruins of his movement. Soviet authorities had every right to claim, as *Pravda* did at the end of 1922, that "kulak banditry" had been effectively suppressed.[55]

What emerged from the repression of the *antonovshchina* and similar revolts in Siberia, the Kuban, and the Ukraine was a modified economic and social order that represented a retreat from the uncompromising principles that had shaped War Communism. Over "a long period to be measured in terms of years," the Tenth All-Russian Bolshevik Party Conference explained at the end of May 1921, the peasant was to be left free to dispose of his surpluses as he saw fit, for the "linchpin of the New Economic Policy . . . [was to be] the exchange of goods."[56] Although this shift did not come soon enough to avert the dreadful famine of 1921–1922, which took millions of lives, the New Economic Policy came close to restoring Russia's supplies of food and consumer goods to their prewar levels before Stalin abolished it in 1928.[57] Such success in the production of food and consumer goods quickly brought new problems, including a dramatic resurgence of what Bolshevik loyalists called the "trading-industrial bourgeoisie," whose numbers, according to the best estimates, soared beyond two million before the end of 1924.[58] Ultimately, these had no more place in the Soviet system of things than did other holdovers from the Old Regime; like the leftovers from tsarist society, the new "trading-industrial bourgeoisie" also would be destroyed before the decade's end.

With more than forty thousand churches, fifty thousand deans and priests, twenty thousand monks, almost seventy-five thousand nuns, and an annual appropriation on the eve of the Revolution of more than sixty million rubles (thirty million dollars at the official exchange rate), the Russian Orthodox Church stood prominently among those Old Regime institutions that the Bolsheviks marked for destruction. For centuries, the Orthodox Church had buttressed the tsar's authority, prayed for his safety, and called upon Russia's faithful to do the same. Orthodox clergy had summoned their flocks to defend Holy Russia against the Poles in 1611, against the invading Swedish armies of Charles XII in 1708, the Grand Army of Napoleon in 1812, and the modern hosts of the Hapsburgs and the Hohenzollerns in 1914. Then, when revolution threatened, the Church had urged the Russians to stand behind the Tsar. "Fear God and honor the Tsar," the Metropolitan Makarii of Moscow had told Russia's people just a month before the February Revolution. "Let us unite around our mighty Orthodox Tsar! Let us stand in defense of the divinely established authorities appointed by the Tsar!"[59] To fight for Tsar and Country meant to fight for God and the True Faith; to take up arms against them meant to stand against God and Christ. The Metropolitan of Moscow had made that clear half a millennium earlier when he had condemned as enemies of Christ those who opposed the conquest of other Russian princes' domains by the grand prince of Moscow. In those long-ago days, the Russian Orthodox Church had punished the tsar's enemies with excommunication. Yet excommunication had remained a weapon in the Church's arsenal long after medieval Russia had disappeared. As recently as 1902, the procurator general of Imperial Russia's Holy Synod had pronounced the sentence of excommunication upon the great novelist Lev Tolstoi.

Despite its wealth, its churches, and its legions of priests, monks, and nuns, the Church influenced the attitudes of the Russian masses toward the Revolution far less than Russian conservatives expected. Ever since Peter the Great had abolished the Patriarchate and shaped the Church into an instrument of state policy, Russia's peasant millions had grown suspicious of Orthodoxy. Linked to the official Church only by the village priest, and dependent upon him for their only access to salvation, Russia's common folk made him the butt of cruel jokes and obscene humor because he spoke too often for the government and too seldom for God. By the beginning of the twentieth century, many Russian country folk reserved their reverence for those holy fools who wandered from village to village and for itinerant holy men, of whom Rasputin was but one—albeit the most accomplished— among many.

Far-sighted clerics knew the need for reforms, but since the Church functioned within the larger framework of the Russian government, they faced difficulties unfamiliar to churchmen in the West. Only after the Revolution of 1905 had they succeeded in convincing Nicholas II to allow them to begin making plans to summon the first Church Council to be called in almost two hundred and fifty years. Hindered at every step by Russia's secular and religious bureaucracy, the council's planners had moved at a glacial pace. Because the February Revolution had come and gone before even proper elections could be held, the delegates faced a very different political situation than any of them had anticipated as they prepared to assemble in Moscow. Revolution therefore had caught the Orthodox Church in a state of flux. It was ill prepared to face the rapidly changing world in which it suddenly had to function when the first Church Council to sit since 1667 assembled in Moscow in mid-August 1917.

Beginning its deliberations just when Kerenskii summoned the Moscow State Conference to hear sober-minded Russians plead for the restoration of law and order, the Church Council found itself at the very vortex of the events that soon would drag Russia deeper into revolutionary turmoil. For more than two months, liberals and conservatives among the clergy squabbled while Russia moved to the brink of armed insurrection.[60] Then, while Bolshevik artillery shelled the Kremlin's Borovitskii Gates at the beginning of November, the council voted to restore the Patriarchate, which had fallen into abeyance in 1700. Of three names placed in an urn and set before the icon of the Blessed Mother of Vladimir, the eldest monk at the council drew forth that of Tikhon Belavin, newly elected Metropolitan of Moscow and the man who had received the fewest votes of the three candidates in the preliminary balloting.[61] Bishop of the Aleutian Islands, Iaroslavl, and Wilno before he became Metropolitan of Moscow in the spring of 1917, Tikhon at the age of fifty-one had every right to be modest about his accomplishments.

His enemies described him as a "humble man, definitely not noted for anything, soft, characterless [and] poorly educated." Although sympathetic churchmen thought him "shining with Russian popular simpleness and modesty,"[62] even they confessed that learning, political acumen, and the gift of words were not among his virtues.

Given the circumstances of his election, the council viewed Tikhon as the choice of God and hoped that he might "inspire a spirit of unity and fraternal harmony among all sons of our suffering fatherland." Some among the delegates still believed that he needed only to speak and the people would answer. "If a strong man should appear, who [spoke] in an authoritative, mighty voice," one priest exclaimed, "millions of Russian people would hear his voice, and peace and quiet would be established."[63] Thus it had been in the past, but the Russia of November 1917 was not the Russia that the council members had known when they had assembled in August. In the world into which Tikhon went forth after the council, the virtues of humility and piety, so loved for so long by the Russian Church, no longer moved men as they once had. "No one gives us our salvation / Not God, the Tsar, nor heroes," the Red Guards who marched through Moscow's streets had sung as Tikhon's name had been drawn from the sacred urn. "We shall strike the final blow for liberation with our hands alone."[64]

Quickly, the blows began to fall upon the Church. Before 1917 ended, the Bolsheviks confiscated all its lands and buildings, removed all schools from its control, transformed marriage into a civil ceremony, and abolished its longstanding prohibition against divorce.[65] Tikhon heaped anathema upon the "enemies of Christ" who now ruled in the Russian land and swore that all "believing and true sons of the Church" would come forth in its defense. Yet this had no more effect upon the Bolsheviks' policies than had the Petrograd Metropolitan Veniamin's earlier promise that "the people would stand like a wall in defense of their holy things."[66] Although the Petrograd crowd on one occasion had prevented Kollontai from taking over the city's great Aleksandr Nevskii Monastery, and although the common folk in other cities supported the Church from time to time, they would not rise up to protect it against the Bolsheviks. When the Sovnarkom announced the complete separation of Church and State at the end of January 1918, the Church Council could only reply with words that showed its appalling failure to come to grips with the world in which it now had to live. "We have cast down the Tsar and subjected ourselves to Jews," one delegate lamented in a speech which showed that adversity had not moderated Russian clerics' anti-Semitism. "The Russian people have now become the plaything of the Jewish-Masonic organizations behind whom is seen Antichrist in the form of an international tsar," the priest concluded. "They are forging for themselves Jewish-Masonic slavery."[67]

Certain that the Church would never be other than a counterrevolutionary force, the Bolsheviks forbade the teaching of religious doctrine to anyone under eighteen years of age, confiscated church treasures, and transformed churches into schools, workers' clubs, and warehouses. Even though they had deadly enemies among Russia's churchmen, the Bolsheviks' quarrel during the Civil War does not seem to have been so much with the personnel of the Church as with its institutions and the role it insisted upon playing in Russian life. More than a few Reds openly cursed the "black magpies" of the Church,[68] and many priests and monks met cruel deaths during the Civil War. But many more churchmen seem to have died at the hands of hostile crowds or as punishment for leading local anti-Soviet uprisings than as a result of capricious executions. Although none of the casualty figures of the Civil War years can be considered accurate, it seems that other social and professional groups may well have suffered more than Russia's priests. A commission appointed by General Denikin to look into Bolshevik atrocities indicated that more than five times as many teachers and professors, and more than seven times as many physicians, died at the hands of the Bolsheviks than did priests.[69]

Although Tikhon refused to bestow the Church's blessing upon them, the Orthodox clergy organized several "Regiments of Jesus," an "Order of the Holy Cross," and a "Brotherhood of the Life-Giving Cross" to fight against the Bolsheviks,[70] and these militant defenders of the Church proclaimed their hatred for Bolsheviks and Jews until the Civil War's final days. Less than a month before Wrangel's final defeat, leading churchmen in the Crimea urged their flocks to launch a pogrom against the Jews "who had enslaved the Russian people through the Bolsheviks." In the Crimean city of Simferopol, it required Wrangel's direct intervention to prevent such a pogrom from breaking out.[71] Such efforts to lead the masses against the Bolsheviks did not alter the fact of the Church's impotence against them. In fact, because the Bolsheviks found the Church less formidable as an adversary than they or Russia's conservatives had expected, they did not turn their full attention to it until after the last of the Whites had been defeated. Then, to help with famine relief in 1921–1922, the Sovnarkom ordered the confiscation of the gold, silver, and precious stones with which the Church adorned its icons and holy relics and severely punished any Church authorities who attempted to stand in its way.[72] Even when Communist Youth League members began to perform antireligious parodies in Russia's streets, the masses did not protest. Other concerns held their attention.[73] Clearly, by the Civil War's end, the Bolsheviks' authority had grown too strong for the Church to challenge.

Against their disorganized clerical and secular opponents, the Bolsheviks used the precepts Lenin had set down nearly two decades before to construct a monolithic, authoritarian political organization that could take full control of Russia.[74] Before 1917, democratic centralism, a key element in Lenin's system of organization, had kept the Party's leaders in touch with the men and women they led and helped them to command efficiently in times of revolutionary upheaval. Yet the discipline imposed from above inevitably came into conflict with democracy that arose from below, and it became all too easy to sacrifice democracy in the name of expediency. The debate over ratifying the Brest-Litovsk Treaty in March 1918 had been the last major policy issue that the Bolshevik Party had decided by a majority vote at a party congress.[75] After that, policy became the province of party chiefs, who argued that only centralized decision making could respond effectively to the Civil War's many crises. "The Party finds itself in a situation where the most strict centralism and the most severe discipline are absolutely essential," the Eighth Party Congress declared in 1919. "Every party decision must first of all be carried out and only after that has been done can it be appealed to the responsible party authority."[76]

The Bolsheviks also turned away from democracy after 1917 because they had grown too large too quickly. There had been fewer than 25,000 Bolsheviks when Lenin had returned to Russia in April 1917. A year later, the number had grown to 390,000, and by March 1921, it had soared to 732,521.[77] Now a massive party, the Bolsheviks ceased to be a party of the masses. By mid-1919, fewer than one party member in nine actually worked in a factory, six out of ten were employed in government or party offices, and a quarter of all party members served in the Red Army, often in positions of political or military authority.[78] Fighting in the Civil War, not conspiring against tsarism, became the key experience in forming the views of these men and women, and it bred in them different priorities. Theirs was not the dogged patience to persevere, the willingness to work for an ideal world of equal opportunity and social justice against overwhelming odds that had been the moral mainstay of the revolutionaries who had dedicated their lives to the struggle against tsarism. Moved too much by self-interest and too little by the spirit of self-sacrifice, too many of these resourceful, brutal men and women were impatient to reap the rewards of power and privilege that only the Party could bestow as the Civil War came to an end. Corruption, greed, and a voracious appetite for personal gain—the very sins that had so stained the government of Imperial Russia—thus appeared very quickly among those men and women who, Lenin once had insisted, must dedicate their entire lives to the Revolution. The party that once had claimed to draw its strength from the masses rapidly became isolated from them by virtue of its members' privileged position in the new order.

As always, privilege bred arrogance and arrogance bred misconduct. "Horrifying facts about the drunkenness, debauchery, corruption, robbery, and irresponsible behavior of many party workers," one Central Committee member complained at the Eighth Party Congress in March 1919, had become so widespread "that one's hair simply stands on end."[79] "The word commissar has become a curse," another added. "The man in the leather jacket . . . has become hateful among the people.[80] Few seemed willing to disagree. "One is beginning to observe very unhealthy signs in the Party's organization," the congress resolved a few days later. "Elements that are not sufficiently Communist and are mainly opportunistic hangers-on are flooding into the Party," it continued. "A serious *purge* in Soviet and party organizations is absolutely necessary."[81]

Although the Bolsheviks hoped to cleanse their ranks, they were not prepared to admit that proletarians could be every bit as corruptible as the men and women of the old regime. The Eighth Party Congress therefore resolved to be extremely careful about admitting nonproletarians, but since "the numerical growth of the Party can be progressive only to the extent that its ranks are infused with healthy proletarian elements from town and country," it insisted that it must continue "to open wide the door of the Party to working men and women." Corruption, the Bolsheviks tried to convince themselves, stemmed from those opportunists who had joined their ranks after the Provisional Government had been overthrown. "So that special measures of control can be applied to those who entered the Party's ranks after October 1917," the Eighth Party Congress announced, all Bolsheviks would be required to reapply for party membership.[82]

The reregistration campaign of mid-1919 removed one Bolshevik in ten from the Party's ranks, and the Whites' victories that summer reduced its membership even more drastically. As party leaders mobilized the rank and file against Denikin, Kolchak, and Iudenich, tens of thousands resigned rather than go to the front. So many who did remain in the Party were killed in the fighting that spring and summer that, by August 1919, the Party had shrunk to less than half of the membership it had boasted in March.[83] "Cowards and good-for-nothings have run away from the Party," Lenin announced. "Good riddance," he went on. "This reduction in the Party's membership represents an enormous increase in its weight and strength."[84] In a series of special "Party Weeks" held between September and November, the Bolsheviks recruited between 160,000 and 200,000 new members from among Russia's workers, soldiers, and peasants.[85] By definition, they promised themselves, these recruits must be reliable because of their proletarian origins and because a new wave of White victories seemed to have made it a poor time for opportunists to proclaim their Bolshevik sympathies. "Only sincere supporters of Communism . . . will join the Party [now]," Lenin explained as Denikin's armies approached Orël.[86] The Central Committee's *Bulletin* put the matter even more directly a few months later. "To get our party card in such conditions," it remarked, "signified, to a certain extent, becoming a candidate for the Denikin gallows."[87]

To assume that workers, soldiers, and peasants would be more honest and more willing than anyone else to sacrifice their personal interests for the sake of building a Communist society exhibited a degree of ideological naiveté that went beyond all bounds of common sense. The simple truth was that the Soviet system—the "iron system" with the "iron discipline," in Lenin's words[88]—opened the way to power. For men and women born and bred to the Russian system, in which power and corruption had gone hand in hand for centuries, the temptations proved too strong to resist. To cleanse their ranks again, the Bolsheviks expelled a quarter of their members during the second half of 1921, but they still could not overcome their own ideological blindness. The Central Committee urged its purge commissions to be particularly wary of party members who came from "bourgeois," "white collar," or "kulak" backgrounds, and they continued to insist that genuine "poor peasants" and workers must be kept in the Party "at all costs."[89]

The Bolsheviks' belief in a Marxian version of the "noble savage" meant that the real targets of the purge with which they celebrated their Civil War victory were not corrupt officials who abused their power as party members, but those who belonged to several emerging opposition groups within the Party.[90] Despite the sense of crisis that had pervaded the Bolsheviks' ranks between 1917 and 1921, and despite the Party's stern discipline and growing centralization, many old Bolsheviks were not yet ready to allow their leaders to decree a permanent end to genuine debate about party decisions. Every member of the the Central Committee had to defend party decisions at the party congresses and conferences that met annually during those years, and the criticisms that lesser members leveled at the views held by their chiefs could be severe. On a number of occasions, even Lenin had found himself in the minority, and it had taxed his genius as an orator and politician to the utmost to win acceptance for his views.

Despite such criticism and debate, the Bolsheviks had remained united against their foreign and domestic enemies. When the Civil War drew near its end and the opportunity came at last to shape Russia's course according to their beliefs, real opposition—the opposition of divergent visions of Russia's future—began to divide Bolsheviks more sharply than at any time since they had broken with the Mensheviks at the beginning of the century. Disagreement about the shape and direction of Russia's future thus became another bitter fruit of the Bolsheviks' victory. Like the peasants and workers from whom they had demanded so many sacrifices, the Bolshevik rank and file felt they had endured the restraints of iron discipline imposed from above for too long. And like the men and women who had chafed at the shortages of food and fuel and endured the indignity of compulsory grain requisitions, they looked for an easing of those restraints as Wrangel's forces retreated from the Crimea. Demands for still more discipline and further sacrifice therefore stirred animosities among them that none of the Bolshevik elders had anticipated.

During 1920 a group made up mostly of intellectuals who called themselves the Democratic Centralists attacked the atrophy of party democracy that had resulted from the Central Committee's emphasis upon centralization during the Civil War. Many of these men once had stood among those daring young Left Communists who, at Nikolai Bukharin's urging, had called for an all-out "revolutionary war" against Germany rather than accept the humiliating terms of the Brest-Litovsk surrender. Now they dissented from the authoritarian manner in which the patriarchs of the Party made decisions and called for a restoration of true democratic centralism. "Comrade Lenin says that the essence of democratic centralism consists in the fact that the Congress elects the Central Committee and the Central Committee manages the Party," Valerian Obolenskii-Osinskii stated at the Ninth Party Congress. "We cannot agree with this 'original' definition," he continued. "We consider that democratic centralism . . . consists of local [party] organs putting the directives of the Central Committee into effect, in the independence of these local organs, and in these organs having to take responsibility for what they do."[91]

As he looked back upon nearly fifteen years of service to the Party, Obolenskii-Osinskii feared that centralization would destroy the Party's ability to respond effectively to crises by separating it from the wellsprings of new talent. More immediately, he thought that Trotskii's call for militarizing Russia's labor force for the tasks of peacetime reconstruction would undermine the very foundations upon which the Bolsheviks hoped to build a just society. A close associate of Bukharin's since those long-ago days when they had organized a student rally at Moscow University in 1910,[92] he now had to face the scorn of his old comrade, who undertook to tutor him in public about the principles upon which socialism must be built. "Militarization is nothing other than the self-organization of the working class and the organization by the working class of other classes that stand close to it," Bukharin explained loftily as he urged the congress to reject his old friend's criticisms. "For us militarization is not self-asphyxiation," he concluded. "For us it is self-organization."[93] Bukharin's defense of militarization in 1920 marked the high point of the extreme centralization that Obolenskii-Osinskii and his comrades feared. Yet they preferred to bear their comrades' scorn than risk splitting the party they had served so long. While other opponents of militarization prepared to challenge its advocates because they threatened to transform Russia's trade unions into institutions that represented the state and not the workers, the Democratic Centralists muted their opposition in the hope of preserving the Party's unity.

Broader support among Russia's workers and a willingness to press their arguments further allowed the Workers' Opposition to pose a more serious challenge to the Party's centralized control than the Democratic Centralists had done. Headed by Aleksandr Shliapnikov, a metalworker who had risen to the post of people's commissar of labor in the first Sovnarkom, the Workers' Opposition drew its main strength from the Communist trade unions that dominated the factories of the Moscow region and the coal mines of the Donbas.[94] Ever since 1917, a confrontation had been brewing between Bolshevik leaders and these trade unions over the latter's belief that the best way to restore Russia's industry was to place her factories in the hands of the workers themselves. Certainly the Bolsheviks' call for workers' control of the factories in which they worked had drawn Russia's proletarians to them before the October Revolution, but the gross incompetence of worker management in practice had stopped Lenin from speaking in glowing terms of the masses' talent for organization, planning, and production very soon after the Bolsheviks had taken power. Worker management, Lenin warned at the beginning of 1920, "involves a tremendous waste of forces and is not suited to the rapid and accurate work demanded by the conditions of centralized large-scale industry." To test performance and hold the men and women in charge of industry accountable for it, he insisted that "the principle of one-man responsibility is the only correct method of work," the only "system [that] best ensures the most effective utilization of human abilities."[95]

Just as Trotskii had drawn heavily upon the tsarist officer corps to command the Red Army during the Civil War's darkest days, so Lenin urged the Bolsheviks to recruit "bourgeois specialists" from the Old Regime to restore Russia's shattered industries. At the same time, his idea of placing Russia's factories under one-man management threatened to deprive the trade unions of any effective control over the factories in which they worked. Faced with that grim prospect, the Workers' Opposition urged the Sovnarkom to transfer Russia's entire economic administration to their trade unions, and when they attacked Lenin's proposals to give "bourgeois specialists" one-man responsibility for the factories' management, Lenin convinced the Ninth Party Congress to support his views. "There must be a better understanding of the complex economic problems facing the nation and the importance of technical education and experience," the congress had resolved in

March 1920. All party members, it continued, must wage "a relentless struggle against the crude conceit of those who think that the working class can resolve its problems without placing bourgeois specialists in the most responsible positions."[96]

Although stilled for the moment, the Workers' Opposition would not remain silent. At the root of their discontent in 1920 lay their outrage at Trotskii's rough and ready attempts to restore Russia's shattered railroad and river transport network. As people's commissar of transport and chairman of the Central Transport Committee, Trotskii had ridden roughshod over the trade unionists' call for workers' control,[97] and he had urged the Sovnarkom to extend his tactics to the rest of Russian industry. This had brought a storm of protest from the trade unions. Without faith in the proletariat, and with the purpose of stifling mass participation in the Revolution, they complained, the Party had begun to cater to the "bourgeoisie" at their expense. Once again, the Workers' Opposition demanded that the trade unions take direct control of Russia's economy. This time, it seemed that they might win support among a Bolshevik rank and file that had grown discontented with Lenin's dictatorial methods.[98]

Toward the end of 1920, Lenin began to lose patience with his critics. "When . . . [opposition] turns into opposition for the sake of opposition, we should certainly put an end to it," he told a Moscow Provincial Party Conference in November. "We have wasted a great deal of time on altercations, quarrels, and recrimination, and we must put an end to all that," he went on. "Otherwise, we cannot exist when we are surrounded by enemies at home and abroad."[99] Unlike Trotskii, Lenin preferred to negotiate rather than throw down defiant challenges to his opponents, but these were ominous warnings nonetheless. "Trade unions have an extremely important part to play at every step of the dictatorship of the proletariat," he assured the assembled delegates at the Eighth Party Congress of Soviets at the end of December. "Trade unions are not just historically necessary; they are historically inevitable." Yet this did not mean, Lenin insisted, that trade unions should control the economic life of Soviet Russia. A trade union "is not a state organization," he told his listeners magisterially. "It is, in fact, a school: a school of administration, a school of economic management, a school of Communism."[100] As he had done so often in the past, Lenin masterfully tempered firmness with flattery and assurance while making no real concessions. But this time, more would be needed to restore peace. Not until the Workers' Opposition had openly challenged his authority at the Tenth Party Congress could their opposition be brought to an end.

When Aleksandra Kollontai, the apostle of women's liberation and one-time commissar of public welfare, joined the ranks of the Workers' Opposition in January 1921, her passion for freedom quickly blended with the masses' hatred for the new aristocracy of privilege embodied in the swaggering figure of the arrogant Bolshevik commissar. The "Workers' Opposition," she wrote in February in a pamphlet published at her own expense,[101] was not the work of self-serving individuals but had sprung "from the depths of the industrial proletariat of Soviet Russia." With more passion than sound understanding of Russia's present situation, Kollontai insisted that "a new, homogeneous, unified, perfectly arranged Communist industry" would emerge most quickly from "the collective efforts of the workers themselves," not from decrees imposed from above. The trade unions, she insisted, must be more than the mere "schools for Communism" of which Lenin spoke. Because only workers could "generate in their minds new methods of organizing labor as well as running industry," the trade unions must be the "managers and creators of the Communist economy" in Russia.[102] Lenin thought that such utopian dreams were utter nonsense. Rather than argue against Kollontai's views, he attacked her personally and hinted nastily that her liaison with Shliapnikov was the reason for her support of the Workers' Opposition.[103] Such attacks showed the depths of his frustration, but they also revealed that the Bolsheviks leadership had become far more sensitive to criticism from below than had once been the case.

When the Tenth Party Congress assembled in Moscow on March 8, 1921, it met under the very dark shadow of the Kronstadt uprising, the most serious revolt the Bolsheviks had ever faced. This revealed the rank and file's deep dissatisfaction with the Party's iron discipline and demonstrated that the Bolshevik leadership would tolerate no opposition to its absolute authority. As a result, when Shliapnikov urged a larger role for trade unionists in the management of Russia's economic and political life, Lenin declared that the time had come for the unions to end their criticism and complaint. "The political conclusion to be drawn from the present situation is that the Party must be united and any opposition prevented," he stated flatly in summing up the report that the Central Committee presented to the congress. The Party faced too many dangers to squander its resources in debate, and it must deal sternly with its critics. "This is no time for an opposition," Lenin warned. "Either you're on this side or on the other, but then your weapon must be a gun, not an opposition. . . . I think the Party Congress will have to draw the conclusion that the opposition's time has run out and that the lid's on it," he concluded bluntly. "We want no more oppositions!"[104]

Lenin let the delegates mull over his stern words for more than a week. Then, on the last day of the congress, March 16, 1921, he introduced resolutions "On Party Unity" and "On the Syndicalist and Anarchist Deviation in Our Party" that were designed to put the lid on the opposition. Taken together, these condemned the Workers' Opposition as "radically wrong," "a radical departure from Marxism," and "an expression of syndicalist and anarchist deviation" that was "incompatible with membership" in the Russian Communist Party, the title that the Bolsheviks had taken in 1918.[105] These closed the last avenues for Bolsheviks to express legitimate dissent and condemned what once had been viewed as honest differences of opinion among comrades as a sign of blatant disloyalty. "All class-conscious workers must clearly realize that factionalism of any kind is harmful and impermissible," Lenin's resolution on party unity stated. Even though criticism of the Party's "shortcomings" was "absolutely necessary," he insisted that "every critic must see to it that the form of his criticism takes account of the position of the Party, surrounded as it is by a ring of enemies." At the very least, criticism that damaged the Party was dangerous; sometimes it could even be equated with treason. The Party Congress must order the Workers' Opposition and the Democratic Centralists to dissolve themselves immediately. "Nonobservance of this decision," Lenin's resolution concluded, "shall entail unconditional and instant expulsion from the Party."[106]

When its delegates adopted Lenin's resolutions by an overwhelming majority, the Tenth Party Congress abolished the last vestiges of revolutionary democracy in Soviet Russia. Henceforth, all opposition stood condemned as counterrevolutionary, no matter whether it came from survivors of the Old Regime, workers, peasants, or loyal party members. Although some delegates at first hesitated to follow Lenin's course, many thought that they would consolidate the power of the Communist Party in Russia and could assure the victory of the Revolution by doing so. "In voting for this resolution, I feel that it can well be turned against us, but nevertheless I support it," one senior Bolshevik declared as he cast his ballot. "Let the Central Committee in a moment of danger take the severest measures against the best party comrades," he continued. "[Let it] even be mistaken! That is less dangerous than the wavering that is now observable."[107] What the Tenth Party Congress had accomplished, in fact, was what one expert termed "the consolidation of power in the central party apparatus,"[108] and the Communist Party in Russia now became more important than ever before. The Party, not the people—not even the workers—ruled Russia. As Stalin's rise to power would make clear, whoever commanded the apparatus of the Communist Party could impose his will upon the Russians more effectively than any autocrat had ever done.

The decisions of the Tenth Party Congress thus began to give a rigid form to the Bolsheviks' new Russia. Soviet Russia had become monolithic, Bolshevik, and undemocratic, with its decision-making processes concentrated at the highest levels of the Party. This meant that the modest concessions of the New Economic Policy that followed less than a week later held no real promise of lessening the rigidity of the Bolshevik system. Precisely because the Party now wielded undisputed control over the upper reaches of Russia's government, it could permit a brief restoration of private initiative at the lowest levels of the nation's economy to quench the flames of peasant discontent that still burned in Tambov, the Ukraine, and western Siberia. In terms of altering the shape of Soviet Russia's political system or the manner in which key policy decisions were made at the top, the New Economic Policy therefore had no real significance.

Lenin and the Bolsheviks had come to power in 1917 with promises of peace, land, and social justice to Russia's poor, hungry, and war-weary proletarians. For a moment at the Second All-Russian Congress of Soviets, they and the masses had shared a vision of a future bright with hope, although its dimensions admittedly had not yet been defined. Three and a half years later, that vision had been darkened permanently by clouds of repression. The Tsar had been overthrown and the Civil War won, but the Bolsheviks' domestic security forces continued to be larger than any their imperial predecessors had ever possessed. So did their bureaucracy. In town and country, the living standard of Russia's masses remained far below what it had been in 1917. The general death rate had doubled, and that grim statistic did not take into account some seven million men, women, and children who had died from malnutrition and epidemics since the Bolsheviks had taken power.[109]

In the cities, some began to mutter that the key to Russia's future could be found by spelling *molot* and *serp* ("hammer" and "sickle") backwards to produce *prestolom*, meaning "to the throne," that is, a restoration of the monarchy. Others insisted that the Russians must bear the burdens of their own stupidity and lack of foresight in allowing the Bolsheviks to take power in the first place. "There is no point in cursing anyone," the historian Iurii Gote wrote with grim fatalism in his Moscow diary not long before the Tenth Party Congress assembled. "A people that has ruined itself has no right to demand anyone's help and sympathy."[110]

In contrast to the peasants, who had never been willing partners of the Bolsheviks and whose resentment still burned in Tambov and other parts of the Russian countryside, Russia's factory workers had borne their burdens more willingly during the dark days of the Civil War. Yet the wave of urban discontent that arose during the weeks before the Tenth Party Congress indicated that the patience of even these Bolshevik loyalists had worn thin and that Shliapnikov, Kollontai, and the Workers' Opposition spoke for a much broader group than the Bolsheviks cared to admit. Neither adroit political maneuvering nor the threat of force could contain the proletarians' bitterness at a dream gone sour. In February 1921 there had been strikes in Petrograd. Then, at the end of the month, the resentment of Russia's proletarians had burst into flame at the Baltic naval bastion at Kronstadt. Kronstadt's sailors had stood in Russia's revolutionary vanguard from the moment the first shots of the February Revolution had rung out in Petrograd's streets. They had been the first to cheer Lenin's return, and they had formed a citadel of Bolshevism ever since. As these dedicated heroes of the Revolution took up arms against the Party in the name of the Revolution, the Bolsheviks faced their gravest domestic threat and the greatest test of their resolve to hold to the course Lenin had set.

CHAPTER FIFTEEN

The Kronstadt Uprising

TWENTY MILES west of Petrograd, almost exactly midway between the northern and southern shores of the Finnish Gulf, Kotlin Island forms an elongated triangle some seven and a quarter miles in length and just over a mile across at its widest point. Kotlin sits with its base facing Petrograd, while its needle-shaped, slightly hooked tip points into the deeper waters of the gulf. Its shores are rocky and difficult to approach by sea. At the beginning of the eighteenth century, Peter the Great had laid the beginnings of a town and fortifications at its eastern end to bar all approaches by water to his new capital of St. Petersburg. Named Kronstadt, Peter's early fortifications had grown into the Russians' key naval base in the Baltic. Until the middle of the nineteenth century, five stone fortresses, each with three tiers of heavy guns, had formed its principal defenses. Then the Russians had extended Kronstadt's defenses across the entire seventeen-mile span of the gulf by building in the shallow waters that separated it from the mainland seven low-lying forts supplemented by thirteen stone and concrete batteries that housed heavily armored six-, ten-, and twelve-inch Krupp guns. All the waters of the eastern Finnish Gulf lay within their intersecting fields of fire. Some fifteen miles to the west, the heavy shore batteries of Krasnaia Gorka on the southern Baltic coast could add their long-range guns to Kronstadt's fire-power if needed. The fortifications of Kronstadt, the editors of

Baedeker's *Russia* informed their readers on the eve of the First World War, "are deemed impregnable."[1]

In one of the many paradoxes that fill the pages of Russia's history, Kronstadt, the impregnable bastion that defended Imperial Russia against the warships of foreign enemies, became one of its most fertile seedbeds of revolution. Home to some twenty-five thousand sailors and artillerymen, Kronstadt harbored a powerful but volatile armed force. Fiercely independent, restless, and quick to anger as seamen often are, these Kronstadt men had a close, unspoken kinship with those free-spirited rebels who had lived on Russia's frontiers in days gone by. *Buntarstvo*, the spirit of spontaneous rebellion, burned in their breasts as hotly as it had among the followers of the great rebel chieftains Stenka Razin and Emelian Pugachev. Trained to fight and die for Russia, they were only slightly less ready to rise against her.[2]

For that reason, Kronstadt's sailors and dockyard workers had close connections with the rising wave of labor unrest that began to sweep across Russia at the beginning of the twentieth century. Men who lived in the grim world that excluded Russian soldiers and sailors from the interior of streetcars, forbade them to walk on the sunny side of the street, and posted signs that closed public gardens to them and to dogs were sympathetic to revolutionary preachings about a better world of equality and opportunity. When, in 1901, Russia's Marxists had begun to publish their newspaper *Iskra* in Germany, some of the first copies to reach Russia came through Kronstadt. After that, revolutionary pamphlets circulated widely among the Kronstadt garrison. To crush the rebellious spirit of the Kronstadt men, the fortress officers became notorious for their brutality. Their cruelty soon earned Kronstadt the name of the "Seamen's Sakhalin," after Russia's island penal colony in the northern Pacific.[3]

In October 1905 the sailors and gunners of Kronstadt joined striking workers all over Russia. For two days they rampaged through Kronstadt's streets, built barricades, and burned buildings. At the cost of nearly a hundred dead and wounded, loyal troops from the Petersburg garrison crushed their rebellion and arrested more than three thousand of them. When Kronstadt again burst into flames less than nine months later, the authorities shot 36, sentenced 228 to hard labor in Siberia, and sent more than 1,000 to prison.[4] For a decade, the rebellious spirit of Kronstadt remained silent, except for one brief moment in 1910, when the authorities had snuffed out an attempted revolt by shooting more than 100 and drowning several boatloads of captured seamen.[5] It exploded with renewed force in February 1917, when the Kronstadt men killed close to 40 of their senior officers in one night. Anchor Square, the huge parade ground that stood in the shadow of the immense Seamen's Cathedral and dominated Kronstadt's center, became the sailors' execution ground and meeting place. In mass meetings there, Kronstadt's sailors and gunners brewed their own mixture of libertarian, anarchist, socialist radicalism, which they quaffed in heady draughts while they proclaimed Kronstadt the Paris Commune of 1871 reborn in 1917.

Disdaining the Provincial Government and recognizing no authority but their own, the Kronstadters proclaimed themselves "the sole power" in revolutionary Petrograd. Kronstadt men played a prominent part in the demonstrations that toppled Russia's first Provisional Government in April, and they stood at the very center of the street violence that nearly cost the Socialist Revolutionary leader Chernov his life during the July Days. Kronstadt sailors were the first to call for General Kornilov's arrest and execution at the time of the abortive Kornilov "uprising" against Kerenskii's government in August. They took part in storming the Winter Palace during the October Revolution, provided the main military force that the Bolsheviks used to break up the Constituent Assembly, and, in one of the most shameful episodes in Russia's revolutionary annals, murdered two of the Provisional Government's fallen ministers in their hospital beds. During the Bolsheviks' tenuous first days in power, Lenin used them as a praetorian guard to defend his government.[6]

Forty thousand black-jacketed sailors from Kronstadt and the Baltic Fleet fought for the Red cause at Pulkovo, at Sviiazhsk, and on scores of lesser-known faraway battlefields during Russia's Civil War. Yet, even as their comrades fought against the Whites, the men at Kronstadt grew fearful that the Bolsheviks had begun to betray the Revolution and to establish a new autocracy. Some Kronstadt men supported those Left Communists who urged the Bolsheviks to declare a "revolutionary war" against Germany at the time of Brest-Litovsk, others fought on the side of the Left Socialist Revolutionaries in July 1918, and still others called for armed resistance against the Germans in the Ukraine. Meetings at Kronstadt's Anchor Square condemned the Cheka's attack against Russia's anarchists in the spring of 1918 and denounced those who took part in the Bolsheviks' grain-requisitioning detachments as "thieves" and "plunderers of the peasants."[7] Always, the Kronstadt men defended proletarian democracy and opposed all forms of political restraint and government coercion. Any departure from the most primitive forms of communal socialism stirred their anger.

As the Civil War took its toll, the Kronstadt men grew more restless. At the beginning of 1921, many of them still had not received their clothing allotments for 1920, their food rations—a traditional cause for complaint in the Russian Navy—were worse than ever, and they had been asked to surrender the last of their oil reserves to Petrograd's fuel-starved factories. Although most of the sailors who served aboard the great warships anchored in Kronstadt harbor that winter had begun their service before the Revolution and, therefore, had fewer ties to the countryside whence they had come, there were considerably more men of recent peasant origin in the Kronstadt garrison itself.[8] Because the Bolsheviks had replaced many of the Kronstadters who had been killed during the Civil War with peasant draftees, the plight of Russia's villages stirred discontent on the island fortress as never before, especially since many of the new men came from the turbulent Ukraine. Every letter bearing a report of hunger, every tale of starvation, every complaint about the arrogance of the Bolshevik commissars who had taken control of Russia's countryside after Wrangel's defeat stirred their wrath.[9]

Party membership at Kronstadt fell by half in less than six months, and Bolshevik speakers complained that they found it particularly difficult to gain a hearing among the Kronstadt men. In some cases, poor planning was at fault, for Party-sponsored lectures about "The Origin of Man," "Italian Art," "Greek Sculpture," and "The Morals and Customs of the Austrians"[10] could hardly be expected to attract much of a following in such tumultuous times. But there was more to the sailors' apathetic response than mere disinterest. "The work of cultural-educational enlightenment has come to a standstill," one party activist reported. "Demobilization of the army, the possibility of going home—that is all . . . [the sailors] want to talk about."[11] As had so many of Russia's soldiers during the summer and fall of 1917, the Kronstadt men now began to desert. During just the first month of 1921, nearly five hundred of its garrison did so.[12] "The soil for an uprising in Kronstadt and in the fleet," one Soviet commentator later wrote, "was fully prepared."[13]

The situation in nearby Petrograd was as explosive as in Kronstadt, perhaps more so. Petrograd suffered such an acute fuel shortage during the winter of 1920–1921 that, by December 1920, the flow of coal from the Donbas had nearly halted, and the supply of fuel oil had fallen to scarcely a quarter of what it had been in October. Petrograd's leaders tried to make up for the shortages of coal and oil with wood, but the city received less than a sixth of the eighteen thousand freightcars of wood needed in January because heavy snows and driving blizzards stalled those few trains that Trotskii's railway repair crews had kept in operation up to that time. In January, the Sovnarkom purchased three hundred thousand tons of coal abroad, but that only delayed the crisis for another month. Between November and the end of January, the Petrograd authorities allowed city folk to raze 175 buildings for fuel; in February they authorized the destruction of 50 more.[14]

None of these efforts could heat the city or fuel its factories in the dead of winter. "In view of the problems that are developing with the transportation of fuel," the Petrograd Soviet's Executive Committee decreed on January 18, 1921, "all factories and mills in the city of Petrograd will be closed from January 19 through January 23."[15] Then, before the middle of February, the Petrograd Soviet cut the workers' rations by a third and closed ninety-three of the city's largest factories. Cold, on short rations, and out of work, Petrograd's workers faced skyrocketing food prices and falling wages. At the end of 1920, real wages stood at less than a tenth of what they had been in 1913, while the price of bread during that single year had risen a thousand percent. Then, just between January and February 1921, the prices of potatoes and rye bread nearly tripled. The price of a pound of butter increased by more than two thousand rubles, and the cost of a pound of sugar rose by a third to nearly twenty thousand rubles in the same thirty-day period.[16] Gold rubles had sold at slightly less than eight times the value of paper rubles in 1918. Now it took 10,000 paper rubles to buy a gold one as gold entered a spiral that would reach a ratio of 240,000 paper rubles to 1 by May 1922.[17]

Petrograd's workers protested these conditions with sporadic work stoppages, but until February 1921 these had been scattered, small, and easily dealt with. Closing the city's largest mills stirred larger protests in the middle of the month as angry workers demanded that the Bolsheviks "answer before the representatives of the people for their deceit, their robberies, and all their crimes."[18] Insensitive to how frayed the workers' tempers had become, the city Soviet called out special detachments of *kursanty*, officer trainees who could be counted on to defend the Bolsheviks at all costs, to break up a street protest by more than two thousand workers on February 24. The authorities followed that order with a declaration of martial law that forbade public meetings, set an eleven o'clock nighttime curfew, and deprived the workers of their rations by closing every factory where a demonstration had occurred, but other workers joined their comrades the following day in protests that seemed ominously reminiscent of the events which had ushered in the February Revolution, four years and a day before.

The differences between these street demonstrations and those that had toppled the Romanovs in 1917 were much greater than the similarities. Weakened by nearly four years of hunger, demoralized by never-ending shortages, and terrorized by the Cheka, Petrograd's workers had no taste for direct confrontation with Russia's new masters. Nor did they have the strength. "The strikers were overawed," the exiled American anarchist Alexander Berkman wrote. "The labor unrest [was] crushed with an iron hand."[19] For any who were not willing to abandon their protests in return for the Bolsheviks' promise of special holiday rations that would include up to four pounds of meat, a quarter pound of chocolate, a can of condensed milk, and two pounds of rice, heavily armed patrols of *kursanty* remained an ever-present reminder that a very large stick loomed behind the small carrot Russia's rulers had offered.[20] So did the armed squads that factory defense committees had organized to keep Petrograd's workers at their benches once the factories reopened. "One might have thought," wrote one of the Kronstadt representatives who visited Petrograd's factories at the end of February, "that these were not factories but the forced labor prisons of tsarist times."[21] Punishment of any who refused to return to work remained the order of the day at the end of February. "The handling of the strikers," Emma Goldman remembered with deep sadness, "was by no means very comradely."[22]

Reports of the workers' demonstrations reached Kronstadt at the same time as did wild rumors about their suppression by Cheka firing squads. Although untrue, these tales deepened the sailors' restlessness.[23] At the same time, the bitter feud that Zinoviev had waged with Trotskii ever since Trotskii had replaced him as Lenin's confidant in 1917 took on new and complex dimensions that added to the tension in Kronstadt. Zinoviev posed as a champion of party democracy and condemned Trotskii (who, as commissar of war, controlled the fleet whose command Zinoviev coveted) as an advocate of dictatorial centralization. Translated into concrete political terms, Zinoviev, as chief of the Petrograd party organization, demanded control of the political administration of the Baltic Fleet, while Trotskii and his deputies resisted. The Kronstadt sailors, whose tradition of resisting any authority imposed from above once had led Trotskii to call them "the pride and glory of the Revolution," now readily supported Zinoviev's call for "democracy" against Trotskii's defense of "dictatorship."[24] Although neither the Petrograd party chief nor the commissar of war had any intention of restoring the sort of "democracy" that had allowed the Kronstadt men to play such a key role in the events of 1917, their feud weakened the Bolsheviks' control just when the island fortress began to feel the full effects of Petrograd's fuel and food shortages at the beginning of 1921.

Frozen into the ice less than a stone's throw apart, their heavy steel hulls connected by a crude ice-bound pontoon walkway, the great battleships *Petropavlovsk* and *Sevastopol* seethed with discontent in Kronstadt harbor. As one of the Baltic Fleet commissars later recalled, "the Communists had absolutely no authority there." Between them, the two ships carried a dozen 350 mm. and sixteen 120 mm. guns, all of them capable of serving as heavy artillery against targets on shore.[25] In 1917 their crews and their guns had been vital to the Bolsheviks' success, but memories of their shared triumph did not mean that they would support the Bolsheviks now. When Bolshevik censorship had cut them off from news of the workers' demonstrations in Petrograd, the crews of these ships had sent a special delegation into the city to learn the fate of the workers' protest, and on February 28, that delegation had reported their observations to a joint meeting of both ships' companies aboard the *Petropavlovsk*. Combined with the impressions that some of the ships' crews brought back from home leaves to their villages, the report heightened the sailors' outrage. "When we returned home," Stepan Petrichenko, the senior ship's clerk on the *Petropavlovsk* later wrote, "our parents asked why we fought for the oppressors. That set us thinking."[26] True to their revolutionary tradition, the Kronstadt men moved very quickly from thinking to making political demands, this time directed against the Bolsheviks.

Presided over by Petrichenko, the meeting aboard the *Petropavlovsk* called for freedom of assembly, speech, press, and the liberation of all peasants, workers, sailors, and soldiers "imprisoned in connection with worker and peasant movements," as well as the freeing of "all political prisoners belonging to socialist parties." The sailors also called for new elections "in view of the fact that the present soviets do not express the will of the workers and peasants," asked that equal rations be given to all working men and women except for those who worked in trades which endangered their health, demanded the abolition of the hated roadblock detachments that interfered with private trade between town and countryside, and called for the abolition of all political education, agitation, and propaganda departments in factories, villages, and military units.[27] Certainly these demands showed no sympathy for the values of the Old Regime. Nor did they embody those "petty bourgeois attitudes" for which the Bolsheviks perpetually blamed the Russian peasants. Aside from attacking those principles of War Communism that Lenin and his associates were about to abandon in any case, the *Petropavlovsk* resolution embodied mainly those revolutionary socialist principles that Lenin himself had advocated in 1917. But 1921 was not 1917. Demands for open elections and freedom of expression for all proletarians in Russia challenged the Bolsheviks' now firm monopoly of power. As such, Lenin and Trotskii insisted, they were counterrevolutionary. Any force that threatened the Bolsheviks as the self-styled guardians of the Revolution could not be thought otherwise.

The Bolsheviks therefore sent "Papa" Kalinin to represent them at the mass meeting that the sailors organized the next day on Kronstadt's Anchor Square. More than Lenin or even Trotskii, Kalinin, who had learned to read and write in a tiny country school and had left his native village before the age of eighteen to work in Petrograd's mills, spoke the language of Russia's common folk. It had been Kalinin who had convinced Petrograd's men to join the Bolsheviks' grain-requisitioning detachments during the hungry spring of 1918, and it had been he, a scant week before, who had persuaded many of Petrograd's disgruntled proletarians to return to work. The Bolsheviks' political high command undoubtedly was counting on him to repeat those successes at Kronstadt, and so, perhaps, were some of the sailors who thought of themselves as the Bolsheviks' loyal opposition, not as counterrevolutionaries. Bands and an honor guard therefore greeted Kalinin at Anchor Square, but all signs of good will disappeared when the sailors who had gone to Petrograd repeated the report they had made aboard the *Petropavlovsk* the previous day. As they heard how armed Bolsheviks had forced Petrograd's hungry workers back to their benches, the men and women on Anchor Square grew more hostile.

When Kalinin began to speak, hecklers drowned his words. "Knock it off," one voice called out. "You're keeping warm enough." "You've got a whole bunch of jobs!" a bearded Red Army soldier called out from another corner of the Square. "I'll bet you're collecting rations for each one of them!"[28] Nikolai Kuzmin, the commissar of the Baltic Fleet, who had accompanied Kalinin, tried to divert the crowd by recalling how they had worked together to defend the Revolution during the Civil War. As he began to speak about Kronstadt's glorious revolutionary traditions, an angry voice shouted: "Have you forgotten how you had every tenth man shot when you were assigned to the northern front?" Kuzmin had served on the Revolutionary Military Council of the Sixth Army on the northern front at the height of the Whites' successes, when it had not been uncommon for commissars to order every tenth man shot when Red Army units fled in battle. Others, including Trotskii himself, had done the same, and in those days the men of Red Kronstadt had approved. Yet, when Kuzmin stirred those memories, he struck a hostile response. "We have always shot traitors to the workers' cause and will shoot them in the future," he replied to the men who had recalled his bloody work on the northern front. In 1919, talk about shooting class enemies would have stirred cheers; now it brought shouts of "Enough! Get rid of him! Run him out!"[29] When Petrichenko read the resolution that had been passed at the *Petropavlovsk* meeting, sixteen thousand voices cheered. Only Kalinin, Kuzmin, and the chairman of the Kronstadt Soviet, who had come with them to the Square, voted against it.[30]

The evening of March 1 brought the sailors at Kronstadt close to an open confrontation with the Soviet authorities. The anarchist Emma Goldman, who, with Alexander Berkman, reported on the Kronstadt events from Petrograd's Astoria Hotel, later wrote that, "even after he and his comrades had attacked the sailors and condemned their resolution, Kalinin had been escorted back to the station in the greatest friendliness,"[31] but other evidence indicates that the Kronstadters held Kalinin for several hours before they allowed him to return to Petrograd. At the same time, thirty delegates whom the crowd on Anchor Square sent to look into conditions in Petrograd were arrested the moment they reached the city.[32] "It was the first blow struck by the Communist Government against Kronstadt," Berkman reported sadly. "The fate of the committee [of delegates]," he added, "remained a mystery."[33]

That night and the following morning, the men from the ships and barracks of Kronstadt chose representatives to elect a new Kronstadt Soviet. When these men met at the House of Enlightenment (formerly the Imperial School for Naval Engineers) on the afternoon of March 2, they posted armed sailors from the *Petropavlovsk* to guard against any outside interference. According to the newspaper that the rebels began to publish the next day, Commissar of the Baltic Fleet Kuzmin again angered the sailors by stating flatly that "if the delegates wanted an open armed struggle they would get it, for the Communists would never voluntarily give up power and would fight to the very last gasp."[34] After several hours of debate about how to ensure that the election for a new Kronstadt Soviet would be truly free and secret, the meeting, with a roar of approval, resolved to arrest Kuzmin and the chairman of the Kronstadt Soviet on the spot.[35] The men of Kronstadt had taken a very long step toward breaking with their government.

As the gulf between the sailors and the Soviet authorities widened, Stepan Petrichenko took control of Kronstadt. A peasant from the Ukraine who had served in the Russian navy since 1912, Petrichenko was a strong, good-looking man of about thirty who spoke in the clear and direct manner of the peasants from whose midst he had come. A natural leader and an experienced seaman, he was a dedicated revolutionary who believed in the system of equal opportunity and social justice that the Kronstadt sailors had defended so stubbornly against the Provisional Government in 1917. Although he had no more than two years of formal schooling, he knew the meaning of words and understood how to use them to sway men's minds.[36] When a seaman from the *Petropavlovsk* burst into the House of Enlightenment during the debates of March 2 to exclaim that fifteen truckloads of well-armed Communists were about to attack the assembly, Petrichenko urged his comrades to establish a Provisional Revolutionary Committee of five (later expanded to ten) to administer Kronstadt until the elections for a new soviet could be completed.[37] "The Communist Party, now ruling the country, has cut itself off from the masses and does not have the strength to pull Russia out of her complete economic collapse," he announced to the people of Kronstadt in the first issue of *Izvestiia Vremennogo revoliutsionnogo komiteta* (News of the Provisional Revolutionary Committee) that appeared the next morning. The Party, he insisted, had lost the confidence of Russia's toiling masses. Only a government which held that confidence could "give bread, firewood, coal, shoes and clothing to those who need them, and pull the republic out of its present blind alley." The soviets must once again be allowed to become the "true representatives of working men and women" by new elections that fairly represented all the toilers of Russia.[38]

Historians have argued about whether the arrests of Kuzmin and the chairman of the Kronstadt Soviet or the formation of the Provisional Revolutionary Committee marked the beginning of the uprising, but the combination of those two incidents in the afternoon and early evening of March 2 left no doubt that the Soviet government must crush the Kronstadt dissidents or lose its monopoly of political power in Russia. As Kronstadt's handful of Bolshevik loyalists began to leave, Petrichenko and his comrades turned the *Petropavlovsk* into a headquarters for the Provisional Revolutionary Committee and occupied all key points on Kotlin Island. The voice of all people, they insisted, must be heard. "The task of the Provisional Revolutionary Committee is to organize, through friendly and cooperative effort in the city [of Kronstadt] and its fortress, the conditions necessary for proper and fair elections for a new [Kronstadt] Soviet," Kronstadt's revolutionary *Izvestiia* announced the next day. "And so, comrades," Petrichenko explained in his first proclamation, the people of Kronstadt must work together "for order, for civic calm, for firmness, and for a new honest socialist organization to promote the welfare of all toiling people."[39]

The Bolsheviks' belief that all challenges to their authority must be treated as counterrevolutionary meant that the Provisional Revolutionary Committee's direct challenge had to be met with armed force, and the retreat of Kronstadt's Communists to the mainland on the afternoon of March 2 drew the lines for Russia's greatest battle of Red against Red. Yet Kronstadt was no mere revolt of the disgruntled and disaffected. Kronstadt's sailors still believed in the Revolution and demanded its defense. Kronstadt "was in the front lines in [the] February and October [revolutions]," they insisted. "Now it is the first to raise the standard of revolt for the Third Revolution of working men and women."[40]

All the old underpinnings of mass movements in Russia—populism, anarchism, and fervent Slavic nationalism—had a place in Kronstadt's revolutionary consciousness as Petrichenko and his comrades preached their messianic doctrine of a Third Revolution.

"The autocracy has fallen," they proclaimed. "The Constituent Assembly has departed to the realm of the damned. The commissarocracy is collapsing. The moment has come for a true government of toilers, a government of soviets."[41] Here once again was the peasant hatred for alien authority and a state imposed from above. It was "Us and Them," a headline in the March 8 issue of the rebels' *Izvestiia* proclaimed—Kronstadt men who told the truth against Communists who spoke falsely, the popular democracy of Kronstadt against the privileged "commissarocracy" of Soviet Russia.[42] Kronstadt championed "equal rights for all, privileges for none," Alexander Berkman remembered. In the soviets, transformed once again into the forums of Russia's working men and women, the Kronstadt rebels hoped to find "the true road of liberation from the oppression of Communist bureaucracy."[43]

Within a week, the headlines of the rebels' *Izvestiia* trumpeted the Kronstadters' revolutionary message:

"ALL POWER TO THE SOVIETS, NOT TO POLITICAL PARTIES!"

"DOWN WITH THE COUNTERREVOLUTION FROM THE LEFT AND THE RIGHT!"

"THE POWER OF THE SOVIETS WILL LIBERATE THE TOILING PEASANTRY FROM THE COMMUNIST YOKE!"

"VICTORY OR DEATH!"

With the Bolsheviks denouncing the Kronstadt sailors as "tools of former tsarist generals who, together with Socialist Revolutionary traitors, [have] staged a counterrevolutionary conspiracy against the proletarian republic," there could be no common ground upon which former comrades could stand.[44] As such influential foreign anarchists as Berkman, Emma Goldman, and Victor Serge pleaded in vain for mediation, the soldiers, sailors, and workers of Kronstadt made ready to face what Berkman later called "the Tatar despotism of the Communist dictatorship."[45]

On February 5, Trotskii stormed into Petrograd to face the men who had been his most loyal allies in 1917. In those days, the Kronstadt men had carried him on their shoulders. They had cheered his speeches and had marched to his defense when the Provisional Government had ordered his arrest. Kronstadt's Red sailors had helped Trotskii turn the tide in the dark days of 1918, when victory had seemed so remote, and he had turned to them the next year, when Iudenich's divisions had approached the suburbs of Petrograd. Now he offered them no compromises or concessions. "Only those who surrender unconditionally," he warned, "may count on the mercy of the Soviet Republic."[46] Angrily, the Kronstadt sailors rejected Trotskii's ultimatum. "The Toilers' Revolution," they replied, "will sweep the foul slanderers and rapists . . . from the face of Soviet Russia."[47] But it was Zinoviev, not Trotskii, who turned the anger of the Kronstadt men to outrage. The day Trotskii arrived in Petrograd, Zinoviev's Petrograd Defense Committee demanded that the Kronstadt insurgents "surrender within twenty-four hours . . . [or] be shot like partridges."[48] They also ordered the arrest of all families and relatives of Kronstadt rebels who could be found on the mainland. "If but a hair falls from the head of a detained comrade," the Petrograd Defense Committee stated in regard to the three Bolshevik officials whom the Provisional Revolutionary Committee had not allowed to return to the city, "it will be answered by the heads of the hostages."[49] Again the rebels met the threat of force with stubborn resistance. "At the price of the blood of toilers and the suffering of their arrested families, the Communists hope to restore their tyranny and force sailors, soldiers, and workers to bow again before them," the rebels replied. "This is enough! The toilers will no longer be deceived! Your hopes, Communists, are in vain and your threats have no force."[50]

These were brave words from fifteen thousand men who faced the armed might of Soviet Russia's multimillion-man armed forces. Certainly Kronstadt's massive fortifications and powerful armaments inspired some sense of confidence, and the fact that attackers would have to cross at least five miles of open ice in the face of heavy machine gun and artillery fire was enough to give pause to the bravest troops. But if Kronstadt had massive emplacements of weapons, its stores of ammunition were small, and its reserves of food and fuel even smaller. Bread supplies might last for two weeks at the most. Potatoes and fuel would not last much longer.[51] But there was still another hope, and it was not an entirely false one. If Kronstadt could hold off its attackers until the ice melted—and in March that could happen at any time—the Bolsheviks would no longer be able to reach it by ice. At the same time, since the Kronstadt rebels commanded the most powerful ships in the Baltic Red Fleet, supplies, ammunition, and reinforcements might be sent to them by sea.

A number of emigré groups had precisely that in mind. Although the Bolshevik charges that the Kronstadt uprising was part of a larger plot hatched by Whites in the West cannot be supported by anything but the most questionable and circumstantial evidence,[52] the Whites did greet the Kronstadt uprising with a jubilation that was strikingly out of keeping with its radical aims. The National Center, now recovered from the Cheka's decimations of 1919 and restored to a semblance of its former political authority among the emigrés that thronged the capitals of the West, saw the Kronstadt uprising as a last chance to liberate Russia. Setting aside for the moment the petty squabbles that had drained their energies, emigré groups worked with uncharacteristic efficiency to collect two million Finnish marks, nearly a million French francs, five thousand pounds sterling, twenty-five thousand dollars, and nine hundred tons of flour for Kronstadt's defenders within two weeks. Although impressive as testimony to the ability of feuding emigrés to work together against the Bolsheviks, these efforts were fruitless in the end. Finland, as an American diplomat pointed out, was "zealous in respecting" the peace treaty she had concluded with the Soviet government in the fall of 1920, and she therefore refused to allow military supplies or food for the insurgents to cross her frontiers. With the Finnish Gulf still frozen, no outside aid ever reached Kronstadt. From the beginning of the uprising until its end, the men of Kronstadt faced their enemies on the mainland alone.[53]

While Petrichenko's Kronstadters patrolled the defenses of Kotlin Island, Tukhachevskii massed the Soviet forces at Sestroetsk and Lisii Nos on the Finnish Karelian coast and at Krasnaia Gorka and Oranienbaum on the southern rim of the Finnish Gulf. Tukhachevskii knew that he must find a way to drive reluctant and fearful men across five to fifteen miles of unobstructed ice against heavy machine gun and artillery fire. Each artillery shell that exploded in their midst would plunge everyone in the vicinity into a watery grave, and each machine gun in Kronstadt's defenses would enjoy an unobstructed field of fire against everyone who advanced against it. Yet the island could be reached in no other way. Tukhachevskii therefore assigned battalions of *kursanty* to lead his assault. Behind them, he placed the best units of Red Army regulars at his command, and at their rear he assembled Cheka machine-gunners to provide supporting fire. He also ordered the Cheka to open fire on any Soviet troops who broke under enemy fire.[54]

At six forty-five on the evening of March 7, Tukhachevskii's guns at Lisii Nos and Sestroetsk fired the first of the 2,435 shells they would send that day against the forts that lay between Kronstadt and the Finnish coast.[55] "Thus the first shots rang out," Petrichenko remembered. "Standing waist deep in the blood of [Russia's] toilers, the bloody Field-Marshal Trotskii opened fire on revolutionary Kronstadt."[56] A few minutes later, the guns of Krasnaia Gorka began to fire from the south. Soon, the heavier guns of the *Sevastopol* and *Petropavlovsk* joined those of Kronstadt's forts in reply. In Petrograd, Alexander Berkman heard the thunder of gunfire and knew its purpose. The battle of Red against Red shattered the last vestiges of his faith in the Bolshevik experiment. "Something has died within me," he confided to his diary that day. "The people on the street look bowed with grief, bewildered. No one trusts himself to speak."[57] The grief and bewilderment would continue, for the sounds that Berkman heard in Petrograd's streets that night marked only the overture to ten days of heavy gunfire. Emma Goldman remembered "the fearful suspense, the days and nights filled with the rumbling of heavy artillery" that followed, and she remembered her friends, the men and women who "had once been revolutionary torchbearers . . . [who] felt too broken by the collapse of all human values" to speak out against the Bolsheviks' assault.[58]

That first night, swirling snow and heavy fog forced the gunners on both sides to halt their shooting, which in any case did little more than damage a few buildings in Sestroetsk and Oranienbaum and injure two soldiers at Kronstadt.[59] This storm was no briefly passing flurry such as those that come so frequently upon cities in the eastern Baltic as winter nears its end. On the night of March 7–8, the men fighting at Kronstadt faced a blinding snow gale—a *metel-purga*, the Russians called it[60]—in which visibility sank to zero and snow piled in drifts that shifted like sand dunes in a desert. Long before dawn, Tukhachevskii ordered an attack, hoping that his men could use the cover of the blinding snow to move closer to Kronstadt. Clad in white shrouds, they advanced from both shores, spread out in thin lines for fear that the ice might give way beneath them. Under the cover of the snow, the *kursanty* from Sestroetsk reached Kronstadt before they were discovered, but they were heavily outnumbered and driven back. Those approaching from the south fared even worse. Exploding shells from the fortress and the nearby battleships shattered the ice and plunged some of the attackers into watery graves. From the end of the breakwater that stretched far into Kronstadt harbor, three Colt machine guns cut great gaps in the attackers' ranks. In desperation, one battalion commander stormed the defenders' positions only to have other machine guns take up the slaughter where the captured Colts had left off. Without reinforcements, the attackers fell back. All along the line, Tukhachevskii's other units suffered a similar fate. Before noon, most of them had retreated, leaving five hundred dead and nearly two thousand wounded on the ice behind them.[61]

Kronstadt's defenders thus celebrated International Women's Day and the fourth anniversary of the February Revolution on March 8 with a victory over their Bolshevik foes. "To the thunder of guns and the sounds of exploding shells, we . . . send greetings from Red Kronstadt, from the kingdom of freedom," they radioed from the *Petropavlovsk*. "Long live the free revolutionary women workers! Long live the World Socialist Revolution!"[62] "There is no middle ground. We must triumph or die!" an article entitled "What We Are Fighting For" proclaimed that day in the rebels' *Izvestiia*. "A great new revolutionary phase is being completed. The standard of rebellion has been raised to free men and women from the Communists' three-year reign of violence and oppression. . . . At last," the article concluded, "the police cudgel of the Communist autocracy has been broken."[63]

These were daring words. A heady atmosphere reigned in Kronstadt in those days as Petrichenko and his comrades worked to take command of their revolutionary destiny. Without program or strategy, they lived and worked from day to day, guided mainly by the vision of absolute freedom that had directed their fight against all forms of government authority in 1917. To them, the euphoria of 1917, when the Revolution had flourished and men and women had worked in common to build a world free of bureaucracy, coercion, and state control, seemed once again within their reach. They spoke of it repeatedly during Kronstadt's last glorious rebellious days. "Victory or Death!" was their slogan, just as it had been in the days when they had marched against the government of Nicholas II. "Let the Whole World Know," they proclaimed. "The power of the soviets frees the toiling peasantry from the yoke of the Communists." Other issues of the rebels' *Izvestiia* rejoiced that "the throne of the Communists is shaking." And on March 12, the fourth anniversary of Nicholas II's abdication, they proclaimed that "today is the anniversary of the overthrow of the autocracy and the eve of the fall of the commissarocracy."[64]

As the Kronstadt men celebrated their liberation from the Bolshevik yoke during the first two weeks of March, Tukhachevskii faced an increasingly difficult situation. The Tenth Party Congress had opened in Moscow on March 8, and the first assault against Kronstadt had in part been an effort to end the uprising before the delegates took their seats. Lenin had been obliged to devote several minutes of his keynote report on the political work of the Central Committee to the "petty bourgeois counterrevolution" in Kronstadt,[65] and every day that its discordant clouds hovered over the congress added to the embarrassment. Eventually, Kronstadt became such a central issue at the congress that, on the evening of March 11, 320 of its delegates, most of whom had extensive experience as political commissars, volunteered to help suppress the uprising.[66] Given their visibility and importance, the departure of these men to join Tukhachevskii's forces on the morning of March 12 transformed the Kronstadt uprising from the comparatively minor incident that Lenin had said would be "put down within the next few days, if not hours"[67] into a centerpiece of Russia's political attention. "This is Thermidor, but we shan't allow ourselves to be guillotined," Lenin reportedly remarked at that time. "We shall make a Thermidor ourselves."[68]

In the meantime, the calendar moved relentlessly toward spring. At any moment the ice around Kronstadt would begin to break up, and with it would disappear Tukhachevskii's best hope of invading the fortress in force. Throughout the second week of March, the Red High Command rushed men, weapons, and ammunition to the "Kronstadt front," but Tukhachevskii faced other problems that massive infusions of men and materiel could not solve. Chief among them, the men who had faced machine-gun fire in the open and had seen their comrades drown beneath the ice on March 8 had little desire to face Kronstadt's guns again. When Tukhachevskii ordered an attack from Sestroetsk and Lisii Nos on March 10, it failed miserably, as did another from Oranienbaum two days later. Heavy artillery bombardments seemed to have no effect on Kronstadt's defenses, nor did clumsy attempts to bomb the fortress from the air. Instead, Tukhachevskii's troops grew more fearful and more doubtful about firing upon men with whom they had fought shoulder to shoulder throughout the Civil War. Sporadic mutinies broke out in Bolshevik units on both sides of the Finnish Gulf. "We're not going to the front," insisted the men of a division in which one man out of every twelve was a dedicated Communist. "There's been enough war. Give us bread!"[69]

In addition to weapons, ammunition, and military units, the Bolsheviks therefore rushed in hordes of Young Communists and *kursanty* from as far away as Smolensk, Riazan, Pskov, and the textile center of Ivanovo-Voznesensk to stiffen the morale of Tukhachevskii's forces. Men singing the "Internationale" marched through Petrograd's streets toward the front. Each of them "deeply felt that some sort of great 'sacred' force stood with them," one of the delegates from the Tenth Party Congress remembered. "[Each felt] that to fail in his duty to the Republic was impossible, that here were the best people of the nation who would not hesitate to give their lives."[70] Some Soviet experts have estimated that, as they prepared for the final assault against Kronstadt, Tukhachevskii's units had the highest ratio of Communists to nonparty fighting men of any forces put into the field during the Civil War.[71] Certainly the proportion was high: from fifteen to thirty percent in some units to as much as seventy percent in others.[72] Even then, there was no certainty that Tukhachevskii's forces would not flee in the face of Kronstadt's guns.

Then, on March 15, Tukhachevskii and his commissars received the moral weapon they needed when Lenin called upon the Tenth Party Congress to abolish the hated forced grain requisitions and substitute for them a tax in kind along with assurances that the peasants could sell the remainder of their produce on the open market. Not even Lenin could have anticipated how quickly the abolition of one of the most despised programs of War Communism would rally the Russians behind the Bolsheviks and against Kronstadt. Almost overnight, Bolshevik commissars began to report a "radical change in mood" among the soldiers who faced Kronstadt's guns.[72] Tukhachevskii's men were no less fearful about facing machine guns and artillery on the frozen waters of the Finnish Gulf, but Lenin's words had given them a sense that three years of Bolshevik promises were about to be realized at last. "The effect," one American scholar wrote some years ago, "was remarkable."[73]

Quickly, the Soviet press and hundreds of Bolshevik agitators built upon this sudden shift in sentiment among Tukhachevskii's troops to emphasize the threat that the Kronstadt rebels posed to demobilization, Lenin's new program, and Russia's economic recovery. Everywhere, Bolshevik political leaders spoke of the danger that Kronstadt's betrayal of the Communist cause posed to Russia's future. Again and again, they emphasized the "counterrevolutionary" character of the revolt and condemned the "petty bourgeois attitudes" that had produced it. "We have suffered three years of hunger, lack of fuel, and the like," one newspaper proclaimed. "Now we'll settle their hash!"[74]

As Tukhachevskii's Red soldiers faced the Red sailors of Kronstadt across the thinning ice, Lenin understood, just as Russia's nineteenth century tsars had understood, that nothing posed a greater threat to the survival of any Russian government than those anarchic waves of mass revolt that had swept the Russian land in the seventeenth and eighteenth centuries. Unlike Russia's tsars, Lenin sensed how deeply that rebellious spirit lay imbedded in the Kronstadt tradition. Yet that spirit had not been kindled at Kronstadt, only nurtured and concentrated there, for the Kronstadt men had carried its flame to the fortress on Kotlin Island from the remote villages whence they had come. That spirit tied the Kronstadt men to Russia's masses and joined them to Russia's villages. Should the fires of rebellion spread from Kronstadt and begin to burn their way back to their sources, Russia would collapse into a jumble of a thousand pieces.

While Tukhachevskii strengthened his forces, a firm belief that their revolt was but the first wave of a flood that would engulf Russia and free her from the Bolsheviks' tyranny sustained the Kronstadt men who patrolled the ice in sandals because they had no boots, and lived on a quarter-pound of rye and potato biscuit a day supplemented by bits of horsemeat and an occasional handful of oats.[75] Certain that their Third Revolution could undo the "three-year bloody destructive work" of the Communists, they summoned all Russians to join their cause. "Kronstadt has begun the heroic struggle against the hateful Bolshevik government for the liberation of the workers and peasants," they announced on March 11. "The Kronstadt men have raised the banner of rebellion and are confident that tens of millions of workers and peasants will answer their call. It cannot be that the dawn which has begun here will not become a bright day for all of Russia. . . . Arise, comrades, for the struggle against the autocracy of the Communists!"[76] Yet Russians had become too beaten and too apathetic to respond. There were no uprisings anywhere in Russia in support of Kronstadt, and even

Petrograd, whose workers' unrest had stirred the Kronstadters to action in the first place, remained quiet. "The Petrograd strikers," Emma Goldman reported, "were weakened by slow starvation and their energy sapped. . . . They had no more fight nor faith left to come to the aid of their Kronstadt comrades, who had so selflessly taken up their cause and who were about to give up their lives for them. Kronstadt," she concluded, "was forsaken by Petrograd and cut off from the rest of Russia.[77]

Kronstadt's time had run out. By mid-March, Tukhachevskii's forces had increased to about forty-five thousand men, led by some of the best commanders that the Civil War's battles had produced.[78] Planes and artillery had been moved in to give them support, and they had shells and bombs in profusion. Urged on by agitators and propagandists drawn from the elite group that had attended the Tenth Party Congress, these soldiers had set their doubts aside and were beginning to blame the Kronstadt rebels for the difficulties Russia faced. As he received reassurances from the commanders of units spread along both shores of the Finnish Gulf, Tukhachevskii prepared his final orders. Dated Petrograd, March 15, 11:45 P.M., they began: "On the night of March 16–17, the fortress of Kronstadt is to be taken by a frontal assault."[79]

At 2:20 P.M. on March 16, the guns of Tukhachevskii's Southern Group opened fire upon Kronstadt from Oranienbaum and Krasnaia Gorka.[80] Precisely two hours and forty minutes later, the artillery of the Northern Group joined in and continued for several hours. Quickly, the guns at Kronstadt and those on the *Petropavlovsk* and *Sevastopol* answered. In Petrograd, Emma Goldman and Alexander Berkman heard the "ceaseless firing" of the guns.[81] The rebels' shelling had little effect on shore, nor did the fortress suffer serious damage from Tukhachevskii's guns. Neither the *Petropavlovsk* nor the *Sevastopol* were so fortunate. During the next twenty-four hours, both rebel battleships sustained direct hits from the heavy guns at Krasnaia Gorka, and although the casualties totaled fewer than a hundred, the explosions of huge twelve-inch shells within close confines of the ships began to break the rebels' spirit.[82] Sleepless nights spent on watch for Bolshevik surprise attacks had taken a further toll upon the defenders' morale, while extra rations, warmer clothing, and incessant exhortations to defend the Revolution against White Guards and counterrevolutionaries had strengthened their enemies. When Tukhachevskii launched his final attacks,

Kronstadt's defenders were not as well prepared to stand firm against them as they had been ten days before.

This time, Kronstadt's defenders faced a three-pronged attack. Starting from Lisii Nos and Sestroetsk on the northern shore of the Finnish Gulf, Tukhachevskii assigned his Northern Group to capture the forts that spread between Kotlin Island and the mainland and, from there, to attack the northern shore of the island itself. At the same time, he ordered the Southern Group to advance in two columns from Oranienbaum on the Russian mainland and attack the island's southern edge and its eastern end. Before them lay the frozen expanses of the gulf, in places covered by water from the beginnings of the thaw. At some points, the water stood only a few inches deep, with solid ice underneath. At others, the surface water masked huge holes in the ice through which entire units could (and would) disappear into the black waters of the gulf. There had been no way to chart a safe course across these treacherous expanses of surface water, whose smooth surface was broken only by patches of yet unmelted snow. Nor did Tukhachevskii's intelligence experts know that the Kronstadt rebels had turned the snow into deadly mine fields.

Early on the morning of March 17, Tukhachevskii's forces moved forward. With shock troops drawn from the ranks of the best *kursanty* in the lead, their uniforms covered by white shrouds and capes to blend with the snow and ice, they began their advance from Lisii Nos and Sestroetsk at 3 A.M. and from Oranienbaum an hour later. At first, heavy fog shrouded their movements. Then, as they approached the forts and batteries that spread out across the gulf, they moved forward on their hands and knees. As the attackers approached the forts, searchlights and flares turned the night into day, blinding them and lighting the way for Kronstadt machine guns and artillery to cut them down. In the face of lesser obstacles, Tukhachevskii's men had broken during the attacks of March 7–8, 10, and 12. Their ranks heavily laced with Communists and *kursanty*, they did not do so now. As they hurled themselves against the machine guns of the outer forts, gunfire tore huge gaps in their ranks. Repeatedly, they regrouped and charged again, using hand grenades to blast their way through the wall of machine-gun fire. One battalion of *kursanty* lost all but eighteen men when it stormed one of the fortified batteries north of Kotlin Island. Others suffered only slightly fewer casualties as death upon and beneath the ice bore them to a glacial Valhalla the likes of which Odin and Siegfried had never imagined.[83]

The fighting grew more intense as the sun broke through the fog that morning. Sunlight caught the Seventy-ninth Infantry Brigade on the open ice of Kronstadt's harbor. The brigade already had taken three fortified batteries south of the city, and as they had begun to sense the closeness of victory, they had stormed ahead. At the harbor, heavy machine-gun fire drove them back. Again they raced forward shouting "Hoorah!"—the same cry with which Russian infantrymen had struck fear into the hearts of their enemies for centuries. Casualties became unimportant. By the time it had broken through the harbor defenses and moved into the streets beyond, the Seventy-ninth had lost half its men. Somewhat further east, to the right of the bleeding Seventy-ninth, the remainder of the Southern Group breached Kronstadt's stone walls and fought its way into the city's center. By noon, it had begun to advance methodically, fighting from house to house and street to street. Gunfire poured from every window, doorway, and rooftop until Tukhachevskii's commanders ordered artillery from Oranienbaum into the city to help their men blast their way forward. By late afternoon, *kursanty* from the Northern Group broke into Kronstadt from the northeast, and the two forces began to converge upon the city center. Just before midnight, *kursanty* captured the *Petropavlovsk* and *Sevastopol* and sent a victory message to Petrograd. The last pockets of resistance held out until the next day. That afternoon, March 18, 1921, the fiftieth anniversary of the Paris Commune, the revolutionary ancestor from which both Communists and the Kronstadt men had claimed descent, Tukhachevskii's commanders announced that the guns of Kronstadt had been stilled.

In Petrograd, on the morning of March 17, Emma Goldman and Alexander Berkman had wondered at the silence when the heavy guns had halted their firing. "The stillness that fell over Petrograd was more fearful than the ceaseless firing of the night before," Goldman remembered. That evening, they learned that Kronstadt had fallen. "We were stunned," Goldman wrote in anguish. "Sasha [that is, Berkman], the last thread of his faith in the Bolsheviks broken, desperately roamed the streets." While Berkman wandered, Goldman sat in her room and looked out on the streets of Russia's revolutionary cradle. "I sat limp, peering into the night," she confessed. "Petrograd was hung in a black pall, a ghastly corpse. The streetlamps flickered yellow, like candles at its head and feet." The next day, Goldman heard some of Tukhachevskii's victorious battalions singing the "Internationale" as they marched through Petrograd. "Its strains, once jubilant to my ear," she concluded sadly, "now sounded like a funeral dirge for humanity's flaming hope."[84]

While Goldman and Berkman lamented Kronstadt's defeat, the arrests began. Petrichenko and most of his colleagues on the Provisional Revolutionary Committee had fled to Finland when Tukhachevskii's forces had begun to fight their way through Kronstadt's streets. During the hours that followed perhaps as many as eight thousand of their comrades crossed the Finnish frontier to live the sad lives of exiles until, lured by false promises of amnesty, many returned to Russia to be sent to concentration camps.[85] In the meantime, the Bolsheviks shot several hundred of the men they had captured in the fighting at Kronstadt and sent several thousand more to the dreaded camps of Solovki on the White Sea. The spirit of Kronstadt, so vital to the Revolution's triumph in 1917, the spirit that had rejected all state authority as oppressive, had been eradicated. The Soviet authorities made certain that it would never revive. To recover from its counterrevolutionary illness, they concluded, the "unhealthy organism" of the Baltic Fleet "required surgical intervention."[86] They therefore dispersed fifteen thousand of its sailors to naval units in the Black Sea, the Caspian, the Far East, and along Russia's river system. Only in that way, one Soviet commentator explained, could Kronstadt and the Baltic Fleet "recover from their wounds" and "become once again the vigilant Red sentinel on the shores of the Baltic Sea."[87]

Their movement crushed, their spirit erased from the pages of Soviet life, the Kronstadt sailors left one last legacy. It fell to them, as their uprising entered its last days, to write the epitaph for Russia's revolutionary dreams. "For three years, the toilers of Soviet Russia have groaned in the torture chambers of the Cheka," Kronstadt's *Izvestiia* announced. "The peasant has been transformed into the lowest form of farm laborer and the worker has become a mere wage slave in the factories of the state. The toiling intelligentsia has come to naught. . . . It has become impossible to breathe," the Kronstadt rebels concluded. "All of Soviet Russia has been turned into an all-Russian penal colony."[88]

Epilogue

The Revolution Consumes Its Makers

TUKHACHEVSKII's brutal suppression of the Kronstadt uprising, Lenin's call at the Tenth Party Congress for the Bolsheviks to put a lid on opposition, and the beginnings of the New Economic Policy all came during the third week of March 1921, and each expressed an important aspect of the Soviet state that had emerged from the devastation of Russia's Civil War. Monolithic and intolerant of diversity, the Bolshevik—now Communist—Party had taken full command of Russia with undisputed power to suppress all dissent. From their old formula of democratic centralism, the Bolsheviks had elevated centralism to an all-important principle. At the same time, they had relegated party democracy to a dark corner from which it was destined never to emerge. "Restrictions on political liberty, terror, military centralism and discipline, and the direction of all means and resources toward the creation of an offensive and defensive state apparatus," the newspaper *Krasnyi Kronstadt* (Red Kronstadt) announced soon after Tukhachevskii's victory, would mark the "initial phase" of restored Communist power in Kronstadt.[1] That became the formula for political action everywhere in Russia.

As Soviet Russia faced the worst famine in a century, her railroads in shambles, her agriculture crippled, and her industry stagnant, such absolute authority seemed all but essential to rebuild the Russian nation. This was in keeping with the "revolutionary-heroic" tradition of Bolshevism, which called for a "fierce assault" against the enemies of Soviet Russia. Trotskii had built the Red Army and stemmed the White tide in 1918–1919 by "fierce assaults." The same principle had motivated the Bolsheviks' efforts to confront the crippling economic crises they had faced during the Civil War, and it had underlain all the radical social transformations that had come in the wake of the October Revolution.[2] But, by definition, the "revolutionary-heroic" tradition suited war much better than peace. It had allowed the government and Party to respond to the rapidly changing circumstances of the Civil War, and it had freed energetic men and women from the constraints of formal procedures and well-established institutions when emergencies required them to act decisively. On the darker side, the Party's readiness to reward those who shot first and asked questions later encouraged arrogance. It made Bolshevik commissars too disdainful of popular opinion and too cynical about popular participation in government. Such men and women had no patience with Lenin's September 1917 promise that the Bolshevik Revolution would "be invincible if it is not afraid of itself [and] if it transfers all power to the proletariat."[3] Indeed, they—and Lenin—at the end of the Civil War intended to retain power firmly within the monolithic, intolerant, highly centralized Communist Party.

For a time, the full consequences of this transformation from democratic centralism to what the Kronstadt sailors had called a "commissarocracy"—unrestrained power wielded by arrogant commissars—were masked by the presence of Lenin, who, even in the Central Committee, never wielded absolute power, and by the dramatic shift to the New Economic Policy, which transformed the social and economic life of Russia. The New Economic Policy embodied what has been called "prudent pragmatism," another, more cautious tradition of "historical Bolshevism."[4] While Trotskii continued to urge the "revolutionary-heroic" tradition upon his Communist comrades after 1921, Lenin and the mercurial Nikolai Bukharin called upon them to follow a more cautious program in which Russia's economy would be changed not "by one stroke of the revolutionary sword," in Bukharin's words, but by more gradual, evolutionary means.[5] "What is new at the present moment for our revolution," Lenin explained, "is the need to resort to a 'reformist,' gradualist, cautiously roundabout method of activity in the fundamental questions of economic construction." "My wish," he told *Pravda* in 1922, "is that in the next five years we will conquer peacefully not less than we conquered previously with arms."[6]

The New Economic Policy, Lenin believed, would move slowly and would take much more time than many Bolsheviks anticipated. Only by restoring private initiative and limited private trade could the peasantry be induced to produce the food and raw materials that could bring Russia's stagnant economy back to life. The coercive policies of War Communism, the tendency to use "fierce assaults" to solve economic problems, had failed to establish the firm union between Russia's workers and peasants that all Bolsheviks agreed was essential in a revolutionary socialist society. "Only agreement with the peasantry can save the socialist revolution in Russia," Lenin told the Tenth Party Congress when he proposed replacing compulsory grain collections with a tax in kind. "[The peasantry] will not continue to live as it has hitherto," he concluded. "The state of affairs that has prevailed so far cannot be continued any longer."[7] In expanding upon Lenin's views, Bukharin argued that only through private trade could that union between Russia's workers and peasants be made sound, and that only a firm and lasting union between proletariat and peasants could ensure the stability of the Party. How to ensure that union, Bukharin insisted in 1922, had become "the fundamental question of our revolution."[8]

The New Economic Policy therefore reopened the avenues to individual initiative, private enterprise, and free trade that the Bolsheviks had closed at the beginning of the Civil War. After turning over about a quarter of their crops to the government, peasants could sell the rest in any manner they saw fit. No longer did roadblock detachments patrol the roads, nor did the police and army confiscate the wares of peasants who traveled between town and country to sell their eggs, meat, grain, and produce. Small industries reappeared to manufacture those small wares that had formed the fabric of everyday life before the First World War, and, once again, they became Russia's chief suppliers of consumer goods. Even large-scale enterprises, which had produced minimal outputs in return for large state subsidies during the Civil War, now had to pay their way, balance costs and sales, and show a profit. Despite Lenin's bitter criticism of piecework as one of the worst forms of capitalist exploitation before 1917, he and the Party's planners now restored it to favor in order to increase productivity among Russia's lackadaisical workforce. These measures cut short the incredible waste and the abysmally low productivity of the War Communism years, but they also made it impossible for Russia's recovering factories to absorb the flood of job seekers that poured into the cities from the countryside and from the hastily demobilized Red Army. With too many people for too few jobs, wages fell so far that, in 1925, coal miners, machinists, and locomotive drivers still earned considerably less than they had in 1914, while prices continued to rise in response to the laws of supply and demand. Still, the overall picture had become brighter. Trade revived. Shops reopened. A sense of normalcy returned. Without the chaos of the Civil War and War Communism, people began to live, or try to live, normal lives.

The dark side of Russian life in the 1920s lay in the political arena, where the seeds that would produce Stalin's dictatorship in less than a decade began to sprout. Beneath the economic and social freedom of the New Economic Policy lay the rigid, undiluted political authoritarianism in all its arrogance, intolerance, and coerciveness set down at the Tenth Party Congress. At the very time when the New Economic Policy encouraged more initiative and looser organization in trade, industry, and agriculture, the Communist Party moved toward still greater centralization and more thorough organization in its own—and hence the Soviet Union's—political affairs. Lenin had always tried to direct the Bolsheviks through a small inner circle of key advisers, but as his health declined in 1921 and 1922, control of the Party moved into the hands of newer administrative bodies that enabled other men to wield power in ways Lenin had never dreamed of. Aside from the Central Committee, the key Bolshevik institution since the Party's beginnings, the Politburo, which, in Lenin's words, "decides policy," the Orgburo, which, Lenin also explained, "allocates forces,"[9] and the Secretariat, which dealt with day-to-day party affairs, emerged to rule the Party.

As Lenin grew more frail, a number of men began to wield power in his stead. Although he had never built a power base within the Party, Trotskii remained commissar of war and continued to rely upon his ability to sway men with passionate words to preserve his authority. Still Trotskii's bitter enemy, Zinoviev ruled Petrograd, and, in a similar fashion, Lev Kamenev, who had sided with Zinoviev in opposing Lenin's plan to seize power in October 1917, governed Moscow. "Iron Feliks" Dzerzhinskii, the strain of ceaseless struggle against counterrevolutionaries having thinned his hair and sharpened his aquiline features even more, still headed the Cheka, now reorganized and renamed the GPU. Aleksei Rykov, two years older than Kamenev, and deputy chairman both of the Supreme Council of National Economy and the Soviet of People's Commissars while Lenin lived, served in Lenin's place throughout 1923 and replaced him as chairman in 1924. These men all wielded immense authority in Soviet Russia, but from 1922 onward there was one, and only one, who held positions on all four of the Party's intricately interconnected key administrative and policy making bodies. Only Stalin sat on the Central Committee, the Politburo, the Orgburo, and the Secretariat. As General Secretary of the Party beginning in March 1922, Stalin had a unique opportunity to manipulate all the key instruments of Party authority for his own ends.

The autocratic authority of the Communist Party thus became the political heritage of Russia's Revolution and Civil War, and in that form, the Revolution turned to consume those who once had dreamed of replacing autocracy with a workers' and peasants' democracy. Martov, Chernov, and scores of those Mensheviks and Socialist Revolutionaries who had shared the Bolsheviks' hatred for autocracy but had debated their vision of socialism languished in prison or exile by the Civil War's end. The first casualties among the Bolsheviks came just afterward, when some of the leaders of the Workers' Opposition slipped from the scene in the wake of the Tenth Party Congress. Although Lenin had insisted in March 1921 that Shliapnikov, his principal lieutenant from 1915–1917, continue to serve on the Central Committee,[10] he demanded his expulsion from that post in August after he privately criticized the foibles and arrogance of Soviet bureaucrats. Likewise Kollontai, whose criticisms of bureaucratic arrogance and Party tyranny had stirred Lenin's anger even more than Shliapnikov's, found herself allowed to make a more graceful exit by accepting an appointment as the Soviet ambassador to Norway.[11]

By mid-1921, Lenin himself had begun to play a more limited role in the Party and the government.[12] He felt sick. He suffered from insomnia, vertigo, and exhaustion. His nerves had grown jagged. He often complained of headaches. The ringing of his telephone disturbed him, and technicians were called in to replace the bells with small flashing lights. Russian medical experts could find no explanation for his poor health and prescribed rest. Specialists summoned from Germany were of the same opinion. Then, on

May 26, 1922, Lenin suffered a stroke that paralyzed his right arm and leg and slurred his speech. "Death," Lenin's physician wrote when he recalled that day, "for the first time clearly wagged its finger,"[13] and its warning was one that Lenin heeded briefly. But he did so only until the iron will and constitution that had enabled him to dominate Russian Social Democracy for thirty years helped him recover. Within six weeks, Lenin had regained part of his ability to write. By October he was back at work in the Kremlin, presiding at meetings of the Politburo, the Central Committee, and Sovnarkom. According to his private secretary's calculations, between the beginning of October and the middle of December 1922, Lenin wrote 224 letters, received 171 official visitors, and presided over 32 meetings.[14] By the end of November this work had begun to take a deadly toll. Lenin again became tired and weak, his temper brittle, his nerves raw and edgy. On December 13 he suffered two minor strokes and, three days later, a more serious one.

After December 12, Lenin no longer governed Russia. During the brief moments when the doctors permitted him to work, he dictated a handful of letters and the series of notes that were to comprise the political testament in which he sketched his vision of the future and commented upon the strengths and weaknesses of the men who had emerged as the Party's leaders. He continued to see Trotskii as a man of "outstanding ability" who was "personally perhaps the most capable man in the present Central Committee." But Trotskii's "excessive preoccupation with the purely administrative side" of government concerned him, as did his "excessive self-assurance." At the same time, he feared Stalin's rapidly growing power within the Party. "Comrade Stalin, having become general secretary, has unlimited authority concentrated in his hands," Lenin warned at the end of December. "I am not sure whether he will always be capable of using that authority with sufficient caution."[15]

In February 1923, Lenin dictated an article for *Pravda* entitled "Better Less, but Better," in which he lamented the growth of bureaucracy, red tape, and corruption in Russia's government and criticized Stalin's failure to curb it. That was his last effort. On March 9 he suffered a major stroke that paralyzed his entire right side and left him unable to speak. Yet he still lived despite advanced cerebral arteriosclerosis, which had so calcified some of the blood vessels in his brain that, in the words of one physician who attended the autopsy, "when struck with a tweezer they sounded like stone."[16] In the fall of 1923, Lenin recovered enough to walk with the help of attendants and a cane. He communicated with slight nods of his head, with his eyes and hands. Eventually, he could mutter "Vot, Vot" ("That's it, that's it"), the only word that his efforts to regain his speech enabled him to speak clearly. Then, Lenin's final decline began, with its moments of hope and its days of deathly certainty. At six o'clock on the evening of January 21, 1924, his temperature rose suddenly and he suffered a massive stroke. Thirty minutes later, Lenin was dead at the age of fifty-three. All the ceremony for a man who hated ceremony, and all the adulation for the man who preferred modesty and simplicity, could not conceal the fact that Russia now had turned onto a very different course.

Others who had helped to make the Revolution followed Lenin in death. Mikhail Frunze, the son of a country doctor and a peasant mother, a Bolshevik since the age of nineteen, and one of the truly brilliant Red Army commanders to emerge from the Civil War, died under suspicious circumstances at the age of forty in October 1925, less than a year after he had replaced Trotskii as commissar of war and navy. Evidently at Stalin's persistent urging, Frunze agreed to an operation for a stomach ulcer that was responding well to diet and rest. "I am feeling absolutely healthy and it is somehow ridiculous not only to go to the hospital but even to think about an operation," he wrote to his wife just a few days before the doctors operated. Clearly, he was reluctant to have surgery, but decided to go through with it anyway. "Stalin insists on the operation to get rid of my ulcers for good," a close friend reported him saying at the end of October. "So I [have] decided to go under the knife."[17] Frunze was a strong man who had borne the privations of war easily and often, but the best guesses are that the sixty grams of chloroform which the surgeons administered (no one knows why they chose chloroform rather than the more easily tolerated ether) for the brief operation which found that his ulcer had healed itself, proved to be too much for his liver to absorb. Thirty hours later, on October 31, 1925, Frunze died, quite probably from liver failure.[18] Although a number of Russians thought him responsible for Frunze's death, evidence of Stalin's connection with it remains circumstantial at best. But Frunze's replacement as commissar of war was Kliment Voroshilov, Stalin's close comrade and political ally ever since the two had been together at the siege of Tsaritsyn in 1918.

Nine months later, Dzerzhinskii succumbed to the immense strains of directing the Cheka against foreign and domestic "enemies." Except perhaps for Lenin, no one had been more dedicated to the Bolsheviks' cause than Dzerzhinskii, who had abandoned his personal comfort, his health, even his family, to serve the Revolution. Even before the Civil War's end, tuberculosis had begun to weaken him, and the strain of having the chairmanship of the Supreme Council of the National Economy added to his duties as head of Cheka-GPU a few days after Lenin's death proved more than his sick body could support. For more than two hours when the Central Committee met in July 1926, Dzerzhinskii spoke angrily against the opposition that had formed against Stalin. Then he left the rostrum, walked into the lobby, and died from a heart attack, five weeks before his forty-ninth birthday, while the men to whom he had spoken so harshly looked on. Dzerzhinskii's death placed the power of Russia's security forces in the hands of his deputies. Chief among them was Genrikh Iagoda, another of Stalin's protégés, who would stage-manage Stalin's first show trial exactly a decade later. Trotskii, Zinoviev, Kamenev, Bukharin, Rykov, and Stalin—the men who had inherited Lenin's power and had begun to struggle for it—carried Dzerzhinskii's coffin to Red Square.[19]

Between 1917 and 1923, Lenin had imposed his vision of Russia's socialist future upon the Bolsheviks. Zinoviev, Kamenev, Bukharin, and Trotskii most of all had challenged this many times, but Lenin's wit, wisdom, and sheer political brilliance had always drawn them back to his side. At times like a patient schoolmaster, at others like an angry priest, and, on occasion, like a stern parent, Lenin had defined Communist orthodoxy and kept the Party behind it. Yet Lenin's vision was far from static, and he changed his definition of Russia's goals and the means for attaining them as conditions changed in Russia and the West. Always, he had an explanation that tied the present and future to the past and even managed (if one does not probe too deeply into it) to present the dramatic shift from War Communism to the New Economic Policy as a continuum in Bolshevik theory and practice. Lenin's subtle shifts in meaning and definition thus cloaked in the mantle of theoretical legitimacy changes made in response to the pressure of events. Soviet leaders continue this practice today. It has enabled them to carry the heritage of the Bolsheviks' victory in Russia's Civil War through the regimes of Stalin, Khrushchev, and Brezhnev to those present-day reforms of Gorbachev which contain vital elements of the too briefly tried formulae of the New Economic Policy era. At the same time, it continues to make it difficult to establish a hard and fast framework of Leninist theory in which to place Soviet experience. Defining Leninist orthodoxy therefore continues to be a serious business in the Soviet Union. As Stalin proved all too clearly, whoever could take on that role in a society and state that claimed to be based upon the precepts of Leninism could exercise immense power as Lenin's true heir and apostle.

The ideological and political unity of the Bolsheviks during and immediately after the Civil War was an artificial creation in which divergent visions and incompatible personalities had been held firmly within the Party's ranks by the powerful will of Lenin. Without his firm hand to control it, the Communist Party quickly polarized. On the Left stood Trotskii, no less brilliant, his speeches and writings as compelling as ever. Of all the men who vied for power after Lenin's second stroke, this man who had led the Red Army to victory against what had seemed impossible odds in the Civil War stood the closest to Lenin in the popular mind. Of all Lenin's successors, none preserved the revolutionary spirit more passionately than he, and none saw the struggle for socialism more in terms of new "furious assaults" against enemies at home and abroad. Although the prospects for revolution in the West looked increasingly dim, Trotskii still insisted that, without world revolution, socialism in Russia would be doomed.

Trotskii's popularity lay among the people, not in the higher reaches of the Party. There, as Lenin feared, he had been too arrogant, too self-assured, too ready to sweep opposition aside with a wave of his hand or a few cutting words. Because those qualities had turned many powerful Bolsheviks against him, Trotskii had no institutional power base within the Party after 1923. What power he had came from his position as commissar of war and as a member of the Politburo, where he faced Zinoviev, Kamenev, and Stalin, all of whom had greater influence within the Party and had formed a "troika" against him during Lenin's last days. Of the three, Zinoviev was by far the most volatile. Almost a caricature of a revolutionary in appearance, his eyes often underlined with dark circles, his black hair flying wildly, Zinoviev had a talent for deluging any audience with passionate speeches filled with outrageous claims. Few could match his endurance at the rostrum, and few found his flawed personality attractive. Most high-ranking Bolsheviks thought Zinoviev a coward, and almost no one trusted him.

"He copies my faults," Lenin was reported to have said on one occasion. Sverdlov, the Bolsheviks' organizational genius who died prematurely in 1919, once called Zinoviev "panic personified."[20] Kamenev, the man whom some have called "a sort of political Siamese twin of Zinoviev's,"[21] was more attractive. Unlike Zinoviev, who despised paperwork, Kamenev liked it. Methodically and precisely, he presided over the Moscow Soviet while Zinoviev reigned flamboyantly, albeit uncertainly, in Petrograd, which the Bolsheviks renamed Leningrad a few months after Lenin's death.

The man who seemed the least dangerous in those days was Stalin. Stalin had carefully, but inconspicuously, built a powerful position within the Party from which he projected himself as the modest guardian and defender of Lenin's heritage. While Trotskii, convalescing in Georgia at the time of Lenin's death, had not returned to Moscow (partly at Stalin's urging) in time for Lenin's funeral, Stalin had stepped forward in the manner of Uriah Heep to proclaim his—and the Bolsheviks'—fidelity to the inheritance Lenin had bequeathed to them. "We Communists are people of a special mold," he told his listeners. "We are made of a special stuff." Stalin vowed that he and all men and women who belonged to "the army of Comrade Lenin" would fulfill the duties with which Lenin had charged them. He spoke in a litany, in the language of the devout and faithful that he had learned during his years as an adolescent seminarian. "Departing from us, Comrade Lenin enjoined us to hold high and guard the purity of the great title of member of the Party," he began. "We vow to you, Comrade Lenin, that we shall fulfill your behest with honor. . . . Departing from us, Comrade Lenin enjoined us to guard the unity of our Party as the apple of our eye," he continued. "We vow to you, Comrade Lenin, that this behest, too, we shall fulfill with honor." Four times more, Stalin intoned Lenin's wish and answered it with the vow of all faithful Communists. The dictatorship of the proletariat, the alliance of the workers and peasants, the union of socialist republics, and the Communist International all would be cherished and strengthened. Each of the men and women for whom there was "nothing higher than the title of member of the Party whose founder and leader was Comrade Lenin" would "spare no effort to fulfill [these behests] . . . with honor!"[22]

Stalin, the disciple of Lenin and the defender of his heritage, occupied the center in the factional struggles that took shape after Lenin's death. Unlike Trotskii, Stalin claimed that the victory of socialism in Russia was possible and probable even without the triumph of revolution in the more advanced industrial states of the West. Certainly that view appealed to men and women who did not want to believe that their long revolutionary struggle had been in vain or that the failure of revolution to emerge in the West would destroy Russia's own revolutionary experiment. The October Revolution, Stalin insisted, was not merely "the first stage of the world revolution" but "a mighty base for its further development." At the same time, he warned of "the great chasm" that separated Trotskii's theories from the teachings of Lenin and condemned Trotskii's theory of "permanent revolution" as "a variety of Menshevism."[23] As he strengthened his position as the interpreter of Lenin and the final authority in defining Leninist orthodoxy, Stalin moved easily between Left and Right. As he did so, he pitted his rivals against each other and eliminated them one after another.

Completing the spectrum of political visions that polarized the Bolsheviks after Lenin's death, Nikolai Bukharin stood on the right. Like Trotskii, the diminutive Bukharin believed that world revolution must one day play a part in the final triumph of socialism in Russia, but he rejected Trotskii's repeated calls for militancy at home. Bukharin feared that any turn away from the compromises of the New Economic Policy would threaten the alliance between the peasantry and the proletariat, without which, he insisted, the victory of socialism in Russia would become impossible. "Our salvation lies in our coming to an understanding with the peasantry," he announced flatly. "The question of the worker-peasant bloc is the central question. It is the question of all questions."[24] Rather than force the pace of industrialization in Russia at the cost of alienating the peasantry, as had been the case under War Communism, Bukharin insisted that the Soviet government must continue the New Economic Policy. His view that the peasant–proletariat alliance held the key to developing socialism in Russia accorded with Stalin's assurances that socialism in one country was possible. Both saw their common enemy in Trotskii's ardent internationalism and his efforts to accelerate the revolution's pace in Russia.

Even though it had seemed that his relations with Zinoviev and Kamenev were about to reach a breaking point soon after Lenin's death, Stalin drew them into his campaign against Trotskii, his most obvious rival for Lenin's mantle, and then betrayed them both. Through a masterful series of maneuvers and countermaneuvers, Stalin drove all three men from the Party at the Fifteenth

Party Congress, which took place at the end of 1927. Exiled first to Alma Ata, deep in Central Asia, Trotskii left the Soviet Union for good in February 1929, while Zinoviev and Kamenev began an appalling series of recantations, after which Stalin readmitted them to the Party and then expelled them a second and third time.

Now triumphant against the so-called Left Opposition, his doctrine of "socialism in one country" officially accepted as Russia's true course against Trotskii's internationalism, Stalin abandoned the New Economic Policy and began a policy of forcing the peasantry to pay the costs of Russia's accelerated industrialization that soon would lead to collectivization. Now Bukharin and the "Right Opposition" became the official enemy of Stalin's interpretation of Leninist orthodoxy. In November 1929, Stalin therefore insisted that Bukharin, Rykov, and the leader of Russia's trade unions Mikhail Tomskii renounce their "erroneous views" as the price for not suffering the disgrace that had fallen upon Trotskii or his unwilling allies Zinoviev and Kamenev. Rykov remained in the Politburo, and Bukharin and Tomskii continued to sit on the Central Committee, although all three had become politically impotent and had no hope of opposing Stalin. At the Seventeenth Party Congress, the "Congress of Victors" that assembled at the beginning of 1934, Stalin stood triumphant before the Party and Russia. "Each thick finger moves like a fattened grub," Osip Mandelstam had written of this "Kremlin mountaineer" a few months before in a sixteen-line poem that would cost him his life. "Each death to him is a sweet-tasting berry."[25]

Not content to see his rivals ruined, Stalin demanded their blood. In August 1936, Zinoviev and Kamenev were brought to trial on charges of plotting with Trotskii. They were convicted and shot. In June 1937 Tukhachevskii, who had fought to victory against Kolchak, Denikin, the Kronstadt insurgents, and the Tambov peasant insurrection, who had led the Red Army to the gates of Warsaw in 1920 and had served as chief of staff of the Red Army until his arrest, was tried for treason and shot. The turns of Rykov and Bukharin came in 1938. Convicted of having plotted with the Germans and Japanese to restore capitalism in Russia, they were shot. Former people's commissars, high officials in the security police, friends of Trotskii and Lenin, and scores of men who owed their rise directly to Stalin's patronage, were tried for espionage and treason, convicted, and shot.

Of Stalin's rivals, only Trotskii remained alive when the armies of Nazi Germany invaded Poland in 1939. After their deportation to Turkey in 1929, Trotskii, his wife, his grown son, and several of their associates had settled in a small villa in the Prinkipo Islands, where they remained until the French government offered them political asylum in 1933.[26] But asylum in France was brief. Forced to take refuge in Norway in 1936, Trotskii had to flee to Mexico at the end of the year, after the Soviet government threatened the Norwegians with economic reprisals if they allowed him to remain. In Mexico, Trotskii, his family, and friends found protection. They had settled in a large house in Coyoacan, built a high wall around its garden, and stationed bodyguards in and around it day and night. There Trotskii worked on his last book, which would bear the title "Stalin." "Lev Davidovich still bore himself as of old," his wife remembered. "His head was held high, his gait was sprightly and his gestures animated. He seemed not to have aged," she added, "though his unruly locks had become gray."[27] Yet the tropical beauty of Trotskii's Mexican refuge held great dangers. On May 24, 1940, assassins attacked the Coyoacan villa with machine gun fire and incendiary bombs from four sides at once. Miraculously, Trotskii and his family all escaped injury. After that, his protectors installed steel shutters on Trotskii's bedroom windows. "This reminds me of the first jail I was in," he remarked to one of his bodyguards after the work had been finished. "This is not a home; it is a medieval prison."[28] After higher walls and watchtowers had been built and steel doors and shutters put in place, there were no more direct attacks upon Trotskii in his "little fortress." Was it possible, he and his wife asked themselves, that they were at last safe? Trotskii joked about it from time to time. "There you are," he would tell his wife in the morning. "We've slept through a whole night and nobody has killed us."[29]

Unknown to Trotskii, his family, or his guards, danger lurked not outside but within. Several months earlier, "Jacson," *alias* Jacques Mornard, *alias* Ramon Mercader, had begun to work his way into Trotskii's inner circle of friends. Almost certainly trained in Moscow, his real name unknown to this day, "Jacson" was slender and small-boned with large green eyes and curly dark hair."[30] Not powerfully built like Trotskii, he was agile and quick. He once had boasted that he could "split a huge ice-block with a single blow of an [Alpinist's] ice-axe."[31] Before the beginning of August, he had visited the Trotskii house several times and, in the middle of the month, prevailed upon Trotskii to look over an article he was writing. On August 20, "Jacson appeared shortly after five o'clock in the afternoon, his article manuscript retyped, and asked Trotskii to comment on his revisions. While Trotskii bent over the manuscript in his study, "Jacson" drew from his coat an alpenstock, the pick-shaped axe used by mountain climbers to cut footings in rock or ice, and drove its steel point three inches into his victim's brain. He expected—almost certainly had been trained to expect—Trotskii to collapse, dead at his feet.

Instead, "Jacson" later told his interrogators, Trotskii uttered "a scream that I shall remember all my life"[32] and threw himself upon his attacker. Within minutes, Trotskii's wife and guards burst into the room, and, while she tried to stanch the bleeding, the guards seized his attacker. "Jacson" was wrestled to the floor, beaten, and beaten again. It was too late. The local doctor who examined Trotskii before the ambulance arrived insisted that the wound was not very serious, but Trotskii sensed otherwise. "I feel . . . here . . . that this is the end," he told one of his bodyguards as he pointed to his heart. "This time . . . they've . . . succeeded."[33] At the hospital, Trotskii kissed his wife three times and fell into a coma. Thirty hours later, at seven twenty-five on the evening of August 21, 1940, he was dead. In the Kremlin, the grayest and most ruthless of the men who had made the Russian Revolution, Iosif Dzhugashvili, the man called Stalin, now stood at the pinnacle of power, unchallenged and alone.

Notes

KEY TO ABBREVIATIONS:

ADAE:	Archives des Affaires Etrangères. Paris.
AHR:	*American Historical Review.*
ARR:	*Arkhiv russkoi revoliutsii.*
ASEER:	*American Slavic and East European Review.*
AG-CV:	Archives de la Guerre. Service historique de l'armée de la terre. Château de Vincennes. Vincennes
B:	*Byloe.*
BA:	*Belyi arkhiv.*
BACU:	Bakhmetieff Archives of Russian and East European History and Culture. Columbia University, New York.
BSE:	*Bol'shaia sovetskaia entsiklopediia.*
BD:	*Beloe delo.*
CSS:	*California Slavic Studies.*
DESSRKP:	*Desiatyi s"ezd RKP(b), mart 1921 goda: Stenograficheskii otchet.*
DEVSRKP:	*Deviatyi s"ezd RKP(b). Protokoly.*
HIA:	Hoover Institution Archives. Stanford.
HSS:	*Harvard Slavic Studies.*
IP:	*Izbrannye proizvedeniia.*
IS:	*Izbrannye sochineniia.*
IWM:	Imperial War Museum Archives. London.
IZ:	*Istoricheskie zapiski.*
IZh:	*Istoricheskii zhurnal.*
JMH:	*The Journal of Modern History.*
KA:	*Krasnyi arkhiv.*
KL:	*Krasnaia letopis'.*

KVR:	L. Trotskii, *Kak vooruzhalas' revoliutsiia (na voennoi rabote).*
Lenin, *CW:*	V. I. Lenin, *Collected Works.*
MERSH:	*Modern Encyclopedia of Russian and Soviet History.*
PR:	*Proletarskaia revoliutsiia.*
PRO:	Public Records Office. Kew.
RR:	*Russian Review.*
SAP:	*St. Antony's Papers*
SEER:	*Slavonic and East European Review.*
SIE:	*Sovetskaia istoricheskaia entsiklopediia.*
SR:	*Slavic Review.*
SS:	*Sobranie sochinenii.*
TsGIAL:	Tsentral'nyi gosudarstvennyi istoricheskii arkhiv SSSR. Leningrad.
VI:	*Voprosy istorii.*
VIKPSS:	*Voprosy istorii KPSS.*
ViR:	*Voina i revoliutsiia.*
VKP:	*Vsesoiuznaia kommunisticheskaia partiia (bol'shevikov) v rezoliutsiiakh i resheniiakh s"ezdov, konferentsii, i plenumov TsK.*
VSRKP:	*Vos'moi s"ezd RKP(b): Protokoly.*

Prologue

1. Sassoon, p. 115.
2. Quoted in Fussell, p. 72.
3. Quoted in Tuchman, p. 348.
4. Bernhardi, pp. 11, 37, 27, 258.
5. Aldington, p. 221.
6. Aleksandra to Nicholas, September 24, 1914, in *Letters*, p. 9.
7. Bernhardi, p. 37.
8. Quoted in Hafkesbrink, p. 64.
9. Ibid., p. 67.
10. Quoted in Ehrenburg (1961), p. 68.
11. Aldington, p. 323.
12. Quoted in Wohl, p. 102.
13. This phrase is Fussell's. See Fussell, p. 36.
14. Quoted in Wohl, third page of the picture insert following p. 100.
15. Quoted in Hafkesbrink, p. 69.
16. Knox, I, p. 319.
17. Golovin (1931), pp. 220–221.
18. Quoted in Polivanov, p. 186.
19. Quoted in Florinsky, II, pp. 1378, 1377.
20. "Voina i Mir," in Maiakovskii (1968), I, pp. 160, 173–175.
21. Ibid., pp. 187, 189.
22. Quoted in Florinsky, II, p. 1365.
23. Quoted in Lincoln (1986), p. 205.
24. Florinsky, II, p. 1364.
25. Paléologue (1921), II, p. 107.

26. Aleksandra to Nicholas, March 2, 1916, in *Letters*, p. 283.
27. Paléologue (n.d.), III, p. 119.
28. M. V. Rodzianko, pp. 141–144; and Paléologue (1921), III, pp. 38–39.
29. Aleksandra to Nicholas, November 10, 1916, in *Letters*, pp. 438–439.
30. Ibid., p. 439.
31. Aleksandra to Nicholas, November 11, 1916, in ibid., p. 440.
32. Purishkevich, p. 6.
33. Shul'gin, pp. 100–101.
34. Paléologue (1921), III, p. 24.
35. "Télégramme secret de M. Paléologue au Ministère des Affaires Etrangères," Petrograd, January 14, 1917, no. 646/78–79.
36. Quoted in Pearson, pp. 132–133.
37. Quoted in Lincoln (1986), p. 311.
38. Quoted in Grand Duke Alexander, pp. 283–284.
39. Quoted in Hasegawa, p. 201.
40. Ibid., p. 200.
41. Paustovskii (1956), III, p. 546.
42. Gippius (1929), pp. 75–76.
43. Maiakovskii, "Revoliutsiia," in *SS*, I, pp. 224–225.
44. Shul'gin, p. 308.
45. Sukhanov (1922), I, pp. 229, 232.
46. "Prikaz no. 1 Petrogradskogo soveta rabochikh i soldatskikh deputatov po voiskam Petrogradskogo voennogo okruga," pp. 17–18.
47. Paustovskii (1966), I, pp. 641, 633.
48. "Pis'mo Aleksandra Bloka k materi, 23 marta 1917 g.," in Blok, II, p. 339.
49. Quoted in Pyman (1979), p. 241.
50. "Pis'mo Aleksandra Bloka k materi, 23 marta 1917 g.," p. 339.
51. "Sekretnyi doklad ego prevoskhoditel'stvu gospodinu tovarishchu ministra vnutrennikh del. Otdeleniia po okhraneniiu obschchestvennoi bezopasnosti i poriadka v stolitse"; "Sekretnaia zapiska otdeleniia po okhraneniiu obshchestvennoi bezopasnosti i poriadka v stolitse."
52. Shul'gin, p. 168.
53. Miliukov (1955), II, p. 304.
54. Kerensky (1927), p. 59.
55. Quoted in Florinsky, II, p. 1387.
56. Paustovskii (1956), III, p. 573.
57. Paléologue (1921), III, pp. 339–340.
58. Lockhart (1933), p. 177.
59. Quoted in Florinsky, II, p. 1387.
60. Quoted in Trotsky (1960), II, pp. 136–137.
61. Ibid., p. 137.
62. Voznesenskii, pp. 33–34.
63. Kerensky (1927), p. 75.
64. Knox, II, pp. 581–582.
65. Paustovskii (1956), III, p. 577.
66. Baklanova, p. 38.
67. Sidorov, pp. 213–220; Liashchenko, II, pp. 632–633; *Rossiia v mirovoi voine 1914–1918 goda v tsifrakh*, p. 30.
68. Fussell, pp. 65–67.
69. Paléologue (1921), III, p. 244.
70. Golder, p. 324.

71. Sukhanov (1922), II, p. 204.
72. Browder and Kerensky, II, p. 1045.
73. Ibid., p. 1098.
74. Kerensky (1927), p. 195.
75. Quoted in ibid., pp. 193–195.
76. Quoted in Denikin (1922), p. 175.
77. Quoted in ibid., p. 257.
78. Quoted in Kerensky (1965), p. 282.
79. Sukhanov (1922), IV, p. 137.
80. Quoted in ibid., p. 153.
81. Browder and Kerensky, II, p. 943.
82. Ibid., p. 968.
83. Bukhbinder, pp. 30, 49.
84. Kerensky (1927), p. 290.
85. Denikin (1922), p. 298.
86. Quoted in Katkov (1980), p. 31.
87. N. Ia. Ivanov, p. 41.
88. For the text of Kornilov's speech, see Pokrovskii and Iakovlev, pp. 61–66.
89. For a summary account of the Kornilov "revolt," see Lincoln (1986), pp. 414–424. For more detailed discussions, see N. Ia. Ivanov, Vladimirova, and Martynov. In English, see especially Alexander Rabinowitch's masterly effort to unravel the tangled skeins of the Kornilov-Kerenskii conflict in Rabinowitch, pp. 116–150.
90. Tolstoi, III, pp. 299, 298, 299.
91. Gorky (1968), p. 83.
92. Quoted in Rabinowitch, p. 180.
93. Lenin, *CW*, XXVI, p. 20.
94. Ibid., p. 77.
95. "Rezoliutsiia Tsentral'nogo komiteta RSDRP(b) o podgotovke vooruzhënnogo vosstaniia, predlozhennaia V. I. Leninym," p. 49.
96. Quoted in Mel'gunov (1953), p. 35.
97. Trotskii (1930), II, p. 59.
98. Pokrovskii and Iakovlev, p. 63.
99. Williams, p. 125.
100. Gippius (1929), pp. 219, 221. See also Polikarpov, pp. 73–90.
101. Published in Pachmuss, p. 199.
102. Gippius (1929), p. 221.
103. Denikin, II, p. 86. See also "Bykhovskii al'bom," pp. 5–8.
104. Lukomskii, I, pp. 266–267; Denikin, II, pp. 85–130; Lehovich, p. 165.
105. Nesterovich-Berg, pp. 44–46; Lincoln (1986), p. 509.
106. Luckett, pp. xv–xvi.
107. This account of the Bykhov prisoners and their escape to the South has been drawn from the following sources: Denikin, II, pp. 85–185; Lukomskii, I, 260–267; Kenez (1971), pp. 49–67; Lehovich, pp. 164–175.
108. Denikin, II, pp. 147–148.
109. Trotskii, *KVR*, I, p. 165.
110. K. N. Nikolaev, pp. 150–151; Denikin, II, pp. 154–155.
111. Quoted in Kenez (1971), p. 66.
112. Robien, p. 206.
113. Denikin (1930), pp. 96–98.
114. Quoted in Chamberlin, II, p. 78.
115. Quoted in ibid., p. 77.
116. Lukomskii, II, p. 206.

Chapter One: The Hungry Spring

1. Paustovskii (1966), I, pp. 641, 653.
2. Knox, II, p. 581.
3. Buchanan, II, p. 114.
4. Gorky (1968), p. 141.
5. Lenin, *CW*, XXVII, pp. 106, 108.
6. Trotskii, *KVR*, I, pp. 29–30.
7. Tolstoi, III, p. 298.
8. Shklovsky, p. 133.
9. Sorokin, p. 133.
10. Gippius (1929), p. 232.
11. Beatty, p. 324.
12. Robien, pp. 220, 186.
13. Trotskii, *KVR*, I, p. 310. See also, Robien, p. 228; Tyrkova-Williams, pp. 386–389; Beatty, pp. 294–301.
14. Tyrkova-Williams, p. 433.
15. Robien, p. 222.
16. Stites, p. 372.
17. See the watercolors in the Vladimirov Collection in the archives of the Hoover Institution, Stanford, California.
18. Tyrkova-Williams, p. 439.
19. Robien, pp. 165–166.
20. Gorky (1968), p. 138.
21. Robien, p. 165.
22. Tyrkova-Williams, p. 395.
23. Lockhart, p. 239.
24. Gorky (1968), p. 140.
25. Antonov-Ovseenko, I, pp. 19–20. A more extensive version of this quote appears in Lincoln (1986), p. 435.
26. Robien, p. 164.
27. Ibid., p. 176.
28. Ibid., pp. 175, 225. See also Tyrkova-Williams, p. 440.
29. Quoted in Serge (1972), p. 97.
30. Chamberlin, I, p. 358.
31. Translation from a Russian poster reprinted in Reed, p. 267.
32. Tolstoi, III, pp. 297, 300.
33. Beatty, pp. 314, 319–321.
34. Robien, p. 147.
35. Quoted in Fraiman, p. 319.
36. Quoted in ibid. See also pp. 320–321.
37. Ibid., p. 289; Davydov, pp. 20–21.
38. Fraiman, pp. 289, 321–322.
39. Ibid., pp. 292–293; Davydov, pp. 23–24; Konev, pp. 114–115.
40. Davydov, pp. 26–27; Konev, pp. 108–110.
41. Fraiman, pp. 295,306, 321.
42. Quoted in Baburin, p. 343.
43. Gladkov, pp. 263, 267; Fraiman, pp. 304–305; Konev, pp. 130–131.
44. *God raboty*, pp. 43–45; Orlov, p. 354.
45. Geresimiuk, p. 81; Keep, pp. 420–421.
46. Karpinskii, pp. 4–5, 17.
47. J. Maynard, pp. 48–52.
48. Sautin, pp. 130–134.

49. Vinogradov, p. 93.
50. Chamberlin, I, p. 417.
51. *God raboty*, p. 47; Davydov, pp. 74–75.
52. Il'ina, pp. 89–90.
53. Quoted in ibid., p. 91.
54. *Statisticheskii sbornik*, pp. 3–4.
55. Lenin, *CW*, XXVI, pp. 257–261.
56. Pershin, II, pp. 157–219.
57. Okinskii, pp. 60–63; Keep, pp. 397–398.
58. Quoted in S. A. Sokolov, p. 25.
59. Strizhkov, pp. 54–55; Davydov, p. 74.
60. Sorokin, p. 234.
61. Chamberlin, II, p. 337.
62. Davydov, p. 75.
63. Quoted in Gulevich and Gassanova, p. 103.
64. Quoted in Konev, p. 108. See also Gimpel'son (1968), pp. 28–36; Gulevich and Gassanova, p. 103.
65. Quoted in Iskrov, p. 77.
66. Quoted in Gulevich and Gassanova, p. 104.
67. Ibid., p. 108.
68. Paustovskii (1966), I, pp. 709–710.
69. *Sobranie uzakonenii*, p. 437.
70. Quoted in Chamberlin, I, p. 426.
71. Bunyan, p. 463.
72. Quoted in Strizhkov, p. 56.
73. Quoted in Keep, p. 429. See also *Sobranie uzakonenii*, pp. 437–438.
74. Trotskii, *KVR*, I, pp. 81–82.
75. Ibid., p. 82.
76. Bunyan, p. 468.
77. Iskrov, p. 77.
78. Quoted in Strizhkov, p. 57.
79. Quoted in Iskrov, p. 80.
80. Quoted in ibid., p. 79.
81. Quoted in Yaney (1982), p. 492.
82. Quoted in Strizhkov, pp. 62–63.
83. Quoted in ibid., p. 69.
84. Quoted in Semanov (1972), pp. 115–116.
85. Quoted in Strizhkov, p. 68.
86. Quoted in Semanov (1972), p. 116.
87. Ibid., pp. 116–117; Strizhkov, p. 68.
88. Trotskii, *KVR*, I, p. 85.
89. Strizhkov, pp. 70–72.
90. Gordienko, p. 162.
91. Trotskii, *KVR*, I, pp. 85–86.
92. Davydov, p. 76.
93. Bunyan, pp. 447–478.
94. Okinskii, pp. 101–104.
95. Kazakov, p. 132.
96. Storozhev, pp. 188–189; S. A. Sokolov, pp. 59–60; Strizhkov, pp. 91–92.
97. Bunyan, p. 481.
98. Shestakov, p. 55.
99. Kon'kova, pp. 139–140.

100. Ibid., pp. 136–138; Atkinson, pp. 191–194; Shestakov, pp. 18–19; Sharapov, p. 162; S. A. Sokolov, pp. 61–63.
101. Orlov, pp. 281–335; Keep, pp. 432–434.
102. Vladimirov, pp. 3–9; J. Maynard, p. 101.
103. Yaney (1982), p. 488.
104. Keep, pp. 423–434.
105. S. A. Sokolov, p. 64; Vladimirov, pp. 12–20.
106. *Sobranie uzakonenii*, pp. 690–691.
107. Sorokin, p. 212.
108. Quoted in S. A. Sokolov, p. 72.
109. Ibid., pp. 74–75.
110. Bunyan, p. 191.
111. Vladimirova (1927), p. 199.
112. Bunyan, p. 277n.
113. Denikin, II, p. 205.
114. Ibid.

Chapter Two: The Fighting Begins

1. Karlinsky, pp. 72–73.
2. Tsvetaeva, "Don," in Tsvetaeva, pp. 47–49. See also p. 46.
3. On the Cossack communities along the lower reaches of Russia's great southern rivers, see Golubutskii; Platonov, pp. 107–114; Borisenko, I, pp. 21–22; Golovin, III, pp. 19–30; and most recently, Gordon, pp. 11–97.
4. *Taras Bul'ba*, in Gogol (1959), II, pp. 48–49.
5. Quoted in Avrich (1976), p. 59.
6. Ibid., pp. 251, 122.
7. K. N. Nikolaev, p. 149; Kenez (1971), pp. 39–40.
8. Lemke, p. 142.
9. M. V. Alekseev (1929), p. 50; M. V. Alekseev (1928), pp. 77–82. See also K. N. Nikolaev, pp. 149–150.
10. Denikin, II, pp. 156–157, 159.
11. Quoted in Polikarpov, p. 68.
12. Quoted in Kirienko, pp. 69–73.
13. Ibid., pp. 61–62. See also pp. 63–64.
14. Rosenberg, pp. 308–309.
15. Denikin, II, pp. 160–161; Lukomskii, II, pp. 276–280.
16. Pokrovskii, pp. 12–14.
17. Smagin, p. 16; Kenez (1971), pp. 38–39.
18. Borisenko, II, pp. 52–54; Dobrynin, pp. 39–42.
19. Denikin, II, p. 173. See also Babichev, pp. 161–165.
20. K. N. Sokolov, p. 4; Zaitsov, pp. 36–38.
21. Rosenberg, pp. 310–311.
22. See Trubetskoi, pp. 3–5.
23. Lukomskii, I, pp. 280–282; Denikin, II, pp. 188–190; Zaitsov, pp. 38–41.
24. Quoted in Denikin, II, p. 198.
25. K. N. Nikolaev, p. 150.
26. Denikin, II, p. 200; Denisov, p. 80; Kenez (1971), pp. 62, 68.
27. Lukomskii, I, p. 287.
28. Denikin, II, pp. 201–202.

29. Dobrovol'cheskaia armiia, pp. 5–18; Nesterovich-Berg, pp. 91, 105–106, 110–112, 116, 129; K. N. Nikolaev, p. 149; Astrov, "Zapiska," p. 7; Lukomskii, I, pp. 289–290; Kenez (1971), pp. 72–73.
30. Kenez (1971), p. 73.
31. On the Allies' continued confidence in Kaledin, see Kirienko, pp. 128–129.
32. Ibid., p. 128. See also Babichev, pp. 157–158.
33. Quoted in Ullman (1961), pp. 46, 52. On the Allies' early sympathy for the Whites, see also Dumov, pp. 88–96.
34. Ullman (1961), p. 56.
35. Vladimirova (1927), pp. 139–140; Denikin, II, pp. 219–220.
36. Kirienko, pp. 202–203.
37. Trubetskoi, p. 3.
38. Lisovoi, "Rol" ofitserov," pp. 4–5.
39. "Mikhail Dmitrievich Bonch-Bruevich"; "Vladimir Dmitrievich Bonch-Bruevich"; Lincoln (1986), pp. 458–459.
40. Lincoln (1986), pp. 239–240.
41. Denikin, II, p. 198.
42. Maliantovich, p. 130.
43. Polikarpov, pp. 348–352.
44. Ibid., pp. 352–353; Kirienko, pp. 138–139.
45. Antonov-Ovseenko, I, 90–92; Kuz'min, pp. 22–24.
46. Antonov-Ovseenko, I, pp. 76–77.
47. Kakurin, I, pp. 172–183.
48. Gul' (1925), p. 22.
49. Quoted in Kenez (1971), p. 79.
50. Quoted in Nesterovich-Berg, p. 96.
51. Quoted in Luckett, p. 97.
52. Lenin, *CW*, XXIV, p. 374.
53. Borisenko, I, p. 70.
54. Denikin, II, p. 206.
55. Ibid., p. 208.
56. Ibid., p. 224.
57. K. N. Nikolaev, p. 153.
58. Ibid., p. 150.
59. Borisenko, I, pp. 110–112, 130–140.
60. Ibid., pp. 138–140; Gul' (1925), pp. 115–120.
61. Quoted in Denikin, II, p. 294.
62. Quoted in ibid., p. 296.
63. Quoted in K. N. Nikolaev, p. 153.
64. Quoted in Denikin, II, p. 295.
65. Bogaevskii, p. 82.
66. Denikin, II, pp. 298, 303.
67. K. N. Nikolaev, p. 165.
68. Kenez (1971), p. 100.
69. Denikin (1953), pp. 21–80.
70. Quoted in Wheeler-Bennett, pp. 268–269.
71. Bunyan and Fisher, pp. 523–524.
72. Lenin, *CW*, XXVII, p. 159; ibid., p. 109.
73. Suprunenko, pp. 21–42; Reshetar, pp. 117–120; Pipes (1954), pp. 130–131.
74. Piontkovskii, p. 355. See also Adams, pp. 7–10; Fedyshyn, pp. 133–135; Reshetar, pp. 125–128.
75. Quoted in Rosenberg, p. 315.
76. Miliukov, "Dnevnik," pp. 20–30.

77. Kenez (1971), pp. 139–140.
78. Krasnov, pp. 206–210. See also Trubetskoi, pp. 38–40.
79. Quoted in Denikin, III, pp. 131–132.
80. Quoted in Miliukov, "Dnevnik," pp. 47–48.
81. Quoted in Rosenberg, p. 315.
82. Quoted in Denikin, III, pp. 67.
83. Quoted in ibid., p. 130.
84. Ibid., p. 132.
85. Quoted in Zaitsov, p. 153.
86. Golovin, X, p. 52; Trubetskoi, pp. 40–43.
87. Denikin, III, p. 130.
88. Quoted in Zaitsov, p. 155.
89. Klevanskii, pp. 10–21; Kalvoda (1985), pp. 420–422.
90. Klevanskii, pp. 128–147; Miliukov (1927), II, pp. 24–25; Vladimirova (1927), pp. 219–223; Kalvoda (1982), pp. 215–238.
91. Maksakov and Turunov, p. 168.
92. Česka družina, pp. 5–8; A. M. Nikolaev, pp. 38–40; Parfenov, pp. 26–27; Antonov, pp. 62–66. For detailed maps of the Czech Legion's positions at a number of points in 1918–1919, see the maps in the file about its movements, in BACU, Denikin Collection, box 23.
93. Gins, I, p. 60.
94. Mel'gunov, I, p. 71.
95. Quoted in ibid., p. 73.
96. Quoted in Ullman (1961), p. 169.
97. Quoted in ibid., p. 186.
98. Quoted in ibid., pp. 169–170.
99. Quoted in ibid., p. 171.
100. J. White, pp. 14–15; Dunsterville, pp. 15–17; Ullman (1961), pp. 92–95; Kennan (1956), pp. 307–309.
101. Quoted in J. White, p. 228.
102. Ward, p. 268.
103. "Ataman Grigorii Mikhailovich Semenov," p. 614a; Stewart, pp. 265–270.
104. Quoted in Unterberger, p. 60.
105. Quoted in J. White, pp. 239–240.
106. Quoted in ibid., p. 71.
107. Ibid., p. 159.
108. "The American Commercial Invasion of Russia," pp. 362–363.
109. Fisher, "The American Railway Mission," pp. 1–6; Stevens.
110. Cumming and Petit, pp. 28–29.
111. Quoted in Kennan (1958), p. 88.
112. Quoted in White, p. 192.
113. Kennan (1958), p. 105.
114. Quoted in ibid., p. 101.
115. Zaitsov, p. 126; Kuz'min, pp. 84–86.
116. K. V. Gusev, pp. 230–233; Gins, I, pp. 74–83, 86–101.
117. Gins, I, pp. 102–131; Maksakov and Turunov, pp. 197–199, 208–209, 224–225.
118. Garmiza, pp. 34–35.
119. Quoted in Chamberlin, II, p. 15.
120. Quoted in Mints (1974), p. 47. See also pp. 54–55, and Gusev and Eritsian, pp. 323–352; Piontkovskii, pp. 219–220.
121. Piontkovskii, pp. 237–238.
122. Bunyan, pp. 288–290.

123. Ibid., p. 292.
124. A. M. Nikolaev, pp. 41–42.
125. Quoted in Chamberlin, II, p. 18.
126. Quoted in ibid., p. 118.

Chapter Three: "The Expropriation of the Expropriators"

1. Trotskii (1930), II, pp. 59–60.
2. Krupskaia, p. 338.
3. Rigby (1979), pp. 238–242.
4. Quoted in ibid., p. 47.
5. Quoted in Yaney (1982), p. 463.
6. Lenin, *CW*, XXVI, pp. 114, 111.
7. Ibid., XXV, p. 421.
8. Ibid., XXVI, pp. 115, 114.
9. Krupskaia, p. 338.
10. "Vladimir Aleksandrovich Antonov-Ovseenko"; "Pavel Efimovich Dybenko"; "Nikolai Vasil'evich Krylenko"; "Viktor Pavlovich Nogin"; "Nikolai Il'ich Podvoiskii"; "Ivan Ivanovich Skvortsov-Stepanov"; "Ivan Adol'fovich Teodorovich"; and Iosif Vissarionovich Stalin (Dzhugashvili)."
11. Gurovich, p. 304.
12. Vasiukov, pp. 207–209.
13. Iroshnikov (1973), p. 63.
14. Gurovich, p. 316.
15. Iroshnikov (1973), pp. 46–66; Yaney (1971), pp. 3–35.
16. Lenin, *CW*, XXV, p. 420.
17. Fediukin, pp. 40–42; Iroshnikov (1966), pp. 258–259. On the way in which these officials were eventually replaced with newly trained Soviet "specialists," see Sternheimer, pp. 316–354.
18. Bryant (1918), pp, 46–47.
19. Trotsky (1941), p. 256. See also Fitzpatrick, p. 18; Fotieva, pp. 138–141.
20. Rigby (1979), p. 56.
21. Atkinson, pp. 155–164; Keep, pp. 200–216.
22. Gaponenko (1958), p. 10.
23. Lenin, *CW*, XXVI, p. 138.
24. Ibid., pp. 257–261.
25. Krupskaia, p. 338.
26. Reed, p. 184.
27. Gor'kii (1922), p. 43.
28. Atkinson, pp. 180–181.
29. "Obzor polozheniia Rossii za tri mesiatsa revoliutsii," delo no. 4/251–252.
30. Crankshaw, p. 369. On Stolypin's program, see Dubrovskii, pp. 65–230, and Robinson, pp. 208–343. The best summary of Stolypin's agrarian reform is Bazyłow, pp. 196–228.
31. See, for example, Shestakov, p. 55; Kachorovskii, pp. 575–576; Atkinson, pp. 191–196.
32. Lenin, *CW*, XXI, pp. 71, 74.
33. Ibid., pp. 329–330. See also Malle, pp. 153–54; Gladkov, p. 114.
34. Lenin, *CW*, XXVI, p. 107.
35. Gindin, pp. 24–26, 32–33; Epstein, pp. 74–95; Carr, II, pp. 134–135.

36. Gindin, pp. 27–29; Lenin, *CW*, XXVI, p. 389.
37. Lenin, *CW*, XXVI, p. 391.
38. Quoted in Gindin, p. 45. See also pp. 41–44.
39. Lenin, *CW*, p. 467. See also Gindin, pp. 47–56.
40. Gindin, pp. 73–79, 89–90; Berkhin, p. 53; Malle, pp. 158–160; Carr, II, pp. 138–139.
41. Quoted in Tyrkova-Williams, p. 375.
42. Got'e, p. 453.
43. Lenin, *CW*, XXVI, pp. 169–173.
44. Cohen, pp. 53–55, 402, note 35.
45. Baklanova, pp. 89–95; Venediktov, I, pp. 44–47.
46. Quoted in Gaponenko, p. 372.
47. Browder and Kerensky, II, p. 725.
48. Quoted in Baklanova, p. 132.
49. Chugaev, p. 291.
50. Egorova, p. 231; Liashchenko, III, p. 31.
51. Rosenberg and Koenker, pp. 323–324. This article provides an exciting new analysis of worker activism and social protest in 1917.
52. Quoted in Wade, pp. 89–90.
53. Freidlin, pp. 115–118; Carr, II, p. 70; Keep, pp. 74–76; Wilton, p. 180.
54. Lenin, *CW*, XXVI, pp. 105, 109, 107, 110.
55. Malle, pp. 93–94.
56. Quoted in Carr, II, pp. 68–69.
57. Lenin, *CW*, XXVI, p. 468.
58. Ibid., p. 413.
59. Malle, p. 55. See also pp. 48–54.
60. Voronetskaia, p. 18.
61. Quoted in Venediktov, p. 171. See also Ankudinova, pp. 41–59.
62. Venediktov, p. 233.
63. Malle, p. 61. See also ibid., pp. 51–68; and Ankudinova, pp. 60–78.
64. Malle, p. 67.
65. Gimpel'son (1974), pp. 28–30; Koenker, pp. 424–425.
66. Lenin, *CW*, XXVII, p. 519.
67. Woroszylski, p. 229.
68. Lenin, *CW*, XXVI, p. 429.
69. Quoted in ibid., p. 431.
70. Quoted in Malle, p. 55.
71. Lenin, *Sochineniia*, V, pp. 478, 438.
72. Radkey (1958), p. 455.
73. Quoted in ibid., p. 457.
74. Ibid., pp. 439–442.
75. Trotsky, III, pp. 304, 302, 306.
76. Sukhanov (1955), p. 635.
77. Reed, p. 131.
78. Sukhanov (1922), VII, p. 203.
79. Ibid., p. 659.
80. See Brovkin's impressive recent study, especially pp. 49–104.
81. Sviatitskii, *passim;* Lenin, *CW*, XXX, pp. 256–257, 261.
82. Serge (1972), p. 131.
83. Reed, pp. 329, 335.
84. Quoted in Serge (1972), p. 133.
85. The foregoing account of the Constituent Assembly's meeting is drawn from the following: Gusev and Eritsian, pp. 195–218; K. V. Gusev, pp. 184–220;

Sokolov (1924), pp. 62–69; Minor, pp. 125–132; Radkey (1963), pp. 386–416; Serge (1972), pp. 125–135.

86. Lenin, *CW*, XXVI, p. 436.
87. Quoted in Tyrkova-Williams, p. 369.
88. Quoted in Radkey (1963), p. 430.
89. Quoted in ibid., p. 438.
90. Brovkin, pp. 49–196; Haimson (1979), pp. 454–473; Haimson (1980), pp. 181–207.
91. Quoted in Serge (1972), p. 358.
92. Lenin, *CW*, XXVIII, pp. 212–213.
93. Ibid., p. 221. See also Brovkin, 285–293.
94. Cohen, pp. 62–65.
95. Quoted in Deutscher (1959), p. 381.
96. Quoted in Wheeler-Bennett, p. 188.
97. Quoted in Deutscher (1959), p. 392.
98. Quoted in Cohen, p. 65.
99. Lockhart, pp. 292–293.
100. Ibid., pp. 294–295.
101. Bunyan, p. 208.
102. Sadoul, p. 395.
103. Ibid.
104. Lockhart, p. 295; Paustovskii (1966), I, p. 721.
105. Ibid.
106. Lockhart, p. 296.
107. Bunyan, p. 210.
108. Ibid., p. 211.
109. Sadoul, p. 397.
110. Lockhart, p. 297.
111. Paustovskii (1966), I, p. 720.
112. Ibid., p. 724.
113. This phrase comes from Palmer (1941), p. 42.
114. Quoted in Carr, I, p. 141.
115. Lenin, *CW*, XXVI, p. 374.

Chapter Four: First Days of Terror

1. Figner, I, p. 207. For the story of these early Russian terrorists, see Footman (1945) and Volk.
2. Quoted in Steinberg (1953), p. 132.
3. Florinsky, II, p. 1195; Footman (1945), p. 137.
4. Steinberg (1953), p. 134.
5. Palmer (1941), p. 44.
6. Ibid., pp. 55–57.
7. Palmer (1957), p. 360.
8. Quoted in Salisbury, p. 218.
9. Quoted in Florinsky, II, p. 1387; Kerensky (1927), p. 59.
10. Lincoln (1986), pp. 393–394; Znamenskii, pp. 77–106.
11. These phrases have been taken from Lenin's writings and speeches, November–December 1917, and from Trotskii's notes for a biography of Lenin. See Lenin, *CW*, XXVI, pp. 255, 250, 253, 319, 374, 404, 411, 297, 342; and Trotsky (1925), p. 133.

12. Gorky (1968), p. 99.
13. Quoted in Bunyan, p. 227.
14. Lenin, *CW*, XXVI, p. 374.
15. Trotsky (1925), pp. 134, 133.
16. Lenin, *CW*, XXVIII, p. 71.
17. Quoted in Trotsky (1925), p. 137.
18. Quoted in ibid., pp. 137, 139; Lenin, *CW*, XXVII, p. 33.
19. Lenin, *CW*, XXVI, p. 501.
20. Quoted in Gul' (1936), p. 12.
21. Quoted in Zubov, p. 179.
22. Bunyan, p. 227.
23. Mel'gunov (1925), p. 47.
24. Lockhart, p. 254.
25. Steinberg (1935), p. 196.
26. Quoted in Gul' (1936), p. 49. See also Drabkina, pp. 198–199; and Dzerzhinskaia, pp. 282–284.
27. Quoted in Leggett, pp. 250–251.
28. Stasova, p. 165.
29. Quoted in Rozvadovskaia and Slutskaia, p. 282.
30. Quoted in Gul' (1936), p. 51.
31. Quoted in Chamberlin, II, p. 76.
32. The foregoing biographical sketch of Dzerzhinskii is taken mainly from: Zubov, pp 34–169; and Khatsevich, pp. 50–219. A map of Dzerzhinskii's Siberian fugitive wanderings is in Elkina and Minshakova.
33. Zubov, pp. 182–184; Leggett, pp. 29–30.
34. Leggett, pp. 35–37; Scott, pp. 4–5.
35. Quoted in Scott, p. 5.
36. Quoted in Steinberg (1953), p. 145.
37. Lenin, *CW*, XXVI, p. 411.
38. The quotations from Lenin cited in the foregoing section come from the following: Leggett, p. 55; Lenin, *CW*, XXVI, p. 501; ibid., XXVII, pp. 33, 35.
39. Steinberg (1953), p. 145.
40. Abramovitch, p. 313.
41. Quoted in Deutscher (1959), p. 109.
42. Quoted in Leggett, p. 252.
43. Ibid., pp. 262–263; Mel'gunov (1925), pp. 248–249.
44. Quoted in *Osobaia komissiia*, p. 149.
45. Quoted in Gul' (1936), p. 84.
46. Lenin, *CW*, XXVII, pp. 263, 268, 269, 271.
47. Makintsian, pp. 197–198.
48. Ibid., pp. 368–370; Vladimirova (1927), pp. 270–271; Katkov (1962), p. 58.
49. Makintsian, pp. 215–218; Katkov (1962), pp. 64–65.
50. Vladimirova (1927), p. 271.
51. Makintsian, p. 365.
52. Ibid., p. 277.
53. The foregoing account of Mirbach's assassination and the Left SR uprising in Moscow is drawn from the following: Vladimirova (1927), pp. 273–281; Bonch-Bruevich, III, pp. 231–256; Makintsian, pp. 279–288, 293–314, 331–366; Piontkovskii, pp. 167–170; Leggett, pp. 70–83.
54. Vladimirova (1927), pp 243–47; Gopper, pp. 297–299.
55. Latsis, "Soiuz," pp. 1–3.
56. Quoted in Vladimirova (1927), p. 255.

57. Gopper, p. 312.
58. Latsis, "Soiuz," p. 119.
59. Vladimirova (1927), pp. 261–264.
60. Aronson (1929), pp. 228–232.
61. Piontkovskii, pp. 161–163.
62. Vladimirova (1927), p. 257.
63. Latsis, "Soiuz," pp. 172–173.
64. Vladimirova (1927), p. 260.
65. Quoted in ibid., p. 261.
66. Aronson (1929), pp. 226–227.
67. Chamberlin, II, p. 56.
68. Quoted in Leggett, p. 104.
69. Quoted in ibid., p. 105.
70. Kerenski (1936), pp. 162–165; Buchanan, II, pp. 90–106.
71. Gilliard, p. 217.
72. Quoted in Kerenski (1936), p. 165. See also pp. 166–167, and Mel'gunov (1951), pp. 162–171.
73. Kerensky (1927), p. 259.
74. Quoted in Leggett, p. 66.
75. Kerenski (1928), p. 268. See also Mel'gunov (1951), pp. 172–179.
76. Quoted in Mel'gunov (1951), pp. 192–193.
77. Ibid., pp. 192–198.
78. Witte, II, p. 292.
79. Massie, p. 449.
80. Gilliard, p. 254.
81. Nicholas II (1934), pp. 176–200; Nicholas II (1928), p. 118; Trewin, p. 101.
82. Lincoln (1981), pp. 741–743; Mel'gunov (1951), pp. 276–296; Massie, pp. 482–484.
83. N. Sokolov, pp. 130–132; Trewin, pp. 106–109; Mel'gunov (1951), pp. 370–374; Alfer'ev, p. 385.
84. N. Sokolov, p. 131.
85. Alfer'ev, pp. 430–433.
86. N. Sokolov, p. 125.
87. Bykov, p. 313.
88. Nicholas II (1934), p. 214.
89. N. Sokolov, pp. 134–136.
90. Quoted in Trewin, pp. 111–112.
91. Leggett, p. 65; N. Sokolov, pp. 132–134; Bykov, pp. 312–314.
92. Trotsky (1963), p. 80.
93. Chamberlin, II, p. 90.
94. Trotsky (1963), p. 81.
95. N. Sokolov, pp. 173–179; 230–231, 233, 235.
96. N. Sokolov, pp. 204–205.
97. Quoted in Trewin, p. 113.
98. The foregoing description of the Romanovs' last hours and execution is particularly indebted to the immensely detailed and carefully prepared report drawn up by Nikolai Sokolov, a talented tsarist criminal investigator who was assigned by Admiral Kolchak to investigate the circumstances of the Romanovs' deaths after the Whites seized control of Ekaterinburg. The entire report is valuable, but see especially the following: N. Sokolov, pp. 142–148, 212–238. This has been supplemented by materials provided by Bykov, pp. 313–315; Mel'gunov (1951), pp. 382–402; Diterikhs, *passim;* Alfer'ev, pp. 395–410; Lincoln (1981), pp. 744–746; Chamberlin, II, pp. 90–92.

99. N. Sokolov, pp. 194–199, 206–218.
100. Ibid., pp. 191–194; Diterikhs, I, pp. 161–162.
101. N. Sokolov, p. 249.
102. Trotsky (1963), p. 81.
103. Vladimirova (1927), p. 291.
104. Quoted in Leggett, p. 103.
105. Quoted in Steinberg (1935), p. 226.
106. Ibid., pp. 226–231.
107. Uralov, pp. 106–117; Golinkov, I, pp. 187–188; Adamovich, Aldanov, and Ivanov, pp. 20–34.
108. Khatsevich, p. 259; Zubov, p. 208.
109. Lenin, *CW*, XXVIII, pp. 90–92; Shub, p. 321.
110. Bonch-Bruevich, III, pp. 275–277, 277–283, 286–290.
111. Quoted in Golinkov, I, p. 188.
112. Semenov, pp. 33–35; Johnson, pp. 236–237; Steinberg (1935), pp. 98–100.
113. Mal'kov, p. 162.
114. Quoted in Steinberg (1935), p. 236.
115. Globachev, pp. 138–139.
116. Bunyan, pp. 238–239.
117. Quoted in Leggett, p. 108.
118. Quoted in Shub, p. 323.
119. Bunyan, pp. 239–240.
120. Ibid., p. 239.
121. Ibid., p. 241.
122. Ibid., p. 242.
123. Leggett, p. 111.
124. Mel'gunov (1925), pp. 5–7.
125. Goldman, II, p. 745.
126. Bunyan, pp. 244–245.
127. Ibid., p. 243.
128. Mel'gunov (1925), p. 10.
129. Bunyan, p. 261.
130. *Osobaia komissiia*, pp. 149–150.
131. Latsis (1920), p. 75.
132. Leggett, p. 116.
133. Quoted in Chamberlin, II, pp. 77–78.
134. Mel'gunov (1925), pp. 62–63.
135. Begletsov, p. 77.
136. Quoted in ibid., p. 38. See also Golinkov, I, pp. 183–192.
137. Gorky (1968), pp. 233–234.
138. Quoted in Leggett, p. 104.
139. Gorky (1968), p. 173.
140. Trotsky (1963), p. 83. See also Trotsky (1971), p. 160.
141. Trotsky (1971), pp. 160–161.
142. Ibid., p. 161.

Chapter Five: The Allies Intervene

1. Francis, pp. 343, 283, 143.
2. Buchanan, II, pp. 255, 196.
3. Lenin, *CW*, XXVIII, pp. 62, 72, 66–67, 65, 75.

4. Kennan (1956), p. 35.
5. Quoted in ibid., p. 36, note 10.
6. Francis, p. 3.
7. Noulens, I, p. 185.
8. Lockhart, p. 246.
9. Kennan (1956), p. 41.
10. Sadoul, p. 127.
11. Quoted in Lockhart, p. 222.
12. *Bolshevik Propaganda*, p. 889.
13. Lockhart, p. 225.
14. Hard, p. 67.
15. Ibid., pp. 70–71.
16. Efremenkov, p. 143.
17. Francis, p. 237.
18. Ibid., pp. 241–242.
19. Lockhart, p. 246.
20. Quoted in ibid., p. 247.
21. Cumming and Pettit, p. 82.
22. "Zasedanie TsK RSDRP," p. 208.
23. Lenin, *CW*, XXVII, pp. 366, 369–370.
24. Ibid., p. 361.
25. Quoted in Kakurin, I, p. 142.
26. Kovalenko, pp. 98–116, 130.
27. Lenin, *CW*, XXVII, p. 79.
28. Lincoln (1986), pp. 349–350, 404. For a more detailed discussion of Order No. 1, see Tokarev, pp. 56–65.
29. Trotskii, *KVR*, I, p. 45.
30. Ibid., pp. 31–45. This quotation comes from the title, *Trud, distsiplina i poriadok spasuiut Sovetskuiu Respubliku*, under which a separate edition of Trotskii's speech was published (Moscow, 1918), see ibid., note 9, p. 402.
31. Trotskii, *KVR*, I, pp. 30, 29.
32. Ibid., p. 125.
33. Ibid., p. 29.
34. Ibid., p. 135.
35. Il'in-Zhenevskii, p. 87.
36. Quoted in Deutscher (1954), p. 412.
37. Trotskii, *KVR*, I, p. 135.
38. Deutscher (1954), p. 411.
39. Trotskii, *KVR*, I, p. 165.
40. On schools for "Red commanders," see Shatagin, pp. 50–52.
41. Efimov, pp. 92–96; Erikson, pp. 31–34.
42. Trotskii, *KVR*, I, p. 151.
43. Erikson, p. 41.
44. Quoted in Shatagin, p. 52.
45. Denikin, III, p. 146. See also Lisovoi, "Rol' ofitserov," p. 4.
46. Zaionchkovskii, pp. 58–75; Rostunov, pp. 355–359.
47. Kovalenko, pp. 116–118.
48. Ibid., pp. 126–139; Movchin, pp. 87–89. See also Douné, pp. 100–103.
49. Quoted in Kennan (1958), p. 46.
50. Efremenkov, pp. 145–150.
51. Long (1972), pp. 38–64; Masherzerskii, pp. 122–135; C. J. Smith, pp. 92–125.
52. Maynard, p. 24.
53. Long (1972), pp. 53–54.

54. Foreign Secretary Arthur Balfour to R. H. Bruce Lockhart, no. 80, April 17, 1918, PRO: FO 371/3307; R. H. Bruce Lockhart to Foreign Secretary Arthur Balfour, no. 163, May 7, 1918, PRO: FO 371/3285–86; Lockhart, pp. 250–252; Churchill, pp. 82–83.
55. Long (1972), pp. 70–73.
56. Lenin, *CW*, XXVII, p. 380.
57. Quoted in Long (1972), pp. 73–74.
58. Quoted in Kennan (1958), p. 270.
59. Quoted in ibid., p. 364.
60. Ibid., pp. 366–367; Long (1972), pp. 53–54, 87–89; Ullman (1961), pp. 175–179.
61. Maynard, pp. 39, 26.
62. Ibid., pp. 27–29.
63. Quoted in Ullman (1961), p. 180. See also p. 181.
64. Quoted in Kennan (1958), p. 33, fn. 3. See also pp. 32–33.
65. Tarasov, p. 67.
66. Quoted in Long (1972), p. 105.
67. Quoted in ibid., p. 106.
68. Quoted in ibid., pp. 106–107.
69. Bunyan, pp. 133–134.
70. Quoted in Kennan (1958), p. 375.
71. Tarasov, p. 73; Kiselev and Klimov, p. 161.
72. Quoted in Ullman (1961), pp. 184–185.
73. Quoted in ibid., p. 185.
74. Quoted in Long (1972), p. 108, note 66.
75. Ibid., pp. 85–88.
76. Golovin, III, book 7, p. 27.
77. Long (1972), pp. 189–191.
78. Kennan (1958), pp. 438–439.
79. Francis, p. 253.
80. Bunyan, p. 305.
81. Sobolev, pp. 5–6.
82. Quoted in Ullman (1961), p. 186.
83. Quoted in ibid., p. 258.
84. Lenin, *CW*, XXVIII, p. 18.
85. Quoted in Kennan (1958), pp. 396–397.
86. "*Aide-Memoire*," pp. 236–237.
87. Baedeker, p. 539.
88. Kuz'min, pp. 84–85; J. A. White, pp. 258–259; Zaitsov, p. 126.
89. Kalvoda (1982), p. 225.
90. Long (1972), pp. 227–236.
91. Quoted in Unterberger, p. 86.
92. Boldyrev, pp. 75, 83.
93. Quoted in Ullman (1961), p. 273.
94. Lenin, *CW*, XXVII, p. 368.
95. Quoted in Unterberger, p. 103.
96. Graves, pp. 55–56.
97. Lenin, *CW*, XXVIII, p. 74.
98. Trotskii (1930), II, pp. 123–125.
99. Ibid., pp. 140–153.
100. Ibid., 145.
101. Ibid., p. 139; Stites, p. 319.
102. Trotskii (1930), II, p. 139.

103. Quoted in Serge (1972), p. 293.
104. Kakurin, I, pp. 244–245.
105. Trotskii (1930), II, pp. 140, 130–131.
106. Mints (1974), pp. 89–95.
107. Gusev, pp. 100–109; Serge (1972), p. 293.
108. Gorelik.
109. Mints (1974), pp. 101–103; Nenarokov, pp. 215–223.
110. Kakurin, I, p. 245.
111. Chernomortsov, *passim;* "Ioakim Ioakimovich Vatsetis."
112. Trotskii (1930), II, p. 127.
113. The foregoing quotations are taken from Trotskii's orders and decrees in August 1918. Trotskii, *KVR*, I, pp. 239, 240, 241, 245, 244.
114. Mints (1974), pp. 94–100; Nenarokov, pp. 210–215; Kakurin, I, pp. 243–245.
115. Trotskii, *KVR*, I, p. 249.
116. Quoted in Mints (1974), p. 98.
117. Trotskii, *KVR*, I, p. 251.
118. Trotskii (1930), II, p. 140.
119. Tolstoi, III, p. 612.

Chapter Six: Denikin and the Cossacks

1. For the troop strengths of the Reds on various fronts in 1919, see Belov (1961), II, pp. 200–202, 326, 375, 377, 500–503. For White estimates, see the classified biweekly *Obshchaia svodka,* with its detailed top secret supplement, *Boevoe raspisanie,* which Kolchak's Supreme Headquarters published in Omsk from late 1918 into late summer of 1919, copies of which are to be found in AG-CV, 17N625, and "Effectif des combattants sur le front vers le 15 avril 1919," also in AG-CV, 17N625.
2. Lenin, *CW*, XXVIII, p. 103.
3. Movchin (1928), pp. 82, 87–89.
4. Aleksashenko, pp. 120–123; Denikin, IV, p. 86. See also "Etat du matériel d'artillérie éxistant aux armées et en depôt au 15 novembre 1918," AG-CV, 17N624; "Etat de situation de l'armée sibérienne au 6 novembre 1918," AG-CV, 17N624; and Belov (1961), II, pp. 299–303, which includes a brief section on credits extended to the Whites by the Allies.
5. Tomilov, pp. 212–215.
6. Quoted in Luckett, pp. 233–234.
7. Il'in, pp.8–9.
8. Denikin, "Rech' . . . v stanitse Egorlytskoi," and "Iz rechi."
9. Lenin, *CW*, XXVIII, p. 54.
10. Trotskii, *KVR*, I, pp. 74, 91.
11. Bunyan, p. 296.
12. Ibid., p. 310.
13. Denikin, "Rech' k rabochim."
14. Smagin, p. 26.
15. Piontkovskii, p. 219.
16. Quoted in Dobrynin, p. 50.
17. Ibid., p. 111. See also ibid., pp. 49–63; Krasnov, pp. 231–235.
18. Quoted in Trotsky (1941), p. 289.
19. "Kliment Efremovich Voroshilov."

20. The preceding summary of Stalin's life and career before 1918 is based upon the following: Tucker, pp. 69–199; Ulam (1973), pp. 16–174; Trotsky (1941), pp. 162–290; and Medvedev, pp. 3–10.
21. Quoted in Tucker, p. 193.
22. Quoted in Trotsky (1941), pp. 288–289.
23. Quoted in ibid., p. 289.
24. Zhloba, pp. 32–34; "Dmitrii Petrovich Zhloba."
25. Dobrynin, pp. 62–63, 111.
26. Krasnov, pp. 244–245.
27. Leonidov, pp. 15–22; Denikin, IV, pp. 74–80.
28. Denikin, "Iz rechi."
29. Denikin, III, p. 262.
30. Denikin, "Iz rechi."
31. Denikin, III, pp. 133, 132.
32. Ibid., pp. 148–149; Sukhorukov, pp. 41–43.
33. Denikin, III, pp. 156–176; Zaitsov, pp. 219–223; Kakurin, I, pp. 249–251.
34. Denikin, II, pp. 308–309, III, pp. 160–161.
35. Ibid., III, p. 160.
36. Shavel'skii, p. 60.
37. Smagin, p. 34.
38. "Protokol 1919 goda," pp. 17–19; Kalinin, p. 35.
39. Shavel'skii, pp. 57–60; "Protokol 1919 goda," pp. 19–22.
40. Denikin, IV, p. 46.
41. Ibid., III, p. 187.
42. Ibid., p. 210.
43. Ibid., p. 200.
44. Pokrovskii, pp. 164–168.
45. Denikin, IV, pp. 46–47.
46. Filimonov, p. 324.
47. Denikin, IV, p. 52.
48. Quoted in Rosenberg, pp. 318–319.
49. Ibid., pp. 320–332.
50. Quoted in ibid., p. 341.
51. Ibid., pp. 320–340; Kenez (1971), pp. 191–210.
52. Shkuro, p. 164.
53. Krasnov, p. 239.
54. Vinaver, pp. 4–16; Gukovskii (1928), pp. 142–144.
55. Quoted in Rosenberg, p. 360. See also Miliukov, "Dnevnik," pp. 20–38.
56. Kenez (1971), pp. 271–277; Rosenberg, pp. 346–351, 361–366.
57. Vinaver, pp. 14–16; Reshetar, pp. 194–204; Lehovich, p. 256.
58. McNeal (1963), pp. 221–236.
59. Ibid.; Miliukov, "Dnevnik," pp. 263–362; Astrov, "Iasskoe"; Kenez (1971), pp. 263–268; Brinkley, pp. 80–86.
60. Carley, pp. 142–158; Ullman (1968), pp. 44–51; Brinkley, pp. 77–103.
61. Trotskii, *KVR*, II, p. 26.
62. Svechnikov, pp. 137–150.
63. Kakurin (1926), pp. 97–100; Denikin, V, pp. 73–80.
64. Wrangel (1930), p. 87.
65. Makarov, p. 17.
66. Denikin, V, pp. 75–85; Kenez (1977), pp. 31–36; Lehovich, pp. 281–284.
67. Wrangel (1930), p. 4.
68. Ibid., p. 59.
69. Quoted in Chamberlin, II, p. 318.

70. Wrangel (1930), pp. 83–88; Vrangel (1928), pp. 158–160.
71. Denikin, "Rech . . . v Tsaritsyne."
72. Denikin, V, pp. 108–109.
73. Wrangel (1930), p. 89.
74. Bubnov, Kamenev, Eidemann, and Tukhachevskii, III, pp. 247–248; "Boevoi i chislennyi sostav iuzhnogo i iugo-vostochnogo frontov," pp. 72–81; Naida, IV, pp. 202–203.
75. Hodgson, p. 181.
76. Kakurin, II, pp. 179–181.
77. Kenez (1977), pp. 64–65.
78. Quoted in Kolesnikov, p. 207.
79. Shavel'skii, p. 8.
80. Lehovich, p. 297; Kenez (1977), p. 63.
81. Quoted in Lehovich, p. 298.
82. Wrangel (1930), pp. 92–93.
83. Shavel'skii, pp. 31–32.
84. Quoted in Lehovich, p. 298.
85. Hodgson, pp. 181–183.
86. Trotskii (1927), XVII, p. 587; Trotsky (1941), p. 312.
87. Erikson, p. 63.
88. Trotsky (1941), pp. 314–315.
89. Eikhe, pp. 190–204.
90. Trotskii (1930), II, pp. 187–188.
91. Trotsky (1941), pp. 313–315; Deutscher (1954), pp. 436–438.
92. Trotsky (1941), p. 314.
93. Quoted in Deutscher (1954), p. 436.
94. "Prikaz komandirovaniia"; Aleksashenko, pp. 148–154; Kenez (1977), p. 43.
95. Lenin "Zapiska . . . v Revvoensovet respubliki."
96. Wrangel (1930), pp. 96–98.
97. Egorov, pp. 114–116, 119–121; Golubintsev, pp. 107–121.
98. Quoted in Chamberlin, II, p. 280.
99. Trotskii, *KVR*, II, p. 279.
100. "Tsirkuliarnoe pis'mo TsK RKP(b)."
101. Quoted in Palij, p. 194.
102. Rakovskii (1921), p. 3.
103. Chamberlin, II, p. 251.
104. Quoted in Rosenberg, p. 328.
105. Palij, pp. 195–208; Kubanin, pp. 79–89; Piontkovskii, pp. 542–549.
106. Aleksashenko, p. 171.
107. Ibid., Egorov, p. 144.
108. Trotskii, *KVR*, II, p. 288.
109. "Semën Mikhailovich Budënnyi"; Erikson, pp. 70–74; Egorov, pp. 182–185; Budënnyi (1928), pp. 108–114. Lehovich, pp. 353–354.
110. Kenez (1977), pp. 220–222.
111. Quoted in Lehovich, p. 381.
112. Quoted in Kenez (1977), p. 254.
113. Quoted in Chamberlin, II, p. 178.

Chapter Seven: Siberia's Supreme Ruler

1. Dmitriev-Mamonov and Zdziarski, p. 71.
2. Kennan (1891), I, pp. 56–57.

3. Tupper, pp. 348–349.
4. Kennan (1891), I, p. 353.
5. Ibid., pp. 78–79; Okladnikov, col. 840.
6. Borzunov, pp. 21, 90–150.
7. Carr (1961), pp. 245–248.
8. Kennan (1891), I, p. 330.
9. Tupper, p. 198.
10. J. A. White, p. 197.
11. Maksakov and Turunov, pp. 49–60.
12. Ibid., pp. 66–87.
13. Mel'gunov (1930), I, p. 193.
14. Gins, I, p. 133. See also ibid., pp. 183–184; and Golovin, VIII, pp. 66–70.
15. Mel'gunov (1930), I, pp. 63–65.
16. Boldyrev, p. 31. See also pp. 33–34.
17. Quoted in Mel'gunov (1930), I, p. 194.
18. Boldyrev, p. 35. For Ufa's population growth between 1900 and 1914, compare Dmitriev-Mamonov and Zdziarski, p. 96, and Baedeker, p. 369.
19. Golovin, VIII, pp. 77–78; Boldyrev, pp. 35–36.
20. Bunyan, p. 340.
21. "Konstitutsiia Ufimskoi direktorii," p. 189.
22. Gins, I, pp. 256–261.
23. Quoted in Golovin, VIII, pp. 99–100.
24. Gins, I, pp. 260–261.
25. Boldyrev, p. 54.
26. Piontkovskii, p. 286.
27. Quoted in Mel'gunov (1930), I, p. 233.
28. Boldyrev, p. 85.
29. Quoted in Gins, I, p. 266.
30. Quoted in Chamberlin, II, p. 177.
31. Bunyan, p. 370.
32. Boldyrev, pp. 73, 91.
33. Quoted in Chamberlin, II, p. 176.
34. Boldyrev, p. 91.
35. Quoted in ibid.
36. Ibid., note 82, pp. 524–525.
37. Boldyrev, p. 87.
38. Varneck and Fisher, pp. 9–148; Taylor, pp. 110–113. See also the excerpt from Kolchak's diary quoted in Lipkina, p. 37, and pp. 36–40.
39. Varneck and Fisher, p. 142.
40. Quoted in Ullman (1961), p. 272.
41. Quoted in ibid., p. 273.
42. Quoted in Ullman (1968), p. 34.
43. Quoted in Mel'gunov (1930), II, p. 165.
44. Zenzinov, p. 191.
45. Quoted in Ullman (1968), p. 34.
46. Mel'gunov (1930), II, p. 113.
47. For a brief discussion of the relative prosperity of Siberia's lower classes compared to those in European Russia at this time, see Long, "Izhevsk-Votkinsk Revolt," pp. 1–7.
48. Quoted in Rosenberg, p. 395. See also pp. 394–396, and Ioffe, pp. 120–121.
49. "Vyderzhki iz rechi . . . Zhardetskogo," p. 207.
50. Janin (1933), pp. 30–34; Janin (1939), p. 233; Rouquerol, pp. 44–45; and the

remarks of Lt. Col. Pichon, another member of the French Military Mission, that are quoted in Mel'gunov (1930), II, p. 109.

51. Avksent'ev, p. 177; Mel'gunov (1930), II, pp. 144–146.
52. Quoted in Gins, II, p. 306.
53. Mel'gunov (1930), II, p. 146.
54. Quoted in Gins, II, p. 308.
55. Ibid., pp. 307–308.
56. Ioffe, p. 145; Golovin, IX, p. 36.
57. Kolchak (1919), p. 11.
58. Ibid.
59. Bunyan, p. 373, note 94.
60. Kolchak (1919), p. 11.
61. Kolchak's press conference of November 28, 1918, quoted in Golovin, IX, pp. 83–87.
62. Lipkina, p. 52.
63. Quoted in Ullman (1968), p. 34.
64. Quoted in Unterberger, p. 149.
65. Quoted in ibid., p. 157.
66. Kolchak (1919), p. 11.
67. Quoted in Unterberger, p. 150.
68. Graves, p. 101.
69. Quoted in Lipkina, pp. 45–46.
70. Kolchak (1925), p. 299.
71. Budberg (1929), pp. 96–97.
72. Luckett, p. 263.
73. Kakurin, I, pp. 243–248, II, pp. 120–122; "Votkinskoe vosstanie" and "Izhevskoe vosstanie," in Markov, pp. 126, 279; Long, "Izhevsk-Votkinsk Revolt," pp. 1–8; Shorin, pp. 147–150.
74. Stalin, IV, p. 202.
75. Ibid., pp. 202–204, 213–214; Kakurin, II, pp. 123–126.
76. Stalin, p. 229.
77. Kakurin, II, p. 166.
78. Shishkin (1960), p. 69; Gai (1926), pp. 11–12.
79. Gins, II, p. 127.
80. Lenin, *CW*, XXIX, p. 244.
81. Ibid., pp. 257–258.
82. Ibid., XXIX, p. 276.
83. Ibid.
84. Ibid., p. 275.
85. Quoted in Shishkin (1960), p. 70.
86. Kakurin, II, pp. 173–174, 191.
87. Piontkovskii, p. 108.
88. Shishkin (1960), pp. 71–73; Naida, IV, pp. 82–83, 92.
89. Quoted in Naida, IV, p. 83.
90. Quoted in ibid., p. 88.
91. Stalin, IV, pp. 202–232.
92. Ibid., pp. 214, 218–219.
93. Golubev, "Frunze"; Erikson, p. 59; Naida, IV, pp. 96–99.
94. Parfenov, p. 72; Gins, II, pp. 94–97; Molotov, pp. 90–97.
95. Mel'gunov (1930), III, pp. 36–43; Kolosov, pp. 61–62; Varneck and Fisher, p. 202. See also ibid., pp. 198–210.
96. Varneck and Fisher, pp. 201, 210.
97. Quoted in Mel'gunov (1930), III, p. 57.

98. Wrangel (1930), p. 6.
99. Shishkin (1957), pp. 13–14, 22–26; Grondijs, pp. 485–489; Komissiia po istorii oktiabr'skoi revoliutsii i R.K.P. (bol'shevikov), I, p. 79; "Ataman Grigorii Mikhailovich Semenov," p. 614; Kavtaradze.
100. Graves, p. 86.
101. Ibid., p. 313.
102. Ibid., pp. 258–264; J. A. White, pp. 272–273.
103. Komissiia po istorii oktiabr'skoi revoliutsii i R.K.P. (bol'shevikov), p. 80.
104. Graves, p. 242.
105. J. White, pp. 265–266.
106. Wrangel (1930), pp. 6–7.
107. Budberg, "Dnevnik," p. 279.
108. Volkov, p. 10.
109. Riabukhin, pp. 12, 2. See also ibid., pp. 1–42; and Volkov, pp. 1–53.
110. On Kalmykov, see Andriushkevich, pp. 120–137, and J. White, pp. 198–199, 266–267.
111. Graves, p. 90.
112. Andriushkevich, p. 131; Budberg, "Dnevnik," p. 263.
113. Budberg, "Dnevnik," pp. 265, 263.
114. Graves, pp. 129–130.
115. Quoted in Chamberlin, II, p. 197.
116. Budberg, "Dnevnik," p. 290; Graves, p. 215.
117. Budberg, "Dnevnik," p. 297. See also Varneck and Fisher, pp. 244–246; J. White, pp. 118–119, 267–268.
118. Budberg (1929), p. 11.
119. Budberg, "Dnevnik," p. 290.
120. Quoted in J. White, p. 119.
121. Graves, pp. 102–103.
122. Gins, II, pp. 294–295.
123. Budberg, (1929), pp. 187, 191, 211, 218.
124. Ibid., p. 97.
125. Ustrialov, p. 1 (entry for February 9, 1919).
126. Ibid.
127. Ibid., pp. 5–6.
128. Ioffe, pp. 221–222; Gins, II, pp. 206, 220–221.
129. Quoted in Vas'kovskii, p. 318.
130. Lipkina, p. 97.
131. Quoted in Khlebnikov, p. 120.
132. Frunze, I, pp. 166–167.
133. Quoted in Vas'kovskii, p. 320. See also pp. 309–310.
134. Frunze, I, p. 198.
135. Budberg (1929), p. 40.
136. Ibid., p. 62.
137. Quoted in Bubnov, Kamenev, Tukhachevskii, and Eideman, III, pp. 202–203.
138. Quoted in ibid., pp. 328–329.
139. Ibid., pp. 326–330; Naida, IV, pp. 117–120, 134.
140. Kakurin, II, pp. 263–269.
141. Quoted in Naida, IV, pp. 116–117.
142. Erikson, p. 64; Bubnov, Kamenev, Tukhachevskii, and Eideman, III, pp. 201–209; Kakurin, II, pp. 270–274.
143. Graves, p. 227.
144. Budberg (1929), p. 156.

145. J. White, p. 120.
146. Ustrialov, pp. 16, 20.
147. Budberg (1929), p. 156.
148. Naida, IV, p. 132.
149. Ibid., p. 133.
150. Budberg (1929), pp. 149, 226, 212, 211.
151. Quoted in Chamberlin, II, p. 199.
152. Molotov, pp. 120–121; Erikson, p. 64.
153. Quoted in Naida, IV, p. 143. See also ibid., pp. 134–148; Zhigalin, pp. 98–114; Erikson, pp. 64–65.
154. Ustrialov, pp. 26–27.
155. Ioffe, pp. 232–233.
156. Budberg (1929), p. 291.
157. Molotov, p. 130.
158. Zankevich, pp. 150–154.
159. Varneck and Fisher, pp. 240–241.
160. Ioffe, pp. 233–256.
161. Ibid., p. 257.
162. Varneck and Fisher, p. 217.
163. C. F. Smith, pp. 72–174.
164. Quoted in Ullman (1968), note 23, p. 261.

Chapter Eight: The Petrograd Front

1. C. J. Smith, pp. 68–91.
2. Churchill, p. 164.
3. "*Aide-memoire*," p. 236.
4. Quoted in Churchill, p. 164.
5. Ibid., p. 166.
6. Ibid., p. 171.
7. Quoted in ibid., pp. 166–167.
8. Quoted in Graves, p. 4.
9. Quoted in Long (1972), p. 229, note 114.
10. Mints (1926), pp. 41–42.
11. Quoted in Long (1972), p. 219.
12. Quoted in ibid., p. 214.
13. See Long's excellent summary discussion of the so-called Chaplin coup, ibid., pp. 220–222.
14. Noulens, II, pp. 180–181.
15. Quoted in Ullman (1961), p. 239.
16. Francis, pp. 272–273.
17. Quoted in Strakhovsky, p. 90.
18. Ironside (1953), p. 55.
19. Ibid., p. 11.
20. Soutar, pp. 64–65.
21. Francis, pp. 294–295.
22. Quoted in Long (1972), pp. 268–269.
23. Ironside (1953), p. 40.
24. Ironside, "Notes," p. 2.
25. Ironside, "Almost Complete Manuscript," p. 2.
26. Ironside (1953), p. 50.

27. Ironside, "Notes," p. 2.
28. Ironside, "Almost Complete Manuscript," p. 9.
29. Ironside (1953), p. 41.
30. Ibid., pp. 50–51.
31. Ironside, "Notes," p. 1.
32. Ibid., p. 2.
33. Ironside, "Almost Complete Manuscript," pp. 12–13.
34. C. Maynard, pp. 183–187.
35. C. J. Smith, pp. 130–133.
36. Ironside, "Notes," p. 3, app. C, p. 2; "Memorandum," administrative app. 5, p. 5; C. Maynard, p. 169; Strakhovsky, pp. 124–125.
37. "Memorandum," administrative app. 6, pp. 1–3.
38. "Unusual Medical Conditions in North Russia," pp. 1–3; Long (1972), pp. 246–247.
39. Published in Naida, IV, p. 185. See also Long (1972), p. 282.
40. Ironside (1953), p. 105.
41. Marushevskii, I, pp. 49–53.
42. Ironside (1953), pp. 112–113.
43. Quoted in Long (1972), pp. 330–331.
44. Ironside (1953), p. 114.
45. Long (1972), pp. 295–296, 320–321, 332–333.
46. Quoted in ibid., p. 302.
47. These quotes have been taken from several speeches that Churchill delivered in England and at meetings of the Supreme War Council in Paris during the third week of February 1919. See Churchill, pp. 164, 176.
48. Quoted in Thompson, p. 136.
49. Quoted in ibid., p. 138.
50. Dobrovol'skii, pp. 24–25.
51. Quoted in Long (1972), pp. 293, note 137.
52. Sokolov (1923), p. 27.
53. Dobrovol'skii, p. 27.
54. C. Maynard, p. 161.
55. Ironside (1953), pp. 115, 123, 127.
56. Ibid., pp. 126–127, 157–158, 161–163; Marushevskii, II, pp. 38, 47–48, 55–56; Tarasov, pp. 254–260; Iakushkin and Polunin, pp. 224–226.
57. Tarasov, p. 260.
58. Ironside (1953), p. 108.
59. Quoted in Strakhovsky, p. 152.
60. Quoted in ibid., p. 158.
61. Mints (1931), pp. 190–196; Long (1972), p. 314.
62. C. Maynard, p. 214.
63. Long (1972), p. 315.
64. Quoted in Strakhovsky, p. 182.
65. Dobrovol'skii, pp. 75–76.
66. Ibid., p. 68.
67. Miller, p. 10.
68. Sokolov (1923), p. 58.
69. Miller, p. 10.
70. Quoted in Mints (1931), p. 236.
71. Sokolov (1923), pp. 67–72; Dobrovol'skii, pp. 134–141; Alakhverdov and Rybakov, p. 234.
72. Quoted in Luckett, p. 318.
73. Gorn, p. 287.

74. Mannerheim, p. 221.
75. C. J. Smith, p. 135.
76. Tomilov, pp. 30–45.
77. Stalin, IV, pp. 172–173.
78. Bubnov, Kamenev, Tukhachevskii, and Eideman, III, pp. 151–156.
79. Mannerheim, p. 207.
80. Smirnov, p. 116.
81. Ibid., p. 121.
82. Tomilov, p. 6.
83. Smirnov, p. 139.
84. A. P. Rodzianko, pp. 3–31; Gorn, pp. 34–39, 48–49.
85. Ullman (1968), p. 256.
86. C. J. Smith, p. 142.
87. Bulak-Balakhovich.
88. Margulies, II, pp. 183–184.
89. Quoted in ibid., p. 120. See also Gorn, pp. 57–58.
90. Tomilov, pp. 160–161, 176–178, app. 7.
91. Ibid., 179–212, app. 8.
92. Ibid., p. 213.
93. Ibid., p. 170; C. J. Smith, p. 151.
94. Quoted in Naida (1958), p. 155.
95. Stalin, IV, p. 269.
96. Quoted in Naida (1958), p. 160. See also pp. 155–159.
97. Ibid., pp. 160, 155; C. J. Smith, p. 143.
98. Tomilov, pp. 152–158; Naida (1958), pp. 162–163; Kakurin, II, pp. 211–216.
99. A. P. Rodzianko, p. 58. See also pp. 56–57.
100. C. J. Smith, p. 144; Luckett, pp. 202–203.
101. Stalin, IV, p. 273.
102. C. J. Smith, pp. 151–159.
103. Tomilov, p. 178.
104. Guchkov, pp. 2–3; Gorn, p. 71.
105. Tomilov, p. 179.
106. Ibid., pp. 336–346; Naida (1958), p. 168.
107. Gorn, p. 86.
108. Ibid., pp. 86–87.
109. The foregoing discussion is based upon material drawn from the following eyewitness accounts, all of which agree in substance, but each of which supplies additional details: Margulies, II, pp. 202–207; Gorn, pp. 106–110; N. N. Ivanov, pp. 95–100; and Kartashev, Kuz'min-Karavaev, and Suvorov, pp. 297–305. The quotations are all taken from Margulies, II, p. 204.
110. Quoted in Ullman (1958), p. 272.
111. Quoted in ibid., p. 270.
112. Quoted in ibid., p. 272.
113. Quoted in Bennett, p. 157. See also pp. 137–156.
114. Bubnov, Kamenev, Tukhachevskii, and Eideman, pp. 159–160; Naida (1958), p. 169.
115. Gough, pp. 199–200.
116. Quoted in Ullman (1958), p. 256. See also Guchkov, pp. 7–11, and Waite, *passim*.
117. Dmitriev, p. 104; Tallents, pp. 362–363; Luckett, p. 315.
118. Dmitriev, pp. 101–126.
119. "Doklad o sostoianii Petrograda," pp. 1–2.

120. "Svedeniia o potrebnostiakh v prodovol'stvii," p. 4.
121. "Memorandum on the Feeding of the Civil Population of Petrograd," pp. 1–2.
122. A. P. Rodzianko, pp. 93–97; Tomilov, pp. 373–374.
123. Quoted in Deutscher (1954), p. 422.
124. A. P. Rodzianko, pp. 103–107.
125. Quoted in Gorn, p. 286.
126. Ibid., pp. 286–287; Tomilov, pp. 380–386; Kakurin, II, pp. 336–338; Naida (1958), pp. 330–334.
127. Quoted in Gorn, p. 286.
128. Trotskii (1930), II, p. 155.
129. Tomilov, pp. 386–387; A. P. Rodzianko, pp. 113–115; Stewart, p. 232.
130. Trotskii (1930), II, p. 155.
131. Trotskii, *KVR*, II p. 383.
132. Quoted in Trotskii (1930), II, p. 156.
133. Ibid., p. 159.
134. Trotskii, *KVR*, II p. 399.
135. Quoted in Deutscher (1954), p. 445.
136. Trotskii (1930), II, p. 159.
137. Trotskii, *KVR*, II, p. 407.
138. Ibid., pp. 441–442.
139. Tomilov, pp. 405–444; Ventsov, pp. 268–272; Kakurin, II, pp. 342–344; Naida (1958), 339–346.
140. Tomilov, pp. 437–438.
141. Trotskii, *KVR*, II, p. 444.
142. Quoted in Tomilov, p. 447.
143. Gorn, p. 355; Stewart, p. 235.
144. "Uzhasy Narvy," p. 343.
145. Ibid.

Chapter Nine: The Ukraine in Ferment

1. Mawdsley, p. 252.
2. Paustovskii (1966), I, pp. 791–792.
3. Billington, p. 4.
4. Quoted in Chamberlin, II, p. 225.
5. Adams, pp. 4–5.
6. Billington, p. 117.
7. Quoted in Chamberlin, II, p. 225.
8. Quoted in Antonov-Ovseenko, I, p. 47.
9. Quoted in Adams, p. 5.
10. Stalin, IV, pp. 7, 14.
11. Ibid., p. 18.
12. Ibid., p. 22.
13. Gol'denveizer, p. 204; Sumskii, p. 103.
14. Quoted in Antonov-Ovseenko, I, p. 155. See also pp. 135–156.
15. Quoted in ibid., pp. 156–157.
16. Quoted in Reshetar, pp. 117–118.
17. Fedyshyn, pp. 91–92.
18. Quoted in ibid., p. 95.
19. Quoted in Reshetar, p. 119.
20. Quoted in Fedyshyn, p. 107.

21. Ibid., pp. 87–104. See also Eudin, pp. 90–105.
22. Quoted in Reshetar, p. 122. See also ibid., pp. 120–121; and Hunczak, pp. 65–67.
23. Quoted in Reshetar, p. 122.
24. Quoted in ibid., p. 124.
25. Quoted in ibid., p. 125.
26. Bunyan, p. 16. See also Hunczak, pp. 67–68; and Reshetar, pp. 145–147.
27. Quoted in Reshetar, p. 130.
28. Quoted in ibid., p. 88.
29. Quoted in ibid., p. 152.
30. Gol'denveizer, p. 219.
31. Gul' (1921), pp. 60–61.
32. Paustovskii (1966), I, p. 757.
33. Quoted in Rosenberg, p. 307. See also pp. 304–306.
34. Quoted in ibid., pp. 320, 317.
35. Quoted in Reshetar, pp. 158, 155, 157.
36. Gol'denveizer, p. 219.
37. Fedyshyn, p. 187.
38. Reshetar, pp. 170–171.
39. Mogilianskii, p. 102.
40. Fedyshyn, pp. 190–194.
41. Quoted in Hunczak, p. 79.
42. Quoted in Reshetar, p. 198, note 58.
43. Mogilianskii, p. 104.
44. Quoted in Vinnichenko, pp. 293, 296.
45. Ibid., pp. 294–295. For a solid summary of the history of the Directory, see Bohachevsky-Chomiak, pp. 82–103.
46. Reshetar, p. 264.
47. Paustovskii (1966), I, pp. 783.
48. Gol'denveizer, p. 232.
49. Paustovskii (1966), I, pp. 783, 791–793.
50. Ibid., p. 785.
51. Suprunenko, p. 106.
52. Paustovskii (1966), I, p. 796.
53. Vinnichenko, p. 300.
54. Trotskii, *KVR*, II, p. 28.
55. Paustovskii (1966), I, pp. 795–796; Ehrenburg (1962), p. 79.
56. Gol'denveizer (1922), p. 236.
57. Leggett, pp. 262–263.
58. Quoted in Kubanin, p. 66.
59. Quoted in Antonov-Ovseenko, III, p. 291.
60. Kubanin, p. 69.
61. For an especially well-drawn portrait of Grigor'ev, see Adams, pp. 147–157. See also Kubanin, pp. 64–70; and Shchadenko, pp. 68–95.
62. The following account of the Bolshevik campaign against Odessa is based upon the following: Carley, pp. 146–181; Kenez (1977), pp. 180–191; Adams, pp. 186–214; Kakurin, II, pp. 78–92; Antonov-Ovseenko, III, pp. 178–250.
63. Quoted in Carley, p. 164.
64. Quoted in Adams, p. 193.
65. Sannikov, pp. 9–24.
66. Quoted in Carley, pp. 177, 176.
67. Quoted in Antonov-Ovseenko, III, pp. 249–250.
68. "Dnevnik i vospominaniia kievskoi studentki," p. 227.

69. Gol'denveizer, p. 259.
70. Quoted in ibid., p. 260.
71. Quoted in Kenez (1977), p. 152.
72. Chernikover, pp. 18–19.
73. Katsnel'son, pp. 183–188; Frederic, p. 200; "Evrei v Moskve," pp. 153–157.
74. Vishniak, p. 136.
75. Davitt, pp. 167–169.
76. Ibid., p. 129; Korolenko, IX, pp. 409, 420.
77. Kuropatkin, p. 43.
78. Published in Davitt, pp. 276–277.
79. Chernikover, pp. 20–21.
80. Iakhontov, p. 57.
81. Quoted in Paléologue (1921), II, p. 16. See also Gruzenberg, pp. 157–158; Greenberg, II, pp. 94–96.
82. "Dokumenty o presledovanii evreev," nos. 30, 32, pp. 260–262.
83. Paléologue (1921), II, p. 37.
84. Heifetz, pp. 175–181.
85. See, for example, ibid., p. 144; and Shtif, p. 28. On the problem of the syphilis epidemic that raged through rural Russia at the end of the nineteenth century, see Shingarev, pp. 263–269; Kushner, pp. 145–147.
86. Heifetz, p. 213.
87. Gusev-Orenburgskii, pp. 40–49.
88. Ibid., pp. 30–39.
89. Heifetz, pp. 148–157.
90. Grigor'ev's "Universal" of May 7, 1919, published in Antonov-Ovseenko, IV, pp. 203–205.
91. Heifetz, pp. 152, 279.
92. "Report of an Assembly of Party Workers and People in Public Life."
93. Ibid. See also Gusev-Orenburgskii, pp. 51–55.
94. Gusev-Orenburgskii, p. 10.
95. Quoted in Shtif, p. 66.
96. Quoted in Kenez (1977), p. 173.
97. Gol'denveizer, p. 268.
98. Quoted in Shtif, p. 65.
99. Heifetz, pp. 112–114; Gol'denveizer, pp. 268–269. See also "Dnevnik i vospominaniia kievskoi studentki," pp. 232–233.
100. Rosenberg, p. 421.
101. Kenez (1977), pp. 174–175.
102. Shtif, pp. 27–28; Heifetz, p. 111.
103. Shtif, pp. 10–12.
104. Gusev-Orenburgskii, p. 137. See also Heifetz, p. 111.
105. Heifetz, p. 113. See also Gusev-Orenburgskii, pp. 138–142.
106. Andreev, Gor'kii, and Sollogub, p. 61.
107. Shtif, p. 42.
108. Kenez (1977), p. 170.
109. Palij, pp. 67–69; Peters, pp. 13–27; Arshinov, pp. 51–53.
110. Quoted in Palij, p. 61.
111. Makhno (1929), pp. 9–11.
112. Quoted in Palij, p. 73.
113. Makhno (1928), p. 16.
114. Makhno (1929), p. 9.
115. Makhno (1937), pp. 7–8.
116. Makhno (1929), p. 64.

117. Quoted in Peters, p. 32.
118. Footman (1961), p. 252.
119. See the dedication in Makhno (1929), and p. 9.
120. Quoted in Palij, p. 60.
121. Ibid., p. 192.
122. Quoted in ibid., p. 59.
123. Ibid., pp. 110–111, 155.
124. Denikin, V, p. 142.
125. Arbatov, p. 94.
126. Hodgson, p. 184.
127. Kubanin, pp. 84–88.
128. Quoted in Palij, p. 201.
129. Quoted in ibid., p. 208.
130. Lenin, *CW*, XXIX, pp. 437, 453, 444.
131. Trotskii, *KVR*, I, p. 402, note 9.

Chapter Ten: In the Red Heart of Russia

1. Quoted in Beatty, p. 380.
2. Lenin, *CW*, XXVII, pp. 263, 271.
3. Quoted in Clements, pp. 147–148.
4. Goldman (1931), II, p. 756.
5. Sadoul, p. 95.
6. Bryant (1973), p. 113.
7. Kollontai (1972), p. 25.
8. Kollontai, "Sexual Relations and the Class Struggle," p. 245.
9. Kollontai, "The New Woman," p. 86.
10. Ibid., p. 94.
11. Ibid., p. 74.
12. Kollontai (1972), pp. 22–25.
13. Quoted in Stites, p. 355. Ably supplemented by the insightful treatments supplied by Clements, Lapidus, and Farnsworth, Stites's truly masterful work still remains the definitive treatment of the women's liberation movement in Russia.
14. Quoted in ibid., p. 355.
15. Quoted in ibid., p. 267.
16. Kollontai, "Working Woman and Mother," p. 134.
17. Ibid.
18. Quoted in Halle, p. 149.
19. Kollontai, "Working Woman and Mother," pp. 84, 96, 90, 86.
20. Quoted in Stites, p. 353.
21. Ibid.
22. Ibid., p. 347.
23. Kollontai (1971), pp. 11–12.
24. Lenin (1966), p. 26.
25. Ibid., p. 30.
26. Quoted in Lapidus, p. 42.
27. Quoted in ibid., p. 61.
28. Lenin (1966), p. 42.
29. Lapidus, pp. 40–50.
30. Lenin (1966), p. 24.

31. Quoted in Clements, p. 122.
32. Quoted in Farnsworth, p. 102.
33. Itkina, pp. 164–176.
34. Kollontai (1971), pp. 37–38; Clements, pp. 126–129.
35. Quoted in Farnsworth, p. 98.
36. J. Smith, p. 172.
37. Kollontai (1974), pp. 331–335; Itkina, pp. 172–173.
38. Itkina, pp. 173–174.
39. Sadoul, p. 96.
40. Kollontai (1974), p. 341.
41. Ibid., pp. 340–344; Kollontai (1971), pp. 37–38.
42. Sadoul, pp. 96, 316.
43. This is Trotskii's phrase. Trotsky (1941), p. 243.
44. Quoted in Palencia, p. 120.
45. Wolfe (1963), pp. 98–99.
46. McNeal (1972), p. 135.
47. Armand, p. 247.
48. Clements, pp. 77–78.
49. Lapidus, pp. 48–49.
50. Kollontai, *Izbrannye*, p. 405, note 75.
51. Quoted in Clements, p. 126. See also Stites, p. 330.
52. Stites, p. 330. See also Kollontai, *Izbrannye*, pp. 254–259; and Itkina, pp. 196–197.
53. Lenin, *CW*, XXVIII, p. 181.
54. Quoted in Stites, p. 330.
55. Quoted in Clements, p. 155.
56. Itkina, p. 202.
57. J. Smith, p. 7.
58. Halle, pp. 220–221.
59. Quoted in ibid., p. 222.
60. Kruze and Krutsentov, pp. 115–120, 142–144; Halle, pp. 218–223; Stites, 182–185, 224–227.
61. Kollontai, "Prostitution and Ways of Fighting It," pp. 262, 265.
62. Ibid., pp. 265–267, 273.
63. J. Smith, pp. 6–7.
64. Farnsworth, pp. 197–202.
65. Quoted in Fitzpatrick, pp. 1–2.
66. Reed, p. 36.
67. Quoted in Wolfe (1948), p. 506.
68. Quoted in Fitzpatrick, p. 10.
69. Chukovskii, p. 171.
70. Quoted in Fitzpatrick, p. 26.
71. Lunacharskii, "Proletariat i iskusstvo," p. 201.
72. Quoted in Reed, pp. 326, 342.
73. Fitzpatrick, pp. 15–16; Rosenberg, pp. 278–281.
74. Lunacharskii (1968), pp. 183, 181.
75. Levidova and Pavlotskaia, pp. 6–38; McNeal (1972), pp. 7–165.
76. Quoted in Fitzpatrick, p. 28.
77. Quoted in McNeal (1972), p. 194.
78. Quoted in Fitzpatrick, pp. 35, 39.
79. Kenez (1985), p. 72.
80. Quoted in Elkina, p. 27.
81. Kumanev, p. 48.

82. Quoted in ibid.
83. Ibid., p. 66.
84. Quoted in ibid., p. 60.
85. Quoted in ibid., p. 34.
86. Quoted in ibid., p. 86.
87. Ibid., p. 94.
88. See especially Lunacharskii (1908, 1911), *passim.*
89. Quoted in Fitzpatrick, pp. 124–125.
90. This is Kornelii Zelinskii's recollection, excerpted in Woroszylski, p. 200.
91. Ehrenburg (1962), pp. 62–63.
92. Ransome (1920), pp. 140–141.
93. Quoted in Rosenthal, p. 111.
94. Quoted in Gippius-Merezhkovskaia (1951), p. 208.
95. Belyi (1933), pp. 321–322.
96. Quoted in Maslenikov, p. 208.
97. Ehrenburg (1962), p. 66.
98. Quoted in Slonim, p. 93.
99. Quoted in Ehrenburg (1962), p. 65.
100. Ibid., pp. 63–64.
101. Quoted in ibid., p. 64.
102. Ibid., pp. 67, 69.
103. My description of the Poets' Cafe has been drawn from the following first-hand accounts: Spasskii, pp. 161–177; Ehrenburg (1962), pp. 38–40, 62–69; and the recollections of Kornelii Zelinskii, Lev Nikulin, and Boris Lavrenev, excerpted in Woroszylski, pp. 200–201, 209–212.
104. Ehrenburg (1962), p. 68.
105. Ibid., p. 40.
106. Quoted in Spasskii, p. 166.
107. Bonch-Bruevich, "Vladimir Il'ich i ukrashchenie krasnoi stolitsy," p. 409.
108. Ehrenburg (1962), p. 55.
109. Bonch-Bruevich, "Vladimir Il'ich i ukrashchenie krasnoi stolitsy," pp. 409–411.
110. Ransome (1920), p. 34.
111. Lunacharskii, "The Preface of the People's Commissar for Education," p. 244.
112. Quoted in Fitzpatrick, p. 157.
113. Quoted from the recollections of Kornelii Zelinskii, excerpted in Woroszylski, p. 246.
114. Maiakovskii, "Vystoplenie," p. 402.
115. *Iskusstvo kommuny*, no. 4 (December 29, 1918).
116. Quoted in Mayakovsky (1970), p. 18.
117. Maiakovskii, "Radovat'sia rano," p. 248.
118. Maiakovskii, "Prikaz po armii iskusstva," p. 246.
119. Maiakovskii, "Levyi marsh," pp. 255–256.
120. Maiakovskii, "150 000 000," p. 51.
121. This description of ROSTA's work is based upon the following: Cheremnykh, pp. 198–204; Maiakovskii, "Doklad," pp. 449–451; Bryliakov, *passim;* Lincoln (1976), pp. 302–309; and Kenez (1985), pp. 111–118.
122. Cheremnykh, p. 202.
123. Quoted in Lincoln (1976), p. 305.
124. The following account of propaganda trains and riverboats is drawn particularly from: Maksakova, *passim;* Sergeev, pp. 93–168; Kenez (1985), pp. 58–62; Gofman, pp. 63–70; Ransome (1921), pp. 108–118.

125. Fitzpatrick, pp. 54–57; Maksakova, pp. 9–20; Gofman, pp. 63–65.
126. See, for example, the views of Kalinin in "Poezdka predsedatelia," p. 98.
127. "Iz besedy M. I. Kalinina," pp. 110–114.
128. "Rechi M. I. Kalinina i M. V. Frunze," p. 141.
129. Figner, I, pp. 153–155.
130. Shklovsky, p. 184.
131. Ibid., p. 193.
132. Got'e, pp. 223, 61, 95.

Chapter Eleven: The Struggle to Survive

1. Lenin, *CW*, XXIX, pp. 437, 436, 444, 453.
2. "Kolichestvo grazhdan."
3. For one dramatic example, see Mawdsley, p. 181.
4. Trotskii (1930), II, pp. 131, 170.
5. Ulam (1973), p. 173.
6. "Boevoi i chislennyi sostav Krasnoi armii."
7. "Vypusk glavneishikh predmetov"; Movchin, p. 87; Kovalenko, pp. 382–394 Vol'pe, pp. 391–392.
8. Mawdsley, p. 185.
9. Chamberlin, II, p. 291.
10. Shklovsky, pp. 176–177.
11. Brailsford, p. 23.
12. Sorokin, p. 218.
13. Got'e, p. 338.
14. Shklovsky, p. 177.
15. Ibid., p. 175.
16. Got'e, p. 310.
17. Ehrenburg (1962), pp. 139–142, 149.
18. Shklovsky, p. 175.
19. Wells, p. 17.
20. Brailsford, p. 24.
21. Ransome (1920), p. 42.
22. Shklovsky, p. 180.
23. Sorokin, p. 220.
24. Shklovsky, pp. 232, 180.
25. Ransome (1920), p. 40.
26. Ehrenburg (1962), p. 139.
27. Got'e, p. 319.
28. Sorokin, pp. 227, 220, 228.
29. Brailsford, p. 26.
30. Goldman (1923), p. 34.
31. Got'e, pp. 307, 317, 329, 342, 315.
32. Lenin, *CW*, XXIX, pp. 521–522.
33. Got'e, p. 304.
34. Chamberlin, II, p. 341.
35. Goldman (1923), pp. 16–17.
36. Paustovskii (1966), II, p. 36.
37. Got'e, pp. 315, 317, 320, 338–339.
38. Shklovsky, p. 176.
39. Chamberlin, II, p. 336.

40. Shklovsky, pp. 174, 176, 235.
41. Sorokin, p. 218.
42. Gerua.
43. Berkman (1925), p. 157.
44. Ibid., p. 146.
45. Ehrenburg (1962), pp. 140–141.
46. Sorokin, p. 222.
47. Rapoport, p. 105.
48. Shklovsky, p. 235.
49. Got'e, pp. 310, 367.
50. Sorokin, pp. 224, 223.
51. "Doklad o sostoianii Petrograda," p. 7.
52. Sorokin, pp. 229–231.
53. Got'e, pp. 337, 339.
54. Sorokin, p. 231.
55. Got'e, pp. 323–325, 327–328.
56. Goldman (1923), p. 170.
57. Goldman (1924), pp 5–6.
58. Berkman (1925), p. 219.
59. Wells, p. 115.
60. Berkman (1925), pp. 167–168.
61. Paustovskii (1966), II, p. 33.
62. Wells, p. 64.
63. Quoted in Chamberlin, II, p. 291.
64. Mikhailov, pp. 96–111; Trotskii, XV, pp. 452–453, 352.
65. Quoted in Chamberlin, II, p. 108.
66. Mawdsley, pp. 236–237.
67. Liashchenko, III, p. 77.
68. Shvittau, pp. 213–226.
69. Lenin, *CW*, XXX, p. 524.
70. Liashchenko, III, pp. 76–79; Carr, II, pp. 191–195.
71. Ransome (1921), p. 26.
72. Ibid., p. 21; Brailsford, p. 30; Got'e, p. 317.
73. Kritsman, p. 162.
74. Strumilin, p. 56, diagrams 2, 3; Ransome (1921), pp. 35–37; Carr, II, p. 194.
75. Bukharin, p. 48.
76. Gimpel'son (1974), pp. 185–186; Strumilin, p. 18; Bergson, p. 183; Malle, p. 179.
77. Berkman (1925), p. 158.
78. Kritsman, pp. 51–52; Gimpel'son (1973), p. 87; Carr, II, p. 195.
79. See Bukharin's speech at the second session of the Seventh Party Congress, *Sed'moi ekstrennyi s"ezd RKP(b)*, p. 25.
80. Cohen, p. 101.
81. See Bukharin's speech at the sixth session of the Tenth Party Congress, *Desiatyi s"ezd RKP(b)*, p. 225. Bukharin's worries about the "peasantization" of the proletariat proved exaggerated in the end. A nucleus of men and women of strong working-class values remained in Russia's main cities to pass the values and spirit of working-class culture on when a new generation of workers began to appear after the Civil War. See Koenker, pp. 424–450.
82. Gimpel'son (1973), pp. 89–90; Carr, II, pp. 194–195.
83. Quoted in Lenin, *CW*, XXIX, pp. 411–414.
84. Ibid., pp. 412, 415.
85. Ibid., pp. 418–419.

86. Ibid., pp. 415, 434.
87. Ibid., XXXI, pp. 125, 123.
88. Goldman (1924), pp. 34–35.
89. Quoted in Gimpel'son (1973), p. 91.
90. "Programma Rossiiskoi kommunisticheskoi partii (bol'shevikov)," p. 290; Gimpel'son (1973), pp. 91–93.
91. Trotskii, XV, pp. 10–14.
92. Ibid., p. 52.
93. Deutscher (1954), p. 493.
94. Trotskii, XV, pp. 5–6, and notes on pp. 523–528.
95. Ibid., p. 325.
96. Ibid., p. 316.
97. Deutscher (1954), p. 495.
98. Quoted in ibid.
99. Quoted in Chamberlin, II, p. 295.
100. Quoted in Deutscher (1954), p. 502.
101. Ibid., p. 496.
102. Gimpel'son (1982), p. 80. See also Rigby (1968), pp. 78, 80–83.
103. Quoted in Chamberlin, II, p. 366.
104. "Rezoliutsiia vos'mogo s"ezda RKP(b)," p. 306.
105. Gimpel'son (1982), p. 87.
106. Lenin, *CW*, XXX, p. 485.
107. Quoted in S. White, p. 68.
108. Lenin, *CW*, XXXI, p. 68.
109. Trotskii, XV, pp. 115–116.
110. Quoted in Chamberlin, II, p. 113.
111. S. White, pp. 68–69.
112. "Obrashchenie TsK RKP(b)," p. 250.
113. Dzerzhinskii, pp. 254–255.
114. Lenin, "Rech' . . . na 4–i konferentsii," pp. 370–371.
115. Quoted in Leggett, p. 187.
116. Quoted in Mel'gunov (1925), p. 265.
117. "Obrashchenie TsK RKP(b)," p. 250.
118. Quoted in Gerson, p. 150.
119. Mel'gunov (1925), pp. 177–186, 214–219.
120. See, for example, Berkman (1925), p. 166.
121. Latsis (1921), p. 9.
122. Mel'gunov (1925), p. 111.
123. Chamberlin, II, p. 75; Gerson, pp. 172–176; Leggett, pp. 466–468.
124. Mel'gunov (1925), pp. 78–81, 172–187.
125. Chamberlin II, p. 83, note 16; Leggett, p. 200; Mel'gunov (1925), pp. 73–74, 174–175.
126. Mel'gunov (1925), p. 176.
127. Ibid., pp. 75–85; Leggett, p. 200.
128. Stites, p. 275.
129. Quoted in *Pravda, stavshaia legendoi*, p. 7.
130. Quoted in Chamberlin, II, p. 495. On Zemliachka, see also *Pravda, stavshaia legendoi*, pp. 7–26; and Stites, pp. 275, 321.
131. Quoted in Mel'gunov (1925), p. 234.
132. Quoted in Leggett, p. 193.
133. Mel'gunov (1925), pp. 229–232.
134. Berkman (1925), p. 57; Paustovskii (1966), II, p. 33.
135. Gerson, pp. 140–141.

136. Quoted in Leggett, p. 193.
137. Ibid., p. 178; Gerson, p. 176.
138. Mel'gunov, (1925), pp. 68, 190; Leggett, p. 180.
139. Mel'gunov, (1925), pp. 189–190, 241.
140. The following account of the Solovetskii concentration camp is taken from: Ibid., pp. 241–244; and Malsagoff, pp. 39–56.
141. Quoted in Gerson, pp. 257–258.
142. Leggett, p. 180.
143. Quoted in ibid., p. 203.
144. Quoted in Mel'gunov (1925), p. 194.
145. Lenin, *CW*, XXXI, pp. 291, 293.
146. *Deviatyi s"ezd RKP(b)*, p. 377.
147. Poliakov, p. 205.
148. Singleton, p. 499.
149. Gerson, p. 182.
150. Poliakov, p. 204.
151. Lenin, *CW*, XXXII, p. 179.
152. Radkey (1976), p. 324.
153. See, for example, "Iz Prikaza No. 41."

Chapter Twelve: "Give Us Warsaw!"

1. Quoted in Riasanovsky, pp. 97–98.
2. Gogol' (1913), VIII, p. 41.
3. Quoted in Kennan (1972), p. 77.
4. Pogodin, p. 254.
5. Quoted in Kennan (1972), pp. 91–92.
6. Quoted in Wandycz (1969), p. 3.
7. Quoted in Komarnicki, p. 84.
8. Quoted in ibid.
9. Quoted in ibid., p. 9.
10. Quoted in ibid., p. 86.
11. Quoted in ibid., p. 114.
12. Quoted in Davies, p. 21.
13. D'Abernon, p. 39.
14. Howard, II, p. 320.
15. Piłsudski (1931), pp. 10–11.
16. Landau, p. 192.
17. Howard, II, p. 333.
18. Piłsudski (1931), p. 11.
19. Dziewanowski, pp. 46–59.
20. Davies, p. 25.
21. Stalin, IV, pp. 187, 189. See also Vaitkiavichius, pp. 49–53, 56–57.
22. Naida (1957), III, p. 293–294; Kakurin (1922), pp. 11–16; "Iz doklada," pp. 156–157.
23. Davies, pp. 41–45.
24. Senn, p. 137.
25. Wandycz (1969), p. 119; Łossowski, pp. 55–68.
26. Quoted in Davies, p. 51.
27. Lenin, "Telegramma."
28. Bubnov, Kamenev, Tukhachevskii, and Eideman, III, pp. 156–158; Kakurin (1922), pp. 19–25.

29. Quoted in Weygand, p. 46.
30. Wandycz (1965), pp. 432–436.
31. Ibid., p. 439.
32. Lenin, *CW*, XXX, p. 78. See also Deutscher (1954), p. 458.
33. Meijer, pp. 764–768.
34. Wandycz (1965), pp. 446–448.
35. Wandycz (1969), pp. 107–108; Wandycz (1965), pp. 447–448.
36. Sosnkowski, "Memoriał," pp. 379–80.
37. Paderewski, pp. 398–399.
38. Davies, pp. 85–86.
39. "Protokół posiedzenia Rady," pp. 352, 355.
40. "Z depeszy przewodnicząciego Rady Obrony RSFRR," p. 613.
41. Quoted in Davies, p. 69.
42. Budënnyi (1960), p. 63.
43. Quoted in Komarnicki, p. 539.
44. Quoted in Falls, p. 225.
45. Kukiel, p. 49.
46. Quoted in Komarnicki, pp. 563–564.
47. Davies, p. 66.
48. Senn, pp. 104–130; 152–198; Łossowski, pp. 55–85, 128–149.
49. Wandycz (1969), pp. 190–191; Kakurin (1922), pp. 39–40.
50. "Umowa"; "Konwencja."
51. Bubnov, Kamenev, Tukhachevskii, and Eideman, III, pp. 327–341; Kakurin (1922), pp. 39–42.
52. Quoted in Davies, p. 111.
53. Quoted in ibid., p. 114.
54. Wollenberg, pp. 58–61, 196–197; Erikson, pp. 57–58, 63–64, 73–75; V. N. Ivanov, pp. 93–168; Budënnyi (1958), pp. 435–437.
55. Tukhachevskii (1964), I, p. 115.
56. Lenin, "Zapiska v Sekretariat TsK RKP(b)," p. 29.
57. Quoted in Davies, p. 136.
58. Quoted in Fedotoff White, pp. 92–93.
59. Quoted in Wollenberg, p. 196.
60. Budënnyi (1965), II, pp. 26–68; Fedotoff White, pp. 104–105.
61. Trotskii (1930), II, p. 173.
62. Quoted in Budënnyi (1965), II, p. 47.
63. This characterization of Budënnyi is drawn from his memoirs (1958, 1965), vols. I and II, *passim;* "Semën Mikhailovich Budënnyi"; and Erikson, pp. 70–71.
64. Budënnyi (1965), II, pp. 97–201.
65. Piłsudski (1941), p. 92.
66. "Aleksandr Il'ich Egorov."
67. Bubnov, Kamenev, Tukhachevskii, and Eideman, III, pp. 352–362.
68. Lenin, *CW*, XXXI, pp. 133–134.
69. Trotskii, *KVR*, II, p. 99.
70. Ibid., p. 131.
71. Davies, p. 135.
72. Bubnov, Kamenev, Tukhachevskii, and Eideman, III, pp. 365–367; Erikson, p. 93; Davies, pp. 142–143; V. N. Ivanov, pp. 182–183. In his lecture to the General Staff Academy some three years later, Tukhachevskii set the total number of combat troops under his command at the beginning of his July offensive at the somewhat higher figure of 160,238. Tukhachevskii (1964), I, pp. 129–131.

73. Davies, pp. 143–144; Koritskii, p. 238.
74. Quoted in Senn, p. 219.
75. Bubnov, Kamenev, Tukhachevskii, and Eideman, III, pp. 365–377; Tukhachevskii (1964), I, pp. 134–142; V. N. Ivanov, pp.181–190.
76. Gai, I, pp. 300–301.
77. Tukhachevskii (1964), I, pp. 142–145; V. N. Ivanov, pp. 189–191.
78. "Deklaratsiia Verkhovnogo soveta Antanty," pp. 431–432.
79. Trotskii (1930), II, pp. 191–192.
80. "Nota narodnogo komissara inostrannykh del RSFSR."
81. "Direktiva Glavnogo komandovaniia o nanesenii," p. 643.
82. Quoted in Dziewanowski, p. 299.
83. Quoted in Davies, p. 149.
84. Bubov, Kamenev, Tukhachevskii, and Eideman, III, pp. 391–405; Tukhachevskii (1964), I, pp. 146–152.
85. Quoted in Carr (1953), III, p. 188.
86. Trotskii, *KVR*, II, p. 166.
87. Suslov, pp. 97–99.
88. Davies, p. 187.
89. "Direktiva Glavnogo komandovaniia Komandovaniiu iugo-zapadnogo i zapadnogo frontov"; Trotskii (1930), II, pp. 192–193; Trotskii (1941), pp. 328–330.
90. Quoted in Erikson, p. 99.
91. Mawdsley, p. 268.
92. Stalin, IV, p. 352.
93. Sosnkowski,"Rech'."
94. Wandycz (1969), pp. 230–231; Davies, pp. 192–194.
95. Quoted in Mawdsley, p. 257.
96. D'Albernon, p. 9. See also pp. 8–12.
97. Piłsudski (1941), pp. 165, 114–115.
98. Kakurin (1922), pp. 56–66; Bubnov, Kamenev, Tukhachevskii, and Eideman, III, pp. 436–461; Piłsudski (1941), pp. 104–145; Kukiel, pp. 61–65; Davies, pp. 198–208; Erikson, pp. 98–102; Tukhachevskii (1964), I, pp. 152–163.
99. Bubnov, Kamenev, Tukhachevskii, and Eideman, III, pp. 462–469; Tukhachevskii (1964), I, pp. 163–167; Davies, pp. 226–237; Budënnyi (1965), II, pp. 340–376; Budënnyi (1960), V, pp. 172–183.
100. Quoted in Davies, p. 238.
101. Quoted in Wandycz (1969), p. 272.
102. Lenin, *CW*, XXXI, p. 321.
103. Komarnicki, pp. 733–737.
104. Lenin, *CW*, XXXI, p. 318.

Chapter Thirteen: The End of the Whites

1. Rakovskii (1920), pp. 223–256.
2. Vrangel', "Zapiski," VI, p. 9.
3. Ibid., pp. 9, 44.
4. Kenez (1977), p. 262.
5. Vrangel', "Zapiski," VI, pp. 6–7.
6. Ibid., p. 219.
7. Ross, p. 49.

8. Rakovskii (1921), p. 45.
9. Golubev (1930), p. 62.
10. This phrase is taken from the title Wrangel gave to the second part of his memoirs.
11. Ross, pp. 66–68; Pipes (1980), p. 282.
12. Vrangel', "Zapiski," VI, p. 16.
13. Ibid.
14. Pipes (1980), p. 285.
15. Quoted in Pipes (1970), p. 319.
16. Pipes (1980), pp. 268–285; Vrangel', "Zapiski," V. pp. 302–303.
17. Quoted in Obolenskii, p. 7.
18. Vrangel', "Zapiski," V, pp. 302–303; VI, pp. 42–44.
19. Ibid., VI, p. 42.
20. Ibid., p. 45.
21. Ibid., p. 44; Obolenskii, pp. 14–15.
22. Quoted in Ross, pp. 144–145.
23. Vrangel', "Zapiski," VI, p. 63.
24. Obolenskii, pp. 20–21.
25. Valentinov, p. 17.
26. Vrangel', "Zapiski," VI, p. 44.
27. Quoted in Treadgold, p. 488.
28. Vrangel', "Zapiski," VI, p. 45.
29. Ibid., p. 39.
30. Quoted in Rakovskii (1921), p. 39.
31. Vrangel', "Zapiski," VI, p. 44.
32. Ibid., p. 52.
33. Obolenskii, p. 60.
34. Vrangel', "Zapiski," VI, p. 51.
35. Obolenskii, pp. 55–56.
36. Treadgold, p. 486.
37. Vrangel', "Zapiski," VI, pp. 52–53.
38. Quoted in Ullman (1972), p. 69.
39. Quoted in Vrangel', "Zapiski," V, p. 305.
40. Quoted in Ullman (1972), p. 71.
41. Quoted in Vrangel', "Zapiski," V. p. 305.
42. Quoted in ibid.
43. Kenez (1977), p. 262.
44. Vrangel', "Zapiski," VI, p. 11.
45. These quotations are taken from the text of the reply that Wrangel sent to the British on April 4, 1920. See Vrangel', "Zapiski," VI, pp. 13–14.
46. Kenez (1977), pp. 289–290; Brinkley, pp. 262–264.
47. Quoted in Brinkley, p. 248.
48. Pipes (1980), pp. 286–287.
49. Bradley, p. 177.
50. Ibid., pp. 172–176; Brinkley, pp. 249–251.
51. Korotkov, p. 31; Golubev, p. 61.
52. Vrangel', "Zapiski," VI, p. 90.
53. Quoted in Valentinov, p. 11.
54. Quoted in Ullman (1972), p. 84.
55. Quoted in ibid., p. 86.
56. Quoted in Brinkley, p. 252.
57. Quoted in Ullman (1972), p. 87.
58. Vrangel', "Zapiski," VI, p. 92; Lipatov, pp. 126–127.

59. Slashchev-Krymskii, pp. 16–21; Korotkov, p. 60; Golubev, p. 65.
60. Rakovskii (1921), p. 62; Korotkov, pp. 61–62.
61. Valentinov, p. 14.
62. Ibid., p. 13.
63. Vrangel', "Zapiski," VI, p. 81.
64. Quoted in Golubev, p. 71.
65. Quoted in Ullman (1972), p. 88. See also Slashchev-Krymskii, pp. 22–24; and Golubintsev, pp. 192–196.
66. Churchill, p. 271.
67. Kenez (1977), p. 263.
68. Vrangel', "Zapiski," VI, p. 151.
69. Ross, p. 82.
70. Brinkley, p. 264.
71. Vrangel', "Zapiski," VI, p. 121; Chamberlin, II, p. 324.
72. Wrangel (1957), p. 63.
73. Ibid.
74. Vrangel', "Zapiski," VI, pp. 138–139.
75. Valentinov, p. 38.
76. Vrangel', "Zapiski," VI, p. 139.
77. Soviet and White estimates of the number of fighting men who took part in Ulagai's expedition vary. According to Wrangel's account, only 5,000 of Ulagai's force were combatants. Soviet accounts set the figure higher, ranging from 8,050 (Korotkov) to 10,000 (Lipatov). Vrangel', "Zapiski," VI, p. 139; Korotkov, p. 140; Lipatov, p. 209.
78. Vrangel', "Zapiski," VI, p. 139.
79. Quoted in ibid., p. 154.
80. Rakovskii (1921), pp. 116–119; Korotkov, pp. 137–140.
81. Trotskii, *KVR*, II, p. 197.
82. Ibid., p. 200.
83. Golubev, pp. 74–78; Korotkov, pp. 141–146; Chamberlin, II, pp. 324–327; Lipatov, pp. 209–225; Rakovskii (1921), pp. 120–129.
84. Vrangel', "Zapiski," VI, pp. 190–191.
85. Ibid., p. 178.
86. Ullman (1972), p. 87.
87. Vrangel', "Zapiski," VI, p. 187.
88. Korotkov, pp. 118–135; Lipatov, pp. 225–228.
89. Golubev, pp. 82–84; Korotkov, pp. 161–165; Vrangel', "Zapiski," VI, p. 178; Mawdsley, p. 266.
90. Trotskii, *KVR*, II, p. 218.
91. Korotkov, pp. 178–183.
92. Quoted in Wrangel (1957), pp. 296–297.
93. Korotkov, p. 206.
94. Quoted in Rakovskii (1921), p. 163. See also pp. 151–154, 162–164.
95. Frunze (1950), p. 114.
96. Korotkov, p. 206.
97. Budënnyi (1960), V, p. 199.
98. Quoted in Korotkov, p. 167.
99. Vrangel', "Zapiski," VI, pp. 208–209.
100. Frunze, "Telegramma," pp. 418–419.
101. Budënnyi (1960), V, p. 202.
102. Vrangel', "Zapiski," VI, p. 224.
103. Lenin, *CW*, XXXI, p. 311.
104. Quoted in Mawdsley, p. 270.

105. Korotkov, pp. 206–245; Budënnyi (1960), V, pp. 195–203; Bubnov, Kamenev, Tukhachevskii, and Eideman, III, pp. 519–534.
106. Budënnyi (1960), V, p. 203.
107. Vrangel', "Zapiski," VI, p. 226.
108. Budënnyi (1960), V, p. 205.
109. Bubnov, Kamenev, Tukhachevskii, and Eideman, III, p. 513.
110. Vrangel', "Zapiski," VI, p. 226.
111. Korotkov, pp. 245–255; Budënnyi, V. pp. 204–206.
112. Vrangel', "Zapiski," VI, p. 229.
113. Quoted in Valentinov, p. 82.
114. Kenez (1977), p. 64.
115. Vrangel', "Zapiski," VI, p. 144.
116. Keeping in mind Richard Luckett's admonition that "it is almost impossible to reconcile Red and White accounts of the assault on Perekop," (Luckett, p. 377), my account of Wrangel's last battles is drawn largely from the following: Korotkov, pp. 255–278; Budënnyi (1960), V, pp. 204–213; Vrangel', "Zapiski," VI, pp. 222–242; Lipatov, pp. 316–333; Rakovskii (1921), 175–183; Luckett, pp. 377–381; and Chamberlin, II, pp. 329–332.
117. Quoted in Korotkov, p. 255.
118. Quoted in ibid., p. 261.
119. Vrangel', "Zapiski," VI, p. 230.
120. Ibid., p. 232.
121. Ibid., pp. 234–235.
122. Ibid., p. 242.
123. Valentinov, p. 98.
124. Quoted in Korotkov, p. 318.
125. Quoted in Budënnyi (1960), V, p. 212.
126. Lenin, *CW*, XXXI, p. 397.
127. For a summary of this region's earlier history, see the pioneering study by Kazemzadeh, pp. 3–7.
128. Lincoln (1980), p. 32.
129. Baedeker, pp. 514–519.
130. Stalin, IV, pp. 174–175.
131. Ibid., p. 170.
132. Meijer, I, p. 625.
133. Safarov, pp. 71–74; Batyrov, pp. 372–386; Pipes (1954), pp. 175–176.
134. Safarov, pp. 75–86; Ellis, pp. 26–48.
135. Chamberlin, II, p. 419.
136. Quoted in Naida (1959), IV, p. 367.
137. Ibid., pp. 333–337, 366–374; Budënnyi (1960), V, pp. 255–279; Safarov, pp. 74–103; Bubnov, Kamenev, Tukhachevskii, and Eideman, III, pp. 542–557; Chamberlin, II, pp. 418–426; Mawdsley, pp. 235–239; Carr, I, pp. 330–339; Pipes (1954), pp. 178–179.
138. Suny, p. 25.
139. Quoted in Chamberlin, II, p. 409.
140. The foregoing summary of the background to the Civil War in Azerbaidjan, Armenia, and Georgia has been drawn from the following: Mints (1971), pp. 16–17; Chamberlin, II, pp. 407–409; Mawdsley, pp. 226–227; Carr, I, pp. 339–340; Suny, pp. 83–88; Kazemzadeh, pp. 54–78.
141. Suny, p. 15; Arutiunov, pp. 33–34, 42–44; Baedeker, pp. 455–458.
142. Broido, pp. 68–69.
143. Quoted in Suny, p. 53.
144. Kazemzadeh, pp. 74–77.

145. Chamberlin, II, p. 408.
146. Suny, p. 234. See also Kadishev, pp. 94–105.
147. Suny, p. 238.
148. Ibid., pp. 288–306; Kadishev, pp. 127–130; Surguladze, pp. 155–165.
149. Quoted in Chamberlin, II, p. 412.
150. Chaikin, pp. 79–81.
151. Dunsterville, p. 250.
152. Ibid., pp. 239–317; Suny, p. 238; Kadishev, pp. 138–156; Surguladze, pp. 180–182; Kazemzadeh, p. 221–222.
153. Budënnyi (1960), V, p. 215.
154. Pipes (1954), pp. 208–210; Kazemzadeh, pp. 167–169, 211–220.
155. Quoted in Pipes (1954), p. 215.
156. Ibid., pp. 210–215; Kazemzadeh, pp. 184–210; Kadishev, pp. 160–177; Mints (1971), pp. 361–373.
157. Pipes (1954), pp. 225–227; Budënnyi (1960), V, pp. 220–231; Mints (1971), pp. 431–448.
158. Quoted in Chamberlin, II, p. 393.
159. Pipes (1954), p. 232.
160. Stalin, IV, p. 426.
161. Kazemzadeh, pp. 286–293; Mints (1971), pp. 480–507; Surguladze, pp. 395–417.
162. Stalin, IV, p. 423.
163. This brief summary of Georgia's history between 1917 and 1921, including the events leading up to the Bolsheviks' victory, is drawn from the following: Kazemzadeh, pp. 184–210, 294–328; Mints (1971), pp. 538–596; Surguladze, pp. 418–454; Pipes (1954), pp. 210–214, 233–240; Budënnyi (1960), V, pp. 242–254.
164. Bechhofer, p. 14.
165. Pipes (1954), p. 236.
166. Quoted in Ullman (1972), p. 474.
167. Quoted in Kazemzadeh, p. 323.
168. Lenin, *CW*, XXXII, p. 160.
169. Ibid., p. 168.

Chapter Fourteen: Victory's Bitter Fruit

1. Lenin, *CW*, XXIX, p. 437.
2. Quoted in Ullman (1972), p. 397.
3. Churchill, p. 164.
4. Quoted in Ullman (1968), p. 99.
5. Lenin, *CW*, XXXI, p. 472.
6. Quoted in Ullman (1972), p. 3.
7. Quoted in Carr, III, pp. 160–161.
8. Trotskii, *KVR*, II, p. 284.
9. Ibid., p. 282.
10. Lenin, *CW*, XXXI, p. 412.
11. Quoted in Carr, III, p. 289.
12. Ullman (1972), p. 454.
13. Carr, III, p. 380.
14. Bubnov, Kamenev, and Eideman, I, p. 360.
15. Fisher (1927), p. 96.

16. Ibid.
17. Ibid., pp. 49–51; Singleton, p. 498; Anfimov, pp. 308–312; Yaney (1982), pp. 411–413; Radkey (1976), p. 34.
18. Fisher (1927), pp. 99, 108.
19. Quoted in ibid., p. 52.
20. Lenin, *CW*, XXXII, p. 174.
21. Kritsman, pp. 189–191.
22. Malle, p. 451.
23. Lenin, *CW*, XXXI, pp. 499–502.
24. Quoted in Malle, p. 451.
25. Quoted in Poliakov, p. 197.
26. Singleton, pp. 498–499.
27. Ibid.
28. Lenin, *CW*, XXXII, p. 172.
29. Ibid., pp. 264–265.
30. Donkov, pp. 15–18; Radkey (1976), pp. 12–16.
31. Donkov, p. 15–16.
32. Robinson, p. 245.
33. Okinskii, pp. 299–300, 311–312.
34. Radkey, (1976), p. 127.
35. Singleton, pp. 501–502.
36. Radkey (1976), pp. 48–52.
37. Singleton, pp. 504–505; Radkey (1976), pp. 204–214; Trifonov (1964), pp. 245–247.
38. Quoted in Singleton, p. 504.
39. Donkov, p. 39.
40. Gor'kii (1922), p. 18.
41. Radkey (1976), pp. 319–320.
42. Quoted in Donkov, p. 40. See also p. 41.
43. Ibid., pp. 90–91.
44. Quoted in Radkey (1976), p. 224.
45. Ibid., pp. 236–237; Donkov. pp. 51, 91; Tukhachevskii (1926), pp. 6–7; Trifonov (1964), pp. 248–250.
46. Trifonov (1964), pp. 238–239.
47. Radkey (1976), pp. 324–329.
48. Quoted in Donkov, p. 41.
49. Lenin, *CW*, XXXII, p. 156.
50. Ibid., p. 364.
51. Ibid., p. 367.
52. Quoted in Radkey (1976), p. 225.
53. Quoted in Donkov, p. 120.
54. Radkey (1976), pp. 284–286.
55. Poliakov, pp. 457–458.
56. *VKP*, I, pp. 396–397.
57. Hosking, p. 125.
58. Trifonov (1969), p. 67.
59. Curtiss (1953), p. 10.
60. Titlinov, *passim*.
61. Struve, pp. 23–24; Spinka, pp. 87–92.
62. Quoted in Curtiss (1953), pp. 38–40.
63. Quoted in ibid., p. 40.
64. Quoted in Paustovskii (1956), III, pp. 598–599.
65. Titlinov, pp. 109–110.

66. Quoted in Curtiss (1953), pp. 48–49.
67. Quoted in ibid., p. 51.
68. Quoted in Fedotoff, p. 39.
69. Miliukov (1927), I, p. 194.
70. Curtiss (1953), pp. 96–99.
71. Obolenskii, pp. 45–46.
72. Struve, pp. 31–36.
73. Titlinov, pp. 183–192; Stratonov, pp. 7–68. In this connection it is particularly interesting to compare the antireligious carnivals witnessed by Georgii Fedotoff during the Christmas holidays of 1922 (Fedotoff, p. 47), with the scenes described by the Austrian diplomat Johann Korb early in the reign of Peter the Great, in February 1699 (Korb, I, p. 256). See also Lincoln (1981), pp. 273–278.
74. Lenin, *Sochineniia*, V. p. 478.
75. The foregoing discussion of early Bolshevik Party organization has been drawn from the following: Carr, I, pp. 184–190; Schapiro (1960), pp. 159–179; Rigby (1968), pp. 57–67; Service, *passim*.
76. *VSRKP*, p. 426.
77. Rigby (1968), p. 52.
78. Ibid., p. 81.
79. Quoted in Carr, I, p. 205.
80. Quoted in Chamberlin, II, p. 364.
81. *VSRKP*, p. 429.
82. Ibid., pp. 429, 423.
83. Rigby (1968), p. 77.
84. Quoted in ibid.
85. Ibid., p. 78.
86. Lenin, *CW*, XXX, p. 64.
87. Quoted in ibid., note 30, p. 540.
88. Ibid., p. 455.
89. Rigby (1968), pp. 96–98.
90. Ibid., pp. 97–99.
91. *DevSRKP*, pp. 121–122.
92. Cohen, p. 12.
93. *DevSRKP*, p. 138.
94. Schapiro (1956), pp. 227–228.
95. Lenin, *CW*, XXX, pp. 310, 309.
96. *VKP*, I, p. 334.
97. Schapiro (1956), pp. 256–257.
98. Clements, p. 186.
99. Lenin, *CW*, XXXI, p. 424.
100. Ibid., XXXII, p. 20, 19, 20.
101. Clements, p. 189.
102. Kollontai, "Workers' Opposition," pp. 159, 160, 182, 184.
103. Lenin, *CW*, XXXII, p. 198. See also Stites, p. 347.
104. Lenin, *CW*, XXXII, pp. 193, 200.
105. Ibid., pp. 246, 248.
106. Ibid., pp. 243–244.
107. Quoted in Schapiro (1956), p. 320.
108. Ibid., p. 359.
109. Ibid., pp. 215–217; Avrich (1970), p. 23; Kritsman, pp. 184–187.
110. Got'e, pp. 400, 398.

Chapter Fifteen: The Kronstadt Uprising

1. This description of Kronstadt is based upon the following: Avrich (1970), pp. 51–53; Zverev; Baedeker, pp. 184–185; "Kronstadt," pp. 927–928; Voline, pp. 5–6; Semanov (1973), pp. 53–54.
2. Avrich (1970), pp. 53–55.
3. Sivkov, pp. 7–24; Getzler (1983), pp. 9–18.
4. Sivkov, pp. 24–46.
5. Voline, p. 9.
6. Quoted in Sukhanov (1955), p. 446. For a very detailed and important study of the revolutions of 1917 in Kronstadt, see Getzler (1983), pp. 19–183. See also Sivkov, pp. 83–336; Avrich (1970), pp 57–63.
7. Quoted in Avrich (1970), p. 64.
8. Semanov (1973), p. 66.
9. Ibid., pp. 64–68.
10. Ibid., p. 69.
11. Quoted in Pukhov, p. 51. See also ibid., pp. 40–50; Avrich (1970), pp. 68–69; and Fedotoff White pp. 139–141.
12. Semanov (1973), p. 56.
13. Pukhov, p. 54.
14. Semanov (1973), pp. 27–31.
15. Quoted in ibid., p. 35.
16. Ibid., pp. 26–27, 34–35; Kritsman, pp. 189–190.
17. Pukhov, pp. 11–12, 23–24; Got'e, pp. 422, 435, 452.
18. Berkman (1922), p. 8.
19. Ibid.
20. Semanov (1973), pp. 42–52.
21. Quoted in Avrich (1970), p. 72.
22. Goldman (1931), II, p. 874.
23. Ibid., p. 875.
24. Schapiro (1956), p. 299; Avrich (1970), pp. 70–71.
25. Semanov (1973), pp. 53–54.
26. Quoted in Avrich (1970), p. 67.
27. *Izvestiia Vremennogo revoliutsionnogo komiteta*, pp. 46–47.
28. Quoted in Semanov (1973), p. 82.
29. Quoted in ibid.
30. The preceding account of the mass meeting on Anchor Square is based on the following: Semanov (1973), pp. 81–83; Katkov (1959), pp. 27–28; Berkman (1922), pp. 8–10; Daniels (1951), pp. 242–243; Pukhov, pp. 60–63; Getzler (1983), pp. 214–216; and (the best overall account) Avrich (1970), pp. 76–80. For the full text of the resolution passed at the meeting, see *Izvestiia Vremennogo revoliutsionnogo komiteta*, pp. 46–47.
31. Goldman (1931), II, p. 877.
32. Pukhov, p. 62; Semanov (1973), p. 83.
33. Berkman (1922), p. 11.
34. *Izvestiia Vremennogo revoliutsionnogo komiteta*, p. 116.
35. Ibid., pp. 115–117; Petrichenko, pp. 7–8; Pukhov, pp. 65–68; Semanov (1973), pp. 85–87.
36. Avrich (1970), pp. 81–82.
37. Daniels (1951), p. 244.
38. *Izvestiia Vremennogo revoliutsionnogo komiteta*, p. 45.
39. Ibid., p. 46.

40. Ibid., p. 128.
41. Ibid.
42. Ibid., p. 82.
43. Berkman (1922), pp. 21, 19.
44. Goldman (1931), II, p. 878.
45. Berkman (1922), p. 39; Serge (1963), pp. 127–128.
46. Quoted in Avrich (1970), p. 144.
47. *Izvestiia Vremennogo revoliutsionnogo komiteta*, p. 68.
48. Quoted in Avrich (1970), p. 146.
49. Quoted in ibid., p. 147.
50. *Izvestiia Vremennogo revoliutsionnogo komiteta*, p. 68.
51. Semanov (1973), pp. 115–116.
52. For a careful analysis of the evidence that has been used to support claims that the Whites plotted the uprising, see Avrich (1970), pp. 102–114.
53. Quoted in ibid., p. 120. See also pp. 116–130 for an excellent summary of the efforts made by anti-Soviet Russian organizations in the West to collect aid for the Kronstadt rebels, as well as Semanov (1973), pp. 122–135.
54. Katkov (1959), pp. 32–35; Avrich (1970), pp. 152–153.
55. Semanov (1973), p. 153.
56. Petrichenko, p. 13.
57. Berkman (1922), p. 303.
58. Goldman (1931), II, pp. 884–885.
59. *Izvestiia Vremennogo revoliutsionnogo komiteta*, p. 80.
60. Pukhov, p. 140.
61. Ibid., pp. 141–143; Semanov (1973), pp. 152–154; Avrich (1970), pp. 154–155.
62. *Izvestiia Vremennogo revoliutsionnogo komiteta*, p. 80.
63. Ibid., pp. 82–84.
64. Ibid., pp. 82, 108, 126.
65. Lenin, *CW*, XXXII, p. 185.
66. Rafael, pp. 4–5.
67. Lenin, *CW*, XXXII, p. 185.
68. Quoted in Serge (1963), p. 131.
69. Quoted in Pukhov, p. 147. See also ibid., pp. 145–155, and Semanov (1973), pp. 158–162.
70. Rafael, p. 8. See also pp. 5–7.
71. Semanov (1973), p. 164.
72. Ibid., p. 150; Pukhov, p. 150.
73. Avrich (1970), p. 198.
74. Quoted in ibid., p. 203.
75. Ibid., pp. 200–201.
76. *Izvestiia Vremennogo revoliutsionnogo komiteta*, pp. 119–121.
77. Goldman (1931), II, p. 884.
78. Semanov (1973), p. 170.
79. Bubnov, Kamenev, and Eideman, I, p. 366.
80. The following account of the storming of Kronstadt is based upon the following: Semanov (1973), pp. 170–183; Voline, pp. 63–66; Berkman (1922), pp. 36–38; Pukhov, pp. 160–170; Avrich (1970), pp. 202–217; Goldman (1931), II, pp. 884–887; Bubnov, Kamenev, and Eideman, I, pp. 367–374; Rafael, pp. 20–26.
81. Goldman (1931), II, p. 886.
82. Pukhov, p. 167.
83. Bubnov, Kamenev, and Eideman, I, pp. 370–371.

84. Goldman (1931), II, p. 886.
85. Avrich (1970), pp. 209, 216.
86. Pukhov, p. 179.
87. Ibid., pp. 179–181.
88. *Izvestiia Vremennogo revoliutsionnogo komiteta*, p. 128.

Epilogue: The Revolution Consumes Its Makers

1. Getzler (1983), p. 245.
2. Cohen, pp. 129–132.
3. Lenin, *CW*, XXVI, p. 127.
4. Cohen, p. 129.
5. Quoted in ibid., p. 133.
6. Quoted in ibid.
7. Lenin, *CW*, XXXII, pp. 215–216.
8. Quoted in Cohen, p. 145.
9. Quoted in Schapiro (1960), p. 240.
10. Schapiro (1956), p. 316.
11. Clements, pp. 222–223.
12. The following account of Lenin's last illnesses and death is drawn mainly from the following: Lewin (1970), pp. 65–75, 91–103; Ulam (1965), pp. 524–579; Fischer, pp. 545–675; Shub, pp. 366–387.
13. Quoted in Fischer, p. 600.
14. Ulam (1965), p. 555.
15. Quoted in Lewin (1970), p. 80.
16. Quoted in Fischer, p. 673.
17. Quoted in Medvedev, p. 48.
18. Ibid., pp. 47–50. I am indebted to Darrell Wiley, a surgeon in DeKalb, Illinois, for information about the side effects of chloroform.
19. Medvedev, p. 50.
20. Quoted in Daniels (1960), p. 174.
21. Ulam (1973), p. 236.
22. Stalin, VI, pp. 47–53.
23. Stalin, VI, pp. 419, 386.
24. Quoted in Daniels (1960), p. 250.
25. Mandel'shtam, p. 130.
26. For the best treatment of Trotskii's last days, see Deutscher (1963), pp. 483–509.
27. Serge and Trotsky, p. 253.
28. Quoted in Deutscher (1963), p. 494.
29. Quoted in Serge and Trotsky, p. 266.
30. Levine, p. 161.
31. Quoted in Deutscher (1963), p. 497.
32. Quoted in Sanchez-Salazar, p. 160.
33. Quoted in Serge and Trotsky, p. 268.

Works and Sources Cited

What follows is not, in any sense, intended to be a bibliography. It is neither an exhaustive compilation of all materials available about Russia during its Civil War nor even a complete listing of all the materials consulted in the research for this book. As the title above states, it is only a list of the works and sources cited in the notes to this book for the reader's reference.

Abramovitch, Rafael R. *The Soviet Revolution, 1917–1939*. New York, 1962.

"Account of the Activities of the Factory Committees and Their Relation to the Trade Union Movement." In Browder and Kerensky, II, pp. 725–726.

Adamovich, Georgii, M. A. Aldanov, and Georgii Ivanov. *Leonid Kannegiser*. Paris, 1928.

Adams, Arthur E. *Bolsheviks in the Ukraine: The Second Campaign, 1918–1920*. New Haven, 1963.

"*Aide-memoire* of the Secretary of State to the Allied Ambassadors," July 17, 1918. Reprinted in Unterberger, pp. 235–238.

Alakhverdov, G. G. and M. V. Rybakov, "Krakh inostrannoi interventsii na severe." In Naida and Kovalenko, pp. 212–235.

Aldington, Richard. *Death of a Hero*. New York, 1929.

Aleksandr Mikhailovich [Alexander], Grand Duke of Russia. *Once a Grand Duke*. New York, 1932.

Aleksandra Feodorovna, Empress. *Letters of the Tsarista to the Tsar, 1914–1916*. Edited by Sir Bernard Pares. London, 1923.

Aleksashenko, A. P. *Krakh denikinshchiny*. Moscow, 1966.

Alekseev, M. V. "Iz dnevnika generala M. V. Alekseeva," edited by Ian Slavik, *Rusky historicky archiv: Sbrnik prvni* (1929): 15–56.

———. "Pis'mo generala ot infanterii M. V. Alekseeva k general-leitenantu M. K. Dideriksu, 8-go noiabria 1917 g." *BD* (1928), pp. 77–82.

Alekseev, S. A. ed. *Nachalo grazhdanskoi voiny*. Moscow-Leningrad, 1926.
———, ed. *Revoliutsiia na Ukraine po memuaram belykh*. Moscow-Leningrad, 1930.
Alfer'ev, E. E., ed. *Pis'ma tsarskoi sem'i iz zatocheniia*. Jordanville, 1974.
"The American Commercial Invasion of Russia." *Harper's Weekly*, 46 (March 22, 1902): 361–363.
Andreev, L., M. Gor'kii, and F. Sologub, eds. *Shchit: Literaturnyi sbornik*. Moscow, 1916.
Andriushkevich, N. A. "Posledniaia Rossiia (vospominaniia o Dal'nem Vostoke)." *BD*, IV, pp. 108–145.
Anfimov, A. M. *Rossiiskaia derevnia v gody pervoi mirovoi voiny (1914–fevral' 1917 g.)*. Moscow, 1962.
Ankudinova, L. E. *Natsionalizatsiia promyshlennosti v SSSR (1917–1920 gg.)*. Leningrad, 1963.
Antonov, A. E. *Boevoi vosemnadtsatyi god: Voennye deistviia Krasnoi armii v 1918–nachale 1919 g.* Moscow, 1961.
Antonov-Ovseenko, V. A. *Zapiski o grazhdanskoi voine*. 4 vols. Moscow, 1924–1927.
Arbatov, Z. Iu. "Ekaterinoslav 1917–1920 gg." *ARR*, XII (1923), pp. 83–148.
Arkhiv grazhdanskoi voiny. 2 vols. Berlin, 1922–1923.
Armand, Inessa. *Stat'i, rechi, i pis'ma*. Moscow, 1975.
Aronson, Grigorii. *Na zare krasnogo terrora*. Berlin, 1929.
Arshinov, Peter. *History of the Makhnovist Movement (1918–1921)*. Translated by Lorraine and Fredy Perlman. Detroit and Chicago, 1974.
Arutiunov, G. A. *Rabochee dvizhenie v Zakavkaz'e v period novogo revoliutsionnogo pod"ema, 1910–1914 gg.* Moscow-Baku, 1963.
Ascher, Abraham. *Pavel Akselrod and the Development of Menshevism*. Cambridge, 1972.
Astrov, N. I. "Iasskoe soveshchanie." BACU. Denikin Collection, box 24.
———. "Zapiska o moskovskikh politicheskikh organizatsii 1917–1918 gg." BACU. Denikin Collection, box 24.
"Ataman Grigorii Mikhailovich Semenov." In Markov, pp. 614–614a.
Atkinson, Dorothy. *The End of the Russian Land Commune, 1905–1930*. Stanford, 1983.
Avksent'ev, N. "Razskaz g. Avksent'eva." In Zenzinov, ed., *Gosudarstvennyi perevorot Admirala Kolchaka v Omske*, pp. 177–185.
Avrich, Paul. *Kronstadt 1921*. Princeton, 1970.
———. *Russian Rebels 1600–1800*. New York, 1976.
Babichev, D. S. *Donskoe trudovoe kazachestvo*. Rostov-on-the-Don, 1969.
Baburin, D. S. "Narkomprod v pervye gody sovetskoi vlasti." *IZ* 61 (1957): 333–369.
Baedeker, Karl. *Russia, with Teheran, Port Arthur, and Peking: A Handbook for Travellers*. Leipzig, 1914.
Baklanova, I. A. *Rabochie Petrograda v periode mirnogo razvitiia revoliutsii, mart–iiun' 1917 g.* Leningrad, 1978.
Balfour, Arthur. Letter to R. H. Bruce Lockhart, no. 80, April 17, 1918. PRO: FO 371/3307.
Batykov, Sh. B., et al. *Pobeda sovetskoi vlasti v Srednei Azii i Kazakhstane*. Tashkent, 1967.
Bazyłow, Ludwik. *Ostatnie Lata Rossji Carskiej. Rzady Stołpina*. Warsaw, 1972.
Beatty, Bessie. *The Red Heart of Russia*. New York, 1918.
Bechhofer, C. E. *In Denikin's Russia and the Caucasus, 1919–1920*. London, 1921.
Begletsov, Nikolai. "V dni 'krasnogo' terrora." In *Che-Ka*, pp. 69–84.
Belov, G. A., et al., eds. *Direktivy glavnogo komandovaniia Krasnoi armii (1917–1920). Sbornik dokumentov*. Moscow, 1969.

———. *Iz istorii grazhdanskoi voiny v SSSR*. 3 vols. Moscow, 1961.

———. *Iz istorii Vserossiiskoi chrezvychainoi komissii, 1917–1921 gg. Sbornik dokumentov*. Moscow, 1958.

Belyi [Bugaev], Andrei. *Lug zelënyi*. New York and London, 1967.

———. *Nachalo veka*. Moscow-Leningrad, 1933.

Bennett, Geoffrey. *Cowan's War: The Story of British Naval Operations in the Baltic, 1918–1920*. London, 1964.

Bergson, Abram. *The Structure of Soviet Wages: A Study in Socialist Economics*. Cambridge, Mass., 1944.

Berkhin, I. B. *Ekonomicheskaia politika sovetskogo gosudarstva v pervye gody sovetskoi vlasti*. Moscow, 1970.

Berkman, Alexander. *The Bolshevik Myth (Diary, 1920–1921)*. New York, 1925.

———. *The Kronstadt Rebellion*. Berlin, 1922.

Bernhardi, General Friedrich von. *Germany and the Next War*. Translated by Allen H. Powles. New York and London, 1914.

Billington, James H. *The Icon and the Axe: An Interpretive History of Russian Culture*. London, 1966.

Blok, Aleksandr. *Pis'ma Aleksandra Bloka k rodnym*. Edited by M. A. Beketova. 2 vols. Moscow-Leningrad, 1932.

"Boevoi i chislennyi sostav iuzhnogo i iugo-vostochnogo frontov v period s 1 iiulia po 15 oktiabria 1919 g." In Dushen'kin, IV, pp. 72–81.

"Boevoi i chislennyi sostav Krasnoi armii k 1 noiabria 1920 g." In Dushen'kin, IV, pp. 220–227.

Boevoe raspisanie voisk protivnika na vostochnom i prochikh frontakh. Biweekly. Omsk, 1918–1919.

Bogaevskii, A. "Pervyi kubanskii pokhod (Ledianoi pokhod)." BACU.

Bohachevsky-Chomiak, Martha. "The Directory of the Ukrainian National Republic." In Hunczak, ed. *The Ukraine*, pp. 82–103.

Boldyrev, V. G. *Direktoriia. Kolchak. Interventy: Vospominaniia*. Novonikolaevsk, 1925.

Bol'shaia Sovetskaia Entsiklopediia. 1st ed. 65 vols. Moscow, 1926–1947.

Bolshevik Propaganda. Hearings before a Sub-Committee of the Committee on the Judiciary, U.S. Senate, 65th Congress. Washington, D.C., 1919.

Bonch-Bruevich, V. D. *Izbrannye sochinenii*. 3 vols. Moscow, 1963.

———. "Kak pisal Vladimir Il'ich dekret o zemle." In Mushtukov, pp. 435–440.

———. "Ubiistvo germanskogo posla Mirbakha i vosstanie levykh eserov." In Bonch-Bruevich, *IS*, III, pp. 231–256.

———. "Vladimir Il'ich i ukrashchenie krasnoi stolitsy." In Bonch-Bruevich, *Vospominaniia o Lenine*, pp. 407–415.

———. *Vospominaniia o Lenine*. 2nd ed. Moscow, 1969.

———. "Vospominaniia o V. I. Lenine, 1917–1924 gg." In Bonch-Bruevich, *IS*, III, pp. 231–418.

———. *Vsia vlast' sovetam*. Moscow, 1964.

Borisenko, I. *Sovetskie respubliki na severnom Kavkaze v 1918 godu*. 2 vols. Rostov-on-the-Don, 1930.

Borzunov, V. F. *Proletariat Sibiri i Dal'nego Vostoka nakanune pervoi russkoi revoliutsii*. Moscow, 1965.

Bradley, John. *Allied Intervention in Russia*. New York, 1968.

Brailsford, Henry Noel. *The Russian Workers' Republic*. London, 1921.

Brinkley, George A. *The Volunteer Army and Allied Intervention in South Russia, 1917–1921*. Notre Dame, 1966.

Broido, Eva. *Memoirs of a Revolutionary*. Translated and edited by Vera Broido. New York, 1967.

Brovkin, Vladimir N. *The Mensheviks After October: Socialist Opposition and the Rise of the Bolshevik Dictatorship*. Ithaca, 1987.

Browder, Robert Paul and Alexander Kerensky, eds. *The Russian Provisional Government, 1917*. 3 vols. Stanford, 1961.

Bryant, Louise. *Mirrors of Moscow*. New York, 1923; reprinted 1973.

———. *Six Red Months in Russia: An Observer's Account of Russia Before and During the Proletarian Dictatorship*. New York, 1918.

Bryliakov, N. A. *Rossiiskoe telegrafnoe . . . (agentstvo)*. Moscow, 1976.

Bubnov, A. S., S. S. Kamenev, R. P. Eideman, and [for volume 3 only] M. N. Tukhachevskii, eds. *Grazhdanskaia voina, 1918–1921*. 3 vols. Moscow, 1928.

Buchanan, Sir George. *My Mission to Russia*. 2 vols. London, 1923.

Budberg, Baron Aleksei. *Dnevnik belogvardeitsa (kolchakovskaia epopeia)*, edited by P. E. Shchegolev. Leningrad, 1929.

———. "Dnevnik." *ARR*, XII, pp. 197–290; XIII, pp. 197–312.

Budënnyi, S. et al., eds. *Istoriia grazhdanskoi voiny v SSSR*. Vol. 5. Moscow, 1960.

———. "Iz istorii Krasnoi konnitsy." In Bubnov, Kamenev, and Eideman, I, pp. 105–122.

———. *Proidënnyi put'*. 3 vols. Moscow, 1958–1965.

"Budënnyi, Semën Mikhailovich." *BSE*, VII, cols. 803–804.

Bukharin, Nikolai. *Ekonomika perekhodnogo perioda: Obshchaia teoriia transformatsionnogo protsessa*. Moscow, 1920; reprinted Letchworth, 1980.

Bukhbinder, N., ed. "Na fronte v predoktiabr'skie dni. Po sekretnym materialam Stavki." *KL*, no. 6 (1923): 9–64.

Bulak-Balakhovich, Major-General. "Prizyv Bat'ki." HIA, Iudenich Collection, file 111, box 17.

Bunyan, James, ed. *Intervention, Civil War, and Communism in Russia, April–December 1918*. Baltimore, 1936.

———, and H. H. Fisher, eds. *The Bolshevik Revolution, 1917–1918: Documents and Materials*. Stanford, 1934.

"Bykhovskii al'bom." *BD*, I, pp. 5–8.

Bykov, P. M. "Poslednie dni poslednego tsaria." *ARR*, XVII (1926), pp. 306–316.

"The Capture of Kazan." In Bunyan, p. 292.

Carley, Michael Jabara. *Revolution and Intervention: The French Government and the Russian Civil War, 1917–1919*. Kingston and Montreal, 1983.

Carr, E. H. *The Bolshevik Revolution, 1917–1923*. 3 vols. London, 1950–1953.

———. *Mikhail Bakunin*. New York, 1961.

Česka družina. Hlavni stab. "The Operations of the Czechoslovak Army in Russia in the Years 1917–1920." HIA, Československy strelecky pulk, xx517–10.v.

Chaikin, Vadim. *K istorii rossiiskoi revoliutsii: Kazn' 26 bakinskikh komissarov*. Moscow, 1922.

Chamberlin, William Henry. *The Russian Revolution*. 2 vols. New York, 1965.

Chapman, Guy. *A Passionate Prodigality: Fragments of Autobiography*. New York, Chicago, and San Francisco, 1966.

Che-Ka: Materialy po deiatel'nosti chrezvychainykh komissii. Berlin, 1922.

Cheremnykh, M. N. "Maiakovskii v ROSTA." In Grigorenko, pp. 198–204.

Chernikover, I. *Antisemitizm i pogromy na Ukraine 1917–1918 (k istorii ukrainsko-evreiskikh otnoshenii)*. Berlin, 1923.

Chernomortsev, A. "Vozhd' krasnykh I. I. Vatsetis." BACU. Denikin Collection, box 20.

Chugaev, D. A., ed. *Revoliutsionnoe dvizhenie v Rossii v mae–iiune 1917 g*. Moscow, 1959.

Chukovskii, Kornei. "Lunacharskii." In Glagolev, pp. 159–185.

Churchill, Winston S. *The Aftermath*. New York, 1929.
Cioran, Samuel. *The Apocalyptic Symbolism of Andrej Belyj*. The Hague and Paris, 1973.
Clements, Barbara Evans. *Bolshevik Feminist: The Life of Aleksandra Kollontai*. Bloomington and London, 1979.
Cohen, Stephen F. *Bukharin and the Bolshevik Revolution: A Political Biography, 1888–1938*. Oxford, 1980.
Crankshaw, Edward. *In the Shadow of the Winter Palace: Russia's Drift to Revolution, 1825–1917*. New York, 1976.
Cumming, C. K., and Walter W. Petit. *Russian-American Relations, March 1917–March 1920: Documents and Papers*. New York, 1920.
Curtiss, J. S., ed. *Essays in Russian and Soviet History*. New York, 1963.
———. *The Russian Church and the Soviet State, 1917–1956*. Boston, 1953.
D'Abernon, [Sir Edgar Vincent] Viscount. *The Eighteenth Decisive Battle of the World: Warsaw, 1920*. London, 1931.
Daniels, Robert V. *The Conscience of the Revolution: Communist Opposition in Soviet Russia*. Cambridge, Mass., 1960.
———. "The Kronstadt Revolt of 1921: A Study in the Dynamics of Revolution." *ASEER* 10, no. 4 (December 1951): 241–254.
Davies, Norman. *White Eagle, Red Star: The Polish Soviet War, 1919–1920*. New York, 1972.
Davitt, Michael. *Within the Pale*. London, 1903.
Davydov, M. L. Bor'ba za khleb: Prodovol'stvennaia politika kommunisticheskoi partii i sovetskogo gosudarstva v gody grazhdanskoi voiny, 1917–1920. Moscow, 1971.
Degras, Jane, ed. *Soviet Documents on Foreign Policy, 1917–1924*. London, 1951.
"Deklaratsiia Verkhovnogo soveta Antanty o vremennykh vostochnykh granitsakh Pol'shi," 8 dekabria 1918 g., Parizh. In Khrenov, II, no. 269, pp. 431–432.
"Deklaratsiia Vremennago sibirskogo pravitel'stva o gosudarstvennoi samostoiatel'nosti Sibiri, 4 iiulia 1918 g." In Maksakov and Turunov, pp. 197–198.
"Dekret Soveta narodnykh komissarov Rossiiskoi Sovetskoi Federativnoi Sotsialisticheskoi Respubliki o priznanii nezavisimosti Litovskoi Sovetskoi Respubliki." In Vaitkiavichius, pp. 56–57.
"Dekret Vserossiiskogo tsentral'nogo ispol'nitel'nogo komiteta sovetov rabochikh, soldatskikh, krest'ianskikh i kazach'ikh deputatov ob organizatsii derevenskoi bednoty i snabzhenii ee khlebom, predmetami pervoi neobkhodimosti i sel'skokhoziaistvennymi orudiiami," 11 iiunia 1918 g. In Shestakov, pp. 52–55.
Denikin, A. I. Collected Papers. BACU.
———. "Iz pis'ma gen. Denikina komanduiushchemu 'Dobrovol'cheskoi' armiei gen. Mai-Maevskomu o demoralizatsii voinskikh chastei armii," 10 sentiabria 1919 g. In Belov, *Iz istorii grazhdanskoi voiny*, II, pp. 518–519.
———. "Iz rechi generala Denikina na kazach'em verkhovnom kruge, 16 ianvaria 1920 g." BACU. Denikin Collection, box 20.
———. *Ocherki russkoi smuty*. 5 vols. Paris and Berlin, 1921–1925.
———. *Put' russkogo ofitsera*. New York, 1953.
———. "Rech' generala Denikina k ofitseram Dobrarmii v kontse maia 1918 g., v stanitse Egorlytskoi." BACU. Denikin Collection, box 20.
———. "Rech' generala Denikina v Tsaritsyne, 20 iiunia 1919 g." BACU. Denikin Collection, box 20.
———. "Rech' k rabochim v Odesse, 27 sentiabria 1919 g." BACU. Denikin Collection, box 20.
———. *The Russian Turmoil. Memoirs: Military, Social, Political*. London, 1922.
———. *The White Army*. Translated by Catherine Zvegintzov. London, 1930.

Denisov, S. V. "Nachalo grazhdanskoi voiny na Donu." In Alekseev, *Nachalo*, pp. 80–108.

Desiataia Vserossiiskaia Konferentsiia RKP(b), 26–28 maia 1921 g. "Rezoliutsii i postanovleniia konferentsii ob ekonomicheskoi politike." In *VKP*, I, pp. 396–399.

Desiatyi s"ezd RKP(b), mart 1921 goda: Stenograficheskii otchet. Moscow, 1963.

Deutscher, Isaac. *The Prophet Armed: Trotskii, 1879–1921*. New York, 1954.

———. *The Prophet Outcast: Trotskii, 1929–1940*. London, 1963.

———. *The Prophet Unarmed: Trotskii, 1921–1929*. New York, 1959.

Deviatyi s"ezd RKP(b). Protokoly. Moscow, 1960.

"Direct-Wire Conversation Between Chicherin and Iurev, Chairman of the Murmansk Soviet, Midnight, July 1, 1918." In Bunyan, pp. 133–134.

"Direktiva Glavnogo komandovaniia Komandovaniiu iugo-zapadnogo i zapadnogo frontov o vkliuchenii 12 i 1 konnoi armii v sostave zapadnogo fronta," 13 avgusta 1920 g. In Belov, *Direktivy*, no. 709, pp. 711–712.

"Direktiva Glavnogo komandovaniia o nanesenii okonchatel'nogo porazheniia protivniku i ovladenii Varshavoi," 23 iiulia 1920 g. In Belov, *Direktivy*, no. 635, pp. 643–644.

Diterikhs, General M. K. *Ubiistvo tsarskoi semi'i i chlenov doma Romanovykh na Urale*. 2 vols. Vladivostok, 1922.

Dmitriev, S. "Doklad glavnokomanduiushchemu vooruzhennymi silami iuga Rossii o polozhenii del na zapadnom fronte voobshche i ob armii polkovnika Bermonta Avalova v chastnosti k 15 oktiabria 1919 goda." In *BA* 1 (1926): 101–126.

Dmitriev-Mamonov, A. I. and A. F. Zdziarski. *Guide to the Great Siberian Railway*. Translated by L. Kukol-Yasnopolsky and revised by John Marshall. St. Petersburg, 1900.

"Dmitrii Petrovich Zhloba." *SIE*, V, col. 556.

"Dnevnik i vospominaniia kievskoi studentki." *ARR*, XV (1924), pp. 209–253.

Dobrovol'cheskaia armiia. Glavnyi kaznachei. "Prikhodnaia-raskhodnaia kniga." HIA, pp. 5–18.

Dobrovol'skii, S. "Bor'ba za vozrozhdenie Rossii v severnoi oblasti." *ARR*, III (1921), pp. 5–146.

Dobrynin, V. *Bor'ba s bol'shevizmom na iuge Rossii. Uchastie v bor'be donskogo kazachestva*. Prague, 1921.

"Doklad o sostoianii Petrograda k 10 iiulia 1919 g." HIA. Iudenich Collection, file 120, box 18.

"Doklad t. Dzerzhinskogo Sovnarkomu o vosstanii 1. s.–r." In Piontkovskii, pp. 167–170.

"Doklad tt. Podvoiskogo i Muralova." In Makintsian, pp. 279–288.

"Dokumenty o presledovanii evreev." *ARR*, XIX (1928), pp. 245–284.

Donkov, I. P. *Antonovshchina: Zamysly i deistvitel'nost'*. Moscow, 1977.

Doune, E. "Zapiski krasnogvardeitsa." BACU. Dune Collection.

Drabkina, Elizaveta. *Chernye sukhari: Povest' o nenapisannoi knige*. Moscow, 1963.

Dubrovskii, S. M. *Stolypinskaia zemel'naia reforma*. Moscow, 1963.

Dumov, N. G. *Kadetskaia kontrrevoliutsiia i ee razgrom (oktiabr' 1917–1920 gg.)*. Moscow, 1982.

Dunsterville, Major-General L. C. *The Adventures of Dunsterforce*. London, 1920.

Dushen'kin, et al. eds. *Direktivy komandovaniia frontov Krasnoi armii (1917–1922 gg.). Sbornik dokumentov*. 4 vols. Moscow, 1978.

Dzerzhinskaia, S. *V gody velikikh boev*. Moscow, 1964.

Dzerzhinskii, F. E. "Stenogramma vstupleniia F. E. Dzerzhinskogo na 8-om za-

sedanii VTsIK," 17 fevralia 1919 g. In Belov, *Iz istorii Vserossiiskoi*, pp. 251–257.
Dziewanowski, M. K. *Joseph Piłsudski: A European Federalist, 1918–1922*. Stanford, 1969.
"Effectif des combattants sur le front vers le 15 avril 1919." AG–CV, 17N625.
Efimov, N. "Komandnyi sostav Krasnoi armii." In Bubnov, Kamanev, and Eideman, II, p. 91–109.
Efremenkov, I. G. "Bor'ba s anglo-franko-amerikanskoi interventsiei na severe v 1918 g." In Naida, *Iz istorii*, pp. 142–170.
Egorov, A. I. *Razgrom Denikina 1919*. Moscow, 1934.
"Aleksandr Il'ich Egorov." *BSE*, 1st ed., XXIV, cols. 422–423.
Egorova, A. G. *Partiia i profsoiuzy v oktiabr'skoi revoliutsii*. Moscow, 1970.
Ehrenburg, Ilya. *First Years of Revolution, 1918–1921*. Translated by Anna Bostock. London, 1962.
———. *People and Life: Memoirs of 1891–1917*. Translated by Anna Bostock and Yvonne Kapp. London, 1961.
Eikhe, G. Kh. "5-aia armiia v bor'be za zapadnuiu Sibir'." In Bubnov, Kamenev, and Eideman, I, pp. 190–204.
Eikhenbaum, Vsevolod. *See* Voline.
Elkina, S. I. *Na kul'turnom fronte*. Moscow, 1959.
———, and I. M. Minshakova, eds. *Feliks Edmundovich Dzerzhinskii: Zhizn' i deiatel'nost' v fotografiiakh i dokumentakh*. Moscow, 1972.
Ellis, C. H. *The British "Intervention" in Transcaspia, 1918–1919*. Berkeley and Los Angeles, 1963.
Epstein, E. *Les banques de commerce russes*. Paris, 1925.
Erikson, John. *The Soviet High Command: A Military-Political History, 1918–1941*. London, 1962.
"Establishment of the Supreme Administration of the North," August 2, 1918. In Bunyan, pp. 304–306.
"Etat du matériel d'artillerie éxistant aux armées et an dépôt au 15 novembre 1918." AG–CV, 17N624.
"Etat de situation de l'armée sibérienne au 6 novembre 1918." AG–CV, 17N624.
Eudin, Xenia Joukoff. "The German Occupation of the Ukraine in 1918." *RR* 1 (1941): 90–105.
"Evrei v Moskve po neopublikovannym dokumentam." *B*, no. 9 (September 1907): 150–161.
Falls, Cyril. B. *A Hundred Years of War*. London, 1961.
Farnsworth, Beatrice. *Aleksandra Kollontai: Socialism, Feminism, and the Bolshevik Revolution*. Stanford, 1980.
Fediukin, S. A. *Sovetskaia vlast' i burzhuaznye spetsialisty*. Moscow, 1965.
Fedotoff, G. P. *The Russian Church Since the Revolution*. London, 1928.
Fedotoff White, D. *The Growth of the Red Army*. Princeton, 1944.
Fedyshyn, Oleh S. *Germany's Drive to the East and the Ukrainian Revolution, 1917–1918*. New Brunswick, 1971.
Figner, Vera. *Zapechatlënnyi trud: Vospominaniia v dvukh tomakh*. 2 vols. Moscow, 1964.
Filimonov, General A. P. "Razgrom Kubanskoi rady." *ARR*, V. pp. 322–329.
Fischer, Louis. *The Life of Lenin*. New York, 1964.
Fisher, H. H. "The American Railway Mission to Russia." With marginal notes and comments by John F. Stevens. HIA, John Frank Stevens Papers, file no. 1.
———. *The Famine in Soviet Russia, 1919–1923: The Operations of the American Relief Administration*. New York, 1927.

Fitzpatrick, Sheila. *The Commissariat of Enlightenment: Soviet Organization of Education and the Arts under Lunacharsky*. Cambridge, 1970.
Florinsky, M. T. *Russia: A History and an Interpretation*. 2 vols. New York, 1968.
Fomin, F. T. "Chelovechnost', skromnost', prostota." In Rozvadovskaia and Slutskaia, pp. 282–292.
Footman, David. *Civil War in Russia*. London, 1961.
———. *Red Prelude: The Life of the Russian Terrorist Zheliabov*. New Haven, 1945.
Fotieva, L. A. *Iz zhizni V. I. Lenina*. Moscow, 1967.
Fraiman, A. L. *Forpost sotsialisticheskoi revoliutsii: Petrograd v pervye mesiatsy sovetskoi vlasti*. Leningrad, 1969.
———, et al., eds. *Istoriia rabochikh Leningrada*. Vol. 2. Leningrad, 1972.
Francis, David R. *Russia from the American Embassy, April 1916–November 1918*. New York, 1921.
Frederic, Harold, *The New Exodus: A Study of Israel in Russia*. New York and London, 1892.
Freidlin, B. M. *Ocherki istorii rabochego dvizheniia v Rossii v 1917 g*. Moscow, 1967.
Frunze, M. V. *Izbrannye proizvedeniia*. Moscow, 1950.
———. *Izbrannye proizvedeniia*. 2 vols. Moscow, 1957.
———. "Obrashchenie k voiskam iuzhnoi gruppy vostochnogo fronta," 10 aprelia 1919 g. In Frunze, *IP*, I, pp. 166–167.
———. "Telegramma M. V. Frunze V. I. Leninu o. podgotovke obshchego nastupleniia na Vrangelia," 26 oktiabria 1920 g. In Belov, *Iz istorii grazhdanskoi voiny*, pp. 418–419.
Fussell, Paul. *The Great War and Modern Memory*. New York and London, 1975.
Gai, G. D. "III Konnyi korpus pod Grodno." In Bubnov, Kamenev, Tukhachevskii, and Eideman, III, pp. 295–301.
———. *Pervyi udar' po Kolchaku*. Moscow, 1926.
Gaponenko, L. S. *Rabochii klass Rossii v 1917 godu*. Moscow, 1970.
———, et al., eds. *Revoliutsionnoe dvizhenie v Rossii v aprele 1917 g. Aprel'skii krizis*. Moscow, 1958.
Garmiza, V. V. "Iz istorii samarskoi uchredilki." *IZh* 8 (1940): 33–43.
Gąsiorowska-Grabowska, Natalia, et al., eds. *Dokumenty i materiały do historii stosunkov polsko-radzieckich*. 3 vols. Warsaw, 1961.
Gavrilov, L. M., ed. *Voiskovye komitety deistvuiushchei armii, mart 1917 g.–mart 1918 g*. Moscow, 1982.
Geresimiuk, V. R. "V. I. Lenin i bor'ba za khleb v pervye mesiatsy sovetskoi vlasti (oktiabr' 1917 g.–aprel' 1918 g.)." *VIKPSS* (January 1966): 75–84.
Gerson, Lennard D. *The Secret Police in Lenin's Russia*. Philadelphia, 1976.
Gerua, Major General. "O sostoianii Petrograda," 16/29 ianvaria 1919 g., Helsingfors. HIA. Iudenich Collection, file 55, box 9, p. 9.
Getzler, Israel. *Kronstadt, 1917–1921: The Fate of a Soviet Democracy*. Cambridge, 1983.
———. *Martov: A Political Biography of a Russian Social Democrat*. Cambridge, 1967.
Gilliard, Pierre. *Thirteen years at the Russian Court*. New York, 1970.
Gimpel'son, E. G. *Rabochii klass v upravlenii sovetskim gosudarstvom, noiabr' 1917–1920 gg*. Moscow, 1982.
———. *Sovetskii rabochii klass 1918–1920 gg. Sotsial'no-politicheskie izmeneniia*. Moscow, 1974.
———. *Sovety v gody interventsii i grazhdanskoi voiny*. Moscow, 1968.
———. *"Voennyi Kommunizm": Politika, praktika, ideologiia*. Moscow, 1973.
Gindin, A. *Kak bol'sheviki natsionalizirovali chastnye banki (fakty i dokumenty posleoktiabr'skikh dnei v Petrograde)*. Moscow, 1962.

Gins, G. K. *Sibir', soiuzniki, i Kolchak, 1918–1920.* 2 vols. Peking, 1921.
Gippius [-Merezhkovskaia], Zinaida. *Dmitrii Merezhkovski.* Paris, 1951.
———. *Siniaia kniga. Peterburgskii dnevnik, 1914–1918.* Belgrad, 1929.
Gladkov, I. A. *Ocherki stroitel'stva sovetskogo planovogo khoziaistva, 1917–1918 gg.* Moscow, 1950.
Glagolev, N. A., ed. *O Lunacharskom. Issledovaniia. Vospominaniia.* Moscow, 1976.
Globachev, N. K. "Pravda o russkoi revoliutsii. Vospominaniia byvshago nachal'nika Petrogradskogo okhrannego otdeleniia." BACU. Globachev Collection.
God raboty Moskovskago gorodskogo prodovol'stvennago komiteta (mart 1917 g.–mart 1918 g.). Moscow, 1918.
Gofman, Ts. "K istorii pervogo agitparakhoda VTsIK 'Krasnaia zvezda'." *VI*, no. 9 (1948): 63–70.
Gogol', N. V. *Polnoe sobranie sochinenii N. V. Gogolia.* Vol. 8, Moscow, 1913.
———. *Sobranie sochinenii N. V. Gogolia v shesti tomakh.* 6 vols. Moscow, 1959.
Gol'denveizer, A. A. "Iz kievskikh vospominanii (1917–1921 gg.)." *ARR*, VI (1922), pp. 161–303.
Golder, F. A., ed. *Documents of Russian History, 1913–1917.* Translated by Emanuel Aronsberg. New York, 1927.
Goldman, Emma. *Living My Life.* 2 vols. New York, 1931.
———. *My Disillusionment in Russia.* Garden City, 1923.
———. *My Further Disillusionment in Russia.* Garden City, 1924.
Golikov, G. N., ed. *Oktiabr'skoe vooruzhënnoe vosstanie v Petrograde.* Moscow, 1957.
Golinkov, D. L. *Krushenie antisovetskogo podpol'ia v SSSR.* 2 vols. Moscow, 1978.
Golovin, [Golovine] N. N. *Rossiiskaia kontrrevoliutsiia v 1917–1918 gg.* 5 vols. Paris, 1937.
———. *The Russian Army in the World War.* New Haven, 1931.
Golubev, A. V. "Bor'ba Krasnoi armii na krymskom fronte." In Gukovskii, *Razgrom*, pp. 55–99.
———. "Mikhail Vasil'evich Frunze." *SIE*, XV, cols. 450–453.
Golubintsev, General. *Russkaia Vandeia: Ocherki grazhdanskoi voiny na Donu, 1917–1920 gg.* Munich, 1959.
Golubutskii, V. A. *Zaporozhskoe kazachestvo.* Kiev, 1957.
Gopper, General. "Belogvardeiskie organizatsii i vosstaniia vnutri Sovetskoi respubliki." In Alekseev, *Nachalo*, pp. 293–321.
Gordon, Linda. *Cossack Rebellions.* Albany, 1983.
Gordienko, I. *Iz boevogo proshlogo (1914–1918 gg).* Moscow, 1957.
Gorelik, Ia. M. "Mikhail Nikolaevich Tukhachevskii." *SIE*, XIV, cols. 599–600.
Gor'kii, Maksim. *O russkom krest'ianstve.* Berlin, 1922.
Gorky [Gor'kii], Maxim. *Untimely Thoughts: Essays on Revolution, Culture, and the Bolsheviks, 1917–1918.* Translated from the Russian with an introduction and notes by Herman Ermolaev. New York, 1968.
Gorn, V. L. *Grazhdanskaia voina na severo-zapade Rossii.* Berlin, 1923.
Got'e, Iu. V. *Time of Troubles: The Diary of Iurii Vladimirovich Got'e, Moscow, July 8, 1917 to July 23, 1922.* Translated, edited, and introduced by Terence Emmons. Princeton, 1988.
Gough, General Sir Hubert. *Soldiering On: The Story of British Naval Operations in the Baltic, 1918–1920.* London, 1964.
"Gramota Vserossiiskogo vremennogo pravitel'stva ko vsem narodam Rossii," 24 sentiabria 1918 g. In Piontkovskii, pp. 284–286.
Graves, William S. *America's Siberian Adventure, 1918–1920.* New York, 1941.
Greenberg, Louis. *The Jews in Russia.* 2 vols. New Haven, 1951.

Grigorenko, V. V., et al., eds. *V. Maiakovskii v vospominaniiakh sovremennikov.* Moscow, 1963.

Grondijs, L. H. *Le Cas-Koltchak: Contribution à l'histoire de la révolution russe.* Leiden, 1939.

Gruzenberg, O. O. *Yesterday: Memoirs of a Russian Jewish Lawyer.* Edited with an introduction by Don C. Rawson. Translated by Don C. Rawson and Tatiana Tipton. Berkeley and Los Angeles, 1981.

Guchkov, A. I. "Memorandum o Russkoi severo-zapadnoi armii." HIA. Iudenich Collection, file 103, box 16.

Gukovskii, A. I. "Krym v 1918–1919 gg." *KA* 28 (1928): 142–181; 29 (1928): 55–85.

———, ed. *Razgrom Vrangelia 1920: Sbornik statei.* Moscow, 1930.

Gul', Roman. *Dzerzhinskii.* Paris. 1936.

———. "Kievskaia epopeia." *ARR*, II (1921), pp. 59–86.

———. *Ledianoi pokhod (s Kornilovym).* Moscow-Leningrad, 1925.

Gulevich, K., and R. Gassanova. "Iz istorii bor'by prodovol'stvennykh otriadov rabochikh za khleb i ukreplenie sovetskoi vlasti (1918–1920 gg.)." *KA* 89–90 (1938): 103–154.

Gurovich, A. "Vysshii soviet narodnago khoziaistva: Iz vpechatlenii goda sluzhby." *ARR*, VI (1922), pp. 304–331.

Gusev, K. V. *Partiia eserov: Ot melko-burzhuaznogo revoliutsionarizma k kontrrevoliutsii.* Moscow, 1975.

———, and Kh. A. Eritsian, *Ot soglashatel'stva k kontrrevoliutsii: Ocherki istorii politicheskogo bankrotstva i gibeli partii sotsialistov-revoliutsionerov.* Moscow, 1968.

Gusev, S. I. "Sviiazhskie dni (1918g.)." *PR* 26, no. 2 (1924): 100–109.

Gusev-Orenburgskii, S. I. *Kniga o evreiskikh pogromakh na Ukraine v 1919 g.* Petrograd, n. d.

Hafkesbrink, Hanna. *Unknown Germany: An Inner Chronicle of the First World War Based on Letters and Diaries.* New Haven, 1948.

Haimson, Leopold. "The Mensheviks After the October Revolution." *RR* 38 (1979): 454–473; 39 (1980): 181–207.

Halle, Faninna W. *Woman in Soviet Russia.* London, 1934.

Hard, William. *Raymond Robins' Own Story.* New York, 1971.

Hasegawa, Tsuyoshi. *The February Revolution: Petrograd, 1917.* Seattle and London, 1981.

Heifetz, Elias. *The Slaughter of the Jews in the Ukraine in 1919.* New York, 1921.

Hillerson, A. I. "Report of A. I. Hillerson." Published in Heifetz, pp. 185–234.

Hodgson, John E. *With Denikin's Armies, Being a Description of the Cossack Counter-Revolution in South Russia, 1918–1920.* London, 1932.

Hoffman, General Max von. *The War of Lost Opportunities.* Translated from the German. New York, 1925.

Hosking, Geoffrey. *The First Socialist State: A History of the Soviet Union from Within.* Cambridge, Mass., 1985.

Howard, Sir Esme. *Theatre of Life: Seen from the Stalls, 1905–1936.* 2 vols. London, 1936.

Hunczak, Taras. "The Ukraine Under Hetman Pavlo Skoropadskyi." In Hunczak, ed., *The Ukraine,* pp. 61–81.

———, ed., *The Ukraine, 1917–1921: A Study in Revolution.* Cambridge, Mass., 1977.

Iakhontov, A. N. "Tiazhëlye dni (sekretnye zasedaniia Soveta ministrov 16 iiulia–2 sentiabria 1915 goda)." *ARR* (1926): 5–136.

Iakovlev, Ia. A., ed. *1917 god v derevne.* Moscow, 1967.

Iakushkin, E., and S. Polunin. *Angliiskaia interventsiia v 1918–1920 gg.* Moscow-Leningrad, 1928.
Iaremenko, A. N. "Dnevnik kommunista." In *Revoliutsiia na Dal'nem Vostoke*, pp. 133–180.
Il'in, I. A. "Belaia idea." *BD*, I. pp. 7–15.
Il'in-Zhenevskii, *Bolsheviki u vlasti.* Leningrad, 1929.
Il'ina, G. I. "Chislennost, sostav i material'noe polozhenie rabochikh Petrograda v 1918–1920 gg." In Fraiman, *Istoriia*, pp. 88–99.
"Ioakim Ioakimovich Vatsetis," *SIE*, II, cols. 1019–1020.
Ioffe, G. Z. *Kolchakovskaia avantiura i ee krakh.* Moscow, 1983.
"Iosif Vissarionovich Stalin (Dzhugashvili)." *SIE*, XIV, cols. 780–785.
Ironside, William Edmund. "Almost Complete Manuscript Draft . . . of the October 1919 Report." IWM. A. E. Sturdy Papers.
———. *Archangel, 1918–1919.* London, 1953.
———. "Notes on Operations from October 1st 1918 to May 26th 1919." IWM. A. E. Sturdy Papers.
Iroshnikov, M. P. "K voprosu o slome burzhuaznoi gosudarstvennoi mashiny v Rossii." In Tokarev, *Problemy*, pp. 46–66.
———. *Sozdanie sovetskogo tsentral'nogo gosudarstvennogo apparata. Sovet narodnykh komissarov i narodnye komissariaty (oktiabr' 1917 g.–ianvar' 1918 g).* Moscow, 1966.
Iskrov, M. V. "O razrabotke V. I. Leninym prodovol'stvennoi politiki 1918 g." *VIKPSS* (July 1963): 74–86.
Itkina, A. M. *Revoliutsioner, tribun, diplomat: Stranitsy zhizni Aleksandry Mikhailovnoi: Kollontai.* Moscow, 1970.
"Ivan Adol'fovich Teodorovich." *SIE*, XIV, cols. 188–189.
"Ivan Ivanovich Skvortsov-Stepanov." *SIE*, XII, cols. 951–952.
Ivanov, N. Ia. *Kornilovshchina i ee razgrom: Iz istorii bor'by s kontrrevoliutsiei v 1917 g.* Leningrad, 1965.
Ivanov, N. N. "O sobytiiakh pod Petrogradom v 1919 godu." *Arkhiv grazhdanskoi voiny*, I, pp. 9–175.
Ivanov, V. N. *Marshal M. N. Tukhachevskii.* Moscow, 1985.
"Iz besedy M. I. Kalinina s krest'ianami Novo-Mainskoi volosti Melekesskogo uezda Samarskoi Gubernii, 13 maia 1919 g." In Sergeev, pp. 110–114.
"Iz doklada glavnogo komandovaniia V. I. Leninu i revvoensovetu respubliki o strategicheskom polozhenii Sovetskoi respubliki i zadachakh Krasnoi armii," 23–25 fevralia 1919 g. In Belov, *Direktivy*, 153–169.
"Iz plana komandovaniia iuzhnogo fronta po razgromu armii Denikina," 24 iiunia 1919 g. In Belov, *Iz istorii grazhdanskoi voiny*, II, pp. 500–503.
"Iz Prikaza No. 41 komanduiushchego voiskami Tambovskoi gubernii M. N. Tukhachevskogo o nagrazhdenii sotrudnikov osobogo otdela brigady Kotovskogo Gazhalova N. A. i. Ogolia S. M. ordenami krasnogo znameni," 25 sentiabria 1921 g. In Belov et al., eds. *Iz istorii Vserossiiskoi*, pp. 467–468.
"Iz svodki operativnogo otdela razvedyvatel'nogo otdeleniia polevogo shtaba revvoensoveta respubliki o sostave voisk protivnika k 20 iiunia 1919 g." In Belov, *Iz istorii grazhdanskoi voiny*, II, no. 339, p. 377.
"Iz svodki operativnogo upravleniia polevogo shtaba revvoensoveta respubliki o boevom sostave armii zapadnogo fronta k 15 iiunia 1919 g." In Belov, *Iz istorii grazhdanskoi voiny*, II, no. 337, p. 375.
"Iz svodki operativnogo upravleniia polevogo shtaba revvoensoveta respubliki o chislennosti voisk Krasnoi armii i sil protivnika na zapadnom fronte k 1 iiuna 1919 g." In Belov, *Iz istorii grazhdanskoi voiny*, II, no. 281, p. 326.

Izvestiia Vremennogo revoliutsionnogo komiteta matrosov, krasnoarmeitsev, i rabochikh goroda Kronshtadta, nos. 1–14, March 3–16, 1921. Reprinted in *Pravde o Kronshtadte*, pp. 45–183.

Janin, General Maurice. *Ma mission en Siberie, 1918–1920*. Paris, 1933.

———. "Note sur la mission en Siberie," Paris, le 20 juin 1920. In Grondijs, pp. 229–239.

Johnson, Richard. "Fania Efimovna Kaplan." *MERSH*, XV, pp. 235–237.

Kachorovskii, K. R. "The Russian Landed Commune in History and Today." *SEER* 7 (1928–1929): 565–576.

Kadishev, A. E. *Interventsiia i grazhdanskaia voina v Zakavkaz'e*. Moscow, 1960.

Kakurin, N. *Kak srazhalas' revoliutsiia*. 2 vols. Moscow-Leningrad, 1925.

———. *Russko-pol'skaia kampaniia 1918–1920 gg. Politiko-strategicheskii ocherk*. Moscow, 1922.

———. *Strategicheskii ocherk grazhdanskoi voiny*. Moscow-Leningrad, 1926.

Kalinin, I. M. *Russkaia Vandeia*. Moscow-Leningrad, 1926.

Kalvoda, Josef. "Czech and Slovak Prisoners of War in Russia During the War and Revolution." *War and Society in East Central Europe* 5 (1982): 215–238.

———. "The Origins of the Czechoslovak Army, 1914–1918." *War and Society in East Central Europe* 19 (1985): 419–435.

Karlinsky, Simon. *Marina Tsvetaeva: The Woman, Her World and Her Poetry*. Cambridge, 1985.

Karpinskii, V. A. *V pokhod protiv tsaria goloda!* Moscow, 1918.

Kartashev, A. V., V. D. Kuz'min-Karavaev, and M. N. Suvorov. "Iz doklada Kartasheva, Kuz'mina-Karavaeva, i Suvorova." In "Obrazovanie," pp. 295–308.

Katkov, George. "The Assassination of Count Mirbach." *SAP*, no. 12 (Soviet Affairs, no. 3, 1962): 53–93.

———. *The Kornilov Affair: Kerensky and the Break-up of the Russian Army*. London and New York, 1980.

———. "The Kronstadt Rising." *SAP*, no. 6 (1959): 9–74.

Katsnel'son, A. "Iz martirologa Moskovskoi obshchiny. Moskovskaia sinagoga v 1891–1906 gg." *Evreiskaia starina* 1 (1909): 175–188.

Kavtaradze, A. G. "Grigorii Mikhailovich Semenov." *SIE*, XII, col. 729.

Kazakov, A. "Vospominaniia." In Iakovlev, pp. 130–133.

Kazemzadeh, Firuz. *The Struggle for Transcaucasia (1917–1921)*. New York, 1951.

Keep, J.L.H. *The Russian Revolution: A Study in Mass Mobilization*. New York, 1976.

Kenez, Peter. *Civil War in South Russia, 1918: The First Year of the Volunteer Army*. Berkeley and Los Angeles, 1971.

———. *Civil War in South Russia, 1919–1920: The Defeat of the Whites*. Berkeley and Los Angeles, 1977.

———. *The Birth of the Propaganda State: Soviet Methods of Mass Mobilization, 1917–1929*. Cambridge, 1985.

Kennan, George. *Siberia and the Exile System*. 2 vols. New York, 1891.

Kennan, George F. *The Decision To Intervene*. Princeton, 1958.

———. *The Marquis de Custine and His* Russia in 1839. London, 1972.

———. *Russia Leaves the War*. Princeton, 1956.

Kerensky [Kerenskii], Alexander. *The Catastrophe: Kerensky's Own Story of the Russian Revolution*. New York, 1927.

———. *La révolution russe, 1917*. Paris, 1928.

———. *Russia and History's Turning Point*. New York, 1965.

———. *La vérité sur le massacre des Romanovs*. Paris, 1936.

Khatsevich, A. F. *Soldat velikikh boev: Zhizn' i deiatel'nost' F. E. Dzerzhinskogo*. 3rd ed. Minsk, 1970.
Khlebnikov, N. M., et al. *Legendarnaia chapaevskaia*. Moscow, 1970.
Khrenov, I. A., et al., eds. *Dokumenty i materialy po istorii sovetsko-pol'skikh otnoshenii*. 3 vols. Moscow, 1965.
Kirienko, Iu. K. *Krakh kaledinshchiny*. Moscow, 1976.
Kiselëv, A. A. and Klimov, Iu. N. *Murman v dni revoliutsii i grazhdanskoi voiny*. Murmansk, 1977.
Klevanskii, A. Kh. *Chekhoslovatskie internatsionalisty i prodannyi korpus: Chekhoslovatskie politicheskie organizatsii i voinskie formirovaniia v Rossii, 1914–1921 gg*. Moscow, 1965.
"Kliment Efremovich Voroshilov." *SIE*, III, cols. 715–716.
Knox, Major-General Sir Alfred. *With the Russian Army, 1914–1917. Being Chiefly Extracts from the Diary of a Military Attache*. London, 1921.
Kochakov, B. M., et al., eds. *Ocherki istorii Leningrada*. 3 vols. Moscow-Leningrad, 1956.
Koenker, Diane. "Urbanization and Deurbanization in the Russian Revolution and Civil War." *JMH* 57, no. 3 (September 1985): 424–450.
Kolchak, Admiral A. V. "K naseleniiu Rossii," 18 noiabria 1918 goda. In Zenzinov, *Gosudarstvennyi*, p. 11.
———. "Manifest Kolchaka, 23 noiabria 1918 g." In Piontkovskii, pp. 298–301.
Kolesnikov, B. *Professional'noe dvizhenie i kontr-revoliutsiia. Ocherki iz istorii professional'nogo dvizheniia na Ukraine*. Kiev, 1923.
"Kolichestvo grazhdan, priniatykh po mobilizatsiiam v Krasnuiu armiiu v dekabre 1918 g.–noiabre 1919 g." In Dushen'kin, IV, p. 276.
Kollontai, Aleksandra. *The Autobiography of a Sexually Emancipated Communist Woman*. Edited with an afterward by Irving Fetscher. Translated by Salvator Attanasio. New York, 1971.
———. *Izbrannye stat'i i rechi*. Moscow, 1972.
———. *Iz moei zhizni i raboty*. Moscow, 1974.
———. "Kak i dlia chego sozvan byl I Vserossiiskii S"ezd Rabotnits." In Kollontai, *Izbrannye*, pp. 254–259.
———. *Love and the New Morality*. Edited and translated by Alix Holt. Bristol, 1972.
———. "The New Woman." Published as an appendix to Kollontai, *Autobiography*, pp. 51–103.
———. "Prostitution and Ways of Fighting It." In Kollontai, *Selected Writings*, pp. 261–275.
———. *Selected Writings of Aleksandra Kollontai*. Translated with an introduction and commentaries by Alix Holt. London, 1977.
———. "Sexual Relations and the Class Struggle." In Kollontai, *Selected Writings*, pp. 237–249.
———. "The Workers' Opposition." In Kollontai, *Selected Writings*, pp. 159–200.
———. "Working Woman and Mother." In Kollontai, *Selected Writings*, pp. 127–139.
Kolosov, E. E., ed. *Sibir' pri Kolchake: Vospominaniia, materialy, dokumenty*. Petrograd, 1923.
Komarnicki, Titus. *Rebirth of the Polish Republic: A Study in the Diplomatic History of Europe, 1914–1920*. London, 1957.
Komissiia po istorii oktiabr'skoi revoliutsii i R.K.P. (bol'shevikov). *Revoliutsiia na Dal'nem Vostoke*. Vol. 1. Moscow-Petrograd, 1923.
Konev, A. M. *Krasnaia gvardiia na zashchite oktiabria*. Moscow, 1978.

Kon'kova, A. S. *Bor'ba Kommunisticheskoi partii za soiuz rabochego klassa s bedneishim krest'ianstvom v 1917–1918 gg.* Moscow, 1974.
"Konstitutsiia ufimskoi direktorii: Akt ob obrazovanii vserossiiskoi verkhovnoi vlasti, 8–23 sentiabria 1918 g." *ARR*, XII, pp. 189–193.
"Konwencja woiskowa między przedstawiecielami Ministerstwa Spraw Wojskowych RP a rządem S. Petlury w sprawie wspolnej ofensywy przeciwko Ukrainie Radzieckiej," 1920 kwiecień 24. In Gąsiorowska-Grabowska, II, no. 381, pp. 749–753.
Korb, Johann Georg. *Diary of an Austrian Secretary of Legation at the Court of Czar Peter the Great.* 2 vols. London, 1863.
Koritskii, N. I., et al., eds. *Marshal Tukhachevskii: Vospominaniia druzei i soratnikov.* Moscow, 1965.
Korolenko, V. G. "Dom no. 13." In Korolenko, *SS*, pp. 406–422.
———. *Sobranie sochinenii v desiati tomakh.* 10 vols. Moscow, 1955.
Korotkov, I. S. *Razgrom Vrangelia.* Moscow, 1955.
Kovalenko, D. A. *Oboronnaia promyshlennost' Sovetskoi Rossii v 1918–1920 gg.* Moscow, 1970.
Krasnov, P. N. "Vsevelikoe voisko donskoe." *ARR*, V, pp. 190–320.
Kritsman, L. *Geroicheskii period velikoi russkoi revoliutsii.* Moscow, n.d. [1924].
"Kronstadt." *Encyclopedia Britannica.* 11th ed. XV, pp. 927–928.
Krupskaia, N. K. *Vospominaniia o Lenine.* Moscow, 1968.
Kruze, E. E. and D. C. Kutsentov. "Naselenie Peterburga." In Kochakov, III, pp. 104–146.
Kubanin, M. *Makhnovshchina: Krest'ianskoe dvizhenie v stepnoi Ukraine v gody grazhdanskoi voiny.* Leningrad, 1927.
Kukiel, General Marjan. "The Polish-Soviet Campaign of 1920." *SEER*, no. 22 (June 1929): 48–65.
Kumanev, V. A. *Sotsializm i vsenarodnaia gramotnost': Likvidatsiia massovoi negramotnosti v SSSR.* Moscow, 1967.
Kuropatkin, A. N. "Dnevnik A. N. Kuropatkina." *KA* 2 (1922): 5–112.
Kushner, P. I., ed. *The Village of Viratino.* Translated and edited by Sula Benet. New York, 1970.
Kuz'min, G. V. *Razgrom interventov i belogvardeitsev v 1917–1922 gg.* Moscow, 1977.
Lampe, A. A. von. *Beloe delo: Letopis' beloi bor'by.* 6 vols. Berlin, 1926–1933.
Landau, Roman. *Piłsudski and Poland.* New York, 1929.
Lapidus, Gail Warshofsky. *Women in Soviet Society: Equality, Development, and Social Change.* Berkeley, 1978.
Latsis (Sudrabs), M. Ia. *Chrezvychainye komissii po bor'be s kontrrevoliutsiei.* Moscow, 1921.
———. *Dva goda bor'by na vnutrennem fronte.* Moscow, 1920.
———. "Soiuz zashchity rodiny i svobody." In Makintsian, pp. 1–196.
Leggett, George. *The Cheka: Lenin's Political Police.* Oxford, 1981.
Lehovich, Dimitry V. *White Against Red: The Life of General Anton Denikin.* New York, 1974.
Lemke, M. *250 dnei tsarskoi stavki (25 sentiabria 1915–2 iiulia 1918 gg.)* Petersburg, 1920.
Lenin, V. I. *Collected Works.* Various translators. 45 vols. Moscow, 1960–1970.
———. *The Emancipation of Women: From the Writings of V. I. Lenin.* With a preface by Nadezhda K. Krupskaia, and with an appendix, "Lenin on the Woman Question," by Clara Zetkin. New York, 1966.
———. "Rech' V. I. Lenina na 4-i konferentsii gubernskikh chrezvychainykh komissii," 6 fevralia 1920. In Belov, *Iz istorii Vserossiiskoi*, pp. 365–371.
———. *Sochineniia.* 40 vols. Moscow, 1952–1959.

———. "Telegramma V. I. Lenina Glavkomu i Revvoensovetu zapadnogo fronta," 24 aprelia 1919 g. In Belov, *Direktivy*, no. 316, p. 365.

———. "Zapiska V. I. Lenina v Revvoensovet respubliki," 10 avgusta 1919 g." In Belov, *Iz istorii grazhdanskoi voiny*, I, no. 462, p. 512.

———. "Zapiska v Sekretariat TsK RKP(b)," aprel' 1920 g. In Khrenov, III, no. 11, p. 29.

Leonidov, O. *Po tylam generala Krasnova*. Moscow, 1939.

Levidova, S. M., and S. A. Pavlotskaia. *Nadezhda Konstantinovna Krupskaia*. Leningrad, 1962.

Levine, Isaac Don. *The Mind of an Assassin*. New York, 1959.

Lewin, Moishe. *Lenin's Last Struggle*. Translated from the French by A. M. Sheridan Smith. New York, 1970.

———. *Russian Peasants and Soviet Power: A Study of Collectivization*. Translated by Irene Nove with the assistance of John Biggart. Evanston, 1968.

Liashchenko, P. I. *Istoriia narodnogo khoziaistva SSSR*. 3 vols. Moscow, 1956.

Liddell Hart, B. H., ed. *The Soviet Army*. London, 1957.

Lincoln, W. Bruce. *In War's Dark Shadow: The Russians Before the Great War*. New York, 1983.

———. *Passage Through Armageddon: The Russians in War and Revolution, 1914–1918*. New York, 1986.

———. *Petr Petrovich Semenov-Tian-Shanskii: The Life of a Russian Geographer*. Newtonville, 1980.

———. *The Romanovs: Autocrats of All the Russias*. New York, 1981.

———. "Soviet Political Posters: Art and Ideas for the Masses." *History Today* 26, no. 5 (May 1976): 302–309.

Lipatov, N. P. *1920 god na Chernom More: Voenno-morskie sily v razgrome Vrangelia*. Moscow, 1958.

Lipkina, A. G. *1919 god v Sibiri*. Moscow, 1962.

Lisovoi, Ia. M., ed. *Belyi arkhiv*. 3 vols. Paris, 1926–1928.

———. "Rol' ofitserov general'nago shtaba v revoliutsii i v belom dvizhenii (statisticheskii ocherk po dannym k 1 dekabria 1918 g.)." BACU.

Lockhart, R. H. Bruce. *British Agent*. New York and London, 1933.

———. Letter to Foreign Secretary Arthur Balfour, no. 163, May 7, 1918. PRO: FO 371/3285–86.

Long, John W. "Civil War and Intervention in North Russia, 1918–1920." Ph.D. dissertation, Columbia University, 1972.

———. "Izhevsk-Votkinsk Revolt, 1918." *MERSH*, 49: pp. 24–29.

Łossowki, Piotr. *Stosunki Polsko-Litewskie w latach 1918–1920*. Warsaw, 1966.

Luckett, Richard. *The White Generals: An Account of the White Movement and the Russian Civil War*. New York, 1971.

Lukomskii, A. S. *Vospominaniia A. S. Lukomskago*. 2 vols. Berlin, 1922.

Lunacharskii, A. V. "The Preface of the People's Commissar for Education to *The Unsifted Word*." Excerpted in Woroszylski, pp. 244–245.

———. "Proletariat i iskusstvo [tezisy doklada dlia Pervoi Vserossiiskoi Konferentsii Proletkul'tov]." In Lunacharskii, *SS*, VII, p. 201.

———. *Religiia i sotsializm*. 2 vols. St. Petersburg, 1908, 1911.

———. *Sobranie sochinenii v vos'mi tomakh*. Moscow, 1967.

———. *Vospominaniia i vpechatleniia*. Edited by N. A. Trifonov. Moscow, 1968.

Maiakovskii, [Mayakovsky] Vladimir. *The Bedbug and Selected Poetry*. Edited by Patricia Blake. Translated by Max Hayward and George Reavey. New York and Cleveland, 1970.

———. "Doklad o khudozhestvennoi propagande na Pervom vserossiiskom s"ezde rabotnikov ROSTA," 19 maia 1920 goda. In *SS*, II, pp. 449–451.

———. "Levyi marsh." In *SS*, I, pp. 255–256.
———. "Prikaz po armii iskusstva." In *SS*, I, pp. 246–247.
———. "Radovatsia rano." In *SS*, I, pp. 248–249.
———. *Sobranie sochinenii v vos'mi tomakh.* Moscow, 1968.
———. "150 000 000." In *SS*, II, pp. 51–100.
———. "Vystuplenie na mitinge ob iskusstve," 24 noiabria 1918 goda." In *SS*, I, p. 402.
Makarov, P. V. *Ad"iutant generala Mai-Maevskogo: Iz vospominanii nachal'nika otriada krasnykh partizan v Krymu.* Leningrad, 1928.
Makintsian, P., ed. *Krasnaia kniga V.Ch.K.* Moscow, 1920. [Typescript copy located in the Hoover Institution Library.]
Makhno, Nestor. *Makhnovshchina i ee vcherashnie soiuzniki-bol'sheviki (otvet na knigu M. Kubanina "Makhnovshchina").* Paris, 1928.
———. *Russkaia revoliutsiia na Ukraine (ot marta 1917 g. po aprel' 1918 goda).* Paris, 1929.
———. *Ukrainskaia revoliutsiia (iiul'–dekabr' 1918 g.).* Paris, 1937.
Maksakov, V., and A. Turunov. *Khronika grazhdanskoi voiny v Sibiri, 1917–1918.* Moscow, 1926.
Maksakova, L. M. *Agitpoezd "Oktiabr'skaia Revoliutsiia", 1919–1920 gg.* Moscow, 1956.
Maliantovich, P. N. "V Zimnem dvortse 25–26 oktiabria 1917 goda. Iz vospominanii." *B* 12, no. 6 (June 1918): 111–141.
Mal'kov, P. *Zapiski kommendanta Moskovskogo kremlia.* 2nd rev. ed. Moscow, 1961.
Malle, Sylvana. *The Economic Organization of War Communism, 1918–1921.* Cambridge, 1985.
Malsagoff, S. A. *An Island Hell: A Soviet Prison in the Far North.* Translated by F. H. Lyon. London, 1926.
Mandel'shtam, Osip. *Selected Poems.* Russian and English texts. Russian translated by David McDuff. Cambridge, 1973.
"Manifest vremennogo revoliutsionnogo raboche-krest'ianskogo pravitel'stva Litvy o provozglashenii v Litve sovetskoi vlasti," 16 dekabria 1918 g. In Vaitkiavichius, no. 23, pp. 56–57.
Mannerheim, Carl Gustav Emil. *The Memoirs of Marshal Mannerheim.* Translated by Count Eric Lewenhaupt. New York, 1954.
Marchlewski, Iu. "Pis'mo Iu. Markhlevskogo k L. D. Trotskomu, 19 noiabria 1919 g." In Meijer, I, no. 426, pp. 764–768.
Margulies, M. S. *God interventsii.* 2 vols. Berlin, 1923.
Markov, Anatolii. "Entsiklopediia belogo dvizheniia." HIA. Anatolii Markov Collection, file 1.
Martynov, E. I. *Kornilov: Popytka voennogo perevorota.* Leningrad, 1927.
Marushevskii, V. V. "God na severe (avgust 1918 g.—avgust 1919 g.)." In *BD*, I, pp. 16–60; II, pp. 21–61.
Masherzerskii, V. I. *Ustanovlenie sovetskoi vlasti v Karelii, 1917–1918 gg.* Petrozavodsk, 1957.
Maslennikov, Oleg. *The Frenzied Poets: Andrey Biely and the Russian Symbolists.* Berkeley, 1952.
Massie, Robert. *Nicholas and Alexandra.* New York, 1978.
Mawdsley, Evan. *The Russian Civil War.* Boston, 1987.
Maynard, Major-General C. *The Murmansk Venture.* New York, 1971.
Maynard, John. *The Russian Peasant and Other Studies.* Vol. 1. London, 1942.
McLean, Hugh, Martin Malia, and George Fischer, eds. *Harvard Slavic Studies.* Vol. 4, Cambridge, Mass., 1957.
McNeal, Robert. *Bride of the Revolution: Krupskaia and Lenin.* Ann Arbor, 1972.

———. "The Conference of Jassy: An Early Fiasco of the Anti-Bolshevik Movement." In Curtiss, pp. 221–236.

Medvedev, Roy A. *Let History Judge: The Origins and Consequences of Stalinism.* Edited by David Joravsky and Georges Haupt. Translated by Colleen Taylor. New York, 1971.

Meijer, Jan M., ed. *The Trotskii Papers, 1917–1922.* 2 vols. The Hague, 1964–1971.

Mel'gunov, S. P. *Kak bol'sheviki zakhvatili vlast'.* Paris, 1953.

———. *The Red Terror in Russia.* London, 1925.

———. *Sud'ba imperatora Nikolaia II posle otrecheniia.* Paris, 1951.

———. *Tragediia admirala Kolchaka: Iz istorii grazhdanskoi voiny na Volge, Urale, i v Sibiri.* 4 vols. Belgrad, 1920.

"Memorandum on R. E. Services, N.R.E.F. Administrative Appendix No. 5." IWM. A. E. Sturdy Papers.

"Memorandum on R. E. Services, N.R.E.F. Administrative Appendix No. 6." IWM. A. E. Sturdy Papers.

"Memorandum on the Feeding of the Civil Population of Petrograd and Its District, After Its Liberation from the Bolsheviks," June 5, 1919. HIA. B. V. Gerua Collection, file 120, box 18.

"Miatezhnym kazanskim voiskam, srazhaiushchimsia protiv rabochei i krest'ianskoi Krasnoi armii, obmanutym chekho-slovakam, obmanutym krest'ianam, obmanutym rabochim," 26 avgusta 1918 goda. In *KVR*, I, p. 240.

"Mikhail Dmitrievich Bonch-Bruevich." *SIE*, II, col. 615.

Mikhailov, I.D. *Evoliutsiia russkogo transporta 1913–1925.* Moscow, 1925.

Miliukov, P. N. "Dnevnik." BACU. Miliukov Collection.

———. "Miliukov's Note on the Policy of the Provisional Government," 5(18) March 1917. In Golder, pp. 324–325.

———. *Rossiia na perelome: Bol'shevistskii period Russkoi revoliutsii.* 2 vols. Paris, 1927.

———. *Vospominaniia, 1859–1917.* 2 vols. New York, 1955.

Millar, James, ed. *The Soviet Rural Community.* Urbana, 1971.

Miller, E. K. "Bor'ba za Rossiiu na severe, 1918–1920 gg." In *BD*, IV, pp. 5–11.

Minor, O. S. "Odin den' Uchreditel'nago sobraniia: Ocherk." *Perezhitoe (v god revoliutsii).* Moscow, 1918. I,. pp. 125–132.

Mints, I. I. ed. "Anglichane na severe." *KA* 19 (1926): 39–42.

———. *Angliiskaia interventsiia i severniaia kontrrevoliutsiia.* Moscow-Leningrad, 1931.

———, ed. *Lenin i oktiabr'skoe vooruzhënnoe vosstanie v Petrograde: Materialy vsesoiuznoi nauchnoi sessii, sostoiavsheisia 13–16 noiabria 1962 g. v Leningrade.* Moscow, 1964.

———, et al., eds. *Grazhdanskaia voina v Povolzh'e, 1918–1920.* Kazan, 1974.

———, et al., eds. *Pobeda sovetskoi vlasti v Zakavkaz'e.* Tbilisi, 1971.

"Minutes of the Ufa State Conference: Opening Session." In Bunyan, pp. 340–341.

Mogilianskii, N. M "Tragediia Ukrainy (iz perezhitogo v Kieve v 1918 godu)." *ARR*, XI (1923), pp. 74–105.

Molotov, Vladimir. *Bol'sheviki Sibiri v period grazhdanskoi voiny (1918–1919 gg.).* Omsk, 1949.

Movchin, N. "Komplektovanie Krasnoi armii v 1918–1920 gg." In Bubnov, Kamenev, and Eideman, II, pp. 75–90.

Mushtukov, V. E., ed. *Petrograd v dni velikogo oktiabria. Vospominaniia uchastnikov revoliutsionnykh sobytii v Petrograde v 1917 godu.* Leningrad, 1967.

Naida, S. F., et al., eds. *Iz istorii bor'by sovetskogo naroda protiv inostrannoi voennoi interventsii i vnutrennei kontrrevoliutsii v 1918 g. Sbornik statei.* Moscow, 1956.

———. *Istoriia grazhdanskoi voiny v SSSR.* Vols. 3–4. Moscow, 1957, 1959.

Naida, S. F., and D. A. Kovalenko, eds. *Reshaiushchie pobedy sovetskogo naroda nad interventami i belogvardeitsami v 1919 g.* Moscow, 1960.
Nenarokov, A. P. *Vostochnyi front 1918*. Moscow, 1969.
Nesterovich-Berg, M. A. *V bor'be s bol'shevikami: Vospominaniia*. Paris, 1931.
Nicholas II. "Dnevnik Nikolaia Romanova." *KA* 20 (1927); 21 (1927); 22 (1927); 27 (1928).
———. *Journal intime de Nicolas II (juillet 1914–juillet 1918)*. Paris, 1934.
Nicholas II. *Letters of the Tsar to the Tsaritsa, 1914–1917*. Translated by A. I. Hynes. London, 1929.
Nikolaev, A. M. "1918: Vtoroi god rossiiskoi grazhdanskoi voiny." BACU.
Nikolaev, K. N. "Moi zhiznennyi put'." BACU. K. N. Nikolaev Collection.
"Nikolai Il'ich Podvoiskii." *SIE*, XI, pp. 238–239.
"Nikolai Vasil'evich Krylenko." *SIE*, VIII, cols. 194–195.
"Nota narodnogo komissara inostrannykh del RSFSR G. B. Chicherina pravitel'stvu Velikobritanii po voprosu o peremirii i mire s Pol'shei," 17 iiulia 1920 g. In Khrenov, III, no. 93, pp. 157–162.
Noulens, Joseph. *Mon ambassade en Russie sovietique, 1917–1919*. 2 vols. Paris, 1933.
"O mobilizatsii. Krest'ianam i rabochim Kazanskoi gubernii," 27 avgusta 1918 g. In *KVR*, I, p. 240.
Obolenskii, Prince V. *Krym pri Vrangele: Memuary belogvardeitsa*. Moscow-Leningrad, 1927.
"Obrashchenie TsK RKP(b) k kommunistam-rabotnikam vsekh chrezvychainykh komissii s otsenkoi deiatelnosti vserossiiskoi i mestnykh chrezvychainykh komissii," 8 fevralia 1919 g. In Belov, *Iz istorii Vserossiiskoi*, pp. 248–250.
"Obrazovanie severo-zapadnago pravitel'stva." *ARR*, I, pp. 295–308.
Obshchaia svodka svedenii o protivnike shtaba verkhovnago glavnokomanduiushchago. Biweekly. Omsk, 1918–1919. AG–CV, 17N625.
"Obzor polozheniia Rossii za tri mesiatsa revoliutsii po dannym otdela snoshenii s provintsiiei Vremennago komiteta Gosudarstvennoi dumy." TsGIAL, fond 1278, opis' 10, delo 4.
Okinskii, A. *Dva goda sredi krest'ian*. Riga, 1936.
Okladnikov, A. P., et al. "Sibir'." *SIE*, XII, cols. 840–850.
Orlov, N. *Prodovol'stvennaia rabota sovetskoi vlasti*. Moscow, 1918.
"Osnovnye zakony vsevelikago voiska donskogo." In Golovin, X, pp. 49–55.
Osobaia komissiia po razsledovaniiu zlodeianii bol'shevikov sostoiashchaia pri glavnokomanduiushchem vooruzhennymi silami na iuge Rossii. Svodka materialov po gorodu Khar'kovu i Khar'kovskoi gubernii. Rostov-na-Donu, 1919. BACU. Denikin Collection, box 24.
Pachmuss, Temira. *Zinaida Hippius: An Intellectual Profile*. Carbondale, 1971.
Paderewski, Ignacy. "Pismo prezydenta Rady Ministrów RP I. Paderewskiego do ministra wojny i lotnictwa Wielkiej Brytanii W. Churchilla o grozbie załamania się frontu antyradzieckiego w wypadku neiudzielenia Polsce pomocy brytyjskiej," 1919 paźdiernik 15. In Gąsiorowska-Grabowska, II, no. 222, pp. 398–399.
Palencia, Isabel de. *Alexandra Kollontay, Ambassadress from Russia*. New York and London, 1947.
Paléologue, Maurice. *An Ambassador's Memoirs*. Translated by F. A. Holt. 3 vols. New York, n. d.
———. *La Russie des tsars pendant la Grande Guerre*. 3 vols. Paris, 1921.
Palij, Michael. *The Anarchism of Nestor Makhno, 1918–1921: An Aspect of the Ukrainian Revolution*. Seattle, 1976.
Palmer, R. R. *A History of the Modern World*. New York, 1957.
———. *Twelve Who Ruled*. Princeton, 1941.

Parfenov, P. S. *Grazhdanskaia voina v Sibiri, 1918–1920.* Moscow, 1924.
Paustovskii, Konstantin. *Povest o zhizni.* 2 vols. Moscow, 1966.
———. *Sobranie sochinenii v shesti tomakh.* Moscow, 1956.
"Pavel Efimovich Dybenko." *SIE*, V, cols. 422–423.
Pearson, Raymond. *The Russian Moderates and the Crisis of Tsarism, 1914–1917.* London, 1977.
Pershin, P. N. *Agrarnaia revoliutsiia v Rossii: Agrarnye preobrazovaniia velikoi oktiabr'skoi sotsialisticheskoi revoliutsii.* 2 vols. Moscow, 1966.
Peters, Victor. *Nestor Makhno: The Life of an Anarchist.* Winnipeg, 1970.
Piłsudski, Józef. *The Memories of a Polish Revolutionary and Soldier.* Translated and edited by D. R. Gille. London, 1931.
———. *Rok 1920.* London, 1941.
Pinson, Koppel S., ed. *Essays on Anti-Semitism.* New York, 1946.
Pintner, Walter McKenzie, and Don Karl Rowney, eds. *Russian Officialdom: The Bureaucratization of Russian Society from the Seventeenth to the Twentieth Century.* Chapel Hill, 1980.
Piontkovskii, S., ed. *Grazhdanskaia voina v Rossii (1918–1921 gg.): Khrestomatiia.* Moscow, 1925.
Pipes, Richard. *The Formation of the Soviet Union: Communism and Nationalism, 1917–1923.* Cambridge, Mass., 1954.
———. *Struve: Liberal on the Left, 1870–1905.* Cambridge, Mass., 1970.
———. *Struve: Liberal on the Right, 1905–1944.* Cambridge, Mass., 1980.
"Pis'ma generala Pula k predsedatel'iu arkhangel'skogo pravitel'stva," 5 i 7 avgusta 1918 goda." In Mints, "Anglichane," pp. 41–43.
Platonov, S. F. *Ocherki po istorii smuty v moskovskom gosudarstve XVI–XVII vv.* St. Petersburg, 1910.
"Poezdka predsedatelia VTsIK M. I. Kalinina (iz stat'i v *Izvestiiakh* 1 maia 1919 g.)." In Sergeev, p. 98.
Pogodin, M. P. *Istoriko-politicheskie pis'ma i zapiska v prodolzhenii Krymskoi voiny, 1853–1856 gg.* Moscow, 1974.
"Points of Dispute Between the Bolsheviks and the Socialist-Revolutionists of the Left." In Bunyan, pp. 205–209.
"Pokazaniia F. Dzerzhinskogo po delu ob ubiistve germanskogo poslannika grafa Mirbakha." In Makintsian, pp. 293–308.
"Pokazaniia Iakova Bliumkina," 8 maia 1919 g. In Makintsian, pp. 367–386.
"Pokazaniia Leitenanta L. G. Miullera," 7 iiulia 1918 g. In Makintsian, pp. 215–218.
"Pokazaniia M. Latsisa." In Makintsian, pp. 308–314.
Pokrovskii, Georgii. *Denikinshchina: God politiki i ekonomii na Kubani, 1918–1919 gg.* Kharkov, 1926.
Pokrovskii, M. N., and Ia. A. Iakovlev, eds. *Gosudarstvennoe soveshchanie: Stenograficheskii otchet.* Moscow-Leningrad, 1930.
Poliakov, Iu. A. *Perekhod k NEPu i sovetskoe krest'ianstvo.* Moscow, 1967.
Polikarpov, V. D. *Prolog grazhdanskoi voiny v Rossii, oktiabr' 1917–fevral' 1918 gg.* Moscow, 1976.
Polivanov, A. A. *Iz dnevnikov i vospominanii po dolzhnosti voennogo ministra i ego pomoshchnika, 1907–1916 gg.* Edited by A. M. Zaionchkovskii. Moscow, 1924.
"Pomnite ob Iaroslavle!" avgust 1918 g. In *KVR*, I, p. 245.
Popov, P. P. "The People's Army." In Bunyan, pp. 288–290.
"Postanovlenie glavnonachal'stvuiushchego Iaroslavskoi gub., komanduiushchego vooruzhennymi silami Severnoi dobrovol'cheskoi armii Iaroslavskogo raiona," 13 iiulia 1918 g. In Piontkovskii, pp. 161–163.
"Postanovlenie Vremennogo sibirskogo pravitel'stva ob annulirovanii dekretov sovetskoi vlasti, 4 iiulia 1918 g." In Maksakov and Turunov, p. 198.

"Postanovlenie Vremennogo sibirskogo pravitel'stva ob ustranenii armii ot uchastiia v politicheskoi deiatel'nosti 23 avgusta 1918 goda." In Maksakov and Turunov, pp. 224–225.
"Postanovlenie Vremennago sibirskogo pravitel'stva o nedopushchenii sovetskikh organizatsii, 6 iiulia 1918 goda." In Maksakov and Turunov, pp. 198–199.
"Postanovlenie Vremennogo sibirskogo pravitel'stva o vozvrashchenii vladel'tsam ikh imenii, 6 iiulia 1918 g." In Maksakov and Turunov, pp. 208–209.
Pravda o Kronshtadte: Ocherk geroicheskoi bor'by kronshtadtsev protiv diktatury Kommunisticheskoi partii. Prague, 1921.
Pravda, stavshaia legendoi. 2nd ed. Moscow, 1969.
"Prikaz komandirovaniia osoboi gruppy iuzhnogo fronta o nastuplenii v raione Khopra, Dona i Tsaritsyna," 15 avgusta 1919 g. In Belov, et al., eds., *Iz istorii grazhdanskoi voiny v SSSR*, II, no. 464, pp. 512–515.
"Prikaz narodnogo komissara po voennym delam o razoruzhenii chekhoslovakov," 25 maia 1918 g. In Maksakov and Turunov, pp. 168–169.
"Prikaz narodnogo komissara po voennym i morskim delam ot 24 avgusta 1918 g." *KVR*, I, p. 239.
"Prikaz no. 1 Petrogradskogo soveta rabochikh i soldatskikh deputatov po voiskam Petrogradskogo voennogo okruga," 1 Marta 1917 g. In Gavrilov, pp. 17–18.
"Prikaz predrevvoensoveta respubliki ot 30 sentiabria 1918 g." *KVR*, I, p. 151.
"Prikaz predsedatelia RVSR i Narkomvoenmora po Krasnoi armii i Krasnomu flotu ot 10 sentiabria 1918 g.," no. 32. *KVR*, I, p. 249.
"Prikaz predsedatelia Revvoensoveta respubliki i Narkomvoenmora ot 24 oktiabria 1919 g." *KVR*, II(2), p. 408.
"Prikaz predsedatelia Revoliutsionnogo voennogo soveta respubliki po krasnym voiskam, srazhaiushchimsia protiv belogvardeiskoi Pol'shi," 14 avgusta 1920 g., no. 233. *KVR*, II(2), p. 166.
"Proclamation of the All-Russian Provisional Government," November 4, 1918. In Bunyan, pp. 368–370.
"Programma Komiteta uchreditel'nogo sobraniia. Deklaratsiia Komiteta chlenov Vserossiiskogo uchreditel'nogo sobraniia," 24 iiulia 1918 g. In Piontkovskii, pp. 219–220.
"Programma Rossiiskoi kommunisticheskoi partii (bol'shevikov)." In *VKP*, I, pp. 281–295.
"Protokol 1919 goda, noiabria 30 dnia." BACU. Denikin Collection, box 24.
"Protokół posiedzenia Rady Najwyzszej Konferencji Pokojowej. Relacja premiera rządu Wielkiej Brytanii D. Lloyd George'a o projekcie prezydenta Rady Ministrów RP I. Paderewskiego wyslania 500-tysięcznej armii polskiej na Moskwe oraz oswiadczenie I. Paderewskiego i dyskusja w tej sprawie," 1919 wrzsien 15. In Gąsiorowska-Grabowska, II, no. 203, pp. 348–356.
"Protokol sobranie bol'shevikov-uchastnikov Vserossiiskogo soveshchaniia Sovetov rabochikh i soldatskikh deputatov," 4 aprelia 1917 g. In Gaponenko, et al., pp. 6–12.
"Protokol soveshchaniia, byvshego 16-go iiulia 1917 goda v Stavke." In Bukhbinder, pp. 19–51.
"Protokol zasedaniia Ts, K.," 24 iiunia 1918 g. In Makintsian, pp. 197–199.
Pukhov, A. S. *Kronshtadtskii miatezh v 1921 g.* Moscow, 1931.
Purishkevich, V. M. *Dnevnik chlena Gosudarstvennoi dumy Vladimira Mitrofanovicha Purishkevicha.* Riga, n.d.
Pyman, Avril. *The Life of Aleksandr Blok: The Distant Thunder, 1880–1908*. Oxford, 1979.

———. *The Life of Aleksandr Blok: The Release of Harmony, 1908–1921.* Oxford, 1980.
Rabinowitch, Alexander. *The Bolsheviks Come to Power: The Revolution of 1917 in Petrograd.* New York, 1976.
Radkey, Oliver H. *The Agrarian Foes of Bolshevism: Promise and Default of the Russian Socialist Revolutionaries, February to October 1917.* New York, 1958.
———. *The Sickle Under the Hammer: The Russian Socialist Revolutionaries in the Early Months of Soviet Rule.* New York, 1963.
———. *The Unknown Civil War in Soviet Russia: A Study of the Green Movement in the Tambov Region, 1920–1921.* Stanford, 1976.
Rafael, M. A. *Kronshtadtskii miatezh: Iz dnevnika politrabotnika.* Kiev, 1921.
Rakovskii, Grigorii. *Konets belykh: Ot Dnepra do Bosfora.* Prague, 1921.
———. *V stane belykh (ot Orle do Novorossiiska).* Constantinople, 1920.
Ransome, Arthur. *The Crisis in Russia.* New York, 1921.
———. *Russia in 1919.* New York, 1920.
Rapoport, I. "Poltora goda v sovetskom Glavke." *ARR*, II, pp. 98–107.
"Rechi M. I. Kalinina i M. V. Frunze na mitinge-parade v Orenburge, 19 sentiabria 1919 g." In Sergeev, pp. 141–146.
Reed, John. *Ten Days that Shook the World.* New York, 1960. Originally published 1919.
"The Regional Government of the Urals. Proclamation of August 20, 1918." In Bunyan, pp. 96–299.
"Report of an Assembly of Party Workers and People in Public Life in the City of Uman, called by the Regional Director of the Head Mission of the Russian Society of the Red Cross, on the Question of the Course and Proportions of Local Pogroms." Undated. Reprinted in Heifetz, pp. 316–336.
Reshetar, John S. *The Ukrainian Revolution, 1917–1920: A Study in Nationalism.* New York, 1972.
"Rezoliutsiia I Petrogradskoi konferentsii fabrichno-zavodskikh komitetov ob ekonomicheskikh merakh bor'by s razrukhoi," 3 iiunia 1917 g. In Chugaev, pp. 290–291.
"Rezoliutsiia Tsentral'nogo komiteta RSDRP(b) o podgotovke vooruzhënnogo vosstaniia, predlozhennaia V. I. Leninym," 10 oktiabria 1917 g. In Golikov, no. 15, p. 49.
"Rezoliutsiia vos'mogo s"ezda RKP(b) po organizatsionnomu voprosu." *VKP*, I, pp. 303–307.
Riabukhin, N. M. "The Story of Baron Ungern-Sternberg Told by His Staff Physician N. M. Riabukhin (Ribo)." HIA. N. M. Riabukhin Collection, file 1.
Riasanovsky, N. V. *Nicholas I and Official Nationality in Russia, 1825–1855.* Berkeley and Los Angeles, 1959.
Rigby, T. H. *Communist Party Membership in the U.S.S.R., 1917–1967.* Princeton, 1968.
———. *Lenin's Government: Sovnarkom 1917–1920.* Cambridge, 1979.
Robien, Comte Louis de. *The Diary of a Diplomat in Russia, 1917–1918.* Translated by Camilla Sykes. London, 1969.
Robinson, G. T. *Rural Russia Under the Old Regime.* New York, 1957.
Rodzianko, A. P. *Vospominaniia o Severo-zapadnoi armii.* Berlin, 1920.
Rodzianko, M. V. "Dopros M. V. Rodzianko, 4 sentiabria 1917 goda." In Shchegolev, VII, pp. 116–175.
Rosenberg, William G. *Liberals in the Russian Revolution: The Constitutional Democratic Party, 1917–1921.* Princeton, 1974.
———, and Diane P. Koenker. "The Limits of Formal Protest: Worker Activism

and Social Polarization in Petrograd and Moscow, March to October 1917." *AHR* 92, no. 2 (April 1987): 296–326.
Rosenthal, Bernice Glatzer. "Eschatology and the Appeal of Revolution: Merezhkovsky, Belyi, Blok." *CSS* 11 (1980): 105–140.
Ross, Nikolai. *Vrangel' v Krymu.* Frankfurt-am-Main, 1982.
Rossiia v mirovoi voine 1914–1918 v tsifrakh. Moscow, 1925.
Rostunov, I. I. *Russkii front pervoi mirovoi voiny.* Moscow, 1976.
Rouquerol, General J. *La guerre des rouges et des blancs: L'aventure de l'Amiral Koltchak.* Paris, 1929.
Rozvadovskaia, M. F., and V. M. Slutskaia, eds. *Rytsar revoliutsii: Vospominaniia sovremennikov o Felikse Edmundoviche Dzerzhinskom.* Moscow, 1967.
Sadoul, Capitaine Jacques. *Notes sur la révolution bolchevique (octobre 1917–janvier 1919).* Paris, 1919.
Safarov, G. *Kolonial'naia revoliutsiia, (opyt Turkestana).* Moscow, 1921.
Salisbury, Harrison. *Black Night, White Snow: Russia's Revolutions, 1905–1917.* New York, 1978.
Sanchez-Salazar, General Leandro A. *Murder in Mexico: The Assassination of Leon Trotsky.* Westport, 1973.
Sannikov, A. S. "Vospominaniia gen.-Shtaba general-leitenanta A. S. Sannikova." BACU. Sannikov Collection.
Sasson, Siegfried. *Memoirs of an Infantry Officer.* London, 1930.
Sautin, N. *Velikii, oktiabr' v derevne na severo-zapadnom Rossii: Oktiabr' 1917–1918 gg.* Leningrad, 1959.
Schapiro, Leonard. *The Communist Party of the Soviet Union.* New York, 1960.
———. *The Origin of the Communist Autocracy: Political Opposition in the Soviet State.* Cambridge, Mass., 1956.
Scott, E. J. "The Cheka." *SAP*, no. 1 (Soviet Affairs, no. 1, 1956): 1–23.
Sed'moi ekstrennyi s"ezd RKP(b), mart 1918 goda: Stenograficheskii otchet. Moscow, 1962.
"The Seizure of the Gold Reserve at Kazan." In Bunyan, p. 292.
"Sekretnaia zapiska otdeleniia po okhraneniiu obshchestvennoi bezopasnosti i poriadke v stolitse," 2 sentiabria 1915 g. TsGIAL, fond 1405, opis' 530, delo 1058/70–71.
"Sekretnyi doklad ego prevoskhoditel'stvu gospodinu tovarishchu ministra vnutrennikh del. Otdeleniia po okhraneniiu obshchestvennoi bezopasnosti i poriadka v stolitse," 13 avgusta 1915 g. TsGIAL, fond 1405, opis' 530, delo 1058/40–42.
Semanov, S. N. "V bor'be protiv inostrannykh interventov i vnutrennei kontrrevoliutsii." In Fraiman, *Istoriia*, II, pp. 113–131.
———. *Likvidatsiia antisovetskogo kronshtadtskogo miatezha 1921 goda.* Moscow, 1973.
"Semën Mikhailovich Budënnyi." *SIE*, II, cols. 794–795.
Semenov [Vasil'ev], G. *Voennaia i boevaia rabota partii sotsialistov-revoliutsionerov za 1917–1918 gg.* Moscow, 1922.
Senn, Alfred Erich. *The Emergence of Modern Lithuania.* New York, 1959.
Serge, Victor. *Memoirs of a Revolutionary, 1901–1941.* Translated and edited by Peter Sedgwick. London. 1963.
———. *Year One of the Russian Revolution.* Translated and edited by Peter Sedgwick. Chicago, New York, San Francisco, 1972.
———, and Natalia Sedova Trotsky. *The Life and Death of Leon Trotsky.* Translated by Arnold J. Pomerans. New York, 1975.
Sergeev, B., ed. "Agitpoezdki M. I. Kalinina v gody Grazhdanskoi voiny." *KA* 86 (1938): 93–168.
Service, Robert. *The Bolshevik Party in Revolution.*

Sharapov, G. V. *Razreshenie agrarnogo voprosa v Rossii posle pobedy oktiabr'skoi revoliutsii*. Moscow, 1961.

Shatagin, N. I. *Organizatsiia i stroitel'stvo Sovetskoi armii v period inostrannoi voennoi interventsii i Grazhdanskoi voiny (1918–1920 gg.)*. Moscow, 1954.

Shavel'skii, G. I. "V Dobrovol'cheskii armii." BACU. Shavel'skii Collection.

Shchadenko, E. A. "Grigor'evshchina." In Bubnov, Kamenev, and Eideman, I. pp. 68–95.

Shchegolev, P. E., ed. *Padenie tsarskogo rezhima*. 7 vols. Moscow-Leningrad, 1924–1927.

Shestakov, A. V., ed. *Kombedy RSFSR: Sbornik dekretov i dokumentov o komitetakh bednoty*. Moscow, 1933.

Shingarev, A. I. *Vymiraiushchaia derevnia*. St. Petersburg, 1907. Republished as an appendix to Shuvaev, pp. 149–347.

Shishkin, S. N. *Grazhdanskaia voina na Dal'nem Vostoke*. Moscow, 1957.

———. "Kontrnastuplenie Krasnoi armii na vostochnom fronte protiv Kolchaka (aprel'–iiun' 1919 g.)." In Naida and Kovalenko, pp. 69–120.

Shklovsky [Shklovskii], Viktor. *A Sentimental Journey: Memoirs, 1917–1922*. Translated by Richard Sheldon. Ithaca and London, 1970.

Shkuro, A. G. *Zapiski belogo partizana*. Buenos Aires, 1961.

Shorin, V. "Bor'ba za Ural (iz boevoi zhizni 2-oi armii)." In Bubnov, Kamenev, and Eideman, I, pp. 136–163.

Shtif, N. I. *Pogromy na Ukraine (period Dobrovol'cheskoi armii)*. Berlin, 1922.

Shub, David. *Lenin: A Biography*. New York, 1948.

Shul'gin, V. V. *Dni*. Belgrad, 1925.

Shuvaev, K. M. *Staraia i novaia derevnia*. Moscow, 1937.

Shvittau, G. G. *Revoliutsiia i narodnoe khoziaistvo v Rossii (1917–1921)*. Leipzig, 1922.

Sidorov, A. I. *Ekonomicheskoe polozhenie Rossii v gody pervoi mirovoi voiny*. Moscow, 1973.

Singleton, Seth. "The Tambov Revolt (1920–1921)." *SR* 25, no. 2 (September 1966): 497–512.

Sivkov, P. Z. *Kronshtadt: Stranitsy revoliutsionnoi istorii*. Leningrad, 1972.

Skoropadskii, Pavlo. "Gramota ko vseukrainskomu narodu." In Piontkovskii, pp. 355–356.

———. "Proclamation of Hetman Skoropadsky," April 30, 1918. In Bunyan, pp. 16–17.

Slashchev-Krymskii, Ia. A. *Trebuiu suda obshchestva i glasnosti (oborona i sdacha Kryma)*. Constantinople, 1921.

Slavin, N. F. "Oktiabr'skoe vooruzhënnoe vosstanie i predparlament." In Mints, *Lenin*, pp. 222–231.

Slonim, Marc. *From Chekhov to the Revolution: Russian Literature, 1900–1917*. New York, 1962.

Smagin, General A. A. "Vospominaniia." BACU. Smagin Collection.

Smirnov, K. K. "Nachalo Severo-zapadnoi armii." In *BD*, I, pp. 109–158.

Smith, C. Jay. *Finland and the Russian Revolution*. Athens, Ga., 1958.

Smith, Canfield F. *Vladivostok Under Red and White Rule: Revolution and Counterrevolution in the Russian Far East, 1920–1922*. Seattle and Washington, 1975.

Smith, Jessica. *Women in Soviet Russia*. New York, 1928.

Sobolev, P. G. "Belyi sever: Protivobol'shevistskaia bor'ba na krainem severe Rossii, 1918–1920 gg." BACU. Sobolev Collection.

Sobranie uzakonenii i rasporiazhenii rabochego i krest'ianskogo pravitel'stva. 2nd ed. Moscow, 1918.

Sokolov, Boris. "Padenie severnoi oblasti." *ARR*, IX (1923), pp. 5–90.

———. "Zashchita Vserossiiskago uchreditel'nago sobraniia." *ARR*, XIII (1924), pp. 5–70.

Sokolov, K. N. *Pravlenie generala Denikina.* Sofia, 1929.

Sokolov, N. *Ubiistvo tsarskoi sem'i.* Berlin, 1925.

Sokolov, S. A. *Revoliutsiia i khleb: Iz istorii sovetskoi prodovol'stvennoi politiki v 1917–1918 gg.* Saratov, 1967.

Sorokin, Pitirim. *Leaves from a Russian Diary.* New York, 1924.

Sosnkowski, K. "Memoriał wiceministra spraw wojskowych gen. K. Sosnkowskiego do rządu francuskiego w sprawie konieczności udzielenia przez mocarstwa koalicji natychmiastowej wydatnej pomoscy dla armii polskiej," 1919 [wrzesień nie później 27]. In Gąsiorowska-Grabowska, II, no. 212, pp. 377–382.

———. "Rech' zamestitelia voennogo ministra K. Sosnokovskogo na konferentsii nachal'nikov otdelov General'nogo shtaba Pol'skoi armii i departamentov Voennogo ministerstva o polozhenii na frontakh i sostoianii armii," 2 iiulia 1920 g. In Khrenov, III, pp. 119–123.

"Sotsialisticheskaia kliatva, utverzhdënnaia Vserossiiskim tsentral'nym ispolnitel'nym komitetom Sovetov rabochikh, soldatskikh, krest'ianskikh, i kazach'ikh deputatov, 22 aprelia 1918 g." *KVR*, I, p. 135.

Soutar, Andrew. *With Ironside in North Russia.* New York, 1970.

Spasskii, S. D. "Moskva." In Grigorenko, pp. 161–177.

Spinka, Matthew. *The Church and the Russian Revolution.* New York, 1927.

"Spravka kolchakovskogo ministerstva finansov o prodazhe za granitsu chasti zolotogo zapasa dlia pokrytiia raskhodov po voennym postavkam," dekabr' 1919 g. In Belov, *Iz istorii grazhdanskoi voiny*, II, pp. 299–303.

Stalin, J. V. *Works.* 14 vols. Moscow, 1953.

Stasova, E. D. *Vospominaniia.* Moscow, 1969.

Statisticheskii sbornik po Petrogradu i Petrogradskoi gubernii. Petrograd, 1922.

Steinberg, I. N. *In the Workshop of the Revolution.* New York, 1953.

———. *Spiridonova: Revolutionary Terorrist.* Translated by Gwenda David and Eric Mosbacher. London, 1935.

Sternheimer, Stephen. "Administration for Development: The Emerging Bureaucratic Elite, 1920–1930." In Pintner and Rowney, pp. 316–354.

Stevens, John Frank. "Memorandum on Russia." HIA. John Frank Stevens Papers, file 1.

Stewart, George. *The White Armies of Russia: A Chronicle of Counter-Revoluton and Allied Intervention.* New York, 1933.

Stites, Richard. *The Women's Liberation Movement in Russia: Feminism, Nihilism, and Bolshevism, 1860–1930.* Princeton, 1978.

Storozhev, V. *Soiuz rabochego klassa i bedneishego krest'ianstva v sotsialisticheskoi revoliutsii.* Moscow, 1954.

Strakhovsky, Leonid I. *Intervention at Archangel: The Story of Allied Intervention and Russian Counter-Revolution in North Russia, 1918–1920.* Princeton, 1944.

Stratonov, Irinarkh. *Russkaia tserkovnaia smuta, 1921–1931.* Berlin, 1932.

Strizhkov, Iu. K. *Prodovol'stvennye otriady v gody grazhdanskoi voiny i inostrannoi interventsii, 1917–1922.* Moscow, 1973.

Strumilin, S. G. *Zarabotnaia plata i proizvoditel'nost' truda v russkoi promyshlennosti v 1913–1922 gg.* Moscow, 1923.

Struve, Nikita. *Les chrétiens en U.R.S.S.* Paris, 1963.

Sukhanov, N. N. *The Russian Revolution 1917.* Edited, abridged, and translated by Joel Carmichael. London, New York, Toronto, 1955.

———. *Zapiski o revoliutsii.* 7 vols. Berlin-Petersburg-Moscow, 1922.

Sukhorukov, V. I. *XI armiia v boiakh na severnom Kavkaze i nizhnei Volge*. Moscow, 1961.
"Summary of Kamkov's Attack on Bolshevik Policies." In Bunyan, p. 211.
"Summary of Lenin's Arguments in Defense of Bolshevik Policies." In Bunyan, pp. 209–210.
Sumskii, S. "Odinadtsat' perevorotov." *ARR*, VI (1922), pp. 99–114.
Suny, Ronald Grigor. *The Baku Commune, 1917–1918: Class and Nationality in the Russian Revolution*. Princeton, 1972.
Suprunenko, N. I. *Ocherki istorii grazhdanskoi voiny i inostrannoi voennoi interventsii na Ukraine*. Moscow, 1966.
Surguladze, A. N. *Zakavkaz'e v bor'be za pobedu sotsialisticheskoi revoliutsii*. Tbilisi, 1971.
Suslov, P. V. *Politicheskoe obespechenie sovetsko-polskoi kampanii 1920 goda*. Moscow-Leningrad, 1930.
Svechnikov, M. *Bor'ba Krasnoi armii na severnom Kavkaze*. Moscow-Leningrad, 1926.
"Svedeniia o potrebnostiakh v prodovol'stvii dlia naseleniia Petrograda, otnosiashchiasia ko vremeni okolo oktiabria 1919 g." HIA. Iudenich Collection, file 120, box 18.
Sviatitskii, N. V. *Itogi vyborov vo Vserossiiskoie uchreditel'noe sobranie*. Moscow, 1918.
"Svodka operativnogo upravleniia polevogo shtaba revvoensoveta respubliki o chislennosti voisk Krasnoi armii i sil protivnika na vostochnom fronte k 1 iiune 1919 g." In Belov, *Iz istorii grazhdanskoi voiny*, II, no. 169, 200–202.
Tallents, Sir Stephen. *Man and Boy*. London, 1943.
Tan-Bogoraz, V. G., ed. *Revoliutsia v derevne. Ocherki*. Moscow-Leningrad, 1924.
Tarasov, V. V. *Bor'ba s interventami na severe Rossii (1918–1920 gg.)*. Moscow, 1958.
Taylor, P. R. "Aleksandr Vasil'evich Kolchak." *MERSH*, XVII, pp. 110–113.
"Télégramme secret de M. Paléologue au Ministère des affaires étrangères," Petrograd, 14 janvier 1917, AdAE. Guerre, 1914–1918, Russie, dossier général 646/78–79.
Thompson, John M. *Russia, Bolshevism, and the Versailles Peace*. Princeton, 1966.
Titlinov, B. V. *Tserkov' vo vremia revoliutsii*. Petrograd, 1924.
Tokarev, Iu. S. *Petrogradskii sovet rabochikh i soldatskikh deputatov v marte–aprele 1917 g*. Leningrad, 1976.
———, et al., eds. *Problemy gosudarstvennogo stroitel'stva v pervye gody sovetskoi vlasti: Sbornik statei*. Leningrad, 1973.
Tolstoi, A. N. *Izbrannye sochineniia v shesti tomakh*. Moscow, 1951.
Tomilov, P. A. "Severno-zapadnyi front grazhdanskoi voiny v Rossii 1919 g." HIA. Tomilov Collection.
"To the Citizens of Archangel! To the Citizens of the Northern Region! [Chaplin's Proclamation, September 6, 1918]." In Bunyan, pp. 309–310.
Treadgold, Donald, "The Ideology of the White Movement: Wrangel's 'Leftist Policy from Rightist Hands.' " *HSS*, IV, pp. 481–497.
"Tret'ii dopros Ivana Ivanovicha Popova," 25 iiunia 1918 g." In Makintsian, pp. 79–81.
Trewin, J. C. *Tutor to the Tsarevich*. London, 1975.
Trifonov, I. Ia. *Klassy i klassovaia bor'ba v nachale NEPa (1921–1923 gg.): Bor'ba s vooruzhënnoi kulakskoi kontrrevoliutsiei*. Leningrad, 1964.
———. *Klassy i klassovaia bor'ba v nachale NEPa (1921–1923 gg.): Podgotovka ekonomicheskogo nastupleniia na novuiu burzhuaziiu*. Leningrad, 1969.

Trotsky [Trotskii], L. *The History of the Russian Revolution*. Translated by Max Eastman. 3 vols. Ann Arbor, 1960.
———. *Kak vooruzhalas' revoliutsiia (na voennoi rabote)*. 3 vols. Moscow, 1923–1925.
———. *Lenin: Notes for A Biographer*. Translated by Tamara Deutscher, with an introduction by Bertram D. Wolfe. New York, 1971.
———. *Moia zhizn'. Opyt avtobiografii*. 2 vols. Berlin, 1930.
———. *Sochineniia*. Vols. 15 to 17. Moscow-Leningrad, 1926–1927.
———. *Stalin: An Appraisal of the Man and His Influence*. Edited and translated by Charles Malamuth. New York, 1941.
———. *Trotsky's Diary in Exile*. Translated by Elena Zarudnaia. New York, 1963.
Trubetskoi, Kniaz' G. N. "Otryvki iz dnevnika, 1918–1919 gg." BACU. Denikin Collection.
"Tsirkuliar Ts.K RKP ob armeiskom stroitel'stve," 23 aprelia 1919 g. In Piontkovskii, pp. 108–110.
"Tsirkuliarnoe pis'mo TsK RKP(b) k partiinym organizatsiiam ob organizatsii otpora Denikiny," 30 sentiabria 1919 g. In Belov, *Iz istorii grazhdanskoi voiny*, II, no. 414, p. 462–463.
Tsvetaeva, M. *Lebedinnyi stan. Perekop*. Paris, 1971.
Tuchman, Barbara. *The Guns of August*. New York, 1962.
Tucker, Robert C. *Stalin as Revolutionary, 1879–1929: A Study in History and Personality*. New York, 1973.
Tukhachevskii, M. N. "Bor'ba s kontrrevoliutsionnymi vosstaniiami: Iskorenie tipichnogo banditizma (tambovskoe vosstanie)." *ViR*, no. 8, (1926): 3–15.
———. *Izbrannye proizvedeniia*. 3 vols. Moscow, 1964.
———. "Pokhod za Vislu." In *IP*, I, pp. 114–168.
Tupper, Harmon. *To the Great Ocean: Siberia and the Trans-Siberian Railway*. Boston and Toronto, 1965.
Turkul, A. V. *Drozdovtsy v ogne*. Munich, 1948.
Tyrkova-Williams, Ariadna. *From Liberty to Brest-Litovsk: The First Year of the Russian Revolution*. London, 1919.
Ulam, Adam. *The Bolsheviks: The Intellectual and Political History of the Triumph of Communism in Russia*. New York and London, 1965.
———. *Stalin: The Man and His Era*. New York, 1973.
Ullman, Richard. *The Anglo-Soviet Accord*. Princeton, 1972.
———. *Britain and the Russian Civil War, November 1918–February 1920*. Princeton, 1968.
———. *Intervention and the War: Anglo-Soviet Relations, 1917–1921*. Princeton, 1961.
"Umowa między rządem Rzeczypospolitej Polskiej a rządem S. Petlury," 1920 kwiecień 21. In Gąsiorowska-Grabowska, II, no. 379, pp. 745–747.
Unterberger, Betty Miller. *America's Siberian Expedition, 1918–1920*. Durham, 1956.
"Unusual Medical Conditions in North Russia," in "Memorandum on R. E. Services, N.R.E.F. Administrative Appendix No. 7." IWM. A. E. Sturdy Papers.
Uralov, S. G. *Moisei Uritskii: Biograficheskii ocherk*. Leningrad, 1929.
Ustrialov, N. V. "Dnevnik." HIA. Ustrialov Collection, box 1.
"Uzhasy Narvy: Iz chastnago pis'ma." Reprinted on Gorn, pp. 342–344.
Vaitkiavichius, B., et al., eds. *Bor'ba za sovetskuiu vlast' v Litve v 1918–1920 gg. Sbornik dokumentov*. Vilnius, 1967.
Valentinov, A. A. "Krymskaia epopeia (po dnevnikam uchastnikov i po dokumentam)." *ARR*, V (1922), pp. 5–101.

Varneck, Elena, and H. H. Fisher, eds. *The Testimony of Admiral Kolchak and Other Siberian Materials*. Translated by Elena Varneck. Stanford, 1935.
Vasiukov, V. S. *Predistoriia interventsii, fevral' 1917–mart 1918*. Moscow, 1968.
Vas'kovskii, O. A., et al. *Grazhdanskaia voina i inostrannaia interventsiia na Urale*. Sverdlovsk, 1969.
Venediktov, A. V. *Organizatsiia gosudarstvennoi promyshlennosti v SSSR*. Vol. 1. Leningrad, 1957.
Ventsov, S. "Geroicheskii gorod: General Iudenich pod Petrogradom osen'iu 1919 g." In Bubnov, Kamenev, and Eideman, I, pp. 256–272.
"Viktor Pavlovich Nogin." *SIE*, X, cols. 299–300.
Vinaver, M. *Nashe pravitel'stvo: Krymskie vospominaniia 1918–1919 gg*. Paris, 1928.
Vinnichenko, V. "Iz istorii ukrainskoi revoliutsii." In Alekseev, *Revoliutsiia*, pp. 277–358.
Vinogradov, A. "Ot burlaka do VUZ'a." In Tan-Bogoraz, pp. 87–104.
Vishniak, Mark. "Antisemitism in Tsarist Russia." In Pinson, pp. 121–144.
"Vladimir Aleksandrovich Antonov-Ovseenko." *SIE*, I, cols. 634–635.
"Vladimir Dmitrievich Bonch-Bruevich." *SIE*, II, cols. 614–615.
Vladimirov, M. *Meshechnichestvo i ego sotsial'no-politicheskie otrazheniia*. Kharkov. 1920.
Vladimirova, V. *God sluzhby sotsialistov kapitalistam: Ocherki po istorii kontr-revoliutsii v 1918 godu*. Moscow-Leningrad, 1927.
———. *Kontr-revoliutsiia v 1917 g. (kornilovshchina)*. Moscow, 1924.
"Vneshniaia politika Komiteta uchreditel'nogo sobraniia, 3 avgusta 1918 g." In Piontkovskii, pp. 237–239.
Voline [Vsevolod Eikhenbaum]. *The Unknown Revolution (Kronstadt 1921, Ukraine 1918–1919)*. Translated by Holley Cantine. London, 1955.
Volk, S. S. *Narodnaia volia, 1879–1882*. Moscow-Leningrad, 1966.
Volkov, Boris, "Ob Ungerne." HIA. Boris Volkov Collection, file 2.
Vol'pe, A. "Voennaia promyshlennost' v grazhdanskoi voine." In Bubnov, Kamenev, and Eideman, II, pp. 371–392.
Voronetskaia, A. A. "Organizatsiia Vysshego soveta narodnogo khoziaistva i ego rol' v natsionalizatsii promyshlennosti." *IZ* 43 (1953): 3–38.
Vos'moi s"ezd RKP(b): Protokoly. Moscow, 1959.
Voznesenskii, A. N. *Moskva v 1917 godu*. Moscow-Leningrad, 1928.
Vrangel' [Wrangel], P. N. *Always with Honor*. With a foreword by Herbert Hoover. New York, 1957.
———. Collected Papers. HIA.
———. *The Memoirs of General Wrangel: The Last Commander-in-Chief of the Russian National Army*. Translated by Sophie Goulston. London, 1930.
———. "Zapiski (noiabria 1916 g.–noiabria 1920 g.)." *BD*, V (1928), pp. 9–311, VI (1928), pp. 5–266.
Vsesoiuznaia kommunisticheskaia partiia (bol'shevikov) v revoliutsiiakh i resheniiakh s"ezdov, konferentsii, i plenumov TsK. 2 vols. Moscow, 1940.
"Vyderzhki iz rechi lidera omskikh k.–d. Zhardetskogo na s"ezde torgovo-promyshlennikov v Omske v iiule 1918 g.," no. 80. In Maksakov and Turunov, pp. 207–208.
"Vypiska iz zhurnala zasedanii 7 iiulia 1918 goda V.Ch.K." In Makintsian. p. 277.
"Vypusk glavneishikh predmetov vooruzheniia armii za 1919 g. po pervuiu polovinu 1920 g. (po sovetu voennoi promyshlennosti)." In Duchen'kin, IV, p. 386.
Wade, Rex A. *Red Guards and Workers' Militias in the Russian Revolution*. Stanford, 1984.

Waite, Robert G. L. *Vanguard of Nazism: The Free-Corps Movement in Postwar Germany, 1918–1923*. Cambridge, Mass., 1952.
Wandycz, Piotr S. "Secret Soviet-Polish Peace Talks in 1919." *SR* 24 (September 1965): 425–449.
———. *Sovet-Polish Relations, 1917–1921*. Cambridge, Mass., 1969.
Ward, John. *With the "Die-Hards" in Siberia*. London, 1920.
Weygand, General Maxime. "The Red Army in the Polish War, 1920." In Liddell Hart. pp. 45–51.
Wheeler-Bennett, *The Forgotten Peace: Brest-Litovsk, March 1918*. New York, 1939.
White, John Albert. *The Siberian Intervention*. Princeton, 1950.
White, Stephen. *Political Culture and Soviet Politics*. London, 1979.
Williams, Albert Rhys. *Journey into Revolution: Petrograd, 1917–1918*. Edited by Lucita Williams. Chicago, 1969.
Wilton, Robert. *Russia's Agony*. London, 1918.
Witte, S. Iu. *Vospominaniia*. 3 vols. Moscow, 1956.
Wohl, Robert. *The Generation of 1914*. Cambridge, Mass., 1979.
Wolfe, Bertram D. "Lenin and Inessa Armand." *SR* 22, no. 1 (March 1963): 96–114.
———. *Three Who Made a Revolution: A Biographical History*. New York, 1948.
Wollenberg, Erich. *The Red Army: A Study in the Growth of Soviet Imperialism*. Translated by Claud W. Sykes. London, 1940.
Woroszylski, Wiktor. *The Life of Mayakovsky*. Translated by Boleslaw Taborski. New York, 1970.
Wrangel. *See* Vrangel'.
Yaney, George. "Agricultural Administration in Russia from the Stolypin Land Reform to Forced Collectivization." In Millar, pp. 3–35.
———. *The Urge To Mobilize: Agrarian Reform in Russia, 1861–1930*. Urbana, 1982.
"Zaiavlenie," 24 oktiabria 1918 g. In Boldyrev, note 82, pp. 524–525.
Zaionchkovskii, A. M. *Kampaniia 1917 goda* [vol. 7 of *Strategicheskii ocherk voiny 1914–1918 gg.*]. Moscow, 1923.
Zaitsov, A. *1918 god. Ocherki po istorii russkoi grazhdanskoi voiny*. Paris, 1934.
"Zakliuchenie obvinitel'noi kollegii." In Makintsian, pp. 331–366.
Zankevich, General. "Obstoiatel'stva, soprovozhdavshiia vydachu admirala Kolchaka revoliutsionnomu pravitel'stvu v Irkutske." *BD*, II (1927), pp. 148–157.
"Zasedanie TsK RSDRP, 22 fevralia 1918 g." In *Protokoly Tsentral'nogo komiteta RSDRP(b), avgust 1917–fevral' 1918*. Moscow, 1958.
"Z depeszy przewodniczącego Rady Oborony RSFRR W. Lenina do Rady Wojenno-Rewolucyjnej RSFRR w sprawie wzmocnienia frontu zachodniego," 1920 luty 27. In Gąsiorowska-Grabowska, II, no. 331, p. 613.
Zenzinov, V., ed. *Gosudarstvennyi perevorot admirala Kolchaka v Omske, 18 noiabria 1918 goda*. Paris, 1919.
———. "Pravda o nepravde (pis'mo V. Zenzinova v redaktsiiu *Obshchago dela*)," 22 aprelia 1919 g. In Zenzinov, *Gosudarstvennyi*, pp. 186–193.
Zhigalin, Ia. "Partizanskoe dvizhenie v zapadnoi Sibiri." *PR* 11, no. 106 (1930): 98–114.
Zhloba, D. P. "Ot Nevinnomyskoi do Tsaritsyna." In Bubnov, Kamenev, and Eideman, I, pp. 28–34.
Znamenskii, O. N. *Iiul'skii krizis 1917 goda*. Moscow, 1969.
Zubov, N. *F. E. Dzerzhinskii: Biografiia*, 3rd ed. Moscow, 1971.
Zverev, B. I. "Kronshtadt." *SIE*, VIII, cols. 175–176.

Index

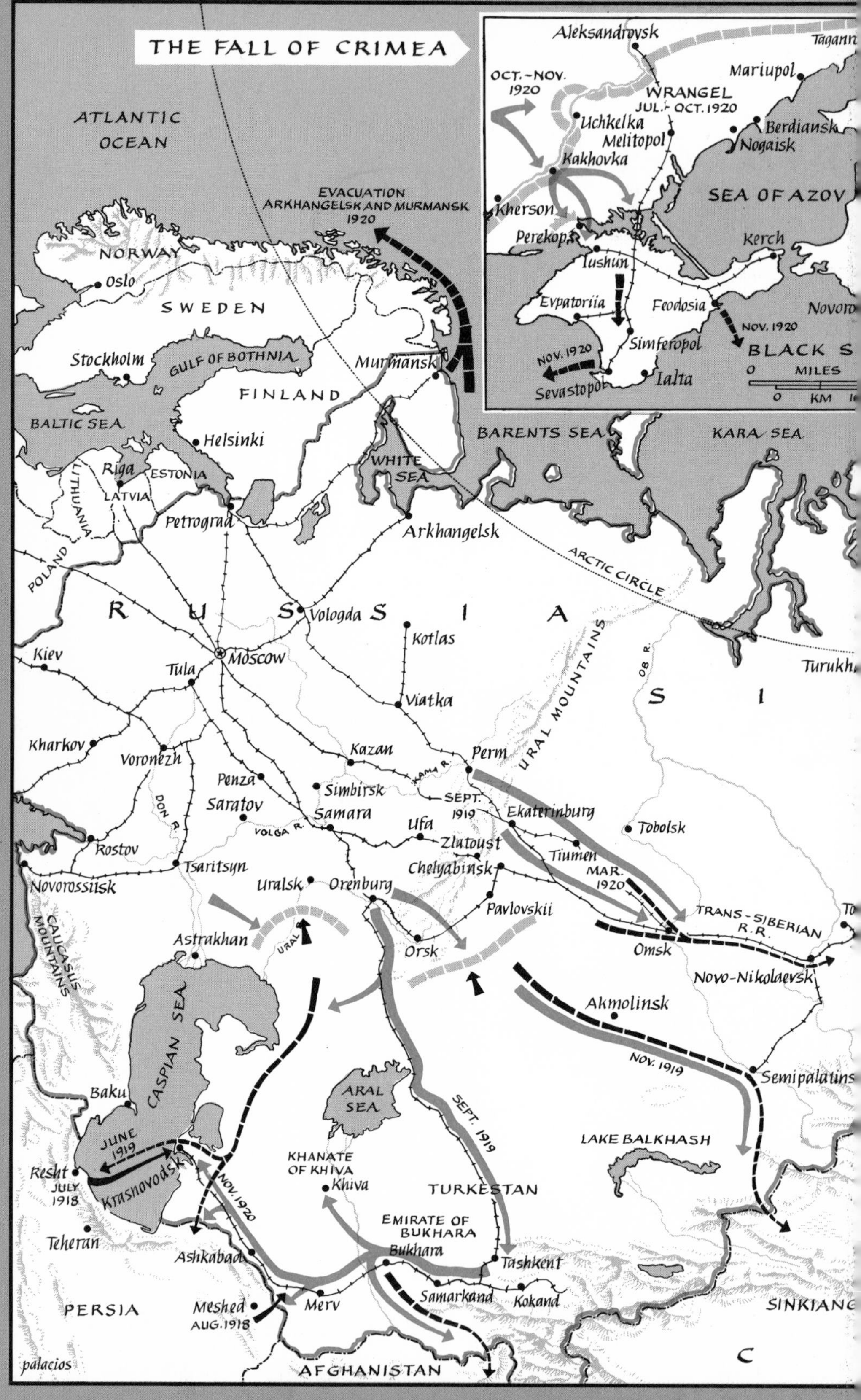
THE FALL OF CRIMEA
ATLANTIC OCEAN
EVACUATION ARKHANGELSK AND MURMANSK 1920
NORWAY
Oslo
SWEDEN
Stockholm
GULF OF BOTHNIA
FINLAND
Murmansk
BALTIC SEA
Helsinki
BARENTS SEA
KARA SEA
WHITE SEA
Riga
ESTONIA
LATVIA
LITHUANIA
Petrograd
Arkhangelsk
POLAND
ARCTIC CIRCLE
RUSSIA
Vologda
Kotlas
Kiev
Tula
Moscow
Viatka
URAL MOUNTAINS
OB R.
Turukh
Kharkov
Voronezh
Kazan
Perm
KAMA R.
Penza
Simbirsk
DON R.
Saratov
Samara
SEPT. 1919
Ekaterinburg
Tobolsk
VOLGA R.
Ufa
Zlatoust
Rostov
Tiumen
Tsaritsyn
Chelyabinsk
MAR. 1920
Novorossiisk
Uralsk
Orenburg
Pavlovskii
TRANS-SIBERIAN R.R.
CAUCASUS MOUNTAINS
Astrakhan
URAL
Orsk
Omsk
Novo-Nikolaevsk
CASPIAN SEA
Akmolinsk
NOV. 1919
Semipalatinsk
Baku
ARAL SEA
SEPT. 1919
LAKE BALKHASH
JUNE 1919
Resht
JULY 1918
Krasnovodsk
NOV. 1920
KHANATE OF KHIVA
Khiva
TURKESTAN
EMIRATE OF BUKHARA
Bukhara
Teheran
Ashkabad
Tashkent
Samarkand
Kokand
PERSIA
Meshed
AUG. 1918
Merv
SINKIANG
AFGHANISTAN
palacios
Aleksandrovsk
Taganr
OCT.-NOV. 1920
Mariupol
WRANGEL JUL.-OCT. 1920
Uchkelka
Melitopol
Berdiansk
Nogaisk
Kakhovka
SEA OF AZOV
Kherson
Perekop
Kerch
Iushun
Evpatoriia
Feodosia
Novoro
NOV. 1920
Simferopol
BLACK S
NOV. 1920
MILES
Sevastopol
Ialta
KM